The
Science and Art
of Branding

The Science and Art of Branding

Giep Franzen and Sandra Moriarty

M.E.Sharpe
Armonk, New York
London, England

Library of Congress Cataloging-in-Publication Data

Franzen, Giep.
  The science and art of branding / by Giep Franzen and Sandra Moriarty.
     p. cm.
  Includes bibliographical references and index.
   ISBN 978-0-7656-1790-3 (cloth: alk. paper)—ISBN 978-0-7656-1791-0 (pbk.: alk. paper)
   1. Branding (Marketing) 2. Brand name products. 3. Consumer behavior. 4. Social values.
5. Branding (Marketing)—Management—Case studies. I. Moriarty, Sandra E. (Sandra Ernst)
II. Title.

HF5415.1255.F73 2008
658.8'27—dc22   2007047066

Printed in the United States of America

The paper used in this publication meets the minimum requirements of
American National Standard for Information Sciences
Permanence of Paper for Printed Library Materials,
ANSI Z 39.48-1984.

| BM (c) | 10 | 9 | 8 | 7 | 6 | 5 | 4 | 3 | 2 | 1 |
| BM (p) | 10 | 9 | 8 | 7 | 6 | 5 | 4 | 3 | 2 | 1 |

CONTENTS

v

ACKNOWLEDGMENTS

The authors wish to express their thanks to a number of people who have made important contributions to this book.

First and foremost to Marieke van den Berg, who co-authored with Franzen the Dutch predecessor of this book. Chapter 10 on brand personality is to a large extent based on her contributions.

Then also to Joke Oppenhuisen, who focused her PhD degree on "values." Chapter 9 is largely based on her dissertation.

Ruth Rose helped us enormously by translating the original Dutch book into proper English.

Henrietta Toth, M.E. Sharpe's editor for our project, made many helpful suggestions as she managed the production proces.

The women from FHV/BBDO—Clary Veenstra, Marieke van de Pol, and Bernadette Daniels—have always been ready to find any piece of information we needed.

There are of course many people without whose efforts you would not now hold this book in your hands. We want to express our heartfelt thanks to all of you.

INTRODUCTION

In 1998, the CEO of the giant aircraft maker Boeing appointed a brand manager for the first time and declared that, from that moment on, brand strategy would constitute an integral element of the company's business strategy. At first, the new official was approached by colleagues with comments like, "You *know* we are an aircraft manufacturer, don't you?"

A lot has changed since then. In 2000, a Boeing brand strategy was formulated and a plan for brand extensions materialized. Boeing reached number 63 on the Interbrand list of financial brand values, priced at $4 billion. Nowadays Boeing sees its brand at a strong competitive advantage. It measures its strength continuously with various stakeholder groups, as well as against other brands like General Electric, Microsoft, and IBM. In short, Boeing has been converted to branding, marking a development in brand thinking that has been progressing at a global level since 1990, apparently at an accelerated pace.

Brand management is an old practice, but a very young science. Brands in their modern meaning originated in the nineteenth century. Up to about 1990 they had not been a subject of scientific study. As a result of the growing realization that brands can be the most valuable assets of companies, they moved to the center of attention on almost every manager's desk. As a result, they are now a key subject for everyone in business administration, marketing, communication, and research.

After fifteen years of theory development, the academic literature is still rather limited. At the same time, brands are gradually entering the curricula of many academic courses, such as business administration, marketing, communication studies, and economic psychology. The subject of branding has also become international—the whole world has recently discovered brands, and investigations into brand strategy have been conducted around the world by both academics and practitioners. An analysis, such as the one in this book, that combines theoretical concepts, findings from large-scale empirical market research, and the best of professional practice from case histories and interviews with brand practitioners can significantly advance our knowledge of brand strategy development.

A growing interest in the working of brands inspired us to write this book. In a way, we have experienced it as a journey of discovery. More than was the case when we started, we have become permeated by the intriguing, complex character of brands and by the difficulty of putting into words the development of such abstract and changeable phenomena. During our journey, new insights kept coming up on the horizon. The most important insight is embodied as the dynamic system theory. This is a theory that assumes that phenomena in the world consist of a fabric of elements with specific properties between which relationships exist. The theory posits that the explanation for the behavior of entities in reality—such as brands—can be found not by researching isolated relationships between the different parts, but by looking at the entire picture. This whole is always more than the sum of its parts and has characteristics that cannot be explained by its separate elements.

But there is more to a brand than science. Branding is also an art. An effective brand manager must be a master of both the science and the art of branding. Addressing those two responsibilities is the focus of this book. This introduction will briefly explain both sides of the brand puzzle by looking, first, at a brand as a system and, second, at a brand as a work of art. The first chapters will introduce the idea of a brand as a system and then relate systems thinking to strategic thinking. The chapters that follow will look at the various brand system components. The final chapters will return to the idea of a brand as a work of art and relate that idea to brand equity and integrated branding.

THE SCIENCE: BRANDS AS A SYSTEM

Celebrating brands is one thing, but knowing what that means in terms of management and strategy is an entirely different matter. Brands are not isolated phenomena; they are inseparably linked to the world in which they exist. This makes their study simultaneously fascinating and complex.

The problem is that current thinking in marketing and brand management is, in some ways, contrary to the practices needed to create and grow strong brands. The dominant business tradition, sometimes referred to as flowchart or spreadsheet thinking, is designed to isolate key variables and locate them on a preplanned form that makes it possible to control a process or tally up costs and predict revenue. Essentially, brand planning is designed to simplify complexity using a bottom-line focus and linear thinking.

A brand, however, is a study in complexity with a number of interacting marketing processes and a relatively murky set of interrelated components. Creating a successful brand, therefore, is an exercise in managing these complex and dynamic systems. Because of the overarching dominance of the spreadsheet approach, far less attention typically is placed on identifying the elements of the system, the various subsystems, and the relationships among the elements, as well as the interaction of the systems. To some degree, the work is done intuitively, as Boeing did in addressing its need for a brand strategy. Most brand managers, however, use bottom-line or spreadsheet thinking for brand management, rather than systems thinking, and they fail to see how a decision in one area (automating customer service) may positively or negatively affect an outcome in a different area (long-time customer value).

The root of the problem is that brand management is mired in one-way, linear thinking. The old information-processing model, which underlies the marketing concept, is referred to in communication studies as a source/message/receiver (SMR) model—both are based on input → process → output. The company is the source and controls the output, which the customer receives. The idea of a "target" market, complete with its gun-to-the-head imagery, reflects this overly simplistic asymmetrical point of view. The marketing concept with its customer focus is a good idea that, in reality, is more of a fantasy operating as a shadow in the background of brand strategy.

What is missing is the notion of circularity and interaction, which, in planning, means an integrated feedback loop—not something added on to the model as an afterthought, as in the traditional communication model, but rather an understanding that the idea of multiple interacting systems and processes redefines the concepts of input and output.

A new mind-set is needed to move away from one-way thinking. What is needed is a new brand development and management philosophy that sees a brand as a complicated system of inputs and outputs and recognizes its multiple interacting systems and subsystems and the various interrelated components that make up the systems. Such an approach favors complexity rather than simplicity, but it is one that is designed to manage the realities of branding in the twenty-first century. The systems approach also recognizes the importance of communication—not one-way from source to receiver—but a two-way approach that encourages interaction throughout the system, particularly between the brand and its stakeholders. A brand is a message—a conversation—and it should be managed as a dialogue with consumers.

The study of brands from the perspective of dynamic system theory is enlightening because it leaves the nature of brands, especially their holistic and dynamic character, fully intact. The second major advantage is that system theory is based on a constant interaction between the various components of the system itself and between the system and its surroundings. Inspired by the possibilities that system theory offers for studying and describing brands and their functioning, we have chosen elements we see as most relevant to strategy development. We are aware of the fact that making a selection from a larger whole inevitably entails limitations: we too are merely presenting our truth.

THE ART: BRAND AESTHETICS

Managing a brand is not unlike composing a symphony or designing a cathedral. Parallel to the brand's bottom-line imperative and functional considerations, there is also an aesthetic dimension. The aesthetics of brand strategy are driven by the classical notion of "good fit," a concept that explains the beauty and parsimony of a "perfect" solution to a functional problem.

Gesamtkunstwerk is a German term that means, literally, "joint art work." Its use, which goes back to the nineteenth century, refers to the aesthetic merging of all the arts involved in a design solution. The concept was originally linked to the operas of Richard Wagner (1813–1883), in which music was combined with theater. Later on it referred to a fully integrated design in architecture and interiors, each element being designed with an artistic intention and the utmost precision, usually by a single designer who was a master of all these design systems.

The idea of a complete design, one that brings order to complexity, as expressed in *gesamtkunstwerk* influenced the concept of "total design" in which the design, manufacture, and sales of products were approached holistically. In today's world we could stretch the idea to include the holistic manifestation of the brand phenomenon and the complexity of the physical, social, and mental framework that surrounds branding.

As Andrew Lyons (2001) states in his article "Gestalt Approaches to the Gesamtkunstwerk," the idea of *gesamtkunstwerk* is Apple's Steve Jobs, Nike's Philip Knight, Virgin's Richard Branson— who are the driving forces behind the success of many of the world's most distinguished brands. With their extraordinary passion and eccentric characters and vision, these visionaries manage to create a climate with the power to touch people's hearts and minds, within and outside the organization.

THE BOOK'S APPROACH

This is not a how-to book, and it is intended as a manual not for brand management, but rather for understanding the brand phenomenon. We do not give instant solutions, but do provide insights into some important core elements within the process of brand development. The idea is to present the research and theory behind branding in order to identify the basic principles that lead to better understanding of how branding works in the real world of business. Depending on the context, for example, a certain type of brand or a problem formulation in the strategy development process can illustrate one or several of these systems, elements, and, ultimately, principles.

We have tried to give a complete overview of the current knowledge on the selected elements, as well as the system of branding, having searched mainly for empirical data—what is known about the influence of these elements on the performances of brands and their markets. These data come largely from databases of market research agencies. The boxes contain abridged descriptions of brands that illustrate specific insights. As you will notice, the book is based on extensive analysis of the literature. We departed from a book that Franzen wrote together with Marieke van den Berg in 2002 for the Dutch market. The chapter on brand personality by Van den Berg was kept for this current publication. For several chapters we were able to base our writings on the work and publications of the Foundation for Scientific Research on Commercial Communication (SWOCC; Stichting Wetenschappelijk Onderzoek Commerciele Communicatie) at the University of Amsterdam. This work has helped us present an up-to-date overview of the knowledge available in our field.

We believe that any book that includes strategic management in its introduction cannot avoid dealing with the concept of strategy. This is where we kick off in the first set of chapters. We end the book with what is perhaps a rather idealistic plea for the brand as *gesamtkunstwerk*, in which the brand's entire body of ideas manifests itself as brand equity. In between you will find a myriad of information about the systems and their core elements that are used in the process of brand strategy development.

The book is organized in four main parts. The first looks at the notion of a brand as a system and brand management as a form of systems thinking. Parts II and III set up the two primary ways of thinking about a brand: from the perspective of the brand manager (Part II) and from the perspective of the brand's customer (Part III). In between is the area where brand strategy intersects with brand perception. Part IV focuses on how the integration of these two perspectives leads to a coherent and integrated brand and, ultimately, to brand equity.

Our aim is to make a substantial contribution to the need for knowledge that still exists when it comes to brand management, and we hope you will derive as much pleasure from reading this book as we had in writing it.

PART I

THE NATURE OF BRANDS

CHAPTER 1

THE BRAND AS A SYSTEM

The statement "Diesel is not my company, it's my life" is a reflection of the passion of Renzo Rosso, founder of and driving force behind the Italian clothing brand Diesel. Intuitively he manages the Diesel brand as a totally focused system of decisions, forces, and stakeholders. The following story briefly reviews the Diesel brand philosophy.

DIESEL: A STATE OF MIND

> Diesel is a state of mind: it means being open to new things, listening to one's intuition and being honest with oneself. We would like to offer consumers a total look which reflects this attitude.
> —Renzo Rosso

The brand Diesel was born more than thirty years ago and is today an innovative international design company, manufacturing jeans and casual clothing, as well as accessories. It is present in over eighty countries with 5,000 points of sale and 270 single-brand stores, 170 of which are company owned. When Renzo Rosso founded the company in 1978, he wanted it to be a leader, a company that took chances and carved out a niche for itself in its field. He surrounded himself with creative, talented people—innovators who, like him, rejected the slavish trend-following typical of the fashion industry. Rosso wanted to come up with a more dynamic and imaginative line of clothing than was available anywhere. He gave his open-minded new designers broad stylistic freedom, hoping they could create a line of clothing perfect for people who follow their own independent path in life—particularly for those who decide to express their individuality also by the way they dress. From the very beginning, Diesel's designers let their own tastes lead them, turning their backs on the style dictators and consumer forecasters of the fashion establishment. And from the very beginning, these designs, as well as the outrageous Diesel advertising, appealed to the iconoclastic tastes of Generation Y.

Ever since the beginning, Renzo Rosso believed in addressing the world with one product and one brand language, and one of his first steps was building a solid, vast distribution platform stretching across all five continents. Most of Diesel's current production is outsourced to small- and medium-sized companies. Production of denim jeans is based exclusively in Italy. All international logistics operations (wholesale and retail) are centrally managed and carefully controlled. Today Diesel is a global brand with a consolidated annual turnover of $1.5 billion in 2005, 85 percent of which is generated outside Italy. The headquarters are located in Molvena, in the northeastern part of Italy, where the company manages twelve subsidiaries across Europe, Asia, and the Americas. Diesel employs over 3,300 people worldwide.

The company views the world as a single, borderless macroculture. The Diesel staff reflects this view: a wide variety of people and personalities from all parts of the globe, creating an unpredictable, dynamic vitality and energy within the company. The style and graphics departments literally work side by side in one huge open space, a creative group strengthening itself through close collaboration. Diesel's stylists come from widely diverse cultures and backgrounds, and they all contribute to the creation of a truly global brand. As Rosso explains, "Diesel isn't just about making clothing and accessories. Its design team is creating Diesel 'spaces' that help communicate the message and the feeling, as well as the personality, of the brand it is selling."

Parallel to its wholesale distribution through multibrand stores and corners (in chain and department stores), in 1996 Diesel embarked on a new adventure: retail. Flagship stores (in New York, London, San Francisco, and Rome) and single-brand stores (from Santa Monica to Milan, Paris, and Antwerp) are the ideal vehicle to bring the Diesel concept to life in its entirety, providing enough space to showcase all Diesel collections. While each individual store is unique, they all share a similar atmosphere. The stores help Diesel's retail and wholesale divisions to grow simultaneously because they strengthen the company's image and increase customer product awareness. They guide the market and help immeasurably in communicating the true vibe of the company to the public.

When advertising is at its best, it expresses the inner feelings associated with the company and the brand. The now famous Diesel advertising campaigns started in 1991 and ever since have been characterized by a single creative execution run in every market of the world, helping the company to become truly global. The ad campaigns are developed by bringing together the work of Diesel's internal creative team and external advertising agencies. The creative team is a small, cross-functional group of people with creative and marketing functions in the company. It is their creativity and knowledge of the brand values, together with the executional skills of advertising agencies, that guarantee that all Diesel communications stay true to the company's particular brand philosophy.

Diesel appropriated the "consumer products make better living" theme (so beloved by advertisers from the 1950s onward) and translated it into the "DIESEL—FOR SUCCESSFUL LIVING" campaigns. Diesel images of a retro consumer paradise must, however, be interpreted very ironically: the standard promise of "success" found in most advertising is exaggerated and made absurd. Serious themes seem to be lurking everywhere in the advertising, but any suggestion of worthiness is undercut by a final admission that it is all just a joke.

The real showcases for the broad range of Diesel collections have been the various eclectic catalogs produced, in which the product often serves only as illustrative, incidental content.

These publications have been celebrated over the years for their radical approach, every edition representing a significant evolution in graphic and photographic technique. New Diesel catalogs feature the product a bit more prominently (a concession to the expansion of the company's range and growing customer base), but still maintain an edgy creativity and high artistic standards. Diesel is also globally recognized in communication circles for its progressive interactive media activities. Diesel was one of the first companies to have a major presence on the Internet (www.diesel.com), launching its site in 1995. Today the site contains information about all Diesel clothing collections, as well as its licensed products, plus a complete archive of all Diesel advertising. Members of the Diesel Club receive new information, exclusive previews, and regular updates via e-mail.

Diesel first entered the world of e-commerce in 1997, selling jeans online in Finland and Sweden. In 1998 Diesel opened an Internet-based virtual store for home delivery of products to customers in selected markets. Creatively using new media, Diesel's communication is no longer a one-way message, but rather a complex, entertaining dialogue between Diesel and its customers that enables active participation and interaction with the brand. Beyond the Internet, Diesel's new media activities stretch into many different areas. The company has produced award-winning CD-ROMs, such as *Digital Adrenaline—55DSL*, a game- and music-filled CD-ROM in support of the 55DSL clothing line. Additionally, Diesel has begun to make a big splash in the world of video games, contributing its logo and creative content to new video game releases.

By 2005 Diesel had become one of the big fashion brands and started to license its brand to other manufacturers. Under its supervision, Diesel Shades (sunglasses), Diesel Footwear, Diesel Time Frames (watches), Diesel Plus Plus, Zero Plus, and Diesel Green (cosmetics and perfumes), and Diesel Jewelry are now being produced. All these products represent the character of the brand, as does its latest marketing communication effort called www.dieselsweeties.com, which is a romantic comedy starring a burned-out porn star and her robot boyfriend. To cement the appeal of the brand to young people, the Web site also features indie rockers and metalheads.

Source: www.diesel.com; www.dieselsweeties.com; T. Duncan, *IMC: Using Advertising and Promotion to Build Brands* (New York: McGraw-Hill, 2002), 345; *Adweek*, "What's New Portfolio," December 22, 1997, 24.

A brand like Diesel comes alive as it takes on meaning for its users. The meaning of a brand, and ultimately the equity of the brand, are an outgrowth of two primary marketing systems operating in parallel and sometimes in conflict. The corporate nature of a brand is manifest in a set of management decisions and strategies; the consumer meaning of a brand is manifested as an integrated perception that is derived from experiences with and messages about the brand.

In traditional marketing, the practice is to give lip service to the idea of consumer power and, instead, focus on brand management as the primary controlling system. As Naumann (1995) observes in his book *Creating Customer Value*, economic power is now in the hands of the consumer rather than the manufacturer. It is the premise of this book that the power of producers of products and owners of brands is equal to and, hopefully, in partnership with their customers who control the meaning of the brand.

The concept of a brand is defined by the American Marketing Association (AMA) as "a name, term, sign, symbol, design or some combination of these elements, intended to identify the goods and services of one seller or group of sellers to differentiate them from those of competitors" (Bennett 1988, 18). This definition focuses on the identification function, which is definitely central.

From our discussion of Diesel, however, it should be apparent that a brand is more than just an identity system. A brand, from our viewpoint, can be defined as a complex system of interrelated management decisions and consumer reactions that creates awareness, visibility, and meaning, as well as distinguishing a product from its competitors. Branding, then, is the strategic process that manages the presentation and influences the perception of a brand.

In Part I of this book, we will discuss the nature of a brand and introduce the concept of brands as systems. The next chapter describes the context within which branding takes place and the external components of the brand system.

> *Principle:* A brand is a complex, interrelated system of management decisions and consumer reactions that identifies a product (goods, services, or ideas), builds awareness of it, and creates meaning for it.

SYSTEMS AND SUBSYSTEMS

What do we mean by a system and how do we apply that to a brand? A system is a complex network of interlocking components, "a group of interacting, interrelated, and interdependent components that form a complex and unified whole" (Pegasus 2005). In addition to the human body, other systems include organizations such as companies and departments, the solar system, and, on a more micro level, such things as the ignition system in your car and the heating system in your home. Most importantly, for our discussion, a brand can be analyzed and managed as a system.

Systems theory is the study of organizational structures and patterns that can be mapped or modeled using the idea of a network, rather than a path, to define the flow of information and decision making. It is the study of the structure that emerges from an analysis of the interconnectedness of components, as well as the complexity of relationships between parts and related networks (Scrivener 2004). Another related concept is system dynamics, which considers the interactions of the components and how self-correction can be a stabilizing process within the system (Pegasus 2005).

Every system represents a specific level in a hierarchy of dominant systems and subsystems. For example, the marketing system has been represented by the convenient phrase "the four Ps," which identifies the components of marketing as product, price, place (distribution), and promotion (marketing communication). Each of those components is also a system with a network of interrelated components. The marketing communication system, for example, includes advertising, sales promotion, direct marketing, and public relations, among other areas and activities. Within advertising there is another subset or network of components, such as strategies and tactics for both messages and media.

A system is characterized as a set of interrelated components in which the condition and behavior of the system cannot be traced back to the specific properties of any of the individual components, but rather can only be understood through the synergistic interactions and relationships of the network of components. This is an apt description of how branding works. For example, the Tiffany brand means far more than stained glass lamp shades, exquisite jewelry, turquoise boxes, upscale retail environments, and premium prices. It is all of these, plus customer service, image-building advertising, and years of tradition—all of which contribute to the meaning of Tiffany as a classy, upscale brand.

Characteristics of a system, then, include the following:

- Systems consist of definable elements (components, the pieces and parts).
- Interrelationships exist between these elements. A system is more than a mere accumulation of elements; there has to be a structure of relationships that exist in a network.
- Systems have a boundary with the surrounding "environment"; this border determines

  - the identity of the system;
  - the contact points where interactions occur.

- Systems are hierarchical, with dominating systems, as well as subsystems.
- Systems are dynamic in that they are adaptive (evolutionary) and self-regulating (through information feedback).

When you unpack all the systems and subsystems of branding, you see the complexity of this business function and the challenge these interrelated networks represent to those who attempt to manage all the components and their interactions.

The Brand Conversation

A brand, like a coin, has two sides. The primary controlling systems involved in branding are found in the corporate (brand management) and consumer perspectives. These are the two actors in the brand-as-conversation model. These systems work in parallel, although as suggested earlier they sometimes exist in a state of tension as the push and pull of decision making rubs against the different interests of these two forces.

Management, for example, aims to control costs and increase revenue (at the consumer's expense) and consumers strive to get the best possible deal for their money (at the company's expense). This system schism is further complicated by the fact that brand managers believe they "own" the brand, when, in reality, a brand is a perception that lives primarily in the mind of the customer and the best a brand manager can do to control the perception is to use appropriate communication cues.

Principle: Brand managers believe they "own" the brand, but a brand is a perception that lives primarily in the mind of the customer.

The mandate in popular marketing literature to distinguish between inside-out and outside-in viewpoints recognizes this schism. Remember, two tracks running in parallel never touch, and therein lies the dilemma of the marketing concept. This tug-of-war between corporate and consumer needs is at the heart of marketing's *exchange* concept. The implications of these two interrelated but conflicting systems are seldom articulated and managed strategically because both parties to the exchange look at the situation through their own blinders. Systems thinking in brand development is useful because it provides a lens that exposes this dual nature of the brand conversation and lays bare the crux of the control issue:

- *Corporate:* the strategic function—marketing research, decisions about brand identity and its presentation product development, and marketing strategy support through the marketing mix. Brand strategy is largely under control of the brand's managers.
- *Consumer:* the perception function—messages and experiences that come together to form a consumer's unique impression of a brand, an impression that is largely beyond the control

of the company. The company, through the strategic decisions of its brand management, can only influence or cue these brand perceptions: it cannot control them.

Both corporate and consumer forces contribute to the identity of the brand through a delicate dance between intended meanings sent by the company and the perceived meanings elicited through consumer response. The interactive nature of brand identity follows logically from the view of a brand as a message and brand strategy as a dialogue.

> *Principle:* Brand identity is a delicate dance between intended meanings sent by the company and perceived meanings elicited through consumer response.

A Hierarchy of Systems

Every system represents a specific level in a hierarchy of systems, the complexity of the levels increasing with their rank. It shows properties that are not present at the lower level and that are the result of the specific makeup of the components. For a macro example, consider the layered systems of (1) economics, (2) the business (strategic business unit management), (3) marketing in general supported by (4) specific areas of the marketing mix, and (5) marketing communication in general supported by (6) specific areas of marketing communication.

Consider how these levels operate and interrelate, all affecting brand strategy development. When looking at this system at the world economy level, for example, we see that it consists of a network of connected systems of national economies. If we put the economy of one of those countries under the microscope, what we see is a concatenation of interrelated market systems, each with its own set of business entities and industries. Within such a market system we also see a network of competing brand systems. Each separate brand system can, in turn, be dissected into subsystems reflecting marketing strategies, such as the corporate and consumer decision-making systems mentioned earlier, as well as specific product lines and brand extensions, and, ultimately, the brand-related subcomponents, such as the systems of identity, image, and personality cues. The system is further complicated by different components and hierarchies that operate geographically and in parallel to the brand's home country strategy—such as local, national, and international or global strategies. A change in any one of the levels can affect subsequent decisions made at all the other levels, as well as decisions made in parallel systems—geographic markets, niche markets, and stakeholder markets, such as channels, suppliers, and employees.

When studying a certain level, it is important to keep in mind that the behavior of the system is influenced by both the dominating and underlying systems. Systems are thus interconnected not only horizontally in a network, as is the case with the brand systems within a specific market system, but also vertically: changes in the system of the world economy, or a corporate financial position, can affect all lower-level systems and vice versa.

The Black Box

Lewin (in Schein 2004) stated as early as 1952 that a system always has forces that stimulate stability and balance, as well as forces that tend toward disruption and change. The presence of these opposite forces keeps the system in balance. Systems can also become disrupted due to changes in component or environmental variables. To an outside observer, these changes often appear to be spontaneous and coincidental because the relationships within systems and within a system and its environment tend to be complex and nontransparent. So many forces can be acting and interacting that it becomes impossible to ascribe a change to one single cause.

A system thus has very much the character of a "black box," an entity that is sensitive to and generates a certain input, but which offers no good overview of the essence of its working. As Schein (2004) explains, systems thinking focuses on "phenomena that are below the surface." Consequently, effective management of the system comes about through a process of trial and error that allows us to obtain information on how the system works.

The clothing brand Benetton is an example of the transparency problem in the workings of the brand system. For years, Benetton used advertising and other promotions to showcase itself as a brand in tune with social issues and contemporary problems, such as a priest kissing a nun. However, the unconventional promotional strategies generated controversy and criticism, which some Benetton managers said reinforced the brand's intended edgy image and its appeal to young people. Eventually, however, the controversy became too much for the brand to manage and it backed away from this public presentation of its inner soul. What did the managers think of the brand's perception? What did consumers think of the brand's image? How did the edginess connect with critical-minded young people? And how did Benetton's management arrive at the decision first to use the provocative strategy and then to dump it and return the brand's focus to its less risky slogan, "The United Colors of Benetton"?

Due to the lack of insight into the inner workings of a brand system, problems can arise when attempting to influence it, as Benetton discovered. Intended changes may not happen—according to Franzen et al. (1999), half of all advertising campaigns have no visible behavioral effects—or the condition of the system may develop in the opposite direction (the market share keeps dropping). Again, the application of systems theory to brands offers a good possibility to escape the linear cause-and-effect thought process.

Principle: A brand system has very much the character of a "black box," whose regulation comes about through a process of trial and error.

BRANDS THROUGH THE LENS OF SYSTEMS THEORY

Marketing is like the human body in its complexity, and marketing scholars and practitioners, like health professionals, often focus on the details rather than the interactions. As Ellen Goodman said about health research, "There's a tendency to study single diseases and small body parts instead of lives." (Or distribution or pricing, rather than a brand.) She continues, "The group concerned with the maintenance of lungs doesn't always do ankles and the cancer-prevention team isn't into cardiovascular diseases. As the last generalists, we, the owners of whole bodies, are supposed to think of ourselves as nothing more than the sum of parts and potential diseases to be taken care of with separate regimens" (in Scrivener 2004).

A similar problem bedevils marketing and brand strategy, which typically focuses on definable, observable, measurable practices and processes, such as research and development (R&D), pricing, distribution, new product launches, and brand positioning. Sometimes these details are the focus of strategy—rather than the health of the brand, which is a better expression of how well all these systems are working together. The result is that branding strategists may get lost in the forest because they focus on individual pieces of a brand, rather than the big brand picture.

Branding is an area, or subsystem, within business. It is the study of how products take on

---

Table 1.1

A Review of Marketing and Brand-Related Systems

Networks of business management cause-and-effect decisions (objectives, strategies, tactics, and evaluation for the various business levels)
• Corporate
• SBU (strategic business unit)
• Brand management strategies
• Marketing: Product, product line, SKUs (stock keeping units)

Networks of information
• Internal and external communication
• Contact points
• Media vehicles
• Formal and informal feedback (research)

Networks of stakeholders
• Customers
• Shareholders
• Employees
• Other key stakeholders: Suppliers and distributors, media, financial, government, community

Networks of branding components
• Brand functions: Product representation, symbolism, purchasing behavior, customer relationship
• Brand strategy: Brand identity, core concept, segmentation, differentiation
• Brand meaning: Brand promise and position, associations, personality, values
• Brand span and brand extension
• Brand integration: Integrity and coherence
• Brand strength: Saliency, prominence, visibility, dominance
• Brand architecture: Brand portfolio, brand equity and financial value

Networks of marketing components
Marketing mix
• Product attributes and design (the physical reality)
• Pricing
• Distribution
• Marketing communication: Advertising, consumer sales promotion, channel (trade) marketing, direct response, public relations, packaging, events and sponsorships, licensing
• Customer service

Networks of marketing and branding contexts
• Personal and psychological (consumer, manager)
• Cultural and social
• Economic, political, environmental
• Technological
• Situational

---

a distinctive character and meaning when a company creates a brand identity and manages the strategy behind the presentation of a brand personality through informed decision making. The concept of systems is not unknown in marketing and branding. Macrae (1996), for example, in his discussion of brand equity, defines a brand as a leadership system; Aaker and Joachimsthaler (2000) refers to the brand identity system as a step in his brand-planning process; and Kay (1993)

Figure 1.1 **The Brand Systems Cube**

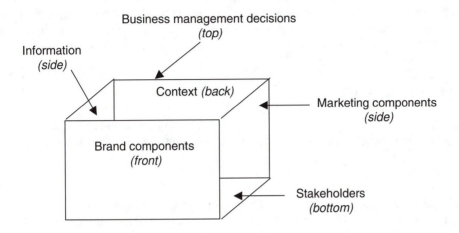

refs to brand architecture as a system of relationships within the firm or between the brand and its stakeholders. Furthermore, the McKinsey Consulting Company (1994) challenges brand managers to adopt "a total system perspective."

A systems approach to branding is based on an understanding of the following marketing-related systems and subsystems. We will summarize this complex system in terms of six key networks, or clusters, of components—business management decisions, information, stakeholders, marketing components, branding components, and the marketing and branding contexts.

Principle: Integrated branding aims at bringing all the components of the brand system together to create a harmonious whole.

Integrated branding is a management philosophy that deals with the problem of bringing all these systems and components together to create a holistic approach to the management of a brand. Brand coherence and integrity exist to the degree that the interaction of the individual pieces and parts is strategically managed as a complex system. Systems thinking is different from other forms of strategic thinking in that it emphasizes the connectedness of components and their resulting interactions (Heylighen et al. 1991). Such an approach contrasts with traditional strategic thinking that attempts to simplify complexity by isolating key variables in order to manage them as independent elements. Systems thinking is a reaction against reductionism and simplification. It takes into account multiple objectives, constraints, resources, agents, risks, and their interrelations.

Since all brand systems are networks, they can be mapped and modeled if the structure of the system can be identified. Typically, marketing structures are modeled using a linear model based on an "input → process control → output" approach. Such thinking tends to ignore the reality of networks and clusters of interactions. The Brand Systems Cube in Figure 1.1 illustrates one way to map the structure of a brand system and its various subsystems. In this figure, each of the six sides of the cube represents a cluster of interrelated activities and relationships. As a holistic representation of branding as a system of networks, the cube depicts the complexity of brand strategy and management. Because each side represents a network or cluster, those activities also can be mapped to identify interactions, as well as the information gaps, between elements in the various systems.

The Agents in the System

In the organization of a company, a brand strategy reflects not just high-level strategies and the vision of senior management, but also the push and pull of other stakeholder interests.

Management

With corporate brands, it is usually the CEO who ultimately gives a focus to the strategy and determines the conditions. At a business level, there are elementary decisions related to management's choice between the use of corporate or individual brands. These decisions are the pivotal premises for the planning of strategic business units (SBUs). A clear choice for full corporate branding means that derivative strategic decisions are usually taken at the top management level.

Corporate leadership and planning departments draw up large plans that give focus to and often entail limitations for the lower levels. Next to this top-down process, there is also a bottom-up process in which opinions and initiatives at lower levels exert an influence on the final brand strategy. In practice, the result is brand planning brought about in consultation between the upper management and the SBU levels.

Companies that have chosen management strategies based on individual brands make decisions at an SBU level. The company's top management only gives frameworks within which this planning is to take place. At Unilever, for example, this strategy is manifest in the guidelines for concentrating development of large brands in the international portfolio. At an SBU level, the decisions are taken on the role of individual brands in the total brand portfolio, and on brand extension measures. Brand managers then implement the strategies at the product level.

It is essential for management strategy choices at the higher levels in the hierarchy to be in harmony. Especially in corporate brands, the brand communication management strategy should be rooted in a deep understanding of the vision of the senior management or C-level executives. In implementing activities at the lower levels, philosophies often arise and programs are developed that may be in conflict with the strategy of the top management. The development of vision and mission statements and their adjustment when needed can help maintain harmony in strategies at the various levels. The problem of conflicting strategies is exacerbated by the practice of using multiple outside agencies at the marketing communication level, all of which want to make their own contributions to strategy development.

Stakeholders

In addition to the managers and strategy developers, other actors are involved in implementing strategies and sharing messages about a brand. A company brand has numerous stakeholder groups—employees, customers, suppliers, distributors and others in the channel, the community, investors and the financial community, the media, regulators and government agencies, activist groups, and others. Each stakeholder group is characterized by its own specific set of interests and values. The most important stakeholder values are the following:

- *Organizational values:* the collective convictions and expectations within the supply-side organization with regard to mutual and common behavior.
- *Employee values:* the individual values of the employees with regard to their personal life and the function of their work in it. What motivates or demotivates them?
- *Leadership values:* What do the top managers find important? What drives them?
- *Shareholder values:* Which values does the brand represent for the shareholders or the financial world in general?
- *Social values:* What does society as a whole find worth striving for or rejecting?
- *Consumer values:* What forces affect how consumers and customers make choices between and among alternative brands?

Campbell and Yeung (1991) found that based on mission statements, company values and their stakeholder focus can be classified into three categories:

- Shareholder values come first: public companies see it as their primary mission to create as high a shareholder value as possible. All decisions are seen in this light. Hanson, a British conglomerate, has the philosophy " The shareholder is king."
- The values of all the stakeholder groups are weighed: the dominance of any one shareholder's value is rejected. In its company principles, Ciba Geigy, for example, stresses four different stakeholder groups:

  - The society and the environment
  - Clients and customers
  - Employees
  - Shareholders

- A high ideal prevails: a common example is the ideal of a better future for humankind, embodied in The Body Shop's guiding principle to make products that are not produced at the expense of animals or the environment.

Strangely enough, in their research Campbell and Yeung did not find companies in which the values of consumers or customers came first. However, the renowned management expert Peter Drucker (in David 1989, 93) made that point when he wrote:

> It is the customer who determines what a business is. It is the customer alone whose willingness to pay for a good or service transforms economic resources into wealth and things into goods. What a business thinks it produces is not of first importance, especially not to the future of the business and to its success. What the customer thinks he/she is buying, what he/she considers value, is decisive—it determines what a business is, what it produces, and whether it will prosper. And what customers buy and value is never a product. It is always utility, meaning what a product or service does for them. The customer is the foundation of a business and keeps it in existence.

Therefore, based on Drucker's reasoning, a fourth category should be added to Campbell and Yeung's three categories of company philosophies:

The Business Balanced Score Card

The business Balanced Score Card (BSC) is becoming increasingly popular for companies in balancing their short- and long-term objectives. Companies adopting the BSC realize that their long-term objectives are not automatically reached by hunting the short-term financial objectives. Certain investments that might reduce short-term profits are encouraged because they serve the longer-term objective of healthy, profitable growth.

The BSC consists of four global perspectives:

1. Financial perspective
2. Customer perspective
3. Business process performance perspective
4. Competence perspective: learning and growth

The financial aspect is considered a "lagging" indicator—it is the result of what has been achieved in the past. Customer satisfaction is also a result from the past, but at the same time is an indication for the future—sales potential, potential price premiums, and new opportunities depend on the perception of the customers. There is a cause-and-effect relationship that can be quantified. Therefore, customer data provide indications of future financial results (or potential). Customer perceptions are caused by process performance. "Process" includes all types of processes—advertisement, production, logistics, sales, quality, and so on. Competences impact process performance by knowledge, leadership, employee motivation, and so on.

From this point of view, competences lead toward process performance, which leads toward customer perception and satisfaction. The financial results are lagging, with a certain time shift. In some cases this time shift can be significant (years), making it more difficult to manage ("check and adjust"). This is one of the benefits of the BSC: shorter feedback loops provide a basis for better controlled processes.

In the design and deployment of the BSC, five key stages can be distinguished:

1. Select critical success factors (CSF) in the four BSC perspectives and explore interrelationships.
2. Identify performance indicators.
3. Set targets.
4. Deploy whole scorecards to sites.
5. Deploy goals within sites.

The BSC provides a measurement tool to evaluate sites and businesses in a balanced way, so it should help to assess improvement opportunities. As such, it is a very useful, advanced way to monitor business performance.

The BSC is not an improvement implementation program. It is the measurement part of the Demming (Plan, Do, Check, and Adjust) Circle. In order to improve performance, structured improvement implementation programs are needed.

Source: Adapted from Kaplan and Norton (1996); Niven (2002); Productivity Factory, www. tpfeurope.com; Value-Based Management, www.valuebasedmanagement.net.

- Consumer values come first: especially with individual brands that are not interwoven with a whole business organization, consumer values are almost always central. McDonald's has summarized its core values in QSC&V (quality, service, cleanliness, and value). Perrier can be summarized as invigorating, healthy, stylish, and French.

From a systems standpoint, the consumer sees a brand as a cluster of experiences that have occurred over time and provide the fragments of impressions that coalesce as a brand image.

Balanced Interests

To balance the interests of the various stakeholder groups, Kaplan and Norton (2000) developed the Balanced Scorecard (see box). This concept is based on the observation that the long-term goals of a company should not depend on the pursuit of short-term profits; a balanced approach is desirable instead. They are right in positing that a client perspective is, in fact, the driving power behind the financial goals of a company. The core of every business strategy is, in their eyes, the proposal of added value to the customer. This is why we propose that a successful brand is dependent upon customer perceptions, as well as management vision.

D'Aveni and Gunther (1994) remark that in the static environment of the 1970s and 1980s, in which sustainable competitive advantages still existed, the tendency arose to subordinate the consumer or customer interest to that of the shareholders. However, in the dynamic environment of more recent decades, there are few competitive advantages to be sustained. Companies that now give the highest priority to shareholder interests risk investing too little in a renewal of competitive advantages that, especially now, have to be found in the motivation and empowerment of personnel. Employees, in other words, may be as important as shareholders in the development of a successful brand. D'Aveni proposes the following order of priorities: the static priorities of shareholders, top managers, personnel, and clients; and the dynamic priorities of clients, personnel, shareholders, and top managers (see Table 1.2).

The value sets of the various stakeholder groups can vary considerably and be in mutual conflict. The top challenge the company faces, then, is creating as much harmony as possible between the expectations of the various stakeholders, given the brand situation. A brand cannot satisfy everyone to the same degree.

There are companies with a very pronounced, distinctive collective value system that resounds in all its manifestations. Such companies make no concessions and follow an explicit inside-out strategy. Examples are The Body Shop, Ikea, Virgin, Nike, Diesel, and Apple. Their pronounced character traits are their strength as well as their weakness. These companies create a bond with people who are attracted to them, but at the same time turn off others. There is almost no possibility of a middle road (May 2000). Other companies have less pronounced values and norms, which are not consciously cultivated internally and thus may not be as well-known as the values of these "superbrands."

With individual brands, values can be more synchronized to consumer needs and wants. The values of these brands should also be matched to the supply-side organization as well. Brand values can never be the sole result of market research and an analytical exercise. All members of the organization have to believe in the values represented by the brand.

External marketing communication has to respect the values that are alive in an organization and linked to a brand. A brand that pretends to have values it does not actually have comes across as phony. External communication, however, can help to revive values that have slipped into the background and become disassociated from the brand.

Table 1.2

Static Versus Dynamic Priorities

Static priorities	Dynamic priorities
1. Shareholders	1. Clients (customers)
2. Top managers	2. Personnel (employees)
3. Personnel (employees)	3. Shareholders
4. Clients (customers)	4. Top managers

Source: D'Aveni (1994).

THE BRAND SYSTEM

Seen from a brand level, we can think of a brand as a system that consists of the physical reality of a brand (e.g., organizations, factories, shops, offices, products, communication, packaging, and the environment where the user encounters the product); the social interpretation of this reality (as depicted by perceptions and attitudes and habits shared within a culture or subculture); and the representation of the mental reality in the form of a brand associative system. On a macro level, a brand system is a holistic system of meaning that consists of physical, mental, and sociocultural components:

1. *Physical nature:* the product, package, marketing communication pieces, identity cues, buildings, trucks, uniforms, and so forth. These communicate the official corporate-determined, or strategic, identity of a brand.
2. *Mental nature:* the representations and meanings associated with the brand and with a customer's brand experiences, as well as the psychology of brand associations that contribute to a customer's internal and individualized brand meaning.
3. *Sociocultural nature:* the cultural context, such as trends, fashions, opinions, values, and attitudes within which a brand and its customers live, and the social context, which includes communication among friends, families, coworkers, and other influencers. A brand also has a set of various stakeholders who affect or are affected by the activities of a brand and also contribute to the brand's meaning. These cultural and social forces impose external meaning on a brand.

In this book, we will approach a brand as a complex phenomenon—a network of interacting systems—that is initiated, steered, and created by manufacturers, and perceived, interpreted, and evaluated by consumers. Although brands are ultimately mental phenomena, their origin is always based on the perception of a physical reality—a product or service—in its broadest sense. Activities started by brand planners to influence directly the representation of the brand in consumers' memories lead to physical stimuli that have to be perceived and mentally processed. When it all comes together, both in presentation and in perception, a brand becomes imbued with meaning.

Principle: The external brand reality is perceived, interpreted, and evaluated by consumers and customers, creating an internal brand perception. Brand strategy development involves both aspects.

Table 1.3

Main Theoretical Concepts in Brand Strategies

Company perspective	Brand reality	Customers/consumers perspective
• Vision/mission (core goal + values)	• Brand core concept	• Consumer expectations (brand functions)
• Strategic positioning	• Physical brand identity	• Brand representation + perceptual positioning
• Brand equity investments	• Market-brand equity	• Consumer brand equity

Brand Theories

In brand theory there are a number of brand concepts and, correspondingly, mental models. Most are personal visions of theoreticians who have succeeded in gathering some degree of following for their concepts. Theoreticians have been dealing with the phenomenon of brands only for a short time, so few concepts are properly crystallized and not many mental models have been sufficiently substantiated with research. We have therefore decided to give an overview of the most important concepts that are relevant to the understanding of brand strategy components—concepts that help explain how brand systems function. Table 1.3 represents both company and consumer perspectives; the middle column represents three factors that define the reality of the brand.

We identify the following three basic concepts that we believe are always present in brand strategies—the critical elements that define the reality of the brand:

- *The brand core concept*: entailing the core meanings of a brand. This is also called the brand essence, the summary of the meaning of a brand in one or several concepts.
- *The physical brand identity*: the all-inclusive concept for all elements in which a brand offers itself for sensory perception and experience, to the degree they answer to the identity criteria of singularity, equality, continuity, and saliency.
- *Market brand equity*: an all-inclusive concept for financial or economic performance of a brand in the market; a standard for the strength of a brand in terms of distribution, penetration, market share, price premium, profit margins, and return on investments.

These three basic concepts can be reinterpreted and rephrased to illustrate the difference between the corporate versus consumer perspectives (or inside-out versus outside-in perspectives). The following "fields of focus" demonstrate the difference in these two parallel perspectives.

The company's perspective includes the following fields of focus:

- *Vision or mission formulation:* determination of the core goal and core values of a brand, as well as the operational functions and goals that should be realized in the longer term.
- *Strategic positioning:* realization of the specific constellation of activities that, in the context of a competitive field, is geared toward transforming the abstract vision into a concrete reality.
- *Brand equity investments:* the quantitative component of brand strategy—making available

the financial means that are deemed necessary for the development of the brand, leading to assessment of its strength and financial value.

The customer's or consumer's perspective includes the following fields of focus:

- *Consumer expectations and brand functions:* identification of the function(s) that a brand fulfills in the lives of customers and consumers; determination of the needs, wants, desires, and values the brand answers or should answer; and the way the brand's promise delivers on those needs and wants.
- *Perceptual positioning:* the development of a brand representation or image in the memory of consumers or customers, the classification of a brand into a category or subcategory of other brands based on their common meanings, and the distinctiveness of this brand and its competitors within that category based on different associations.
- *Consumer brand equity:* the strength of a brand in the perception and behavior of consumers through which they include it in their purchasing repertoire and the brand acquires a certain share of their expenditures in the category (share of wallet).

Brand Strategy Concepts

To better understand how branding works, let us first identify the key brand strategy concepts that operate as components in a branding system. Brand concepts are generalized mental constructions in which the main characteristics of a perceived phenomenon are brought together and given a label, such as a brand name. These are the fragments of brand impressions that coalesce to create a brand perception.

It is clear from a review of the brand literature that a brand has multiple components and features. Furthermore, various writers use common, as well as proprietary terms to describe these components. It is also clear that there is a great deal of confusion in the use of these terms. Various writers using the same terms are not referring to the same concepts; in other words, the same term is used to mean two different things and the opposite is also true—various writers use different terms to refer to the same concept. For example, consider brand identity and brand image.

Brand identity is a critical brand concept, one that has a dual meaning. The strictest and most literal meaning refers to the physical identification cues used to make a brand distinct and recognizable in the marketplace. This is the meaning found in the American Marketing Association definition of a brand that we referred to earlier in the chapter: a name, term, design, symbol that identifies one seller's good or service as distinct from those of other sellers. These identity signals, which are usually trademarkable, include such elements as the name and how it is presented as a logo (Coca-Cola's script), distinctive graphics (Altoid's layout that looks like its distinctive metal box package), color (IBM and the color blue), distinctive music (NBC's three notes), and characters (Jolly Green Giant, Maytag's lonely repairman). These cues signal a brand identity as they are learned over time by consumers.

These are the standard elements managed in a brand or corporate identity program, and a company has complete control over how they are presented. The consumer does have a role, however, in perceiving identity. From the reception viewpoint, identity comes with awareness and knowledge of these signs and leads to recognition, which is a learned cognitive response by the customer or stakeholder. But still, the establishment of the identity is a corporate responsibility.

On another level, some brand experts also use the phrase *brand identity* to refer to a deeper level of brand meaning. Kapferer, for example, says that "a brand is a symbol, word, object, and concept—all at one and the same time" (1992, 149). But other brand experts propose to extend the meaning of identity to include not just the recognition cues but also the larger social and psychological meaning of the brand with all of its associations, emotions, experiential, and cognitive dimensions. This deeper meaning, the core values, character, or essence of a brand, is what Upshaw (1995) refers to when they use the term *brand identity*. However, that expansion of the meaning of brand identity causes some confusion because it overlaps with other common branding terms, such as brand image, brand personality, and brand meaning.

Consider how this broader use of brand identity relates to *brand image*. The concept of "image" was borrowed from psychology in the middle of the twentieth century to indicate the total mental picture or impression of a brand in the consumer's mind. What it means in practice, however, is somewhat unclear (see Franzen and Bouwman 2001). In contrast to Kapferer and Upshaw, this deeper level of brand meaning is what the AMA refers to in its definition of *brand image*, which it describes as "the perception of a brand in the minds of persons." The definition continues: "The image is a mirror reflection (though perhaps inaccurate) of the brand personality or product being. It is what people believe about a brand—their thoughts, feelings, expectations."

Some marketing experts criticize the idea of brand image as a superficial or shallow facade. The problem comes from the interchangeable use of the phrases *brand identity* and *brand image* for this deeper level of meaning, as well as the resistance by some to the idea of image-building as a manipulation of consumer perceptions.

A common view is that consumers select brands on the basis of an image or impression, and thus brand strategy is essentially building or cuing this image. Combining the two concepts of identity and image, a definition emerges of a brand as a way to identify a product, organize a consumer's experiences with the product, and, if successful, build a long-term relationship between the brand and the consumer. It works on two levels: first is the identification function and second is the creation of the meaning, or image, of the brand.

> *Principle:* Brand image is the generalized perception of a brand in people's minds.

As managers rush to create and strengthen their brands in hotly competitive markets, it is important to anchor the basic branding concepts with more carefully defined meanings. *Brand identity* and *brand image* are only two of the buzz words that are used and confused by brand experts and brand managers. Consider the following list of branding terms, which was compiled from a list of current books on branding by major authors in the field:

brand architecture	brand culture
brand asset	brand differentiation
brand associations	brand equity
brand awareness	brand essence
brand character	brand extension
brand charisma	brand focus
brand contract	brand function
brand core, brand core concept	brand loyalty
brand covenant	brand mantra

brand meaning
brand mission
brand perception
brand personalty
brand physique
brand picture
brand portfolio
brand position
brand power
brand promise
brand relationships

brand reputation
brand saliency
brand segmentation
brand soul
brandsphere
brand strength
brand value
brand values
brand vision
brandwidth

It is pretty obvious that this list of brand concepts is a collection of apples and oranges, in that they represent different dimensions of branding. In order to systematize brand strategy, we need a semantic logic that sorts out these concepts and groups them based on their related dimensions in order to identify the key components that must be considered by brand managers. A content analysis of these terms leads to the emergence of a simple organizational structure. This logic is as follows:

- *Nature or deep structure:* core concept, essence, soul, character, core, vision;
- *Strategy (intention):* identity, function, mission, focus, segmentation, differentiation, position, promise, culture;
- *Meaning (perception):* awareness, function, image, associations, personality, position, charisma, picture, values, culture;
- *Relationship:* reputation, covenant, promise, contract;
- *Structure:* architecture, physique, extensions, portfolio, brandwidth, brandsphere;
- *Power or leadership:* strength, saliency, equity, loyalty.

Deconstructing the Branding Lingo

There are hundreds of books and articles on branding. Here is a collection of books whose authors make a special effort to sort out the concepts of branding and articulate the meaning of various common, as well as proprietary, terms. These books were consulted in the search for key brand concepts:

Aaker, D. 1991. *Managing Brand Equity.* New York: Free Press.
———. 1996. *Building Strong Brands.* New York: Free Press.
———. 2004. *Brand Portfolio Strategy.* New York: Free Press.
Aaker, D., and R. Joachimsthaler. 2000. *Brand Leadership.* New York: Free Press.
Bedbury, S. 2003. *A New Brand World.* New York: Penguin.
Chernatony, L.D. 2001. *From Brand Vision to Brand Evaluation.* Oxford, UK: Butterworth Heinemann.
Davis, S. 1995. *Brand Asset Management.* San Francisco: Jossey-Bass.
Franzen, G., and M. Bouwman. 2001. *The Mental World of Brands.* Henley-on-Thames, UK: World Advertising Research Center.
Gobé, M. 2001. *Emotional Branding.* Garsington, UK: Windsor Books.
Gronstedt, A. 2000. *The Customer Century.* New York: Routledge.
Ind, N. 1997. *The Corporate Brand.* London, UK: Macmillan.
———. 2001. *Living the Brand.* London, UK: Kogan Page.
Kapferer, J.N. 1992. *Strategic Brand Management.* New York: Free Press.

Keller, K.L. 2003. *Strategic Brand Management.* 2nd ed. Upper Saddle River, NJ: Prentice Hall.

Kunde, J. 2000. *Corporate Religion.* Harlow, UK: Pearson Education.

LePla, F.J., S.V. Davis, and L.M. Parker. 2003. *Brand Driven.* London: Kogan Page.

Lindstrom, M. 2005. *Brand Sense.* New York: Free Press.

Macrae, C. 1991. *World Class Brands.* Workingham, UK: Addison-Wesley.

———. 1996. *The Brand Chartering Handbook.* Harlow, UK: Addison-Wesley.

Rust, R.T., V.A. Zeithaml, and K.N. Lemon. 2000. *Driving Customer Equity.* New York: Free Press.

Taylor, D. 2003. *The Brand-Gym.* Chichester, UK: John Wiley.

———. 2003. *The Brand-Stretch.* Chichester, UK: John Wiley.

Temporal, P. 2002. *Advanced Brand Management.* Singapore: John Wiley.

Upshaw, L. 1995. *Building Brand Identity.* New York: John Wiley.

Weilbacher, W. 1993. *Brand Marketing.* Lincolnwood, IL: NTC Business Books.

Wreden, N. 2005. *Profit Brand.* London: Kogan Page.

The Primary Components of a Brand System

Looking specifically at a brand as a complex system, we can identify certain key brand components from the brand logic that emerged as a result of the analysis of brand concepts and detail their relationships in order to construct a model of the brand system. Note that this list of components also recognizes the difference in perspective between the corporate view of a brand and the consumer's view. Furthermore, it recognizes the role of brand cues—what the company uses as devices to signal various aspects of brand meaning, meanings that come to exist in the consumer's mind. This is the point of interplay between the intended meaning and the perceived meaning of the brand.

- Brand strategy (the company perspective)
- Brand functions
- Brand core concept
- Brand identity strategy
- Brand segmentation strategy
- Brand strategy meets brand perception
- Brand differentiation and positioning strategy
- Consumer needs and values
- Brand personality
- Brand meaning: image, function, culture
- Brand relationships: reputation
- Brand equity: expansion and integration
- Brand strength: saliency
- Brand span and brand extensions
- Brand portfolio and architecture strategy
- Consumer brand equity
- Market brand equity
- Brand financial value
- Brand integration: The brand as *gesamtkunstwerk*, a work of art whose components relate perfectly and synergistically to one another, creating brand integrity.

The brand components on this list will be addressed later in the book, with specific chapters on each topic. Figure 1.2, which is a model of how branding works, details the components of the brand system.

Figure 1.2 **How Branding Works**

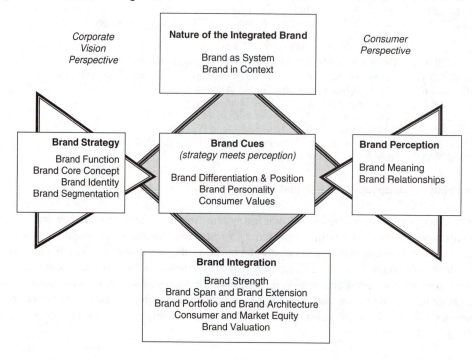

Applying the Concepts of Branding

Brand strategy, which is the subject of Chapter 4, involves weighing the importance of the various brand components and deciding which are most relevant to the particular marketing situation. Every strategy development is a question of defining the repertoire of brand components that are most critical to the brand system. James Moore (1993, 76) explains: "Business communities, unlike biological communities of co-evolving organisms, are social systems. And social systems are made up of real people who make decisions; the largest patterns are maintained by a complex network of choices, which depend, at least in part, on what participants are aware of. As Gregory Bateson (1991) notes, changing the ideas in a social system, changes the system itself.

In practice, all elements are seldom of equal concern. The limitation of cognitive capacities plays a role here. It is impossible to weigh a large number of elements in working memory. Besides, the relevance of an element is not always clear; there are often things that cannot be known. Therefore, strategy development for a complex brand system has the character of repertoire choice and issue management, as it takes place on the basis of a limited, often reduced number of critical components and their relationships.

Similar to systems thinking, strategic management is like steering a truck or piloting a ship or plane. In the management process, steering powers are executed by influential actors—pilots, drivers, or brand managers—and the management process is defined by the situation. Put simply, a small number of people determine what is under discussion, what is taken as a given, what gets attention, what is believed, and thus which strategic framework drives the operation of a brand system. This group of people itself is part of the "brand system," often the most influential part.

Brand strategy development can therefore never consist of a simple set of standardized rules that are applied all the time and everywhere. There will always have to be objective identification of the issues that are important, given the specific brand in its specific context and marketing situation. It will also be necessary to consider the contexts within which a strategy is developed, becomes accepted, gets support, and ultimately recruits commitment. The role of context, therefore, is the topic of the next chapter as it provides the framework within which brand strategy development takes place.

THE DIESEL BRAND AS A SYSTEM

Systems thinking provides a philosophical foundation for understanding how knowledge is organized and managed in complex settings. Branding is an example of a complex set of activities, programs, strategies, decisions, agents, and stakeholders, as well as the interrelationships among them.

The opening story about Diesel illustrates how these marketing complexities can be managed as a total brand system. Under the guidance of its founder, Renzo Rosso, Diesel has developed a highly coordinated brand management approach that is global in scope. The marketing mix, including centralized production and complex distribution logistics, delivers on the brand promise of innovation and creativity. The retail spaces communicate the personality of the brand, as do the advertising, catalogs, Web site, and other novel communication contact points, such as video games.

In terms of interacting systems, Diesel exhibits an understanding of various stakeholders and their needs—employees, designers, customers, suppliers, distributors, and retailers. The brand is governed by a specific sense of style relevant to fashion-conscious, but independent thinkers. The design system is reflected in a full line of fashion products supported by a broad distribution system that reaches across five continents. The marketing communication is a system of image-building activities anchored by catalogs and edgy advertising that project a unified Diesel vision and style.

The Diesel brand represents a single borderless culture, one that is a good example of a brand managed as a system of interconnected components and interactions.

BRANDING IN CONTEXT

Chapter 1 discussed the brand as a system, but it is important to remember that every brand strategy is developed within a context that impacts brand decisions. As Macrae explains in his *Brand Chartering Handbook* (1996, 207), "All branding and leadership decisions need to be context specific." He points to two factors that contribute to a strong brand, both depending upon an ability to monitor and respond to environmental factors. The first is providing leadership in world-class quality and value and the second is marshalling local buy-in and feedback on consumer relationships and the brand's business development (205).

The environment in which powerful brands emerge is not a system—at least not one that can be controlled, but rather a set of specific forces that restrict brand operations or create brand development opportunities. The environment is a controlling influence that limits the activities of the system and also provides expansion opportunities.

It is not possible for companies to ignore developments in the wider business community, such as the advent of the Internet or the concentration of retail outlets and the enormous influence these can have on the brand system itself. As Naumann (1995) explains in *Creating Customer Value*, "Virtually every aspect of the business environment is experiencing accelerating change, particularly the consumers, customers, technology, and globalization of markets." Companies have to look not only at developments within the direct competitive surroundings, but also at the changes and forces outside the brand's "world of consumption," such as those illustrated in the following story about the revitalization of the Lego brand.

LEGENDARY LEGO®: BACK TO BRICKS

Ole Kirk Christiansen was a carpenter in Billund, Denmark, who opened a woodworking shop in 1916. In 1932 he started to make wooden toys, which brought him moderate success. In 1934 he dubbed his business Lego, a contraction of the Danish words *leg* and *godt*. *Leg godt* means "play well" in Danish.

When plastics came into widespread use, Lego bought the first plastic injection-molding machine in Denmark to make toys. In 1949 Lego began manufacturing toy bricks made of cellulose acetate with four protrusions on the top and a hollow bottom. In 1953 these were renamed Lego Bricks and the brand Lego was officially registered. In 1958 the stud-and-tube configuration of the Lego brick was invented and patented.

After the founder died in 1958, Godtfred Kirk succeeded him. He formed a team to design new sets of bricks—the beginning of a continuous release of exciting new Lego sets during the decades that followed. In 1961 Lego wheels and a new plastic, ABS, which was more stable, held colors better, and was nontoxic, were introduced.

Introducing new line after line, the Lego company became much larger. Lego sets included building instructions, train sets, larger Duplo bricks, tow trucks, police cars, fire engines, floating boats, and doll houses. In 1968 the first Legoland Park was opened in Billund, Lego's hometown. Since then Lego has made many leaps forward. In 1977 the Expert Builder range was launched, with special elements such as gears, joints, beams, and pegs that allowed users to build complex, realistic models.

In 1984 the first pocket computer games came into the market and managed to immediately cut Lego's worldwide sales by 30 percent. Despite this clear warning, Lego did not change its strategy. For more than twenty years the plastic bricks had remained basically unchanged in the face of competition from Playmobile, Tyco, Matchbox, and later PlayStation, Nintendo, and Sega.

Kids no longer considered it cool to play with Legos; and over the years the Lego brand name had become absolutely synonymous with "plastic bricks." To compensate for the lost sales, Lego did what many companies in similar situations had tried before—mostly with mixed results: it began to diversify. It introduced children's clothing, computer games, children's books, and opened new Legoland amusement parks in California, England, and Germany. Most of the new ventures did not match Lego's one-dimensional brick image.

Lego was also caught off-guard by the rapid acceleration of globalization in the 1990s. In the late 1970s its last patents expired, and Mega Bloks, a Canadian company, immediately took advantage of this, producing its blocks in Asia at a fraction of the costs of Lego in Denmark. The growth of discount retailers, such as Wal-Mart, and the decline of specialized toy shops also had a negative influence on Lego sales and margins.

In 1996 SPV Darwin was established to develop software related to Lego products. In 1997 Lego attempted to recapture market share by introducing the first Lego CD-ROM with building instructions. But it was a bit too little and much too late. Lego's staff was drastically reduced from 5,000 in Billund in 1998 to 2,400 in 2006 and to an estimated 1,500 in 2009. In 1999 LEGO made its first-ever loss with 48.5 million euros in the red. In 2000 losses more than doubled. In 2004 they amounted to 259 million euros. Lego had a real problem.

"Getting into the clothing and publishing businesses was a mistake and it contributed to Lego losing its direction," said company director Kjeld Christiansen, grandson of the Lego founder, in 2001. "We lost focus. Lego will introduce the basic brick and toy-parts concept to the universe of IT." The company sold its theme parks, teamed up with Microsoft, and introduced an interactive CD-ROM series based on the *Harry Potter*, *Star Wars*, *Jurassic Park* stories and Mindstorms, a popular line of robot tool kits. But the new ventures did not yet stop the bleeding.

Hope is now focused on Lego Digital Designer, a piece of free software that lets children create their own three-dimensional models, and on Lego Factory, which allows them to share their personal designs with the world and order the bricks to build custom models. The Digital Designer Web site attracted 1 million visitors in 2004. "We have 100 designers in-house," says Lizbeth Pallesen, a Lego spokesperson. "Maybe we should have 300,000 designers who don't work for Lego. The company should be run by consumers."

In 2004 Jörgen Vif Knudstorp, a former McKinsey consultant, took over as CEO. He started to cut 3,500 jobs in Billund alone, outsource manufacturing to cheaper locales in Eastern Europe, and cut the number of "elements." In 2005 Lego made a moderate profit again and in 2006 and 2007 its profit further expanded. New games built around Batman, *Star Wars* movies, and Ferrari race cars seemed to be connecting with children again. But Lego's more traditional games still generate about two-thirds of sales, with the traditional Lego City Line as the most popular series. "Lego is a niche product, with 2% to 3% of the global toy market. Our vision is based on the Lego brick—that is our heritage and our future," says Knudstorp.

Lego customers are, in fact, very much involved in the company through Lugnuts, the international fan-created Lego Users Group Network, where Lego enthusiasts of all ages find information, meet each other, and share ideas. The Web site, www.lugnet.com, is also a valuable source of customer information for the company, and this level of fan support and participation is a good sign for the company's future.

Source: www.lego.com; "Lego Legends in the Making," *Business Week Online*, August 24, 2005; Spencer Ante, "For Lego, An Online Lifeline?" *Business Week Online*, August 23, 2005; "Is Lego Losing Out to Computers?" *BBC News*, April 12, 2005, http://news.bbc.co.uk/go/pr/fr//2/hi/uk_news/magazine/4434057. stm; Schwartz (2006b); F. Baltesen, "Een futuristische politie-auto verkoopt niet," *NRC Handelsblad*, December 2, 2006.

THE BROADER CONTEXT OF BRANDING: THE EXCHANGE BETWEEN A BRAND SYSTEM AND ITS ENVIRONMENT

The environment surrounding a marketing effort is as complex as the marketing program itself, with a network of forces that creates both opportunities and threats for the brand. The Lego story illustrates the difficulties one high-flying toy manufacturer faced in trying to keep up with the changing tastes of its customers, as well as competitive actions and serious threats brought on by technological change.

The situations within which brands are created, distributed, purchased, and used provide the environmental context. Four basic situational contexts surround the brand: the product category, the company, its network of suppliers and distributors, and consumers. These four context parameters define the boundaries of brand strategy and create a set of mandates:

- No brand can exist independently of its product category.
- No brand can exist independently of its company producer (source).
- No brand can exist independently of its suppliers and distributors.
- No brand can exist independently of its customers.

Principle: No brand can exist independently of its category, company, suppliers and distributors, and buyers.

Similar to the exchange concept in marketing, there is an exchange between a system and its environment. This can be related to material, means and agents, and information. The exchange influences the system, as well as the environment. The core idea of a dynamic system is that an entire entity can and must adjust itself and survive in a changed environment. Thus, many brand systems must adjust in order to survive in the dynamic business environment of today.

In his book *Brandscendence*, Clark (2004, 17) identifies three stages in which brands interact with their environment. The reflective nature of brand strategy changes to become adaptive and then dominating as a brand gains strength within its category.

- *Stage 1:* The brand reflects its surroundings and reacts to the environment.
- *Stage 2:* The brand proactively adapts itself to the world to increase its success.
- *Stage 3:* The brand projects itself to the world and changes the environment.

Developments in the world, the market, and with consumers have forced brands to be more flexible, alert, nimble, and interactive. Rigid brand systems jeopardize their own chances of survival. For example, the big cigarette brands are finding ways to adapt to a consumer population that is becoming more concerned about health issues. In the United States, there is much less advertising to recruit new smokers and, instead, more emphasis on database programs that keep the brands connected with their loyal customers. That adaptation process has also meant focusing more marketing efforts on countries and parts of the world where the health concerns have not surfaced. However, as consumers become more informed, inevitably the health issue will spread even to third-world countries. So the cigarette brands will have to continue to adapt to this long-term negative force that affects their business plans.

Principle: Changes in a brand's context means it has to be flexible, alert, nimble, and interactive in order to adapt to the new environment

---

Adjustment to a changed environment, such as Lego faced, needs a feedback process that informs the system about the reactions of the environment. Adequate processing of and reaction to this feedback is vital to the system and integral to the development of adaptation strategies for a brand. That is why many large companies employ futurists either on the staff or as consultants. Their learning is a source of predictions about change that is fed back into the strategy development process.

One problem in analyzing the environmental context of branding is how a brand system's boundaries can be delimited so that its behavior can be understood. To specify a system, however, requires that the brand system be distinguished from its environmental system. That can sometimes be difficult because domains of control and effect overlap.

THE BRAND'S ENVIRONMENT

The "environment" is a very broad concept, within which we can distinguish between the macroenvironment, the microenvironment, and the internal environment of the brand (Kotler 2003). These are depicted in Figure 2.1.

The Brand's Macroenvironment

The macroenvironment includes eight networks of external forces, all of which can impact upon a brand strategy:

Figure 2.1   **The Environment of Branding**

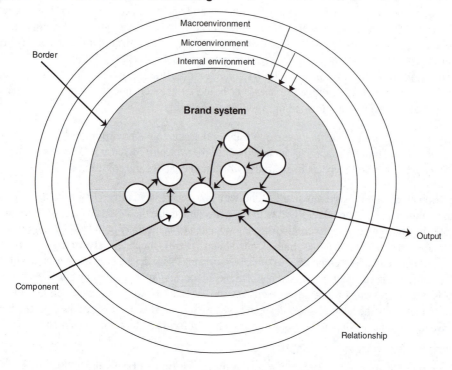

1. *Demographic:* trends in size and composition of the population.
2. *Natural:* availability of natural resources; developments in the natural environment.
3. *Technological:* development of new technological know-how and resources; speed of these developments.
4. *Economic:* economic developments; personal income; income distribution; buying-power.
5. *Political and legal:* political developments; legislation; influence of pressure groups.
6. *Ecological:* effects of production and consumption on the environment.
7. *Cultural and social:* development of values, perceptions, attitudes, and behaviors in the society.
8. *Communicative:* development of media availability and media usage in the society.

Not all developments influence every individual brand, but the fate of most brands is at least partly dependent on a combination of these macrodevelopments. Thus, companies have to constantly monitor the macroenvironmental forces (see Figure 2.2), which represent both opportunities and threats.

The technological context, for example, has been an important factor in marketing since the Industrial Revolution and its introduction of mechanization to production of all kinds. One of the first major brands was Procter & Gamble's Ivory Soap, which in 1837 took the lump of soap out of a grocer's barrel and put it on a shelf wrapped in a pristine package. Eventually its label proclaimed its technological superiority to other types of soap: "99 and 44/100ths percent pure"—so pure that it floats. In 2005 Ivory is still the market leader in the soap market in the United States.

Other important technical advances, such as electricity, railroads and airplanes, telephones,

Figure 2.2 **The Macroenvironment**

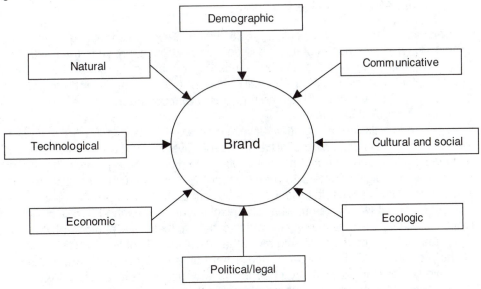

computers, and the Internet, have followed, each one affecting the production, marketing, and branding of products. Big brands have come and gone or adapted to survive in a new world of changing technology, as the Lego story illustrates. As a result of digitalization, Polaroid went bankrupt, and Kodak is having great difficulty adapting itself.

Principle: Brand managers need a good understanding of the developments in the macroenvironment of the brand.

Economic forces are just as important as technological ones in understanding the context within which a brand system operates. Railroad companies in the United States lost their way because of advances in other forms of transportation. Subsequently, the high-flying airline industry has been dragged down by costs and pricing strategies, leading to the loss of major carriers such as TWA and Pan Am. The major carriers like United, British Airways, and Delta struggle to balance their books given the inroads of low-cost carriers like Easy Jet, Southwest, and Ryan Air and the recessionary events of the early years of the twenty-first century.

Political action can also negatively or positively affect brands—for example, when a company wins a major government contract. When the rebuilding of the oil industry in Iraq was given to Halliburton (the company formerly headed by U.S. vice president Richard Cheney), that company's fortunes rose along with all its suppliers and other partners. The solar industry in the United States, which was a promising growth industry in the 1960s, was totally devastated when the government eliminated the tax credits that had subtly motivated consumers to consider alternative energy.

The ecological environment is another issue that became a force in marketing in the late twentieth century. Consumer and governmental concerns about pollution, water and air quality, and other types

Kodak From Pictures to Pixels

The history of Kodak goes back to 1888, when George Eastman put the first simple camera in the hands of a world of consumers. Since that year, the Eastman Kodak Company has created an abundance of products and processes to make photography "as convenient as a pencil." It became the absolute world leader in photographic film and one of the leading camera manufacturers. In the late 1990s it employed 130,000 people.

In 1975 one of its young engineers developed the first digital camera that captured a black-and-white image on a digital cassette tape. Over the next two decades Kodak received 1,000 patents on technologies related to digital photography, although it never moved a digital camera to market. In 1981 Sony launched the first digital camera, the Mavica. It could produce images with up to 60,000 pixels. Sales were modest for about twenty years, when the pixel count had reached 5 million. But a majority of Kodak's middle managers could not believe that digital photography would supersede film, since they still sold more than 1 billion rolls of film in 1999.

Its previous CEO, Daniel Carp, had a hard time convincing them that digital technology would fundamentally change the way people take and use pictures. Consumers can take as many photographs as they want, see them immediately, manipulate them on their computer, print them at home, and send them to their friends by e-mail. As soon as consumers began to understand these higher intrinsic values, they bade farewell to their suddenly outdated film cameras.

In 1999, 5.5 million digital cameras were sold worldwide. In 2004 this number had exploded to 53 million units. Kodak had totally underestimated the speed at which digital technology spread around the globe. It took Kodak twenty-six years to introduce its first digital camera in 2001. It met a number of newcomers that had entered the camera market with a succession of new sophisticated models—Sony, Hewlett Packard, Panasonic, and Samsung, for example—next to the traditional camera brands, such as Canon and Nikon. The competition was so fierce that in 2005 reputable brands such as Minolta and Konica decided to get out of the camera market altogether. Kodak had hoped that developing countries, such as China and India, would first use the traditional film camera and then switch to digital cameras. The truth is that these consumers chose digital cameras right from the start. About one-quarter of Kodak's consumer film business was disappearing each year.

Kodak still is in a difficult position. It is closing down factories and laying off tens of thousands of workers, having reduced its workforce to 51,000 in 2006. At the same time it is working hard to develop and strengthen its position in the digital world. Kodak managed to capture third place in the worldwide market of digital cameras in 2005, after Canon and Sony. It entered the markets of inkjets, picture frames and professional digital photo printing systems. In 2005 digital sales made up 54 percent of its total revenue which still continued to drop however, by 3 percent in 2007. Its C.E.O. since 2006, Antonio Perez said in an interview: "The dream when we started was that we will wake up in 2008 with a digital company that we wanted and we are very close to that." Carp estimated that the transformation process might have cost Kodak as much as $16 billion.

Perez now aims to make Kodak do for photo's what Apple does for music: help people to organize and manage their personal libraries for images. Its like reinventing the company. It is still far from clear how Kodak's story will play out.

Source: www.kodak.com; *Digital Tech News*, "Kodak's Future of Digital Photography and Imaging," January 7, 2006, www.digitaltechnews.com/news/2006/01/kodaks_future_o.html; B. Dobbin, "Kodak's Future," *Cincinnati Post*, October 22, 2005; B. Dobbin, "Eastman Kodak to Wrap Up 4 Year Overhaul this Year," Associated Press, February 2008; "Kodak: Mistakes Made on the Road to Innovation," September 2007, www.businessweek.com; "A Tense Kodak Moment," October 2005, www.businessweek.com.

of ecological impact forced companies to reconsider many of their business practices. Combining environmental concerns with political action, the Green Party became a major political force in northwestern Europe, where brands are now much more likely to proclaim their environmental sensitivity.

The cultural and social contexts, which are seen in the macroenvironment, are particularly important for brand strategy, and these will be developed in more depth after this discussion of macro, micro, and internal forces.

The Brand's Microenvironment

The microenvironment of a brand consists of all the specific stakeholder groups the brand is dependent on, which is determined by the specific product category within which the brand is marketed. Let us consider first the stakeholders, then the product category.

The interests, perceptions, opinions, attitudes, and behaviors of the various groups that have a stake in a brand's success influence the development of the brand's sales and market position. Corporate brands, in particular, are dependent on a large number of groups with very different and often conflicting interests. The following networks of markets and stakeholders are crucial:

1. *Labor market:* availability of labor with the necessary qualifications; position of the brand versus its competitors in this market.
2. *Financial market:* developments in the financial market and among its constituents—stock market, banks, investors, venture capitalists, and middlemen; position of the corporate brand with these groups.
3. *Suppliers:* developments among suppliers whose cooperation is essential for the brand's success.
4. *Trade channels:* developments in the distribution structure and in the relative power of the players in the distribution systems.
5. *Governmental bodies:* the legislative, managerial, and controlling bodies on the international, national, regional, and local levels that occupy themselves with the brand's behavior.
6. *Nongovernmental organizations:* the international, national, and local organizations that concern themselves with the field(s) in which the brand operates.
7. *Market and competition:* definition of the domains and domain developments; identification of competitors and their relative strategic positions and developments.
8. *Customers or consumers:* needs, values, perceptions, and attitudes; behavior of (potential) buyers of the category, and the trends in this behavior.

Within the microenvironment, the trade channels are a force of special importance which has a large influence on the brand's distribution possibilities. Both the producer and the distributors

Figure 2.3   **A Brand's Microenvironment** (Stakeholders)

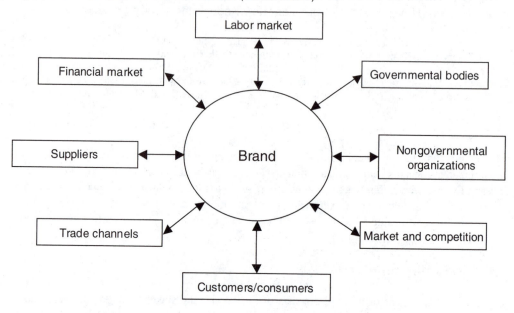

must have the same understanding about the nature of the brand and its strength so they are both able to judge its appropriateness for specific distribution channels.

Brand systems are linked with one another by a common domain. Such domains are most commonly known as *product categories*, which often include a set of levels or subcategories. For example, the restaurant category includes both sit-down restaurants and fast-food places. These groupings are important when the execution of one specific system influences the behavior of another. For example, the development of a brand of tea can be influenced by that of a brand of mineral water. Both brand systems fall within the domain of thirst quenchers.

This category domain can in turn be seen as a system that is located at a higher level in the hierarchy, producing a link between different systems—such a sum of linked systems can be seen as a system in itself. An example is the emergence of a new category from the merging of two existing categories, as was the case with Lipton Iced Tea and its identification with tea and flavored mineral water. Managers who identify the competitors have to take a broad view—they should be aware of the different levels of categories.

Principle: Brand managers need a broad view of the market and awareness of different levels of categories in order to identify the real competitors.

The Brand's Internal Environment

The development of brands is to a large extent dependent on the characteristics and resources of the organization itself. Of course, this applies especially to corporate brands, but the destiny of individual brands is also dependent on a company's qualities. An accurate analysis of these qualities is a pre-

Figure 2.4 **The Brand's Internal Environment**

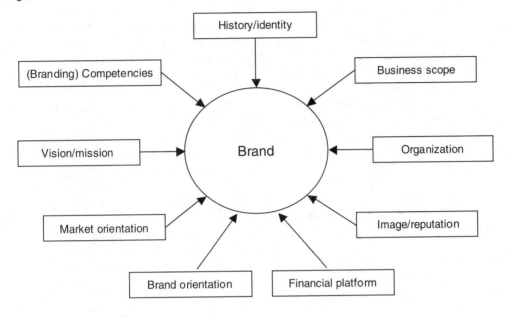

requisite for effective brand management. On a highly abstract level, we can distinguish a number of important company attributes that influence the development of its brands and their position:

1. *History and identity:* the origins of the company and the role and legacy of its founders; the "corporate DNA" and the company's self-image.
2. *Competencies and brand orientation:* the company's strengths and weaknesses; its know-how and core competences, especially its brand orientation.
3. *Vision and mission:* the company's reason for existing; its contribution to society; its long-term view; its operational goals and strategies.
4. *Market orientation:* the company's commitment to the implementation of its marketing philosophy; placement of the customer in the center of its beliefs; dedication to the continuous creation of superior customer values; consideration of the competences and strategies of its competitors.
5. *Brand orientation:* the company's abilities in and dedication to the creation and development of strong brands, with the aim to foster their brand equity; establishment of its brands as the hub around which its strategic processes circle.
6. *Business scope:* the relative size of the company (leader, challenger, or follower); its growth strategy; its geographical coverage.
7. *Organization:* the company's degree of centralization or decentralization; its power structure; its locus of branding responsibility; its marketing organization.
8. *Image and reputation:* the company's image with the different stakeholder groups; its reputation in important areas of activity.
9. *Financial platform:* the assets of the company, physical as well as intangible; financial goals; financial performance.

Clearly, the boundaries between a system and its environment are not easy to delineate, as the people in any given example are sometimes also part of a brand system, or part of the internal context, or both. In the case of Heineken, for example, Founder Alfred Heineken may well have been the most essential component of the "Heineken system," since his initiatives and views for many decades have determined everything that has happened to the brand. The same applies to many founders of successful companies, who usually have very outspoken views on the world at large and their product domain in particular, and who continue to mold their organization according to their own visions. Some brands have become almost synonymous with their founders, as is the case with Richard Branson of Virgin and Steve Jobs of Apple.

A factor of special importance in the internal environment is the brand orientation of a company—the degree to which a brand is seen as the strategic hub around which all processes of a company are being managed, with the aim of giving the brand meaning and value. That was the central issue in the Martha Stewart headlines about her jail sentence—the association with the person built the brand, but the connection could also destroy the brand if the person's problems splash distrust all over the brand reputation.

In companies with a high level of brand orientation, the brand becomes a symbol in its ongoing interaction with its environment rather than a mere identifier for its offerings. Research among the 260 largest Swedish companies showed that the companies with a strong brand orientation on average generated a profit (earnings before interest, taxes, depreciation, and amortization) almost twice that of the companies with a low degree of brand orientation (Melin 2005).

CULTURAL CONTEXT

We identified cultural and social factors as part of the macroenvironment. We will discuss both of them here in more detail because they are so important to brand strategy development, as well as to consumers' brand perceptions.

The Cultural Environment

Culture is defined by Hofstede (1991) as the collective spirit of a group of people that distinguishes them from other groups of people. A culture is a way of living that distinguishes one group of people from another; it is learned and passed on from one generation to another by family, school, and religious organizations. Values and attitudes, along with language and religion, form the core of a culture. The process of growing up as citizens, of becoming "acculturated," takes place in constant interaction with a person's surroundings, not only the natural physical environment, but also a specific cultural and social environment—the society, group, family, organization, and so on, that a person belongs to. This constant interaction with others influences the construction of every person's individual reality and affects how people relate to other people, as well as to products and brands.

Principle: Culture is the collective programming of the spirit through which the members of one group distinguish themselves from other groups and determine how they relate to products and brands.

Culture is a force deep in the psyche of a consumer; however, people contribute on a daily basis to building the world of which they are part. All human activity is subject to habit, and anything that is repeated regularly becomes a specific pattern—a type of cultural knowledge that gives order to our everyday activities. (We also call this a schema, which is a learned pattern of behavior or way of thinking.) Such a pattern provides stability and direction in the complex world of possible choices, resulting in psychological peace of mind. These habits belong to the history and fixed expectation patterns of a (sub)culture and underlie such varied phenomena as emotional displays, food preferences, architecture, graphic design styles, musical tastes, art appreciation, and fashion.

A simple everyday example of the behavioral indications of acculturation is what occurs when you have an appointment to meet with someone. What do you do first? You shake hands and introduce yourself. This is a habit no one in the Western world would give a second thought to. Nonetheless, there are countless other ways to greet people, such as bowing. People follow such a behavior pattern not so much because it works, but because in the culture they grew up in they were taught that these things are proper. Likewise, brand messages have different ways of greeting people depending upon the culture within which they are offered. Some advertisements, for example, address their audience directly, even using personal pronouns. This is particularly prevalent in a U.S. message format known as "hard sell." Advertisements in other cultures, such as Japan, may be more oblique and subtle.

Cultural conventions determine how appropriate attitudes and behaviors are learned—the process through which a person becomes acculturated. People are cultural beings who grow up with a cultural fluency that lets them navigate their own culture or subcultures or become part of the counterculture if they strive to live outside their mainstream. Advertising usually signals this cultural orientation by either presenting mainstream values (Rolex as a status symbol) or flaunting counterculture styles and nuances of meaning (grunge fashions for skateboarders and snowboarders).

From a marketing perspective, culture is what determines wants—the way people define their needs. Wants are culturally based and are shaped by the environment in which people live and grow up. People in some cultures, such as Korea, may eat the meat of dogs and horses; in other cultures, such as the United States, eating those forms of meat is taboo. Like a fish swimming in water, most of the activities of our daily lives are embedded in a cultural context that we rarely recognize. Marlboro is a successful brand because its appeal is based on symbols of the pioneer West, such as the independence of cowboys, and these values are embedded seamlessly in their cultural context.

> *Principle:* Consumers' wants are culturally determined and shaped by the environment in which the consumers live.

Cultural Values and the Realities of Branding

The United States is a culture that values action and independence; many of the Asian cultures value deliberation and collective decision making. Brand strategies often have to be modified in international marketing to accommodate these differences in values. Since values are the core of culture, research on cultural values is particularly important to brands that seek to immerse themselves in an appropriate value system. Edward Hall and Geert Hofstede are two important theorists in this area whose work relates directly to brand strategy.

Edward Hall classifies cultures as either high-context or low-context (1976). By context, we mean that the nonverbal elements surrounding the message carry meaning and are a significant part of the message. In high-context cultures, such as many Asian countries and France, people depend on the context to signal the appropriate message. Their behavior is to a great extent determined by social roles and expectations. People are usually spoken to in order to motivate them to behave differently from what they would otherwise probably do. Speakers emphasize emotion. In commercial communication, drama and imagery are often appropriate message design tools.

In low-context cultures, such as the United States and the Nordic European countries, people do not rely as much on the context to interpret a message. A speaker expects to influence listeners by providing enough information to enable them to take an appropriate decision by themselves. Rational information prevails over social information. In commercial communication, an informational approach often is successful.

Another useful approach used in evaluating brand strategy is to analyze the components of culture as Geert Hofstede has done and use them to develop brand (message) strategies. In a study of fifty countries, Hofstede identifies five basic components of culture (Hofstede 1980, 1991):

- *Power distance* (PD): the degree of equality or inequality in a society. A high power distance indicates that inequalities of power and wealth have been allowed to grow within a society. Upward mobility of citizens is hampered. Countries with a low power distance deemphasize the difference between citizens' power and wealth.
- *Individualism* (IDV): represents the degree of interpersonal relationships. Individuality and individual rights are the norm in a highly individualistic society. Low individualistic societies are characterized by close ties between individuals and responsibility for fellow citizens.
- *Masculinity* (MAS): represents the degree to which a society reinforces or does not reinforce the traditional masculine role model of male achievement, control and power, and discrimination between genders.
- *Uncertainty avoidance* (UAI): focuses on the level of tolerance for uncertainty and ambiguity. A high uncertainty avoidance country has a rule-oriented society that institutes laws, rules, regulations, and controls. A low uncertainty avoidance country has more tolerance for adverse opinions and readily accepts change.
- *Long-term orientation* (LTO): focuses on long-term devotion to traditional values and long-term commitments. In a low long-term orientation society, change can occur more rapidly.

The differences in business style created by these factors can be major. Ihator (1999) observes that rugged individualism is essentially an American trait. He explains that the individualistic U.S. business culture values self-determination, achievement, a future orientation, optimism, and problem solving. In contrast, collectivistic cultures, such as most Asian countries, value maintenance of the status quo, harmony, and collaboration.

How can understanding Hofstede and Hall help in planning brand strategies? Researchers have found that Hofstede's individualism factor corresponds to Hall's high- and low-context cultures: low-context cultures are individualistic; high-context cultures are collectivist. Further, high-context, collective societies are mostly Asian and South American, cultures that value social harmony and selflessness. Low-context, individualistic cultures are mostly European and North American; people in these cultures tend to value self-realization and see themselves as independent, self-contained, and autonomous. Such an analysis helps to explain why different brand message strategies are needed for different cultures.

Figure 2.5 adapts Hall's context categories and five of Hofstede's cultural dimensions—each one presented as a continuum—to set up a chart for evaluating the cultural dimensions of a target

Figure 2.5   **Cultural Profiling**

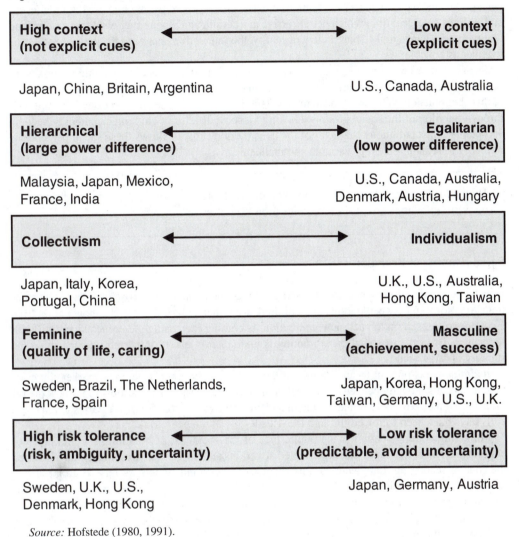

| High context (not explicit cues) | ⟷ | Low context (explicit cues) |

Japan, China, Britain, Argentina   U.S., Canada, Australia

| Hierarchical (large power difference) | ⟷ | Egalitarian (low power difference) |

Malaysia, Japan, Mexico,   U.S., Canada, Australia,
France, India   Denmark, Austria, Hungary

| Collectivism | ⟷ | Individualism |

Japan, Italy, Korea,   U.K., U.S., Australia,
Portugal, China   Hong Kong, Taiwan

| Feminine (quality of life, caring) | ⟷ | Masculine (achievement, success) |

Sweden, Brazil, The Netherlands,   Japan, Korea, Hong Kong,
France, Spain   Taiwan, Germany, U.S., U.K.

| High risk tolerance (risk, ambiguity, uncertainty) | ⟷ | Low risk tolerance (predictable, avoid uncertainty) |

Sweden, U.K., U.S.,   Japan, Germany, Austria
Denmark, Hong Kong

Source: Hofstede (1980, 1991).

market. This chart assigns countries to opposite ends of the spectrum in order to demonstrate how they differ on these dimensions. In planning a campaign, however, brand managers would need to conduct research to plot the actual positions and develop cultural profiles for specific target groups in different countries.

SOCIAL AND PERSONAL CONTEXT

"No man is an island," wrote the English poet John Donne in 1624. Every decision a person makes is in part a reaction to social, as well as cultural, influences. The social moderators include social role, social class, reference groups, and notions of status. The mutual interactions between individuals can lead to a situation of balance—the interactions construct shared views about (or perceptions of) reality that serve as truth within the group. When people interact for a while, social systems emerge within which people arrive at a certain agreement over what they understand reality to be. Thanks to the shared view of reality, the interactions between the participants come together as a whole.

Such processes can manifest themselves in trends. Certain brands can suddenly become very popular within certain subcultures, for no apparent explainable reason. Fashion is a good example of this phenomenon. When we look at new collections, they might seem quite ridiculous, but seen through the filter of the social group we belong to, some articles of clothing can quickly become acceptable. The continuous character of the construction process allows these social perceptions of reality to remain relatively variable and malleable.

> *Principle:* People are not passive recipients of an independent brand reality, but construct it within an interaction with their social environment.

Social Realities of Branding

How the world functions as we know it is knowledge that is transferred to our children. The emotional relationship between parents and children strengthens this effect. This is how habits from a culture are passed on to each new generation, becoming increasingly entrenched and difficult to change. This type of social programming is undoubtedly a very important factor behind the stability of large brands.

Its influence is present to an extreme in the Dutch beer market, where the market shares of brands vary gigantically per region (as shown in Table 2.1). This distribution still reflects the regional provenance of these brands in the nineteenth century, and the patterns established in those early days have been followed through the decades by Dutch beer drinkers.

Marketing communication is the public face of the social art of branding. It communicates cultural and social messages that are directed at various audiences that, presumably, have learned the code of marketing. Language with its shared meanings and symbol systems is an important factor in the socialization process. Communication theory has long believed in the necessity for shared fields of experience in order for communication to be successful (Schramm 1954).

Beyond family, people who have similar backgrounds derived from their interactional subgroups and communities may respond to a brand in predictable ways and derive similar interpretations for marketing communication. People from a different background may find a brand presentation distressingly inappropriate or even incomprehensible. Think about the difference in the mind-set and communication styles between computer geeks and some of their non–computer-literate clients. The ability to understand the language, symbols, or other aspects of the brand strategy is totally dependent upon shared cultural experiences.

The knowledge that we have about our reality has to keep being reconfirmed as proper. This can be done, among other things, through symbolic objects, sanctions, symbols, or rituals (e.g., military symbols, parades, laws, the police and the legislative power, and brands). Symbols, like brands, confirm consciously and unconsciously how our reality is put together. They reactivate our behavioral pattern, and social definitions of reality end up having a certain self-fulfilling potential. According to social constructionist theory, one of marketing communication's roles is to teach people how to act and respond in different consumption situations (Deighton and Hoch 1993).

Table 2.1

Market Shares per Beer by Region

Brand	Beer district						
	1	2	3	4	5	6	7
A	54	100	38	12	97	24	9
B	32	49	32	100	71	31	13
C	100	35	77	3	65	20	18
D	5	15	5	4	26	100	12
E	40	85	35	9	77	100	9
F	48	71	32	9	100	16	7
G	18	26	10	3	30	24	100

Source: ACNielsen, Netherlands (2001).
Notes: Highest regional, market share of a brand is put at 100. Market shares in other regions are indexed against this region. Brand A's market share in region 7 is only 9 percent of its market share in region 2.

Peer Groups and Brand Communities

We can sum up the social context by stating that people are born into a world that they experience as *the* world. But the world as they experience it is only a social construct. Habits from this social reality are passed on from one generation to another. Children internalize this social reality so it becomes *the* reality for them.

Besides the social programming of children by their parents, people are exposed throughout their lives to all kinds of influences from the members of (consumptive) subcultures they are attracted to. The same socialization process that characterizes child-parent relationships takes place with members of (sub)cultures, for instance the way children learn from each other about the popular, cool, or trendy brands of clothes and shoes to wear.

With young people, this social influence can manifest itself in the diverse clothing styles that are experienced as proper by the different groups. Peer groups have tremendous impact on the brand choices of young people, particularly for trendy products, such as clothing, music, movies, and electronics. Such social influence can be death for a brand that is not favored by peer-dominated groups such as teenagers, who use social consensus information to arrive at judgments and brand evaluations.

Brand communities are a twentieth-century phenomenon that reflect the power of a social relationship to confirm the value of a brand. Harley-Davidson and its grassroots HOG (Harley Owners Group) is one of the most well-known examples of a brand community and the model for Lego's Lugnuts group. Less formalized groups are those loyal, almost cult-like owners of Apple computers and Saab and Volvo cars. Muniz and O'Guinn (2001) have found three characteristics of these communities: consciousness of being connected not only to the brand but to other members of the community; legitimacy achieved through rituals and traditions that distinguish real members from marginal members; and oppositional brand loyalties.

Unconsciously, social reality becomes the subjective reality of the individual. The individual then propagates the common norms through the process of social influence. This externalization strengthens the course of the process. Symbolic objects, such as favorite brands, enhance and confirm knowledge of this social reality. New situations for which the history of the society has no ready-made answer, however, offer a chance to explore new roads.

Social Change

Social reality is not a constant—it is subject to change. In general, small, short-term changes are involved that are perceived only by those who desire the change ("our market share has gone up again by 0.1 percent") or are part of it ("another six hundred jobs lost at Philips"). Outsiders notice changes only when they take on the character of historical trends (individualization, technological literacy) or have a revolutionary character, such as mobile phone usage spreading into every area of our lives.

Most societies are pluralistic. Different ideologies exist next to each other within a shared universe. Factors such as tolerance, cooperation, division of labor, and economic surplus make this pluralism possible. Pluralism is another source of renewal. New ideas and changes are also part of the social fabric and buttressed by social judgment theory (Sherif and Hovland 1961), which explains how individuals confront new ideas through a frame of reference based on prior socially determined attitudes. The frame provides a point of comparison for new, incoming information; serves as an anchor for the adaptation process; and identifies boundaries of acceptability by establishing a latitude of acceptance surrounding the new idea.

Successful changes of a brand reality are therefore possible, but a social and conceptual basis is important to understand the change processes. In other words, the new alternative has to be

plausible and legitimated within the old reality; the easiest change to manage and accept is usually not too radical. Only then can the alternative be confirmed by others, establishing a basis for a new course. New media, for example, have traditionally been launched in the trappings of older, familiar media—television was radio with pictures, for example.

Change stems from people's reactions to the prevailing social structure. These reactions can consist of maintenance, adjustment, or distortion. This is a continuous social process that is done by people, lived by people, and, which, in turn, produces people's perceptions of a social artifact, such as brands.

The purpose of this section is the understanding of the human dimension of brand reality, one which is socially constructed. Understanding a brand as a social construct raises the question of the degree to which brand strategies are socially "fluent." Successful brands are capable of penetrating a person's social experience and embedding the brand in the network of social forces that surround brand selection in a specific product category. If marketers can integrate brands into the sociological building stones of the constructed reality, success may be easier to manage.

Personal or Psychological Context

A later chapter will discuss the psychological processes consumers use in formulating a brand response; however, it should be noted here that the personal context within which both managers and consumers live their lives also affects their decision making. At the psychological level, physical states (fatigue, arousal), moods, attitudes, emotions, knowledge levels, and motivations play a role in deciding on brand choices, as well as perceiving and forming impressions about brands.

These personal and psychological factors also intersect with the sociocultural factors to further compound the external complexity surrounding branding. A brand manager in the middle of a difficult divorce may have a hard time critiquing a message strategy for selling diamond rings. The conceptual fluency (Whittlesea 1993) that drives human judgment is always colored by personal, subjective experiences, as well as social experiences.

THE SITUATIONAL CONTEXT

We have presented the context of a brand from a number of different perspectives, including the macroenvironment, the microenvironment, and the internal environment. We have also outlined the key environmental factors that create a brand's marketing situation. They are as outlined in Table 2.2. These are all important forces that define a brand's marketing situation.

In addition to the factors in Table 2.2, there are other types of situations that also affect brand strategy. For example, with regard to brand-communication:

- What is the involvement situation? Are the consumers, as well as the product category and marketing communication messages, low or high involvement? In other words, is there something in the situation that demands shallow or deep processing of information?
- What is the exposure situation? Can the brand and its messages be seen and perceived or not? Does it or can it have a visible presence? Are there media or points of contact where customers can come in contact with the brand?
- What is the temporal situation? Is there a timing dimension for the brand message? How much time is needed for exposure, understanding, adoption, repeat purchase? Are there seasonal factors or events on the horizon that make a marketing strategy current, late, or cutting-edge?

These are just a few of the numerous situational factors that brand strategists must consider in their decision making. Again, all these business and marketing situations—as well as the social,

Table 2.2

Environmental Forces That Impact on Brand Strategy Development

Macroenvironment	Microenvironment	Internal environment
Demographics	Labor market	History/identity
Natural	Financial market	Competencies
Technological	Suppliers	Brand orientation
Economic	Trade channels	Vision/mission
Political/legal	Governmental bodies	Culture/philosophy
Ecological	NGOs (nongovernment organizations)	Business scope
Cultural/social	Market/competition	Organization
Communicative	Consumers/customers	Image/reputation
		Financial platform

cultural, technological, political, and economic contexts—constitute the surrounding complex environment within which a dynamic brand system operates.

THE LEGO ENVIRONMENT

Lego and its plastic toy bricks dominated the toy industry in the last half of the twentieth century. Lego bricks have won awards as the best plastic toy ever made. The company's Web site informs us that there are fifty-two Lego bricks for every person on earth and that children spend 5 billion hours a year playing with Lego bricks.

Lego is a business empire, as well as a cultural icon. But everything changed for Lego at the end of the century. Competitors made look-alike products and sold them cheaper. It found itself in a stagnant market, under assault from computer games and other electronic toys such as Nintendo. But a bigger problem was the brand mission—Lego was so linked with plastic bricks that its attempts to diversify into new markets failed. Losses mounted and the once high-flying company found itself searching for a new brand vision in a rapidly changing marketplace.

As a result of digitalization, Lego's environment also has changed dramatically. Children have not given up on traditional toys altogether, but the use of computers, mobile phones, MP3 players, iPods, and other electronic gadgets by younger and younger children means that the competition for their playtime has become much fiercer, causing a severe impact on the plastic brick-business.

Despite its new emphasis on computer- and customer-designed toys, Lego is not yet out of the danger zone. To further reduce costs, the distribution of the blocks was transferred to the Czech Republic. The company managed to cut its costs in 2004 by 20 percent. Although its sales fell by another 7 percent, it succeeded in making a moderate profit again. In 2006 it announced that it would shift part of its production capacity to Mexico and eastern European countries. So the company continues to struggle to find its place in the modern world of kids and toys.

Unfortunately, it took the legendary LEGO company exactly twenty years to realize the changes in its marketplace and begin to create programs that will allow it to adapt to the digital age. So it is too early to declare LEGO's turnaround plan a success, but early results suggest it might be working.

PART II

BRAND STRATEGY DEVELOPMENT

THE COMPANY PERSPECTIVE

BRAND STRATEGY DEVELOPMENT

Part I of this book looked at the basics of branding from a systems perspective. Now in Part II we will turn to the perspective of the marketer and consider the factors that the brand manager controls in planning brand strategies. First we will consider how brand strategies are developed.

Some companies are negatively limited by the image they have of themselves and the way they think. A certain self-image can result in automatically shutting out other viewpoints. These are systems that strive to form themselves according to their own image—good or bad. Examples of this limitation of vision are companies that used to make watches and typewriters. They kept making their traditional products in a conventional way and failed to understand that their identity was no longer relevant or even realistic for consumers. Swatch used a new way of thinking about itself and its brand to engineer an amazing turnaround for the company and the Swiss watch industry.

SWATCH: THE TURNAROUND OF THE SWISS WATCH INDUSTRY

In the early 1980s, Swiss watchmaking was on the brink of disaster. According to Nicolas G. Hayek, president of SMH, the parent company of Swatch, "It was a chaotic jungle. An absolute mess." Hayek described the problem: "Most people who analyze the destruction of the Swiss watch industry in the 1970s emphasize price and technology. They point to the arrival of hundreds of millions of cheap quartz watches from Japan and Hong Kong and our decision to ignore quartz, a technology we invented. But we had huge problems beyond technology. There were problems of strategy, structure, and management."

The two companies that became SMH were the flagships of the Swiss industry. One was SSIH, a company that had Swiss-French origins, with Omega and Tissot as its prestige brands. Omega was so successful for so long that it ruined SSIH. The company got arrogant. It also got greedy. It wanted to grow too fast, and it diluted the Omega name by selling too many watches at absurdly low prices. SSIH had no discipline and no strategy.

The other company was ASUAG, of Swiss-German origins. ASUAG was a manufacturing company with the brands Rado and Longines. But its heart was a very capable operation called Ebauches S.A. that supplied components to the whole Swiss watch industry. Over the years, however, various small Swiss brands faltered. By 1982, ASUAG owned more than 100 separate companies—some big, some small, some modern, and some backward. Most of these companies did their own marketing, their own research and development, their own assembly.

When Hayek joined the company, it had already developed, under the leadership of Dr. Ernest Thomke, an inexpensive, non-repairable watch, which today is known all over the world as Swatch. In interviews, Hayek explained the genesis of Swatch, the watch and the brand:

> We merged SSIH and ASUAG to create SMH. It was time to sort through the jungle. We began with the products themselves. We had to understand our strategic positioning, where we stood in world markets. We conducted a big study that became known as the Hayek Report. In the report, we drew a diagram to describe our competitive environment. It looked like a three-layer wedding cake. Back then, the world market for watches was about 500 million units per year. The low-end segment, the bottom layer of the cake, had watches with prices up to $75 or so. That layer represented 450 million units out of 500 million. The middle layer, with watches up to $400 or so, represented about 42 million units. That left 8 million watches for the top layer, with prices from $400 into the millions of dollars. The Swiss share of the bottom layer, 450 million watches, was zero. We had nothing left. Our share of the middle layer was about 3 percent; our share of the top layer was 97 percent.
>
> We were cornered. The Swiss spent much of the 1970s reacting to quartz by retreating. Why should we compete with Japan and Hong Kong? They make junk, and then they give it away. We have no margin there. Of course, as we retreated, the Japanese moved up to the next layer of the cake. Then the retreat would start again. I decided we could retreat no longer. We had to have a broad market presence. We needed at least one profitable, growing, global brand in every segment, including low-end.
>
> Ten years ago, the people on the original Swatch team had asked a crazy question: Why can't we design a striking, low-cost, high-quality watch and build it in Switzerland?
>
> I understood, Hayek said, that we were not just selling a consumer product, or even a branded product. We were selling an emotional product. You wear a watch on your wrist, right against your skin. You have it there for 12 hours a day, maybe 24 hours a day. It can be an important part of your self-image. It doesn't have to be a commodity. It shouldn't be a commodity. I knew that if we could add genuine emotion to the product, and attack the low end with a strong message, we could succeed. In 1983 the first Swatch watches were released in the United States.
>
> It is not just turning a functional product into a fashion-article. The people at our Swatch Lab in Milan and our many other designers do beautiful work. The artists who make our Swatch special collections design wonderful watches. But take a trip to Hong Kong and look at the styles, the designs, and the colors. They make pretty watches over there too.

We are not just offering people a style. We are offering them a message. This is an absolutely critical point. Fashion is about image. Emotional products are about message—a strong exciting distinct authentic message that tells people who you are and why you do what you do. There are many elements that make up the Swatch message. High quality. Low cost. Provocative. Joy of life. But the most important element of the Swatch message is the hardest for others to copy. Ultimately, we are not just offering watches. We are offering our personal culture.

I am talking about everything we do. Everything we do and the way we do everything sends a message. Each brand is different, so each message is different. My job is to sit in the bunker with a machine gun defending the distinct messages of all my brands. I am the custodian of our messages. I review every new communications campaign of every single brand.

In the mid-1980s Swatch started collaboration with famous artists such as Keith Haring and Alfred Hofkunst and later with fashion designers such as Paco Rabana and Vivian Westwood and with photographers such as Annie Leibowitz, David La Chapelle, and Helmut Newton. They participated in product design, as well as the design of promotional materials.

Since the introduction of the Swatch brand, the Swiss watchmaking industry as a whole has recovered. In 1998 SMH was renamed "The Swatch Group." Today it is the number one manufacturer of finished watches in the world, marketing eighteen watch brands in all price categories. The group employs over 20,000 people in more than fifty countries. Gross sales in 2005 amounted to 4.5 billion Swiss francs (approximately $3.9 billion in 1995) with a net profit of 14 percent.

Sources: W. Taylor (1993); www.swatchgroup.com; *gWatchers* (1995) "Fun of Swatching," vol. 4, no. 1 (January); C. Koopman (2006) "Kunst kijken met Swatch," *Villa d'Arte*, April.

Hayek explains the thinking behind the Swatch brand by emphasizing his understanding that everything the brand does sends a message. In order to manage the brand, he has to see and review every message—meaning every component of brand management and every customer experience with the brand. That is an entirely new way of thinking about the Swatch brand strategy. This chapter will explain how the process of strategic thinking is similar to—and informed by—the concept of systems thinking.

SYSTEMS THINKING AND STRATEGIC THINKING

In Chapter 1, Ellen Goodman was quoted on the tendency to look at the human body as parts rather than as a human life, as a system. The same problem can occur in branding when too much attention is directed to details of the marketing mix—the pricing problems, market share, competitors—rather than the health of the brand as a whole. Systems thinking forces managers to look at complexity, interrelationships, and the need for integration as a management tool.

We have talked about systems, but what exactly is systems thinking? As Ossimitz (1997) describes it, systems thinking is focused on the analysis of components that influence each other, thus producing the ability to see the interrelationships in a complex network of components. Systems thinking, in other words, distinguishes itself from more traditional analytical approaches by focusing on the interactions and connectedness of the different components of a complex system, such as a brand (Heylighen et al. 1995).

Systems thinking is valuable to brand managers because it helps identify brand reality and the natural forces governing a situation, as well as providing a mechanism for decision making based on a long view. The problem, in terms of brand management, is that in our schooling we tend to focus on simplistic solutions by finding key variables and exercising a tight linear logic to simplify processes and decision paths. The messiness of real systems, with their circularities in logic, crossover links that make matrix organizations look overly simple, and overlapping and sometimes conflicting forces, is probably not as appreciated in business and formal education as it is in the esoteric world of fuzzy math. As Scrivener (2004, 3) explains, "Our tradition of education has a blind spot when it comes to complexity, interconnectedness, and relationships, and the properties that emerge from them."

Strategic thinking in marketing and branding is often equated with determining the best way to achieve something. Typically, it is path-oriented, but paths and linear processes do not do justice to the complexity of the activities involved in managing a brand. Systems thinking, which is the focus of the most recent writings in systems theory, is a more useful approach to strategic thinking. It calls for an analysis of an entity, such as a brand, by looking at its systems and subsystems and their components in terms of how they influence each other and produce interrelated effects (Ossimitz 1997). This is described by Heylighen et al. as a form of thinking that "applies systems principles to aid a decision-maker with problems of identifying, reconstructing, optimizing, and controlling a system (usually a socio-technical organization), or set of systems, while taking into account multiple objectives, constraints, and resources. It makes it possible to better specify possible courses of action, together with their risks, costs, and benefits" (1995, 14). That description of systems thinking is also a good description of how strategic thinking operates in brand development. Strategic brand thinking, to be effective, is also concerned with managing complexity and interrelationships.

In systems thinking, rather than a path metaphor, strategy might be seen as steering or piloting a complex integrated system with multiple and sometimes conflicting objectives, forces, and outcomes. A metaphor we referred to in Chapter 1 is piloting a plane. In this situation, decision making is based on information from multiple sources, the interaction of complex physical and technological forces, sometimes conflicting goals (keep the plane level, avoid bad weather, arrive on time, save costs), and personal, social, and cultural frames of reference (ethics, individual achievement, social responsibility).

In a sense, strategy always involves the notion of arriving somewhere, but the arrival is predicated on negotiating how all the many systems and parts can work in concert, given their varied and sometimes conflicting interests and demands. Strategic thinking employs systems thinking to the degree that it identifies and accommodates the various systems, subsystems, and components, as well as all their interrelationships. Strategic thinking in branding, in other words, is always systems thinking if it is to deliver strong brands. To better understand how systems thinking and strategic thinking relate, let us look first at the history and theory of strategy.

STRATEGY DEVELOPMENT

The concept of strategy has an important place in the daily language of marketing professionals, as well as communication specialists. Complex management decisions are made on the basis of alleged "strategies." Brand strategy, for example, involves decisions about business and marketing plans (objectives and strategies to achieve them), information networks and research, stakeholders (suppliers, distributors, employees, shareholders, the public, and customers, to name a few), and the more traditional marketing mix components—product, pricing, distribution, and marketing communication.

But what is a strategy, really? And how does it arise? Providing a satisfying answer is not a simple task. During the writing of this book about brand strategy development, these questions stared us in the face too. Here are the results of our search for answers.

What Is Strategy?

In daily life, the word *strategy* indicates the road taken to reach certain goals. The word stems from *strategos*, the title of military authorities in ancient Greek cities, and it entered Western vocabulary through military theory. Carl Von Clausewitz (1780–1831), a Prussian army officer and expert in military strategy, proposed in his classic 1832 book on war that a strategy is concerned with drafting a plan of war by shaping individual campaigns, and within these, deciding on the individual engagements (Rapaport 1982). Helmuth Von Moltke (1800–1890), a renowned Prussian field marshal, proposed that strategy is a matter of understanding correctly at every moment a constantly changing situation and then doing the simplest and most natural thing with energy and determination (Abegglen 1995).

Beyond the military meaning, strategy is a general notion used in numerous other areas of society wherever goals are set and plans forged to achieve them. However, when the concept of strategy is linked to specific areas, such as business, confusion over the meaning arises. For one thing, there is no consensus on the definition of the concept of business strategy other than that it relates to plans and goals.

- *The plan or path aspect:* Mintzberg (1987) describes strategy as a consciously intended course of action, a guideline or set of guidelines to deal with a situation.
- *A position:* Porter (1996) defines strategy as the creation of a unique and valuable position, involving a different set of marketing activities; it is about making trade-offs whose essence is choosing what not to do. This notion of trade-offs underlies the concept of decision making.
- *A goals orientation based on integrative thinking:* Glueck (1980) defines strategy as a unified, comprehensive, and integrated plan designed to ensure that the basic goals of the enterprise are achieved.
- *Coherence:* Quinn (1980) sees strategy as the pattern of the plan that integrates the main goals, policies, and series of actions into a coherent whole. A well-formulated strategy helps unite and allocate the resources of an organization into a unique and executable situation, based on relative internal competencies and deficiencies, expected changes in the environment, and potential reactions of intelligent adversaries.

The integrative aspect of strategy, complete with Quinn's delineation of all the contexts and elements that become decision points, comes very close to being a definition of systems thinking.

Mintzberg (1987) believes that the *plan-and-goals* definition of strategy is too limited because it puts a one-sided emphasis on conscious behaviors defined a priori, before the actions are taken. He proposes distinguishing four additional meanings:

- Strategy as a *pattern* in a *flow* of activities. The consistency of the manifested behavior is what makes it a strategy. The common belief that an all-encompassing plan is hidden behind it is just an assumption that could turn out to be wrong. Sometimes there are deliberate strategies that cannot manifest themselves in behavior. The key element is behavioral consistency, but the question is how this consistency comes about.

- Strategy as a (chosen) *position* that the company assumes in its environment. This involves the power structure between the organization and its competitive environment, bridging an organization's internal operations and its outside world. Such a position can be the result of conscious strategy development (e.g., Swatch) or of a historically grown situation (e.g., Hershey's).
- Strategy as *perspective*, an embedded manner in which the company looks at the world, a worldview. Examples are the habit of using technological capacities as a basic premise against the focus on external expectation such as those of customers and consumers.
- Strategy as a *concept*, in the sense that it only exists in people's minds, constituting a company's personality, value system, and ideology. This meaning is comparable to the personality of individuals, in which little is chosen consciously. A company usually has shared ways of thinking and acting (e.g., Diesel).

All four of these definitions improve on conventional definitions because they move away from the linear cause-and-effect pattern and permit consideration of complexity. They better support an integrative, or systems, approach. Understanding patterns is similar to identifying systems, and consistency is the result. But consistency is also derived from the other three—position, perspective, and concept—which act as anchors for integration and mechanisms that keep the various patterns and systems aligned.

Mintzberg points out that in most companies there are no complete pronouncements on a total business strategy, but this does not mean they are not there. Such a strategy can be present implicitly and manifest itself in the results of current decision-making processes. For an objective observer, such a strategy can be quite visible, even when obscured for those directly involved.

Whether a strategy is deliberate (explicitly formulated in advance) or emergent (having become visible only in the decisions taken and the main programs emanating from it), it remains a real strategy. Strategies can arise gradually, as time passes, without having to be formulated explicitly beforehand. Mintzberg indicates that none of his strategy definitions has precedence over another. In reality, there will often be a combination of several activity dimensions that are ultimately developed. Even when there is a conscious, structured plan development, making choices can be highly influenced by perspective, position, and concept approaches.

Principle: A strategy is the road taken to achieve formulated goals. It can come from a well-considered plan, but also can be implicitly present, manifesting itself in behavioral patterns.

What Are the Characteristics of Effective Strategies?

In the course of time, general criteria have emerged to identify the key characteristics of strategies. Some come from the military field, some from the development of theories in the business world (Tilles 1986; Day 1986; Quinn 1980). Every strategy has at least one of the elements described below:

- *Clear and decisive goals:* Everyone involved in the implementation of a strategy must be aware of the goals. At the central level there are only a few goals from which subgoals could be derived for parts of the management strategy. Goals ensure coherence and continuity. Wherever possible, they are quantified and linked to a moment in time.

- *Simplicity:* Strategies that are too complicated lead to inconsistent interpretations, confusion, and weak follow-up.
- *Motivating impact:* Goals should speak to people; employees, for example, should find them worthy of devotion.
- *Committed leadership:* The top management should identify with the strategy and support fully those who have to implement the activity plan. There is nothing worse than a halfhearted attitude from the company top.
- *Feasibility:* The goals should be feasible, given the financial, organizational, and professional means available.
- *Consistency:* The strategy should correspond to the individual character of the organization or the brand; it should "fit."
- *Concentration:* The strategy should be focused and aimed at what makes the company or the brand superior to its competitors in actual critical dimensions. There should not be any distracting or even marginal activities being developed.
- *Enterprising:* This means being proactive, not just reacting to events in the environment. A strategy that is focused on incidents is bad for morale and creates chances for the competition.
- *Flexibility:* The strategy has buffers and dimensions that allow reacting to new developments and possibilities without losing sight of concentration.
- *Surprise:* The strategy makes it possible to surprise opponents with new elements. This has proven to be a decisive criterion in the military.
- *Security:* There is an information system with which developments can be followed, so that steering is possible and surprises from competitors can be prevented.

What Does a Strategy Contain?

There is no consensus on the contents of a strategy either, especially regarding whether goals and objectives should be considered as part of it. It is clear that without goals there can be no strategy, as both are as closely related as yin and yang. The familiar expression "If you don't know where to go, any road will take you there" applies here. However, strategies are generally seen as the road that is taken to realize long-term goals. A goal is where you want to go; a strategy is how you will get there.

Strategy, in other words, comprises the most important, essential decisions that give focus to goal-oriented activities. It is a broad plan of action, of identifying and doing the right things that will best deliver the desired goals. Following the logic of Porter and Quinn, then, the essence of strategy is a set of decisions framed as a plan that leads to desired goals. In addition to objectives, brand strategy decisions also can include such specific factors as target audience, competitive advantage, brand position, and the selling proposition.

Tactics are about the short-term execution details, taking care that things happen "the right way." Military vocabulary posits that tactics are decisive to winning on the battlefield and strategy to winning a war. Seen this way, strategy would only be applicable at the highest levels of decision forming. Strategy gives focus to tactics, but tactics in turn exert an influence on strategy. In practice, they sometimes are so interrelated that they cannot be clearly distinguished from each other.

Objectives, strategies, and tactics cascade from one level to another. A goal and strategy at the business level, for example, may be supported by a set of marketing objectives, strategies, and tactics, which, in turn, are supported by a set of pricing, distribution, product development, and marketing communication objectives, strategies, and tactics. Upper-level tactics are intimately related to those at subordinate levels. In this cascading relationship, it is sometimes difficult to make a clear distinction between one level's objectives and another level's strategies and tactics.

Levels of Strategy in Brand Management

Since strategic thinking affecting brand management takes place at nearly every business level, it might be useful to map these levels and their typical decision points. Table 3.1 presents an overview of the strategy levels that create the systems-based decisions involved in brand development and management. Specific components of brand strategy are identified in Levels 4–7.

At a business level, there are elementary decisions related to the choice between the use of corporate or individual brands. These decisions are pivotal for the planning of strategic business units (SBUs). A clear choice for full corporate branding means that derivative strategic decisions are usually taken at the top management level.

Corporate leadership and planning departments draw up plans that give a focus to—and often entail limitations on—actions at the lower levels. Next to this top-down process there is also a bottom-up process in which opinions and initiatives at lower levels exert an influence on the final brand strategy. In practice, therefore, brand planning occurs in consultation between the upper management and the SBU levels.

Companies that have chosen management strategies based on individual brands make brand decisions at an SBU level. The company top management only gives frameworks within which this decision making is to take place. At Unilever, for example, this is manifest in the guidelines for concentrating development of large brands in the international portfolio.

At an SBU level, the decisions are made on the role of individual brands in the total brand portfolio and on brand extension measures. This will be discussed further in Chapter 15. It is essential for management strategy choices at the various levels to be in harmony. Especially in corporate brands, the brand communication management strategy should be rooted in a deep understanding of which approaches the upper management believes in and aims for. When the guard changes, philosophies often arise and activities programs are developed at the lower levels that may be in conflict with strategies articulated by those at the top management levels. The development of vision and mission statements and their adjustment when needed can help maintain the harmony in strategies at the various levels.

A brand communication strategy, or any brand strategy, can never stand completely on its own; it is always a reflection of, and designed to support, higher-level strategies. With corporate brands, it is usually the CEO who ultimately gives a focus to the strategy and determines the conditions. But, overall, brand strategy is a complex system of goals and objectives, programmatic decisions, and performance evaluations to determine if the programs achieved the objectives. All these are interdependent because performance on one level is inevitably impacted by performance on another level.

THEORIES OF STRATEGY DEVELOPMENT

The development of theories of business strategy started in 1960; that on brand management strategy only since 1990. In terms of theory development, the complexity of context factors has resulted in a great divergence of approaches and viewpoints. One of the problems is that theory development is rarely based on the study of concrete, practical cases. This has led to several mental models whose relation to reality is dubious (Banens 2000).

The useful theories we do have at our disposal are highly influenced by research and mental

Table 3.1

Levels and Components in Brand Strategy Management

Level	Strategic brand decisions
1. Corporate	• Corporate goals • Choice of markets • Environmental surveillance • Formulation of vision/mission • Choice of corporate/individual branding • Brand portfolio planning • Endorsement planning • Arrangement into SBUs (strategic business units) • Choice of development directions • Allocation of means among SBUs • Corporate communication management strategy • Corporate performance evaluation
2. Strategic business unit (SBU) management	• Business objectives • Identification of prospective markets • Competitive surveillance • Choice of brands • Product-brand combinations (brand extension management) • Allocation of means among brands • Evaluation of business objectives
3. Marketing management strategy	• Marketing mix objectives • Marketing research • Selection of target groups • Development of databases • Segmentation strategies • Marketing mix decisions: product design, SKUs, pricing, distribution, marketing communication functions • Scheduling and budgeting • Evaluation of marketing strategies
4. Brand strategy	• Consumer insight research • Setting brand objectives • Brand concept planning • Brand positioning planning • Brand communication planning • Brand architecture planning (endorsement and sub-brands) • Evaluation of brand strategies
5. Brand contact point strategy	• Setting marketing communication objectives • Choice of communication target audiences and key stakeholders • Choice of means • (Mass) media communication • Individual or two-way communication • Other types of touch points • Message strategies • Budget Allocation • Evaluation of message effectiveness
6. Media communication strategy	• Setting media objectives • Choice of medium vehicles • Scheduling (burst-drip) • Budgeting • Evaluation of media effectiveness
7. Individual communication strategy	• Selection of target groups • Identification of contact points • Choice of means • Word-of-mouth • Personal sales • Interactive • Corporate response; listening • Evaluation of individual contacts

models from the world of daily consumer products. The literature on the effects of brands in the markets of business-to-business marketing, as well as professional products and services, is still extremely scarce—particularly as it relates to some areas of marketing communication—and very rarely empirically substantiated. In the field of communication strategy development, there is a large lacuna in our knowledge of interactions between the various media types and marketing communication functions.

According to Mintzberg et al. and others, all theory can do is provide points of connection, concepts, outlooks, mental models, and techniques from which the strategist must make a choice. The idea is to identify those elements that help a manager understand properly the situation of the brand itself. Theories such as those presented in this book are not aimed at telling a strategist what to do, but at opening windows and offering new perspectives.

Mintzberg, a pioneer in the field, made it his life mission to develop an all-encompassing theory for business strategy. Still, he did not succeed in bringing about a synthesis. In his last publications, he ended with a list of ten schools of strategy development (Mintzberg et al. 1998, 1999). His last book had the self-explanatory title *Strategy Safari: A Guided Tour Through the Wilds of Strategic Management.*

Six Perspectives on Strategy Development

In the process of strategy development, countless factors play a role, resulting in an endless number of decision combinations and options. That is why strategizing involves systems thinking. Still, some specific configurations can be seen as clusters of insight. In a study of 1,174 managers and 141 organizations in Great Britain, Bailey and Johnson (2001) found six archetypical forms of strategy development processes. The characteristics of each of these perspectives are summarized in Table 3.2.

Four Approaches to Strategy Development

These six perspectives on strategy development are useful in analyzing the way strategy is approached in general. Other approaches are more specific in highlighting the tensions implicit in Porter's view of the trade-offs in decision making. One common view of the oppositional structure of strategy involves rational and analytical approaches versus creative and intuitive approaches. A variation on those oppositions is knowledge-driven versus experience-driven approaches. This creates a set of four strategic approaches.

The Rational/Analytical Approach

The rational/analytical process is based on research and quantitative analyses whose goal is to explain the current situation, isolate the relative influence of individual variables, and, if possible, calculate their impact. Inherent in this approach is the conviction that strategies should come about via a rational order of thinking and working (single-loop learning), as shown in Figure 3.1.

It consists of six stages, which have to be passed through on a recurrent basis. The model suggests that brand strategy development has to be executed in a planned and sequential order. In reality, all six stages usually get continuous attention. The six stages are:

1. *What or who is the brand?* Analysis of the physical, mental, and social components of the brand, regarding their centrality, durability, and salience.
2. *Where is the brand?* Analysis of the technological, cultural, social, political, economic, and competitive environment in which the brand operates and of its position within each

Table 3.2

Six Perspectives on Strategy Development

1. Planning perspective
   - Strategies are the outcome of rational, sequential, planned, and methodical procedures.
   - Strategic goals are set by senior organizational figures.
   - The organization and environment are analyzed.
   - Definite and precise goals are set.
   - Precise plans for implementation are developed.
   - The strategy is made explicit in the form of detailed plans.

2. Incrementalism perspective
   - Strategy is continually adjusted to match changes in the operating environment.
   - Strategic options are continually assessed for fit.
   - Early commitment to a strategy is tentative and subject to review.
   - Strategy develops through experimentation and gradual implementation.
   - Successful options gain additional resources.
   - Strategy develops through small-scale changes.

3. Cultural perspective
   - A "way of doing things" in the organization impacts strategic direction.
   - Strategies are evolved in accordance with a set of shared assumptions that exist in the organization.
   - A core set of shared assumptions based on past experience and history guide strategic actions.
   - Organizational history directs the search for and selection of strategic options.
   - Strategy that does not fit with the culture is resisted.

4. Political perspective
   - Strategies are developed by negotiation and bargaining between interest groups.
   - The interest groups seek to realize their own desired goals.
   - Their influence on strategy formulation increases with power.
   - Power comes from the ability to create or control the flow of scarce resources.
   - Interest groups form coalitions to further their desired strategy.
   - The control and provision of information is also a source of power.
   - A strategy acceptable to the most powerful interest groups is developed.

5. Command perspective
   - An individual is the driving force behind the organization's strategy.
   - Strategy is primarily associated with the institutional power of an individual or small group.
   - The strategy represents the individual's aspirations for the organization's future.
   - The individual becomes the representation of the strategy for the organization.
   - An individual has a high degree of control over strategy.
   - A "vision" belonging to the whole organization is not seen.

6. Enforced choice perspective
   - Strategies are prescribed by the operating environment.
   - Strategic choice is limited by external forces that the organization is unable to control.
   - Strategic change is instigated from outside the organization.
   - Organizations are not able to influence their operating environments.
   - Barriers in the environment severely restrict strategic mobility.

Source: Bailey and Johnson (2001).

Figure 3.1   **Single-Loop Learning According to the Rational/Analytical Approach**

of these spheres. Analysis of the category and the brand users, their motivation, purchasing behavior, and product and brand perceptions. Analysis of the distribution forces.

3. *Why is the brand there?* Diagnosis of environmental developments and the brand's history, to uncover the basis of its current position. Analysis of factors that are responsible for its market position and for recent developments (growth, stability, decline) in its market position.

4. *Where could the brand be?* Definition of the goals that seem attainable given environmental forces and the resources available for the development of the brand. Consumer perception and consumer behavior objectives and channel objectives.

5. *How can the brand get there?* Strategies that could (and should) be followed to reach these goals. Decisions on the balance between push and pull strategies. Decisions on advertising framework media strategy and message strategy.

6. *Is the brand getting there?* Development and application of a brand monitoring system covering the essential market development and brand performance factors and relating these to the actions of the brand and its competitors.

In the rational/analytical approach, SWOT analysis (see box) is the most well-known example of field analysis. The letters of the acronym SWOT stand for strength, weakness, opportunity, and threat, and SWOT analysis involves examining the strengths and weaknesses in the internal environment of the company or the brand as well as opportunities and threats in the external environment. According to the SWOT analysis, a strategy is effective if it takes advantage of the opportunities, leverages strengths, ducks threats, and corrects or compensates for weaknesses.

In the 1980s, under the influence of the competition theories of Porter, there was a major focus on the external side. In the 1990s, Hamel and Prahalad (1994) shifted the focus to the internal side,

The Development of SWOT Analysis

SWOT analysis, developed by Kenneth Andrews, is probably the most commonly applied method of analysis in strategy development. It is an approach in which the internal strengths and weaknesses of an entity (company, product, brand, etc.) are linked to the opportunities and threats of the outside world. The analysis is done not only when evaluating entire businesses, but also when analyzing parts of a management strategy, such as:

- the opportunities of a specific product market;
- the position in a specific segment;
- the position of a specific brand;
- the evaluation of competitors' positions;
- the evaluation of communication programs.

The appeal of a SWOT analysis lies in the simplicity and plausibility of the basic premise and its applicability by managers and planners. It allows structuring of a diversity of qualitative and quantitative information, allowing a better grasp of such a situation. It especially lends itself to team applications, because it integrates personal orientations and views into a greater whole to arrive at a consensus.

When carrying out a SWOT analysis, the company should concentrate on its relevance for customers and consumers (Piercy and Giles 1989). The only sources and capacities of a company or brand to qualify would be those recognized and valued by customers and consumers. This criterion helps determine what is a strength and what is not, thus preventing all kinds of internal issues that could be seen as strengths, but that make no difference to customers, from determining the evaluation.

All opportunities and threats in the environment relevant for the company or the brand should therefore be taken into account. Each item should be evaluated against the following criteria:

- a realistic estimate of the damage to the brand equity when a weakness or threat is not tackled;
- a realistic estimate of the advantages of using a strength or chance;
- the real capacity to make use of or tackle the identified SWOTs;
- the related costs and efforts;
- the time that is available to make use of or tackle each SWOT.

The information derived from the internal and external analysis becomes meaningful when it is compared using a confrontation matrix (Table 3.3). The confrontation matrix shows to what extent the company can take advantage of the opportunities in the business environment, using its own strengths, or whether it will be undone by its own weaknesses. Threats that are reinforced by a company's own weaknesses are the main concern.

Sources: Based on Piercy and Giles (1989); Johnson and Scholes (2002); Kotler (2003).

Table 3.3

Confrontation Matrix

		Opportunities			Threats		
		01	02	03	T1	T2	T3
Strengths	S1						
	S2						
	S3						
	S4						
Weaknesses	W1						
	W2						
	W3						
	W4						

Ratings in the cells: ++ = Very favorable; + = Favorable; 0 = Neutral; – = Threat; — = Big threat

emphasizing the influence of resources and capacities. These scholars are seen as the heralds of a new era of business strategies, an era based more on daring and less on analysis, control, and security. This new era is also more open to intuitive approaches to strategy development, rather than relying exclusively on the rational approach.

The Creative/Intuitive Approach

In the creative/intuitive process, the situation is dealt with more intuitively, and choices may be made more unconsciously than consciously. In this process, those questions presented in previous models may not be discussed at all. Managers may realize only after a long time and by coincidence what the essence of the company is and how it fits in the world. They make decisions based on their intuition and their power; they carry out decisions on a trial-and-error basis. Richard Branson and his leadership of the Virgin conglomerate of companies and brands is an example.

Vision and daring are the most important characteristics of the creative/intuitive approach. Strategies are based on visions formed with powers of imagination that can see patterns in complexity. It is a creative process that can lead to innovative concepts. The creative/intuitive approach can lead to unpredictable results and a more differentiating positioning.

Fabian (cited in Coomans and Van Veen 1999) makes a comparison between rational and intuitive approaches (see Table 3.4).

The Integration of Rational and Intuitive Approaches

Mintzberg (1994) says that an obsession with the rational/analytical approach leads to an aversion to risk, which means that creative ideas get less of a chance because they have unpredictable effects. He argues for supplementing the rational/analytical process with a creative/intuitive think tank where imaginative powers get the space to create new chances. Rational/analytical and creative/intuitive approaches are complementary, and together they can ensure balance in strategy formation. Strategic thinking demands a combination of analytical methods and mental elasticity.

Table 3.4

Rational/Analytic and Creative/Intuitive Strategy Development

Elements	Rational/analytic	Creative/intuitive
Way of thinking	Reductive Step-by-step Analyzing (SWOT)	Expansive Simultaneous Intuitive
Way of acting	Searching for the proper way	Searching for various ways
Requirements	Precision Control	Approach Let go

Sources: Mintzberg (1994).

Research and analysis can give an idea of the present and the past, but they seldom lead to un-equivocal cause-and-effect relations. Besides, the future is not just an extrapolation of the present; discontinuities in observed trends are not predictable. Too much analysis can result in too little synthesis. For this reason, Kenechi Ohmae—former head of the McKinsey consulting firm's Japan office and an authority on strategy, also known as "Mr. Strategy"—argues for a synthesis of both approaches. He proposes replacing the concept of strategic planning with strategic thinking.

In strategic thinking, as Ohmae states:

> One first seeks a clear understanding of the particular character of each element of a situation and then makes the fullest possible use of human brainpower to restructure the elements in the most advantageous way. Phenomena and events in the real world do not always fit a linear model. Hence the most reliable means of dissecting a situation into its constituent parts and reassembling them in the desired pattern is not a step-by-step methodology such as systems analysis. Rather, it is that ultimate non-linear thinking tool, the human brain.
>
> True strategic thinking thus contrasts sharply with the conventional mechanical system approach based on linear thinking. But it also contrasts with the approach that stakes everything on intuition, reaching conclusions without any real breakdown or analysis. No matter how difficult or unprecedented the problem, a breakthrough to the best possible solution can come only from a combination of rational analysis, based on the real nature of things, and imaginative reintegration of all the different elements into a new pattern, using non-linear brainpower. This is always the most effective approach to devising strategies for dealing successfully with challenges and opportunities, in the market arena as on the battlefield. . . .
>
> No proper strategy can be built on fragmentary knowledge or analysis. If such a strategy happens to produce good results, this is due to luck or inspiration. The true strategist depends on neither the one nor the other. He has a more reliable recipe for success: the combination of analytical method and mental elasticity that I call strategic thinking. (Ohmae 1982)

Principle: Brand strategy development benefits from the balanced combination of a rational/analytical approach to a situation combined with an intuitive, nonlinear approach in which the powers of imagination are used to create surprising solutions and new opportunities.

The Knowledge- Versus Experience-Driven Approaches

Similar to the difference between rational and intuitive approaches to strategy development are the knowledge- and experience-based approaches. In knowledge-based strategy development, it is assumed that there is sufficient knowledge in the organization to arrive at effective strategies. One's own insights and evaluation capacities are trusted. In experience-based strategy development, the emphasis is on continuous interactivity with market channels and end users and on creativity in the development of new propositions and communicative approaches.

The enormous success of the Dutch supermarket chain Albert Heijn, which realized a growth in market share from 13.5 percent in 1982 to 29 percent in 2007, can be largely attributed to monthly interviews by top executives with consumers. Test shops continuously experimented with new concepts, and consumer reactions were gauged in direct meetings between the management and the shoppers. Of course, this was not the only source of information for the development of a strategy, but it was undoubtedly the most influential.

McKenna (1991b) argues for a new form of marketing that integrates the clients into the company, thus making use of knowledge-based as well as experience-based marketing.

Knowledge-based marketing requires a company to master a scale of knowledge—of new sources of technology that can alter its competitive environment and provide business opportunities, and of its own organization, capabilities, plans, and way of doing business. Armed with this mastery, companies can put knowledge-based marketing to work in three essential ways: integrating the customers into the process to guarantee a product that is tailored not only to their needs and desires, but also to their strategies; generating niche thinking to use the company's knowledge of channels and markets to identify segments of the market the company can own; and developing the infrastructure of suppliers, vendors, partners, and users whose relationships will sustain and support the company's reputation and technological edge.

The other half of this new marketing paradigm is *experience-based marketing*, which emphasizes interactivity, connectivity, and creativity. With this approach, as McKenna explains, companies listen to their customers, monitor their competitors, and develop a feedback-analysis system that turns this information into new product intelligence. At the same time, these companies both evaluate their own technology and partner with other companies to create mutually advantageous systems and solutions. These encounters—with customers, competitors, and internal and external technologies—give companies the information they need to invest in market development and to take intelligent, calculated risks (McKenna 1991b).

In this time of exploding choices and unpredictable change, marketing has to find a way to integrate the consumer into the company. It has to synthesize the company's technological capability with market needs. Marketing has to shift focus from customer manipulation to customer involvement.

> *Principle:* Brand development strategy demands the deployment of the knowledge available in the organization, combined with knowledge that becomes available through integration of the consumer or customer into the strategy process.

THE MANDATES OF STRATEGY DEVELOPMENT

Mandates are requirements, and perhaps that word is too strong for this section. Nevertheless, there is a set of conditions surrounding the development of effective strategy:

- strategy seen as a shared process;
- strategy understood as a mental model;
- strategy expressed as thinking in time;
- strategy as ambition or intent.

Strategy as a Shared Process

From these discussions, it appears that strategy development is best seen as an integration of rational thinking and intuition combined with knowledge-based information and personal experiences. But more than that, strategy may best be developed through a shared process that brings together the analytical thinking, intuition, knowledge, and experiences of a group of committed managers who are informed by customer viewpoints.

Liedtka (1998) sees strategy development not as an abstraction that takes place at the desk of a specialized planner, but as a social process (planning dialogue) that is permanently taking place in a business. It involves a group that arrives at common insights at a certain point in time, making decisions and developing activities on this basis. Implicitly, Liedtka supports Mintzberg's view of the increasingly open character of strategies. In this context, Stacey (1992) suggests that strategic intention focuses, not on achieving something known, but rather the discovery of

> what, why, and how to achieve innovation and insight. Strategic intention comes not from what managers predict but from what they have experienced and understood.
>
> The dynamic systems perspective thus leads managers to think in terms, not of the prior intention represented by goals and visions, but of continuously developing agendas of issues, aspirations, challenges, and individual intentions.

Cross-Functional Planning

The dialogue on strategy issues should take place between people with a multidisciplinary background whose contributions reflect their experiences and insights without restraints. This is the case in the development of communication strategies in which the input of creative people is undeniably as productive as that of managers, planners, and researchers. The dialogue contributes to the insight of the participants, increasing support as well as the chance of getting effective results. On the sense of dialogue, Dixon (1996) says the following:

> Dialogue has the potential to alter the meaning each individual holds and, by doing so, is capable of transforming the group, organization, and society. The relationship between the individual and the collective is reciprocal and is mediated through talk. People are both recipients of tacit assumptions and the creators of them. In this way, dialogue results in the co-creation of meaning . . . the common understanding engendered by dialogue is one in which each individual has internalized the perspectives of the others and thus is enriched by a sense of the whole.

Studies on successful product development teams have shown that the participation of persons with different talents and experiences contributes to increased creativity. In strategy development it is important that those at the highest decision level, which will ultimately have to sanction the strategy, make time to participate in the development process as well.

> *Principle:* Brand strategy development should have the character of a continuous dialogue between all the involved actors rather than an isolated planner's activity. This increases support and chances of effective results.

Strategy as a Mental Model

Brand strategy development is based on a mental model of what a brand is and how it functions in its environment. Strategy developers almost always hold a hypothesis or mental image of a means-end chain and of the mutual dependencies of the variables in such a chain. These management strategy heuristics are explanations of the workings of the underlying mental model with assumptions about characteristics of phenomena. In systems thinking, they are especially important because they include assumptions about the relationships between phenomena.

Argyris and Schön (quoted in Hoogerwerf 1984) distinguish between a theory of action (which can be summed up as "when one wants to get result R in situation S, under assumptions of the type 'if . . . , then . . . ,' then do D") and a theory of practice (a system of interconnected theories of action). The mental model and the hypotheses on which it is based are views of the cohesion between means and goals and between cause and effect. Liedtka (1998), a dedicated supporter of the strategic thinking approach, underlines that learning is more important than knowing.

> Liedtka says the assumptions on which actions of brand strategists are based can, of course, be borrowed from scientific or academic insights, but are often based on personal observations of the market. Failure of many a management strategy, seen as failure to reach the aimed-for goals, can be partially explained by the fact that management strategy is often based on flawed assumptions. For a well-balanced strategy development process and an increase in strategy effectiveness it is necessary to articulate the most implicit assumptions, make them part of the strategic dialogue, and attempt to test them with research. Leidtka explains that it is his personal belief that the ability to work well with hypotheses is the core competence of the best consultancy firms.

> *Principle:* All brand strategy development is based on mental models and hypotheses, which should be, if possible, tested in the course of time.

Strategy as Thinking in Time

A book series containing case histories of strong brands has appeared in fifty-one countries under the title *Superbrands*. The brands are selected by committees of experts. What is striking is that most of the discussed brands already existed between 1850 and 1950. Many market leaders in the Netherlands go back more than half a century, with a significant number from before 1900. The success of these brands can probably be ascribed to the feeling of familiarity they induce in consumers—we saw them as children in the world where we grew up. They formed a self-evident element in our environment, a natural part of our lives. They are a small part of us, like people we have known for years or seen in the media for a long time.

In strategy development for brands, the historical context always plays an important role.

Strategic thinking is always what Neustadt and May refer to as "thinking in time" (1986). They say it is a constant exchange between past, present, and future.

> According to Neustadt and May, thinking in time [has] three components. One is recognition that the future has no place to come from but the past, hence the past has predictive value. Another element is recognition that what matters for the future in the present is departures from the past, alterations, changes, which prospectively or actually divert familiar flows from accustomed channels. A third component is continuous comparison, an almost constant oscillation from the present to the future to the past and back, heedful of prospective change, concerned to expedite, limit, guide, counter, or accept it as the fruits of such comparison suggest.

In their analysis of forty-six successful businesses, Brown and Eisenhardt (1998) also arrive at the conclusion that in strategy formation it is essential to pay attention to the connection between past, present, and future. "Stretch out the past, live in the present, reach into the future," they state (see Figure 3.2):

> Managers who compete on the edge learn more from the past than their counterparts who don't compete on the edge. They keep their product and service platforms in the market longer than others, exploit derivative products more effectively, and extend their offerings into new geographies and customer segments more frequently. They often selectively use the past to jump-start new opportunities. The past is often the competitive advantage when chasing new opportunities. Wise use of the past diminishes risk and frees resources to focus on new ideas.
>
> The present is the most important time frame. Today's product launch, today's manufacturing performance, and today's sales bookings matter most . . . Managers who compete on the edge structure their business as little as possible, paying attention to what is not structured as well. Structure is found in priorities that everyone can recite and responsibilities that everyone knows.
>
> Managers who compete on the edge reach further into the future. They manage in a longer time horizon than most others. Driven by a belief that the future is unpredictable, they launch more experimental products and services, create more strategic alliances with a focus on nascent markets and technologies, and employ more futurists than other firms. Driven by a paranoia that the future is constantly changing, they revisit their plans often.

Strategy development is by definition geared toward the future, but will always be rooted in the past. An understanding of its history, therefore, is indispensable if one is to know the actual strength of a brand. First and foremost, brands demand continuity. The key question is, what does the future of the brand we want to realize look like, and what must be maintained from the past in order to achieve that? What is sacred and what can be renewed? The image of Betty Crocker on the package and in advertising has constantly been updated over the years in order that the personality reflected in the image continues to look modern.

Most psychologists see the content of people's memory as permanent (see Franzen and Bouwman 2001)—that is, we can add new elements but cannot remove existing ones. In particular, the mental images of large, long-existing brands are so embedded in public memory that changing them would be extremely time-consuming and costly. Deciding to change them anyway should

Figure 3.2 **Strategy as Thinking in Time**

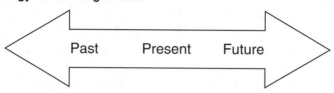

only be undertaken for very good reasons. A gradual adjustment to the spirit of the times, without losing sight of the past, is the secret of strong brands.

> *Principle:* Brand strategy is oriented toward the future but, at the same time, must be rooted in the past. The secret of a strong brand is constant renewal that preserves its historical essence.

Strategy as Ambition

Strategic thinking is driven by the ambition of reaching a higher goal and the willingness to make personal sacrifices for that sake. This was the ambition of Canon's "Beat Xerox," and Virgin's "Beat British Airways." Hamel and Prahalad (1994) define this concept of strategic intent as chasing a main goal to which everything else is subordinated:

> Strategic intent is our term for such an animating dream. . . . It also implies a particular point of view about the long-term market or competitive position that a firm hopes to build over the coming decade or so. Hence, it conveys a sense of direction. A strategic intent is differentiated; it implies a competitively unique point of view about the future. It holds out to employees the promise of exploring new competitive territory. Hence, it conveys a sense of discovery. Strategic intent has an emotional edge to it; it is a goal that employees perceive as inherently worthwhile. Hence, it implies a sense of destiny. Direction, discovery, and destiny. These are the attributes of strategic intent.

Strategic ambition is focused on the essence of wanting to win and motivating people through communication of the value of the main goal. It provides the focus that enables individuals in an organization to connect to a higher goal, direct their energy, and resist distractions. An example from history is the American Apollo program, whose main goal was to reach the moon before the Russians.

Liedtka (1998) draws a comparison with the concept of psychic energy—directing energy toward a single goal, as professional athletes do. This kind of focus entails the capacity to be enthusiastic and dedicated to achieving the goal. The danger lies in setting goals that are not clear or realistic, as Durk Jager did as CEO of Procter & Gamble (in Smit and Ligtenberg 2000): Jager, who reached the top of P&G in 1998, developed a very ambitious plan to shift the organization of the company from a regional-based to a product category–based structure. Under the motto "Organization 2000," his program praised "speed, innovation, and stretch" as core values. As financial goal, he proposed a profit growth from 15 to 17 percent. However, he underestimated the resistance of an organization that had existed for 163 years and was used to tight, rooted procedures. Within a short period he had to adjust the 15 to 17 percent profit growth to 1 to 2 percent, the share price crumbled by 50 percent in six months, and Jager was replaced by a new CEO who promised immediate improvement by emphasizing the organization's existing assets.

What Makes a Strategy Successful?

The characteristics of effective strategies give some idea as to how to assess the effectiveness of strategy development in a general way. It is definitely useful to test the formulation of strategies against this checklist of criteria:

- clear and decisive goals
- simplicity
- motivating impact
- committed leadership
- feasibility
- consistency
- concentration
- enterprise
- flexibility
- surprise
- security

Managers have to be able to attest to the success of their strategies. That usually means meeting measurable goals, so the criteria, in most cases, are rational and knowledge-based. There is a place for intuitive and experience-based assessment, particularly for the big picture of how various systems are interacting and reinforcing one another, but most business decisions in Western countries are evaluated on the basis of quantitative information, which addresses the pieces and parts of the strategy rather than the big picture. There is a need for brand evaluation systems that go beyond tracking studies.

BRAND STRATEGY

We started this chapter by suggesting that the concept of strategy is sometimes unclear, particularly in the area of branding. Part of the problem lies in two different ways the concept of strategy is used in marketing. On one level, the term has a big-picture meaning and refers to philosophical approaches used in managing a brand. For example, we might refer to a brand extension strategy as opposed to a new product strategy. On a more programmatic level, however, strategy refers to specific plans designed to accomplish specific, usually short-term goals—the activities needed, in other words, to accomplish the brand's objectives.

In Chapter 1, we mentioned a review of branding literature that led us to identify the buzzwords and key concepts of branding. A similar review of the leading books on branding finds a dearth of definitions or even explanations of what the authors mean when they use the phrase *brand strategy*. In most cases, the concept of strategy seems presumed to be widely understood so a definition is not needed. On the big-picture level, however, it appears that these experts all have personal philosophies of brand strategy that are radically different in their focus. For example, compare the approaches to brand strategy summarized below:

- Focus on integration as the strategic process for building brands—Leslie de Chernatony, *From Brand Vision to Brand Evaluation*; Tom Duncan and Sandra Moriarty, *Driving Brand Value.*
- Focus on brand asset management strategy—Scott Davis, *Brand Asset Management.*
- Focus on leadership systems and strategic integration of core competences in order to create added value—Chris Macrae, *Brand Chartering Handbook.*
- Focus on brand identity; focus on the brand covenant with customers—Lynn Upshaw, *Building Brand Identity.*
- Focus on customer relationships—Stewart Pearson, *Building Brands Directly.*
- Focus on brand equity—David Aaker, *Managing Brand Equity*; Kevin Keller, *Strategic Brand Management.*
- Focus on emotional connections and product innovation—Scott Bedbury, *A New Brand World.*
- Focus on employees who translate brand strategy into reality—Nicholas Ind, *Living the Brand.*
- Focus on communication as a brand strategy driver—Tom Duncan and Sandra Moriarty, "A Communication-Based Marketing Model for Managing Relationships."
- Focus on consumer satisfaction—William Weilbacher, *Brand Marketing.*
- Focus on brand experiences—Chris Macrae, *World Class Brands.*
- Focus on stakeholder expectations and brand experiences—James Gregory, *The Best of Branding.*
- Focus on social responsibility—Marc Gobé, *Citizen Brand.*

In terms of elements and components of brand strategy, these various authors refer to brand architecture, brand relationships, brand stakeholders, brand reputation, brand personality, brand promise, brand position, brand differentiation, brand image, brand reputation, brand values, brand identity (recognition cues, as well as brand meaning), brand essence, brand character, brand soul, and brand culture, among others.

This analysis of philosophies, elements, and components provides a framework for analyzing how brand strategy development works, which is the subject of the remaining chapters in this book. The chapters that follow discuss the essential components of a brand system, which we have identified not only from reviewing the literature on branding, but also from personal experience in managing brands.

THE STRATEGIC THINKING BEHIND SWATCH

Strategic thinking, in the Swatch case, meant moving from a vision of the product as a watch made of finely engineered components to seeing the brand as a fashion statement. In other words, Swatch is not about the pieces and parts of a watch or the technology that makes them run, no matter how well engineered. Instead, the Swatch brand is an emotional message that attests to the creativity and fantasy of its imaginative designers and embodies the attitude and innovative culture of the company, as well as the fashion culture of its buyers.

Like the Swatch brand image, the company's president found a powerful brand strategy in the emotional/intuitive area, rather than the rational/logical approach. The brand strategy reflected an understanding of all the critical criteria—the goals were clear and well understood; the approach was powerful in its simplicity and powerful, also, in its motivational impact; the leadership commitment was evident, as was the strategy's feasibility, consistency, and focus; the effort was enterprising, surprising, and flexible enough to move the brand in a different direction, surprising competitors and bringing security to the brand's future.

CHAPTER 4

THE NATURE OF BRANDS AND BRAND FUNCTIONS

The first step in brand strategy is the determination of the function of the brand and how it relates to consumers' basic decisions about the product category. It is very hard to disassociate brands from the products, services, and categories they are linked to. Xerox is copying machines, Vick's is cough drops, and 7-Eleven is a convenience store. The combination of brand and product is a process of symbiosis—two different organisms living together in a close relationship for the benefit of both. Gillette, for example, is strongly linked to shaving products and dominates the shaving category.

GILLETTE: THE BEST A MAN CAN GET

In 1895, King C. Gillette got the idea to make a disposable razor blade. He encountered the expected incredulity: people did not think it would be possible to make a thin slice of metal so sharp that it could serve as a razor blade. Gillette persevered, and in 1902 he managed to develop a machine that could roll out extremely thin slices of steel with a cutting edge. In 1903 he sold the first fifty sets of razor blades.

Since then, the Gillette Safety Razor Company has kept developing the product, which is now the worldwide market leader in the shaving category, with a market share of about 65 percent. The following is an overview of the most important technological innovations in the shaving category during the last fifty years:

1960	Polymer coating on the shaving surface to prolong blade sharpness
1967	The Techmatic, the first razor in a plastic holder
1971	The GII, the first razor with two blades
1975	The Contour, the first flexible blade, whose position adjusts to the face
1986	Addition of the Lubrastrip, which eases the shaving process
1991	The Sensor, with elastic blades, and the Sensor for Women
1994	The Sensor Excel, with a strip that precedes the blades, tightening the skin
1998	The Mach 3, the first razor with three blades, which shaves more smoothly and quickly
2002	The Mach 3 Turbo, with antifriction blades and Vitamin E lubricating strip
2004	The M3 Power, a battery-operated, pulsating model
2006	The Fusion, with five closely spaced blades, a chip giving micro-pulsing power, and a trimming blade for sideburns

Even though Gillette has dominated the shaving category, it hit on some hard times in the 1980s when disposable razors became popular and competitors like Bic were making inroads on Gillette's business. Gillette answered with the Good News disposable; however, consumer research found that the new subcategory was beginning to shift Gillette's image from engineering excellence to the production of razors described as "hollow, plastic, and blue."

To redefine its place as the leader in shaving technology, the company asked its advertising agency, BBDO, to develop a repositioning campaign that would reassert Gillette's quality. The answer was the legendary campaign expressed in the well-known slogan, "Gillette: The Best a Man Can Get." The campaign, launched in 1989, underscored the idea that Gillette understands what it takes to make a man feel good as he shaves. It has been cited as one of the most successful advertising campaigns ever.

But Gillette did not rely exclusively on a great advertising campaign to turn its image around. The company also turned to its research-and-development heritage and followed the successful "Best a Man Can Get" campaign in the 1990s with such product developments as the Sensor, the Sensor for Women, the sensor Excel, and eventually the Mach 3. Each of these was launched with a fully integrated campaign managed by BBDO, the keeper of the Gillette brand image, but led off by a public relations campaign that made news of the successive engineering breakthroughs. The PR efforts were designed by Porter/Novelli, BBDO's partner, and involved a team of other agencies that provided sales promotion and direct marketing support for the brand launches. To paraphrase the slogan, the marketing communication efforts were also "the best a brand can get."

Sources: Superbrands (2003); Burnett and Moriarty (2000); Reuters (2005).

BRANDS AS SERVICE PROVIDERS

What is it that the symbiosis between a brand and a product does? What is the role of a brand—its mission in life? When we speak about a brand's function, in essence, we are saying that all brands are service providers. By fulfilling this function of providing service, as well as delivering familiarity that reduces risk, brands acquire value for their users. We call this service brand function the "binding factor" between brands and consumers.

But brands not only provide a service function for customers, they also provide a service function for their manufacturers. Franzen et al. (1999) make a distinction between the function of the brand for the company and its function for the consumer, which reflects the approach we use in this book. A core function can always be identified as the primary representation of the brand's right of existence. This core function is the most important reason for the company to produce the product, as well as for the consumer to buy the brand.

The Complexity of Brand Functions

As in other areas of systems thinking, brands can have several simultaneous functions, and a brand can also have several functions for several groups of people. Or, more simply put, the same brand can have different functions at different moments—for instance, before, during, or after the purchase, during use, and so on.

Not all functions are equally important for brand preference. Some functions are experienced by consumers as self-evident. These functions will not earn the brand any added value against competing brands. Still, insight into these functions is not superfluous because they often constitute an entry requirement if a brand is to enter a category at all. They form the basis of the brand's relation to its product category.

In addition to functions that competing brands have in common, there are functions in which brands in the same category differ from one another. Although cigarette brands are often automatically allocated a symbolic function, research has shown that the brand Marlboro has a different core function for its users than the brand Gauloises Blondes. Probably thanks to its leadership position in the market and its ubiquitousness, the function Marlboro fulfills is not so much symbolic as it is about security. Gauloises Blondes, precisely because of its smaller market share, is more suitable to fulfill a symbolic (or expressive) function (Berg 1999).

Since the emergence of the very first brands, brand functions have developed further. Brands have kept expanding their services—not only can they help consumers recognize the producers, but nowadays they often pretend to be able to accompany people on their way to self-fulfillment (Sony's "go create," Nike's "just do it," and Siemens's "be inspired"). The range of human needs, desires, and values that brands think (or hope) they can supply is ever expanding.

A real understanding about the functions of brands is that they only make the brand valuable when their users identify and recognize the function. One could easily question to what degree people buy and use the brand Siemens to provide for their need for self-fulfillment. In other words, a brand function cannot be invented; the function must be discovered in the way the customer perceives the brand (and its relationship to the product category). As soon as the (potential) core function of a brand for a specific group is found, it can give direction to the development of brand and communication strategy.

> *Principle:* Brands are essentially service providers. They have a function for both consumers and producers—brand strategy development requires primarily an awareness of the essential functions a brand fulfills for both groups.

The Historical Development of Brand Functions

This chapter begins with a description of the historical development of the phenomenon of brands and their function, from a primal identification function in the Middle Ages to the concept of the brand as a relationship in our times. Based on the evolution of the concept of a brand, we distinguish several brand functions for consumers and producers.

1850: The Identification Function of Brands

The concept of brand originally stood for an article branded by a manufacturer or merchant. As early as the Middle Ages, artisans put initials on their merchandise to enable customers to repeat the purchase if they were satisfied with the product. Later on, distributors took over the custom, and shopkeepers put their names on products they bought from smaller manufacturers.

When production became separate from trade during the Industrial Revolution, these recognition signs from entrepreneurs—usually family names—served as a guarantee of the provenience of the products. This is how brands like Philips, Citröen, Knorr, Nestlé, Maggi, Cointreau, Heineken, Wedgwood, Levi Strauss, Bayer, and countless others came into being. With their name, these companies implicitly offered security to consumers. This primal function of a brand—the identification and recognition of its maker—is still current and important. In fact, many marketing manuals still discuss the brand only within this meaning. Table 4.1 shows some examples of well-known brands from that period that still carry the name of their long-deceased founders.

1900: The Benefit Function of Product Branding

The meaning of brands is becoming increasingly broader. At the end of the nineteenth century, brands emerged that were linked to individual products. On that basis, buyers knew which product they were looking for and what the products' specific characteristics were. This is how Americans learned that Ivory soap floated in water and was 99 and 44/100 percent pure, and consumers in the Netherlands found out that Blue Band was a margarine with vitamins, minerals, and carotene.

The brand represented one specific product or a number of related products with certain specific attributes. As products and services became more differentiated, producers started selling more brands together, each brand representing a specific package of attributes. From pure product identification, brands developed into stenographic signs for products or services with very specific characteristics and benefits.

1950: The Symbolic Function of Branding

In the middle of the twentieth century, the belief emerged among marketers that brands were not only bought for the functional characteristics of the products and services they were linked to, but also for the symbolic meanings that they represented. Product quality was increasingly relegated to a basic condition that was no longer an effective means to distinguish the brand from its competitors.

As developing and maintaining product differentiation became increasingly difficult, companies began to create differentiated symbolic brand meanings. Thanks to the symbolic meanings they are linked to, brands have a great influence on how people perceive products. Brands add emotion to the world of functional products. Brands can represent lifestyles and values (Lexus, Rolex), function as symbols of interpersonal role play (Nike, Gap), and transform the consumer experience of the naked product into a pleasurable event (Starbucks, Bloomingdale's). Thanks to these symbolic meanings, on the basis of a brand people ascribe a level of quality to a product that cannot always be proven in a laboratory.

The emotional experience of the brand has become just as important—sometimes even more so—than the instrumental function of the product. The brand differentiates the product and the services from similar products that technically may be just as good, but appeal less to the imagination. Nike's marketing managers discovered when the brand became a status symbol among kids, that young people all over the world would cut each other's throats for the newest pair of

Table 4.1

Brand Names and Their Founders

Brand name	Inventor/founder	Country	Year	Original product
Bols	Lucas Bols	NL	1575	Liquor
Douwe Egberts	Douwe Egberts	NL	1753	Coffee and tobacco
Schweppes	Jakob Schweppe	USA	1780	Tonic ("Indian tonic water")
Van Houten	Coenraad Johannes van Houten	NL	1828	Cacao in powder form
Colt	Samuel Colt	USA	1835	Revolver ("six shooter")
John Deere	John Deere	USA	1837	Steel plough
Levi Strauss	Oscar Levi Strauss	USA	1850	Jeans (working clothes)
Singer	Isaac Meritt Singer	USA	1850	First working sewing machine
Honig	Klaas Honig	NL	1867	Starch
Grand Marnier	Louis Alexandre Marnier	F	1872	Liquor
Linde	Karl von Linde	D	1872	Cooler (with ammonia compressor)
Heinz	Henry Heinz	USA	1876	Tomato ketchup (bottled)
Heineken	Gerard Heineken	NL	1879	Beer
Gestetner	David Gestetner	H	1881	Duplicating machine
Benz	Karl Benz	D	1883	Automobile in its current form
Maggi	Julius Maggi	D	1886	Soup flavoring
Spalding	Albert Goodwill Spalding	USA	1886	Baseballs, tennis balls, etc.
Dunlop	John Boyd Dunlop	GB	1888	Air tire
Michelin	Edouard and André Michelin	F	1889	Demountable bicycle tire
Philips	Anton and Gerard Philips	NL	1891	Light bulbs
Browning	John Moses Browning	B	1896	Firearms (model 1900)
Gillette	King C. Gillette	USA	1901	Disposable razors
Kellogg's	Will Keith Kellogg	USA	1906	Corn flakes
Cartier	Louis Cartier	F	1904	Jewels/wristwatch
Evinrude	Ole Evinrude	USA	1909	Outboard motor
Boeing	William Boeing	USA	1916	Airplanes
Birds Eye	Clarence Birdseye	USA	1930	Frozen foods
Tupperware	Earl W. Tupperware	USA	1938	Plastic storage boxes

Nikes. It was not because of the quality of the product, but rather the power of a youth movement searching for badges and status symbols.

According to Yasin, consumers also seem willing to pay for the perceived added value. Compared with generic brands, leading brands in England benefited from a 40 percent higher surplus value (Luik and Waterson 1996). It is therefore not surprising that brands have taken a more central position in the minds of producers. Unilever has a policy that it is in the business of marketing brands, not products.

Managers began to see brands primarily as elements in the memory of consumers. The literature was dominated by concepts such as brand familiarity and brand image, and building brands became synonymous with advertising and promotion. Brand and brand strategy management became autonomous focal issues.

1990s: The Relationship Function of Branding

Until about 1995, consumers' behavioral loyalty to the brands they were buying and using was regarded as the ultimate goal of branding. But then a novel way of looking at branding began to take hold, based on the metaphor of interpersonal relationships. The brand and the consumer were now seen as partners in a dyadic relationship conceptually similar to the relationships established between two people.

Regis McKenna wrote about this phenomenon in *Relationship Marketing* (1991b), and Terry Vavra's book on *Aftermarketing* (1992) argued that customer relationships (and the databases that made corporate memory possible) were important long after the sale was made. The relationship metaphor seemed to accurately describe many aspects of customer-brand interaction—such as the use of nicknames and personal terms of endorsement for one's favorite brands—and led to an emphasis in brand strategy on brand personality.

Don Peppers and Martha Rogers (1993) proclaimed *The One-to-One Future*. Instead of trying to sell a brand to as many customers as possible, the new "share of customer marketing" would concentrate on one customer at a time. Instead of using mass media to expose an audience to a brand message, a brand would now have a conversation with each of its customers.

1990s: The Societal Branding Function

In the late twentieth century, business faced many challenges. It seemed that bottom lines and shareholder value had become the overriding principles for corporate management. In 1984 gas leaked from a Union Carbide plant in India, killing 8,000 people. In 1989 the *Exxon Valdez* grounded in Alaska, spilling 11 million gallons of oil. Lowering costs had become the primary focus of management. Production was shifted to low-wages-countries, where workers, often children, had to do their jobs in sweatshops under abominable circumstances for starvation wages and with total disregard for environmental pollution. Naomie Klein (2000) pilloried a number of world-famous brands in her best seller *No Logo*, which created a great stir in the media and among union leaders, advertising practitioners, and corporate directors. Not that they wholeheartedly agreed with her indictment, but it at least made them think about the social responsibilities of their brands.

Companies had seen branding only as a marketing tool and had been blind to the societal context in which it took place. But now brands got the blame for all the negative influence that a firm's behavior had on society as a whole and on each of its stakeholder groups. Philip Kotler and Gerald Zaltman (1971) began working with the concept of social marketing as early as the 1970s. With such efforts, branding began to take a societal view—brands would not only have a function for consumers, but would have to make contributions to society. They would have to become what Gobé called in his 2002 book "citizen brands."

1990s: The Integrated Branding Function

In concert with the movement toward societal branding, business leaders became aware that their brands had become a summary of everything a business is, says, does, and wants to be. Furthermore, everything a brand does and sometimes what it does not do sends a message, according to Duncan and Moriarty, who examined the concept of integrated branding in *Driving Brand Value* (1997a).

Brands describe and shape how an organization works and they define the customer's experience. Customers judge brands holistically—they expect the producers to be good citizens, good employers, and trustworthy bookkeepers. A brand should guide all actions within a company—in senior management, product or service development, human resources, operations, marketing, and customer service. Without company alignment and execution—referred to as "living the brand"—all branding efforts are doomed to fall short. A brand is only as powerful as its total package. "Brand-based strategic management" is the new idea, with the brand as the point of departure for the business strategy. Vision and mission are the leading branding principles. Scott Davis and Michael Dunn articulate that brand-as-vision model in their book, *Building the Brand-Driven Business* (2002).

2000: The Experience Branding Function

The 1990s could be considered the decade of abundance, when product performance and even psychosocial meanings became commodities. Pine and Gilmore (1999) welcomed consumers to a new "experience economy" in their book of that name. Brands now had to offer multisensory experiences, not just functional and/or symbolic meanings. Brands used to manifest themselves primarily in sight and sound, but now also had to appeal to taste, smell, and touch. Product and packaging design became the new branding power tools, and producers started to create environments in which their brands would be optimally experienced. They opened brand stores on the high streets in the world's leading cities and redesigned and opened their factory buildings for an intense and fascinating brand experience.

In contemporary times, the brand now acts as an integration instrument, internally by steering development programs, capacities, and personal orientations, and externally by developing common ground with suppliers, vendors, and other stakeholder groups. McDonald's is not just a restaurant where you can eat hamburgers—it is a total experience in which the personnel's friendly faces contribute as much to brand evaluation as does the quality of the hamburgers. The contracts that McDonald's employees sign even have a clause that requires them to radiate cheerfulness.

The brand no longer represents only brand familiarity and brand image; it has become a way of living for the company. It is not just a new advertising campaign or a new promotion—it is now the core of all activities, a part of everyone's job description, from the receptionist to the chair of the board.

This direction-giving role is most clearly self-evident when there is a personal relationship between producer and consumer, as is the case in the services sector, which includes retail. A brand is less about standardized products that leave the factory with a brand label on them, and more about performances that have to be delivered every day, often by thousands of employees. Employees have to be motivated to present themselves naturally as service-oriented to customers and are led by clear goals, guidelines, and principles that emanate from the mission of the brand.

From Identification to Relationship

This short historical overview shows the development that the brand phenomenon has undergone in the last 150 years. In the last decade, the relationship function has become the center of marketers' interest. A brand is thus back to where it started—in the Middle Ages, the things that consumers bought had the name of the manufacturer on them. In the twenty-first century, the brand continues to be, more than anything else, a symbol for the relationship entered into between producer and consumer.

Principle: In the nineteenth century, brands emerged as a means of identifying their makers. In the twenty-first century, they remain symbols of the relationship entered into by producers and consumers.

Relationship marketing, however, is not as straightforward as it sounds. Not all users have what, with some brands, can be called a relationship. The number of brands people have this connection with and its duration and quality are limited. Fournier (1994) identified a large variation in relationship quality, even with well-known brands such as Coca-Cola, Nike, and Levi's.

In fact, relationships between people are no different. Most people have only a few real friends with whom they have an intense, long-term relationship. By far, their relationships with most others tend to be superficial and temporary. That does not mean, however, that the goal of creating a strong bond between a brand and its customers is not an important management objective. The stronger the bond, the higher the loyalty and the greater the brand equity. It may be harder in some categories than in others, but any increase in the strength of the brand relationship will ultimately increase profits.

We will now analyze in more detail each of the functions that evolved for consumers and customers, as well as for producers, and indicate their consequences for brand management.

THE CORPORATE VIEW OF BRAND FUNCTIONS

As we have said, the functions of brands differ if you are looking at them through the lens of a brand strategy or through the eyes of consumers. First, let us consider the corporate perspective of brand functions.

The Brand as Driver of Revenue

A basic function of a brand is to establish a point of competitive difference among similar products in a category. That is done primarily through the ability of a brand to create meaning and transform a product into something special with its own unique identity. This ability translates into a brand's equity: the influence it exerts on the category buyers' purchasing behavior.

By building, maintaining, and strengthening a brand's equity, a company can attain a number of economic advantages, which can be summarized as follows:

- Within the category or categories in which a brand is present, it will create a set of buyers (the "consumer franchise") who have a certain degree of preference for the brand. They tend to reduce their information search and switching behavior.
- The preference of the consumer franchise of a brand will influence the trade to stock the brand. The brand's distribution creates opportunity for consumers to buy the brand.
- The consumer preference leads to a market share of the brand, which tends to be proportional to its relative strength. The number 1, 2, and 3 brands in a category tend to take up on average more than 60 percent of the total sales in that category, in a ratio of 4:2:1.

- The high sales volumes of strong brands lead to cost advantages in production and marketing, which have a positive effect on the brands' profitability.
- The consumer preference for the brand leads to increased marketing communication effectiveness.
- The consumer preference leads to stability of future cash flows. Market shares of strong brands tend to be relatively stable over time, reducing the risk of weakening the future cash flows of the company and hence the discounting rate of these cash flows.
- The brand positively influences the quality and value perceptions of its users, who are willing to pay a higher price as a result. Studies have demonstrated that strong brands tend to sell at a 25 percent premium to weaker brands and at a premium of up to 200 percent to private labels.
- The combination of a relatively high market share, a premium price, and low production and marketing costs leads to a relatively high profitability for strong brands.
- Strong brands can deliver strong revenue growth.
- Companies with strong brands in their brand portfolios tend to be more profitable than companies without brands or with only weaker brands in their portfolio. Brand-driven companies on average reach an operational profit that is almost twice as high as their category's average.
- The combination of higher sales volumes and higher profitability leads to a higher shareholder return at brand-dominated companies compared to the market average and to lower shareholder return at companies with weaker brands.
- The combination of risk reduction of future cash flows and high profitability has a positive influence on the company's stock-performance.

Brand Orientation: The Corporate Mind-Set

In Chapter 13 we will see that there are both big and small, strong and weak brands. With a view of the tremendous economic advantages that a strong brand has for companies, we should expect that strategic brand management would be given a high priority in company management. That is not always the case.

Companies that have come to realize the real power of their brands tend to place them at the center of their organization and strategy. They treat them as true symbols in an ongoing interaction between the company and its customers. We call this attitude the "brand orientation" of a company. Urde (1999) defines it as an approach in which organization revolves around the creation, development and protection of brand identity. This happens in an ongoing interaction with target consumers with the goal of achieving a competitive advantage. True brand-oriented companies constantly work to keep their brands alive and relevant. They continually build integrated strategies to support this focus. They work hard to build brand competencies and they make sure to gain sufficient market-based information to ascertain that their strategy implementation is effective.

But there also are numerous companies that only pay lip service to the management of their brands. Their approach is merely to have or own brands—even spending advertising for them, but without a deeper understanding of the brand phenomenon and without building true branding competence. Gromark and Melin developed a brand orientation index consisting of eight factors, which together explain the variation in brand orientation value:

1. *Approach:* awareness of the relationship between branding and profitability, development of strong brands as a natural part of the business model, approaching brand

building as a core competence, seeing brand advertising as an investment rather than a cost.

2. *Implementation:* degree to which the brand is used as the guiding star for the development of a value-driven organization and for the motivation of employees to live up to the brand promise.

3. *Goals and follow-up:* the capacity of the company to define clear goals for the branding activities and measure their performance.

4. *Relationships:* using the brand not only as a means to create relationships with consumers, but also more broadly as the pivot in the company's relationships with other stakeholder groups.

5. *Identity development and protection:* paying attention to the brand's legal protection, visual identity, and mental positioning.

6. *Operational development:* the company's ability to employ the brand's core value as a point of departure for developing activities such as product development, internal communication, and marketing communication.

7. *Top-management participation:* ensuring that top management is really involved in brand strategy development and acting as ambassador for the brand.

8. *Responsibility and roles:* ensuring that brand responsibilities are well defined, clarifying who is responsible for strategic, executional, and tactical matters.

Gromark and Melin interviewed 263 Swedish companies to measure how they performed on each of these factors. A cluster analysis of the scores produced four different types of companies:

1. *Leaders:* companies with a high level of brand orientation; the brand is the heart of strategy development and implementation.

2. *Educators:* companies that see their brand as the bearer of culture; branding is primarily seen as culture development within the company.

3. *Salesmen:* companies that see their brand as a tactical sales instrument for products; branding is focused on consumers; internal branding is absent.

4. *Skeptics:* companies with a hesitant attitude toward branding issues, a lack of true branding expertise, and a lack of a clear direction in brand development.

An analysis of the profitability of companies within each of the groups (Figure 4.1) showed that the leaders on average scored an "ebitda" (earnings, or operating profit, before interest, tax, depreciation, and amortization) of 14.4 percent, the skeptics only 8.0 percent (Gromark and Melin 2005). This Swedish research project is a strong demonstration of the effects of branding on the economic performance of companies. Brands are clearly assets that generate (future) economic benefits and should be managed as such.

Another advantage that a brand can have for a company is the possibility of business growth through such activities as brand and line extensions, as well as diversification. These can be new variants of the same product (line extensions), similar or related products (brand extensions), or products that have little or no affinity with what exists under the brand (brand diversification). These possibilities are discussed in more detail in Chapter 14.

There is a legal function to a brand, which means that a company can establish ownership over a unique product entity through trademarkable devices such as logos. These trademarks protect the company from misappropriation of the unique features of the product and brand, although that is sometimes a problem in developing countries where there is less respect for international laws.

Figure 4.1   **Profitability of Companies With a Brand Orientation** (in percent)

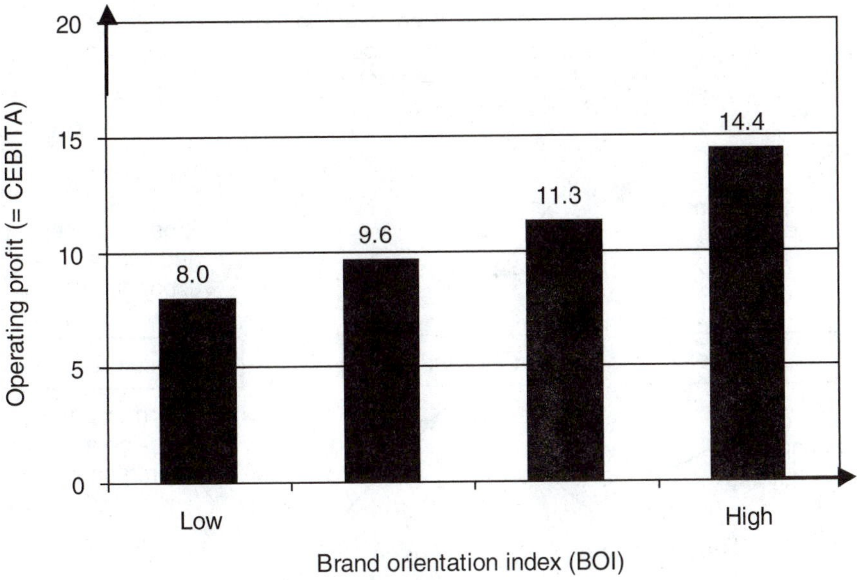

Source: Gromark and Melin (2005).

Principle: The level of brand orientation of a company has a big influence on its financial performance. Leaders with a high level of brand orientation are, on average, twice as profitable as skeptics.

The Relationship Function

For producers of fast-moving consumer goods (package goods in the United States), the brand is the point of departure for strategy management in other areas (see Figure 4.2). In effective branding, the brand integrates the consumer into the development and design of the products and services in a systematic process of interaction that gives content to the relationship with the company. The brand has become a well-organized way of living. The degree to which this can be accomplished depends partly on the meaning of the product in the life of the consumer—it is still difficult to have a deep emotional relationship with an insurance company whose premium invoices are the only manifestation of the relationship. Deep relationships will not easily develop with brands that are used briefly (Band-Aid, Alka-Seltzer) either.

Figure 4.2 expresses the independent position of the brand as a bridge between producers and consumers. It distinguishes between the brand as a container of rational product or service meanings and as a representation of emotional symbolic meanings. The producer supplies two types of input—the products and services it attaches to the brand, and the marketing-manifestations it surrounds the brand with. The consumer perceives both and constructs two different types of brand meanings. The brand leads a life of its own, however, because a producer can supply input, but cannot control the brand perception. The consumer is the sovereign over the construction of the

Figure 4.2   **The Brand as a Bridge Between Producers and Consumers**

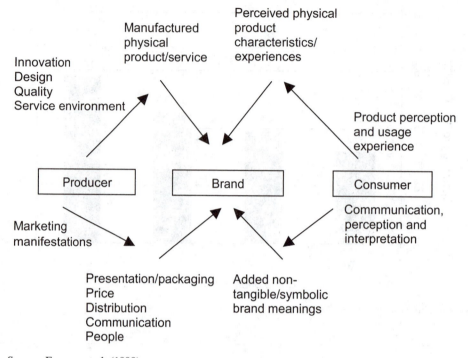

Source: Franzen et al. (1999).

brand's meaning. These meanings are not constant during the life of most brands because there are periods when a brand meaning does not conform to the producers' intentions. Changing the meanings of the brand (sometimes called repositioning) can be a difficult and sometimes impossible task, as we will see in the following chapters.

The idea is to develop a mutual relationship that is felt by producers and consumers (Figure 4.3). A brand gets a deeper meaning when the consumers have an idea that the people behind it are determined to give the customer a positive experience. Companies want to give their customers the feeling that their brands are authentic and available whenever necessary. For example, one of Unilever's many brands, Pond's, now has the Pond's Institute, which appeals to a small number of Pond's users, although they may be the ones with the most valuable brand relationship with Pond's.

Because a brand relationship is the link between a consumer and a brand, by definition there are two parts to it—the corporate perspective and the consumer perspective.

The function of the brand for the consumer emanates from their private motivations, and their relationships with their social environment, which is composed of an inner circle of close friends, colleagues, and relatives, and a wider circle of acquaintances. For the producer or manager, the brand also represents relationships with other stakeholders such as employees, trade partners, capital providers, and society at large. The nature of these relationships can assume many different forms, depending on the many components involved. The significante of all these relationships can vary depending upon the product category, brand heritage, stakeholder experiences and interac-

Figure 4.3 **The Brand as Relationship Concept**

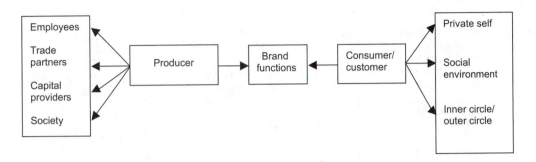

tions with the brand, and the brand's communication. The end result of the successful creation of a relationship between brand and customer is brand loyalty. We will discuss this relationship concept further in Chapter 12.

Principle: A brand relationship is characterized by an ongoing interaction between the producer and the customer. It is reciprocal and based on a company's appreciation of and behavior toward the consumer. It culminates in the strength of the brand's equity

The Brand Equity Function: The Culmination of Brand Relationships

The properties of a brand that have an influence on its market performance all come together in a concept known as brand equity, which is discussed in depth in Chapters 16 and 17. Brand equity is reviewed briefly here to establish this important function of brands, at least from the company's perspective.

The enormous amount of recent literature on brands provides countless definitions of this concept, but the most common understanding is that brand equity represents the strength of a brand, at the level of both the consumers and the market. Underlying these perspectives is the strength of the brand's relationships with all its myriad stakeholders, particularly employees, its suppliers and distribution system, and the financial community. Brand equity is the crystallization of the nature of the many and varied relationships between producers and their stakeholders (Duncan and Moriarty 1997a).

On the level of the consumer ("consumer brand equity"), we distinguish mental brand equity— the strength of the mental representation of a brand—as well as relationship brand equity and behavioral brand equity—the strength of brand purchasing habits and brand purchasing patterns (see Figure 4.4). The strength of the brand in the market refers to the distribution position and market dynamics, such as price premium, market share, and profit of a brand. The equity of a brand translates into its financial value (see Chapter 18).

These areas of brand strength detailed in Figure 4.4 are a set of interrelated systems. The goal of strategic brand development is to strengthen the position of a brand in all four areas. The systems through which a brand operates cannot be disconnected from one another: fundamental strengthening in one area will permeate into the other areas over time.

Figure 4.4 **The Concept of Brand Equity**

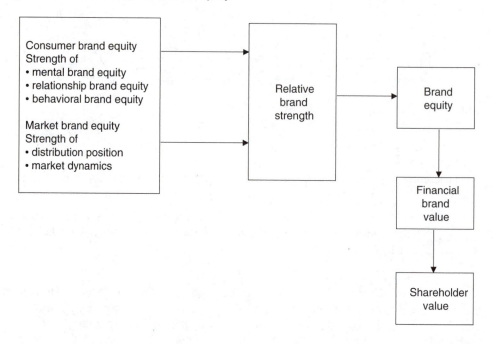

BRAND FUNCTIONS FOR CONSUMERS

Brands exist because humans innately want to name and categorize things. To make sense of our lives, we reduce the millions of information bits around us into objects and concepts. By doing so, we are able to share information—for example, we can talk about chairs and bananas and feel confident that others understand us—and make quick decisions—we know we sit on chairs but we do not sit on bananas. This is true for both corporate executives and consumers who go to the store to buy specific products that they like. How can they repeat that purchase if they find only a barrel of unlabeled bottles of shampoo or boxes of cereal? Perfume is perfume; cars are cars, right? Obviously that is not so for most consumers buying most products in most product categories.

In addition to the name and identification function, brands also exist because people are inclined to adopt a certain brand or set of brands as their favorite products in a given category. This elicits an affective response to a brand, as well as the cognitive one of identification. Just as brands perform various functions for a company, brands also play critical roles in the lives of consumers. We will talk briefly in this chapter about the brand choice, purchasing behavior, product representation, and symbolic functions.

The Brand Choice Function: Simplifying Consumer Decisions

Naming and categorizing depend on grouping objects and concepts according to similarities and separating them from other concepts according to differences. The more pronounced the similarities or differences, the easier it is for us to process information about the product and identify its category. The fewer ambiguities we have to deal with, the better, since subtlety forces us to discern more layers of attributes, which takes time and mental energy.

Figure 4.5 **Brand Functions**

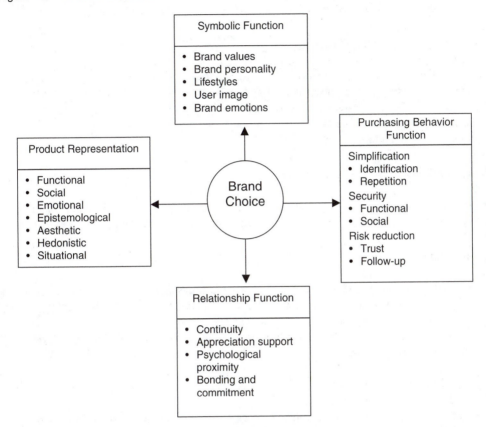

Through branding, product managers simplify the consumer's decision making by setting up the categorization process and separating one product from another. Chairs are chairs but Henredon is a particular type of chair, as Chiquita is a particular type of banana. Not only do brand names separate products in a category, they also add a cachet. As Arnold (1992) explains, a brand is a form of mental shorthand. It removes the need to devote a lot of effort to interpret the choices in the market. It carries all the meanings one needs to make a dependable and risk-free choice in only a few seconds.

For purposes of brand strategy development, it is necessary to have a clear notion of the functions that a specific brand has for consumers or customers. When we know that Ariel or Tide gets sold because of its functional performance, the communication will be geared primarily toward strengthening these associations. However, with brands chosen by consumers mainly to support their self-image, symbolic brand associations are the most important. For consumers, these meanings represent positive values that are instrumental to the achievement of their goals.

Four important groups of brand functions can be distinguished (Franzen and Bouwman 2001) in Figure 4.5, providing for many types of consumer needs:

1. *Purchasing behavior function:* the functions of brands in the purchasing behavior itself.
2. *Product representation function:* the brand as container of product meanings.

3. *Symbolic function:* the brand's ability to add symbolic meanings to the product.
4. *Relationship function:* the brand's ability to provide the value of long-term relationships.

The Purchasing Behavior Function

The primary group of functions that brands perform is found in the functions they fulfill in purchasing behavior, such as facilitation and risk reduction. These are the primal functions of brands. When we see purchasing behavior (e.g., shopping) as an important human activity, related functions can also be distinguished. The most important ones are understanding, simplification, security, optimization, trust, and follow-up.

Understanding

The brand is an authority that functions as a guide to help consumers to understand what is happening around them and to inform them which behavioral ways are normative.

Simplification

- *Identification:* The brand name is a container of meanings that facilitates the identification of the specifically sought product. Metaphorically speaking, brands in the purchasing environment function as signposts of a touring club on the highway. Brands tell us where something is (the detergent shelf), what something is (a product for washing delicate textiles), how something is (high-quality). This way we can consider price versus value and make a quick decision.
- *Optimization:* The brand helps to decide what is the best product in the category, the best performer for a particular purpose.
- *Repetition:* Brands make it possible to repeat a previous purchase without having to make the same cognitive effort all over again. This can even lead to an automation of the purchasing behavior. Thus brands save us an enormous amount of time.

Security

- *Functional security:* A brand provides security because of the continuity of the supply. The composition, amount, quality, and user experience are constant. A consumer knows exactly what to expect of a brand.
- *Social security:* In the social sphere, a brand offers security through its approval by colleagues or friends. It reduces the social risk of the purchase because it has a meaning within a group.

Risk Reduction

- *Trust in the producer:* When it comes to major single purchases, consumers may experience feelings of risk. Familiarity with a provider that inspires trust (Toyota's "Get the feeling") can reduce or even remove the perceived risk.
- *Follow-up:* Consumers assume that they can contact the producer and get help when they are not satisfied with the functioning of the product. Especially with products that require

maintenance (cars, some domestic appliances), consumers are confident that parts will be immediately available and that they will get quick service. With products for which information, education, or even training is necessary, the expectation is that the brand will provide for these services adequately.

Principle: A brand is a container of meanings whose primary function is to simplify consumer decision making.

The Product Representation Function

Some brands are bought mainly because of the value of the product they are associated with. In this type of brand, the product-brand association is very important, as here brands are primarily representatives of the product categories they are linked to (which is often the case in fast mover or package goods brands). The value of a brand for consumers would then be largely determined by the degree to which the product meets their expectations.

Consumer behavior experts have tried to categorize the functions that products have in people's lives. This seems to be more complicated than we might think. The most well-known classification was suggested by Seth et al. 1991 under the title "Why We Buy What We Buy." The authors distinguish five basic categories of product values, or reasons why, to which Lai (1995) added three more. On the basis of both classifications, we can distinguish the following eight values or purchasing reasons:

- *Functional values:* the capacity of products to carry out instrumental, utilitarian, or physical functions. These emanate from concrete, tangible characteristics of the products as an instrument. Some such products that make it possible to avoid or solve problems or to improve the material situation are detergents, medicines, insurance, means of transportation, kitchen appliances, and computers and software.
- *Social values:* the cultural values that the use of the product represents, especially the associations with social groups. These are symbolic meanings that are associated with a product in a specific culture, like wearing jeans at the office or sneakers with a suit, rolling one's own tobacco during meetings, or driving a motorcycle. These are socially visible products through which consumers give out a statement to their environment.
- *Emotional values:* the ability of products to activate emotions and influence moods, like video cameras, drinks, some food products, motion pictures, and greeting cards.
- *Epistemological values:* the role products play in knowledge development and intellectual stimulation by arousing curiosity, gathering new experiences, and expanding knowledge. Books, newspapers, magazines, certain television programs, the Internet, exotic vacations, and CD-ROMs are some examples.
- *Aesthetic values:* the ability of a product to satisfy our feeling for beauty and our style preferences. These flow out of the design and style marks of products such as clothing, interior decoration products, jewelry, and watches.
- *Hedonistic values:* the capacity of a product to provide sensory enjoyment, give pleasure, or evoke a feeling of well being and comfort. These are mainly the pleasures of life that stimulate the senses of taste, smell, hearing, and touch. Some products in this category are cigarettes and drinks, sweets, ice cream, food products, perfume, restaurant meals, certain hotels, and resorts.

- *Situational values:* the contribution of products to experiencing specific usage situations, and the capacity of influencing the experience of these situations. These are products used at feasts and special occasions, like champagne, the experience of drinking a cup of coffee together, or serving snacks at parties.
- *Holistic values:* the value of the product's harmony in all its aspects, the "coolness of the whole thing." This is the ideal combination of the preceding values as they take form in the total product constellation, as in the user-friendliness combined with design of Apple's iMac and iPod.

Of course, several functions can be present at the same time in products. To some degree, brands are associated with the functions of the product categories to which they are linked. Brands whose associations with the products represent the core product or category associations are positioned in memory on the basis of these product values. In this type of brand, the product-brand association is essential and should be carefully maintained in the communication process. In contrast, brands can also give a focus to the perception of the product functions and influence the value for the corresponding product performance. A piece of clothing of an expensive brand is often attributed better quality than a similar no-brand product. Just as the product influences brand perception, the brand influences product perception.

The Symbolic Function

Thanks to their symbolic meanings, brands can be used as a means of communication. This is known as the symbolic function. This group of brand values is formed by the symbolic meanings associated with certain brands. Symbolic meanings come about through a process of interaction between members of a culture or subculture and the messages delivered by the brand. Advertisers try to influence the process of symbolic meaning formation via mass communication.

Richins (1994) indicates that the value of possessions (in this case, brands) emanates from private as well as public meanings. The private meaning refers to the meaning the user of the brand allocates to it. The public meaning is the one allocated by groups in society or by society in its entirety. A meaning is generally not fully private or public; instead, there is a gradual transition between the two. This implies that the meaning of a brand for a consumer is influenced by the personal meaning that the consumer attaches to it, as well as by the meaning others give to it. Consumers derive symbolic meanings from seeing how brands manifest themselves, how others react to them, how brands are used and by whom. The following symbolic meaning categories can be distinguished:

- *Brand values:* the association between a brand and abstract values, such as individualism versus bonding (see Chapter 9).
- *Brand personality:* the associative link between a brand and certain human personality characteristics, such as sincerity, honesty, liveliness, or toughness (see Chapter 10).
- *User image:* the association between a brand and the perceived socioeconomic and personality characteristics of the stereotypical user (or user group) of the brand (see Chapters 10 and 11).
- *Lifestyles:* the association of a brand with a certain lifestyle, a way in which people prefer to live, spend their time; the interests and opinions they have.
- *Brand emotions:* the cognitive association of brands with specific emotions or with more holistic affects (positive, negative); the awareness that certain emotions "belong" with a brand (see Chapters 10 and 11).

Based on these meanings, brands can have a symbolic function for the consumer in different ways. Franzen et al. (1999) distinguish the three following variants:

- *The expressive or self-identification function:* Consumers use some brands to communicate certain messages about themselves—who they are, what they stand for, what values they consider important, and what they consider worthy of aspiration or rejection. Such brands are used as personality extensions, chosen only if they fit the image that someone wants to project to the outside world. In some circles it makes a big difference whether you drive a BMW or a Nissan or wear Diesel or Levi's jeans.
- *The social-adaptive function:* People like to look at others, out of curiosity or a desire to find out what their own position is. In this game of mutual observation, positioning, and evaluation, brands can play a role. Some brands (and products) serve as symbols that allow consumers to conform to the demands set by a subculture, thus assuming the desired identity and gaining acceptance by that specific social group. An example is the acceptance at school of new classmates based on their wearing a certain popular brand of clothing or athletic shoes.
- *The impressive function:* This function is about the emotions of satisfaction, self-fulfillment, or self-confidence that emanate from the possession or use of a brand. The meaning of the brand has developed in a cultural context (e.g., through advertising), but the feelings that its use or possession invoke are individual. For example, when a person is preparing for a job interview, the right clothing and makeup can provide a certain professional feeling, as well as increasing self-confidence. Choosing a brand based on social values, such as caring for the environment, can also be classified under the impressive function. For example, by buying products from The Body Shop, consumers can express sympathy with third-world farming cooperatives that supply the company with raw materials. Although this is about a social ideal, the consumers get a good feeling about the choice they make. The impressive function is about satisfying the private self. Sensory and intellectual satisfaction also contributes to this function. A brand can please its owner and others through its design, color, taste, or fragrance.

In brands that are primarily characterized by their symbolic meanings, the choice can also be highly determined by the perceived popularity of the brand. In Chapter 15, which discusses brand saliency, we see how important this principle is—for instance, in the beer market.

> *Principle:* The symbolic meanings of a brand can have a stronger influence on the consumer's buying behavior than its product meaning. They can have an expressive, social-adaptive, and impressive function.

STRATEGY IMPLICATIONS

Brand strategies emanate from the basic functions of brands for consumers and suppliers. It is therefore important to get as clear a picture as possible of the primary functions of a brand. We can distinguish five basic strategies that evolve from this analysis of brand functions:

1. *Signaling strategy:* Communication is geared mainly toward the function of the brand as a sign of identification for products. The brand name, the external characteristics of a brand, and packaging are central.

2. *Confidence strategy:* Communication is geared toward the reliability of the supplier.
3. *Product-focused strategy:* The product's properties and their function for the user are central to communication of the brand. The brand is the primary representative of the products to which it is linked.
4. *Symbolic strategy:* Communication is geared mainly toward the development of symbolic brand meanings. The product tends to play a role at the margin and is sometimes entirely absent.
5. *Relationship strategy:* The user is central. The brand is geared directly toward the consumer and aims at creating a feeling of relationship, trying to convince users that the brand is interested in them.

Within each of the basic strategies we can define more specific substrategies. By classifying product functions, several strategic directions emerge. The most important distinction here is that between utilitarian or instrumental products and ritual or transformational ones. Schmitt (1999), an exponent of experience marketing, makes a subclassification into the following basic strategies:

1. *Sense:* Communication emphasizes the aesthetic and epistemological values of a product (brand) by offering experience possibilities. An example is the campaign for Absolut Vodka, in which every expression incites a sensory or aesthetic experience.
2. *Feel:* Communication is geared toward activating product-related emotions with the intention of linking them associatively to the brand. This is the case with communication in Hallmark greeting cards.
3. *Think:* Communication appeals to intelligence, as is usual for many high-tech products.
4. *Act:* Communication is based on physical experiences, showing consumers alternative ways of doing things or stimulating participation. An example is Nike's "just do it."
5. *Relate:* Communication emphasizes a social setting that is central to the meaning of the product use. The Harley-Davidson HOG Club in the United States is a striking example.

In his classification, Schmitt does not include the utilitarian or instrumental direction, in which products are nothing more than problem solvers. The sixth strategy therefore would be:

6. *Problem-solving:* This strategy is based on the ability of a brand to solve the consumer's problems. An example would be a campaign for a new Gillette shaving line.

Marketing Communication Implications

The symbolic strategy is particularly important for marketing communication. It can be subclassified into several substrategies:

1. *Brand personality strategy:* Communication is geared toward developing personality associations with the brand.
2. *Value-oriented strategy:* Communication aims at creating associations between the brand and an end value, like those between American Maxwell House or Dutch Douwe Egberts coffee brands and images of family togetherness.
3. *Affective strategy:* Communication aims at linking a positive feeling to the brand.
4. *User image strategy:* Communication is aimed at linking a stereotypical image of the users to the brand.

A brand fulfills several functions, which can make an univocal choice difficult. Several strategies can go together. A certain balance will always be necessary between the brand as a representative of a product or service and the brand as an independent carrier of meanings that are added to the product. After all, people buy products and services. Brands can add symbolic meanings to them, but they can never be seen separately from the product. In the eyes of their creators, products must always retain an important role in brand communication.

GILLETTE AND THE FUNCTION OF THE BRAND

Historically, the primary function of a brand was to identify the product. It also served to differentiate the product from its competitors. Because of the familiarity that comes from previous and repeated use, a brand also anchored a relationship with a customer. All those functions continue to be central to the evolution and development of the Gillette brand.

The Gillette name, which honors the founder and inventor of the disposable razor blade, has been the leader in the shaving category ever since it launched the first disposable blade. The meaning of the brand has changed over the years as competitors made inroads on the brand's market share with new products like cheap disposable razors. Gillette fought back, however, protecting its leadership position by using its excellence in shaving technology to engineer a series of new products in the 1990s that separated it from the cheap, commodity products represented by the disposable razor. The Gillette product line, heralded in its famous slogan "The best a man can get," once again took on meaning as the recognized leader in the category.

And with the renewed research-and-development efforts behind new products such as the Sensor and the Mach 3, Gillette was able to shift the category from disposable razors back to well-engineered razors and the innovative blades they used. Not only did the company launch these innovative new products, such as the Mach 3, globally, but it also extended them to new categories, such as the Venus for Women, and used the power of this sub-brand to extend the business to even more new markets.

CHAPTER 5

BRAND CORE CONCEPT

The brand's core concept, sometimes called the essence, soul, or DNA of a brand, is a very important component of the system of brand strategy decisions because it tells the consumer precisely what the brand stands for—what it is all about. After identifying the brand function, the next step is defining the core or essence of the brand, as Red Bull did when it moved to dominate the energy drink category. The core concept could be compared with an admission ticket to enter the mental competition world, and it is also the weapon with which the brand enters the field of battle against the other brands.

RED BULL: THE PROTOTYPE OF ENERGY DRINKS

In 1984 Dietrich Mateschitz saw that rickshaw drivers in Thailand drank a beverage, Krating Daeng (translation: "red water buffalo"), to keep them energized throughout the day. He adapted it, translated its name into Red Bull, and packaged it in a small, blue-and-silver 8.3-ounce can.

Before launching the new brand, Mateschitz had Red Bull's acceptance tested with a catastrophic result: people did not accept the taste, the logo, or the brand name. "I had never before experienced such a disaster," he confesses. Nevertheless, he launched the drink in Austria in 1987 with the slogan "Red Bull gives you wings." The brand took off. After the first success in Austria, the brand was introduced in Germany in 1994, then in all western European countries, and in 1997 in the United States.

The lightly carbonated drink has a sweet, lemony taste, like a melted lollipop. Each can, which initially cost about two dollars in a convenience store, contains eighty milligrams of caffeine (more than twice as much as a similar serving of Mountain Dew and about the same as a strong cup of coffee) along with B vitamins and taurine, an amino acid.

Red Bull's prime consumers are young adults, better known as kids in their twenties. The company courts the college crowd and has also established itself in the black-and-blue world of extreme sports. The core tactic: Company reps target key neighborhoods, nightspots, and gyms city by city, region by region, relying on local scene-makers to spread the word.

Initially the drink of choice among extreme athletes and all-night ravers, Red Bull has worked its way into the local supermarket. In the process, it has spawned a new beverage category that has Coca-Cola and the other big companies rushing to catch up. With Red Bull leading the way, domestic sales of energy drinks in the United States since 1999 have grown by an impressive 68 percent a year.

Energy drinks are just a drop in the $80 billion beverage industry bucket, but the major players have learned to heed such fledgling trends. Mighty Gatorade started as a niche drink in 1967. To acquire the brand and become a sports drink superpower, Pepsi paid nearly $14 billion for Quaker Oats, which owns Gatorade. Determined not to miss out on the next breakout hit, Pepsi, Coke, and Anheuser-Busch have rolled out energy drinks. Busch went national with 180 (supposed to turn your energy around 180 degrees), and Coca-Cola introduced KMX (according to Coke, the letters do not mean anything but have an energetic sound) in several key markets. Pepsi, meanwhile, bought the South Beach Beverage Company and now counts the bluntly named Adrenaline Rush among its brands.

In 2005 Coke tapped the energy market with Full Throttle, a sugar-free drink, a clear indication of the potential further growth of the market. However, the Coca-Cola Company still trails Red Bull, which in 2007 had 47 percent of the U.S. market for energy drinks. "If you appreciate the product you want the real one, the original, not a Rolex made in Taiwan," Mateschitz declares. In Western Europe, Red Bull has continued to be the leading energy drink.

In just twenty years, Red Bull has developed into the absolute category prototype.

Sources: Noonan (2001); BeverageDaily.com (2003, 2005); Dolan (2005); Energy Fiend (2007).

CORE CONCEPT: THE ESSENCE OF THE BRAND

The mental representation of the most basic defining characteristics of a brand is what we call a *brand concept*. For example, Cadillac's brand concept is built on the core concept of ultimate luxury; the Cadillac brand name is even used to describe other products in unrelated categories that aspire to this standard, such as the Cadillac of power tools. A company's brand or corporate mission statement sums up the core concept and expresses the values that guide the company's business operations.

The Category Prototype

The core concept of a brand provides the organizing framework the brain uses to categorize the brand in a mental set of other brands that have corresponding characteristics and meanings. Based on the core concept, the brain then determines how well the brand represents the category-specific meanings. The brand that does this best goes, as it were, to the top of the list—it is the best example of the category, the *prototype brand*. In addition to the characteristic meanings that define the category and that the brand has in common with other brands in the mental category, the brain also looks for meanings with which it distinguishes one brand from the other competing brands in the category.

For brand concept development, it is important for managers to have insight into the system of meanings that gives the brand access to a category—the typical properties or category drivers that identify the category. Brands without these meanings run the risk of not being allowed to participate in the category because they are not perceived as a viable alternative. When consumers think of vodka, for example, they probably first think of prototype brands like Absolut, Smirnoff, and Stolichnaya instead of a vodka brand like Virgin. In most categories there are such prototype brands that tend to be the market leaders.

The brand that succeeds in making the strongest link with these category meanings has an enormous advantage over the others (often these others are the market leaders that were once part of the beginning of the category but have now fallen behind), and this advantage may lead to category dominance. It is important to realize that this dominance is always relative as meanings shift. The brain asks itself time and again what the best representation of the category is. It is therefore essential to keep these meanings fresh and updated. When they are neglected, the brand is at risk of losing not only dominance, but also legitimacy (its admission ticket to the category).

One of the most difficult questions regarding the core concept is how "different" a brand can be without becoming so deviant that the mental product category is thrown out by the brain and ends up in a segment or niche position. This problem will be analyzed further in Chapter 8, which discusses brand positioning.

Principle: The core concept is the most important element of the brand strategy system because it tells the consumer precisely what the brand stands for. It serves as an admission ticket to the mental competition field and is a weapon with which the brand enters the battlefield against other brands.

Typology of Brand Concepts

We have defined core concept in abstract terms, but it is useful to also explore its system of components. The contents of the brand core vary from brand to brand, but several basic brand concept categories can be identified. *The Mental World of Brands* (Franzen and Bouwman 2001) describes the most common components. This typology is useful because it lets a brand management team identify the logic of the brand's core concept and provides ideas about how to sharpen, refine, or strengthen it.

- *Brand as product:* The brand represents only one specific product within one category. It is the name of one object. The brand-product association stands at the brand's core as the brand immediately evokes the product it is linked to: Sensodyne is toothpaste, Oreos are cookies, and Chiquita is bananas. Such brands do not raise any questions as to what is in the package; the brand tells consumers exactly what they can expect. Some brands fall together with such a specific product that the brand name serves as an indicator of the product—there is no generic product name for the Post-it product category. Post-its are post-its, although they are sometimes referred to as little yellow sticky notes.
- *Brand as product category:* The brand is linked to one product category, offering within this category several product variants. Coca-Cola is a soft drink that encompasses Coke Classic, Diet Coke,

Cherry Coke, Caffeine-Free Coca-Cola, and others. A category brand is generally associated primarily with the basic category—in the case of Coca-Cola, that is a carbonated soft drink. This association often complicates the attempt to position the brand in subcategories, especially when another special brand serves as prototype within such a subcategory. That was the problem 7-Up faced when it tried to establish itself as the "un-cola" as a way to contrast its clear-colored drink against Coke. Red Bull created a whole new category—energy drinks—and has become this category's prototype.

• *Brand as product attribute:* The brand is strongly associated with a special product attribute or with a consumer advantage. It encompasses various product categories in which consumers experience this attribute as relevant. The letters in the name Becel (a European margarine brand) stand for Blood Cholesterol Lowering, indicating precisely what Becel stands for: it has "nonsaturated fat" as an attribute and "cholesterol-lowering" as a consumer promise and brand advantage. This type of brand usually comes about as a basic product in which the attribute is central and is then linked to another product category. Becel started with margarine and followed with Becel oil, salad dressing, coffee creamer, and cheese. The extension of the brand was limited by the degree to which the attribute was looked for in other products. Becel cheese, for example, seems to have been a less successful brand extension.

• *Brand as domain:* The brand is primarily associated with a certain domain—a market space inside which it enjoys specific expertise, such as the Home Depot retail brand. A domain can be narrowly delimited or broadly defined. It is generally a categorization at a higher abstraction level than the product category. However, domains can be defined in many different ways. A very common one is based on common applications and complementariness. Gillette is shaving in the broadest sense, including equipment and toiletries to be used in the shaving process. Gillette has tried to develop its brand into an ever-higher abstraction level, offering everything a man needs in the bathroom, including deodorants.

Nivea (from the Latin *neveus*, or snow-white) started out in 1912 as a product brand, a simple facial cream in a blue tin, to which Nivea talcum powder and Nivea hair lotion were added. The 1970s saw the introduction of a large number of body care products for all kinds of target groups, which expanded Nivea's association with body care into related core meanings, such as caring, protective, natural, fresh, uncomplicated, and relatively cheap. In 1997 Beiersdorf announced it would also introduce a cosmetics line under the brand name Nivea Make-Up to further cross its domain boundaries.

• *Brand as provenience:* With some brands, the country or region of provenience forms the most important association (Moet et Chandon champagne, Perrier water), constituting the core of the brand concept. With car brands, provenience is a primary categorization variable (Volkswagen and BMW are German and carry with them the German associations of quality engineering). Singapore Airlines is intensely associated with Singaporean stewardesses, their appearance and character traits. Buitoni represents eating Italian-style with an emphasis on pasta dishes.

• *Brand as people:* The brand chiefly represents a person or a combination of several persons, such as the Walt Disney company. In its purest form, such as the Disney brand, it is the name of someone known for outstanding performance in a certain field: an artist, musician, television personality, athlete, or engineer (Ford). When the activities take the shape of an enterprise, the brand represents primarily the founders who are still active. This is generally the case in the initial phase of all kinds of consulting firms, like advertising agencies, law firms, and organizational consultants. When the organizations become older and their namesakes have stepped down, these brands tend to develop into a different type of concept. By keeping the founder's legend alive, these "people brands" can prolong their original core for a long time. This is the case with brands like Chanel and Versace.

• *Brand as design:* The brand is no longer linked to a specific product category or domain, but is perceived as an authority in the area of design. It is known for its taste and design talents. The most well-known example is Swatch, originally linked to watches only, but with design as its core meaning. Swatch claims to offer people more than a watch, as it is not just about the mechanical side of the product, but also about the message behind it: high quality, low cost, the joy of living, a provocative personal culture (W. Taylor 1993). By now, Swatch has branched out from watches to Swatch telephones and Swatch skis. Other style brands are Laura Ashley and Alessi.

   • *Brand as emotion:* The brand is intensely linked to certain emotions. The Douwe Egberts coffee brand in the Netherlands is primarily associated with the warm-hearted feelings of people who enjoy being together and caring for their loved ones. Hallmark is linked to the sentiments expressed in greeting cards at the most personal and momentous occasions of life.

   • *Brand as personality:* Although most brands are associated with certain personal traits, some brands are defined by such traits. The meaning core for the brand consists of associations with human personality traits. Harley-Davidson is associated with an outlaw personality; Virgin is irreverent. The brand personality of Marlboro is characterized by masculinity and the freedom and individualism of the American West. Besides cigarettes, clothing collections, trips, and memorabilia are sold that fit this Marlboro brand essence. Chapter 10 is devoted to the brand personality concept.

   • *Brand as value system:* The core of this type of brand is formed by a set of values that are intensely experienced by the people directly involved with the brand who exert a power of attraction in broader circles. This is seen with political parties, churches, and charity institutions. Consumption brands can also be primarily defined with a set of values. Apple computers have always been about simplifying and demystifying computers so people who are not computer nerds can use them. With the launch of the Macintosh, the Apple brand meaning was expanded to include creativity, expressed not only in the functional attributes of the computer but also in its product design. Chapter 9 analyzes the value concept in depth.

   • *Brand as ideology:* The brand is a representation of a social ideal, a vision of how the world could be improved and a higher quality of life attained. The brand is always aspirational—it intends (or pretends) to contribute toward reaching a better situation than that of today. The Body Shop is not merely a shop for toiletries, one that has nothing to do with glamour; it also evokes a feeling of identifying with distant peoples, of being good citizens of the world, of an altruistic lifestyle. The Body Shop refuses to carry out tests on animals and donates money to oppressed Indian tribes. Whoever buys there is doing a noble action. Nike is passionate about sports and athletic performance. It wants to make the best sporting shoes and fitness articles in the world. This means close cooperation with top athletes in order to give them the best technology possible in the field. It means constant innovation. At the same time, Nike stimulates amateur athletes and weekend joggers to expand their boundaries: to "just do it."

   • *Brand as low price:* The brand is primarily perceived as the cheap alternative in this category or as offering the cheapest or most cost-effective products (the best price-value). This brand concept is linked to products or series of products that perform adequately on the generic functions, but that usually lack special added properties. Presentation (packaging) and service tend to be minimal. Examples are Aldi, Kmart, Wal-Mart, Easy Jet, and generic store (house) brands.

   • *Brand as luxury:* The brand is perceived as the luxury variant in its category. It is linked to a product or a series of products of exceptionally high quality that signal high status. It is an expensive brand. Research shows that these brands cue a set of complex meanings that are associated with luxury brands to various degrees (Kapferer 1998). Important elements are the beauty or excellence of the product and the magic of the brand: its uniqueness, tradition, creativity, exclusivity, or avant-gardism. All these factors can be combined to classify luxury brands into four main subcomponents, based on the following elements:

- *Object brands:* These are luxury brands strongly associated with a certain product (Chanel No. 5, Porsche 911, Corvette) whose beauty and excellence are the most valued characteristics of the brand.
- *Creativity brands:* Here excellence is not the main issue: it is sensuality and creativity. Examples of this group are Hugo Boss and Gucci.
- *Magical brands:* The magic they radiate makes these brands the great classics. They are not fashion-sensitive. Examples are Dunhill, Louis Vuitton, Hermes, and Mercedes.
- *Exclusive brands:* Here the emphasis lies on a small number of people who possess these brands or can afford them. These are brands that serve as functions for the privileged, the very rich. Rolls Royce, Chivas, and XO cognacs are examples.

- *Brand as organization:* With some brands, the supplying organization, such as IBM, is central to customers' perception of what the brand stands for. These are often brands of service-providing businesses whose product itself is not tangible. Even though IBM sells hardware and systems, it also excels in providing a broad range of IBM expertise and far-reaching solutions for the customer's entire business. Consultancy firms fall into this category, especially when they are active in different markets. Large consultancy firms have emanated from traditional accountancy firms like Accenture and Ernst & Young. Their brand DNA captures characteristics like competency, reliability, and authority from their source brand.

Managing the Abstraction Level

In addition to this system of brand core meanings, there is also a system of abstraction levels that helps in further defining the core of the brand. The brand concepts discussed in the typology differ from each other in the abstractness of their core meanings, varying from associations with concrete products to associations with highly abstract values and ideologies.

There are various opinions as to the degree to which it is desirable to raise the abstraction level of brand core meanings to unexplored heights. Brands whose core meaning lies at a higher abstraction level (personality, value, or ideological brands) have more room for extensions than brands at lower abstraction levels (product, category, attribute). However, brands whose core meanings are too abstract are less successful as internal information cues for choices in individual product categories. This weakens the position of such brands against competing brands within the category that do have a stronger product-brand association.

BRAND VISION AND BRAND VALUES

The core concept of a brand is a handle on which to hang the meaning of the brand in terms of its category and purpose. More informative, however, is the identification of the brand's vision or values, which is the ideological platform upon which the identity of the brand and its social posture can be constructed.

The concept of vision as a requirement for the development of a brand identity has taken an important place in management literature and in the language of managers and their consultants. Little consensus has been achieved about the content of this concept, though. Thornberry (1997) defines it simply as an image of the future, something that is not there yet but that we imagine: what the organization (the brand) could or should look like, part analytical, part emotional. Inherent in a vision is a sense of the values that animate the brand, the qualities that management believes are central to the distinctiveness of the brand. Red Bull, for example, has a vision of itself

Figure 5.1 **Brand Mission**

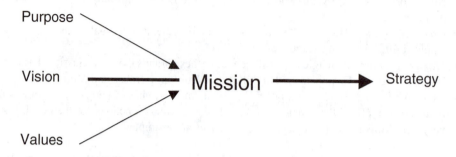

as a leader in the energy beverage category. The values and qualities that reflect that leadership position include its association with the health and sports markets, but most importantly with the energy boost that comes from caffeine.

The identification of the brand's values and the statement of its vision relative to competing brands is a central responsibility of top management and something over which a company has complete control. Brand management is largely based on activities within the brand's own organization, particularly for corporate brands. Collins and Porras (1997) go as far as to claim that it is impossible to make up or fabricate a core ideology: they believe it can only be discovered. A contemporary example of research into vision explores the views of Stephen Case, founder of America Online.

Vision and Core Purpose

We can distinguish two basic components in the literature on visions—a formulation of the core purpose of the brand in terms of its future direction and identification of the core values that the brand actually represents. In the case of AOL, the vision is clearly to be the global leader in the development of a medium that has become universal in people's lives. The values include technical sophistication, ease of use, and trustworthiness.

> *Principle:* A vision statement, which puts into words what a brand wants to be in the future, consists of the brand's core purpose and values.

Similar to a brand's core concept, the most important element of a company's brand vision is a sense of the purpose of its existence: "What is our place in the world? What would society lose if our company brand ceased to exist tomorrow?" Clarity on the subject can be inspiring, since it can open the eyes of those working behind the brand to the essential contribution of their work to other people's lives. This goal is sometimes hidden behind superficial everyday reality.

Collins and Porras (1997) suggest the use of the "five whys" method, a laddering technique that will expose the company's purpose. The technique starts with the descriptive statement, "We make X products" or "We deliver X services" and then asks, "Why is that important?" five times. After a few whys, one gets down to the fundamental purpose of the organization.

Getting America Online

When working for Pizza Hut managing pizza development, Stephen Case spent many evenings exploring one of the first online services, the Source. Fascinated with the possibilities of the online world, Case became marketing director of Control Video, which provided an online gaming service. He believed that the future for the company would be to create its own branded online service—which he named America Online (AOL). AOL emphasized ease of use in a friendly, well-designed environment that attracted average consumers, who had not warmed to the high-tech aura of the corporate service companies. In 1993 Case became CEO, and AOL came to the fore as the leading provider of branded online content. Throughout his career, Case says, he held onto one idea: "To build a global medium as central to people's lives as the telephone or television—and even more valuable. . . . Our attention is on creating a great medium and making sure that it has a positive impact on the economy and on society."

In 2000 Case stated that he wanted to double the number of AOL's subscribers by 2005, with a heavy emphasis not just on the United States but also abroad; to develop services that would encourage users to triple their time online with AOL companies, to about three hours per day; and to deliver services not just via computers but also via televisions, cell phones, and others devices that might be embedded in cars or kitchens. Case wanted to combine sophisticated technology with simple delivery and ease of use.

One of his most important goals was to establish a brand that consumers would trust. "We will continue to innovate, of course, but we'll do it in stages so that every time you sign on, we don't force you to download a new browser, for example. We know people want innovation. We also know they don't want the screens to look different every day." He underlined the concepts of choice, convenience, flexibility, immediacy, interactivity, and personalization.

In 2005 AOL was the world's largest Internet provider, with over 24 million subscribers in the United States and Europe. However, with intense competition the once dominant online provider has dropped to 10 million subscribers in 2008.

Sources: Adapted from Carter (2005); Academy of Achievement, "Getting America Online," October 13, www.achievement.org; Time Warner Web site, www.timewarner.com.

Collins and Porras used this method to deepen and enrich a discussion about the purpose of a certain market-research company. The company executives first generated the following statement of purpose for their organization: "To provide the best market-research data available." They were then asked, "Why is it important to provide the best market-research data available?" After some discussion, the executives answered in a way that reflected a deeper sense of their organization's purpose: "So that our customers will understand their markets better than they could otherwise." Further discussion led the team members to realize that their sense of self-worth came not just from helping customers understand their markets better, but also from making a contribution to their customers' success. This introspection eventually generated a new statement of purpose: "To contribute to our customers' success by helping them understand their markets." With this purpose in mind, the company now frames its product decisions not with the question, "Will it sell?" but with the question, "Will it make a contribution to our customers' success?"

A core purpose does not consist of aimed-for turnover, market share, profits, or growth in shareholder value. These are merely calibrators to measure a company's success. The core purpose of a corporate brand is an abstract formulation of its contribution to society as a guiding star far above the horizon. This is how some companies state their core purposes—for example, 3M sees its purpose as an uninterrupted search for innovative solutions for tough problems (Collins and Porras 1997).

> *Principle:* The most important element of a brand vision is the core purpose: "What is our place in the world?"

The second element of a vision consists of the values and convictions that the company brand represents. Chapter 9 looks at the values concept from a consumer perspective. For now, we will work with Rokeach's (1973) definition of values as durable convictions that a specific mode of behavior or an ultimate existential ideal is personally or socially preferable to the opposite mode of behavior or existence.

Expressing the values that drive a corporate brand is what constitutes the ideology of the brand. Also called brand philosophy, it represents the values of the sender in a communication situation or of the manager in a brand strategy. Seen from a recipient's perspective, the values that the brand is associated with form a part of the brand personality. Sony provides an example of a core ideology that has been stated in many different ways over the company's history.

Sony at the Service of Progress

At its founding in 1946, Masaru Ibuka described two key elements of Sony's ideology: "We shall welcome technical difficulties and focus on highly sophisticated technical products that have great usefulness for society regardless of the quantity involved; we shall place our main emphasis on ability, performance, and personal character so that each individual can show the best in ability and skill." Four decades later, this same concept appeared in a statement of core ideology called Sony Pioneer Spirit: "Sony is a pioneer and never intends to follow others. Through progress, Sony wants to serve the whole world. It shall be always a seeker of the unknown. . . . Sony has a principle of respecting and encouraging one's ability and always tries to bring out the best in a person. This is the vital force of Sony."

In 2006 Sony declared itself a company devoted to the celebration of life:

> We create things for every kind of imagination. Products that stimulate the senses and refresh the spirit. Ideas that always surprise, and never disappoint. Innovations that are easy to love, and effortless to use. Things that are not essential, but hard to live without. We're not here to be logical. Or predictable. We are here to pursue infinite possibilities. We allow the brightest minds to interact freely, so the unexpected can emerge. We invite new thinking, so even more fantastic ideas can evolve. Creativity is our essence. We take chances. We exceed expectations. We help dreamers dream.

Sources: Adapted from Collins and Porras (1997); Sony Web site.

Values are enduring and have a pledge-like character: you cannot get around them. Core values as embodied in the brand vision form the essential, durable basic principles that people in the organization believe in. They provide principles for the development of the brand and for day-to-day behavior. The wishful character of the brand is anchored in core ideology. It rises above the life cycle of products, above technological developments, fashion trends, and the views of the managers who come and go. The core values manifest the permanent contribution a brand wants to make to the quality of life. This provides an inspiring focus for the organization behind the brand.

Companies usually do not have many core values—three to five at the most. In the research of Collins and Porras (1997), none of the companies with vision seemed to express more than five, and most had three or four. If more than five or six are described, there is a risk that the values will be overlooked or forgotten or mixed with views susceptible to change. Values have to be made salient—they should be top-of-mind in the internal organization as well as in the brand perception of consumers. The real core values should also be able to endure the passing of time, developing a sort of "eternity value."

Several years ago, Xerox had a vision/mission document that described a strategic direction, two vital goals, three company-wide initiatives, four priorities, and five values. People at Xerox admitted they had fifteen messages, and which was the most important one depended on which manager was communicating with the organization (Gronstedt 2000). Such a list of priorities was synonymous with a lack of priorities. Xerox cut it down to four core messages: "The Document Company," "Customer First," "Empowering Work Environment," and "Growth and Productiveness." For each of the four, an icon was designed that is now added to all internal communications as a visual reminder. Every six months, Xerox examines whether these core messages are familiar, understood, relevant, and credible.

But even having three or four core values may lead to a drifting strategy. There are very strong arguments to declare only one core value, one key message, one promise central in the brand strategy, and give the other ones a subordinate and if possible a supporting role. In Chapter 19 we will see how making "driving pleasure" central to its strategy for decades helped make BMW the most admired car brand in the world.

Discovering Core Values

The question is not "which core values are we going to choose?" but "which core values do we have and will never let go of because they are embedded in our hearts?" This is not about the made-up values that an advertising agency feels should be alive in a company (but which often are not)—it is about values that are actually experienced in a brand's daily business operations and customer interactions.

A core ideology cannot be created—it can only be discovered. Company values should exist in the organization and be brought to the surface through a process that very much resembles "soul examination." An ideology has to be lived; it has to be authentic and passionately held by an organization. When values have weakened over time, they still can be revived. If they are to be accepted throughout the firm, senior employees must actively participate in their creation and communication. The following four steps should ensure the kind of sharing necessary to gain acceptance for a statement of core values (Osborne 1991):

- *Step 1:* The entrepreneur or CEO, drawing on his or her own set of principles, should write a tentative list of core commitments.

- *Step 2:* Key employees, without seeing the owner's statement, should do the same. The deeper this process penetrates the organization, the better.
- *Step 3:* Both statements—employee and management—should be discussed with the board of directors or advisory board. If these groups are not present in some functioning form, the entrepreneur may wish to test the statements with trusted outsiders, including the public accountant and corporate lawyer who serve the company.
- *Step 4:* In meetings between senior managers, the tentative core values should be evaluated to assure compatibility with the strategic intention of the company. For example, value statements about product quality and service must consider the marketplace's need and willingness to pay.

At the very least, a shared process to identify and agree upon the firm's basic beliefs gives entrepreneurs a chance to audit the clarity with which they have articulated and communicated their corporate value system. More often, if the CEO permits it, such a process leads to sharpened or new fundamental emphases in the company.

Principle: The permanent contribution of a brand to the quality of society manifests itself in a small number of core values, which have to be discovered through a process of self-examination.

Vision Development

In a changing marketplace, a brand cannot always move into the future with values from the past. Sometimes it is necessary to make a fresh start by determining what drives the current organization. A possible approach, as proposed by Richardson (2000, 275–280), is holding brand vision workshops with key executives from the organization: "They can be asked to imagine themselves inside this company in its future guise, being asked first to create a future picture as if looking through their own eyes, hearing the sounds they would hear, and feeling the feelings they would have. They are then asked to remove themselves from the picture and see themselves in it, as if watching a movie."

Visualizing this outcome in this way has several advantages. "Stepping into" the vision makes the goal seem real and thus more compelling and achievable. Even though the process is commonly referred to as visualization, individuals can be encouraged to imagine the outcome in whatever modalities are most appropriate for them (e.g., visual, audio, kinesthetic). Further, when participants discuss the detail of their own visualization or representation of the future, they are starting to generate and discuss possible behavior and actions that could underpin the vision. Finally, this process programs the participants to recognize when they start to achieve their goals (so they actually notice their own success).

Criteria useful in deconstructing or critiquing a company or brand's current values are as follows:

- What are the prevailing values in the organization?
- On which implicit assumptions are the values based?
- To what degree are the values distributed or presented fragmentarily?
- To what degree are the values mutually consistent?

- To what degree are the values internalized (in other words, how strongly are they experienced)?
- To what degree are the values radiated into the market (products or services, market manifestations, corporate communications)? (May 2000)

When defining consumer or customer values, a description of the market segment these values are relevant to is not entirely out of place. The chapters on segmentation, positioning, and brand equity development deal with this issue in more detail. With large, established brands, the focus should be on the values that are important to the existing brand users (the brand's loyal following or the brand's fan club) and on relationship development; with younger brands, the focus may be on potential buyers whose personal value system fits with the identity the brand radiates.

In vision development, there is always a danger that the formulation of the core values will get stuck at a high abstraction level; as a result, those involved with the brand will have difficulty imagining what these values mean in their daily lives. A vision statement should be a simple description (Collins and Porras 1997)—lively, memorable, inspiring, concrete, meaningful, and short. The point is not the words but the content of the message those words embody. A good vision points an arrow to the brand's future. It is not real yet, but it is what the brand would like to be. It is a dream, but one that lies within the range of feasibility; the vision should not lie at too great a distance from actual reality. I. Wilson (1992) gives a number of criteria he believes a vision should fulfill:

- A vision should be coherent, integrating the goals, strategy, and working method of the company.
- A vision should be strong, motivating, and convincing. It should be realistic, and the market potential for the company should be researched properly.
- The vision should fit with the values and ambitions of the company's management.
- The vision ensures that the company is collectively aware of the future image and of how it must be achieved.
- The vision can "freshen" a corporate culture, becoming a driving force for the company strategy.

Wind and Main (1998) merge function and vision. A vision should define a clear, specific goal that may well be challenging, but is also achievable. This goal should differentiate the company from its competitors, and bring about a change in the market developments and inside the company itself. A vision should also incorporate a definition of a company's core competencies, and provide a reason why the customer should buy from this company.

Principle: Vision statements should be feasible, lively, memorable, inspiring, concrete, meaningful, and short.

THE MISSION OF A BRAND

There is as little consensus about the concept of mission as about that of vision. The word *mission* is defined by both Webster's and the Dutch Van Dale dictionaries as reflecting the goals of a group of persons whose specific tasks serve a particular goal. Sometimes the vision is seen as part of a mission; sometimes vision guides the mission. As we have presented it, however, a vision is a future statement—"where we want to be"; a mission is a reflection of the current core purpose—"the way we do things around here and the reasons we do what we do."

The mission of a company or brand is usually expressed in a simple statement that encapsulates the core purpose. Based on an analysis of 200 mission statements, the Ashridge Strategic Management Centre developed the Ashridge Mission Model, consisting of four components: reason for existence, values, strategy, and behavioral standards (Campbell and Yeung 1991).

Vision and Mission

It is best to see vision and mission as a connected whole. Figure 5.2 sums up the components of our model of vision and mission. Vision provides the overarching direction to the long-term brand strategy. The core purpose forms the core of the vision concept, in which the contribution of the brand to the business is central. Decisions about the target audience, core values, behavioral standards, and operational goals evolve from the sense of mission and help implement the mission. Mission lies within the organization; vision, however, may rest on perceptions of the needs, values, and problems of a group of consumers or customers or society as a whole and therefore can be situated outside the company.

The vision is an idea about the future; the mission contains the fundamental guidelines for the implementation of that idea. The mission is not the distant horizon expressed in the vision; rather it is more operational and specifies the concrete tasks of the organization behind the brand that contribute in the short term toward the realization of the vision.

The operational goals supporting a mission statement should not be confused with the core company goals. The brand or corporate core purpose has no end point: according to Collins and Porras (1997), it should remain valid for at least a century. A corporate mission statement is something companies engrave on their conference room walls. It does not change from year to year. ConAgra's mission, for example, is "feeding people better." Merck's is "We are in the business of preserving and improving human life." The operational goals in a brand's mission statement, however, are time-bound fixed points used to measure the success of the brand's operations in delivering on its mission.

Principle: A brand mission contains the concrete task for the organization behind the brand regarding the contribution to be made in the short term toward the realization of the vision.

Strategy and Mission

Strategy is the way in which, and the road along which, a goal is to be reached. Thus, brand strategy is the mechanism by which a brand mission is accomplished. When a company wants to be the best in its category, the strategy has to verbalize how this goal is to be accomplished. When shareholders' value is the primary aim, the strategy will have to indicate how the company thinks it will realize this goal in competition with other businesses. For example, Egon Zehnder wants to be the most professional, though not necessarily the largest, executive search firm. For this reason, in its strategy, the development and application of methods and systems are central to the "one firm culture" it deliberately strives for (Campbell and Yeung 1991).

Figure 5.2 **The Vision and Mission Model**

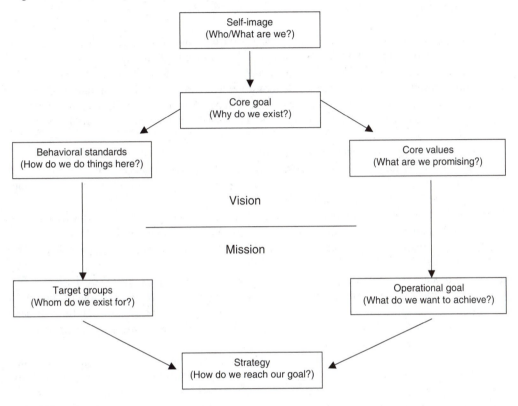

Mission and Behavior

Goals and strategies are just words when they are not turned into concrete behavior. Because a brand mission has an operation component, by definition, it can be observed in the brand's public behavior, in its operations, and in its interactions with its key stakeholders. This is crucial, particularly for large service-providing organizations.

British Airways, whose goal is "to be the best and most successful company in the airline industry," implemented an extensive training program under the motto "Putting People First." Egon Zehnder developed a systematic consulting approach, which entails, among other things, that the company does not accept assignments that cannot lead to success and that behind every consultant there is a second one involved in the assignment in order to assure maximum quality (Campbell and Yeung 1991). Converting values and strategy into a limited number of essential behavioral standards, such as "putting people first," can lend great power to the mission statement.

Similar to how a company changes constantly in a turbulent environment, a mission may also undergo development and modification to meet changing times. Young companies often lack an explicitly stated mission, since a mission is mostly present in the minds of the founders. As an organization grows, it becomes necessary to write down guidelines and make them measurable. This leads in particular to the specification of behavioral standards as expressed in the Ashridge model.

The Ashridge researchers observed that two approaches could be distinguished within the 200 mission statements they studied:

- *The cultural school:* Here the emphasis lies on the company's philosophy, values, and norms—in our terms, the vision of the brand. This movement emphasizes cooperation and teamwork. The mission here has mainly a philosophical character and is intended to help employees interpret things from a common framework and to speak a common language.
- *The strategic school:* Here the mission is the first step within the strategy development process. The goals to be achieved are indicated, and the desired behavior of employees is specified.

The two approaches are not necessarily conflicting, but rather they can be seen as complementary. A qualitatively high mission can only work if the elements form one coherent whole. Campbell et al. (in Waalewijn et al. 1996) believe that a strong mission exists when the elements of a mission are closely interrelated and strengthen each other.

Research by Brabet and Klemm (1995) indicates that mission statements are, in a way, culture-dependent. In France, the emphasis lies strongly on the vision component, in establishing higher ideals (values), while British companies stress their specific goals and the means to realize them. In English companies, missions tend to have a pragmatic purpose: they are intended for internal use, often quantified in time, and are concrete with regard to the goals that must be aimed for and the performance expected of employees. It is assumed that such concrete touchstones will have a greater influence on the organization than the often-lofty expressions of cultural values. The French missions tend to express management's ideals; English statements serve primarily as criteria for the ideal brand situation that has to be realized.

In market practice, the development of value-based mission statements has become fairly common. The use of mission statements, geared toward the relationships of a company with all its stakeholder groups, is currently prevalent in corporate brands. Although the function for customers is usually central, many of the formulations are too general to offer a footing in daily brand management activities. Analyses of the literature by Pearce and David (1987) and by Bart (1997) have produced the components of mission statements as summarized in the following list. In this sense, a brand mission could be seen as an essential element in the overall brand system.

Components of Mission Statements

- Definition of the business scope (which business are we in?)
- Identification of the core offer (what is our focus?) or a very general description of the products or services
- General goal or reason of existence (why do we exist, why are we doing it?)
- More specific company goals
- Description of the self-concept (who are we?)
- Statement of values or philosophical views (what do we believe in, what binds us?)
- Identification and description of the most important buyer or client groups (whom are we there for?)
- Identification of specific competencies and strengths of the company (what are we good at?)
- Identification of core competencies and core technologies (what do we ultimately consist of?)
- Identification of the competitive advantage (what are we better at?)
- Competitive position to be aimed for (where do we want to go?)

- Competitive strategy (how do we compete and how do we deal with competitors?)
- Description of good relations with providers (how do we deal with our suppliers?)
- The desired image (how do we want to be seen?)
- Description of efforts to retain customer satisfaction and loyalty (how do we keep our clients happy?)
- Description of methods to ensure the validation and well being of employees
- Identification of other relevant stakeholders (especially shareholders)
- Specific behavioral standards and policy that must be observed (what is expected of us?)
- Description of efforts to strive toward growth
- Specific financial norms and goals
- Description of methods of rewarding shareholders
- Description of methods of establishing good relations with society
- Commitment to survive

Missions and Perceptions

Simply stating a mission does not make it so. A statement from the management as to how it would like clients to look at the company or brand may have little to do with the actual image. There also tends to be a comparable distance between the self-image in the organization and the ideals expressed in the mission statement. Furthermore, the stated mission may not be consistently expressed by all the key stakeholders. Employees, for example, may see the brand's mission as entirely different from the shareholders' view of the mission.

On the one hand, focusing is a function of the mission statement. After all, it is an instrument designed to influence reality and to bring performance in line with that reality. Against it stands the fact that too great a distance between the actual perceptions of employees or customers and the mission is counterproductive: "That's not true at all; we don't deliver that by a long shot," is the general reaction. If negative elements in image forming are present to a large degree, they could be listed as points of departure for the mission.

Bastmeijer (1997) says that, in general, there is a major difference between mission statements in the Netherlands and the perceived brand reality. He analyzed the mission statements and codes of behavior of forty-eight Dutch companies with more than 500 employees in order to find out to what degree these statements contribute to the validation of the organization's members as expressed in the question, "What am I actually doing this for?" In the statements, it was the profit principle that was prominent, with the principle of personal development always subordinate to it. Only four companies had a formulation of principles from which a personally satisfying answer could be obtained to the question, "What am I doing it for?"

Mission Statements and Marketing Communication

As a steering element for marketing communication, most mission statements do not come up to the mark, as the following example of the corporate culture of Ahold (the Dutch mother corporation of Albert Heijn supermarkets), based on the Ahold corporate brochure illustrates. Although Ahold is not a brand that operates in the consumer market, this document also serves as a guideline for the employees of Albert Heijn supermarkets. The six-item summary is printed on a card that employees carry. These items are so generic, though, that they could apply to practically any company at random. The development can hardly be called specific either. This is a general problem for many mission statements.

The Corporate Culture of Ahold

Ahold has laid down its basic principles in a small brochure. The core principles are summed up as follows:

- Strive for healthy continuity
- Client is number one
- Grow in current and new markets
- Development possibilities for employees
- Quality and innovation
- Society-oriented

The items "Client is number one," "Development possibilities for employees," and "Quality and innovation" are developed in the brochure as follows:

Consumers

Our point of departure is that we offer consumers value for their money, always and everywhere. Consumers should see the choice in our shops as logical and self-evident, and still be pleasantly surprised time and again. The sophisticated combination of quality, price, assortment, and service should ensure that they are and remain loyal customers. Ahold's customer-oriented character is clearly anchored in our operational management, but is sometimes held back by systems, procedures, and collective market approaches. To promote individually oriented customer service, a flexible approach is necessary in which there is space for personal initiative. One should keep in mind that being customer-oriented is not the same as being market-oriented. These are two separate issues, both greatly important at different levels of the organization.

Consumers should be convinced that offering service and quality in our shops is a priority for us. A consumer can only become and remain convinced of that if he is approached and treated in a personal manner. At all levels of the organization, motivation and flexibility should be present in order to bind consumers to our shops. This is also the best way for our employees to find more challenges and satisfaction in their work.

Employees

Caring for the individual is one of the cornerstones of the corporate policy. Every employee has a right to fair treatment. Employees of Ahold at all levels should be allowed to develop, provided this fits within the context of the company's goals. We expect of our employees a high degree of integrity and ethic norms awareness. Employees should be stimulated to take initiatives, develop their entrepreneurial sense and be proactive in striving toward the corporate goals. We want them to have a sense of loyalty and pride for the company and/or for the part of the company they work in. The necessary motivation and involvement should be fostered by positive attention from those in top positions.

Employees should be able to make mistakes. As long as there is mutual respect, conflicting meanings can be very useful and contribute to better decision making.

Team spirit and comradely cooperation should be stimulated and tasks should be determined accordingly. Such a corporate culture demands a flat, decentralized organization in which every-one knows his specific responsibilities. We also believe it is of great importance to have effective management development programs at our disposal. Such programs are geared toward putting the right people in the right places. This is one of the ways of stimulating the self-development of employees and increasing pleasure in work at the same time. Schooling and training programs, at work and outside, are among the most important instruments of the MD programs.

Quality and Innovation

We strive toward top quality in everything we do. The priority lies in the quality of the products and the services provided to our clients. Consumers should be able to trust blindly the quality we offer. We also strive for quality in the relationships with our employees and other interested parties. Ahold is also oriented toward innovation, and modern technology forms an excellent aid. We expect from our employees a certain passion and natural curiosity in order to fully put their efforts into the development and implementation of new ideas. The company should be widely well known for its high-quality standards and its strong orientation toward innovation.

Source: Ahold corporate brochure (1998).

The often-meaningless generalities of mission statements are a consequence of the fact that most of them concern the entire company, all its parts, and all the important stakeholder groups. This is the reason they have little influence on how things go within specific business units and departments. A solution would be to develop "missions within a mission"—developing high abstract principles from the corporate mission statement into specific sub-missions that are applicable to parts and partial activities of a company. Such a sub-mission could also be formulated for brand communication strategies. The following table shows the basis of such a sub-mission, formulated for Albert Heijn in 1983. These values remained a guideline in Albert Heijn's marketing communication for more than a decade.

Collins and Porras (1997) remark that it is not what is written that determines success, but the consistency with which all parts of business management are aligned with the deep values and goals of a brand. Writing down a mission is only the very beginning of an entire management process that is geared toward actually realizing the formulated goals.

Operationalizing a mission involves putting words into action, and if a company's words proclaim some allegiance to socially responsible marketing, then the mission becomes a rallying point for all the brand's stakeholders. In other words, it becomes a platform for the development of brand strategy. Duncan and Moriarty (1997a) provide the following guidelines for this "mission marketing":

1. *Institutionalize the mission:* This means having staffing and infrastructure that will allow the mission to continue to be executed.
2. *Measure its contribution to the organization:* One way to guarantee that a portion of an organization's energy and resources are used for a certain program is to measure that program's performance ("What gets measured gets done"). There are several ways to evaluate the performance of the people assigned to run the program:

- Awareness of the organization's mission activities among key stakeholders.
- Evaluation by key stakeholders of the program's benefits to society in relation to other, similar corporate sponsorships and involvements.

Table 5.1

Mission and Marketing Communication at Albert Heijn

The values of Albert Heijn	Consequences in marketing communication
Albert Heijn is innovative:	
We want to familiarize consumers with new products, new ways of cooking, and new ways of shopping.	We strive toward constant innovation, in the development of our own media (the Allerhande monthly), as well as in the use of existing media (such as weekly promotions on television).
Albert Heijn is inspiring:	
We want to give consumers ideas about being able to serve something delicious every day.	In the communications, we pay attention to the final result.
Albert Heijn is aware of quality:	
We have an eye for detail, and are always looking to make improvements.	Our expression will radiate quality, for example through the quality of photography and through typographic design.
Albert Heijn is honest and close to people:	
We put ourselves in the situation of our clients, and attempt at honesty in our relationship with them.	We do not use bombastic language, we "talk to the neighbor."
Albert Heijn is "king of food":	
We are mental market leaders and try to remain a step ahead, both in our assortment and in our shops.	We ensure dominance in the media, for instance by using 1/1 pages.
Albert Heijn is proud and self-assured:	
We are proud of what we are and of our role in society.	We are sometimes a bit arrogant in the tone of our communications.
Albert Heijn can put things into perspective:	
We realize that there are more important things in life than daily shopping.	Still, we do this with a tone that reveals such a capacity to put things into context. Where relevant, we make use of restrained humor.

Source: Floor (1983).

- Evaluation of news clips, taking into consideration where they ran, the audiences they reached, and their degree of positive link to the organization.

3. *Make it a top management responsibility:* Mission marketing must be directed by top executives.
4. *Appoint a representational executive committee:* Establish an executive committee made up of representatives from all levels of the company to ensure that the effort does not have an internal, elitist image. Make membership on this committee a prestigious assignment by providing executive perks such as special dinners and trips.
5. *Incorporate the mission's essence into all departmental plans:* If a sporting goods company adopts a mission of "ensuring that the fun and excitement of sports are available to

everyone," it should include in its marketing plan certain events that provide underprivi-
leged youth and adults an opportunity to participate in something more than backyard
basketball.

Principle: For corporate brands it may be necessary to develop a "mission within a mission" in which the contribution of a brand to the well being of customers is further developed. A mission should be brought to life first at an internal level.

RED BULL AND ITS CORE BRANDING CONCEPTS

Red Bull's core concept is tied to the category it created—energy drinks. The energy is derived from its formulation, which includes caffeine. But Red Bull is also a health and sports drink, honoring the values of those categories as well with its B vitamins and amino acid formula. The combination of good-for-you and high-energy speaks to the values of its young adult consumers, but even more so to its extreme sports users.

The extreme sports connection works as an aspirational cue for the rest of its consumer market, who may not be into sports at this level, but would like to think that they could belong in this world. It is an interesting combination of values that seems to work well for the target market.

Although energy drinks became one of the most dynamic soft drink markets, with a continuous proliferation of new product formulas and new brands by huge companies, such as Coca-Cola and Pepsi, Red Bull remained the undisputed global market leader. It is the prototypical energy drink.

BRAND IDENTITY

A brand is not a product but rather a means of representing and identifying a product or range of products. Branding is the process of creating a unique identity for a product and the system of cues that make it recognizable to its customers. An easily recognizable brand is the secret behind the phenomenal success of McDonald's and Coke over the years. The hamburger maker and soft drink producer have familiar, comfortable identities, their products are easy to recognize, and consumers know from experience that they offer dependable quality at a reasonable price. Branding creates this cuing system that consumers use to identify, recall, and select a company's product or service. Branding also identifies the source or maker of the product, as the Jack Daniel's story explains.

JACK DANIEL'S: THE POWER OF A BRAND STORY

Welcome to Lynchburg, Tennessee, home to about 400 souls and the world-famous Jack Daniel's distillery. Over yonder is the Moore County Courthouse, which you may have seen in magazine ads for Jack Daniel's whiskey. Across the square are the Farmer's Bank, the Ladies' Handicraft Shop, Lynchburg Hardware, and the White Rabbit Saloon. It is not really a saloon since Moore County has been dry for as long as anyone can remember, but you can eat your lunch there.

In the 1990s Roger Brashears was the proprietor of the White Rabbit, and also the promotion director for Lynchburg and the spokesman for the distillery. Like many people and places in and around Lynchburg, Roger appeared in a number of Jack Daniel's ads over the years. He dutifully took all the tourists—about 275,000 of them during the tourist season—to see the sights of Lynchburg: the county jail, the soda shop, and the distillery. Most of the tourists are Jack Daniel's drinkers who have come to this out-of-the-way spot to pay homage to the distillery. You cannot see the distillery from town but you can see the smoke from the burning ricks. These are specially laid piles of hard maple wood that are burned and their charcoal used in the famous mellowing process that Jack Daniel's Tennessee Whiskey goes through—drop by drop. Jack Daniel's whiskey, and its ads, has not changed much over the past 100 years.

Jack Daniel's is an example of a brand whose consistent development of a brand identity gradually gained it a unique position in the minds of consumers. The identity is based on a story about the origin of the brand—and the community that produces it—that expresses the unique style and traditions of Jack Daniel's.

Jack Daniel's was founded in 1866. It is the oldest whiskey distillery in the United States. After a difficult first ninety years, during which the brand struggled against the prohibition movement in the United States, it has managed to develop since 1960 into one of the largest world brands in the alcoholic beverages market. The motor behind the brand is a communication strategy established in 1954. The strategy reads that Jack Daniel's will be identified in the minds of consumers with the quiet old times in a small community, typical of the American South, where honest people make whiskey with diligence and pride. The advertising copy is not sales talk, but tells about the world of Jack Daniel's in Lynchburg. Photography has the character of historic snapshots, showing life as it happens in and around the company.

For more than fifty years now, this campaign has been running and no one has fiddled with it. Every advertisement is merely a new chapter in the continuing story of Jack Daniel's and its people, telling about the ducks in Lynchburg or the new stoplights, the cool water of the town's own well or the burning of heaps of maple blocks used to make charcoal to filter the whiskey. Jack Daniel's has built a database of whiskey drinkers, each of whom has been given a small piece of ground in Lynchburg, documents and all. These whiskey drinkers are informed several times a year about town events and the condition of their tiny bit of property. In the course of the years, a collection of merchandising articles—clothes, glasses, trays, and so forth—has been built that fits into the nostalgic world of Jack Daniel's. They are, of course, sold through a catalogue of the Lynchburg Hardware & General Store.

Consistency has been the strength of the company. Nostalgia and country life are much appreciated in modern society. Jack Daniel's advertising and promotion do not demonstrate brilliant creative insight because there is nothing to create—everything is very real and very ordinary, demonstrating the brand's down-home identity.

In 1954 Jack Daniel's produced only 160,000 fourteen-liter crates, which went up to 700,000 in 1970 and 3.5 million in 1981. Between 1982 and 1987, sales increased to 5 million nine-liter crates per year. Between 1997 and 2000, sales reached 6 million crates annually. In the twenty-first century, Jack Daniel's continued to grow year after year to more than 9 million crates in 2007.

Jack Daniel's is more than a brand. It has become a legend, a piece of history. It is typical of an American culture of earlier days, a symbol of everything that touches Americans and makes them nostalgic and proud.

Sources: Adapted from Yonovich (1981); Gay (1983); Jack Daniel's (2001); Brown-Forman (2007).

The primary brand identity elements under the control of a brand manager include devices that can be trademarked, such as the brand name; the logo and other distinctive symbols associated with the brand, such as Nike's swoosh; brand characters (the Jolly Green Giant); slogans ("the ultimate driving machine"); jingles; and packages (Coca-Cola's distinctive hourglass bottle). These are the functional tools of identity. As we mentioned in Chapter 5, brand identity is sometimes referred to as including all the meanings a consumer has acquired about a brand. Brand meanings at this deeper level will be discussed in Part III of this book when we turn our attention to consumer response to brands. The discussion in this chapter, however, will be focused on those elements that a company controls and manages as identity cues.

THE CONCEPT OF BRAND IDENTITY

The word *identity* has two possible origins in Latin (Bernstein 1984): First, it is a merger of *idem* (the same) and *entitas* (the being, existence) and, second, it comes from *identidem* (time and again). The first source indicates that something has the right to exist by staying the same. An entity has an identity if it remains the same over a certain period. The second origin seems to point out that repetition, continuity, and consistency are needed in order to establish an identity.

The word *identity* occurs frequently in our daily language and is surrounded by its own field of meanings. Webster's English dictionary covers the following connotations—the state or fact of remaining the same one (as under varying aspects or conditions); the condition of being oneself and not another; the sense of self; exact likeness in nature or qualities. The word is a synonym for individuality, personality, distinctiveness, and uniqueness, thus denoting a singular character, an individual feature.

An analysis of these definitions also determines that the linguistic concept of identity has three characteristics that something or someone has to comply with:

- *Equality:* identity indicates that something or someone is the same over a certain period. The identity characteristics form the essence of the self. Without this sameness, the identity is not recognizable.
- *Continuity:* identity is only tangible if it is displayed over an extended period of time.
- *Singularity:* an identity is unique. It belongs to something or someone. Identity is linked to whatever or whoever possesses the identity and offers a certain degree of distinction.

The fact that these three aspects are characteristic of an identity does not say much in itself. They only become significant when we examine which aspects actually distinguish something or someone. For example, a brand name has to be anchored to a product or company in order to meet the requirement of equality. The Jack Daniel's label on a bottle of whiskey means the product is equivalent to the essence of Jack Daniel's; it has to be used over a period of time in order to have the continuity necessary for recognition; and, finally, it has the ability to distinguish a bottle of Jack Daniel's from other whiskeys.

Three Levels of Brand Identity

The concept of identity has been borrowed from psychology, with Erik Erikson (1963) as its most important contributor. He distinguished three levels of components: physical, social (relationships with others), and mental (the ego and self-identity).

• *The physical level:* This level encompasses all aspects related to physical appearance. The clearest dimension of identity, it includes all external and bodily characteristics of a person. There is a physical dimension to brand identity, as well. Products are the most important elements of brand identity, but buildings, shop displays, offices, interiors, cars, packaging, and other presentation can (and should!) be part of the brand identity. The physical level is usually consciously managed, with the help of extensive manuals. Later in the chapter we will elaborate on this physical dimension of branding.

• *The social level:* This is a person's self-concept, derived from perceived membership in social groups and nonmembership in other groups. It defines *us* as opposed to *them*, which is the basic way our brains work, but also the source of stereotyping. We categorize people, for example, as being black or white, old or young, wealthy or poor, female or male, Christian or Muslim, Irish or Italian, student or teacher, taxi driver or cop. We figure out things about ourselves and others by knowing what categories we do and do not belong to.

Brands also tend to have typical social characteristics. These can stem from the brand organization itself, from what it does or does not do, from what is undertaken and how it is done in relation to the environment. Brand identity presumes stable modes of behavior of both management and employees. The social identity can also be a result of the perception of the typical users of a brand (the user image) with which people identify or which they reject. In extreme cases a "brand community" can come into being, defined by Carlson (2005) as a perceived social bond that exists among a collective group of users of a brand. Such a brand-driven affiliation results from a congruency between the beliefs, attitudes, and values held by an individual, those held by other users of the brand as a collective group, and those projected by the brand itself.

Individuals who acknowledge membership in such a brand community will share a common social identification with other users of the brand and a sense of differentiation from non-users. They openly acknowledge their membership in the brand community and define themselves through their membership. A brand community may function as an aspirational group for current non-users of the brand (Carlson 2005). An example of such a brand community is Airstream RV owners who travel together in groups and wave to each other on the highway.

• *The mental level:* The psychological level—sometimes called self-identity or "Who am I?"—is often seen as the most important part of a person's identity. This seems logical, given that the outwardly oriented psyche is the component that steers a person. This level, related to genetic programming and the learned experiences that are unique to the individual, manifests itself in character traits, social views, and cultural values. For a brand, the mental dimension lies in the vision and values of the company and its brand management. It finds expression in the brand's personality, which we will discuss extensively in Chapter 10. How management sees the brand determines the way the brand's identity is presented. Jack Daniel's, for example, is seen as a very authentic brand, having its roots in a small community and quiet old times.

The three levels cannot be separated from one another because they are interdependent. They are central to the brand identity and are enduring and important, or salient, to both the brand managers and the brand users.

Principle: Brand identity is the unique combination of the physical, social, and mental components of a brand—central, durable, and salient.

Several authors have applied the concept of identity to brands, attempting to give it meaning in this framework. The fact that these efforts lead to very contrasting visions is an indication that we are only at the beginning of knowledge development in this field. The differences in insights are not so much about the interpretation of the abstract concept of identity as about the components of a brand that are distinguished in the process and the perspective in which these are placed. Dealing with an enormous diversity of types of brands seems to make it difficult to arrive at a satisfying, all-encompassing framework, although this book will try to do so by making use of the notion of a brand as a complex system.

INTERNAL AND EXTERNAL PERCEPTIONS

For many years, the counterculture magazine *Rolling Stone* ran a campaign based on the contrast between the way its readers were perceived and the reality of their lives. The point of the "Reality/ Perception" campaign was that the readers were not all hippies and their real identity differed dramatically from the image that other people had of them.

Organizations always have some form of identity awareness ("Who are we?") and sometimes an identity crisis when there is confusion about the nature of the real organization. This awareness is present in a more implicit form in individual brands and tends to be relevant only to the external brand characteristics. Unilever, for example, never uses the concept of brand identity for any of its brands (Sanders 2000). And it is easier to take stock of a monobrand such as After Eight than of a corporate brand such as Philips, whose reality is so unimaginably complex that it is hard to understand the company's philosophy of brand identity strategy.

Authors in the field of (corporate) brand identity also differ in their interpretation of the concept. Aaker (1996b) defines brand identity as a set of brand associations in the memory of consumers, whereas Rekom (1997) sees it as situated within the brand organization itself.

There is even less of a consensus on whether identity is related to the objective reality of a brand (the real person who reads *Rolling Stone*) or to the ideal situation aimed for by management (how the editors of *Rolling Stone* would like to describe its readers). Some authors see brand identity as a collective self-image of an organization, others as the result of a process of vision, mission, and ambition formulation by the management.

In earlier chapters we noted that a brand has a dual function—it represents the values and characteristics that the company attempts to bring out in its products and services, and, at the same time, it represents the ideas that consumers and customers have formed about it. As a result, there is an internal perception (the brand as the supplier sees it) and an external one (the brand as it is present in the memory of consumers and customers). However, both are merely perceptions— subjective images that people have formed of something outside their own body, something they have perceived through their senses. A brand, after all, also has an objective reality, its material reality as it presents itself to the observer.

Six Approaches to Brand Identity Strategy

In sum, there are three fields in which a brand has a presence: the brand as internal perception of the sender, as objective reality, and as external perception of the recipients. These three fields can be subclassified into two layers: that of actual reality of the brand identity as it is and the ideal representation that those involved have of the brand. This is represented in Table 6.1.

The diagram leads to six fields in which brand identity manifests itself in a complex system of intentions and perceptions. Each of these also functions as a focus of strategy development:

- *The self-identity:* the identity that a brand has for those working on it—the internal brand perceptions. This is an important component, especially with corporate brands and in service organizations. It overlaps with the concept of the corporate identity. In individual brands, the question of how those involved in production and marketing perceive the brand remains relevant.
- *The management's brand ideal:* the ideals of management with regard to the brand, as usually expressed in a vision and mission statement; a confirmation of belief that serves as a guideline for the actions of those involved, with the purpose of influencing the external reality of the

Table 6.1

Brand Identity Strategies

	Internal perception (management/personnel)	Objective reality (observed/experienced through senses)	External perception (consumer/customer)
Actual	Self-image	The external brand reality	Brand representation (image)
Ideal	Brand ideal (vision/mission)	The desired external brand reality	Brand expectation (self-ideal needs/values)

brand positively. To an increasing degree, mission statements are also being formulated to express the ideals behind individual brands.

- *The external brand reality:* the material reality of a brand as brought about by the sender of the brand message and presented as an object to the senses of consumers and customers. Here the concept of object denotes any capacity in which a brand can be present in the physical world and present itself for perception. It includes concrete products, service, personnel, and perceptible "property," such as branches (factories, shops, and offices), as well as expressions of communication and the appearance of spokespersons. An important part of it is what is known as visual identity—the combination of external brand characteristics such as writing style, brand logo, color, and visual stylistic traits.
- *The desired external brand reality:* the standards that external brand reality should comply with in the view of the brand management. It is the conversion of the vision statement into controllable standards related to crucial aspects of the brand's reality. As the vision statement expresses the aims at an abstract level, what is central here is the degree to which those aims have to be realized in concrete terms—that is, the operational goals.
- *The brand representation (image and associations):* the presence of the brand in the memory of consumers and customers in the form of emotional and cognitive associations (as will be described in Chapter 11).
- *The brand expectations:* the expectations of consumers and customers, the needs and values that they expect the brand to fulfill, and the dimensions of their self-ideal to which the brand can contribute (as described in Chapters 4 and 9).

Most of the literature on brands sees brand identity as an internal construct, constructed by the brand manager. In our model, this is referred to as the self-image or the ideal representation. A brand operates, however, in a reciprocal environment with meaning attached to it by the consumer. Thus external identity can be steered only indirectly. The image the brand manager has is only one way of looking at the brand, just as the consumer can have an image of a brand. In both cases there is a desired, as well as a perceived identity.

The objective reality of the brand is perceived by the consumer and may not match the management's perceptions of the brand's identity. Ideally, this reality would correspond with the ideal aimed for by the management, being perceived thus by consumers and customers and processed into an image that matches the manager's intended identity. But that ideal is not feasible. Steering that reality so that it answers to the expectations of consumers and customers is precisely the task that brand management faces. And it can be accomplished only through the application of the appropriate cues that, if they work correctly, will suggest the desired brand identity.

Fields of Tension

There are relationships in the six fields that are often characterized by inconsistencies. Brand management can thus be confronted with the following fields of tension:

- *Brand ideal versus self-image:* Management has formulated a brand ideal and is then confronted with a self-image in the organization that does not correspond—in other words, employees may not see the brand the same way as top management or identify in the same way with management's ideals.
- *Brand ideal versus the actual identity:* What the brand is, makes, does, and communicates corresponds insufficiently with the brand ideal envisioned by the management.
- *Brand ideal versus brand image:* Brand image in consumers and customers is at odds with the formulated brand ideal.
- *Brand representation versus brand expectation:* The image of a brand does not fit with the needs and values of consumers and customers.
- *Self-image versus brand representation:* The image that consumers and customers have of the brand does not correspond with the self-image present in the brand organization.

Principle: A brand has a presence at three levels: as internal perception of the producer, as external reality, and as mental representation of this reality with consumers and other stakeholders. At each level, a distinction can be made between an actual and a desired situation, and there may be inconsistencies in between.

Ours or Theirs? Brand Identity Ownership

The concept of brand identity lies at the heart of the systems schism between managers and customers. Brand identity as projected by the manager may or may not match the external reality of the brand identity as perceived by the consumer. The ultimate test of successful brand management, then, is the measure of the match between the intended and perceived brand identities and the systems of cues and perceived meanings.

The motives and competencies of the management and the organization behind the brand are influential—but only partly—in the creation of the external brand reality. The management conundrum concerns the location of the point of departure between intention and reality: Is it in the supplier's own ideals and capacities? Or in the expectations of customers? It is not possible to give a categorical answer to this question. In principle, however, the right of existence of a brand—the reality of the brand identity—lies outside the supplier's organization, in the heart and mind of the customer.

Brand management is essentially nothing more than looking after the proper coordination of the ideals and expectations of producers and consumers. Likewise, brand strategy is based on the understanding of a brand's basic functions for consumers and customers, as well as the more specific objectives that management wishes to give to these brand functions.

BRAND IDENTITIES AND TARGETING

A brand must always find a group of customers willing to put down money for it. But that does not necessarily mean that defining this group—and its needs and values—is the only point of departure for brand management. Formulation of a target group can also be an experimental result of a strategy that is primarily rooted in the values and views of the supplier. A brand that emerges this way, as is the case to an extreme degree in signature brands (Chanel, Jill Sander, Hugo Boss, Alessi, Prada), attracts its own buyers on the basis of its own identity.

With brands that are strongly driven by technological development, the ideas of product developers also tend to assume that a solution will find its problem—the brand awaits to see who will feel addressed. Historically that has been the motivation behind product-focused marketing, but it also has been the pattern for recent developments in the new technology industries. As Rijkenberg (1998) contends, "concepting" demands a different vision of (groups of) consumers, and the concept of follower group is sometimes more appropriate nowadays than that of target group.

> Rijkenberg explains that a new mentality concept needs the creation of a consumer group, a group of "followers" who feel attracted to the body of thought. The term *target group* does not fit anymore, because marketers no longer formulate in advance a well-defined socio-demographic or purchasing behavior group on which we focus (just as the immediate competitors). In concepting, the description of target group is actually very simple: Everyone that feels addressed by the body of thought of (the new) brand X.
>
> In Rijkenberg's view the concepting team feels and registers which movements exist and emerge and develop, corresponding with and anticipating a new body of thought that is then spread by the brand. The concepting team probably has met the new spiritual need more in some groups than others, but will not fall to the temptation of immediately fixing on those groups. The need to describe that group in great detail is not there if the concepting team is convinced of potential of fellow believers, kindred minds, followers. They will tend to describe a target group more in terms of e.g., 'I know for sure that there is an increasing group of people that feels at home with . . . ; feels attracted to . . . ; has had enough of . . . ; is looking for . . . ; that just likes our idea, etc.'
>
> It all seems vague, but it isn't. Those groups are real. After all, don't masses of people think that everyone in the world should have equal chances, as Benetton does? Or that there should be television without games and soap operas, as the Discovery Channel does?
>
> In these post-materialistic times, follower groups could have more opportunities than the described traditional target groups.

Outside-In or Inside-Out Brand Strategies

In this context we can distinguish two basic types of components, which we refer to as outside-in and inside-out strategy drivers. The outside-in approach reasons from the consumer's angle, using as point of departure segments that can be distinguished on the basis of the brand expectations of buyers or prospects in those segments, as well as which values and instrumental characteristics the brand has to represent for them, how these can be realized, and the best way to link these meanings to the brand through communication. This approach is highly valued for customer-focused brand management strategies. Although it is tempting to say that this is the philosophy that brand managers should follow, there is reason also to value the inside-out approach.

The inside-out approach is based on an understanding of the core meaning of a brand and a commitment to maintain the essence of the brand. This can be achieved either by using a "followers" strategy (as opposed to targeting) or a strategy that is historically determined, as is the case with most established brands that have built a solid image over time. As we will see in Chapter 8, most brands are in a minority position in their categories—they appeal only to a small part of all

Table 6.2

Identity-Driven Brand Strategy Components

	Focus	Strategic challenge
Outside-In	Meeting customer needs and expectations	Brand identity consistency
Inside-Out	Brand core concept and meaning	Salience to customer

category users. This is especially common for niche brands, which means brands are continually searching for ways to reinforce and strengthen their identities in order to appeal to prospective new customers. The outside-in and inside-out components that affect brand strategy are identified in Table 6.2.

In both approaches there is a defined view of the contribution that a brand wants to make to a part of society. The difference lies only in the origin of that view—to what degree it is the result of the personal ideas of brand leadership regarding societal needs or the result of research and analysis of the underlying needs and values of consumers and customers. The first case requires self-examination—what is the real reason for the brand's existence, what are the brand's core values, and how do they reflect societal needs? In the second case, the primary questions refer to potential buyers—what is the basis upon which consumers make a choice and how can the brand address their needs, thereby influencing that choice?

The inside-out approach entails the risk of using management's own values and views as initial premises; if they are not valid or relevant to consumers, customers could react with "so what?" The strategic challenge is to recognize the degree of recognition, interpretation, and relevance—that is, the salience—of the internal ideal for an external group of customers.

The outside-in approach, as respected as it is, can lead to friction with the values and culture that live in the organization, causing an identity crisis. For example, an organization may not recognize itself in a new course set by the results of customer positioning research. An outside-in approach that, in the eyes of the consumers and customers, does not correspond with the brand reality can also lead to lack of trust or authenticity.

Consequently, companies need to strive for harmony between their internal value systems and the external expectations of customers and consumers. There are, however, important strategic differences between corporate brands and individual brands that guide the internal/external focus. Likewise, there are differences between long-established brands and new brands. With individual brands, the point of departure lies primarily with consumers and customers. The products, as well as the identity elements, tend to be constructed based on the result of lab research, product development processes, and standardized production methods. These are largely reactions to the needs of the market. Brand management is very much externally driven.

With corporate brands, the identity characteristics come mostly from within the company itself. With service providers, the possibilities for standardization are limited. The performance and attitudes of the personnel play a dominant role. They have to make the product again every day, often in complex forms of cooperation. The attention of brand management is then internally focused.

The difference between corporate and individual brands is not black-and-white. The phenomenon of house brands is an example of an in-between position, as formally speaking they are not corporate brands, whereas in consumers' eyes Sikkens and Organon (both subsidiaries of Akzo

Nobel) do fall into that category of corporate brands. Although brand managers in this category of brands have greater freedom of movement than is the case with fully corporate brands, they must nonetheless take into account such consumer experiences and expectations.

> *Principle:* There are two basic strategies used in identity targeting: inside-out and outside-in. Successful brand strategy requires a joining of internal values and external expectations.

ELEMENTS THAT DETERMINE IDENTITY

Brand reality is composed of all the ways in which a brand manifests itself, including definable elements like identity cues, but also intangibles like perceptions. The fact that brand identity embraces what a brand is in objective reality makes the concept difficult to manage because the control over the identity lies, to some degree, outside the organization. The question, then, is which are the most relevant characteristics of brand identity. As a point of departure, the definition of identity given previously suggests that we are dealing with elements that can be characterized as follows:

- *Unique and distinguishing:* A brand has to take its own place in society in order to have a right to exist. By distinguishing itself from other brands, what is characteristic of a brand becomes clear, thus making consumers and customers willing to invest.
- *Durable:* The identity is formed by that which the brand displays over an extended period of time. There cannot be identity development without consistency. Weber (in Rekom 1998) defines corporate identity as the essential structures with whose help an organization can be identified during a long period of time as the same organization.
- *Central:* The identity is determined by the elements that make up the soul or DNA of the brand—the essence, that which represents the brand's core characteristics. Weber defines corporate brands as the structure of rules based on the actions of the members of the organization who create the visible and tangible reality of the organization. This element is about the common characteristics seen in the manifestations of the brand that are interpreted as typical of the brand.
- *Salient:* The identity is determined by the noticeable, distinct elements that are important, frequently present, and drive people's attention—things that stand out. For certain brands, some products are more identity defining than others.

The Stepping Stones Brand Identity System

In collaboration with the Centre for Integrated Marketing and Corpus Angeli, the British marketing consultancy Stepping Stones has developed a brand identity system called Stellar. The two principal developers were Professor Angus Jenkinson and the analyst Richard Leachman. The system consists of a set of interlocking insights, of which eight represent the internal perception of an organization and three the consumer perceptions.

Internal Perception

- *Customer motivations:* core customer needs and values satisfied by the brand
- *Profound purpose:* why the company exists; its profound value for the world

- *Business model:* the system of strategic synergies that creates sustainable profits
- *Vision:* the potent imagination of the future
- *Cultural values:* the organizational values and principles that best serve life in the company
- *Unique competence:* the unique ability to create value deriving from systemic expertise
- *Product:* distinguishing product concepts and design principles
- *Integrated dashboard:* dynamically related key performance indicators of health and progress

External Perception

- *Brand essence:* the heart of the unique brand experience
- *Brand character:* values, archetypal personality, image, style
- *Brand positioning:* strategic ownership of exclusive value in the customer's mind

Stepping Stones arranged these insights as coordinates on a circle, with opposites balancing complementary principles. The system has been applied across many categories, becoming a leadership tool that gets an organization's members focused together on the successful creation of value. The application for Nokia is discussed in Chapter 19.

The Elements of Physical Identity

The elements of a brand's physical identity, including the appearance dimensions or a brand's physique, comprise every object in which a brand offers itself for sensory perception and experience, to the degree it fulfills the criteria of uniqueness, equality, and continuity described earlier. Jack Daniel's is an example of a brand whose physique is coherent and consistent. Needless to say, the breadth of the physical identity package can produce a very diverse collection of identity cues. They can be grouped in seven categories, as shown by Figure 6.1.

Each main category can be further subdivided. Basic elements of products are the product and service categories a brand is linked to, as well as their characteristics and design. The principle of equality implies that there should be a connection between the products that are brought to market under one brand. The greater the connection, the clearer the brand identity. The connection can take many forms, such as technology, application area, or user characteristics. We will return to this topic in the chapters on brand span and brand architecture.

The second element—buildings and interiors—contains all the offices, factories, warehouses, and shops.

The third element—properties—contains all the buildings, offices, shops, vehicles, and other property. The brown UPS truck riding through the city is an important brand identity element.

The fourth element—advertising—contains all the persuasive messages in print, mailings, outdoor advertising, TV, radio, Internet, and other media.

The fifth element—presentations—contains all those items geared toward supporting visual brand recognition. Packaging is the most cogent example, because it usually responds to the criterion of continuity. Illuminated neon signs and other permanent or semi-permanent presentation items, point of purchase materials, and exhibitions also fall into this category.

The sixth element—publications—includes all sorts of temporary communication manifestations, such as annual reports, news releases, electronic publications, information brochures, forms, and Internet sites.

The seventh element—people—consists of the people behind the brand. Company founders (Richard Branson *is* Virgin), other contact persons, and celebrities who appear in advertisements for a

Figure 6.1   **The Set of Physical Identity Elements**

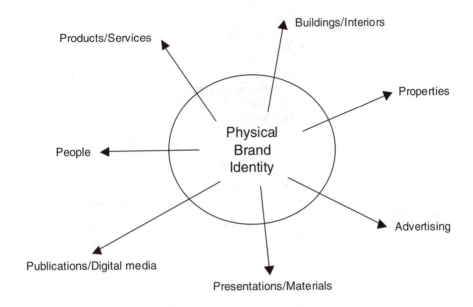

brand fall into this category. For years, actress Catherine Deneuve was the face—that is, an important identity element—of Chanel. But salespeople, receptionists, and customer service agents can also become familiar, personal links with the brand. Uniforms can be important identity elements.

An audit of the physical identity elements in the brand's recent past (for instance, in the last ten years) could be useful in analyzing a company's strengths and weaknesses. When weak management strategy is implemented through a lack of brand vision or the identity shows a lack of uniqueness, reformulation of the identity should be the focus of the brand strategy.

> *Principle:* Brand strategy should focus on reformulation when it has been driven by a weak brand vision or an indistinctive brand identity.

Style Characteristics

Style denotes a unique, distinguishing, and consistent form of expression; according to Webster's dictionary, it is "a quality that gives distinctive excellence to something." Style is the distinguishing content or message, the concept or big idea, as understood in the advertising world. Style has to do with all seven categories of physical identity elements—including such things as the way employees act, the design of shops, the graphic features of advertisements (e.g., typography, layout, use of color, and the character of illustrations), and the behavior of people affiliated with the brand.

Style is formed by the characteristic properties of identity elements. It is about the unique combination of visual codes, sound, material, taste, smell, and language. The diagram in Figure 6.2 illustrates this.

Not all elements are equally relevant for all brands. For Nivea, color and smell are identity

Figure 6.2 **Elements of Brand Style**

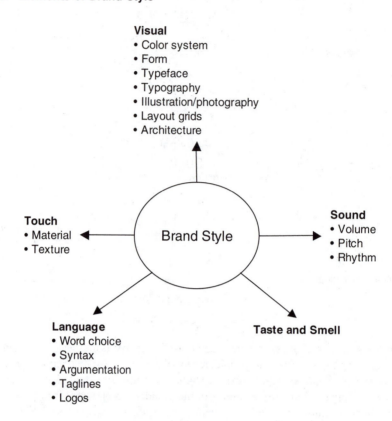

Visual
- Color system
- Form
- Typeface
- Typography
- Illustration/photography
- Layout grids
- Architecture

Touch
- Material
- Texture

Brand Style

Sound
- Volume
- Pitch
- Rhythm

Language
- Word choice
- Syntax
- Argumentation
- Taglines
- Logos

Taste and Smell

determinants; for Absolut Vodka, the form and shape of the bottle are primary. Management of identity and style elements contributes to creating the *actual* personality of a brand. It is communicated through advertising and processed by the recipients into a *perceived* brand personality as measured in market research. This issue will be analyzed further in Chapter 10.

In general, identity management is aimed one-sidedly at the graphic design of the elements. With the help of house style manuals, a unity is attempted. The importance of this unity is particularly evident with corporate brands of international and decentralized companies. Still, unity is only one aspect of physical brand identity. Coordination of the products' style and the behavior of employees toward consumers and customers are, certainly, no less important.

Principle: Style is a unique, distinguishing, and consistent form of expression. Applied to all the physical elements of brand identity, style is about the synchronization of all the manifestations of a brand.

A consistent style of verbal expression—as in a certain tone of voice—can also exert great influence on how brand identity is processed by recipients into an image, giving a total impression. A tone of voice applies literally to written text—how radio and television commercials are spoken, for example. The need to attract attention, however, can lead to a way of expression that is at odds with the self-image of a company. Yelling to get attention may not match a brand's sophisticated, low-key personality. Style contributes highly to brand recognition. Advertising manifestations of McDonald's are immediately recognizable on the basis of their visual and verbal characteristics.

Milka: The Identity of a Violet Cow

The story of Milka goes back to 1901, when the inventor of milk chocolate, Carl Russ-Suchard, launched a chocolate bar based on milk from the Alpine regions under the brand of Suchard-Milka. The candy was sold in a violet-colored package with the picture of a farmer and his cow against a snow-white Alpine background.

In 1971 the Y&R advertising agency proposed to use the same violet color for a living cow from the Swiss Simmental Valley in Milka's advertising. The name Suchard was eliminated and the violet cow and Alpine scenery became the distinguishing elements in Milka's identity. They represent the brand's core values, which have been defined as tenderness, authenticity, naturalness, simplicity, and lucidity. The violet cow is seen as sympathetic, believable, good-natured, and patient. She has acquired loyal friends all over the world.

The association with the Alpine world has been supported with public relations and promotional programs, such as snowboarding competitions and pedagogically equipped ski runs with a lot of violet color.

Since 1971 the basic elements of Milka's identity have not changed, making it the most distinguishing brand on the supermarkets' confectionery shelves. Ninety-six percent of the population in Western Europe knows the brand. Milka is now part of Kraft Foods, which sells 400 million violet chocolate bars annually in more than 155 countries.

Sources: www.milka.deLivre des Grandes Marques; Lepeu (2005).

To a great extent, the purpose of marketing communication is to showcase the brand identity, making it recognizable to its customers as well as prospective customers. Advertising campaigns are developed over time, as Jack Daniel's whiskey and the Milka cow illustrate, to establish, maintain, and reinforce the brand's enduring identity.

Principle: Advertising campaigns are not only about a brand—they are primarily an expression of the brand style and thus an important component of the brand identity.

JACK DANIEL'S: A LIGHTHOUSE IDENTITY

"Build a lighthouse identity" is one of the credos that Morgan (1999) formulated for small and beginning brands that have to take on large, dominant market leaders. By "lighthouse identity" he refers to brands with the following characteristics:

- They have a strong awareness of what they are and who they are, based not on the perspective of consumers but on a sense of internal identity.
- They express their internal identity in all they do, consistently following an inside-out strategy.
- They are distinctive in their physical appearance as well as in the body of thought they represent.
- They are penetratingly present: nobody in the market can avoid noticing them.
- They are emotional, aimed primarily not at the instrumental functions of their products but at creating an emotional relationship with their customers.

Many lighthouse brands are the creations of founders with very self-willed ideas: for example, Anita Roddick (The Body Shop), Ben Cohen and Jerry Greenfield (Ben & Jerry's), Philip Knight (Nike), Giorgio Armani (Armani), Steve Jobs (Apple), Nicholas Hayek (Swatch), and Bill Gates (Microsoft). In brand literature, these founders are quoted endlessly and presented as role models. Other companies can undoubtedly learn much from them and certainly be inspired by them.

But the reality of most brands is that they are already 50 to 150 years old; their founders have long been forgotten; their identity is the product of a long history; they are part of complex, often multinational, organizations; and their managers are relatively young people who are primarily expected to keep increasing the quarterly profit figures. Giving shape to a new identity, as these lighthouse founders did, is not a possibility. In such a situation, it is essential to analyze properly the history of a brand and to identify those elements of its identity that may have been overlooked, but that could constitute once again a point of departure for a current interpretation.

This is the secret to the longevity and strong brand identity of Jack Daniel's. It uses nostalgia and country life as a frame for a brand story based on a small Southern town and an earlier time. The story, however, is timeless even as its events unfold at the slow pace of a carefully crafted quality whiskey.

CHAPTER 7

STRATEGIC BRAND SEGMENTATION

The old neighborhood grocer knew the customers—knew where they lived, how much money they made, their age, their family situation, and other details that helped the grocer create a personal relationship with customers. That one-to-one form of marketing may be most effective, but it is not efficient, or even possible, for most contemporary producers and retailers. New technology and databases make it possible to approximate that level of knowledge, but even with that information, modern marketers are more likely to identify their customers and prospective customers not as individuals, but as groups of people who are alike in some way.

The essence of marketing, therefore, is identifying the differentiated segments or groups of people within the general market for a product. Once these groups are identified, the company then develops customized product and service variations, brand images, and communication programs that speak to the various instrumental and psychosocial needs of these groups of people. In an existing market, this process should lead to differences in the user profiles of the different brands, as well as of the different segments. Harley-Davidson is an example of a dominant brand in the motorcycle category, but within that motorcycle market, it also addresses the interests and needs of different segments.

HARLEY'S BIKERS

For a long time, motorcyclists were seen as members of a subculture that was at the fringes of society. Everyone knows the stereotypical image of the Hell's Angels. However, increasing numbers of "regular" people ride motorcycles. What leads them to start? As a rule, their motive is not the instrumental function of a means of transportation for commuting between home and work—it is more than that. In a study in the United States (Swinyard 1998), "spiritual solace" appeared to be the core function of motorcycling. While riding, most motorcyclists experience a feeling of freedom and peace, a meditative state, a transcendent awareness, magic power, the feeling of being close to nature, relaxation, and an escape from everyday worries. These experiences become stronger as they spend more time, money, and mileage—in short, as motorcycling takes a more important place in their lives.

In addition to this commonly shared meaning of motorcycling, different types of riders put their own stamp on this central meaning:

- *Hard-core riders*, whose whole life revolves around their motorcycle. When asked in an interview on Dutch television whether he would choose his wife or his motorcycle if he had to give one up, one motorcyclist said without even blinking that he would, of course, never give up his motorcycle. These hard-core drivers embody the stereotype of the dark, fringe-group biker.

But Harley's market is more than the hard-core bikers. A study in the late 1990s found five other types of motorcycle riders, whose experience of motorcycling presented different secondary motivations next to the common one of spiritual solace:

- *Social riders*, who distinguish themselves from the others because they like to have a woman riding with them on the backseat and do not like to ride alone.
- *Solitaires*, who prefer riding on their own and for whom the motor is chiefly a meditative vehicle (and possibly a means to escape from spouses, kids, and hassles).
- *Trip-drivers*, who like to cover long distances and enjoy taking someone on the backseat.
- *Part-timers*, who get pleasure out of their motorcycle without its taking an important place in their lives.

Table 7.1

Harley Davidson and Market Segmentation

Market segments	In percent		
	Share in sample	Share of Harley	Share of Honda
Social riders	10.9	5.0	47.5
Solitaires	15.6	5.4	48.2
Trip-drivers	18.3	23.9	47.8
Hard-core riders	6.6	75.0	8.3
Part-timers	20.8	21.1	34.2
Neutrals	27.9	11.8	34.3

Source: Adapted from Swinyard (1998).

• *Neutrals*, who do not really feel involved with their motorcycle, which they consider merely a means of transportation. They sometimes ask themselves why they still have the motorcycle.

Table 7.1 demonstrates that three-quarters of the hard-core drivers chose a Harley-Davidson, but only 5 percent of the social riders and the solitaires. The picture is the complete opposite for Honda: only 8 percent of the hard-core drivers choose this brand, against 48 percent of the socials and the solitaires. These differences lead to different positioning strategies or are, in fact, already a result of these different strategies.

The Swinyard study also provides insight into the demographic characteristics of the motor-cyclists: 93 percent were men, with 40.6 as average age; 66 percent were married; they had on average one child; 37 percent worked in a professional or leadership environment; and 32 percent had a manual occupation.

The study did not include a measurement of the brand associations, for which reason the connection between the different brand images and the differentiated motivations cannot be determined. For the rest, the study is a good example of domain-specific market segmentation. It illustrates how the motivations of different groups of consumers within a category can differ, leading to different brand choices.

In the early twenty-first century, Harley realized that the average age of Harley riders had increased from thirty-seven to forty-six years. Although younger bikers liked the Harley, they were not buying it because of their perception that it was high-priced. So age had become a defining factor of the Harley rider. In order to reach this younger group, Harley promoted its lower-priced, entry-level bikes, creating an edgier image that still reflected the freedom of spirit and individualism of the Harley brand but in a more youthful way.

Sources: Swinyard (1998); "What's Holding You Back," Harley-Davidson Attainability Campaign, 2003 International DMA Echo Award brief; "Authentic Harley Riding Gear," 2003 Effie Award brief.

SEGMENTATION AND BRANDING

Most theories of consumer behavior have moved away from the idea of a mass market in which all the people in the market are seen as similar. In fact, using the tools of segmentation, a brand's market can usually be divided into several different segments of people based on (1) their similarities within the group and (2) their differences from others in the market. For example, although most of Harley's market appreciates the spiritual solace of biking, they still differ in key ways, meaning that their relationship with the brand will be different as well. Furthermore, because they have different values and a different brand relationship, the way Harley communicates with them will differ. Most brand managers, then, make the following assumptions about their markets:

- A brand's consumers or customers differ in certain ways from each other and are in different circumstances and situations, as a result of which their functional and psychosocial needs, wishes, and desires with regard to the product category differ.
- Products and brands consist of different combinations of attributes, through which they meet the needs of various types of consumers in varying degrees.
- As a result, different groups of consumers can have a preference for different attribute combinations of a product or brand. These segments are homogeneous in themselves and heterogeneous versus other segments.
- Segments can be distinguished from the rest of the market, making it possible to reach a certain segment and fit the product-brand attribute combination to that segment.

Segmentation Hierarchy

In order to better understand the implications of those four assumptions, we must first review the basics of segmentation. Consumer brand segments can be defined and classified on the basis of countless characteristics. Sometimes the characteristics reflect basic demographics, sometimes needs and lifestyle, sometimes behavioral patterns that relate to the product or brand.

Consumers can be identified and analyzed in terms of a hierarchy of four worldviews, beginning at the top with the most general characteristics that are associated with a person as a citizen and ending with the role a person plays as a user of a specific brand. That hierarchy can be found in Figure 7.1.

This complex system of personal relationships with the world of products establishes an organizational hierarchy for deconstructing the types of variables used in segmenting, which is elaborated in Table 7.2. Beginning again at the top with the most general, person-as-citizen characteristics, we can see that that category includes geographic, demographic, and socioeconomic variables and other lifestyle indicators, such as psychographic variables and activities.

Next comes variables that define the person as a consumer, such as consumption-related attitudes and values, and then as a consumer of a particular product category, and finally as the user of a specific brand. These are the characteristics that can be used to define and profile a segment. Not all characteristics are equally important, and they vary in their predictive power based on the marketing situation.

Identification and Measurement

The reason it is important to profile consumers according to these segmentation variables is that they make it possible to identify the specific group most likely to buy the brand and then predict the extent to which they will become good customers. These segmentation variables are useful as predictors of a consumer's brand relationship potential only to the degree that they can be measured.

It goes without saying that the insight obtained with segmentation research depends very much on the characteristics obtained with the measuring instrument. For example, the previous example of the motorcyclists in the United States showed how little their social-demographic characteristics

Figure 7.1 **Brand Segmentation Hierarchy**

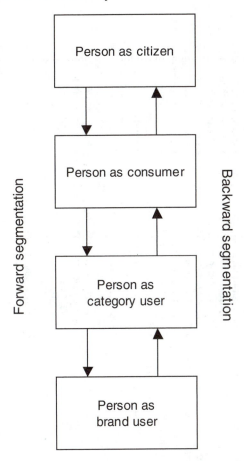

tell us. These characteristics may be useful in order to establish a relationship with other databases (such as the corresponding media consumption), and they can color further the image of the users, allowing for better customization of communication, but they do not usually give any explanation of the choice of a product, a product variant, or a brand.

Market research agencies and media operators offer many measurement instruments that lead to standardized segmentations that are applied to all consumers, products, and services. Although they can certainly contribute to insight into the composition of user groups and the positioning of brands, they carry with them the danger of ignoring important discriminating variables, giving a much too unidimensional or generic view of category users.

Market segmentation should be based, for example, on a selection as wide as possible of personal traits, after which the most discriminating variables can be identified that truly characterize a prime group of prospects. Examples of techniques that help with these decisions are the use of consumer panels, which include a large number of personal characteristics (usually already present) in the form of a database. By supplementing them with category- and brand-related characteristics, a base rich with relevant variables can be created that makes insightful segmentation possible.

Table 7.2

Segmentation Hierarchy and Variables

1. Person as citizen	2. Person as consumer	3. Person as category user	4. Person as brand user
Geographical • Postal code • Region • Degree of urbanization *Demographic* • Sex • Age • Education • Size of family • Composition of family • Phase of life • Ethnic background *Socio-economic* • Education • Occupation • Income • Social class • Type of dwelling *Psychographic* • Basic needs • End values • Personality • Lifestyle • Interests • Opinions • Adoption categories *Activities* • Hobbies *Media consumption*	*Values and general attitudes to consumption-related issues* • Availability of time and money • Quality sensitivity • Price sensitivity • Focus on convenience • Environmental awareness • Health awareness • Attitude toward household work *Domain-specific values, interests/attitudes/ behavior in consumption domain* • Food/drink • Clothing • Technique • Transportation, etc. *Purchasing and shopping behavior* *Media consumption*	*Mental level* • Need-states • Product motivation • Product involvement • Product awareness *Knowledge/perceptions* • Product experience • Product problems • Product attitudes • Sought product attributes • Sought product benefits *Behavioral level* • Product purchasing behavior • Channel choice • Product ownership/used • Moments/occasions • Situations • Variants • Frequency • Use intensity (light/heavy)	*Mental level* • Brand awareness • Brand associations • Brand positioning • Brand feelings • Brand attitude • Consideration set • Brand preference • Buying intention • Satisfaction • Bonding • Brand relationship *Brand behavioral level* • Purchasing history • Brand repertoire • Share of customer • Brand loyalty

Strategic and Descriptive Variables

A distinction should be made between strategic and descriptive variables. Strategic variables explain how—and why—consumers behave in relation to a specific product, service, or brand. Descriptive variables describe who these consumers are.

The real value of segmentation is in delivering understanding of why consumers behave in different ways, especially why they prefer one brand to another. Most segmentation studies, however, are based on descriptive variables, such as demographic and socioeconomic data, because they are easy to obtain, understand, and apply. They can provide useful information about who the users are in order to implement strategy, such as how and where to reach them. But this type of information does not explain much and does not help much to develop a brand strategy.

The real challenge of strategic segmentation is to find out which functions a product fulfills in the lives of consumers and how these functions vary. Which functional, psychosocial, or experiential attributes do consumers expect in the products they buy? And how do these expectations correlate with their brand choice? Afterward, it is possible to find out how specific subgroups of category users can be distinguished and described. Here are the core questions that have to be answered in segmentation research for a brand:

1. What purchasing and usage behavior do consumers show?
   - at a category or subcategory level
   - at a brand level
2. On which motivational and attitudinal variables is this behavior based?
   - category-related needs/values/benefits sought/attitudes (domain-specific segmentation)
   - brand saliency/perception/attitude/behavioral intention/relationship
3. Which general personal traits go together with this behavior?
   - consumption-related needs/values/attitudes/lifestyles
   - sociodemographic characteristics

The central strategic issue in segmentation is not just understanding and describing a segment, but selecting segments for effort and concentrating resources on them to the exclusion of alternatives.

> *Principle:* A distinction should be made between strategic and descriptive segmentation variables. Strategic variables explain how consumers behave in relation to a product and why. Descriptive variables describe who these consumers are.

Forward and Backward Segmentation

We can distinguish two different segmentation approaches. One is a classification of consumers and customers based on their personal characteristics, determining the connection between the found segments and their purchasing behavior (forward segmentation). For example, which brand of toothpaste do people with high educational levels buy—what are these people like and would they buy this toothpaste brand? The other classification of consumers and customers is based on the purchasing behavior of brand customers, determining the connections with their personal characteristics (backward segmentation). For example, who buys Buitoni fresh pasta? What is driving these people? How would you profile them? With forward thinking, you focus on the consumers as category users first, and with backward thinking you focus first on the brand users.

Planners who believe that segmentation is first a product decision tend to believe that market segmentation should be based primarily on category and brand purchasing behavior. Only afterward should a determination be made of whether and the degree to which there are differences between the buyers' group of a brand and the characteristics of other buyers of the category. In established markets for existing brands, segmentation should be aimed mainly at a category and brand level, after which the backward connections with more general personal characteristics can be determined.

DEFINING THE BRAND'S CATEGORY

The first question that a brand manager faces in developing a segmentation strategy is how to define the market within which the brand competes. Answering such a question seems easier than it is.

The starting point is often the way suppliers themselves look at a market, but segmenting also involves thinking from the consumer's perspective, and consumers appear to classify markets rather differently than do producers and retailers. For this reason, it is necessary to do preliminary research in order to find out how consumers categorize products and brands. As soon as it becomes clear how the consumer classifies the market, the purchasing behavior at a market level can be analyzed, for instance on the basis of the following questions:

- Which products and brands form a category in the perception of the consumer?
- What defines this category (what are the category drivers)?
- How are the different products and brands within the category positioned by the consumer in relation to one another?

For large market leaders, their main competitors often lie outside their own product category. In the Netherlands, Douwe Egberts coffee competes not only against Kannis & Gunnik or Perla coffee brands, but also with soft drinks like Coca-Cola and in some cases even with Cup-a-Soup by Unox (instant soup-in-an-envelope mix for one person). What do such brands have in common in the perception of consumers? They provide for the same need—a pep-up. For years, a cup of coffee—and thus Douwe Egberts—had more or less the sole rights to satisfy such a need, but since Coca-Cola and Unox took over the Dutch workplace with its automated vending machines, the status quo has been shattered.

This example shows how important it is to look at brands from the consumers' perspective, to find out what is the essence of their need and which options (products and brands) are available to them to provide for this need. *Those* questions identify the layers in the competition field.

It is very possible that, as a result of the specific goal that a consumer aims for—in this example, a pick-me-up during working hours—Douwe Egberts, Coca-Cola, and Cup-a-Soup together could end up forming a temporary, constructed need-based mental category. They are all considered by the consumer. The best representatives from various mental categories (coffee, soft drinks, and soup) compete with each other in this example. There are many ways to categorize such options (products and brands), and a distinction can also be made between more permanent and ad hoc categories.

The definition of a category was derived from the company's perspective in Chapter 1, but the category also is defined in the consumer's mind according to brand and category meanings. In fact, the brand's meanings have to be linked to the category in order to be perceived by consumers as an acceptable alternative within that category. These meanings, which serve as an admission ticket to the category, are known as category drivers. The brand's associations with these category drivers have to be established, but in principle do not provide the brand with any extra appeal compared with other brands within the category. In general, they offer no basis to compete, considering the fact that the other brands are also linked to these category meanings.

An exception is the prototype brand (often the market leader), which, in a way, is the ultimate representative of the category. The big strategy question is how a brand can, in some way or other, distinguish itself from the others without distancing itself from the category.

Hierarchical Categorization Schemas

The relationships that people establish between and among the various products, services, and brands they perceive enable them to form categories and subcategories and store them in long-term memory for easy retrieval. These categories are important in segmentation strategies because they provide a structure for analyzing users and the way they think about brands.

Classical categorization theories assume that categories are hierarchically organized. The top of the hierarchy is formed by an abstract representation of the categorized phenomenon. As we descend in the hierarchy, more characteristics are added and the concepts become increasingly concrete. A middle level serves as a basic level, which optimizes the balance between the richness of the representation and the degree to which it differentiates itself from other categories at the same level. The basic level, representing most easily how we perceive a category, contains the most information on all the entities that fall under it. Thus, all the characteristics of the more abstract higher level apply to all the categories under it.

Figure 7.2 represents a hierarchical structure of means of transportation in which the categorization of car choices is specified down to the brand level.

Subcategories

Under a product category we usually find subcategories that add specific meanings to the category and, therefore, help to identify and profile its users. For example, consumers seem to define private automobiles first on the basis of their class and then on their provenience. The categorization of personal automobiles in Figure 7.2 is based on research in Belgium (Sampson 1992). It shows that the brands are first categorized into top-class, middle-class, and lower-class brands. The middle-class brands are then subdivided according to their provenience, into French brands, Japanese brands, and German brands. Within the Japanese brands, Honda occupies a position of its own, Mazda and Nissan are grouped together, and so are Toyota and Mitsubishi. This categorization means that Japanese brands are primarily competing against each other. Similar hierarchically structured concept categories are found in many other markets.

Categorization by Product Function

Figure 7.3 shows the results of a study of how consumers in Austria categorize detergents. They first split them into "universal" (for regular wash) and "special" (e.g., for delicate fabrics). This basic (first-level) distinction represents the main differences that these consumers perceive among detergents. The special detergents are in turn categorized into hand-wash and washing machine detergents. The special machine detergents are subclassified into detergents for wool and delicate fabrics, and detergents for color fabrics. The universal detergents are subclassified into traditional

132

Figure 7.2 **Hierarchical Structure of Means of Transportation**

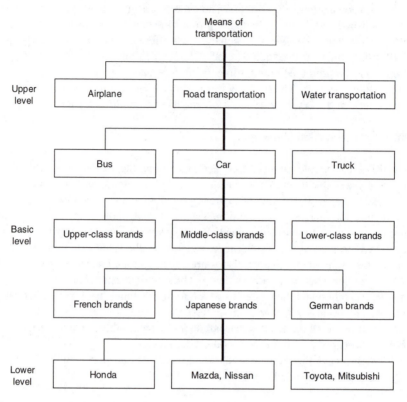

Figure 7.3 **Categorization of Detergents by Austrian Consumers**

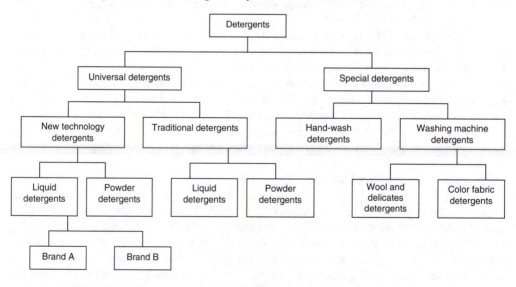

Source: BBDO Austria (1993).

and new technology (with solvents), the last ones into powder and liquid. Finally, brands fall under this categorization, forming the most specific level.

In both the preceding examples, consumers categorize products on the basis of the function of specific types of products and product variants. In the early days of branding, brands were mainly representative of product categories (see Chapter 4 on brand functions). The large majority of the strong brands that exist today were traditionally linked in this way to a product category. These brands, often market leaders, were once at the cradle of the product category and are primarily defined by the product with which they have been linked for generations. The product association is the core association of the brand: Philadelphia = cream cheese, Coca-Cola = carbonated soft drink, Duracell = alkaline batteries.

Not all brands, however, are primarily defined by their product category linkage. Virgin, for example, is not. Except for the "brand = product" category, we can also distinguish other basic brand concepts, as we did in Chapter 5, leading to other categorization schemas.

Categories have traditionally been seen as stable structures that are stored in hierarchical connections in long-term memory. However, Barsalou (1993) believes that temporary constructions in working memory are involved too. In his view, categories are very flexible. Someone who wants to lose weight may form a mental category of low-calorie products including a brand of diet soda as well as a brand of low-calorie jam. This explains why one product can often be found in two different places at the supermarket (e.g., canned tomatoes may be located in both the canned vegetable and the pasta sections). Retailers take great pains with the categorization system when organizing their products along the aisles and shelves.

In addition, associations have different strengths, as a result of which the accessibility of concepts also varies. Strong associations lead, within the same context, to the formation of the same categories time and again. This indicates that there probably are relatively stable subsets of entities that are united in permanent concepts in long-term memory, and also very flexible, ad hoc subsets in working memory based on the situation in which consumers find themselves and the task they are facing.

Affective and Formal Categorization

Next to categorization based on product functions, there are affective and formal categories. Affective categories are a person's collections of entities that have a mutually affective relation; they are based on distinctions between good and bad, beautiful and ugly, enjoyable and unpleasurable. Formal categories are formed on the basis of more abstract brand meanings, like brand personality and value associations; examples are youth brands and status brands.

Principle: People place products and brands in categories on the basis of similar perceived attributes. The categorization can be based on all kinds of different attributes and can have a permanent or an ad hoc character.

Natural Groups

Before segmentation research can be carried out, there should be insight into the way consumers themselves categorize brands and product categories. A method developed to do this is called "natural grouping." A respondent is asked to split a collection of brands (usually depicted in photographs) into two groups. In turn, each subgroup is split in two. With every split, the respondent is asked to indicate the reasons and to describe the new subgroups. These actions are repeated until the respondent can think of no more reasons to make new groups. The researcher thus gains insight into the brands that the respondent seems to believe are similar and the reasons behind those similarities. The process sets up a natural schema based on the distinctions that consumers feel are important—and sometimes this scheme may be different from how managers analyze a category and its brands. The categorization of detergents by Austrian consumers in Figure 7.3 is the result of such a natural grouping study.

Techniques such as natural grouping not only provide insight into the way consumers classify products, but also reveal which other brands consumers compare a given brand to. This knowledge constitutes the foundation of the positioning concept, which is discussed in the next chapter. When insight is obtained into the way consumers categorize products and brands, a market definition can be formulated.

PURCHASE BEHAVIOR SEGMENTS AT THE CATEGORY LEVEL

It is essential to know as much as possible about the purchase and use behavior of consumers and customers. The most important aspects are the penetration and the purchasing frequency of the category. On the brand level, it is the brand repertoire (a consumer's set of favorite brands) and the share of customer (the percentage of the customer's expenditure spent on any one brand in the repertoire) of the individual brands. As we will see, the result of the combination of these two aspects is that a large part of the sales of most brands depends on a relatively small minority of consumers. It is therefore important to establish who they are and then to identify, as far as possible, other characteristics in the segment that could explain the behavior, as was done for the motorcyclists example. This behavior can be analyzed at two levels of decision making—the category level and the brand level.

Category Penetration

Brand managers always want to know where their sales come from—for instance, the degree to which the sales come from consumers who have been (sub)category users for a long time or from new entrants. For almost every category, the answer is a combination of both factors. When an entirely new category is created, the contest between competing brands will concentrate on reaching the maximum penetration with the incoming new users. The development of the market of mobile telephony was a spectacular example of this.

As a category grows, a condition of balance sets in that is expressed in a greater stability in the penetration of the category. This is the case with nearly all fast-moving consumer goods (FMCG, also called "package goods" in the United States) and durable products that have been available for a long time. By way of example, the penetration of breakfast cereals among U.S. households has been stable at about 90 percent for more than a decade, and the usage frequency also has been stable at around five times a week (Jones 1992).

An important factor in situations like this cereal example is the entry of new generations into the market, which heavily impacts the long-term development of the market. The large brands are particularly dependent on this process. In the Dutch coffee market, for example, the use of coffee by young people is decreasing in favor of mineral water and soft drinks. For a market leader like Douwe Egberts, this problem is a primary focal point of brand strategy. The short-term growth of brands in stable markets is only possible at the expense of competing brands (brand switching).

Table 7.3

Hallberg Rule: One-third of Buyers Account for Two-thirds of Sales

	Percent category buyers	Share category sales	Average amount per buyer
Heavy users	33	67	2.0
Light users	67	33	0.5

Source: Hallberg (1995).

Principle: Developed markets are generally characterized by a condition of balance in which the penetration and the usage frequency of a category are stable.

Purchasing Frequency in the Category

Every user is different. A "real" beer drinker may drink twenty beers in one day; an occasional drinker may order just one beer at an outdoor cafée on a warm summer evening. Almost every category has light, medium, and heavy users, which is another way to segment the market based on usage levels. As early as the nineteenth century, the Italian economist Vilfredo Pareto established that, seen over many markets, about 50 percent of buyers account for 80 percent of sales and the other 50 percent for only 20 percent of sales. This is referred to the 80–20 rule (which is often quoted inaccurately as meaning that 20 percent of consumers are responsible for 80 percent of the category consumption).

Hallberg (1995) makes a plea for concentrating marketing efforts on this heavy buyer segment. In the early 1990s, an analysis by the Marketing Research Corporation of America (MRCA) over diverse categories shows that about 33 percent of buyers account for 67 percent of sales. They buy on average four times as much as the other 67 percent of buyers do (Table 7.3). MRCA determined a similar ratio for different categories—the top 33 percent of buyers account for 77 percent of the sales volume for clothing, 66 percent of credit card payments, 68 percent of long-distance calls, and 90 percent of restaurant visits.

It goes without saying that, for purposes of marketing and communication strategy, it is crucial to gain insight into the profiles of the heavy buyer segment of a category. First, an inventory is made of all the relevant user characteristics, such as goal of use (product function), sought attributes and benefits, product-related attitudes, and usage moments and situations. In addition, connections with underlying socioeconomic and psychographic characteristics are investigated. This serves a dual purpose: to learn how a product or product variant fits exactly into the life of these segments (the why of the use), and to identify mid-heavy and heavy category segments in databases, like those related to media reach.

Principle: Nearly every category has light, medium, and heavy users. According to the Pareto Principle, in many markets, 50 percent of buyers account for 80 percent of sales, and the other 50 percent of buyers account for only 20 percent of sales.

PURCHASE BEHAVIOR AT THE BRAND LEVEL

Although the category is the primary factor affecting consumer choice, the brand itself also functions as part of the selection schema. The idea of a repertoire, or set, of acceptable brands is the most important concept to understand in segmenting a market, and parallel to that is the concept, or ideal, of brand loyalty. Similar to heavy users, brand-loyal customers are, of course, a critical segment to profile and serve.

As soon as it becomes clear how the consumer classifies the category, the purchasing behavior at a brand level can be analyzed—for instance, on the basis of the following questions:

- What is the field in which the brand has to compete, and who are the players?
- Does the brand distinguish itself from the other brands in the category, and how?
- In terms of a competitive analysis, who in this field of brands gives the strongest challenges to the brand?

The Brand Repertoire

In many markets, most people alternate between two, three, or four different brands. In some markets, the number of brands that the consumer uses is even larger. The snacks market is one in which consumers are willing to try new products. This makes trial use easier to realize, but individual brands will always have only a small part of the purchases of a consumer in the category.

In other markets, such as cigarettes, razors, cosmetics, and toothpaste, consumers focus on one main brand that has a high share of their individual purchases. These are generally products in which strong sensory (taste, smell, feel) habituation plays a role. It is very difficult for new brands to realize trial use in such markets, because a strong preference relationship exists between consumers and their current brand. Even if a marketer succeeds in getting consumers to try a brand once, chances are they will fall back to their old brand afterward. Often they just forget the tried brand.

In most categories, consumers form what is known as a *brand repertoire*, a collection of brands within a product category over which their purchases are distributed. A brand repertoire goes together with the consideration set, but is not the same thing. The *consideration set* is a mental response—the brands that are being considered for choice when the consumer thinks of a category—whereas the brand repertoire points to a behavioral pattern.

A study by Jones (1995) of ten product categories revealed that in the United States, 43.5 percent of consumers alternate between three or more brands, and 33 percent buys only one brand. This last group consists of two subgroups:

- consumers who do not purchase much in the category and thus have little opportunity to alternate between several brands;
- consumers who have a really strong preference for one brand and will postpone their purchase when a shop does not have their favorite brand that day.

Unfortunately for most brands, the first subgroup, the light buyers in the category, forms the largest part of the 100 percent loyal buyers.

However, there are meaningful deviations from the averages in the Jones study that generally represent differences in how consumers relate to the various categories. For example, 55 percent of the consumers bought only one brand of mayonnaise (Hellmann's), whereas only 18 percent of the tissue buyers bought only one brand. The 29 percent of the detergent buyers that bought four or more brands were responsible for 47 percent of the sold category volume, whereas the 33 percent of the total buyers who bought only one brand accounted for only 18 percent of the category volume.

Another study by MRCA over twenty-seven product categories in the United States showed that the number of brands purchased alternately by mid-heavy buyers averages 3.9, and as much as 5.7 for heavy buyers (Hallberg 1995). These figures fit in a general sense with the analyses of Jones.

The studies of Jones and of Hallberg and others register behavior per household and not per individual consumer. The fact that, for instance, several brands of shampoo are bought per household could be related to the different wishes of the separate family members—the father wants Head & Shoulders because he has dandruff, the mother wants the more expensive Nexxus for her permed hair, and they buy Johnson & Johnson for their baby. Even in the detergents market, the purchase of different brands can be explained in terms of different functions required by individual consumers—people will buy one detergent brand for delicates, one for color fabrics, and yet another for whites.

The share that a brand represents in all purchases of the individual consumer within a product category during a specific period of time is known as *share of customer*, *share of wallet*, or *share of requirements*. The share of the customer's wallet is present in different levels and that provides a basis on which different brand behavior typologies can be distinguished.

Principle: Most category users have a repertoire of two to six brands over which they distribute their purchases. Buyers who stick to one brand only are mostly the light category users.

The Field of Brand Purchasing Behaviors

Various brand segmentation schemes have been developed on the basis of purchasing behavior patterns. James McQueen proposes a classification into six brand behavior typologies (as presented in Franzen 1994):

1. *One-time buyers:* These consumers buy the product one time in order to try it out. They do not buy it again, perhaps as a result of a negative brand experience or because the purchase was motivated by strong trial advertising or packaging. Sometimes they simply forget.
2. *Repeated trial buyers:* These consumers buy the brand just a few times, perhaps because they have not formed a clear judgment about the product yet. The premature halt of an introductory campaign could play a role here. New users have no bond yet with the brand and quickly fall back into their old buying behaviors.
3. *Now-and-then users:* A brand that reaches this position in the client's behavior rarely accounts for more than 20 percent of the brand purchases in the product category. There can be all kinds of explanations for this incidental use, such as product attribute–related factors—for example, the product might be a variant suitable for special situations. Or customers may have such a strong bond with the main brand that they buy a different brand only in exceptional situations—for example, when the preferred brand is not available. Or the brand could be a young brand that has not yet managed to reach a preferential position. Or incidental use could be the result of the consumer's price sensitivity.

Figure 7.4   **The Importance of Brand Loyalty** (in percent)

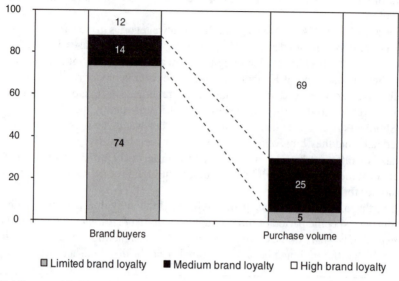

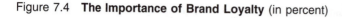

Source: Baldinger and Rubinson (1996).

4. *Repertoire buyers:* This group of buyers purchases the brand in question as regularly as several others. Repertoire buyers are those whose purchase of the brand represents 20 to 50 percent of all their purchases in the relevant product category. This purchasing behavior appears often in the categories in which alternating is important, such as snacks and desserts. It could also be an in-between phase building toward main brand status.

5. *Main brand buyers:* Main brands are those brands that account for more than 50 percent of the purchases of a consumer within the category in question, even if many other brands are available. Main-brand buyers purchase this brand at least 50 percent more often than any other brands.

6. *100 percent brand-loyal buyers:* These are consumers who want absolutely nothing else. They form the fan club of a brand. If the brand is not available, they postpone the purchase or look for it in another shop.

Brand Loyalty

The buyers in the last two groups, for whom a brand is a main brand or even the only brand they will accept, represent a high share of brand sales. An analysis of the purchasing data of twenty-seven brands in the United States showed that the segment of consumers with a high degree of loyalty to a brand amounted to an average of 12 percent of the category users, but accounted for an average 69 percent of the sales of the individual brands (Baldinger and Rubinson 1996). This is illustrated in Figure 7.4.

Principle: The sales of a brand are largely determined by the heavy-use category segment for which the main brand is within their brand repertoire. An average of 12 percent of the category users accounts for an average of 69 percent of the sales of a brand.

Figure 7.5   **Market Share Versus Loyalty**

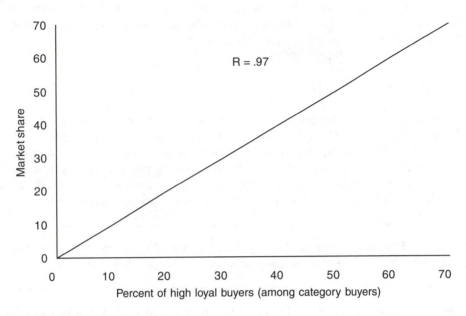

Source: Baldinger and Rubinson (1996).

Baldinger and Rubinson (1996) also determined a considerable shift from year to year among the segments. The growth of brands would thus be mainly the result of conversion of users from groups 2 and 3 to the segment with high brand loyalty. On average, it appeared that half of the users with high brand loyalty in a specific year also belonged to that segment in the preceding year. At the same time, almost half the users with high brand loyalty in a specific year seemed to slide off to a medium or low brand loyalty in the following year.

For an average brand within the fast-moving consumer-goods category, the share of customer amounts to an average of between 25 and 30 percent, and for the heavy user segment in a category in the United States only 18 percent (Hallberg 1995).

Research by a Dutch management-consulting firm has shown that the average share of wallet in the financial services sector is 36 percent (Geurtsen and Lodders 2001) and that clients switch service providers about every fourteen years. Consequently, the lifetime share of wallet of financial brands does not exceed 7 to 9 percent.

In the Netherlands, brand loyalty toward car brands, defined as the percentage of new-car buyers who buy the same brand they had before, fluctuates between 65 and 75 percent and varies per brand. In France it lies between 28 and 64 percent and in Italy between 29 and 59 percent (Pikaar 2000). Seen over four consecutive purchases, brand loyalty (share of customer) in the Netherlands is close to 45 percent on average. For domestic appliances, brand loyalty (new brand bought as percentage of the previous brand) for Philips lies between 29 percent for vacuum cleaners, 36 percent for irons, and 88 percent for electric razors (Pikaar 2000).

An analysis of sixty packaged goods brands in the United States (Baldinger and Rubinson 1996) showed that there is a nearly perfect correlation between the percentage of high-loyal users and the market share of a brand (see Figure 7.5). For large brands, the high-loyal segment accounted for 80 percent of the sales volume, for small brands 56 percent.

> *Principle:* Brand loyalty is lower for irregularly purchased consumer goods than for fast-moving consumer goods because no regular purchasing habit has emerged. The choice process is started anew each time.

Loyalty and Usage

The classification of category buyers according to share of customer (loyalty level) can now be combined with the classification of brand buyers according to purchasing intensity (frequency level). The connection of a high purchasing intensity with a high share of customer leads to a very high share of a relatively small group of the category's buyers in the sales of a brand. This segment represents the proverbial needle in the marketing haystack; successful brands are unusually effective at identifying and targeting this segment with appropriate marketing communication strategies.

> *Principle:* High purchasing intensity and high share of customer means that the brand has a high share of a relatively small group of loyal consumers.

Consider the situation for a brand of instant coffee in the United States. Let us assume research determined that the segment of heavy buyers with a high SoC (i.e., greater than 50 percent) comprises only 8.7 percent of all buyers, but this small segment in fact accounts for 61.3 percent of the sales of the brand in question. If we also include the 45 percent heavy-buyer segment—those with a SoC from 20 to 50 percent, then 54 percent of the category buyers account for 90 percent of the brand sales. Obviously these two types of heavy buyers are the segments that should be targeted in planning marketing communication strategies that are designed to maintain and reinforce the brand relationship (the first group) and to grow the SoC (the second group).

In another example of how brand and category data can be combined to identify promising segments, Barlow (2000) identifies and classifies business clients into four segments. The four categories that are crucial to database marketing are nonbuyers, a SoC segment less than 20 percent, a SoC of 20 to 50 percent, and a SoC of more than 50 percent. Based on Barlow, several general strategy consequences can be formulated for the four segments:

- *Segment 1—nonbuyers and light buyers:* These buyers offer few prospects although claiming a disproportionate portion of the marketing costs. In customer databases they are characterized by relative inactivity. According to Barlow, the goal is to lead them away from the marketing program activities, gradually but effectively, and to limit communication with them or even reduce it to nil.
- *Segment 2—loyal and light buyers:* These buyers may be profitable but offer little growth potential. Barlow sees the goal here as maintaining low costs and ensuring regular communication so these clients keep feeling special and continue their current level of purchase behavior.
- *Segment 3—nonloyal and heavy buyers:* These are the customers with the greatest growth potential, although they may be more loyal to competing brands. Strong stimuli would be necessary to increase the share of this customer for the brand. They should get the feeling that they are considered important and should be tempted toward higher loyalty with attractive offers.

Figure 7.6 **Classification of Category Buyers Into Four Segments**

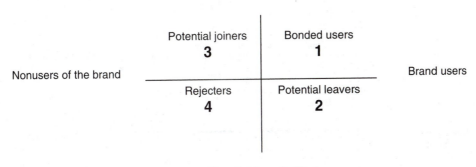

- *Segment 4—loyal and heavy buyers:* These clients are the crown jewels of a brand. They are usually loyal to it, but also constitute the primary target group of competing brands (where they fall into segment 3). There is not much to be gained with this group, but everything to lose, as there is a danger of overspending on it. These clients should get the feeling that they are considered important, but they tend to need less material reward. Personalization, access to information, attention, and recognition of their status will maintain their loyalty.

SEGMENTATION BASED ON BRAND ATTITUDE AND BRAND RELATIONSHIPS

Loyalty is one factor affecting the brand behavior of a segment, but so is a positive or negative brand attitude. In other words, the purchasing behavior of different loyalty segments can be cross-tabulated with their attitude in order to accurately profile a segment to target. Category buyers can be classified into a field of four different segments based on positive or negative attitudes toward the brand (see Figure 7.6).

Here is how the four segments in the matrix in Figure 7.6 can be distinguished from one another:

1. *Bonded users:* Every brand has users that feel a bond with it. Small portions of these users are the real ambassadors of the brand. They love the product and serve as advocates, talking with other people about their favorite brand. Another portion is constituted by the loyal buyers who have a small brand repertoire, show a relatively high degree of loyalty toward their favorite brands, and feel little need to switch in the short term. However, the attached users are often *not* the heavy category users, but the light and medium-heavy ones. Heavy category users are often very experienced consumers who are always open to (new) alternatives.

2. *Potential leavers:* A brand usually has an important group of habitual buyers who have a relatively low involvement in the category and perceive little difference among brands. They are ambivalent about their choice, have an above-average price sensitivity, and switch easily to other brands—not necessarily because they are dissatisfied but because another brand makes a more attractive offer. These are *switchers*, the potential leavers of

Figure 7.7   **Reclassification Into User Subsegments**

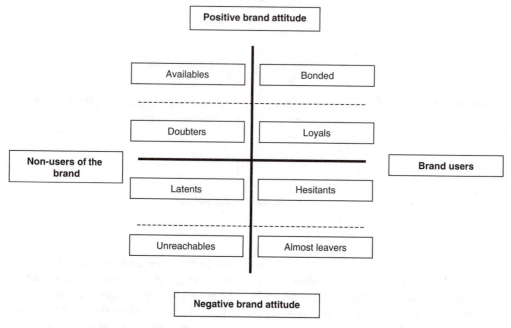

Source: Rice and Hofmeyr (2000).

a brand. In some categories, the variation *searchers* also fall under this category—they like to keep trying new variants and thus show a low degree of brand loyalty. Among the potential leavers are also, of course, those who are not satisfied with their brand.

3. *Potential joiners:* The third important group is the potential joiners of a brand—they are not buying the brand (yet), but already have a positive feeling about it. Some do not (yet) buy the brand for financial reasons ("We cannot afford a Lexus") or lack of availability ("There is no Ikea store in town"). Others are category buyers who have been led to doubt their current brand but have not (yet) made the switch to another brand.

4. *Rejecters:* These are category buyers who have attached themselves emotionally to another brand and will remain loyal ("I am loyal to my Saab and will not buy any other type of car"). These also can be buyers who do not feel any connection to the brand ("You will never catch me in a Hummer") or have been disappointed by the brand in the past ("I had one of those cars once and it was a lemon").

The bonded users segment forms the core of the consumer equity of a brand and is the group referred to as the brand-loyal segment. The potential leavers and the potential joiners account for the growth or decline of sales in the short term.

The Conversion Model

Hofmeyr (1990) classifies each of these four segments into another two subsegments. This results in eight groups—four of brand users and four of non-users (Figure 7.7). Hofmeyr's conversion model is based on a simple measuring instrument that focuses on measuring the strength of the bonding

Table 7.4

The Field of Loyalty Segments

	Brand users	Brand bonding pattern	
1	The Bonded	Tend not to change in the near future, remain loyal to the brand through thick and thin	100 percent loyal
2	The Loyals	Tend not to change in the short term, have so much attachment that they will not switch easily	Safe buyers
3	The Hesitants	First hesitations can be detected, loyalty is below average and attention begins to focus on other issues/brands	Potential switchers
4	The (Near) Leavers	Are at the crossways, about to change	Potential leavers
	Non-brand users	**Brand bonding pattern**	
5	The Availables	Have a greater inclination toward the brand or the organization that is subject of research than to their current brands	Potential joiners
6	The Doubters	Have been brought to doubt between current brand and brand that is subject of research	Switchers
7	The Latents	Will probably remain loyal to their current brand(s)	Non-available buyers
8	The Unreachables	Strong preference for current brand(s)	Rejectors

Source: Rice and Hofmeyr (2000).

of buyers with their brand and the degree to which nonbuyers of a brand feel any attraction to the brand. Table 7.4 follows with an analysis of the strategic implications of these segments.

In order to develop brand segmentation strategies, it is useful to combine our understanding of the field of category buyers (bonded users, potential leavers, potential joiners, and rejecters) with the field of brand purchasing behaviors (one-time buyers, repeated trial buyers, now-and-then users, repertoire buyers, main brand buyers, and 100 percent brand-loyal buyers). Insight into these categories helps us identify a set of eight loyalty segments that demand different brand communication strategies. Table 7.4 outlines these groups and describes the nature of their bonds with the brand.

It is possible to profile or map a brand based on an analysis of these eight segmentation factors. By comparing the profiles of competing brands, it becomes clear which brands will grow in the near future and which will lose. Figure 7.8 shows such a comparison for three brands in a category as a method of identifying market potential for a hypothetical Brand A. Let us just compare Brand A with Brand C. Note that the users of brand A have a much stronger attachment to the brand (bonded, loyals) than users of brand C even though there are more users of Brand C. In addition, 4 percent of the non-users of brand A are potential joiners to that brand, versus 1 percent of the non-users of brand C to that brand, and there is a higher level of available non-users identified with Brand A who might be open to conversion.

A large number of validation studies of the conversion model have investigated how the behavior of the interviewees developed six to twenty-four months after the first measurement. These studies support the assumptions upon which the conversion model is based (Rice and Hofmeyr 2000). These analyses confirm that the chance of losing users decreases as their bonding with a brand becomes

144

Figure 7.8 **Market Potential for Different Brands**

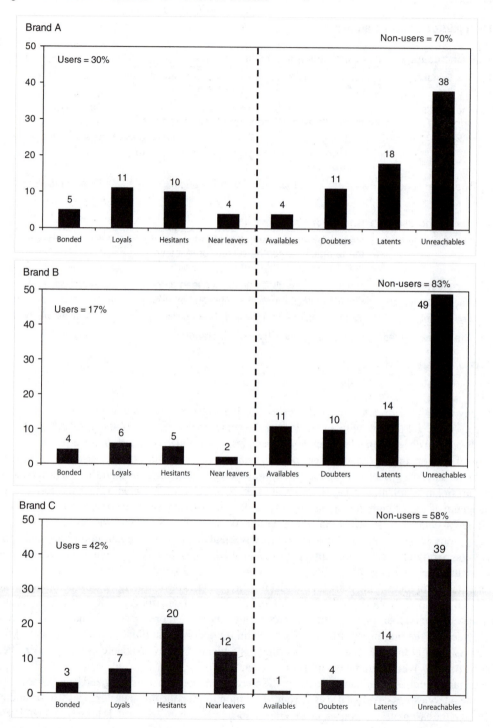

stronger and that the chance of attracting non-users increases as their attitude becomes more positive about a brand. The extensive research carried out with the conversion instrument (1,500 studies in the 1990s, with about 500 studies a year in the early 2000s) confirms in general lines the insights of Ehrenberg, which come down to the position that it is usually not the differentiation of a brand that constitutes the key to success, but its saliency, or importance to the customer. Using a brand leads to positive feelings about it, with some of the usage resulting in bonding.

> *Principle:* The growth of a brand in the short term depends on increasing the percentage of potential joiners and decreasing the percentage of potential leavers.

Four Relationship Factors

The bonded brand users segment can be described in terms of four aspects of their relationships with brands that define the nature of the brand relationship. These are the factors that are analyzed to diagnose the strength of the link between brand and customer:

1. *Meeting expectations:* One cannot underestimate the relevance of satisfaction derived from the degree to which a brand meets product expectations and brand values of a consumer. However, satisfaction is usually an insufficient condition for brand-loyal purchasing behavior, as it often has the character of a mere precondition. There is hardly any correlation with future purchasing behavior. As the correspondence between brand expectations and perceptions decreases, so does attachment to a brand.

2. *Involvement in the category:* Buyers who are not involved in a category are usually not very interested in brands either. Their brand association networks are extremely limited or even nonexistent. They do not care too much about what they buy. Their choice is based on heuristics (a way of making a decision using rules, even "rules of thumb"): they buy "what everybody buys," whatever is easy to find, or whatever is on sale at the moment. They tend to buy the dominant brand in their surroundings. They may be relatively loyal buyers of a brand, but they do not feel attached to it. They switch in their purchases easily to another brand when the situation arises, such as when the competitor has a sale or when the brand in question is out of stock.

In much of the literature, product categories are classified according to the involvement of consumers in general, but, in fact, nearly every category—even detergents—has users with high and low degrees of involvement. On the other hand, there are people buying cars who are not concerned with brands. The conversion model assumes that, without involvement in the brand choice, there can be no bonding to the brand and that no strong relationship can be developed with someone for whom the brand choice is not really relevant. In other words, it is users, and not product categories, that should be classified according to their degree of involvement.

3. *Attractiveness of alternatives:* The degree to which customers feel attracted toward an alternative brand could be an explanation for why some satisfied consumers leave a brand. As a (new) alternative is found more interesting, the attachment to the previous brand declines.

4. *Ambivalence:* Some consumers like two or three brands about the same. Sometimes the brand matters little to them. The market leader maintains its position thanks to its strong distribution. In highly involved choices, ambivalence can create a dilemma. As the ambivalence grows, attachment to the brand diminishes. One of the reasons to keep buying a brand is the feeling that

Table 7.5

Bonded Users and Association Scores for the Brand

Brands	Percentage of users who claim the brand possesses characteristic X	Percentage of bonded users
1st	73	88
4th	59	69
7th	31	46
6th	43	42
8th	39	41
5th	40	29
2nd	31	22
3rd	25	17

Source: Campbell (1998).

other brands are equally bad. Especially when it comes to higher switching costs, as can be the case when switching banks, the feeling of having to choose between a rock and a hard place can be enough to make people stay where they are.

Insight into the distribution of the category users according to their brand attitude and behavioral profiles, as well as their four bonding levels, makes it possible to predict the way users and non-users move from one brand to another. Hofmeyr's (1990) conversion model claims to provide good predictions on the development of market shares, having allegedly predicted correctly the decline of Marlboro in the United States in 1991, a brand crisis known as Marlboro Friday (Heath 1997). The conversion model helps to answer the following types of questions (Rice and Hofmeyr 2000):

- What is the overall position of a brand in the market—which segment is bonded, and which is uncertain?
- How strong and how weak are the competing brands? Which category users are attracted to or repelled by each?
- Will the brand grow or lose in the near future?
- Which non-users of a brand are possible joiners, and which are unreachable?
- To which competing brands does a brand risk losing users, and from which brands can new users be won?
- What motivates category users? What are the most important associations? How does a brand score on these characteristics? What undermines the connection to a brand, and why are some non-users unreachable?

Usage and Image

The user segment of the various brands usually has a similar image for the brand it uses—in other words, the essence of the category determines the image, and all the various brands use that as their touchpoint with their customers. Campbell (1998) proposes that in some markets there is a strong connection between the percentage of bonded users and the association scores for brands (see Table 7.5).

Just as Ehrenberg (1996), Hofmeyr and Rice (2000), arrived at the conclusion that differentiation is more the exception than the rule, bonding creates perceptions, not the other way around.

Consequently, direct stimulation of bonding with the brand user segment is an important strategic option. The limitation is that for a portion of the brand users this is not a feasible goal because they are not involved with the category.

Principle: Bonding creates perceptions—much more than the other way around.

Benefit Segmentation

Brands are chosen because they promise to fulfill specific human needs. Any branding strategy needs to integrate fundamental consumer needs with the psychosocial and functional benefits of the brand. We will discus the issue of needs more extensively in Chapter 9. Different needs are activated in different situations or on different occasions, resulting in different benefits sought. Understanding choice behavior requires occasion-based benefit segmentation in which the needs experienced and the benefits sought in different usage situations are considerations in brand choice (Dubow 1992).

In a famous article in the *Journal of Marketing* in 1968, Russell Haley first used the term *benefit segmentation*, which he described as "an approach to market segmentation whereby it is possible to identify market segments by causal factors rather than descriptive factors. The belief underlying this segmentation strategy is that the benefits which people are seeking in consuming a given product are the basic reasons for the existence of true market segments. They determine their behavior much more accurately than do demographic characteristics" (Haley 1968). Haley was clearly referring to desired or sought functional and psychosocial benefits, reflecting the fundamental human needs of consumers.

To understand how a specific brand fits in with the needs of consumers, their brand perceptions have to be measured. (We shall deal with this issue in Chapters 10 and 11.) All in all, this requirement leads to pretty extensive and complicated research designs. The difficulty can partly be overcome with the application of standardized values and lifestyle instruments, to which we will now turn.

VALUES AND LIFESTYLE SEGMENTATION

As was shown earlier in this chapter, consumer segments can be defined and classified on the basis of countless characteristics. It is common to segment on the basis of values and lifestyles. Most research companies and advertising agencies offer standard research instruments in this area, and most professional advertisers apply them in order to understand consumer choices.

For example, Heylen et al. (1995) postulate that people in Western societies use two dimensions to give meaning to the world around them. On the one hand, their behavior is determined by innate needs. On the other hand, they learn at a young age that they have to adapt themselves to the norms, values, and lifestyles of their social environment and of society at large. There is a constant tension between these innate needs and the demands of a culture and a society. People are constantly confronted with the choice of expressing or repressing their needs and values, as well as how to do this in either an active, self-assured manner or in a passive, sensitive, manner. Social integration and harmony are the ultimate goal.

Though they have slightly different labels, their content shows great similarity, even in their opposition meanings.

Figure 7.9   **Basic Dimensions of Value Measurement Systems**

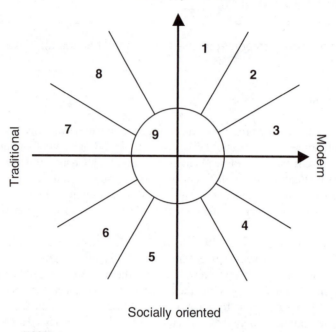

Source: Hansen (1998).

Two Basic Dimensions of Human Needs and Values

Human needs and values can be grouped in a space defined by two basic qualities relating to personal expressiveness and social orientation. Having compared a number of different measurement systems, Hansen (1998) concluded that these two dimensions appear regardless of what questions are being asked.

- *Dimension 1:* Expression versus repression
  - modern versus traditional
  - open versus resistant to change
  - preferring change/preferring stability
  - pragmatic versus faithful
- *Dimension 2:* Social integration versus individual orientation
  - individual versus social
  - action-oriented versus principle-oriented
  - hedonistic versus ethical
  - humanistic versus materialistic
  - self-transcendent versus self-enhancing

Likewise, Hansen found nine segments, based on needs, of more or less similar size groupings in the Denmark population (see Figure 7.9 and Table 7.6).

Table 7.6

Nine Needs Segments

Segments	Percent of respondents (Denmark)
1. The individually oriented	11.0
2. The modern socially oriented	10.1
3. The moderns	11.8
4. The modern individually oriented	10.9
5. The traditional socially oriented	10.0
6. The socially oriented	12.6
7. The traditionals	11.5
8. The traditional individually oriented	10.0
9. The center (neutral)	12.4

Source: Hansen (1998).

Lifestyle Segmentation in Europe

One example of such a research instrument is the Euro-Socio-Styles system, a pan-European research approach created by the GfK research agency (GfK 2005). It incorporates values, attitudes, and consumer behavior in order to identify eight lifestyle segments (see Figure 7.10). These are mapped in a space defined by two dimensions:

1. *Reality versus illusion* (or materialism versus post-materialism, or price-orientation versus quality orientation);
2. *Present versus future* (or personal security versus living one's own emotions, or puritanism versus hedonism).

In this system, eight characteristic lifestyles can be identified, which, despite individual national characteristics, show the same basic value orientations across national borders. The eight lifestyles are described as follows:

1. *Secure world* (11 percent of population). Conformist, hedonist families of simple origin who live in isolation, dream of an easy life, and are committed to playing traditional roles. They are simultaneously materialistic and price-oriented. They want a high standard of living and fashionable brands. They want to buy branded products at the lowest possible prices.
2. *Steady world* (19 percent). Tradition-oriented, conforming middle-class senior citizens who are making full use of their retirement. Their purchases are carefully considered and based on need. This segment also attaches a lot of importance to price.
3. *Standing world* (14 percent). Educated, conscientious people who are faithful to their convictions and tradition-oriented. They have a realistic attitude in their purchases and a preference for timeless things.
4. *Authentic world* (15 percent). Rational, moral, cocooned families with good incomes who are socially committed and looking for a harmonious, balanced life. They have an attitude of practicality and prefer timeless products and organic, additive-free foods. Their style of consumption is critical in its approach.
5. *New world* (11 percent). Hedonistic, easy-going intellectuals with an above-average standard of living who seek personal harmony and social commitment. For them, price is less decisive than ambience and quality.

Figure 7.10   The Eight Euro-Socio-Styles® and Their Position in the "Map of Personal Values"

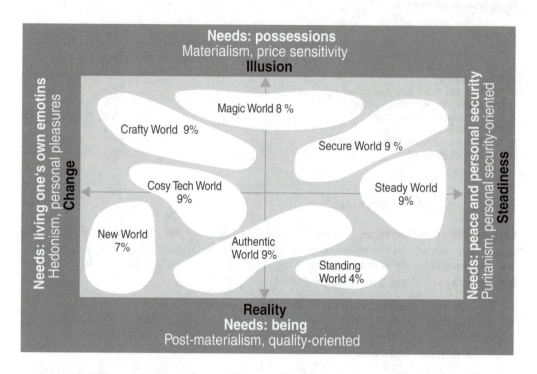

Source: Adapted from GfK magazines for staff and clients 2(2004: 16–19); www.gfk.de/lifestylesresearch.

6. *Cosy tech world* (9 percent). Active, modern, middle-aged couples with above-average household equipment who are seeking personal development.
7. *Crafty world* (13 percent). Young, dynamic, opportunity-seeking people from simple family backgrounds who are looking for success. They are materialistic and fashion-oriented and want to achieve something worthwhile. They prefer things that are innovative, new, and powerful.
8. *Magic world* (8 percent). Intuitive, young, materialistic people with children and a small income who are longing for a better life. They have an extreme orientation toward fashion. They want brands that help them fulfill their personal dreams and get noticed.

The differences between the lifestyles are greater than the national differences between the countries.

Lifestyle Segmentation in the United States

In the United States, lifestyle research has been dominated since 1978 by the VALS™ system, originally developed by SRI International and now owned and operated by SRI Consulting Busi-

Figure 7.11   **The Eight Consumer Segments in the VALS Framework**

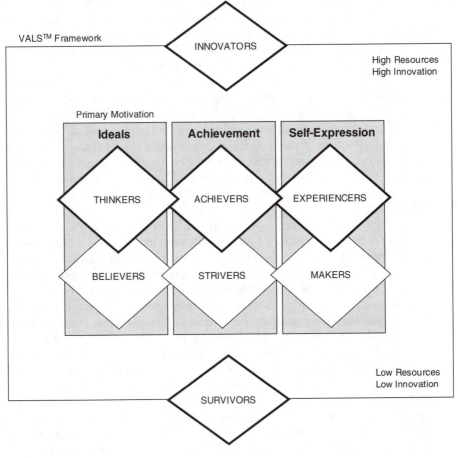

Source: SRI Consulting Business Intelligence (SRI-BI), www.sric-bi.com/VALS.

ness Intelligence (SRI-BI). In 1989 VALS was revised to maximize its ability to predict consumer behavior. The original system grouped consumers based on their attitudes toward social values such as military spending and abortion rights. Research conducted by SRI, Stanford University, and the University of California, Berkeley, found that psychological characteristics with several key demographics were better predictors of consumer behavior than social values were. The new VALS system, called VALS 2 for a short time but now known again as VALS, has psychology at its core and is therefore known as a psychographic segmentation system. VALS systems for Japan and the United Kingdom have also been developed using the same methodology. The U.S. VALS system places U.S. adult consumers into one of eight segments. The two main dimensions of the framework are *primary motivation* (the horizontal dimension) and *resources* (the vertical dimension).

The SRI premise is that consumers are inspired by one of three primary motivations: ideals, achievements, and self-expression. Consumers who are primarily motivated by ideals are guided by knowledge and principles. Consumers who are primarily motivated by achievement look for products and services that demonstrate success to their peers. Consumers who are primarily motivated by self-expression desire social or physical activity, variety, and risk.

Energy, self-confidence, consumerism (propensity to buy), age, education, and income define an individual's resources. Different levels of resources enhance or constrain the expression of a person's primary motivation. VALS distinguishes the following eight segments; each segment represents between 10 and 17 percent of the U.S. adult population:

1. *Innovators* are successful, sophisticated, active, take-charge people with high self-esteem and abundant resources. They are interested in growth and seek to develop, explore, and express themselves in various ways, sometimes guided by principle and sometimes by a desire to have an effect or to make a change. Image is important to innovators not as evidence of status or power but as an expression of taste, independence, and character. Their consumption patterns reflect a cultivated taste for the fine things in life. They are receptive to new products, new forms of distribution, and new technologies.

2. *Thinkers* are mature, satisfied, comfortable, reflective people who value order, knowledge, and responsibility. Most are well educated and in or recently retired from professional occupations. They are content with their careers, families, and status in life, well informed about the world and national events, and alert to opportunities to broaden their knowledge. They have little interest in image and prestige. They tend to base their decisions on strongly held principles and consequently appear calm and self-assured. While their incomes allow them many choices, thinkers are conservative, practical consumers, concerned about functionality, value, and durability in the products they buy.

3. *Believers* are conservative, conventional people with concrete beliefs based on traditional, established codes: family, church, community, and the nation. Many believers express moral codes that are deeply rooted and literally interpreted. They follow established routines, organized in large part around their homes, families, and social or religious organizations to which they belong. As consumers, they are conservative and predictable, favoring American products and established brands. Their education, income, and energy are modest but sufficient to meet their needs. They look for bargains.

4. *Achievers* are successful career- and work-oriented people who like to and generally do feel in control of their lives. They value structure, predictability, and stability over risk, intimacy, and self-discovery. Their social lives are structured around family, church, and business. Achievers live conventional lives, are politically conservative, and respect authority and the status quo. As consumers, they favor established products and services that demonstrate their success to their peers. They are attracted to premium brands.

5. *Strivers* seek motivation, self-definition, and approval from the world around them. Unsure of themselves and low on economic, social, and psychological resources, strivers are deeply concerned about the opinions and approval of others. Money defines success for strivers, who do not have enough of it. Strivers are image-conscious and sensitive to the tastes and preferences of the persons with whom they live and socialize.

6. *Experiencers* are young, vital, enthusiastic, impulsive, and rebellious. They seek variety and excitement, savoring the new, the offbeat, and the risky. Still in the process of formulating life values and patterns of behavior, they quickly become enthusiastic about new possibilities but are equally quick to cool. Experiencers combine an abstract disdain for conformity and authority with an outsider's awe of other people's wealth, prestige, and power. Their energy finds an outlet in exercise, sports, outdoor recreation, and social

activities. Experiencers are avid consumers and spend much of their income on clothing, fast food, music, movies, and video. They follow fashion.

7. *Makers* are practical people who have constructive skills and value self-sufficiency. They live within a traditional context of family, practical work, and physical recreation and have little interest in what lies outside that context. Makers experience the world by working on it—building a house, raising children, fixing a car, or canning vegetables. They are unimpressed by material possessions other than those with a practical or functional purpose (e.g., tools, pickup trucks, or fishing equipment). They value durability and comfort and buy the basics.

8. *Survivors* endure constricted lives. With limited economic, social, and emotional resources and often in poor health, survivors experience the world as pressing and difficult. Because they are so limited, they show no evidence of a strong self-orientation, but are focused on meeting the urgent needs of the present moment. Survivors are cautious consumers. They represent a very modest market for most products and services but are loyal to favorite brands. They watch for sales.

The VALS categories that consumers fit into are determined by the way they answer a list of attitude items known as the VALS questionnaire. This battery of items is integrated into larger questionnaires about products or media so marketers can see the kinds of products that appeal to different consumer types. For instance, survey research confirms that makers are more likely to buy hunting equipment, full-size trucks, and Western boots than other consumer groups, while achievers are more likely to own SUVs and Mp3 players and use online banking services. VALS is used for targeting, positioning, advertising, and new product ideation.

General segmentation studies like these combined with brand perception measurement based on the same variables can give insight into the underlying motivations of brand choice. The predictive power of segmentation systems varies widely. Systems based solely on demographics tend to have relatively low predictive power. Systems based on demographics and psychological characteristics correlated with purchase behavior are substantially more predictive.

TO SEGMENT OR NOT?

The most important strategic question is when and to what degree segmentation is needed or even useful. To determine this, Kennedy et al. (2000) analyzed the buyers' profiles of the top ten brands in forty-two product and service categories in England. The personal data of the buyers included demographic information, media consumption data, and scores on 200 attitude and lifestyle statements. For each brand, the researchers established to what degree the user characteristics deviated from the profile of all users of the category—for example, to what degree do Visa users deviate from all credit card users? The results were surprising: fewer than 5 percent of the user characteristics seemed to deviate by more than 5 percent from the category averages. In other words, in 95 percent of the scores, hardly any difference seemed to exist between the characteristics of users of an individual brand and the characteristics of all users of the corresponding product category.

On the surface this finding may sound like an argument against segmentation. The point is that, unless there are real attribute- or price-related differences in their products, many brands are really involved in a nonsegmented, competitive mass marketing. Segmentation is a second-level strategy that operates only as the brand takes on power in and of itself and creates distinction where there is otherwise none in the product. In other words, the brand becomes an important segmentation tool only if it creates a point of differentiation within the category. The results of the Kennedy analysis also correspond with theories on saliency-driven brand choice, as discussed in Chapter 13.

The basic idea behind market segmentation is that the differences in the need patterns of consumers provide the basis on which preferences develop for differentiated products and brands. Differentiated products mean that there are real differences in their attributes. In reality, though, it seems that many marketplaces contain product and/or brand variants that are nothing more than acceptable alternatives for something that already exists. The findings of Kennedy et al. (2000) could indicate that brand choice is made primarily on the basis of the strength of the mental connection between brand and product category—that is, brand saliency.

Another explanation could lie in the fact that perceptual differentiation of brands is very much dependent on the constant confirmation of that differentiation in communication. Brands in which this happens to an insufficient degree gradually lose their distinctiveness and fall back into a "me too" perception, at which point any brand will do.

The power of the brand, then, lies in the communication effectiveness of its brand message. Brand-relevant segmentation strategies (as opposed to attribute-relevant segmentation) are totally dependent on the consumer perception of the brand symbolism as expressed through the marketing communication, and that argues for the important role that advertising and other types of marketing communication play in maintaining brand differentiation and the brand's appeal to different segments.

Principle: Many markets are nonsegmented. They contain product and/or brand variants that are nothing more than acceptable alternatives for something that already exists.

Components of Segmentation Strategies

We have discussed a number of ways to identify segments, but what are the components of segmentation—the segmentation factors—that affect brand strategy? Analyzing all the fields and types of buyers in a market segmentation system, we have arrived at the following as the key components that determine the strategic approach to be used in brand segmentation strategies:

- *Information:* brand knowledge or lack thereof, knowledge about competitive brands;
- *Personal characteristics:* needs, values, lifestyles, benefits sought;
- *Attitude:* liking, doubting, satisfaction, dissatisfaction, preference, loyalty;
- *Behavior:* trial, buy, repeat buy, switch, leave, return.

Let us turn now to a review of the development of a system of segmentation-based brand strategies that reflect these opportunities.

BRAND STRATEGY OPTIONS

Assuming that a brand manager has decided that a segmentation strategy is achievable for the brand, a set of subsequent strategic decisions can be derived from that decision. On an abstract level, we can distinguish the following four options in the development of brand segmentation strategies: penetration, frequency, continuity, and winning back.

Figure 7.12   **A Brand With More Available Non-users Than Nonbonded Users**

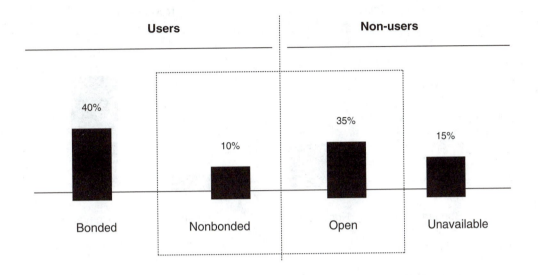

Penetration Strategy

A penetration strategy means increasing the percentage of category users that use the brand. This includes four substrategies:

1. *Inflow or acquisition strategy:* attracting new category users for the brand. In developed markets, this involves primarily the newly entering generations. In the Netherlands, for instance, Gillette sends each year a Mach 3 to 50,000 youngsters as they turn eighteen.
2. *Switching or conversion strategy:* attracting users of competing brands (brand switch).
3. *Retention strategy:* keeping potential leavers. There are two different groups—consumers who have made one or a few test purchases of the brand but have not adopted it yet, and consumers who have been using the brand for a while already but have not become attached to it.
4. *Winning-back strategy:* detecting defectors and reinstating trust.

   For the decision between conversion strategy and retention strategy, insight is needed into the classification of the category users in terms of their attachment to the brand and the degree to which they see other brands as acceptable alternatives. The most important fact is the relationship between potential leavers and potential joiners. The larger the percentage of potential joiners, the more appropriate a conversion strategy is. The larger the percentage of potential leavers, the more a retention strategy deserves consideration. The brand in the hypothetical example of Figure 7.12 is characterized by a high percentage of attached users and potential joiners. A conversion strategy is an obvious choice here. Figure 7.13 shows an opposite example of a brand with a high share of potential leavers and a low percentage of potential joiners. Here a retention strategy would be appropriate. Measurements such as those of the conversion model can help brand managers make a rational choice.

Figure 7.13   **A Brand With More Available Potential Leavers Than Potential Joiners**

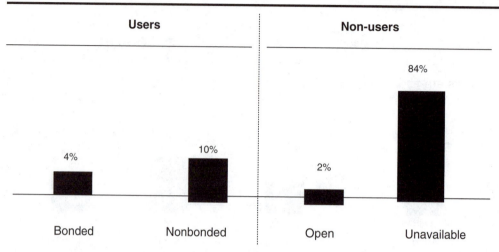

Frequency Strategy

The goal here is to increase the share of customer of a brand. As we have seen, the purchasing frequencies of brands in a developed market often are close together with a small correction for the market share. The chances of success of a frequency marketing strategy (mostly in the form of a so-called savings program based on amount used or spent) are probably not too high.

Based on analyses of practical cases, Dowling and Uncles (1997) arrive at the conclusion that saving programs tend not to be very successful in changing the already existing purchasing behavior patterns of customers. In an analysis of six saving programs in Australia (Sharp and Sharp 1997), no effects on purchasing frequency were found. Only two programs showed an increase in the share of requirements, a factor present to the same degree with participants and nonparticipants in the program.

Research by the McKinsey consulting company (Cigliano et al. 2000) shows that the first retailers that introduced saving programs in the United States and Europe recorded an average sales increase of 1 to 3 percent for groceries and 5 to 8 percent in department stores. However, competitors who followed later with their own saving programs ensured that a large part of this initially modest growth was cancelled out. Saving programs are also characterized by several tough problems, as described in the box.

Continuity Strategy

This strategy is about maintaining and strengthening the brand relationship with already attached brand users. The primary goal is the consolidation of brand-loyal purchasing behavior through the years, and the secondary goal is attaining a higher share of customer or the customer's wallet. There is thus a certain overlap with the frequency strategy—the latter is aimed primarily toward increasing the share of customer and makes use of rewards, while the continuity relationship strategy is aimed toward developing and reinforcing the mental commitment of the customer and aspires to maintain a long-term relationship.

The Trouble With Saving Programs

- *Saving programs are expensive.* Research reveals that sixteen major European retailers had a total of some $1.2 billion tied up in annual discounts to customers, with several supermarket chains devoting some $150 million each to these programs. Costs are about the same in the United States. Given large sales volumes, even programs with modest rebates (up to 1 percent) can cost a great deal of money. Then come the costs of marketing and managing a program investment in systems, fulfillment support, and so forth, which usually run well into the millions.

- *Saving programs take on a life of their own.* Once they start, mistakes can be very difficult to correct. Even programs with low benefits become entrenched in the minds of customers, who must be informed when they change or come to an end. Customers react negatively to any perceived "take away" once a program is in place, even if they are not actively involved in it. Curiously, the successful launch of a program worsens the problems of ending it. And a negative experience with a program heightens the skepticism of consumers when they are offered a follow-up program, even further undermining their trust in the retailer.

- *Saving programs often fail to increase customers' loyalty.* In fact, 79 percent of customers in casual apparel and 70 percent in grocery say they are always seeking alternatives to their current retailers, percentages that far exceed the percentage of customers actively seeking alternatives in other categories. Nor do consumers who join a saving program necessarily increase their spending. These saving programs operate within the context of shoppers who are frequently re-evaluating their loyalty to a particular retailer or brand and, if they work, cement a bond with the customer.

Percent of shoppers by category who "frequently reassess" their choice of retailer:

Apparel	79
Grocery	70
Cellular-phone service	57
Auto insurance	48
Home equity loan	48
Credit card	47
Soft drinks	39
Long-distance telephone service	34
Life insurance	32

Source: Based on a McKinsey survey of 1,200 consumers across sixteen product categories conducted in October 1999 (Cigliano et al. 2000).

In practice, this strategy is also followed for the nonbonded users, but as has become clear, it is often difficult—if not impossible—to develop a deeper relationship with people who are not involved in the category or who do not easily become attached to things.

A brand relationship strategy that encourages continuity should be tailored to the relationship needs of the users. For some customers, the product or service is important enough in their lives to merit spending energy in gathering knowledge about it. Other users, however, experience no involvement whatsoever in the process, so for them a relationship strategy would be a waste. The less they are bothered by brand-related information, the happier they are. For a responsible relationship strategy, it is necessary to have insight into the involvement of buyers in the category so that a relationship program can be fitted as well as possible to the needs and aversions of the individual users. Very little empirical data are available about the effect on continuity of the relationship program (Schijns 1998). These findings also indicate that a relationship program, like a customer club, does not significantly strengthen the relationship between suppliers and participants.

Established brands in developed markets usually use a combination of the above-mentioned strategies, in which a certain balance has to be found.

Winning-Back Strategy

In spite of all efforts to maintain and strengthen the relationships with their customers, companies do lose customers every year. Estimates range from 20 to 40 percent of them. Almost half of all marketing managers do not know how many customers their firm loses annually and do not have a system in place for detecting them. Research has shown that often a company has a better chance of winning back a former customer than creating a new one (Griffin and Lowenstern 2001).

Winning back customers requires insight into why they defected. Were they dissatisfied with the brand, for instance, or just lured away by a competitor offering a better price? Companies should not wait until the relationship is completely broken to develop a winning-back strategy—and such a program should make it easy for customers to return. This strategy calls for a well-aimed, well-planned effort based on sound information from the brand's own database. Typical diagnostic questions include the following:

- What are the sources of dissatisfaction?
- What can be done to ameliorate these feelings before they cause a rupture?
- Are these customers worth the extra effort to retain them?
- How much damage can they do to brand perceptions if they leave?

The main goal is to reinstate trust. The company has to let customers know that it values their business. Perhaps things have changed on the company's side; perhaps it can make a special offer for a retrial. Following a complaint registered through customer service, a personal note from a senior executive may be sufficient to convince a customer that the company cares, listens, and is willing to improve. If nothing else, such a personal contact leaves customers with a better feeling for the company, which should try to keep in touch with them for a better chance in the future. Also the new supplier may make mistakes, which might encourage consumers to return to the original relationship.

HARLEY-DAVIDSON AND SEGMENTATION

What factors identify the segment of people who would be in the market for a motorcycle? For a Harley-Davidson? How does an understanding of those factors lead to an effective segmentation strategy for Harley-Davidson?

The hard-core biker, for example, makes up only 14 percent of the overall market, which is shared with five other segments: social riders, solitaires, trip-drivers, part-timers, and neutrals. Harley is the choice of most hard-core motorcyclists, but only 5 percent of the solitaires and social riders. The Honda market is just the opposite. Obviously, these differences in the attitudes and characteristics of the segments buying the two brands lead to different brand and marketing communication strategies.

The three most important factors determining Harley's segmentation strategy, then, are consumers' behavior and attitudes relative to the category, consumers' behavior and attitudes relative to the brand, and the behavior and attitudes of consumers of the competing brands.

PART III

BRAND STRATEGY MEETS
BRAND PERCEPTION

BRAND DIFFERENTIATION AND POSITIONING

Part II of this book focused on the components of branding that can be managed by a marketer. Part III looks at the other half of the brand system—the consumer—and considers how the values of consumers affect their perceptions of a brand, as well as the construction of other customer-focused perceptions, such as brand position, brand meaning, and brand personality.

The concept of positioning refers to the strategy companies follow to reach a favorable, sustainable competitive position in a market. Positioning of a brand by companies refers to the choice of the customer groups to be served, the structure of the activities necessary to answer to their needs and desires, and the competitive advantage a brand has over its competition. The importance of understanding the target market's needs and wants relative to the product's competitive advantage is illustrated in the story of how Levi's, which in the early 1990s was still an example of successful positioning, got into trouble in the late 1990s.

LEVI'S: WILL THEY EVER BE COOL AGAIN?

Levi's is a huge brand, with more than a century of image and tradition behind it. In 1853 Levi Strauss (1829–1902), a Jewish immigrant from Bavaria in Germany, went to San Francisco to produce waist-high overalls, which were roomy, practical, and almost indestructible. Gold miners who bought them called them "Levi's."

Using a sturdy serge fabric made in Nimes, France—that is, *de Nimes*, which was anglicized eventually to *denim*—the shopkeeper also introduced the idea of riveting the pocket corners for added strength to handle the weight of gold nuggets. Thus was the birth of the legendary jeans and the global Levi's brand. Levi's owned the position of a tough, durable jean with a tradition that gave it a cachet.

The enterprise prospered splendidly. By 1961 Levi's had grown into a $40 million business, selling mainly to farmers and cowboys, primarily west of the Mississippi. Levi's president, Walter Haas, the grandnephew of Levi Strauss, promoted the original 501 button-fly denim jeans to rodeo fans, using a cowboy image.

In the 1960s Levi's was discovered by the Woodstock generation, becoming one of its symbols of rebellion. Hippies had to wear jeans by definition. Levi's became their uniform. In that decade Levi's also spread to international markets. The brand had become a youth icon—which it remained up to the 1990s. At that point the style preferences of teens began to deviate radically from those of the baby boomers, on whom Levi's had largely become dependent for sales of its traditional models—like the 501, Levi's flagship product. The company seemed to be trying to appease children and at the same time keep adults happy. Even into the early twenty-first century, Levi's was still searching for a link with the teen market again.

Analysts believe that the market share of Levi's has declined since the mid-1990s from 31 to 17 percent, thanks to brands like Gap, Old Navy, Tommy Hillfiger, and Diesel, which have positioned themselves as designer jeans for young people. The year 1996 was the last in which Levi's sales increased. Since then, its sales slumped from more than $7.1 billion to $4.1 billion in 2002.

To fight back, Levi's came up with jeans with pressed creases, Star, which flopped. People liked the advertising with the comic figure Flat Eric, but did not like the product. In 2002 the company introduced a modernized line called Engineered Jeans. Levi's practically revived the pants models with five pockets, side seams that followed the leg line, and a hem that was a little shorter in the back so the pants would not drag over the ground. The pants pockets were also a little bigger, so things like mobile phones could fit into them. The redesigned styles were intended for niche stores that were currently stormed by youth. But those shops and their customers were not prepared for a radical switch to Engineered Jeans, considering that Levi's had always been known for its tight, average-Joe jeans and the classic Red Tab denim pants. The Engineered Jeans reached a bare 10 percent of Levi's sales in Europe.

Levi's cannot allow itself to alienate the core group of baby boomers. "It is dumb to aim at the under-25 market only, because that market is too capricious," says Harry Bernard, a San Francisco marketing consultant. In new advertisements, the product itself is central, and no attempt is made to sell a "mentality." In television ads for cut-off, short, frayed pants, a young woman throws her jeans at an oncoming train. The wheels cut them into short, frayed pants. This is a remarkable difference compared with the newspaper advertisements—showing teenagers strolling around with exposed navels—that had earned Levi's Silver Tab pants much praise. "The brand Levi's is too big to aim at such a limited market," says Phillip Marineau, chair of the board at Levi's.

As a result of slumping sales, Levi's has closed down a large number of its factories. In 2003–04 it closed its last two remaining plants in the United States and Canada, including its landmark

Valencia Street plant in San Francisco. In 2003 the company took a desperate step: it rolled out blue jeans into 2,864 Wal-Mart discount stores in the United States at about half the price of the Red Tab 501 pants, which are sold at department and specialty stores. The Wal-Mart jeans carried the Signature sub-brand, but the Levi's label was firmly stitched on the back. They were made with lighter-weight, lower-quality fabric and cheaper dyes than the other Levi's jeans, which showed. By 2007 Levi's total sales were just over $4 billion, $3 billion less than during its peak in 1996. Its sales had declined in nine of the ten preceding years.

For Levi's the dilemma remains: How can the company sell a hip image without losing its older target group?

Sources: Lee (2000); Van Dijk (2000); Knobil (2003); Pfannenmüller (2003); Robinson (2003); Ginsberg (2003); Fishman (2003).

THE BASICS OF BRAND POSITIONING

A position is a mental concept, a location of a brand relative to its competitors that exists in the mind of the consumer—cheaper, higher quality, more durable, cooler, and so forth. There are two sides to positioning. The first is the strategy developed by the company to claim a position that provides a competitive advantage in the marketplace. The Levi's story demonstrates the efforts of the managers of the Levi's brand to maintain its leadership position in denim jeans. The problem Levi's face is keeping in touch with its consumer market. And that brings us to the second face of positioning.

"Positioning is not something you do to a product, it's what you do to the mind of the prospects." This is a much-quoted one-liner by Al Ries and Jack Trout, the inventors of the positioning concept. It is a one-sided or consumer-focused definition of the concept of positioning as a process that takes place only in the memory of consumers. The principle is that consumers classify a brand in a group or subgroup of other brands on the basis of the most salient category characteristics and distinguish the brand from the other brands in the group or subgroup on the basis of its most differentiating characteristics.

So how do brand managers manage this difficult process of positioning a brand, which seems to take place primarily in the black box of the consumer mind?

The marketer—the source of the product—is a central focus in most theories about company business strategies, whereas in marketing theory and consumer behavior literature, the key figure is the customer—or, in communication theory, the receiver of the brand message. There is a direct relationship between the two approaches, just as there is a direct connection between the sender and the receiver of a message. A position can be defined in terms of how its elements are presented in a message, but the position itself is a perception. It can be cued, but not controlled by a brand's managers. Figure 8.1 illustrates the sender and receiver perspective on positioning.

Principle: Positioning has a strategic and a perceptual meaning. Strategic positioning by companies relates to the choice of customer groups and the structuring of activities to answer to their needs. Perceptual positioning involves the placement of a brand in a category or subcategory by customers based on differentiating the brands in a category according to characteristics that are important to the consumers.

Figure 8.1 **Positioning From the Consumer and Competitor Perspectives**

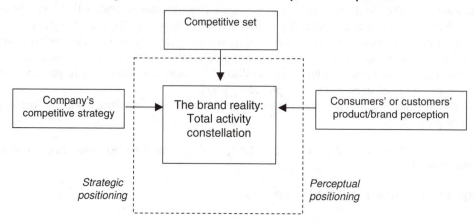

Brand Positioning and Market Segmentation

Brand positioning is rooted in the brand's core concept, in the definition of the market that a company wants to serve, and in the activities that will achieve the ultimate values for the consumers or customers. The basic principle behind positioning is depicted in Figure 8.2.

Positioning is always relative in that it sets up a location (a place in a customer's mind) relative to other brands, a place that is important primarily to a particular group of people. Positioning, then, is a combination of three factors:

- the category or subcategory definition;
- the target group or segment definition;
- the definition of properties, attributes, or differences that create a brand's advantages (relative to a certain segment).

How is positioning done? First, the category is defined and the brand is placed within a field of competing brands within the category. To know which brands these are, the category must be carefully identified. What is the product all about? Product categories can be classified by the degree to which brand preference is influenced by product-related or symbolic perceptions.

The second step is to define the target group, identifying the boundaries of the segment. Does the brand aim at "all coffee drinkers" or "the entire work force," or is there a more specifically described target group? Depending on the span or breadth of the target group, we can distinguish the following basic strategies.

1. Broad Positioning, Aimed at All Category Users

This comprises two substrategies:

- *The monobrand strategy*, in which the market is covered as well as possible with only one product variant that answers optimally to the generic expectations for the category. The brand Heineken is a typical example of this strategy.

Figure 8.2   **Basic Principles of Positioning**

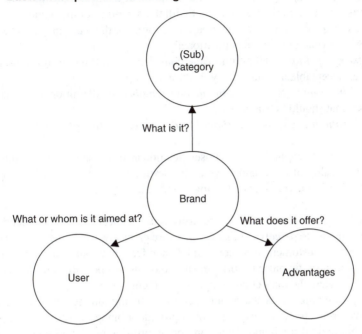

- *The variety strategy*, in which a possibly wide assortment of product variants is offered under a brand, meeting the varying needs and expectations of different user groups at different moments and in different situations. The special beers of Grolsch exemplify such a strategy.

2. Segment Positioning

This is based on the selection of one or several market segments, with specific, deviating needs and expectations that the activities of a brand are painstakingly adjusted to. The skin-care brand Clinique illustrates segment positioning because it appeals to those women who are concerned about the latest scientific improvements in skin care.

3. Niche Segment Positioning

The very specific needs of a small group of buyers constitute the basis for this type of positioning. Individual customers are central here, with one-to-one marketing as the ultimate consequence. The Russell Moccasin Company of Wisconsin, which has been making custom-made footwear for the great outdoors for more than 100 years, is an example of a distinct niche brand.

The Position Statement

Positioning, in its meaning of the marketer's influence on the consumer's perceived brand position, relates to the strategy decisions the manager makes regarding the definition of the "ideal" positioning situation:

- *Who is the target group?* (target market): description of the best (potential) buyers of a category, whose choice criteria are congruent with the meanings of the brand
- *What is the category?* (frame of reference): description of the typifying characteristic of the category within which the brand is positioned
- *Who are the competitors?* definition of the consideration set: the group of brands that are evaluated as acceptable alternatives by the target group
- *Which typifying brand associations should be strengthened?* definition of the typifying core associations that should be supported
- *Which differentiating associations should be developed or strengthened?*

How *credibility* can be created for the chosen position also can be included in this list: which elements from the reality of the brand serve as supporting proof? Some companies summarize these choices in what is known as a positioning statement.

> When we think about positioning we are really getting at how we want an intended audience (be it one or many) to perceive our situation. More precisely, we define brand positioning as the way we want customers to perceive, think, and feel about our brand versus competitive entries. It's the specific piece of turf we want to occupy in potential customers' minds and hearts as they view the market landscape before them.
>
> Brand positioning states the brand's reason-for-being among select customers versus competitive products or services. It should provide a blueprint for the development and franchise building of the brand. Therefore, brand positioning should precede the development of all sub-strategies such as pricing, distribution, packaging, and advertising, to name just a few of the many marketing-mix elements. Brand positioning that firmly takes hold in the marketplace becomes brand equity. It creates value for the brand that goes beyond the mere physical properties of the product, sales and/or market share position. (Czerniawski and Maloney 1999, 18–19)

The positioning a brand intends to occupy is often verbalized in a statement, containing the following seven elements:

To _____ buying _____,
        (target customer group)   (category)

the brand _____ offers _____
           (brand name)   (benefit)

over _____.
                           (competitors)

The reason is _____.
                        (reasons why)

The brand character can be described as _____.
                      (brand character and personality)

Figure 8.3   **Loyalty by Uniqueness Scores** (in percent)

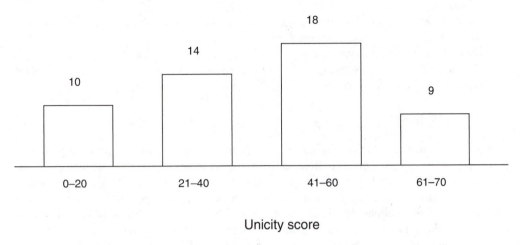

Unicity score

Source: Davenport and Hallward (1999).

THREE BASIC APPROACHES TO BRAND POSITIONING

People categorize brands on the basis of their similarities and distinguish them from each other on the basis of their differences. As the similarities increase, so does the brands' resemblance to each other in the perception of the consumer, and they become to a larger degree alternatives for each other. They are interchangeable, a situation known as "parity." Through similarity with competitors, a brand acquires greater legitimacy: it becomes easier for consumers to accept it as a justified choice within the category. As a brand differs strongly from similar brands, it is less affected by exchangeability and thus competition. At the same time, a large degree of differentiation ensures that fewer consumers will consider the brand as a choice alternative, and thus the brand risks losing legitimacy. In short, a field of tension exists between the need for a brand to be the same and the advantages of being differentiated.

> *Principle:* A legitimacy problem can arise when a brand does not sufficiently fit the generic product expectations, deviating too strongly from the prototype.

The Theory of Strategic Balance

The effects of these two factors are brought together in the theory of strategic balance, which states that brands that only differ from other brands to a limited degree are in the most favorable position. The difference should not be so great that the legitimacy of the brand feels pushy to others. An analysis of brand equity scores of 200 brands (Davenport and Hallward 1999) showed that with extreme scores for uniqueness, the loyalty of buyers decreases (see Figure 8.3).

Based on an understanding of this theory of strategic balance, we can distinguish three basic positioning strategies:

- *the prototype approach*, in which a brand strives to be the ultimate example of the category or subcategory;
- *the differentiation approach*, in which a brand strives to distinguish itself from the prototype in one or several dimensions relevant to the consumer;
- *the category values and attitudes modification approach*, in which a brand aims to influence the choice criteria of consumers, thus expanding the preference for the characteristic meaning of the brand.

The Prototype Approach

In their choice between alternatives, the great majority of consumers try to find a compromise between general, generic characteristics that they expect from a (product) category and more specific, singular characteristics that identify a specific brand. They are tolerant toward brands that are somewhat different, but do not easily accept brands that deviate greatly from the optimal, general product expectations. As a result, all major brands are positioned in what Marchand et al. (1994) call a limited zone of viability. Most consumers choose among brands that are positioned in this middle ground. Consequently, the positioning of these brands is not the most determinant factor for their choice—it is their saliency or visibility.

Brands within a category or subcategory always have a number of common meanings. The degree to which a brand has these typifying characteristics determines the degree to which it is seen by consumers as a better or not-so-good representative of the category. These meanings serve as preconditions to consider a brand as a choice alternative. When a brand has these typifying characteristics to an insufficient degree, it will probably be eliminated from the consideration set and the choice process. As the typifying meanings of a category are increasingly associated with a brand, it will be evaluated as being "better" and will have more of a chance of being chosen. Brands in a category can be classified according to a gradation structure, from most representative to least representative for the category.

In many categories or subcategories, one single brand serves as the prototype, the most original, most representative example for all brands in the corresponding category. In marketing practice, a category often arises from a specific brand that is the first one to be linked to new or different meanings and that then serves as the prototype for brands that follow in its tracks with similar characteristics. Such prototypical brands can be encountered in many product fields. Their emergence usually goes back decades, even generations. Levi's jeans, introduced in 1850, serve as the prototype for denim pants; Moët & Chandon (since 1743) for champagne, Speedo for swimwear. These prototypical brands tend to be market leaders in their category or subcategory and are perceived as the most authentic—Coca-Cola is proclaimed "the real thing"; Budweiser, "the king of beers."

The choice process is divided into two phases: an evocation phase and an evaluation phase. In the evocation phase, a consumer determines from which brands a choice is made (the consideration set), in the evaluation phase what (which brand) is finally chosen.

The relative strength of the mental connections between choice cues and brands largely determines which brands are part of the consideration set and which position they take in the rank order. Central to the prototype strategy is the strength of the association between the category and the brand—e.g., instant coffee (Nescafé), sunglasses (Ray-Ban). In addition, associations with the characteristics that are central to the functional or symbolic expectations of the category users play an important role in brand choice. For example, the emphasis in the communication of the brand Rolex lies strongly on the customer's financial success in life and ability to afford the brand.

The prototype strategy is a clear-cut strategy for market leaders. Their goal is to position themselves as much as possible as "the real thing." They are dominant category leaders because they own the association between the generic mental product concept and the brand. A prototype strategy for numbers two or three in the market, which is also based on the generic product expectations, tends to lead to a "second best" perception.

Principle: In the prototype strategy, the brand serves as the most typical, original, and representative example of a category or subcategory.

A prototype strategy usually consists of some or most of the following elements:

- *Pioneering spirit:* A great many brands have become prototypical because they stood at the cradle of their product category. Their origins often go back to the nineteenth and first half of the twentieth centuries. Many brands that have originated new developments in recent decades have also grown to be prototypes in their categories: Xerox for photocopiers, Hewlett-Packard for desktop laser printers, Kleenex for paper tissues, Post-it for self-adhesive notes, Bayer Aspirin for pain relief, McDonald's for fast-food hamburger restaurant chains, Duracell for alkaline batteries, Tupperware for plastic containers—the list is endless.
- *Authenticity:* Whoever is first, or is perceived first, is seen as the original. Whoever comes afterward is a follower. The feeling of authenticity clings to the first one: it is the "real thing." Evian presents itself in France as "l'original."
- *Familiarity:* Prototypical brands are usually close to the consumers, who feel that they know the brand very well. To some degree, it is a self-evident part of their lives—like a very good acquaintance who asks no questions. People know what to expect of these brands.
- *Speciality:* Prototypical brands tend to aim with their entire soul at one product category, and within that category they provide a broad line of product variants with which they meet the diverse wishes of different user groups. Following the development of mobile telephones, Nokia ended the production of television sets in order to fully position itself as specialist in digital telecommunications ("connecting people").
- *Perfectionism:* Prototypical brands have almost always a basic product that optimally fulfils the core functions of the category. It tastes the way people expect, shaves flawlessly, glues inimitably, copies perfectly, etc.
- *Technological leadership:* The prototypical brand makes certain it is ahead of the technological developments in the category. These are generally gradual product improvements, and the brand ensures it is always one small step ahead of its competitors. A characteristic example of a prototypical brand is Gillette, which introduced the first disposable razor as early as 1903 and has now been working for a century on innovations to further improve the shaving comfort of men (see opening story in Chapter 4). The advertising theme of Gillette expresses its prototype strategy well: "Gillette: the best a man can get."
- *Image of competency:* Prototypical brands get high scores on the personality dimensions of reliability, sobriety, efficiency, and balance. In the twenty-seven years that the brand Oral-B existed before being taken over by Gillette, it did not introduce a single new toothbrush. Gillette deployed a team of 150 people to tackle the problem of plaque removal. The result was a flood of new products and product improvements. Competency can usually be translated into a competitive advantage because it reflects supremacy in technology, as well as an authentic attribute.

- *Pervasive presence:* Prototypical brands are unavoidable. Coca-Cola's strategy is aimed at being "everywhere people are thirsty." Visa also dominates the credit card market by "being everywhere."

It should be clear that the prototype strategy is not the most recommended for every brand. As we mentioned before, such a strategy is mainly suitable for market leaders, and other brands in a category will have to distinguish themselves from the Goliath in some other way.

> Companies pursuing product leadership continually push products into the realm of the unknown, the untried, or the highly desirable. Reaching that goal requires that they challenge themselves in three ways. First, they must be creative. More than anything else, being creative means recognizing and embracing ideas that may originate anywhere inside the company or out. Second, they must commercialize their ideas quickly. To do so, all their business and management processes are engineered for speed. Third and most important, they must relentlessly pursue ways to leapfrog their own latest product or service. If anyone is going to render their technology obsolete, they prefer to do it themselves. Product leaders do not stop for self-congratulation. They are too busy raising the bar. (Treacy and Wiersema 1995, 52)

The Differentiation Approach

Brands that aim at distinguishing themselves from the prototype brand in one or several dimensions relevant to a specific consumer segment use a differentiation strategy. Differentiation from the prototype brand is not without risks, though. After all, in the perception of consumers, prototype brands are the best representatives of the generic mental product concepts. If a nonprototype brand removes itself from this benchmark, consumers may no longer perceive it as a full alternative within the category. This is what happened initially to the European car brand Smart, owned by the Daimler Company. Smart cars were placed by consumers in the category of very small private vehicles. They had an initially weak position because they deviated in too many ways from a prototypical car. They had two seats only ('Fortwo') and looked like toy cars. This perception has changed, as energy efficiency and environmentalism have become more of a concern. Smart cars were officially launched in 2008 into the U.S. market, and consumers are on waiting lists for these novel little cars.

> *Principle:* When using the differentiation strategy, a brand aims at distinguishing itself within a category on a prototype dimension relevant to consumers.

The goal of differentiation is to create a brand concept that distinguishes itself from the generic product or the prototypical brand in dimensions that are important for at least one specific market segment, as Miller Lite was able to do. The basis for the differentiation is the congruency between the brand concept and the needs and values of a specific user segment. When a brand succeeds in being the only one to provide for these needs, the result should be that the user profile of a differentiated brand differs from the profile of all category users on those dimensions.

Keller (1998b) stresses:

[T]he key to positioning is not so much in achieving a point of difference as in achieving necessary or competitive points of parity! For example, consider the introduction of Miller Lite beer. When Philip Morris bought Miller Brewing, its flagship High Life brand was not competing particularly well, leading the company to decide to introduce a light beer. The initial advertising strategy for Miller Lite was to assure parity with a necessary and important consideration in the category by stating that it "tastes great," while at the same time creating a point of difference with the fact that it contained one-third less calories (96 calories vs. 150 calories for conventional 12-ounce full-strength beer) and was thus "less filling."

As is often the case, the point of parity and point of difference were somewhat conflicting, as consumers tend to equate taste with calories. To overcome potential consumer resistance to this notion, Miller employed credible spokespeople, primarily popular former professional athletes who would presumably not drink a beer unless it tasted good. These ex-jocks were placed in amusing situations in ads where they debated the merits of Miller Lite as to which of the two product benefits—"tastes great" or "less filling"—was more descriptive of the beer. The ads ended with the clever tagline, "Everything you've always wanted in a beer . . . and less."

In Chapter 7, on segmentation, we showed that a comprehensive analysis by Kennedy et al. (2000)—which included 280 variables and 42 categories—revealed that there was hardly any difference between the user groups of different brands and the average user of a category. However, image research nearly always evidences differences between brands. The explanation for this paradox can be found in theories of choice behavior, which are based on motives, needs, and values. People use brands whose characteristics best fit their personal needs and values, and thus people with different needs choose other brands. This constitutes the basis for the differentiation principle.

Still, we do know that many choices are made on the basis of pure saliency or visibility. Consumers choose among brands that are visibly present in their surroundings. Brands become salient because they somehow distinguish themselves from their surroundings. They are noticed because they are simply different, a quality that can manifest itself, for example, in a special visual identity or a charismatic, unique brand personality.

Sometimes, unique communication is the only thing that serves as a distinguishing brand characteristic, in which case we speak of advertising positioning. This can happen in situations in which the consumer has an extremely low involvement in the choice between alternatives, such as toilet paper or carrots.

It follows that the basis of "being different" does not have to be congruent with the needs and values of a group of consumers, as it is not the same as segment-based differentiation. Brands can be attractive to people because of their singularity and uniqueness without content corresponding with characteristics of their user groups. People do not always relate to others on the basis of personality similarities either—in fact, they often relate to very different types (opposites attract).

Carpenter et al. (1994) examine the effects of "irrelevant attributes" that appear frequently in advertising campaigns, such as the "Pure Extract of Thermal Plankton" in the Biotherm skin-care line or Folger's "mountain grown." The researchers conclude that this ostensibly irrelevant—but unique—information leads to increased attention for the brand, resulting in greater saliency, and believe that this approach has a disturbing effect on the rational choice model. When an evaluation of brand value depends on the information consumers have at their disposal, the notion of competition can take on an entirely different character. This research shows that there is differentiation in characteristics that seem to offer functional advantages but in fact do not—instead, such characteristics just make the brand more unique and more salient.

> *Principle:* Distinguishing characteristics of a brand that do not answer to needs of a market segment ("irrelevant attributes") can contribute to the saliency of the brand.

To its marketer, a brand is like a snowflake, unique in composition. To consumers, alas, competing brands are all but indistinguishable. That is the message of a study by Copernicus and Market Facts, discussed in *Adweek* (2001, 22):

> In category after category, "most companies have commoditized their products and services," even while spending tons of money to achieve the opposite result. And the problem is getting worse. "None of the 51 product and service categories studied are becoming more differentiated over time, and 90 percent are declining in differentiation," the research firms conclude. Based on a poll of consumer differentiation in particularly leading brands, the highest "similarity scores" went to Visa and MasterCard; Staples and Office Depot; Pets.com and Petsmart.com; and L'Oréal and Clairol. In the middle of the pack were such rivals as United and American Airlines, Nike and Adidas, Tylenol and Advil, and Budweiser and Miller.
>
> Given the effort brands make to distinguish themselves, why do consumers see so many as being so similar? Perhaps people don't want brands to differ significantly. When rival brands are alike (or perceived as such), the psychic opportunity cost of forgoing the unchosen one is slight. Even if you're brand loyal in a category, it's easier to enjoy your favorite if you feel the alternative wouldn't be much different. Commoditization frustrates marketers, but it suits consumers just fine.

The Category Values and Attitudes Modification Approach

Besides the positioning strategies aimed at influencing brand perceptions, there is also a strategy that aims to directly influence the choice criteria of consumers. The idea is to develop a new segment or increase the scope of an existing segment by introducing new choice criteria. This is, in fact, about expanding the preference for the characteristic meanings of a brand. When a brand is strongly linked to characteristic X, expanding the "need for X" could benefit the brand's sales. When X is about fundamental issues such as core functions of a product or values in the choice process, we are dealing with goals that are difficult to realize and tend to lie outside the (financial) reach of individual brands. This can only be an attractive option for market leaders in categories represented by high monetary sales, such as the market of personal-care products. In this market, Dove sets an example of influencing the basic beauty perception and attitudes of women around the world.

When dealing with less fundamental characteristics, this strategy can be part of a differentiation, subcategory, or even niche strategy. For example, Daimler's tiny Smart car could emphasize the parking problem in such a way that, conceivably, consumers would be more receptive to its extremely reduced length of only eight feet, compensating for the disadvantage of only two seats ("Smart—reduced to the max").

> *Principle:* The category values and attitudes modification strategy aims at influencing the choice criteria of consumers. This strategy costs a great deal of time and money.

Dove Changes the Rules of Female Beauty

Unilever launched Dove in the United States in 1957 as a bar of soap that was clinically proven to be mild for dry, sensitive skin, a problem that half of all women faced. Since the 1980s the brand was extended to a large number of other personal-care products, such as deodorants, body lotions, face lotions, shampoos, and conditioners. It also was launched in a large number of other countries and currently is a true global brand. This expansion meant that by 2000 the Dove brand had fundamentally changed. What had been a soap brand had become something else. Unilever stopped thinking about Dove as a soap brand and started thinking of it as a beauty brand.

But the world already was awash with beauty brands. The type of beauty promoted by these brands was all about physical beauty, which almost all woman fall short of: "if you believe what the beauty industry tries to tell us, beautiful is only beautiful if it's 5'11", eight stone, with long hair, ideally blond, with a perfectly symmetrical face, flawless complexion and under the age of 30. And yet, all around us is evidence to the contrary." Research showed that just 12 percent of women was very satisfied with their physical attractiveness, only 2 percent described themselves as beautiful, and 68 percent strongly agreed that the media set unrealistic standards of beauty.

Dove decided to change the beauty rules. Its mission became "to make more women feel more beautiful every day, by widening today's stereotypical view of beauty and inspiring them to take great care of themselves." It developed "Dove's beauty theory": "Dove makes it clear it sees beauty in imperfections and doesn't worship stereotypes. Dove's beauty is self-defined, beauty with brains, democratic. Dove recognizes not only the exterior, but also the woman within. There is depth of character behind the eyes, a strength and vitality of personality showing through." The proposition became a call to action: "Seeking your own version of beauty will get you much closer to beauty than seeking flawless stereotypical perfection."

To advance this idea, the company decided to use "real ordinary" women, as opposed to models, in its advertising. Its advertising campaigns feature groups of real women in their underwear, celebrating their unique individual curves. Dove offers a democratized view of beauty to which all women can aspire.

Insisting that beauty comes in all shapes, sizes, and ages, Dove is actively trying to address the root of the problem of negative self-image. It founded the "Dove Self-Esteem Fund" to fund programs to raise self-esteem in girls and young women. It sponsors a partnership called "Uniquely Me" with Girl Scouts in the United States and supports the "Body Talk" education programs in the United Kingdom and Canada.

Sources: www.campaignforrealbeauty.com; Howard (2003); Hoggard (2005, 4).

BRAND DIFFERENTIATION STRATEGIES

In theories of competitive strategies (e.g., Porter 1996; Levitt 1991) as well as in marketing theories, a strong emphasis is put on the need for product differentiation, which continues to be the most accepted route to defining a position. *Differentiate or Die* is the title of one of Jack Trout's books (2000). (He and his coauthor Al Ries were the originators of the positioning concept in their classic book, *Positioning: The Battle for Your Mind.*) Differentiation is closely tied to segmentation, so these strategic decisions are interrelated. More than forty years after their first publication on positioning and differentiation, Trout complains that many organizations still fail to appreciate the importance of differentiation:

> For what seems like several lifetimes, my partners and I have been preaching the importance of being different. In *Positioning*, being different meant differentiating yourself in the mind of your prospect. In *Marketing Warfare*, being different meant using a differentiating idea to defend, attack, flank, or become a guerrilla. In *The 22 Immutable Laws of Branding* being different meant using a differentiating idea to build a brand. In *Power of Simplicity*, being different meant using a strategy that was all about differentiation.
>
> Being different is at the heart of everything we've done for almost thirty years. You might assume that by now the message has been delivered. Everyone is busy building "differentiation" into his or her plans. And no one would leave home without his or her differentiating idea. Right?
>
> Wrong! What we tend to see are two types of organizations. One type still doesn't get it. They're out there doing battle with "higher quality" or "good value" or good old "better products." They feel that they are better than their competitors and that truth will out. They surround themselves with gurus who talk about quality, empowerment, customer orientation, and various forms of leadership. Unfortunately, all of their competitors are surrounded by the same cast of "you can get better" gurus. Nothing different. The other type of organization understands the need to be different. But after some prodding, they will admit that they just don't know how to do it. Their excuse: Our product or sales force just isn't that much different from our competitors. . . .
>
> But in a sea of choice, a prospect has the problem of figuring out what to buy or not to buy. In other words, alternatives are but the raw material of decision making. And decisions must be made. . . . Choosing among multiple options is always based on differences, implicit or explicit. Psychologists point out that vividly differentiated differences that are anchored to a product can enhance memory because they can be appreciated intellectually. In other words, if you're advertising a product, you ought to give the consumer a reason to choose that product. (Trout 2000, 35)

David Aaker (1996b) states that differentiation is the bottom-line characteristic of a brand. Everything can be differentiated, even parity products like sand, concrete, copper, grains, money, air cargo or ship insurance, credit cards, soap, beer, and investments. Harvard professor Ted Levitt (1991), another pioneer of marketing theory, also emphasizes the need to differentiate as one of the most important strategic and tactical activities that companies can pursue. Levitt claims that there is no such thing as standard products: there are only people who see them as a commodity. He insists that everything can be differentiated—no company has to stay put in a commodity or parity position.

The big question, then, is how different a brand can be without losing its legitimacy as an acceptable alternative within the category. Successful brands are generally able to combine a high degree of legitimacy with a limited degree of difference. This makes them acceptable to many consumers and at the same time represents a reason for a positive choice. As long as the legitimacy is not compromised, a larger degree of difference tends to lead to better performance in the market. When the perceived difference becomes large, a brand finds itself in a subcategory or niche situation. Many brands have ended up in such a situation without intending to. A well-known example is Apple, whose willful approach never allowed it to reach a large share of the computer market as Dell and Compaq managed to, thanks to their cooperative approach to marketing partners. Apple ultimately has become a niche brand with a U.S. market share of about 4.4 percent in 2005. Since then it has surged to 9 percent in 2007, and is expected to rise further to about 14 percent in 2008.

> *Principle:* Successful brands often combine a high degree of legitimacy with a limited degree of difference.

For a successful differentiation strategy, a brand has to answer to the preconditions set by the expectations of the category buyers. In addition, a limited perceptual difference can lead to an advantage in the choice process. Sometimes this advantage is based on a distinctive attribute, but it may also be primarily perceptual.

By and large, the problem of a differentiation strategy is not the achievement of a certain degree of differentiation, but the assurance that the brand perception remains within the preconditions of the generic product expectations. Of course, the differentiation should be relevant for consumers and the brand should live up to it. In 1997, the brand 7-Up brought on the market a clear cola drink that failed pitifully. Not only did the extension not answer to the core expectations of a cola drink (it should at least be brown), but also the differentiation (clarity) was not relevant.

Trade-Offs

The essence of a differentiation strategy is that a fabric of impressions is realized that is different from that of the competition. By definition, this means that trade-offs have to be made. In many product categories, for example, a weighing-out takes place between effectiveness and safety: in pain relief tablets, for example, between fast acting and "safe for the stomach"; in detergents, between stain removal and fabric protection. Nearly always, a product's safety is a precondition to win over an important market position. A perception of effectiveness can also provide differentiation, as long as it remains within acceptable boundaries of safety.

Different positioning strategies require different research programs, core competencies, product compositions, means of production, types of employees, skills, management systems, and communication strategies. However, if a brand competes in a focused way, it becomes clear to everyone where the brand's priorities lie. Porter goes a step further in maintaining that the choice of what a company or brand should *not* do is the essence of strategy development. As an example, he refers to Neutrogena's decision to avoid attributes and distribution that were conflicting with its basic positions:

> Neutrogena Corporation's variety-based position is built on a "kind to the skin," residue-free soap formulated for pH balance. Neutrogena uses a slow, more expensive manufacturing process to mold its fragile soap. With a large sales force calling on dermatologists, Neutrogena's marketing strategy looks more like a drug company's than a soap maker's.
>
> To reinforce its position, Neutrogena originally focused its distribution on drugstores and avoided price promotions. It advertises in medical journals, sends direct mail to doctors, attends medical conferences, and performs research at its own Skincare Institute.
>
> In choosing this position, Neutrogena said no to the deodorants and skin softeners that many customers desire in their soap. It gave up the large-volume potential of selling through

supermarkets and using price promotions. It sacrificed manufacturing efficiencies to achieve the soap's desired attributes. In its original positioning, Neutrogena made a whole raft of trade-offs like those, trade-offs that protected the company from imitators. (Porter 1996, 77)

Principle: An important dimension of strategy development is the choice of what a brand should *not* be or do.

The System of Differentiation

There are a number of ways to analyze the systems of brand differentiation. The following is a brief review of eight ways managers create differentiation as part of brand positioning strategies. Four of them reflect a company perspective, and four are more reflective of a consumer perspective.

Company Perspective on Differentiation

Intrinsic product differentiation. A unique product characteristic or a combination of product characteristics is central to this positioning strategy. The characteristic has to provide a relevant advantage for a segment of the category users, giving the brand a strong competitive advantage. The following characteristics, for example, are central to the positioning of different car brands:

Volkswagen	reliability
BMW	driving pleasure
Volvo	safety
Mercedes	engineering, perfectionism
Peugeot	comfort
Alfa Romeo	speed, sportiness
Citröen	willfulness
Lancia	style
Lexus	luxury, exceptional quality

Within the differentiation strategy there can be an adjustment of the product proposition to a specific usage goal or a specific use situation. Gatorade positioned itself as a drink for athletes who have to supplement their body fluids in the summertime and during competitions. It was so successful at creating this new position that it became the most important brand for Quaker Oats and led to the takeover of the company by PepsiCo.

Design or style differentiation. Brand differentiation based on intrinsic product characteristics is becoming increasingly difficult to accomplish. The differentiation possibilities based on design and styling are inexhaustible, though. Styling is normally developed as an added dimension to other differentiation strategies. The entire strategy revolves around it, however, with brands that choose design as a central positioning strategy.

Design and styling are, in principle, two different disciplines. Design is holistic and functional; it involves problem solving and seeks to simplify the essence of the total product. Typical design brands are Bang & Olufson audio systems, Artemide Italian lighting systems, Gaggenau European-styled kitchen appliances, and Apple's iMac.

Styling, on the contrary, is involved with superficial treatment and the external—the expressive outside of things. Most of what is considered "design" is, in fact, limited to styling. This category includes many appliance brands whose "cabinets" are the only things that are styled. An example of successful styling is the vodka brand Absolut.

Absolut: Success of a Bottle Design

In 1879 a young Swede, Lars Olsson Smith, introduced a new kind of vodka in his country. He used a revolutionary distillation method, called rectification—a method Absolut still uses today—and named his product Absolut Rent Brännvin (Absolute Pure Vodka). Toward the end of the nineteenth century, Smith started to export his spirits. He died in 1913, but his technical know-how did not die with him.

In the 1970s, a successor to Smith, Lars Lindmark, CEO of the V&S Vin and Spirit AB, a liquor manufacturer, set about modernizing the respected old company—and decided to introduce Absolut to the United States. His advertising man found an old Swedish medicine bottle in an antique shop. It was decided that there should be no pasted-on label to hide the crystal-clear contents. After much discussion and several prototypes, the design team came to the conclusion that some kind of colored lettering was required. Blue was decided upon as the most visible and attractive color, the color that is still used today for the famous Absolut Vodka logo. Thanks to its cylindrical simplicity and transparency, the Absolut bottle, though solid and heavy, is elegant and utterly distinctive. Pure, strong, blond, Swedish—so runs the chain of associations.

In the first year on the U.S. market, only 10,000 nine-liter cases of Absolut Vodka were sold. The product was launched first in Boston, then in New York, Chicago, Los Angeles, and San Francisco, and eventually all over the country. Its success in America took on sensational dimensions in the 1980s when the yuppie generation accepted Absolut as a cool lifestyle drink. By 1982, Absolut Vodka had passed a major Finnish competitor that had entered the U.S. market ten years earlier. In 1985, the biggest Russian competitor was overtaken, making Absolut Vodka the leading imported vodka in the United States.

An advertisement contributed by the pop artist Andy Warhol (captioned "Absolut Warhol") sparked the marketing campaign. He was followed by more than 400 artists, mostly from the United States, as well as by a series of additional campaigns that helped the company penetrate the cult-filled region between art, advertising, and fashion. Absolut's marketing is all about design, for most of the advertisements are original, contemporary picture puzzles featuring the distinctive outline of the bottle. The 80 proof grain distillate from the Swedish province of Skåne today has cornered more than 60 percent of the U.S. vodka market.

Sources: Polster (1999); www.Absolut.com, "About Absolut;" Howard (2006).

Channel differentiation. In channel differentiation, the strategy revolves not around the physical end products but around the communication and distribution interactions between a brand and its customers (Moenaert and Robben 1999). Relationship development is the most important characteristic of this differentiation strategy, with one-to-one marketing as its outcome. Direct marketers such as mail-order companies, Reader's Digest, and direct campaigns at certain insurance companies are traditional examples of this strategy. The advent of the Internet has led to a parade of new brands that attempt to differentiate themselves from brands that are still distributed through traditional channels. Examples of such Internet brands are Amazon and Dell.

Price differentiation. Almost every category has brands in different price classes. A low price can form the basis for the differentiation strategy of the entire organization. This strategy is characterized by a reduction of the product or service to its basic function and the avoidance of any expenditure that is not absolutely necessary to exercise that function. In the Netherlands, an excellent example is the discount supermarket chain Aldi, followed by Hema (comparable to Kmart). Brands that opt for price differentiation are at great risk of being insufficiently differentiated. Inevitably, a price position requires a trade-off with quality. The former Dutch supermarket chain Edah illustrates the problem: it exchanged price differentiation and quality differentiation several times, and because it never drew the ultimate consequences of the chosen strategy, it found itself in a clear middle-of-the-road position and was eventually closed down. Examples of successful price differentiation are Wal-Mart, easyJet, and Motel 6 hotels.

Consumer Perspective on Differentiation

Differentiation through saliency. A saliency strategy is not about fitting the brand to the specific functional or psychosocial needs of a segment, but about having as strong a presence as possible within the category by placing the brand in the foreground of the consumers' perception. This strategy is particularly important with parity products. As noted in the previous chapter, after numerous studies with the conversion research instrument, Hofmeyr and Rice (2000) concluded that real differentiation is more the exception than the rule: they claim that it is quite improbable for the small differences in consumer attitudes between brands to account for large differences in market shares.

Visibility and noticeability are two ways to create and reinforce saliency and activate brand memory in the mind of the consumer. The analyses of Kennedy et al. (2000), discussed in the previous chapter, which found that the user profile of a brand hardly seemed to distinguish itself from the profile of all category buyers, demonstrates a saliency problem. The primary tool is marketing communication that gives consumers a little nudge so they will recognize the brand. Hofmeyr and Rice believe that, for many markets, "Here I am" and "Remember me" advertising is the right way to develop brand saliency because it contributes top-of-mind awareness and gives buyers the feeling that they are choosing a popular brand, while it develops a feeling of brand security.

Symbolic differentiation. Many brands have symbolic associations that do not necessarily form the core of a rational differentiation strategy. Instead, the differentiation is based on symbolism and associations. These associated meanings will be discussed extensively in later chapters on brand values, brand personality, and brand meaning. Imaging is absolutely central to a strategy choice based on symbolism, and communication plays a dominant role in the process. In such cases, products are materializations of the symbolic brand meanings, as illustrated by brands like Ralph Lauren, Perrier, Louis Vuitton, and Davidoff.

Customer service differentiation. For many product and service brands, differentiation based on intrinsic product characteristics or symbolic brand meanings is difficult to achieve, because the brands have a commodity-like character and fulfill no important function in the social relationships between people. Differentiation based on customer service can sometimes be an option, but here the same rule applies regarding the need for it to be central to the thoughts and actions of the entire company. Some hotels succeed in giving their guests the feeling of having landed in a warm bath. In the United States, Nordstrom's department stores are recognized for their exceptional customer service.

Although customer satisfaction is a high priority for many companies, it has taken on the character of a precondition and hence no longer forms a sufficient basis for differentiation. A study in the services industry in the United States showed that 20 to 30 percent of the clients scoring highest on satisfaction tended to switch companies anyway (Mittal and Lasser 1998). Moreover, Reichheld (1993) points out that as many as 65 to 85 percent of customers who changed brands were quite satisfied with the previous brand. In the automobile industry, these figures were as high as 85 to 90 percent. Mittal and Lasser's research indicates that customer service involves not only the technical quality of the service itself, but primarily the attitude of the service provider. Differentiation based on service demands an exceptional degree of service orientation, which consumers should experience as special and which is sometimes referred to as "surprising" the customer.

Customer intimacy differentiation. In this type of differentiation, the point of departure is not what the market expects or is looking for but whatever it is that the individual customers want. The strategy focuses on recruiting, establishing, and using detailed knowledge about individual consumers in order to anticipate and answer to their needs and expectations. Companies attempt to develop as personal a relationship as possible with customers by giving them the feeling that the brand is behind them and will help in any way possible to achieve optimal results and solve any problems (Tracey and Wiersema 1995). An intimacy differentiation is not reactive, as service differentiation is, but proactive. It applies mostly to niche marketing and instances that involve continuous interaction between supplier and consumer, as is usually the case with retailers and service brands and business-to-business marketing.

The operating model of the customer-intimate company is quite different from that of businesses pursuing other disciplines. Its features include:

- an obsession with helping the customer understand exactly what is needed and ensuring the solution gets implemented properly;
- a business structure that delegates decision making to employees who are close to the customer;
- management systems that are geared toward creating results for carefully selected and nurtured clients;
- a culture that embraces specific rather than general solutions and thrives on deep and lasting client relationships. (Tracey and Wiersema 1995)

Combinations of Differentiation Strategies

Differentiation is not as simple as the typology might suggest because people's interests and needs sometimes overlap. A McKinsey consulting company study (Court 2000) of four branches of industry—cars, cosmetics, credit cards, and telephony—shows that consumers can be segmented on the basis of the primary advantages that they look for in a category, but also that different groups of people look for different combinations of these elements. For cars there was even an "I want it all" segment of buyers.

Combining different advantages, however, can lead to large numbers of segments. The McKinsey study indicates that in the American credit card market alone, the number of different combinations adds up to more than 100. A marketer who does not know exactly which specific values clients attach to which specific combinations of product advantages are vulnerable to competing brands whose supply is geared exactly toward extremely detailed microsegments (niches). Airlines have taken this strategy to the limit with different price, service, destination, and loyalty packages that appeal to various niches.

Colgate Total offers a spectacular case of the combination of differentiation strategies.

How Colgate Grabbed the Lead Over Crest Again

The Colgate-Palmolive Company was founded in 1806 by William Colgate. In 1873 it was the first company introducing toothpaste in jars, followed in 1896 by the first toothpaste in a collapsible tube. Since then it has worked hard to convert the whole world to Colgate. In the United States in the 1950s, it was the market leader with a share of about 35 percent. It became the undisputed champion in the global market with market leadership in more than 170 countries.

Then, in 1955, Procter & Gamble launched Crest, a therapeutic toothpaste containing stannous fluoride, which protected against cavities. In 1960 Crest became the first brand of toothpaste to receive an endorsement from the American Dental Association. Within two years Crest became the market leader, with a share of over 30 percent. Nine years after Crest, Colgate obtained a similar endorsement, but by then it already lagged fourteen percentage points behind Crest. For about thirty years Crest remained the market leader with a share of about 35 percent, while Colgate remained in second position with about 20 percent.

In the 1990s cavities ceased to be a big issue thanks to fluoridated municipal water. The aging population became more and more plagued by gum disease. In 1997 Colgate introduced Colgate Total, an all-in-one formula with triclosan, the first toothpaste in the United States to fight the gum disease gingivitis. It obtained the Food and Drug Administration's approval as the only toothpaste that reduces this disease. Colgate soon became the category leader again. Crest fell to the number two position within two years after the launch of Colgate Total.

Colgate took this lesson to heart by trying to exploit the latest dental needs. It now sells a line for sensitive teeth and for whitening. Colgate Total now does everything—fights cavities, fights gum disease, cleans, and whitens. In 2007 it reached record highs for market share, maintaining the brand has category leadership in its home country.

Sources: Miskell (2005); Brady (2001); Procter & Gamble, www.pg.com; Colgate-Palmolive Company, www.Colgate.com/history.

Principle: Small market segments often search for combinations of several differentiations.

Differentiation Positions That Endure

Differentiation strategies are effective only when they are fitted to the specific wishes and needs of a clearly described market segment, formulated in a crystal-clear fashion, fine-tuned to the entire constellation of activities of a supplier (and its competition), and kept up for many years. Pepsi-Cola, for example, has a long-standing position focused on the youth culture, crystallized many years ago in the phrase "The Pepsi Generation." Even more mature audiences are comfortable with Pepsi's position because they still would like to think of themselves as belonging in that generation. According to Porter (1996, 77):

> Strategic positions should have a horizon of a decade or more, not of a single planning cycle. Continuity fosters improvements in individual activities and the fit across activities, allowing an organization to build unique capabilities and skills tailored to its strategy. Continuity also reinforces a company's identity.
>
> Conversely, frequent shifts in positioning are costly. Not only must a company reconfigure individual activities, but it must also realign entire systems. Some activities may never catch up to the vacillating strategy. The inevitable result of frequent shifts in strategy, or of failure to choose a distinct position in the first place, is "me-too" or hedged activity configurations, inconsistencies across functions, and organizational dissonance.

USING DIFFERENTIATION TO SELECT A POSITIONING STRATEGY

The strategic goal of differentiation is to integrate segmentation and positioning—a brand should be positioned in such a way that it is maximally effective in attracting the targeted segment. At the same time, the chosen position should correspond with the brand's strengths and the core capacities of the organization behind the brand. An effective differentiation strategy can be described as

- *relevant:* it should have meaning in light of the goals that a group of consumers aspires to,
- *important:* it should play a role in their choice,
- *understandable:* it should be easy to communicate,
- *distinguishing:* the brand should really distinguish itself on the chosen dimension,
- *confirmed by experience:* the brand should make good on its promise,
- *maintainable:* the difference should be maintained over a sufficiently long period.

It should be clear by now that it is not always possible to find a characteristic that meets all these conditions. Maintenance is not always feasible, especially at the level of physical product characteristics and performance. The difference is therefore sought increasingly in one of the other differentiation strategies.

Market Leaders and Challengers

A positioning strategy is built on a good SWOT (strength, weakness, opportunity, threat) analysis of the brand and its competitors. A small brand that is going against a dominant market leader faces tough choices. Emphasizing central product values, which are almost always covered by a market leader, tends to lead to a weak me-too position. The question is whether the market leader has weak points and whether the smaller brand can make up for them. Can the emphasis lie, for example, on a problem-solving meaning, which allows differentiation strategy to become a possibility? Or can and should brand managers look into a niche strategy or a more distinctive image or emotional connection?

For decades, the coffee brand Van Nelle tried to achieve a position in the middle of the Dutch coffee market, where it played against the dominant Douwe Egberts. It never reached more than 11 percent market share and ended up being taken over by Douwe Egberts, after which the market share became even more fragmented. Nestlé, the world's largest coffee marketer, was always shy of direct competition with Douwe Egberts in the Netherlands. In the 1990s it used a niche strategy that resulted in a successful market introduction of a series of special instant-coffee products in individual sachets including Cappuccino, Espresso, in addition to Nespresso, a complete coffee-making system, all under the Nestlé brand.

A market leader (or segment leader) faces a twofold task: the association strength of the brand should be maintained with the core values, but any vulnerable points have to be strengthened. Research should show whether potential segments exist that have to be covered with an extension. Honig, for example, was for decades the market leader in the Netherlands for traditional noodle products like macaroni and spaghetti. Its position became threatened with a new segment development that we now call "pasta" and was taken over by the brand Grand'Italia. Honig looked for a solution by introducing a new sub-brand, Fiorenza, but has not succeeded in achieving a share in this segment that even comes close to its historic position in the traditional noodle market.

Principle: A market leader or segment leader faces a twofold task: to maintain the strength of the core values and at the same time cover the vulnerable points with extensions.

Market leaders, such as Procter & Gamble's Crest, tend to take their position for granted, as self-evident or even a "legitimate property." They may be awakened from their dream—more frequently than they would like—by a new challenger with a very fresh look at the possibilities. This is how Starbucks managed to shake the American coffee market in a short time (see Starbucks box in Chapter 11). Morgan (1999, 83) maintains that number-one brands have to learn to think as the runner-up:

> We tend to talk about Brand Leadership as if it were only true of one brand in each category—the largest. In fact, there are two kinds of brand leaders in each category. One is the market leader, the biggest player, the brand everyone lives with and, chances are, the brand they probably grew up with.
>
> But there is also another type of brand leadership: the Thought Leader, the brand in the category that everyone talks about. While not the biggest, it is the brand that is getting the most attention. It's the one that is seen to be picking up momentum, entering the popular culture. At one distant point in its life, the existing market leader was this brand. But with very few exceptions, once the brand leader reaches the top, it stops making waves. . . . If we are the Number One brand, the Big Fish that threatens to eat us is ourselves—our own success. The apparent security and real profitability lent by being number one in the market makes us loss-averse and protective: we cease to behave in the way that made us successful and took our brand to leadership in the first place. This confidence, the arrogance of the brand leader, walking the marketplace as if there was no other, no longer applies. Today, to

stay Number One you have to think like a Number Two, like the challenger. This suggests four things:

- Challenger thinking may have an important role even within companies who at face value appear to be comfortable brand leaders.
- A key value of the Challenger is, therefore, to think of it as a mindset. This does not mean, as already noted, aggression per se. It means an active dissatisfaction with your existing position, having ambitions that outstrip your current resources, and the preparedness to embrace the marketing implication of that gap.
- This in turn suggests that perhaps the most useful way to define and differentiate brands is not so much by market position but by their emotional and mental status: are they Establishment brands and companies or Challenger brands and companies by nature?
- And the fourth implication is surely this: that the volatility and speed of the current business and marketing environment demands that a brand leader needs to think and even behave like a Number Two to remain Number One.

Niche Positioning Strategies

In market segmentation, a large market is subdivided into smaller parts in which the choice criteria of the buyers deviate from those of the large middle segment. It is a top-down approach in which the total market is the point of departure. By contrast, in niche strategy the very specific and deviating needs and desires of a small group of buyers constitute the point of departure—this is a bottom-up approach in which individuals or individual customers are central. The ideal niche answers to the following characteristics (Shani and Chalasani 1992):

- It consists of a small group of consumers with very specific, unfulfilled needs. The niche has been ignored or neglected by competitors.
- It has sufficient scope and purchasing power to allow for a profitable brand operation.
- It has growth potential.
- It is not attractive to the major suppliers.
- It has high introduction barriers that make a brand less vulnerable to competition from category leaders.

A successful niche operation demands special resources and capacities from the supplier. The product or service is usually very different from the more standardized products in the large segments. The brand concept is generally based on very different product expectations or on very specific symbolic meanings. The niche tends to require a very special and personal approach in which the use of databases is a more logical choice than the use of mass media.

An example of a large company that follows mainly niche strategies is Johnson & Johnson. It consists of 170 business units, nearly all focusing on small niches (Dalgic and Leeuw 1994). Under pressure of worldwide competition, many category leaders (IBM, Coca-Cola, Douwe Egberts) are switching their aim to niches also. In the large middle segments, a company has to be a low-cost producer by definition. This requirement plays less of a role in the niche, as serving a small group of customers optimally is central.

According to Piercy (in Dalgic and Leeuw 1994), being a niche leader involves nothing less than placing clients above the management agenda: focusing on clients, specializing in their unique needs, coming up with better ways of finding out what they really value, giving them knowledge

The Rover Ghetto

Rover is an example of a brand that has found itself in a ghetto situation. It began in 1877 as a three-wheeler factory. To rove means to roam, to wander. The first Rover car was launched in 1904. By the 1930s Rover had become a prominent carmaker aimed at the sophisticated middle class. It was the brand for the family doctor and the veterinarian, with a "pipe and slippers" image. In the mid-1960s the brand became part of British Leyland, which had a hodgepodge of brands, including Austin, Morris, Triumph, Mini, and Rover. British Leyland, a company fully focused on production, saw the brands merely as identification marks placed on the bodywork. Parts of the various brands were freely interchanged, and there was no strategy whatsoever behind the brands. All the types of the other brands were put together under the brand Rover. This is how the Austin Metro became the Rover Metro.

After a short period in which Honda acquired an interest in the company, British Leyland was taken over by BMW in 1994. In six years, this company invested 13 billion DM in the Rover brand. A whole new model series was brought into the market: the Rover 25, 45, and 75. The latest model harvested worldwide admiration and as many as twelve international distinctions, including being chosen as car of the year. The 75 was expected to turn around Rover's fortune; but the brand became a problem that BMW miscalculated. It saw Rover as a second brand next to BMW in the higher class: "BMW was to be the finest rear wheel drive car in the world, and Rover was to be the first front wheel drive car in the world" (Mitchell 2000).

Some managers had indeed become aware of the weakness of the Rover brand and wanted to continue only with the brands Land Rover, Mini, and MG. Two years of discussions did not lead to a consensus. One manager said, "Once you start pushing the Rover 75, it is competing head on with other luxury brands, which becomes very hard work." In the first year, 1999, only 25,000 were sold and as many remained behind, waiting for a customer. Survival became the goal, with everything else subordinated to it. A sort of Dunkirk spirit emerged, but even mere survival turned out to be a mission impossible.

In March 2000, BMW decided to sell the company to the English investment firm Phoenix Venture Holdings, which again tried to revive the brand. The brand MG was added to the company name.

According to Jeremy Clarckson, host of the BBC car program *Top Gear*, however, Rover remained "one of the least cool brands in the market. With Rover, you think at best of a doctor in a tweed suit." He added, "Rover is a name for a dog." The *Daily Mail* commented, "The English Patient is past help. Let it rest in peace."

The end came in 2005, when MG Rover succumbed to huge debts and sought bankruptcy. Britain lost its last major domestic automobile brand when Nanjing Auto, a Chinese car manufacturer, bought the rights to the models and the complete assembly lines and factory instruments. The Rover brand was acquired by the Indian company Tata Motors in 2008.

Sources: Steketee (2000b); Mitchell (2000); Business Strategy (2005).

and information, involvement and care. The idea is to think small and act small in order to develop customer brand relationships.

Principle: Niche positioning strategy aims at answering very specific needs of a relatively small group of buyers. It is a bottom-up strategy in which a personal approach is the goal.

A Ghetto Position

Sometimes, a brand ends up in a ghetto situation. It has a small circle of buyers and a large group of consumers who do not want to hear about the brand. They may have had negative experiences with it in the past, or its symbolic meanings (for snobs) may be in conflict with their personal values.

Niche brands, as well as major brands in main segments, can be confronted with the problem. The underlying question is whether the ghetto is the consequence of a product problem or of a perception problem. To solve it, drastic measures usually have to be taken. An image that is already established does not lend itself easily to be steered by communication alone—the product reality has to be tackled. But even that does not always offer a solution, as the Rover example shows.

REPOSITIONING STRATEGIES

A brand can find itself in the position where its core concept answers less and less to the changing value-patterns in the market. The last decades of the twentieth century were characterized by increasing individualization. In the Dutch concept of the beer brand Heineken, it was social values that stood central. Thanks partly to the strength of this brand value, Heineken had built a dominant leadership position with a 45 percent share of the Dutch market. This situation changed in the early 1980s, when individualization became a dominant value. The brand managed less well to win over new generations, thus losing a 1 percent market share annually for years. Heineken is still the market leader, but it has lost its dominant lead.

It is difficult for one brand to be able to answer to value systems in very different, conflicting market segments, as is the case with Heineken and Levi's. Another dramatic example is the failed repositioning of GM's Oldsmobile brand.

In fact, when consumers' value systems shift, brand strategy intervention usually becomes necessary. Sub-branding—creating a new brand with the endorsement of the parent brand—can sometimes offer a solution. An example is Donna Karan, a high-fashion brand with an exclusive image that introduced DKNY as a more accessible design brand. The new target group knows the provenience of the brand, and the Donna Karan brand itself has not been affected. A brand should therefore be constantly alert to value and taste changes in the market and make sure it is not seen as outdated or dead. Sometimes, a creative breakthrough in communication can update a once-great brand that has become dusty over time.

Repositioning is often a difficult and precarious enterprise, however. It is difficult because brand associations are, in principle, enduring (see Franzen and Bouwman 2001). Repositioning is always about developing new associations. When these associations conflict with the old ones, a brand irrevocably goes through a phase in which the exact meaning of the brand is unclear to buyers. When there is coordination instead of conflict between the new and the old meanings, a solution can sometimes be found in elements that link the new with the old.

Oldsmobile: The Decline of the Oldest Car Brand

Oldsmobile is the oldest car brand in the United States. The company, founded in 1897 by Ransom Olds, acquired a legendary reputation. The Oldsmobile was the first car whose serial production in 1901 already made use of a conveyor belt. In 1908 Oldsmobile became part of General Motors. Oldsmobile was the first brand to apply automatic transmission in 1939, and in 1966 it was one of the first cars in the United States with front-wheel drive. In the 1970s, the Oldsmobile Cutlass was the best-selling car in the country, and into the 1980s Oldsmobile remained GM's showpiece.

In 1985 Oldsmobile had record sales of 1.6 million cars, but by then the brand had earned the image of a "gasoline glutton for seniors." By the late 1980s, the average Olds driver was sixty years old. Changing track, GM introduced a series of sports models for younger drivers, who saw little difference between Chevrolet and Buick models. The shift did little to overcome the old-man image. The slogan "Not your father's Oldsmobile" did not help but rather called attention to the problem. At the same time, traditional Olds drivers did not like the new models and stayed away en masse.

A desperate investment of $3 billion to give a new face to the brand did not succeed. By 2000 sales had dropped to about 300,000 cars, resulting in a market share of 2 percent, even less than new market entry Hyundai. In December 2000, GM announced it was giving up the Oldsmobile brand, once the crown jewel of the conglomerate.

Sources: Oldsmobile, "Proud American History," www.Oldsmobile.com; Oldsmobile Club of America, www.oldsclub.org; Wikipedia.com, "Oldsmobile History"; money.cnn.com, "General Motors Announces Phase-out of Oldsmobile," December 12, 2000.

Sutherland (1993) cites Volvo as an example of a difficult repositioning problem. For decades, the core meaning of the brand has been safety. Let us say that Volvo wants to switch to durability as a central meaning. Its heavy construction could serve as a connecting link between the two meanings. The message would be something like this: "You know Volvo for its safety features. Volvos are so safe thanks to their sturdy construction. This heavy construction also ensures the durability of Volvos. Volvo, the car that lasts longer." Such a solution has the advantage that the old positioning is not radically abandoned while the new one is being communicated.

Principle: In repositioning, a brand always goes through a dangerous phase in which it answers to a reduced degree to the expectations of existing customers and to a still insufficient degree to those of potential new customers.

POSITIONING RESEARCH

Developing a positioning strategy is dependent upon understanding the basic principles of positioning research. When thinking over the positioning of their brand, managers often imagine a two-dimensional space in which the brand takes a certain position relative to competing brands on two critical decision factors. Such images usually emanate from positioning research, whose results are depicted in what is known as a perceptual map. This is a management-driven approach but is based on consumer research and customer insights.

Research into brand positioning basically comes down to determining:

- which brands form a category with each other,
- which typical associations and characteristics this category is based on,
- to what degree these meanings are associated with the individual brands,
- which additional differentiating meanings a brand has,
- how a market can be segmented on the basis of these meanings,
- how this segmentation relates to purchasing behavior.

Herk et al. (1995) groups positioning research into compositional and decompositional approaches. In compositional techniques, respondents are asked to evaluate products and attributes; in decompositional techniques, statements are requested that respond to preferences and/or similarities between pairs of two brands. Most positioning research follows a compositional method. It consists of the following steps:

- putting together as complete a list as possible of characteristics or attributes that consumers link to the category;
- establishing the relative importance of these characteristics;
- evaluating the brand and the competing brands on each of these attributes;
- establishing whether respondents see these attributes sufficiently realized already in their current brand;
- analyzing the differences between the evaluation of various brands on the relevant dimensions;
- measuring the choice-motivating power of the attributes.

With this information, a perceptual market-map can be constructed in which brands can be located relative to one another on the basis of relevant attributes. Finally, the positioning of brands against each other in a perceptual space can be developed for different target groups or target situations. For further reference, see Franzen and Bouwman (2001), Herk et al. (1995), and Myers (1996).

Issues for Positioning Research

Some of the steps and procedures mentioned above deserve further comment in order to clarify the varied dimensions and the complexity of the strategic decision making.

Attribute Lists

It is important to put together a comprehensive list of all possible attributes that are important to consumers, including product-related as well as symbolic characteristics. Such a list is usually compiled from individual interviews with consumers and/or group discussions. Insights from product development departments, the marketing organization, and the creative department of advertising agencies can also be added to the list. These discussions can result in lists of hundreds of characteristics that, in interim phases, have to be reduced to a maximum of seventy-five to a hundred items, which will form part of the quantitative research.

In order to avoid missing the critical product- and brand-specific associations or measuring certain associations that have little or no relation to brand perceptions, it is preferable to start out by making an inventory of the category- and brand-specific associations via qualitative preliminary research and then to quantify this inventory via survey research. This inventory can, of course, involve the items from standardized instruments, as well.

Desirability of the Attributes

There are different ways to ask consumers what they consider important in the category. Clancy (1991) argues for the replacement of "important" by "desirable," because it would allow respondents to express symbolic meanings. He also proposes replacing the most common five-point scale with a nine-point scale, which would allow respondents to express their negative evaluations as well. The desirability scale would read as follows:

9   Exceptionally desirable
8   Very desirable
7   Somewhat desirable
6   Slightly desirable
5   Neither desirable nor undesirable
4   Slightly undesirable
3   Somewhat undesirable
2   Very undesirable
1   Exceptionally undesirable

Evaluation of the Brands

A great deal of positioning research tests all brands in a market for a large number of meanings. Consumers do not choose among all models of all brands, though, nor do marketers see all brands in the category as competitors. The set of brands is therefore reduced to a limited number that consumers consider acceptable alternatives or direct competitors. The positioning strategy of brands is also based on this categorization. It would, therefore, be worthwhile to consider aiming positioning research at the subcategory within which the competition actually is taking place and to test only those brands that really belong to the competitive set.

An example is the TOMI (Top of Mind Image) method (Leeuwen 1998), in which brand images are measured only for those persons for whom the brand is part of their consideration set. Such a research focus also benefits strategy development, which becomes less abstract and moves closer to the evaluation criteria of the consumers in the corresponding segment.

Methods of Analysis

Many different methods of analysis are used to map out the positioning of brands on the basis of the data presented above. It is not within the scope of this book to review all these methods, but a global overview can shed light on the positioning issues. Here is a brief description of the most important methods.

Quadrant Analysis

The simplest method of analyzing and depicting the positioning of brands in relation to the evaluation dimensions is quadrant analysis, in which the performance of a brand is related to the importance of the attributes. This leads to a matrix in which the vertical coordinates represent the relative importance of key predictor characteristics, and the horizontal coordinates the evaluation of the brand. The matrix can then be distributed into quadrants by bisecting the horizontal and vertical spaces with lines. This is how we make a graphic representation of a retail firm, as shown in Figure 8.4. It is usually best to base the positioning strategy on the relative importance of the properties in the upper right quadrant, allowing proper evaluation of the brand.

A danger of quadrant analysis is that the evaluation of the importance of characteristics leads to predictable results: these are often the characteristics that every brand provides to a sufficient degree, for which reason they no longer exert any influence on the choice process. Therefore, the measurement is sometimes expanded with a question about the degree of uniqueness of the characteristics. Both scores can then be depicted in a matrix, as shown in Figure 8.5 for body oil. The attribute "protects against dry skin," which combines a high score for importance with a high score for uniqueness, could form the basis for an effective brand positioning.

Gap Analysis

Another simple method to determine the potential of an attribute is gap analysis, in which the importance evaluation of a series of attributes is compared with the evaluation scores of the brand that respondents themselves use.

Aggregation of the scores over the total sample could obscure the fact that an attribute has considerable potential with a portion of the buyers. To find this out, the sample is taken apart on the basis of importance levels to segments, and the evaluation of the currently used brand is compared.

A gap analysis can also be used to explore competitive advantage by comparing consumers' ratings of importance and performance for both the marketer's brand and key competitors. Competitive advantage lies in the area or areas that are rated as important or desirable by consumers and where the marketer's brand is rated higher than the competition. Similarly, a brand's points of weakness relative to the competition can also be determined through gap analysis.

Cube Analysis

Further expansion of this method entails measuring the consumer's behavioral intention, allowing for a better determination of the motivating power of an attribute. The research now comprises not only a quest for the desirability of an attribute, but also the degree to which the used brand delivers, as well as the intention to buy if another brand were to offer this attribute. The scores at the three levels can be represented in a cube. Ideally, this method could lead to the identification of attributes that have a high motivating power and on which a brand can be properly evaluated. In strategic cube analysis (Clancy and Krieg 2000), the connection between brand preference, importance of the different meanings, and evaluation of the brands can be analyzed.

Perceptual Maps

Finally, with the help of advanced multivariate techniques it is possible to construct perceptual spaces in which the position of meanings, as well as that of brands, is established. Figure 8.6 gives an example of Dutch investment institutions. It is the result of a principal component analysis, a form of factor analysis in which factors are extracted that explain as much as possible of the total variance in the dataset (Brandmarc 2000). The example indicates that the Rabobank is clearly an old-fashioned investment institution that is statistically linked to attention, privacy, and personal. The Postbank is customarily associated with high interest and returns. Fewer people seem to know Van Lanschot

Figure 8.4   **Quadrant Analysis: Attribute Importance and Brand Evaluation**
(Hypothetical retail example)

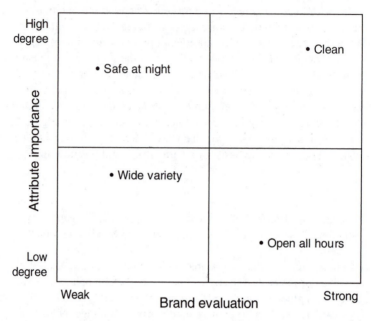

Figure 8.5   **The Degree of Importance and Uniqueness of Characteristics**
(Hypothetical body oil example)

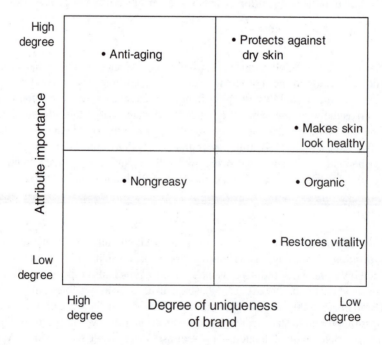

Figure 8.6   **Perceptual Map of Dutch Investment Companies**

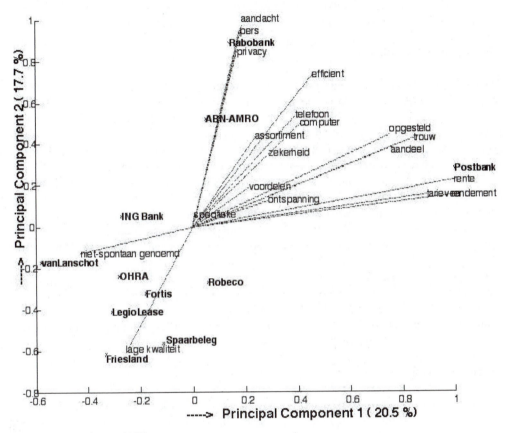

Source: Brandmarc (2000).

spontaneously. This applied, albeit to a lesser degree, to ING and Ohra too. Robeco is placed as a specific investment institution in the direction of Legiolease and Spaarbeleg. The new distribution channels play no special role yet, unless the major labels (banks) are connected to them.

In a full perceptual map, the preferences of user segments are also depicted. The charm of perceptual maps is that they immediately show the following:

- which associations are the most distinguishing for the different brands;
- which associations are the most characteristic for each of the brands;
- which brands compete with each other;
- which segments can (ideally) be distinguished in a market.

The coordinates of a perceptual space are strongly determined by the most distinguishing associations—that is, the characteristics through which consumers see large differences between the individual brands. The two dimensions of a perceptual map frequently explain between 80 and 90 percent of the data. The coordinates do not always provide neat verbal opposites (modern versus old-fashioned), but coordinated dimensions. The technique does not lead to false opposites. At the same time, the absence of clear opposites makes it difficult to do a pure interpretation of the positions in the space. The interpretation of a perceptual map takes place from the center—the more removed brands and associations are from the center, the more distinguishing or discriminating they are. The least distinguishing characteristics end up in the middle.

The Realities of Positioning

The idea that all brands in a category are evaluated on the basis of the same criteria does not correspond with the practice of marketing, according to Trommsdorff and Zellerhoff (1994). What brands try to do is profile themselves on very different dimensions. Some brands emphasize technical innovation, others a specific symbolic meaning, another focuses on price, and so on. In such a market, there is no common perceptual space. The dimension on which one brand profiles itself does not have to be relevant to the same degree, or relevant at all, for another brand.

There are also differences in the perception of brands in different segments: a perceptual map of the car market among young people probably looks very different from one for the middle-aged. Ideally, a positioning analysis requires first a segmentation of the market on the basis of the choice criteria to be distinguished, followed by an analysis of the positions of the brands in the consideration set of the segments to be distinguished on the relevant dimensions. Ultimately, a marketer needs to know about purchasing behavior, not about perception. A positioning analysis cannot ignore this need. When the purchasing behavior itself is difficult to measure, an attitude measurement, such as the constant-sum method, can serve as a surrogate.

In this process it is essential to involve the relationship between brand perceptions and brand attitude and, whenever possible, brand purchasing behavior. This does not happen in much positioning research as only the brand associations are measured.

Brand Positioning Strategy

Whichever method described above is used, in the end it should lead to an identification of the best brand positioning strategy to be followed. The key questions that have to be answered are below.

Segmentation Factors

- Is the market really segmented?
- Are there different groups of consumers who also buy different brands on the basis of diverging needs, desires, and values?

Competition Factors

- Which other brands is a brand competing with?
- What are the most relevant attributes or dimensions on which these brands are evaluated?

Attribute Factors

- Which of the attributes or dimensions have a high choice-motivating effect, which have a low one, and which play no role?
- How is a brand evaluated on these attributes or dimensions as against the competing brands? Better, equally, less well?

Symbolic, Affective, and Experiential Factors

- What symbolic meanings and associations do consumers associate with the brand? With competing brands?
- How are the brand experiences (buying, using) unique to this brand?

The strategic alternatives that can be considered on the basis of the results of the process are as follows:

- Strong brand evaluation on important attribute: good positioning option.
- Average brand evaluation on important attribute: improve product, or correct perception.
- Weak brand evaluation on important attribute: consider repositioning.
- Strong brand evaluation on less important attribute: consider stressing the attribute importance or reposition.
- Average brand evaluation on less important attribute: consider repositioning or cost reduction.
- Weak brand evaluation on less important attribute: consider withdrawing.

LEVI STRAUSS: A COMPANY IN A POSITIONING CRISIS

On one hand, jeans are a classic style, one that has been cultivated for a century by the Levi Strauss Company in its tough, red-seamed, hot-riveted denims. Worn by teenagers and adults alike, the brand began to lose its cachet in 1990s when the fashion sense of young people moved away from Levi's to more hip brands such as Diesel.

Levi's differentiation has always been clear, with the distinctive styling of its signature 501 line reflecting rugged durability, as well as its traditional leadership position as the brand that invented the category. The image of the gold miner or cowboy in the distinctive jeans, their rivets reflecting in the sunlight, has been a powerful Western icon. The button fly and the five-pocket style with the red stitching are recognized around the world. The Levi brand position has always been strong because of its authenticity, and its management has carefully controlled the way its image is presented to maintain that authenticity.

But classicism is a fashion statement that has its ins and outs. There is no segment more responsive to the whims of fashion than young people, which is also the biggest market segment for jeans. The position in the mind of the Levi's brand manager is not necessarily the position in the mind of a young fashionista. No matter what the company does, the decision about whether Levi's is in or out, cool or not, is made by the fashion-conscious youth market.

Levi's desperate step in 2003 to sell its Signature sub-brand at Wal-Mart stores (and somewhat later also at Target and Kmart) will doubtless have a tremendous impact on both the brand and the company. Wal-Mart has a reputation of putting tremendous pressure on its suppliers to continually lower their prices. It sells its own house brand of jeans, Faded Glory, for $16 a pair and does $3 billion in sales, not much less than famous Levi Strauss. Three months after introduction, Wal-Mart cut the price of a basic pair of Signature jeans to $19. In 2008 Levi's is selling a lot of jeans through Wal-Mart and by 2007 was again said to be profitable.

Moving downscale will not help to reclaim the company's standing as the trendsetter for youth. There is also the question of how the traditional outlets for Levi's jeans will react in the long run. Some department stores immediately reacted by reducing orders, and sales of the Red Tab lines resumed their decline.

CHAPTER 9

BRANDS AND CONSUMER NEEDS AND VALUES

Brand values, what a brand stands for, are an area where the two systems—corporate and consumer—must mesh. Although all people share a set of universal basic needs, major differences can be observed between the values they hold in life. Some people find it important to form a family, buy a house, and surround themselves with as much security as possible as early as possible. Others roam the world unattached, searching for the ultimate feeling of freedom. Anyone who has been to a high school reunion knows how similar people can end up in totally different worlds within a lapse of ten years. Although you may be a single, successful, world-traveling urban executive, your closest high school friend has become a wife and mother of two children, with a third on the way, leading a contented life in the suburbs.

There are huge differences between the ways similar people give content to their lives and the choices they make. Why, for example, do some people only drink Pepsi-Cola and others maintain a to-die-for loyalty to Coca-Cola?

PEPSI-COLA: THE VALUES OF A NEW GENERATION

Pepsi-Cola was "invented" in 1898 by Caleb D. Bradham, a pharmacist in North Carolina. This was eleven years after John Pemberton developed the formula for Coca-Cola and came up with the brand and the logo (1887). The two brands have remained entangled in a constant struggle ever since. Until long after World War II, price was Pepsi's main weapon. In 1934, when Coke was sold in a six-ounce bottle for ten cents, Pepsi offered a twelve-ounce bottle for a nickel. Yet Coca-Cola had built an enormous lead by advertising for decades that it was the first quality cola, had the best taste, and was the most refreshing— that is, "the real thing." Coke was the brand for everyone and stood for traditional American values.

Starting in 1960, Pepsi changed its course. It began focusing explicitly on the younger generation, who were the heavy users, and consciously polarized the choice between Coke and Pepsi. From Pepsi's perspective, Coca-Cola was universal, traditional, conformist, predictable, and, especially, linked to the past. Pepsi-Cola itself was young, independent, adventurous, leading-edge, future-oriented, and entertaining—in short, "the choice of a new generation."

In the course of the following decades, Pepsi deployed a whole series of singers and movie stars, including Madonna, Michael Jackson, Michael J. Fox, Lionel Ritchie, Ray Charles, Cindy Crawford, and the Spice Girls, to give shape to this new identity. At the same time, wherever possible it presented Coca-Cola as a brand from the distant past.

The period from 1960 to 1990 became known as the cola wars. The success of the new Pepsi positioning was so great that its market share in home use in the United States from 1975 to 1987 was larger than that of Coca-Cola. This success tempted Coca-Cola to modify its legendary formula and introduce New Coke in an attempt to compare more favorably with the sweeter taste of Pepsi, which research consistently found to be preferred by customers in blind taste tests. However, Coke's loyal users, the ones who believed strongly in "the real thing," saw the formula adjustment as a betrayal that seemed to contradict everything the brand stood for. Coke's managers discovered not only the depth of loyalty of its customers, but also that a brand is owned as much, if not more, by its loyal users than by its marketing strategists. The new soft drink was recalled within a year and the original Coke was reintroduced as Coca-Cola Classic. This has become a standard case study of brand strategy failure in marketing textbooks.

There is hardly any difference between the products Coca-Cola and Pepsi-Cola, but the difference between the meanings of each brand is gigantic, and the meanings lie in the values the two brands represent.

Sources: Based on Troeken (1994–1995); www.Pepsi.com.

THE ROLE OF A BRAND STORY

Storytellers throughout history have been the carriers of culture and social values. Similarly, successful brands add a story to the bare, physical product. The theme of this story varies with the brand. Swatch tells a passionate story about design. Nike encourages people to transcend their personal boundaries with its motto "Just do it." IBM advertises an image of service and competence that seems to go beyond lifestyles, geographies, and cultures. Sanex tells us that its mission is "to keep skin healthy." Amstel beer shows how important friendship is. Vodaphone addresses ease of international communication and cosmopolitan sophistication.

Some brand stories are profound, philosophical, or involved; others are to the point and nonsense; some emphasize the brand's utilitarian value (as in the American Express slogan "Don't leave home without it"). Other brands have a weak story or no story at all. In the worst case, competing brands all tell the same story. At the beginning of this new century, which is characterized in the West by enormous wealth and overabundance, self-actualization seems to be the magical word. Notice how many brands today tell us that we must or will be "inspired" by the brand.

Of course, the idea is to attract consumers by the stories the brands are telling because the story expresses how the brand relates to its customers' needs and desires. A brand's story has to inspire and motivate, but, more important, it has to activate and incite consumers toward purchasing behavior. This is only possible when the story is authentic. Nowadays, consumers are extraordinarily cynical and can see through a story that is not "right." Superficial, cosmetic stories do not work anymore.

Interest in the person to whom the story is being told is normal, but with brands, this interest is not always evident. Some brands shout out what they have to say without asking themselves whether there is any consumer who wants to listen. This type of arrogance often affects larger, established brands. Beyond the general question of what motivates a person, brands should ask themselves what motivates consumers and, more specifically, what motivates the consumers to whom the brand wants to tell its story and with whom the brand wants to enter a dialogue. Part of the answer lies in understanding needs and values and how they relate to brand differentiation. Let us begin with consumer needs.

WHAT ARE NEEDS?

All human behavior, including brand behavior, is ultimately the product of the interaction of people's physiological and psychological needs with their values and their physical and social environment. Henry Murray, a famous psychologist who developed an early taxonomy of basic needs, defined needs as "the representation of a brain force that energizes, directs, selects, and organizes human perception—a process of thinking that transforms an unsatisfying situation into a more satisfying one" (quoted in McAdams 2004).

In marketing we talk about a need as something necessary for life—such as food and shelter. These innate needs are called basic needs or *primary* needs. Acquired needs, those we learn about from our culture and environment such as taste in food and fashion, are *secondary*. There is still uncertainty about how many basic needs there are.

Needs can be also characterized as *utilitarian*, which refers to something functional or practical, or *hedonic*, which refers to pleasurable experiences or emotions (Solomon 2004). These distinctions are particularly useful in the development of brand strategy whereby brands are designed to appeal to various types of needs and wants.

Taxonomies of Needs

Over the past century, a succession of philosophers and psychologists has attempted to develop a broader taxonomy of basic human needs. The best known of these taxonomies is certainly Abraham

Figure 9.1 **Maslow's Pyramid**

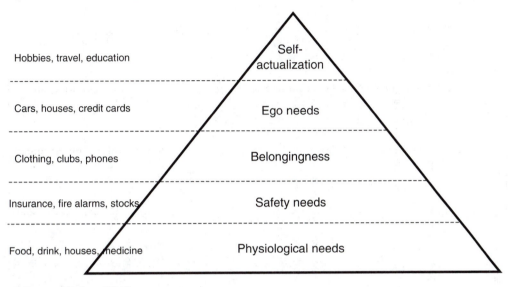

Self-actualization — Hobbies, travel, education

Ego needs — Cars, houses, credit cards

Belongingness — Clothing, clubs, phones

Safety needs — Insurance, fire alarms, stocks

Physiological needs — Food, drink, houses, medicine

Source: Maslow (1943).

Maslow's (1943) need pyramid, but even this has met with serious scientific criticism. Maslow organized needs with physiological or survival needs as the base and hedonic needs at the top. He postulated that the physiological needs have to be satisfied before hedonic needs can be addressed. Figure 9.1 illustrates Maslow's theory and orients it to common product categories.

Although Maslow's ideas are intuitively very appealing, his proposal of a hierarchy of needs has been abandoned. The modern view is that the activation of needs is person- and situation-dependent. When people who have reached a satisfactory level of self-actualization, for instance, experience an illness, they will most strongly experience the physiological need of health. Human behavior also tends to be activated by a constellation of different needs—so Maslow's pyramid is less useful as a tool to develop brand strategy because so many of the motivations and needs addressed by branding move beyond the basic needs in Maslow's hierarchy.

In the last decade, therefore, scientists have tried to derive a more comprehensive list of basic needs. The number of independent needs they distinguish, however, still varies from three to twenty-two. A recent attempt by Stephen Reiss and Susan Havercamp involved a measurement instrument with 300 statements representing needs and solicited judgments on them by 6,000 respondents. A factor analysis of the answers produced sixteen factors that the researchers called "basic desires." Reiss and Havercamp claim that the list is comprehensive and that there is no overlap or hierarchic relationship between the needs (Reiss 2002). In his book *Who Am I?* Reiss relates almost all the needs to evolution and argues that they are coded in the DNA of all humans, albeit to varying degrees. We must be aware, however, that culture has a large influence on their expression.

Franzen (2008)—expanding on the work of Reiss and Havercamp and of earlier specialists in the field, such as Martin Ford, Clay Nichols, Jeffrey Vancouver, and James Austin—developed a list of twenty-three needs. This list, which is presented in Table 9.1, includes the sixteen basic needs of Reiss and Havercamp, which are identified in the last column.

We must be aware that people have different needs in different situations. Brands may project

Table 9.1

A Taxonomy of Needs

		Reiss/Havercamp
1. Certainty of existence	Meeting essential physiological needs for food, drink, and shelter; being healthy	X
2. Safety and relaxation	Absence of threats, tranquility	X
3. Order and control	Need for stability and organization, tidiness, predictability, and control over the environment	X
4. Physical well being	Need for bodily activity, fitness, vitality, sport; feeling energetic	X
5. Individuality	Having own identity, feeling unique	
6. Sexuality	Need for romance, sex, lust, and beauty	X
7. Knowledge and understanding	Satisfying curiosity, gaining knowledge, learning new things; need for understanding and truth	X
8. Competence	Improving one's performance and self-effectiveness, expanding one's limits	
9. Achievement	Meeting achievement standards, doing well, getting ahead, reaching goals, being successful	
10. Recognition	Getting attention, being known, accepted and liked, obtaining approval from others, being popular	X
11. Parenthood	Having children, spending time with family, nurturing	X
12. Belonging	Bonding with those who care for you; psychological proximity, companionship, friendship, empathy, and love	X
13. Play	Need for play and entertainment, having fun, seeking sensations	
14. Self-determination	Freedom to act and make one's own choices, being master over one's life; being free and independent	X
15. Loyalty and integrity	Being loyal, showing character, being conscientious and responsible, meeting obligations	X
16. Self-esteem	Having a positive self-image, self-respect, self-confidence, and pride	
17. Status	Wealth, reputation, being prestigious, having high rank and titles	X
18. Possessions	Acquiring tangible goods or money, leading a luxurious life, defending one's possessions	X
19. Power	Having influence over others, authority, control	X
20. Vengeance	Aggression, competitiveness, getting even with people, seeking revenge	X
21. Idealism and transcendence	Promoting fairness, justice, equality, and reciprocity; being altruistic; experiencing extra-ordinary states of functioning; experiencing oneness with people and nature	X
22. Self-realization	Full development of one's potential, making life meaningful, achieving inner peace.	
23. Happiness	A state of well being characterized by relative permananes.	

Figure 9.2 **Car Brands and Universal Needs**

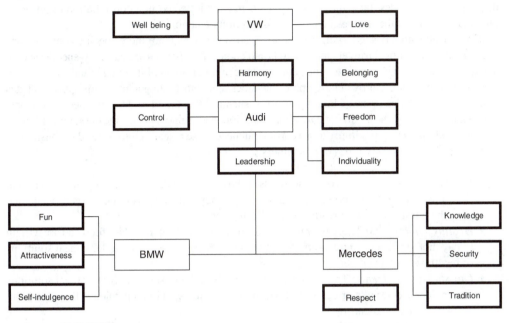

Source: Hall (2002).

an ability to meet one, several, or a constellation of these human needs, but the choice of a brand is dependent on which needs are activated in the specific circumstance.

In order to understand why people choose different brands in different circumstances, we have to look at needs from the perspective of the brand, rather than from the perspective of individuals. Of course, we can segment a population on the basis of its claimed basic needs and try to establish a fit between the associations of the brand and the need scores of a segment, but often this fit turns out to be imperfect or even nonexistent. Different people are drawn to different brands in different situations. Nevertheless, it is useful to focus on the basic needs with which brands in a category are associated. Hall (2004) developed a measurement instrument consisting of fifteen universal needs and showing similarities to the preceding list (see Figure 9.2). For example, a German automotive study based on it shows that all brands ultimately tap into the basic need for leadership (for example, having the best, the sexiest, the trendiest, the most technical, or the highest-status car), but do so in very different ways. With BMW you get a car that satisfies the need for a fun ride as well as the need to feel that you look attractive to others. At the same time it allows for some true self-indulgence. By contrast, the traditional heritage of Mercedes means that you will gain the respect you deserve and the security that comes not just from a solidly built car, but also one that will maintain its value over the years. Audi taps into the needs for individuality, freedom, and belonging; Volkswagen into the needs for well being, harmony, and love.

Need-States

Basic needs, as defined and described here, are drivers of a highly abstract nature, which find their expression depending on the situation consumers find themselves in at a particular time— involving, that is, not only their own experience, role, problems, mood, and attitudes, but also the dynamics in and around the shopping experience. When consumers find themselves in very different circumstances, their unconscious needs may be reflected in a constellation of attitudes that finally manifest themselves in actual consumption behavior.

This consideration has led to the concept of need-states, which are more specific constellations of rational and emotional triggers leading to brand choice. Need-states are category-specific sets of needs and attitudes that interact to guide consumer behavior. Instead of defining brands by category (carbonated soft drinks) or by demographic consumer segments (young adults), this approach leads to needs- and attitudes-oriented brand platforms, such as "this brand satisfies the needs of people who want something cheap, do not care about nutrition, and cannot spend time cooking at home."

The Food Marketing Institute (2000) carried out need-state research into American consumers' attitudes and identified six types of consumers:

- *On-the-go jugglers:* These are time-stressed, busy people who rely heavily on retailer meal solutions to meet their food preparation needs. They will pay even more for services that save them time. They like ready-to-eat offerings best.
- *Healthy family cooks:* These people focus on the nutritional value of their food and are willing to pay more for better ingredients. This group may be attracted to a retailer's meal solutions or healthy ethnic meal choices.
- *Gut-stuffing indulgents:* These eaters want fast, filling food, such as pizza or meal solutions that include free drinks or desserts. They are more interested in convenience than nutrition. They want ready-to-eat foods.
- *Meat and potato cooks:* This is a significant group that wants to feed their families comfort foods, such as lasagna, pot pies, and other traditional offerings. Ready-to-prepare or ready-to-create meal solutions are best for these cooks.
- *Strict food monitors:* This is the largest segment of consumers, who focus on what is in their food and tend to be interested in choices that are light or low in fat. They often choose ready-to-eat or ready-to-heat solutions.
- *Thrifty food balancers:* This group is characterized by people who plan their meals and watch their wallet. They want value from the food they purchase as well as nutrition for their families. These cooks normally pick ready-to-prepare or ready-to-create meal solutions.

Such a need-state segmentation and positioning approach can be an effective platform for brand strategy development. Mapping brands against the need-states in a category is a helpful starting point. This relationship between the things customers value in a given need-state and the attributes that differentiate the brand or sub-brand can produce valuable insights into the opportunities for brand differentiation and extension.

Needs, Desires, and Wants

The need taxonomies of Reiss and Havercamp and of Franzen begin with physiological needs but then move to the hedonic needs. In other words, these lists of needs are most useful in a socioeconomic situation where basic survival needs have been met. People are motivated not only by their innate basic needs, but also by the autonomous attractiveness of the options they encounter during their life. We then speak of "desires" or "wants." Of course, these options may appeal to people's basic needs, such as status or play, but the activation is triggered by the things and experiences they encounter in their physical and social environment. Needs are abstract and often unconscious inner drives; desires and wants are object-bound, conscious longings for mostly very concrete and specific things: "I want an iPod." Needs are push-processes; wants and desires are pull-processes. In a sense, wants are manifestations of desires (Solomon 2004), but there is a difference in degree. Needs are requirements; desires and wants are wishes. In both cases, there is a strong feeling that a drive needs to be fulfilled; however, a need is more urgent than a desire or want. "I want to eat" is less compelling than "I need to eat."

Wants and desires tend to come into play when the basic physiological needs—health, shelter, food, and clothing—have been satisfied. In other words, poor people may be more concerned with stretching their budgets to cover the essentials of life than with the brand of bread they buy. Branding becomes more important when there is a surplus—both of products (marketplace) and discretionary income (consumer). When a market offers a variety of brands of bread with prices that vary from cheap to expensive and the consumer has the wherewithal to make a choice among them, then branding strategies are designed to reflect what people want, rather than just their basic needs. That is why generic brands position themselves as appealing to basic needs without consideration of brand image. Brand strategies, then, tend to be focused on wants and desires, rather than basic needs. That is also why the Reiss and Havercamp analysis of needs is transformed into a list of desires once it moves beyond the survival essentials.

The analysis of wants and desires provides more useful insight into the motivation structure of consumers as they make product selections in a time of abundance. Motivation—the drive to satisfy a need, want, or desire—has two dimensions: *direction*, which refers to the focus of the tension, and *strength*, which refers to the degree of pull, compulsion, or impulse that characterizes the drive. A hungry consumer may buy a candy bar on impulse or look up restaurants in the Yellow Pages. The direction—candy bar versus restaurant—and the strength—now versus later—tell planners how consumers make choices and where a brand fits in that consumer schema.

WHAT ARE VALUES?[1]

When consumers make brand choices, the selection is driven by needs and wants but the decision factors are framed through the consumers' personal set of values. Beyond primary needs, brand selections are based on what consumers consider important, and those factors are a product of their values. In the bread example, important factors could be safety (organics), nutrition, price, taste, convenience, availability, or more general trends in food (multigrain, low-carb, eco-packaging).

Determining what a value is can be complicated. The various scientific disciplines use different definitions. In general, values are ideas in the human mind that make it possible to evaluate all kinds of things in life and to choose between alternatives, thus guiding people's behavior. At a highly abstract level, values are forms of knowledge about what is good and what is not; they are strongly anchored views about what is meaningful in life, what is worth aiming for, a sort of ideal. Milton Rokeach, the most famous scientist in the field of human values, defines a value as an enduring belief that a specific mode of conduct is preferable to an opposite mode of conduct (Rokeach 1973).

Values are an essential element of the human mind that determine what people expect of other people and things in their life. Values influence how people think and act, how they deal with information, how they collect, store, and use it. Values form criteria by which people judge all kinds of information. So how does the concept of values relate to needs?

Needs and Values: What Is the Difference?

Needs and values are complicated concepts that are not always clearly defined and distinguished from each other. We could say that needs are drivers of behavior, such as impulses, and values are beliefs that enable people to choose between alternative modes of behavior. Needs have a conative or cognitive character; values are views on what is good or bad that help people evaluate things. Nevertheless, the difference is sometimes difficult to see. Suppose, for instance, that consumers attach a high value to indulgence. That could motivate them both to buy organic products and to visit expensive gourmet restaurants. In such situations, it is unclear without deeper probing what is driving the evaluation of good and bad that characterizes a value judgment.

Brands and Values

As the story of Pepsi-Cola illustrates, a brand has to stand for something that its customers value. Value is derived from the brand's function and position, both as determined by the management and as perceived by the customer. Pepsi is an example of a brand that matches its mental brand to consumer values. That process is a common practice in successful brands that dominate their categories. In most cases, managers develop strategies that orient supply exactly toward the needs of different types of users.

Tracey and Wiersema (1995) explain that today's market leaders know they have to redefine value by raising customers' expectations in a critical factor used in decision making about the product. No company can succeed today by trying to be all things to all people. In other words, a brand must instead identify the unique value that it alone can deliver to a chosen market or segment.

Consider the views of Ray Ozzie, who became Microsoft's chief technical officer after his firm Groove was purchased by Bill Gates. Ozzie's company was respected for its workplace integration and collaboration tools, but he confides that although Microsoft's engineering culture builds great technology, sometimes he wonders if the technology is packaged in such a way that people see the value of it (Battelle 2006). How many people who use Microsoft Word, for example, use most or even a few of the tools provided by that software? Even a big company like Microsoft struggles to match its corporate values to the values of its customers.

Customer Values

So how does a marketer go about matching the brand's point of difference to consumer needs and values? The answer is to identify and address those things that are important (salient) to consumers. The iPod is successful not just because it is a beautifully designed product, but also because it meets the needs and values of its music-listening consumers. Apple designers approached the iPod with a scenario-based design process. In other words, the designers started with the consumers' experience of listening to music in all their different lifestyle situations and then designed a product that delivered what they valued—portability and ease of use with a high cool factor.

"Customers today want more of those things they value," say Tracey and Wiersema (1995, 52). "If they value low cost, they want it lower. If they value convenience or speed when they buy, they want it easier and faster. If they look for state-of-the-art design, they want to see the art pushed forward. If they need expert advice, they want companies to give them more depth, more time and more of a feeling that they're the only customer."

Naumann (1995), in his book *Creating Customer Value*, identifies the three components of customer value as product quality, service quality, and value-based pricing. He calls this the "customer value triad." Naumann has developed five lessons that he says strong brands have mastered:

1. The customer defines the appropriate product quality.
2. Customer expectations are formed relative to competitor alternatives.

3. Customer expectations are dynamic; companies cannot rely on research that provides a snapshot of just one point in time.
4. Product and service quality must extend throughout the channel.
5. In order to maximize customer value, the whole organization must be involved.

Viewed another way, brands also derive their value(s) from the brand meanings that are experienced as relevant by consumers to the degree that brands fulfill their basic needs. These needs can be purely functional, purely symbolic, or a combination of both. Brand values thus can be mainly at the level of product attributes or at the level of symbolic meanings, but generally will combine both. These values steer the communication and, ideally, the behavior of the brand as well.

In Chapter 5, values were mentioned as central elements in the visions of companies in relation to the contributions that their brands make to the quality of society and, more particularly, to the various interest groups with which they are connected. Values thus take a central place when thinking about brands. When we speak of brand values, we are referring to brand meanings that match values of (groups of) people, thus allowing positive evaluation of a brand. In other words, there are brand values and there are customer values—synchronizing the two is the objective of brand strategy. Brand meaning is expressed in customer interactions that come together to create meaning as a story.

The Value System

The concept of value is inseparably linked to the names of Milton Rokeach and Shalom Schwartz. Mapping the concept in 1973, Rokeach made an inventory of values in American society. According to Rokeach, the behavior people show is the result of the relative importance of the constellation of values that play a role at that moment. He sees values as classified in a value system. This is an acquired classification of principles and rules that can help people choose between alternatives, solve conflicts, and make decisions. Rokeach does not believe that the entire value system gets activated all the time—only those values that are necessary at a certain moment to make a decision or give an opinion play a role. The rest is ignored as irrelevant. Rokeach's theory also assumes a high degree of conscious behavior, but values are functional at an unconscious level too.

> *Principle:* Behavior is the result of the relative importance of all values that play a role at that moment.

More recently, Schwartz (1992, 2003a, 2006a) has proposed a conception of values that specifies six main features that are implicit in the writings of meaning theorists:

1. *Values are beliefs* linked inextricably to affect. When values are activated, they become infused with feeling. People for whom independence is an important value, for example, become aroused if their independence is threatened, despair when they are helpless to protect it, and are happy when they can enjoy it.
2. *Values refer to desirable goals* that motivate action. People for whom social order, justice, and helpfulness are important values are motivated to pursue these goals.
3. *Values transcend specific actions and situations.* Obedience and honesty, for example, are values that may be relevant at work or in school, in sports, business, and politics, with

family, friends, or strangers. This feature distinguishes values from narrower concepts like norms and attitudes that usually refer to specific actions, objects, or situations.

4. *Values serve as standards or criteria.* Values guide the selection or evaluation of actions, policies, people, and events. People decide what is good or bad, justified or illegitimate, worth doing or avoiding, based on possible consequences for their cherished values. But the impact of values in everyday decisions is rarely conscious. Values enter awareness when the actions or judgments that a person is considering have conflicting implications for different values that the person cherishes.

5. *Values are ordered by importance* relative to one another. People's values form an ordered system of value priorities that characterize them as individuals. Do they attribute more importance to achievement or to justice, to novelty or to tradition? This hierarchical feature also distinguishes values from norms and attitudes.

6. *The relative importance of multiple values guides action.* Any attitude or behavior typically has implications for more than one value. For example, attending church might express and promote tradition, conformity, and security values at the expense of hedonism and stimulation values. The trade-off among relevant, competing values is what guides attitudes and behaviors. Values contribute to action to the extent that they are relevant in the context (hence likely to be activated) and important to the actor.

The above are features of *all* values. What distinguishes one value from another is the type of goal or motivation that the value expresses.

At the risk of being redundant, we would like to point out once more that values are not the only factors influencing behavior, but are part of a complicated system of internal and external factors that influence behavior.

Values as Drivers of Choice

What drives people in making decisions? The answer is not simple. The value system of people is largely influential in the way they see and define themselves in relation to the world that surrounds them, but it is too simplistic to assume that people are driven only by values. Biological instinct also plays a role, and if we are to believe Freud, Jung, and Adler, there are myriad other, deeper drives behind human behavior. We also know that people are not only driven from the inside, but also triggered by things surrounding them. Human behavior is the result of a continuous interaction between a person (with instincts, needs, emotions, personality, values) and the physical and social environment. Sometimes internal motives are the decisive ones; sometimes the external ones are the drivers.

The choices people make in their lives are thus determined to a certain extent by their values. The assumption that underlies the concept of brand values is that it also applies to the choices of products and brands that people make in their role as consumers. Values generate specific (consumer) needs, motivate behavior, and influence choice processes. Someone who loves renewal and innovation may be interested in striking product design, switching products frequently as the design changes and technical improvements are offered; a person who values security may prefer to buy the same brand of coffee or razor over a lifetime.

Values and Culture

Values are carriers of culture. Everyone has certain patterns of values that determine thoughts, feelings, and actions. Many of these patterns are acquired in early infancy, when the individual

Figure 9.3 **Hofstede's Three Levels of Mental Programming**

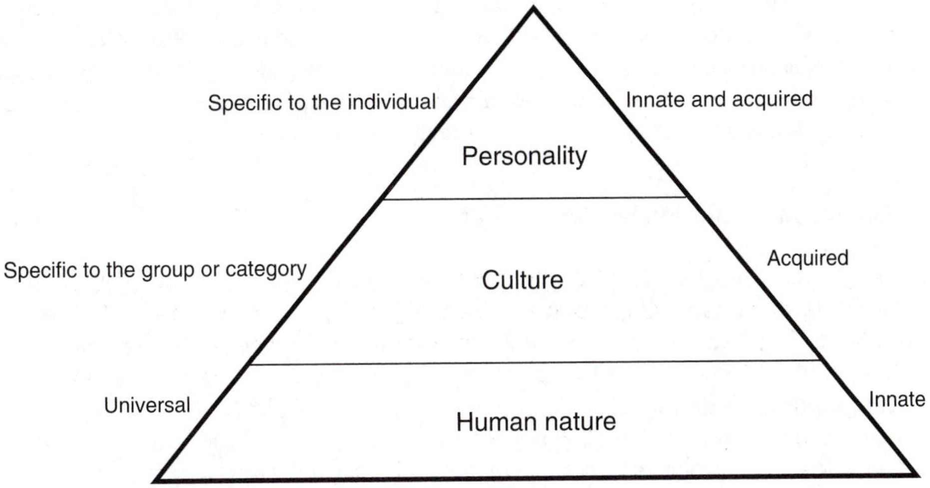

Specific to the individual

Personality

Innate and acquired

Specific to the group or category

Culture

Acquired

Universal

Human nature

Innate

Source: G. Hofstede (1991).

is most receptive to learning and absorbing new things (Engel et al. 1990, G. Hofstede 1991; Rokeach 1973; Oppenhuisen 2000). This learning process happens implicitly. When children are about ten years old, their value pattern is more or less fixed, and it is subsequently very difficult to change.

We described the cultural context within which branding operates in Chapter 2; however, let us take another look at culture in this chapter as a driver of values. G. Hofstede (1991) calls people's value patterns "mental programs," a term that corresponds with the concept of culture. The transfer of values takes place through culture. Values are also transferred by experiences people have in their early years and by their surroundings.

Culture can be distinguished from human nature and from personality (see Figure 9.3). By human nature we understand that which all people have in common. It is hereditary and it determines the physical and primary psychological functioning of the person. Human nature includes the ability to feel fear, love, anger, joy, and sadness; the need to relate to other people, play with them, and measure oneself against them; the possibility of looking at one's surroundings and talking about them with other people. How people deal with these issues—that is, how people show they are happy, sad, or angry—is determined by culture (G. Hofstede 1991). In contrast, the personality of an individual is a unique combination of "mental programs." The personality is not shared with anyone; it is a combination of character traits that are inherited or learned under the influence of culture and personal experience.

Values form the core of a culture. We can derive these values from the manner in which people behave (G. Hofstede 1991). However, Prensky and Wright-Isak (1997) and Kahle et al. (1997) believe that values are not predictors of specific behavior, because how they determine the behavior of people depends on the community to which a person belongs. People's surroundings partly determine how values are transformed into behavior. It is therefore not enough to just look at values; the culture and subcultures that surround consumers and contribute to their attitudes have to be studied in order to know how a consumer will behave.

This is important in the context of the globalization of brands. In a way, globalization and values produce a certain field of tension. Although people—especially the younger generations—are in contact with the world more than ever before, thanks to the globalization of mass media, the advent of the Internet, and the light-speed developments in the field of communication technology, a strong "local awareness" seems to exist simultaneously. Sulin Lau (2001) studied the effects of the globalization of mass media on values within Asian youth culture and concluded that young Asians are much less Westernized than a superficial observer would assume and that the strength of the local culture was one of the most important explanatory factors in this phenomenon (see box below).

"I Want My MTV, But in Mandarin, Please"

Globalization of mass media and the explosion in Internet activity are two of the most visible engines of change in the lives of youngsters growing up in today's wired Asia. The natural question, then, for marketers is whether to sell to them as Asians or as Westerners. The answer is—as always in the shadowy world of psychographics—it depends.

Many magazines would have you believe that Asian teens—in appearance, attitude, and posture—increasingly resemble American and European teens. However, this convergence view of global teen lifestyle overlooks the reality of Asian cultural diversity.

The befuddling paradox is that, as Asian teens have become more globally aware, they have also grown increasingly confident in their local identity. This conflict between global and hyperlocal is becoming more and more important, being reflected in food, music, language, and brands. Marketers struggle to understand a generation of teenagers who worship angst-ridden musicians with names like Lazy Mutha Ferr by night and study religiously for mid-term examinations by day; who aspire to be individuals in their own right, and yet curiously express that individualism en masse; and who seek newer, bigger, and better delivery devices for fun, but also the comforts of familiarity. As a teen research respondent put it: "I want my MTV, but in Mandarin, please."

Source: Lau (2001).

A matrix can be developed that compares different cultures in terms of their relationships with mass media and the globalization forces embodied in modern media. Table 9.2 looks at the teenagers in various cultures and their acceptance of global lifestyles and values.

Values Throughout Time

Values are more or less stable but can change through time, albeit slowly. Research by Abramson and Inglehart (1995) shows a shift from 1970 to 1993 of so-called materialistic values such as economic security and personal safety toward postmaterialistic ones like freedom, self-expression, and improving the quality of life.

In time, societal values can slowly switch their importance. In the 1950s, submissiveness, self-sacrifice, and attachment were highly valued as attributes of the ideal woman. In the 1970s, major social changes turned those values into a negative image of how *not* to behave. Those values were replaced by others, such as equality between men and women, standing up for yourself, and being free so you can develop. A brand must keep up with the current values in a culture and the changes it undergoes if the brand is to properly fit its story into the world and experiences of the consumers.

Table 9.2

Culture Mix Matrix: Culture Strength Versus Media Absorption

Strength of the culture	Absorption of global media	
	Low	High
Porous (dynamic language and value system)	Vulnerables (sensitive to Western values but interpretation is distinctly non-Western): South Korean, Vietnamese, Malaysian (Chinese speaking), Japanese teens	Internationalists (display signs of both global lifestyles and values): Singaporean, Hong Kong, Taiwanese teens
Rigid (established language, institutionalized value systems)	Nationalists (resistance to external attitudes and values): Chinese, North Korean, Arabic, Malaysian (Malay speaking) teens	Tasters (acceptance of external lifestyles but retention of traditional values): Thai, Indian, Filipino teens

---

Principle: Values are not permanent—they can change over time but do show a certain stability.

CATEGORIZING VALUES

A categorization of values inevitably leads to discussions. For people who are involved in market research, positioning brands and brand extensions can be quite enlightening. Different authors distinguish different categories of values. Rokeach (1973), for example, makes a distinction between instrumental values and terminal values. We make the following distinctions because they seem most relevant for brand strategies:

- *Impressive values:* the feelings that a brand or product evokes during its use: cozy, intimate, cheerful, and so on.
- *Expressive values:* the symbolic brand values that consumers find important for themselves and want to express to their social environment, aided by the brand: for example, young, individualistic, no-nonsense.
- *End values:* the ideal representations of the personal life, like freedom and independence, health and wisdom, which the brand is linked to.
- *Social values:* the ideal representations of the society consumers live in and with which they associate the brand: peace in the world, a cleaner environment, a fair society, for example.

Principle: A means-end chain explains how a product or brand brings closer the attainment of an aimed-for, supreme way of living.

Values Inventories

In the late 1960s, drawing on dictionaries, Rokeach made an inventory of the values of the residents of the American Midwest. He arrived at eighteen instrumental values (modes of conduct or personality traits) and eighteen end values (terminal values that define the quality of our existence, such as a longing for peace). The lists have become guidelines for nearly all the value research that has taken place since then. Although Rokeach's research was indeed groundbreaking, there is much in it that can be subject to criticism—for instance, the assumed universality of its thirty-six values. It is quite possible that the values that Rokeach found were only applicable in the middle of the United States in the early 1970s. A more important point of criticism was admitted by Rokeach himself: the limited empirical foundation.

Because of the trend from local to global brands, it is important to ask to what degree values are culture- and time-dependent. Based on the Rokeach values, Schwartz and Bilsky (1987), and Schwartz (1992, 2003a, 2006a) developed a measurement instrument, now known as the Schwartz Values Survey (SVS), which has been translated into forty-seven languages. To that he added the Portrait Values Questionnaire. It includes short verbal portraits of forty people, describing their goals, aspirations, or wishes that point to the importance of a value.

The application of these two instruments in over seventy countries identified ten basic values that individuals in all countries recognize, specifying the dynamics of conflict and congruence among them. These dynamics yielded a structure of relations among values in culturally diverse groups, suggesting a universal organization of human motivations.

Figure 9.4 presents a theoretical model of values relative to the ten motivational types of values. Each of the ten basic values is represented by a set of value items that share a common primary motivational goal.

Some value items included in the SVS have multiple meanings and express the motivational goals of more than one basic value. Some value items have different meanings in different cultures. Only items with meanings clearly expressive of one basic value that also show considerable consistency of meaning across cultures are used to generate value priority scores. Schwartz has clarified these meanings as described in the following list (Schwartz 2003a, 2006a):

1. *Self-direction:* Defining goal: independent thought and action—choosing, creating, exploring. Self-direction derives from organismic needs for control and mastery and interactional requirements of autonomy and independence.
2. *Stimulation:* Defining goal: excitement, novelty, and challenge in life. Stimulation values derive from the organismic need for variety and stimulation in order to maintain an optimal and positive, rather than threatening, level of activation. This need is probably related to the needs underlying self-direction values.
3. *Hedonism:* Defining goal: pleasure or sensuous gratification for oneself. Hedonism values derive from organismic needs and the pleasure associated with satisfying them.
4. *Achievement:* Defining goal: personal success through demonstrating competence according to social standards. Competent performance that generates resources is necessary for individuals to survive and for groups and institutions to reach their objectives. Achievement values emphasize demonstrating competence according to prevailing cultural standards, thereby obtaining social approval.
5. *Power:* Defining goal: social status and prestige, control or dominance over people and resources. A dominance/submission dimension emerges in most empirical analyses of interpersonal relations, both within and across cultures. To justify this fact of social life

Figure 9.4   **Theoretical Model of Relations Among Ten Motivational Types of Value**

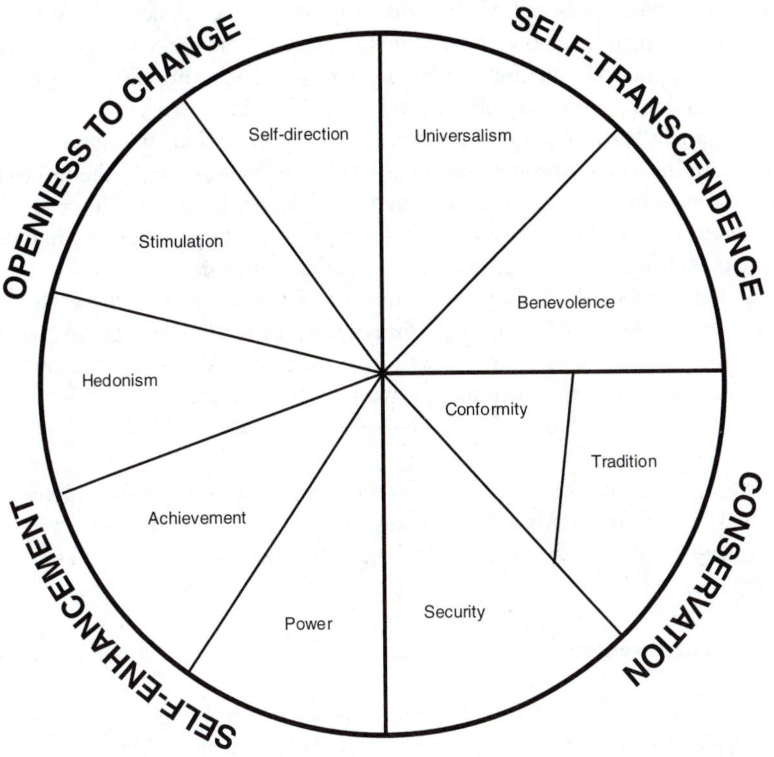

Source: Schwatz (2006a).

and to motivate group members to accept it, groups must treat power as a value. Power values may also be transformations of the individual needs for dominance and control.

6. *Security:* Defining goal: safety, harmony, and stability of society, of relationships, and of self. Security values derive from basic individual and group requirements. There are two subtypes of security values. Some security values serve primarily individual interests (e.g., cleanliness), others primarily wider group interests (e.g., national security). Even the latter, however, express, to a significant degree, the goal of security for self (or those with whom one identifies). The two subtypes can therefore be unified into a more encompassing value.

7. *Conformity:* Defining goal: restraint of actions, inclinations, and impulses likely to upset or harm others and violate social expectations or norms. Conformity values derive from the requirement that individuals inhibit inclinations that might disrupt and undermine smooth interaction and group functioning. They emphasize self-restraint in everyday interaction, usually with close others.

8. *Tradition:* Defining goal: respect, commitment, and acceptance of the customs and ideas that one's culture or religion provides. Groups everywhere develop practices, symbols, ideas, and beliefs that represent their shared experience and fate and that become sanctioned as valued, group customs and traditions. They symbolize the group's solidarity, express its unique worth, and contribute to its survival. They often take the form of religious rites, beliefs, and norms of behavior.

9. *Benevolence:* Defining goal: preserving and enhancing the welfare of those with whom one is in frequent personal contact (the in-group). Benevolence values derive from the basic requirement for smooth group functioning and from the organismic need for affiliation. Most critical are relations within the family and other primary groups. Benevolence values emphasize voluntary concern for others' welfare.

10. *Universalism:* Defining goal: understanding, appreciation, tolerance, and protection for the welfare of *all* people and for nature. This contrasts with the in-group focus of benevolence values. Universalism values also derive from survival needs of individuals and groups. But these needs are not recognized until people come into contact with those outside the extended primary group and until they become aware of the scarcity of natural resources. People may then realize that failure to accept others who are different and treat them justly will lead to life-threatening strife. They may also realize that failure to protect the natural environment will lead to the destruction of the resources on which life depends. Universalism combines two subtypes of concern—for the welfare of those in the larger society and world and for nature.

These values are highly abstract convictions that enable consumers to evaluate things such as products and brands. Implicitly a brand's associations and meanings are tested against the consumers' value-system, which enables consumers to make choices, such as which brands to prefer or reject.

The SWOCC Value Inventory

Sikkel and Oppenhuisen (1998a) did a values inventory for the Foundation for Scientific Research on Commercial Communications (its acronym SWOCC is based on the Dutch name) that applies to the Dutch population of 1997. As far as we know, it is the only bottom-up inventory based on a scientific approach. It was done by means of qualitative interviews of twenty respondents. The interviews lasted three hours, the topics being twenty-two photos and photographic collages that together illustrate many aspects of life (birth, friendship, career, death, etc.).

The typed texts of the interviews were screened for anything that could contain a value. In this qualitative phase, 1,371 descriptions of values were found. These were merged into 160 values, which were then presented to a panel of 2,400 consumers in order to determine the distances between the values. Factor analysis was carried out on these distances, producing six dimensions that, in a general sense, lend themselves well to interpretation as basic values.

A striking phenomenon that this study reveals is that all the dimensions have the same contrast in them, albeit in different ways. What the factors have in common is a recurring element of freedom against binding, or restriction, although the object of the binding differs according to the factor. The binding in factor 1 is social relations (even though wanting to perform can obviously be seen as binding), in factor 2 fellow human beings, in factor 3 society, in factor 4 security, in factor 5 family life, and in factor 6 approval of others.

The interpretation of the dimensions corresponds more or less with the idea behind the model of Vinson et al. (1997) and with the laddering theory—values are attachments to very global objects such as "the other," "family," "homeland"—that become gradually more specific as the object they apply to becomes more concrete and less global. The contrast, the absence of such a binding, is a value too—the absence of family, for example, connects to homeland and conformism, as well as freedom. Table 9.3 presents an overview of the dimensions linked to the most characteristic values discovered in the SWOCC Value Inventory study.

Table 9.3

Dimensions Based on the SWOCC Value Inventory

Factor	1 Relations oriented	2 Socially oriented	3 Tradition oriented	4 Safety	5 Family life	6 To be conformistic
Bonding	To cuddle	To listen to someone	Patriotism	Neatness	To be a mother	To look well-groomed
	Friendship	To be understanding	To be distinguished	To be rich	To have children	To be attractive
	Love	To be helpful	Pride	To be clean	To cuddle	To have prestige
	Coziness	To be responsible	To be sturdy	Safety	To look after	Neatness
	A good atmosphere	To have knowledge of human character	To be attractive	Rest	To spoil	To be distinguished
	To do things for others	To be considerate with someone	To be immortal	Luxury	To have a partner	To have authority
Freedom	To be self-opinionated	To look well-groomed	Expertise	Tension (desired)	To lack for nothing	To be thrifty
	To be tenacious	To have sexual intercourse	To have fun	To be sturdy	To be independent	To be alone (voluntarily)
	To go your own way	To get a kick	To solve (something)	To be broad-minded	Simplicity	To have a place of your own
	Expertise	To have fun	To be creative	Humor	To be not jealous	Freedom
	To achieve	To relax	To be active	To be a hero	Humor	To be idealistic
	To have ambitions		To relax	To have an opinion of your own	To be content	To protect
Factor	Achievement oriented	Individually oriented	Contemporary oriented	Challenge	Freedom	To go your own way

Source: SWOCC, Sikkel and Oppenhuisen (1998a).

Table 9.4

Main Dimensions From Different Values Research Methods

Research	1. Dimension	2. Dimension
VALS	Modern/Traditional	Action-oriented/Principle-oriented
RISC	Openness/Resistance to change	Ethics/Hedonism
CCA	Change/Stability	Material/Spiritual works
Grunert/Schwartz	Openness to change/Conservation	Self-enhancement/Self-transcendence
Valuescope	Change to Modernity/Stability	Pragmatism/Loyalty
		Materialism/Humanism
Kompas	Modern/Traditional	Individually oriented/Socially oriented
Danish attitudes	Modern/Traditional	Individuality/Collectivity
Minerva	Modern/Traditional	Social/Individual

Source: Hansen (1998).

The first three dimensions from the SWOCC Value Inventory can be compared with those found in other values research such as the Schwartz inventory. Factor analysis on value distances, however, produced another three dimensions that supplement the existing three that were found in other research. The six dimensions are all different. This means that many of the dimensions available are there in order to differentiate products and brands.

People thus vary with regard to the importance they give to various values. It is very important to realize that every two-dimensional representation of value systems is a (necessary) simplification of reality. A person is a complex, multidimensional, contradictory being. Someone can be very social in one situation yet introverted in another. It would also be useful to relate the interpretation of value research to the context within which the values are evaluated by respondents.

The Structure of Value Relations

In Figure 9.4, Schwartz's ten basic values are organized along two bipolar dimensions (Schwartz 2003a, 2006a). One dimension contrasts *openness to change* and *conservation* values. This dimension captures the conflict between values that emphasize independence of thought, action, and feeling and readiness for change (self-direction, stimulation) and values that emphasize order, self-restriction, preservation of the past, and resistance to change (security, conformity, tradition). The second dimension contrasts *self-enhancement* and *self-transcendence* values. This dimension captures the conflict between values that emphasize concern for the welfare and interests of others (universalism, benevolence) and values that emphasize pursuit of one's own interests and relative success and dominance over others (power, achievement). Hedonism shares elements of both openness to change and self-enhancement.

The circular arrangement of the values represents a motivational continuum. The closer any two values in either direction around the circle, the more similar their underlying motivations; the more distant, the more antagonistic their motivations.

Comparative research, for example, into methods of value research in the international marketing world by Hansen and Kvaerk (1998) also has found that two dimensions—modern versus traditional—consistently emerge (see Table 9.4), plus another dimension that represents the tension between individual orientation and a society orientation. Only the Valuescope research method expresses these values as three dimensions, splitting the individual/society dimension into two: pragmatism/loyalty and materialism/humanism.

Trade-Offs Between Opposing Values

Schwartz (2003a, 2006a) found that his circular structure of relations among values (Figure 9.4) emerges across countries and measurement instruments. People everywhere experience conflict between pursuing openness to change values and conservation values. They also experience conflict between pursuing self-transcendence and self-enhancement values. Almost any behavior has positive implications for expressing, upholding, or attaining some values, but negative implications for the values across the circle in opposing positions.

Behavior is a result of trade-offs among competing values. To understand the impact of values on behavior, people have to consider the influence of the values that promote the behavior and also those that will be harmed by the behavior. The probability of a behavior depends on the relative priority a person gives to the relevant, competing values.

CONSUMER VALUES AND BRAND CHOICES

The premise in this chapter is that values affect to some degree and in some way consumer choices. This is most apparent in the cause marketing and mission marketing programs that link brands with good causes, such as The Body Shop's support of sourcing from subsistence farmers as a matter of business ethics.

In another example, one that illustrates the power of a storyline to convey values, Gillette, which we discussed in Chapter 4, linked up with the WB television network in the broadcast of the final episode of the teenage-oriented program *Dawson's Creek*. The story encouraged teens who are living with a female family member who has been diagnosed with cancer to seek emotional help. Gillette, of course, wants to reach young people who are forming loyalties around razors and shaving products, but it also took this opportunity to align itself with organizations that help women fight cancer, particularly breast cancer, recognizing that this is an issue that affects everyone in the family (Elliott 2003).

The point is that, as William Band (1991) points out in *Creating Value for Customers*, without value there is no business and without value there is no reason for customers to choose one brand over the large number of competitors crowding the marketplace. Value creation, however, is not a project undertaken in isolation. As Band explains, integrated change is difficult because different parts of the firm have different keys to product improvement, customer satisfaction, quality management, and integrated communication. A shared brand vision is required, one that recognizes that customer value is the goal of all these new models and philosophies of business.

Principle: Without value there is no reason for customers to choose your brand over competitors.

Consumer Value Levels

Various consumer behavior researchers have distinguished three levels within the value system of a consumer: general values, domain-specific values, and product attributes as values. General values can influence or even determine the whole life of a person. These values are so strong that they can affect domain-specific and product-related values. Domain-specific values are related only to a certain consumption domain and are described in terms of this domain. Product attri-

Figure 9.5   **Three Groups of Values**

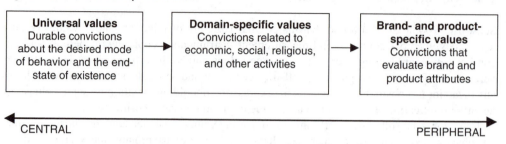

Source: Based on Vinson et al. (1997).

butes are related only to the product category and are visible mainly in the form of a consumer's expectations of certain attributes of products and brands that may be available or unavailable in the market (Franzen and Bouwman 2001).

Vinson et al. (1997) assume a hierarchical link between values at a high general level that could influence more domain-specific values, and these would in turn lead to peripheral values through which aspects like product attributes are evaluated. They define values as centrally held cognitive elements that stimulate motivation for behavioral response, existing in an interconnected hierarchical structure in which global values are related and connected to generalized consumption-related values that are, in turn, similarly associated with product attributes. The researchers also distinguish three groups of values (see Figure 9.5):

1. *Universal values:* These form the core of a person's value system. They are elementary values that determine actions and evaluations in all kinds of situations. They are also called end values or central values.
2. *Domain-specific values:* These values are acquired by a person through experience in specific situations or certain activities. Behavior can be understood or accurately predicted only in the context of specific surroundings. Economic values, for example, are learned through economic transactions, social values by relating to family and friends, consumption values by consuming, and so on.
3. *Product-specific values:* These values are the least abstract but also the most superficial. They are the preferred attributes, which are used, among other things, to form an opinion about brands or products. For example, further into this chapter it will become clear that newspapers are sold based on their specific attributes.

Means-End Chains and Consumer Choices

On a more theoretical level, Gutman (1982) believes that the classification of Vinson et al. fails to indicate how the values of the various levels can be linked to the evaluation of brand and product attributes. He believes that the linking of choice behavior to values can be seen as a means-end chain, in which brands or products are seen as means through which the consumer wants to reach end values. Gutman defines a means-end chain as a model that seeks to explain how the selection of a product or service (brand) facilitates the achievement of desired end-states; such a model consists of elements that represent the major consumer processes that link values to behavior. Gutman's means-end chain model is based on four assumptions:

- Universal values (end-states) play a dominant role in choice processes.
- People must choose from an enormous availability of brands and products, so they group them to make their choice easier.
- Everything the consumer does has consequences (physical, mental, social, or financial).
- Consumers learn to combine certain consequences with certain choices.

The means-end chain allows us to look not only at the large goals that a consumer has in his life, but also at how goals influence choices in very specific situations, like the choice of a brand of beer, car, or housing community. These are derived goals, which are often quite specific and detailed. The most important aspect of the model is that the choice that the consumer makes produces the desired consequences (benefits) and excludes the undesired consequences (disadvantages) as much as possible.

For example, at Ladera Ranch, a large housing development in California that has grown into a community of more than 16,000 people, different villages are tailored to what the developers call "values subcultures." For the conservative-minded "Traditionalists," Covenant Hills provides homes with big classic architecture and big family rooms. For the green, soul-searching "Cultural Creatives," developers built Teramor, with houses that boast of green building technologies. The marketing head explains, "A community is a collection of symbols and images," and at Ladera Ranch these symbols and images are matched to values people use as lenses through which to see the world (McCrummen 2006).

According to this theory, consumers choose products and brands because they assume, consciously or otherwise, that the specific attribute of the product or brand can help them reach their desired end values via the benefits or consequences of its use (Gutman 1982; Reynolds and Gutman 1984). Figure 9.6 shows a diagram of this theory. The following should be remarked:

- *Concrete attributes* are the characteristics perceived through the senses (tactile, visual, functional, taste, and smell attributes) of the brand or product—for example, having a car with four-wheel drive.
- *Abstract attributes* are the summary of the former in abstract, inclusive meanings; with cars, these would be "family cars," "sports cars," and so on.
- *Consequences* refer to what the brand or product does for or gives the consumer at a functional, mental, or social level. For example, four-wheel drive may make a consumer feel safe. Positive consequences are known as advantages.
- *Values* are the intangible results of a higher order that relate to the cognitive images of the most basal and fundamental needs and goals of the consumer (G. Hofstede 1991), like acquiring prestige. There is a difference between end values and personality ideals.

Research into means-end hierarchies takes place with what is known as laddering technique, in which people are continuously asked why they find an attribute given to a brand important and why they consider the chosen answer to be important, and so on, until the person cannot give any more answers to the "why" question. This way, the association process is steered into increasingly higher and more abstract levels of meaning. The technique is regularly used in market research to discover the underlying motivations upon which the purchasing of products and brands is based.

Mark and Pearson (2001) compare the technique with the behavior of a three-year-old, as the idea of going "up the ladder" is as elementary as the behavior of a three-year-old. Any parent would recognize the following routine:

Figure 9.6   **The Means-End Chain**

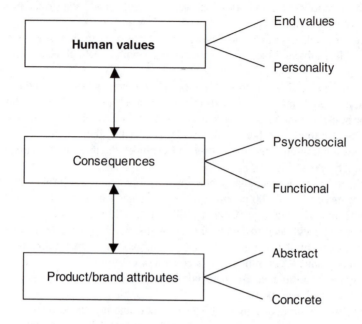

Parent: It's time to go to bed.
Three-year-old: Why?
Parent: Because it's eight o'clock and you need sleep.
Three-year-old: Why?
Parent: So you can grow to be big and strong.
Three-year-old: Why?
Parent: So you can play for the Yankees and get rich!

The three-year-old has just laddered the parent from attributes to benefits to revealing the parent's ruling values. This type of analysis is equally useful in exposing the values associated with brands and how they contribute to brand strength.

Brand Values and Brand Essence

In addition to classifications, the functional values are also important. The strength of a brand is partly determined by the degree to which it represents values that the consumer is looking for in the corresponding product or service. As Naumann (1995) says, a strong brand is a product that conveys to customers value that they desire.

Principle: A strong brand is a product that conveys to customers value that they desire.

Brands are evaluated by consumers partly on the basis of a number of category-typifying attributes. Brands that best represent attributes (those having the strongest associative link with these meanings) are seen by consumers as prototype brands. Mark and Pearson (2001) call them archetypal brands: these are the brands that represent the deeper essence—the core concept—of the product category (see Chapter 5). Mark and Pearson believe that every contemporary category that has stood the test of time has an antecedent from the preindustrial age that reveals its true, deep meaning, purpose, or function. Before cars, we had horses and donkeys; before washing machines, streambeds; before television, radios; and before radios, criers in the street.

Understanding the original purpose or function of a product in the life of an individual or civilization gets us closer to its primal meaning, as well as the identification of its critical values. Furthermore, "branding" the primal meaning and claiming it as your own gets your brand closer to market dominance. This is because category meaning is like a strong tailwind or current. It is not the engine of the brand, as is relevant differentiation, but it can be the force that accelerates the brand's power and increases its momentum. This idea goes far beyond the old concept of owning the category benefit, which ordinarily was perceived in objective, functional terms. Archetypal brands instead come to represent the meaning beneath the benefit—the wind beneath the wings of a brand.

With the help of the laddering technique, we can investigate to what degree the brands in the corresponding (product) category best represent the values of that category. Such research consists of the following phases, which can themselves be seen as a form of strategic laddering:

1. *Defining* the (product) category.
2. *Exposing* the deeper essence of the defined (product) category.
3. *Determining* which brands are the competitors within the defined category.
4. *Examining* the hierarchical meaning structures of these brands.
5. *Determining* which of the brands has the strongest link with the primal meaning of the category, the category essence.

Compared to the other brands within the category, the mental scheme of prototypal or archetypical brands has a relatively strong associative link with the product scheme in the memory of the consumer. When an element of the product scheme is activated, chances are greater that spread of the activation will cause the prototypal brand to be the first to emerge into consciousness.

BRAND VALUES AND BRAND STRATEGY DEVELOPMENT

Values like those we have been describing are attributes of people. Every person has a personal value system. Marketing and market research also use the concept of brand values, aimed at brand meanings that may or may not correspond with the values of individuals or groups. A meaning that falls together with one person's values can be irreconcilable with another person's value system. The same brand meaning can thus represent a value and an antivalue. It is more helpful, therefore, to use the concept of valued brand meanings.

Brand values research asks which brand meanings are seen as brand values by (groups of) consumers, and whether and with which personal values they go together. We will elucidate the attributes of brands, on the basis of which consumers evaluate brands as to the degree to which they are compatible with their personal value system.

Brand Evaluation

We assume that values serve as choice criteria for consumer decisions. Consciously and unconsciously, people test product and brand values against their own value system to see if they fit. Human values—the choice criteria—have been explained extensively.

When brands are evaluated on the basis of different types of brand meanings, the most important question is how values are experienced as important in a certain context by the consumer (or segment) and involved in the choice process. This can vary considerably according to category, consumer (segment), and usage moment or situation. Sometimes brands are evaluated according to the value of the products they are linked to, but it is also possible that consumers will find the symbolic meanings of the brand much more important.

In most cases, all brand meanings will play a role to a greater or lesser degree, but for insight into the primary right of existence of a brand it is important to distill the most decisive ones from the whole. These brand values form the backbone of the brand and communication strategy. For the rest, in the end, it is consumers who determine which brand meanings can be labeled as brand values. A brand meaning that is found to be irrelevant or unimportant by consumers produces no value for either the consumer or the brand. Those brand meanings that meet the core function the brand fulfills for consumers are the ones that can be characterized as the most important values for that brand.

Connection Between Personal and Brand Values

Theories of means-end chains, like those of Reynolds and Gutman (1988) and Pieters et al. (1995), are based on a hierarchical connection between the microlevel of the concrete product attributes (the means) and the macrolevel of the abstract end values (the goal). The researchers are vague, however, about how this connection is created. Hufman et al. (2000) reacted by developing a theory about target hierarchies as a basis for choice processes. They distinguish six hierarchically classified target levels:

1. *End values and life themes:* ideals with regard to personal existence. Life themes include objectives related to the development of the self, like achieving a certain position and having a circle of friends. They are linked to personal history rather than abstract end values.
2. *Life projects:* constructing and maintaining an identity and the different roles that someone fulfills in a society, such as being a good parent, a loyal employee, or a top-class athlete. They change gradually as a person goes through different life phases.
3. *Current interests:* short-term activities, tasks, or explorations a person wants to participate in. They are time- and situation-dependent: people see them as something that needs to happen—for example, following a course, going on vacation, writing a journal. They have the character of personal projects that people want to do.
4. *Consumption intentions:* the need and longing of a person for a specific consumption experience—digital photography, drinking special wines, eating out at a special restaurant, celebrating certain life events, and so on.
5. *Sought product advantages:* corresponding to the previously discussed consequences of having and using a product or service.
6. *Attribute preferences:* the preference for specific, concrete attributes of a product or service, like air-conditioning in a car or memory capacity in a personal computer.

The strength of this theory of the hierarchy of choice is that it depicts behavior close to the lives of regular people. Hufman et al. posit that a connection does not necessarily have to be top-down;

it can equally be bottom-up. Low-level goals can lead to an implicit notion of which higher-levels goals are served. The theory leaves the possibility open that behavior may not necessarily be steered from higher-end values, but may also emanate from lower-level goals. It offers a solution for the fact that research is sometimes far from finding a connection between product and brand choices and the higher, abstract end values of consumers.

The link between high, abstract end values, peripheral values, and consequences at a brand and product level is not found in all product categories. Based on the SWOCC values inventory, Sanoma, a very large magazine publisher in the Netherlands, constructed a value-measuring instrument, the Sanoma Value Monitor. This instrument measured which values respondents associated with forty-nine magazine titles, eleven clothing stores, and six coffee brands. The personal importance the same respondents attached to the distinguished values was measured using a report mark.

A correlation larger than 0.5 with the personal value scores of the readers was found for twenty-five magazine titles; the correlation was smaller than 0.5 or even negative for the other twenty-four titles. A similar analysis for the eleven clothing stores shows that for only five did the value associations correlate by more than 0.5 with the personal values of the respondents (people who shop at those stores); for coffee brands this was the case in two out of six.

This study indicates that strong links are indeed possible between end values and, for example, magazines people subscribe to, but that this link is absent or even negative in nearly half of the titles. Applied to brand choice, values tell only part of the story at the most central, most abstract personal level. In many markets and segments, brands and products seem to be evaluated primarily on the basis of their concrete (physical, functional) attributes and the emanating consequences, without these clearly matching the end values measured. This seems to be particularly the case with many magazines. It could also be that at an individual level the ladders are so different that the resolution does not lend itself to statistical analysis.

Even if we accept the hypothesis of the hierarchical structure of brand meanings, we have to ask at which level does the hierarchy stop. Certainly not all brands and products are linked to the most central end value—happiness. The question is topical in relation to the following: What are the boundaries of an associative network of a brand? When are these boundaries surpassed? That may be difficult to determine, but marketers could at least take into account the function of products and brands in consumers' lives. The associative network of a brand and the value system can be two separate systems in the memory of consumers, with no need for a link between them. However, a successful brand will connect the two value systems in a meaningful way.

Principle: A hierarchical connection between product or brand attributes and the life ideals and associations of people is not always present.

Central Values and Evaluation Points

For brand management and communication, it is important to research the concrete goals underlying consumer evaluation of products and brands. Values tend to be expressed only verbally by brand strategists and are therefore highly abstract. To communicate values properly, it is useful to depict them visually as well, with key visuals (mood boards) combined with verbal descriptions.

The finding of points of disconnect between strategists and users suggests a need for a model of the connection between central values and the evaluation of brands and products (see Figure 9.7). The model indicates that functional and symbolic brand values are or can be evaluated inde-

Figure 9.7   **Connection Between Central Values and Evaluation of Brands**

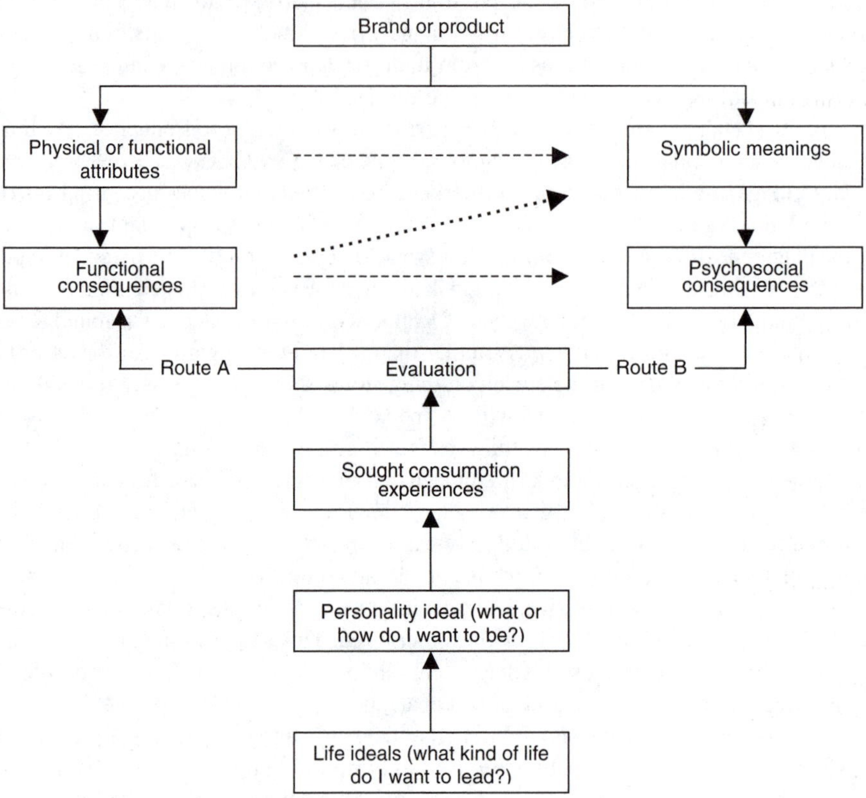

pendently. When research is oriented toward route B, as was the case with the Sanoma research, but the brand evaluation goes mainly through route A, no connection is found.

Values, Segmentation, and Positioning

Buyers are also spread over the different quadrants per product category. Segmentation and positioning research can shed light on the connections between the values of different segments and brand values, as we discussed in Chapters 7 and 8.

When evaluating alternatives, brands are evaluated one way or another on the basis of the degree to which their meanings answer to the values (choice criteria) of the consumer, compared to other brands. There is much theory on how such an evaluation process can take place. The various choice models have the following as a common point of departure: the relative importance of values, the relative knowledge of alternatives, and the perceived attributes of alternatives.

Evaluation Is Relative

Consumers make choices based on, among other things, their value system and the importance of individual values against other values. Value-based evaluation is situationally relative. Different values can be activated according to the choice situation. Consumers do not usually base their choices on one single value, nor have the mental disposition to involve many values in their evaluation process. What is generally involved is a small number of key values. The balance between product-related values and symbolic values in the choice process differs according to the product category and the person.

In order to make an evaluation, consumers usually choose from alternatives they already know and about which they have sufficient information. The relative familiarity with brands (saliency) determines which are involved in the evaluation and which are not.

The Perceived Attributes of Alternatives

Consumers evaluate alternatives against one another based on the strength (saliency) of their perceived attributes (the various elements in their association network) in relation to the relative importance of the values. In marketing and research practice, this leads to the following elementary questions and analyses:

1. Which end values, product-related values, and symbolic values play a role in the category?
2. What is the relative influence of these values? How important does the consumer consider them?
3. What is the relative familiarity of the brands?
4. By which brand associations are brands characterized? Which brand meanings are salient?
5. Which brands are being considered on the basis of their familiarity and their attributes?
6. How are the brands evaluated against each other in light of the values that are relevant in the category?
7. What is the resulting degree of preference (overall evaluation) for the various brands?
8. How can consumers be classified (segmented) into homogeneous groups on the basis of previous evaluations?
9. To what degree are the brands seen as alternatives for one another?

Such questions lead to the observation that brand attributes are reinterpreted based on the values of segments, the purchase situation, the category, the attributes of competitors, as well as the relevance of the brand's attributes and values. Such an analysis does not lead to easy predictions of brand values that connect with personal values.

> *Principle:* Values are attributes of people. A brand meaning that represents a value for one person may be an antivalue for someone else.

Brand Values Research

Every study of the choice process of consumers should begin with as wide an inventory as possible of product-related meanings and values (choice criteria) that can play a role in a category. These meanings or values should not be formulated too abstractly, but expressed as much as possible in

Table 9.5

Sporty New Car Attributes and Benefits

Attributes	Benefits
Tangible	
Removable hard-top	Like two cars in one
Short-throw, five-speed transmission	Better engine efficiency
Two seats	More fun to drive
Tonneau cover	Protects interior from weather
Rear spoiler	Gives aerodynamic performance
Headrest speakers	Improved stereo sound
Intangible	
Manufacturer known for quality	Believe car will not break down
Selected as Motor Trend Car of the Year	Makes you feel smart for buying it
Distinctive design	Everyone will look at it and envy you
Pace car at Indianapolis 500	Feel like a race-car driver
Sporty, youthful design	Recapture your youth
Looks more expensive than it is	Reward yourself without going broke

Source: Clancy et al. (1995).

product-relevant attributes and advantages. This procedure can lead to lists of 20 to 200 product-related meanings, symbolic values, and end values. An example of such an inventory can be seen in Table 9.5.

When this list becomes too extensive to be used on a large scale, it can be brought down to manageable proportions with the help of research in which a smaller quantitative sample survey is used to determine how important the respondents consider each of the items. The battery of resulting items forms the basis for large-scale measuring of choice criteria and brand perceptions. It is supplemented with measurements of brand familiarity, consideration set, brand attitudes, purchasing intentions, and brands purchased in the (recent) past. The data are subsequently analyzed in order to expose the connection between the different variables. The quality of the results is largely determined by the quality of the values and attributes list and of the final analyses carried out on the scores. Both tend to be lacking to a high degree. Chapter 8 provides a closer look at the analysis methods.

An important strategy consideration is the relative weight allocated to the product-related values as opposed to the symbolic values. In Chapter 13, which discusses brand strength, we will show that a great deal of importance must be attached to associations between the brand and the products or product categories it is linked to. Brand communication must pay particular attention to these associations when there are innovations: when new products are brought out or existing ones are improved under a brand name. Even with brands that are linked to products that are consistent throughout time, like Coca-Cola, Heineken beer, and Nivea skin lotion, it is important to keep supporting product perceptions.

Principle: The preference for brands is almost always based on a varying combination of product-related and symbolic meanings.

BRAND STRATEGY AND BRAND COMMUNICATION IMPLICATIONS

In Chapter 2 we distinguished four important groups of brand values: product-related values, added symbolic values, purchasing behavior values, and relationship values. The purchasing behavior values and relationship values emanate from the functions a brand can have during the purchase of a brand article (e.g., simplification) and the need to have relationships and continuity (e.g., appreciation support). They tend to be expressed in the longer term and can lead to automated purchasing behavior and a high degree of brand loyalty.

Still, for each new brand that consumers learn about and each new or renewed product choice they make, a brand is evaluated mainly on the basis of the first two value groups: product-related brand values and symbolic brand values. There are seven product-related brand values: functional, social, epistemological, aesthetic, hedonistic, conditional, and holistic. The four symbolic brand values are brand "values," brand personality, user image, and brand emotions.

The first group represents all the attributes that are inherent to the product the brand is linked to and the functional consequences that stem from it. These are issues like quality, reliability, user friendliness, aesthetic experiences, and sensory experiences. The second group represents the psychosocial (symbolic) meanings connected to the brand. These brand associations can be the result of the attributes of the products that are brought into the market under the brand, but which in the course of time have generally become direct brand meanings.

Although with most established brands there is a historical connection, product-related and symbolic values are essentially independent. According to the "concepting vision"(Rijkenberg 1998), they can even be disconnected completely. Supporters of this vision contend that the symbolic meanings of a brand can be developed independently of the product and are more important for consumers than the product attributes. They believe that marketing from product attributes does not work anymore because society has shifted from materialism to "mentalism." Consumers are allegedly saturated in the physical sphere and are therefore more likely to look for mental riches (Rijkenberg 1998). Right now it is difficult to say whether the future will have brands that are completely unconnected to products.

In Chapter 13 we will show how successful brand introductions for the period 1999 to 2000 in the fast-moving consumer goods channel in the Netherlands can be traced back to product innovations. Most existing brands have always been linked to certain product categories. The product-brand link is usually strong and product meanings are an important part of brand representation. Regardless of whether it is desirable, in practice it will be very difficult for these brands to release themselves from their product-related associations, thanks to the unchangeability of the brand representation—what is already in memory is there permanently.

Most brands exist by the grace of the synergy between product and product-related values and symbolism (symbolic values). Consumers seldom base their choice on only one of the two value dimensions. There is almost always a combination of the two dimensions—product values and symbolism—in a brand representation. On the basis of these two groups, choice processes and brand meanings can be put into a matrix, as shown in Figure 9.8.

In quadrant 1 we have the choice situation in which product-related as well as symbolic values (brand values) are important. Brands that are positioned in this quadrant are associated with high-standing product attributes and are also evaluated largely on the basis of their symbolic values. Brands that exemplify this position are Audi, Nike, Nokia, and Swatch.

Quadrant 2 includes choice processes and brands that are very much driven by symbolic values and in which product-related values have a subordinate meaning. Examples can generally be found in categories that are socially visible but present few observable differences at a product level—for example, Heineken, Marlboro, and Perrier.

Figure 9.8   **Matrix of Choice Processes and Brand Meanings**

Instrumental values and meanings	High	Quadrant 3: instrumental values	Quadrant 1: instrumental and symbolic brand values
	Low	Quadrant 4: commodity values	Quadrant 2: symbolic brand values
		Low	High

Symbolic brand values and meanings

In quadrant 3 product values are predominant. These brands (and products) have no important symbolic function (not yet, anyway). Many new "digital" brands, such Google, Amazon, Compaq, and Vodaphone, fall into this category.

Quadrant 4 is the quadrant of commodities (basic products), which have hardly any symbolic function and in which product differentiation is only possible to a very limited degree. It is the quadrant in which private labels, like Dannon yogurt, Kleenex tissues, and Doritos tortilla chips, reach high market shares (Chernatony and McDonald 1994).

It is important to realize that symbolic brand function is not the same as symbolic brand association. Many brands are associated with symbolic meanings but have no symbolic function. In these brands, the symbolic associations probably have little influence on the choice and purchasing behavior of consumers. The associations are there, but are not part of the attributes on which consumers evaluate the brand. They are not relevant to the function that consumers allocate to the brand—i.e., the yellow in Yellow Pages. Brands have a symbolic function when they are chosen, purchased, and used primarily to express the consumer's identity.

Consumer and Brand Values in Brand Strategy Development

Values are cultural in that they are learned early in life. They address issues of what is good and what is not. They determine what we expect of people, as well as the products we buy and use. A manager must ask to what degree the brand's values are cultural and how are they learned.

Consumers' value systems are largely influential in the way people see and define themselves in relation to the world that surrounds them. Brands acquire strength as their primal or functional meanings connect with the category and, ultimately, the consumer's value system. But how does that happen?

Brands derive their value(s) from the brand meanings that are experienced as relevant by consumers in the degree to which the brands fulfill their needs. These values steer the communication and, ideally, the behavior of the brand as well. Values are expressed best in brand stories that resonate with consumers. Values speak to specific consumer needs, motivate behavior, and influence choice processes. Values affect product choices by establishing personal goals and benefits that a consumer expects a product to meet.

PEPSI AND BRAND VALUES

The Pepsi story illustrates how a position and segmentation strategy can be merged through an understanding of how a product's values connect with consumer values. Coke dominated the cola market with its tradition and history as "the real thing" and its iconic value as a symbol of Americana. Unable to compete directly against this global powerhouse, Pepsi identified a new position in the 1960s that resonated with the values of a younger population who, incidentally, are the biggest purchasers of soft drinks. "The Pepsi Generation" proclaimed the values of young people and, in so doing, also repositioned Coke as a traditional, old-fashioned product that, in comparison to Pepsi, only appealed to older people.

The new campaign successfully repositioned the competition at the same time that it staked out a preemptive claim to a target market that represented the greatest growth opportunity. Pepsi's advertising since then has continued to celebrate the values and lifestyles of young people.

NOTE

1. This chapter's overview on the values literature is based on the dissertation of Dr. Joke Oppenhuisen.

BRAND PERSONALITY

Previous chapters have explored the nature of brand meaning as it relates to consumer values, associations, and the mental idea of a brand, which we refer to as the brand image. In this chapter we will discuss the meaning of the concept of personality and how it becomes part of the meaning structure of a brand, as the Volkswagen Beetle story illustrates.

Although everyone knows intuitively what brand personality means in general terms, understanding the construct becomes more difficult when it comes to the exact difference between brand personality and related concepts. For this reason, this chapter will discuss the differences between brand personality and brand image, brand identity, brand values, and user self-image. In addition to identifying the boundaries of the concept, the process of brand personality perception is examined and the different dimensions of brand personality are considered.

VOLKSWAGEN BEETLE: THE ERA OF THE INNOCENT

Perhaps one of the best contemporary illustrations of brand personality is the Volkswagen Beetle, both in its early life in the United States in the 1960s and in its recent reincarnation forty years later. The 1960s counterculture brought an interesting dilemma to the theater of automotive marketing. Cars, especially the big living-room-on-wheels variety of the postwar generation, represented all that the children of the decade rejected: excessive comfort, overt appeals to status, elaborate swept-back fins, an abundance of chrome and other forms of excessive ornamentation, and high rates of fuel consumption. Yet they valued mobility, and hitchhiking could get them only so far. So how were they to live without a car in such a culture?

The answer for the lost souls of the 1960s came in the form of a little car called the Volkswagen Beetle, or "bug," which spoke directly to the counterculture instincts of its American users because it was the exact opposite of everything that Detroit and the mainstream car-buying public represented. The car was tiny by then-Detroit standards, and its lines were so round that it was almost cuddly. It had no frills or fins of any kind. It was wonderfully fuel-efficient. It was cheap to buy, easy to fix, and seemed to run forever. And its style never changed.

It was an innocent in an era of excess. The brilliant advertising of Bill Bernbach (one of the founders of the Doyle Dane and Bernbach advertising agency) positioned this new "anticar" in ways that captured its unique spirit and delivered on the innocence principle in every way. His clever, humorous, award-winning commercials showed the innocent bug outwitting the gas-guzzlers: Little David getting the better of big Goliath. With headlines such as "Lemon" and "Ugly is only skin-deep," the self-deprecating humor helped make the Beetle a huge marketing success story. Some commentators even equated its unpresuming innocence stance to the appeal of Charlie Chaplin's "everyman" character. And the Beetle's starring role as Herbie in the sitcom *The Love Bug* define its personality even more clearly.

Today, we look at the highly successful reincarnated version of the Beetle and want to smile. We may not know exactly why, but we feel that it would be really great to own and drive one. And we celebrate the 1960s spirit symbolized by the flower vase on the dashboard. The new Beetle, like the original, has a personality that many find enchanting. For an inexplicable reason, we are attracted to its bright, bold colors, like those on the color chart we first saw in kindergarten. As consumers, what we intuit but sometimes cannot express is our delight that the personality of innocence has been resurrected in such a clever new way.

How can this wholehearted expression of a relevant and, in its time, highly differentiating brand personality be compared with that of some other product upon which an archetypal identity has simply been grafted? The answer lies in the annals of marketing history. The best archetypal brands, such as the Beetle, are first and foremost iconic products, created to fulfill and embody fundamental human needs. The Beetle expresses a common archetype in its reference to the David and Goliath story and to Chaplin's everyman. That archetype found its expression in a quiet revolution of counterculture design. And this expression is manifest in or, rather, defines the personality of the brand—what sometimes is referred to as the brand's soul, aura, or essence.

Sources: Adapted from Mark and Pearson (2001); S. Brown et al. (2003).

BRANDS AND PERSONALITY

The personification of brands appeals to our imagination. The brand-as-person metaphor also makes understanding these invisible, abstract mental constructions easier and more fun. Countless human concepts have entered the world of brands through personification—identity, personality, charisma, relationship, trust, integrity, birth, death, soul, awareness, and even karma and reincarnation. All these concepts come together to create a brand personality. They also make brands and working with brands literally more alive. Although a brand is not a person but a man-made artifact—a psychological construction—the comparison with dimensions of human life is embraced everywhere. Brand personality is something everyone talks about, but what are we really talking about?

When concepts like personality are applied to people, the interpretation of such concepts is highly subjective. Although there is a general idea of what the concept means, any attempt to define the exact content gets inevitably bogged down in a psychophilosophical discussion. The same occurs with the interpretation of these concepts in relationship to brands. The same terms are often explained in ten different ways.

In most cases, the definitions of brand personality are superficial. In practice, the concept is often used synonymously with brand image or brand identity, and the difference remains blurred. The substantive meaning is also unclear: are brand values also part of the brand personality? In most literature, the emphasis lies with the tactical effects of brand personality. Its strategic effects are hardly ever discussed, and a relationship with other basic concepts like brand concept, brand positioning, or brand function is almost never established.

Brand personality seems to be an orphan child in scientific research too. An exception is the work of Jennifer Aaker who in 1997 carried out fundamental research in this field in an attempt to develop a valid and reliable measuring instrument to map out brand personality. Her research produced the Brand Personality Scale, a measuring instrument with five basic dimensions that can be used to describe the personality of brands, at least in the United States.

Despite Aaker's work, there is still a great deal of terrain to be explored regarding brand personality. The following questions will be discussed in this chapter:

- What is brand personality?
- How does brand personality work?
- What are the building stones of brand personality strategy?
- How does one research brand personality?

Before dealing with these questions, we first will look at the root of the concept of brand personality—that is, the science of human personality. Since it would be impossible to reveal all the secrets of human personality, as discussed by countless philosophers and psychologists, we will limit ourselves to several key aspects that are relevant to the comparison between a brand and a person. The most important aspects that will be discussed in the following sections are diversity, recognizability, predictability, consistency (stability), and differentiation (flexibility). All these concepts of human personality are also related to brands.

WHAT IS PERSONALITY?

The concept of brand personality is borrowed from the psychological theory of human personality. People have personalities and personality has been studied for centuries. Not that we have gotten too far with it—human personality remains a constant puzzle.

The concept of personality is quite complicated, and a journey among a number of authorities in the field of personality studies does not bring much order to the complexities. The journey goes from Freud's ideas about unconscious motivation and development phases, via Jung's collective unconscious and Skinner's behaviorism, to Kelly's idea of the personality as a system of cognitive constructs. The theories and ideas on personality that have been formulated since Aristotle can be classified into eight basic movements: psychoanalysis, the neopsychological approach, modern psychoanalysis, behavioral and learning theories, dispositional theories, humanistic and existential theories, cognitive theories, and non-Western approaches.

Despite the lack of scientific consensus about what personality means and how it develops, we can confidently say that it has something to do with the way individuals differ. This basic premise is found in nearly all theories of personality. Personality is related to the way people differ from each other with regard to their inner attributes, as well as their behavior. It has to do with individual variations from person to person, and it is experienced from the inside by the persons themselves and from the outside (for instance, through behavior) by those around the person. Although people usually do not deal with it consciously, they realize that they have certain consistent characteristic traits and that their behavior has a particular singularity. Thanks to this singularity, people recognize themselves and are recognized by other people around them.

Scroggs (1994) posits that personality is that part of the individual that is unchangeable and durable. This does not mean that a person cannot change, but when important changes take place in a person's character, we have to say that the personality has changed too. For this reason, he claims that any adequate definition of personality must point in some way toward consistency, thus making a person predictable for others and giving that person the feeling of being one and distinct, of forming an integrated, ordered, and stable whole person. Scroggs emphasizes consistency, predictability, integration, order, stability, and controlled behavior as the features of personality. He even links "predictable and controlled behavior" to mental health, claiming that without this consistency people would become unpredictable and disintegrated and thus unrecognizable to themselves and others.

> *Principle:* Personality is about the durable, consistent, characteristic inner traits of a person and the singularity and predictability of behavior that makes the person different from others. Personality makes every individual unique and recognizable.

Personality Attribution Cues

Lippa (1994) asks you to imagine a world in which you do not form an impression of the people we see, which would be the same as imagining a world in which your heart does not beat. He states that perceptions of people—the process through which you form a judgment about someone else's character traits—form an integral part of daily life.

From job interviews to your most routine interactions with people, the way you see others influences what you feel about them and how you behave toward them. The assigning of traits is known as personality attribution. It is one of the mechanisms the brain uses to manage your social environment. In this way you determine your position and attitude in relation to other people in your surroundings, and these instantaneous personality evaluations steer your behavior.

When you meet someone for the first time, you form an image of that person—nice or moody, pleasant or obnoxious, cool, distant, calculating. In others words, as soon as you meet, you relate to someone. But how does this come about? Is it a result of objective, observable information that you gather? You do see how old the person is, how tall or short, thin or heavy, and hair and clothing signals: you can observe this physical identity—six feet tall, wavy brown hair, and so on. This is the way you relate to people—and brands—as a result of objective, observable information.

People tend to think of the self in the singular, yet there are strong arguments against this position of singular conceptualization of the self (Gergen 1991). For one, if people are asked to describe themselves, they will typically use a large number of different concepts that may have little or no relationship to each other. Former president Lyndon Johnson once described himself as "a free man, an American, a United States Senator, a Democrat, a liberal, a conservative, a Texan, a taxpayer, a rancher," and "not as young as I used to be nor as old as I expect to be." Gergen says that the assumption of a single or global concept of self seems misleading: rather than speaking of the self, self-concept, or self-image, it is much more productive to speak of multilayered self-concepts.

Consistency and Flexibility

Is human personality consistent and unchangeable? Is the absence of these features a sign of mental unhealthiness? How much flexibility can the personality of mentally healthy people present? According to Antonides and Van Raaij (1994), people have a fixed repertoire of character traits on which they continue to draw. Depending on the social context in which they find themselves and the social roles they assume, specific character traits become visible that can remain invisible in other situations.

We could say that personality is internally stable or consistent but manifests itself in different ways depending on the context. The same person can therefore behave differently in different social situations. For example, someone can be very shy and subdued in the company of strangers, but exuberant and extroverted among good friends. To make any statement about personality, it is therefore useful to take into consideration the social context involved. This may also be true for brands, since communication that reflects a brand personality may vary with the situation. The messages sent to partners in the distribution chain may be different in tone and style from the messages sent to customers.

Interaction With Social Environment

One of the reasons people never succeed 100 percent in going through life as stable, consistent, integrated, and predictable beings is that they are constantly interacting with their environment. People do not function as separate, isolated units, but as part of a social context—not a single context either, but a concatenation of interchanging contexts in which a person plays different social roles. One person can be simultaneously mother and daughter as well as colleague, friend, patient, tennis player, and treasurer of the bridge club. In all those different situations, different parts of the personality can be manifest.

Research confirms that there is an interaction between individual personality traits and situations (Lippa 1994). This flexibility makes it possible for people to hold their own in different social situations. People vary not only as far as their character traits are concerned, but also especially in the way these character traits interact with the social situations in which they find themselves. This individual way of reacting to a situation is a dimension of personality.

In sum, we can state that personality is not an isolated and uniform phenomenon, but one that interacts with the situation in which people find themselves. Personality stability provides integrity. Variation in the way the personality manifests itself in various social situations, however, provides flexibility, growth, and adaptation.

> *Principle:* Individual personality traits interact with the social situations in which people find themselves. The individual way of reacting to a situation is characteristic of the personality.

Interaction With Objects

People interact not only with other people, but also with objects. Just as relations between people are the result of perceived personality characteristics, the personality characteristics of products and brands seem to influence the relations between consumers and products or brands.

Where does the "soul" of brands and products come from? It should be clear that objects do not have inner or internal dynamics. The dynamics of the soul and personality that objects, products, and brands obtain are assigned to them by people. According to Cary (2000), people's mental operations are designed so that they gather insight into other people and animals—and inanimate objects such as brands—with a mind and a personality. People consequently attribute a personality to all living entities. Cary goes on to quote the gestalt psychologists Fritz Heider and Thomas Simmerl, who pointed out in 1944 that people even allocate personality traits to moving triangles and rectangles in simple animated movies. In psychology this is known as projection. Observers project an internal dynamic onto the object, which enables them to determine their relation to the object—it is how people have always animated the world around them.

This phenomenon forms the basis of the brand personality concept. According to Cary (2000), because we attribute personality to brands we can have a relationship with that personality, and our tendency is to develop emotional relationships with brands, acting as though they were living entities.

> *Principle:* Brand personality is a projection of human traits onto a brand, through which people can determine their relationship toward that brand and can maintain a relationship with it.

Personality Profiling

Throughout the centuries, scientists have tried to classify people according to their personality traits. This has resulted in different categorizations associated with the different theories. Five basic personality dimensions were developed from dispositional or traits theory. For each dimension, both high-scoring and low-scoring traits were defined:

1. *Extroversion*—High-scoring: talkative, active, assertive, energetic, outgoing, outspoken. Low-scoring: quiet, reserved, shy, silent, withdrawn, retiring.
2. *Agreeableness*—High-scoring: sympathetic, kind, appreciative, affectionate, softhearted, warm. Low-scoring: faultfinding, cold, unfriendly, quarrelsome, hard-hearted, unkind.
3. *Conscientiousness*—High-scoring: organized, thorough, efficient, responsible, reliable. Low-scoring: careless, disorderly, frivolous, irresponsible, forgetful.
4. *Emotional stability*—High-scoring: stable, calm, contented, unemotional. Low scoring: tense, anxious, nervous, moody, worried, and touchy.

5. *Openness*—High-scoring: wide interests, imaginative, intelligent, original, insightful, curious. Low-scoring: commonplace, simple, shallow, unintelligent.

Key Factors in Personality Theory

As we have shown, answers to the questions on personality vary, depending on the theoretical movement within which the concept is described. There is no single answer—there are many. Which answers are "true" is a personal issue. Still, some aspects can be seen in nearly all theories of personality:

- *Individuality:* Personality is that which distinguishes one person from another.
- *Singularity:* Personality makes an individual unique.
- *Durability:* Personality is unchangeable and durable.
- *Personality concerns:* Personality involves characteristic inner traits and characteristic behavior (consistent behavioral pattern).
- *Internal:* Personality is experienced from the inside by the person.
- *External:* Personality is regarded from the outside by others.
- *Social:* Personality plays an important role in the social process (mutual coordination between people).
- *Context:* The social role triggers the manifestation of specific personality traits.

In short, personality is something that distinguishes an individual from others—in the case of humans, from 6 billion others. Personality makes every individual unique and recognizable. Naturally, a phenomenon with such a strong distinguishing power catches the imagination in a world that revolves around being distinctive, as is the case with the world of brands.

Principle: Personality is what distinguishes one person from another. It makes every individual unique and recognizable.

WHAT IS BRAND PERSONALITY?

Sony, a finalist in the 2003 Account Planning Group (APG) Awards (APG 2003), was described as being dogged by a personality problem, one uncovered in international research by its agency, Fallon. The problem was described in a planning document as a "humanity gap." In other words, Sony is well known and has respect, but little affection. Fallon's strategy was to try to close the gap by communicating that Sony and its customers need each other in order to achieve their potential. The strategy statement for this new personality-focused campaign explained that "the consumer is the final component of every Sony" and specified a campaign theme: "You make it a Sony." In other words, Sony is a friend, as well as a partner.

Brand personality is named quite often in the literature on brands, but is rarely conceptualized in a meaningful manner because of confusion with brand image. Patterson (1999), in a major study of the literature on brand research for the period 1950 to 1999, concluded that insight into brand image is inhibited by weak concept development. Although brand image has been the most important focal point of brand research since the 1950s, much confusion remains over what brand image is precisely. Patterson believes that, in particular, many writers have neglected to emphasize the difference between the concepts of brand image, brand personality, and user image, as a result of which the three concepts tend to be used interchangeably.

In order to be useful for research, concepts must be clear and there has to be consensus about their meaning. Both preconditions are lacking when it comes to brand personality. The following list, adapted from work by Patterson (1999), attempts to pin down the many definitions of brand personality that are in circulation.

- A mentality, a tone of voice, and a series of values. (King 1973)
- The degree to which consumers perceive a brand as owner of various human features or character traits. (Alt and Griggs 1988)
- The way a consumer perceives a brand on aspects that have always defined human personality. (Batra et al. 1993)
- Personality consists of a unique combination of functional traits and symbolic values. (Hankinson and Cowking 1993)
- The brand personality shows the core properties of a brand, embodied, described, and experienced in human personality characteristics. (Restall and Gordon 1993)
- Brand personality embodies all the attributes of the brand, which stand out above the primary attributes and the functional objective of a brand. (Tennant 1994)
- Brand personality is a reflection of the emotional response of the consumer to a company and the product of that company. (Triplett 1994)
- The type of human traits attributed to the brand. (Blackston 1995)
- The "external image" of a brand, the tonal attributes that lie closest to human traits. (Upshaw 1995)
- The personification of a brand, which makes visible the radiation of the essential emotional character toward the consumer and especially the reaction of the consumer to it. (The Research Business 1996)
- The group of human attributes that is associated with a brand. (J. Aaker 1997)
- A metaphor for the emotional relationship between consumer and brand. (Gordon 1996)
- Human personality traits that are attributed to a brand. (Franzen and Bouwman 2001)
- The emotional response of the consumer to a brand through which brand attributes are personified and which is used in the differentiation between various purchasing options. (Patterson 1999)

The various authors' interpretations of the concept of brand personality differ in several points:

- the perspective from which brand personality is described: a marketer, brand, or consumer perspective;
- the substantive meaning of brand personality: human character traits, end values, functional attributes, and symbolic values;
- the sources of brand personality associations: product category, communication (style), user image, etc.;
- the (un)changeability of the brand personality: consistency versus flexibility and dynamics;
- the relationship between and among concepts such as brand identity and image, user image, values, etc.

Regarding these issues—all essential aspects of brand personality—different researchers' views are sometimes miles apart. A first step in the direction of clarity consists in formulating a definition that meets the following criteria:

- a clear perspective,
- clarity in relation to substantive meaning,
- distinction in relation to definitions of akin concepts,
- reference to the brand preference–related effect.

To arrive at a new definition, we will examine how brand personalities are commonly profiled, what people base their brand personality perception on, how brand personality is related to other concepts like brand identity, brand image, user image, and brand values, and from which perspectives brand personality can be observed.

Components of Brand Personality

The traits theory approach was discussed in the preceding section as the basis of most personality theory research. It was also the point of departure for a similar identification of the "Big Five" brand personalities, constructed in 1997 by Jennifer Aaker. She was the first to develop a conceptual structure that gives insight into the personality of brands in the United States. By brand personality, Aaker (1997) understands the human character traits associated with a brand. She carried out research based on the "Big Five" personality traits, a recognized list from the theory of personality. Her research led to the conclusion that brand personality also consists of five dimensions: sincerity, excitement, competence, distinction (sophistication), and ruggedness. Each dimension is made up of several factors (a total of fifteen):

1. Sincerity
   - Down-to-earth—family oriented, small-town, conventional, blue-collar, and all-American
   - Honest—sincere, real, ethical, thoughtful, caring
   - Wholesome—original, ageless, classic, old-fashioned

   Examples of brands are Kodak, Campbell's Soup, and Maxwell House coffee.

2. Excitement
   - Daring—trendy, exciting, off-beat, flashy, provocative
   - Spirited—cool, young, lively, outgoing, adventurous
   - Imaginative—unique, humorous, surprising, artistic, fun
   - Up-to-date—independent, contemporary, innovative, aggressive

   Examples of brands are Porsche, Benneton, and Absolut.

3. Competence
   - Reliable—hard-working, secure, efficient, trustworthy, careful
   - Intelligent—technical, corporate, serious
   - Successful—leader, confident, influential

   Examples of brands are IBM, American Express, and ABN AMRO.

Table 10.1

The SWOCC Personality Scale

Dimensions	Facet 1	Facet 2	Facet 3	Facet 4
Competent	Self-assured	Likeable	Precise	Solid
	Successful	Nice	Accurate	Stable
	Determined	Honest	Safe	
	Focused		Careful	
	Sure		Efficient	
Exciting	Alert	Active	Creative	
	Happy	Energetic	Inventive	
	Cheerful	Lively	Original	
		Enthusiastic		
Annoying	Unfriendly	Childish		
	Unpleasant	Silly		
Gentle	Mild-mannered, feminine, amiable			
Rugged	Rough, masculine, firm			
Distinctive	Unique, non-conformist, daring			

Source: SWOCC, Berge (2001a).

4. Distinction
   - Upper-class—glamorous, good-looking, sophisticated
   - Charming—smooth, sexy, gentle
Examples of brands are Mercedes, Revlon, and Lexus.

5. Ruggedness
   - Outdoorsy—Western, active, athletic
   - Tough—rough, strong, no-nonsense
Examples of brands are Levi's, Marlboro, and Nike.

Based on Jennifer Aaker's brand personality scale, SWOCC, the University of Amsterdam-based marketing communication research institute, developed a brand personality scale for the Dutch market (Berge 2001a). To this end, the personality characteristics of Aaker's scale were supplemented with a selection of personality characteristics that were found in previous scientific research in the Netherlands (the Brokken list).[1] This produced a list of 100 brand personality characteristics, with which the SWOCC team measured the personality of a selected group of ninety-three brands and applied factor analysis to the results. The result was seven Dutch brand personality factors that are different from the ones found by Aaker. On each of the factors SWOCC found a factor analysis was carried out again, which led to a further splitting up of three of the factors into facets. Table 10.1 gives an overview of the factors, facets, and the highest-ranking items.

A similar study carried out in Korea produced two factors, which were not comparable to the Aaker factors (Sung and Tinkham 2005). They reflected the importance of Confucian values in Korea's social systems. They were labeled "passive likableness" and "ascendancy." The first connotes warmth and gentleness and reflects the Confucian value of close human relatedness, tradition, family, and harmony. The ascendancy factor is consistent with the paternalism and authoritativeness in Korean business, requiring an employee's obedience and wholehearted loyalty.

Another study by Supphellen and Gronhaug (2003) in Russia, using Aaker's scale, also produced important differences with the American factors; the largest Russian factor turned out to be "successful and contemporary," reflecting a stereotype of the new economic upper class in Russia. The four other factors were more similar to Aaker's factors, but they also contained several different traits.

Research by J. Aaker (1997) already showed that only four of her five dimensions were found in Japan. In Spain, only three of the five found factors corresponded with the American ones (J. Aaker et al. 2001). Not one of the American dimensions was found in Germany (Bauer et al. 2001). So to a certain degree, brand personality factors seem to be culture-dependent.

We have reviewed a number of studies into the constructs of brand personality. By comparing and compiling these efforts, we have created a list of personality constructs that can be considered in brand strategy development. This compilation identifies key constructs, as well as other terms used to characterize that type of personality. This is not a comprehensive list, but it does represent the key personality characteristics that have been observed in brand personality research and should provide brand researchers and managers with relevant adjective descriptors to use in articulating the desired personality of their brands.

Exciting	• Energetic—spirited, young, outgoing, active, lively, enthusiastic, extraverted, surprising
	• Daring—trendy, flashy, provocative, adventurous
	• Creative—imaginative, artistic
	• Distinctive—unique, nonconformist, one-of-a-kind, original
Competent	• Accomplished—influential, self-assured, successful, determined, focused, efficient, organized, responsible, assertive, solid
	• Intelligent—technical, serious, thoughtful, analytical,
Likable	• Nice—honest, friendly, fun, open, kind
	• Charming—mild-mannered, amiable, gentle, warm, agreeable, calm
Sophisticated	• Glamorous—upper-class, good-looking, wealthy
Sporty	• Rugged—athletic, outdoorsy, rough, strong
Sincere	• Genuine—down-to-earth, family-oriented, conventional, sympathetic
	• Reliable—trustworthy, careful, hard-working, dependable
Traditional	• Classic—original, old-fashioned, ageless, wholesome, all-American
	• Honest—Real, ethical, caring, trustworthy, concerned
	• Simple
Modern	• Up-to-date—contemporary, innovative, modern
	• Complex
Annoying	• Unpleasant—bad-mannered, childish, silly, pretentious, condescending, careless, irresponsible, unfriendly, cold, distant, overly formal

Perception of Brand Personality

The differences in the personality-profile characteristics of brands suggest that although everyone uses key personality factors to describe brands, the way they perceive these personality traits is quite varied. People are always trying to make estimates of the personality of people around them. But they also tend to project human traits onto nonliving objects, thus determining the human aspects of their relationship to their surroundings. This constitutes the basis for the brand personality

Figure 10.1 **Brand Personality Perception**

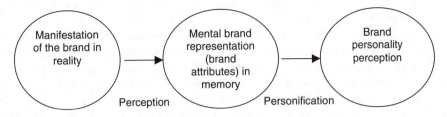

Source: SWOCC, Berge (2001a).

concept. People use human concepts when talking about brands: Grolsch beer is individualistic, ABN-AMRO is businesslike, KLM is reliable, Volvo is solid and safe. How do people arrive at these perceptions and associations?

Principle: People project human traits onto nonliving objects. This is the basis for the brand personality concept—people use human concepts when talking about brands.

Plummer (1985) posits that the perception of brand personality is formed by every direct and indirect contact between people and brands. Although human attributes and brand personality traits have a common concept formation, there is a difference in how they take shape. The perception of human personality traits is derived from an individual's behavior, external features, attitude, convictions, and demographic characteristics. Plummer believes that, against this, the perception of brand personality can be formed and influenced by all types of direct and indirect contact that the consumer has with the brand, but it is primarily through communication and brand-related experiences that such perceptions are formed.

These contacts lead to association formation in memory. The meanings the brand is associatively linked to in the memory of consumers are called brand attributes. As discussed in the previous chapter, the entire set of associatively linked brand attributes is designated by Franzen and Bouwman (1999) as the brand associative system. This system is the residual of all brand perceptions and brand experiences that a consumer has had in the course of time. To a greater or lesser degree, all these meetings between manifestations of the brand and a person leave traces behind in memory. These traces are the foundations upon which people personify the brand. Consequently, there are two mental processes underlying brand personality: a perception process and a personification process. Input for both processes comes from all the manifestations and materializations of the brand. This is illustrated in Figure 10.1.

Sources of Brand Personality Associations

All brand attributes in memory can contribute to brand personality perception (see Figure 10.1). In a small-scale study into the brand personality of cigarette brands in the Netherlands, respondents indicated that their brand personality associations were based, among other things, on the package (color and typography), the popularity of the brand as a result of the market share (Marlboro is seen as a large brand that is present everywhere, thanks to which it is associated with, e.g., the "leader type"), product attributes (the heaviness and taste of the cigarette), user situations and memories of these, the function of smoking (comfort, relaxation), and advertising. Based on the attributes "large," "smoked by many people," "masculine," "red," and the "hard typography on the package," Marlboro has come to be personified as "dominant" and a "leader type" brand (Berg 1999).

Certain types of brand attributes probably have a relatively large influence on the brand personality perception because they are easy to personify. A brand can be associated, for instance, with (stereotyped) users of a brand (user image), with a cranky customer service employee, with charismatic CEOs (Richard Branson of Virgin, Bill Gates of Microsoft), with spokespeople (Krite Kanawa for Rolex), or with characters (Ronald McDonald) used in advertising and other forms of communication. The personality traits of these people shine through to some degree in the brand personality perception.

Associations with nonhuman objects, like the product and the packaging, and less tangible aspects, such as the advertising style and tone of voice, can also trigger specific brand personality traits. If we turn this around, we could state that all these things are used to construct a certain brand personality, and the possibilities for personality cues are not limited to such obvious solutions as those described above.

Principle: Brand personality is the result of a perception and personification process. The perception connects all the previous sensory and observable manifestations of a brand. The traces it leaves in memory form the basis of the personification of a brand.

The Theoretical Boundaries of Brand Personality

At least as important for the formulation of a clear concept is determining the reach of the concept. In their overview of brand meanings within the category of symbolic brand meanings, Franzen and Bouwman (2001) distinguish these subcategories—brand personality, user image, brand values, and associated brand notions—remarking that this distinction is in fact artificial and that the subcategories are intrinsically intertwined. That is not so strange, given the difficulty involved in concretizing the character of symbolism. Still, research forces us to set boundaries. We will now describe brand personality in relation to brand image, brand identity, user image, and brand values.

Brand Personality Versus Brand Identity

Next to brand personality, brand identity is one of the most central concepts from brand theory. What is the difference between the two concepts? In essence, brand identity is the answer to the question, "Who am I?" This question can be answered from an organizational or internal perspective by looking at the *actual* situation as described in Chapter 6. Brand identity is about the brand's internal identification experience as crafted by management. It is about the awareness of what the brand is, what it stands for, and what it can do and what it does at a certain moment in time. The history of the brand is essential to this awareness. Brand identity is emphatically not about "Who would I like to be?"

Identity can serve as a point of departure for the development of thoughts, visions, and strategies for the future. Awareness of the identity of a brand is the basis of all marketing and communication activities of the brand. Without this awareness, it would be difficult for a brand to present itself to the external world and for others (consumers, shareholders, retailers, etc.) to be convinced of its right to exist.

Brand identity is a foundation for the development of a brand personality. Brand personality is directed toward the external world, where it comes into being as a perception by consumers. It is the radiation of identity. To let others see who you are, you yourself have to know who you are first. The same applies to brands. When the brand personality concept is not carried by the brand identity, chances are it will seem unnatural and contrived to external parties (consumers) and will be discounted as a marketing trick. Brand personality, then, can be seen as more cosmetic than the actual face of a brand.

Principle: To let others see who you are, you yourself have to know who you are first.

Brand identity concerns everything a brand is, says, does, and shows. In Chapter 6 we distinguished three main components: a physical component (sensory, observable manifestations of the brand), a mental component (a collection of character traits and values), and a social component (relationships the brand maintains). The mental component of brand identity corresponds with the sender concept (internal perception) of brand personality by management and employees. Consumers perceive the manifestation of the three components of brand identity—the *actual* personality—directly or indirectly. The mental and social components are perceived indirectly—for example, in communication. The physical component is perceived directly through experience. On the basis of these perceptions of and experiences with the brand, associations are formed with the brand in consumer memory. What emerges is a brand associative system: a neural network of all kinds of associatively linked brand information. Ideally, all manifestations of a brand are a reflection of the brand's identity and contribute to the personification of the brand as a friend or a relationship partner.

Based on all their experiences with a brand and the traces that these experiences have left behind in memory, people attribute certain personality traits to the brand. Brand personality is thus a subjective phenomenon that is derived from the objective, sensory, observable manifestation (materialization) of the three components of brand identity (see Figure 10.2).

Brand Personality Versus Brand Image

A brand image is the total, global impression of the information that accumulates in the memory of consumers in relation to a brand. It is the consumer's brand perception and includes identity and values, as well as brand and user personality cues. This total impression is shared by the members of a culture or subculture. Brand image is therefore the impression or perception that the outside world has of a brand (Bouwman 1999b).

Timmerman (2001) did research into the representation of brands in memory, what we call brand image. He distinguished brand attributes and brand attribute values. Brand attributes are the building stones of the brand image, and the attribute values are the associations within the brand associative system. Brand personality is therefore one of the attributes within brand representation; brand personality associations (young, dynamic, etc.) are the attribute values that contribute to the brand image.

Brand image is synthetic to a certain extent because it is often based on cues provided by the

Figure 10.2   **Brand Identity Versus Brand Personality**

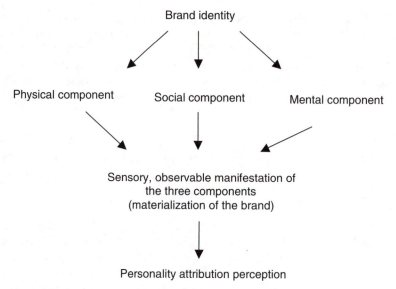

Source: SWOCC, Berg (1999).

brand through advertising and other marketing communication. In that sense, it may be more a mask than the face of a brand. That is the reason some scholars and managers tend to disparage the concept of brand image. Brand personality, on the other hand, is reflected in the perception of customers based on their experiences with a brand, as well as in the strategic decisions by a brand's managers.

Brand Personality Versus User Image

Who uses the brand and how does that association with a person or lifestyle contribute to the meaning of the brand? Although the theoretical concepts of brand personality and user image are sometimes hard to distinguish, such a distinction is important. There may be a correspondence, but this is not always the case. Albeit unjustly, brand personality and user image are often used interchangeably, in science and in practice. This is because both brand personality and user image are described in terms of human personality traits. In brand personality, these traits are partly the result of a personification process of nonhuman attributes; in user image, brand personality is influenced by the perceived personality traits of users of the brand. During research, respondents are asked to express their associations in words. In both cases, this will result in descriptions made in similar terms, which makes it difficult to find out which association category is being addressed.

In theory, the difference between brand personality and user personality becomes clear when we study the definitions that J. Aaker (1997) gives of both concepts. She defines brand personality as a set of human personality traits that are associated with the brand itself, and user image as a set of human personality traits that are associated with the stereotyped user(s) of the brand. As an example of a brand with a strong user image, Pepsi has built its brand image on "The Pepsi Generation" as the image of youthfulness, which it projects as characteristic of its users.

Table 10.2

Brand Personality and User Image (Netherlands based)

	Brand personality	User image
Marlboro	Masculine	Feminine
	Power	Youth
	Roughness	Extraversion
Levi's	Mine worker	Urban
	Durability	Hip
	Simplicity	Contemporary
	Toughness	Female and masculine
Mercedes Benz	Wealth	Amsterdam taxi driver
	Prestige	

Source: Adapted from D. Aaker (1996a), and Franzen and Bouwman (2001).

As mentioned, the brand personality can correspond with the user image. The brand personality of Nike is very much determined by the slick profile of top athletes who can be seen in its campaigns. In this case, user image steers the brand personality (D. Aaker 1996a). The fact that this is not always the case is illustrated in the examples presented in Table 10.2.

In general, a brand personality strategy should be as consistent as possible (D. Aaker et al. 1996). At the same time, D. Aaker and Biel (1993) observe that the idea that user image and brand personality are or should be the same and that the task of consumer research is to bring these two together is a flawed assumption of many psychographic segmentation analyses. According to these authors, user image and brand personality correspond when the brand choice is a direct manifestation of personal values or lifestyles, such as often happens when consumers choose newspapers and cars, but this is rarely the case for most packaged goods.

It is plausible that the influence of user image on the perception of brand personality is partially dependent on the sort of brand and the type of product. Brands of products that are used in public and whose users are thus visible would logically call to mind lively and strong user associations. One sees people wearing Nike footwear, smoking Gauloises Blondes, or driving a Smart car or a Lexus. In these cases, brand personality associations are probably dominated for the most part by user image.

It is important to realize that brand personality and the personality of the user of a brand do not have to correspond. A brand that has a modern, sexy, hip, youthful personality is not necessarily used exclusively by young people whose self-image corresponds with the brand personality. The opposite is often the case: many strong brands are attractive because they represent an aspirational world. Older people drink Pepsi even though they are not in "The Pepsi Generation." Axe deodorant is another good example: the brand positions itself consciously as leading edge and contemporary, but Axe users are certainly not all hip young people. On the contrary, Axe users are largely consumers who do not resemble the Axe man at all, but who do aspire to (Pawle 2000). The difference between identification and aspiration is relevant to this point.

Principle: User image is the generalized personality traits that are attributed to stereotyped users of a brand—user image, in turn, becomes a brand personality cue.

Brand Personality Versus Brand Values

The concept of brand values has been discussed in Chapter 9. Brand values are the brand meanings in memory that consumers consider valuable and that play an important role in the choice between different brands in a category. Brand personality is not the same as brand values, but associations with certain values in the memory of the consumer can serve as a basis or driver for the process of personification of the brand by the consumer. A brand that is primarily associated with career making and self-development will probably make consumers think of a different type of personality than a brand associated with family life and security.

Consistency between the values that a brand wants to represent and the profile of the desired brand personality attributes has an enhancing effect in both directions. Value systems can constitute a basis for the development of a brand personality concept (Sikkel and Oppenhuisen 1998).

The difference between associations with values and associations with personality traits is not always clear in research. In the much-quoted basic research into values by Rokeach (1973), the characterizations of "ambitious," "tolerant," "cheerful," and "courageous" are called instrumental values. In research into brand personality, similar concepts are called personality traits and are considered part of the brand personality. The research of Sikkel and Oppenhuisen (1998a) does not make explicit mention of the difference between brand personality attributes and brand values either.

Although it is useful to put user associations, brand personality associations, and associations with values into separate theoretical categories, it is important to keep in mind that, in reality, they most probably interact with each other intensively. As mentioned, user associations are a source of brand personality associations and sometimes fall together. It seems that values that a brand is associatively connected to can also be a source of brand personality associations. Pure and exclusive measuring of brand personality associations is therefore difficult to the point of being, in all likelihood, impossible. The questions may result in increased chances of activating a number of user associations or values in the process.

Principle: The values a brand is associated with can also be a source of brand personality associations, and vice versa.

STRATEGIC DIMENSIONS OF BRAND PERSONALITY

We talked earlier about the perception of brand personality; now we will look at that phenomenon in terms of its strategy implications. The perception of brand personality, just like the perception of the personality of a person, is a mental process and thus subjective. This implies the need to always indicate from which perspective one is looking at brand personality. Is the focus on the perception of consumers or on the intention of marketers? And is the latter case about the perception of reality or about an ideal or desired brand personality?

The observable reality, the manifestation of the brand in the world—everything the brand says, does, and shows (product, communication, service, buildings, personnel, packaging, sponsoring, events, publicity, etc.)—is the source of all brand perceptions. In short, it is the *actual* situation as described in the six-field model in Chapter 6. When applying this model to brand personality, we come up with the following dimensions:

- *Sender concept:* the personality of a brand as it is perceived within the organization by the management and employees;
- *Receiver concept:* the personality of a brand as it is perceived by external parties (consumers, stakeholders, etc.);
- *Sender ideal:* the brand personality desired by the management;
- *Consumer need:* the brand personality desired by the consumers.

This model can provide brand managers with insight into the weak points of a brand, in this case with regard to brand personality. For example:

- The external perception (receiver concept) deviates from the internal perception (sender concept). In others words, consumers see the brand personality differently than brand managers do. In many cases, brand managers have a relatively more positive image of "their" brand than people who are less involved with the brand. This can lead to an overestimation of the potential of a brand.
- The perceived concept deviates from the consumer need. In that case, the perceived brand personality fits insufficiently or not at all with the needs of consumers. Consumers do not care about the brand because they do not find it relevant. The brand personality will probably have no influence on brand preference.
- The sender ideal deviates from consumers needs. This can happen when brands do not have enough synchronicity with the needs of their potential user groups. This type of diagnosis can serve as a point of departure for steering and strategy development in relation to brand personality.

Individual and Shared Brand Meanings

Brand personality acquires content through the interaction between manifestations of the brand and the people who perceive it. The brand shows what it is by means of its exterior, its stories, and its behavior. These brand signals may or may not be noticed and interpreted. During the interpretation process, all brand signals pass through the personal mental filter of the observer. These various personal interpretation processes can result in different perceptions of the personality of the same brand by different people (brand managers, advertisers, users of a brand, users of a competing brand, etc.). This is why, to some extent, companies all see their own brand with the unhappy likelihood that the perceived personality does not match the intended personality. Instead of brand personality, we are better off speaking of brand personality perception, indicating whose perception we are talking about.

Although the interpretation of a brand—and thus of brand personality—is highly subjective, image research shows that personal perceptions are often very similar. Therefore, in addition to personal or private brand meanings, we can distinguish shared or public brand meanings. Such shared perceptions are known in mass psychology as social representation or collective perception (see, e.g., Ginneken 1993, 1999). For the shared perception of brand meanings, Bullmore (1998) introduces the term "consensus of subjectivity," stating that each of the many millions of people gathers a set of feelings that are to some extent autonomous but which further research shows to be closely related. This connection is present to such a degree that consumers delude themselves into thinking that they have arrived at an objective truth, but that is not the case. Bullmore does not see a shared brand image as objective—it is a consensus of subjectivity, just like a shared image of Elle MacPherson or Matisse.

Public brand meanings influence private ones. People let themselves be influenced by their surroundings, even—or perhaps *precisely*—when it comes to brands. This is especially the case with brands that have a primarily expressive function. For such brands, shared brand meanings are important because they are used by people to communicate about their own values and self-image. The first condition for nonverbal communication through brands is that those people one addresses understand what is being communicated. For this reason, public brand meanings often play a lead role in this type of brand.

Principle: Public brand meanings influence private ones. Shared brand meanings help people communicate about themselves.

To summarize, we can say that brand personality points to the experience and/or description of a brand in terms of human personality traits. These traits are the result of the personification of the brand on the basis of an entire set of brand attributes (brand associations) in the memory of a consumer. These are accompanied by an emotional response. The way the consumer experiences the brand personality determines the relation between consumer and brand. In turn, the relation between consumer and brand determines the experience of brand personality. People who love a brand perceive it differently and tend to ascribe to it more positive personality attributes than people who have no emotional ties to it.

It is important to indicate from which perspective the brand personality is seen. It is not self-evident that consumers see the personality of a brand the same way as marketers, because consumers derive the personality of a brand on the basis of all their experiences with the brand. A brand personality that is carefully communicated through advertising and other forms of brand communication may not correspond to the way a brand is actually experienced in real life. This is a particular danger for service brands that involve direct contact between brand employees and consumers.

Although the holistic character of brands makes it difficult to distinguish between symbolic brand meanings, a theoretical distinction can be made between brand personality, brand image, brand identity, user image, and brand values.

The Workings of Brand Personality

Individuals have personalities—colorless or sparkling, attractive or irritating. Inner character and outward behavior reveal certain traits that make people different from each other, making them recognizable to themselves and to others. How does this work with brands? In general, it is assumed that brands have a personality. Most brands want to have a strong personality. This aspiration stems from the assumption that brand personality works as an anchor in the relationship between customer and brand. Indeed, brand personality can play a primary role in the development of a strong brand.

Given the great interest in brand personality, it is remarkable that the literature on brand management presents hardly any information on how brand personality works or could work. There are four areas in which brand personality could play a role:

- brand personality in the memory of the consumer;
- brand personality in the relation between brands and people;

- brand personality in the communication between brand and people;
- brand personality in the relationships between people.

Because the way brand personality works has not really been scientifically studied, some of the arguments in this chapter are hypothetical.

Brand Personality in Memory

If requested during a research interview, people can associate most brands with certain personality attributes. However, the fact that people can typify brands in terms of human personality traits in a research situation does not automatically make brand personality a variable that explains mental brand preference and purchasing behavior. Although the preference for a brand is a mental response, the emotional response is partly determined by how the brand is represented in the psyche (Franzen and Bouwman 2001).

In order to have any direct or indirect positive influence on brand attitude and, ultimately, on purchasing behavior, brand personality associations must first be present in the memory of a consumer. This presence is thus the first condition for the workings of brand personality. In addition, their dominance within the brand representation is important. Brand personality can be part of the mental brand representation in several ways. The potential working of the brand personality is related to it. In theory, we can distinguish the following possibilities, which will be elaborated upon further in the chapter:

- *Brands without personality:* These are brands in which brand personality associations do not constitute a part of the mental brand representation.
- *Brand personality = brand attribute:* Brand personality is part of the brand representation but does not belong to the core meanings of the brand and has no influence on the positioning of the brand in memory.
- *Brand personality = core concept:* Brand personality is part of the core concept of the brand and determines the positioning of the brand in memory.
- *Brand personality = brand asset:* Brand personality is part of the core concept and has a direct influence on brand purchasing behavior.

Brand Personality as Brand Attribute

Do all brands have a personality? An important question is whether brand personality associations are part of the brand associative system (mental brand representation) in the memory of consumers. In other words, do people associate the brand with human personality traits? If they do not, or if they do only when they are asked, for example, during research, many questions arise regarding the added value of brand personality. It sounds logical that something that is not there cannot be expected to work as a memory anchor.

Research by Timmerman (2001) for SWOCC indicates that not all brands are associated spontaneously with personality traits. His analysis shows that the associative structure of brands can differ considerably within one single product category. When people are asked to carry out a free association task with only the brand name as cue, the types of associations that they mention seem to vary per brand. For example, Heineken generates a different type of brand associations than Grolsch. The following box shows which brand associations differentiate these brands from each other in the perception of Dutch consumers.

Table 10.3

Relevance of Brand Attributes

The relevance of the following attributes are scored from high to low.

Heineken	Grolsch
Reputation	Psychological/symbolic function and attitude
Use: conditions	Reputation
Buying behavior	Product sales
Product appearance	Personality
Advertisement	Product appearance
Use: effects	Use: conditions
Product sales	Advertisement
Psychological/symbolic function and attitude	Buying behavior
Personality	Use: effects
Origin	Origin

Source: SWOCC, Timmerman (2001).

Heineken Versus Grolsch

There are a number of attributes on which the brands seem to be differentiated in memory. Timmerman provides a number of tables that present statistically significant differences between mean scores or rankings of individual attributes. When these attributes are gathered, the following attributes differentiate the two brands:

- Acquaintance (differentiates in favor of Heineken)
- Reputation (differentiates in favor of Heineken)
- Advertising (differentiates in favor of Heineken)
- Brand attitude (differentiates in favor of Grolsch)
- Feelings (differentiates in favor of Grolsch)
- Personality (differentiates in favor of Grolsch)
- Impressive function (differentiates in favor of Grolsch)
- Brand relation (differentiates in favor of Grolsch)

Source: SWOCC, Timmerman (2001).

It is obvious that personality is relevant to the distinctiveness of Grolsch against Heineken and that Heineken distinguishes itself from Grolsch on the basis of familiarity, reputation, and advertising. Besides the fact that Heineken and Grolsch differ in the type of associations with which they differentiate themselves in the perception of consumers, the SWOCC study indicates that the associations differ with regard to dominance within the mental representation of the brand in question. Table 10.3, in which brand attributes are categorized according to their relevance, shows that brand personality seems to be more important for the Grolsch brand when it comes to its mental distinction in contrast to Heineken.

At this point we should mention that it is difficult to say with certainty whether the results of this type of research mean that there are brands in which brand personality associations are entirely absent or whether the research methods to measure them do not deliver. Not everything can be measured, but that certainly does not mean it is not there. At least in part, the personification of brands could be taking place unconsciously, for which reason it becomes very difficult, if not impossible, to bring it into consciousness in order to express it in words or images. This remains a problem when studying symbolic brand meanings.

Brand Personality as Core Meaning of the Brand

After the question whether brand personality associations are part of the brand representation in the memory of consumers, we could ask about the mental status of those associations. Do they belong to the core meanings of the brand? Do they have an influence on the positioning of the brand against competing brands in memory? In other words, are brand personality associations part of the core concept of a brand?

Although most brands are associated with one or several personality attributes, there are brands that are primarily defined by personality attributes. In such brands, the core meanings consist of brand personality associations. The brain position of these brands (their competing position in memory) is primarily determined by their personality.

Franzen and Bouwman (2001) list "brand = personality" as one of the thirteen basic brand concepts they distinguished. These types of brands are no longer representative of products; rather, the products are expressions of abstract, inner characteristics of the brand. In this type of brand, personality associations are seen by consumers as the most typical attributes of the brand.

The fact that people position a brand in their memory on the basis of brand personality associations does not necessarily mean that these associations are relevant in relation to brand preference and brand purchasing behavior. Being familiar with a brand and its personality and knowing what it stands for do not automatically mean that people prefer it. Only when the brand concept, the core meaning of the brand, is valued as positive—for example, because it fits the consumers' expectations or needs regarding the category, or because the brand has created a new need—can there be a relation between brand personality and brand preference and brand purchasing behavior. Brand personality associations that succeed in doing this are brand assets. Brand assets have a direct influence on the strength of the brand. They are drivers of mental brand equity.

Brand Personality as Brand Asset

The core meanings of a brand that have a direct positive relation with brand preference and purchasing behavior are identified as brand assets. Brand assets are the associations that play the lead role in the purchasing and choice behavior of consumers. In fact, they are the most positively valued characteristic attributes of the brand (in the perception of the consumer).

Which brand attributes are potential assets depends, among other things, on the core function of the brand. With brands that are primarily bought for their symbolic function, the symbolic brand meaning is relatively important. Brands like Nike, Absolut, and Diesel probably derive a great deal of their power of attraction from their charismatic personality. Brand personality associations (part of the category of symbolic brand meanings) can become assets with these types of brands. The brand asset is the highest mental status the brand personality can acquire.

To summarize, we can state that in order to indicate the relevance and potency of brand personality for a specific brand, one must first examine whether and how brand personality associations are part of the brand associative system in the memory of consumers. The following questions can serve as steps in this process:

- Are brand personality associations part of the associative structure of the brand? In other words, do people associate the brand with human personality traits?
- Do brand personality associations belong to the core concept of the brand? Are they one of the determinants for the positioning of the brand against competing brands in memory?
- Do brand personality associations have the status of brand assets? Do they have a direct influence on the choice between alternative brands within the category? Do they influence purchasing behavior?

Brand Personality and the Construction of Brand Relationships

Personality plays a central role in relations between people. It regulates social interactions. A logical question that follows regards the role played by brand personality in relations between brands and people. Indeed, if a brand is a special relationship, as McKenna (1991b) says, then it is incumbent upon a brand manager to understand the relationship-building functions of a brand.

The interest people have in brands does not come out of nowhere. People have all kinds of motivations to enter relationships, as indicated, among other factors, by the functions those relationships fulfill for those involved. Fournier (1994) calls this the tie that binds or the binding factor. In relationships between brands and people, just as in relationships between people, there is indeed a binding factor. Brands gratify needs, they do (or are supposed to do) something for people, and they have a function. The function that binds brands and persons can be purely instrumental, focusing exclusively on achieving specific goals, or it can be social-psychological, in which case it is ego- and socially oriented.

In Chapter 4 we distinguished four groups of brand functions. They meet several types of consumer needs:

- *Product representation function:* The brand represents product meanings.
- *Symbolic function:* The brand adds symbolic meanings to the product.
- *Buying behavior function:* The brand simplifies the buying process.
- *Relationship function:* The brand meets the need to have long-term relationships.

In most cases, brands will have a combination of the preceding functions, but a core function can always be determined. It is important to realize that it is the users who have to recognize and acknowledge the function and that only then does the brand acquire value for them.

It is useful to have insight into the core function that a brand has for consumers. The brand function is the binding factor in the relationship between brand and consumers, and it is partly responsible for the type of relation that emerges. Brand personality can strengthen the experience of the brand function for consumers, contributing to the development of the relationship between them and the brand.

Brand Functions and Types of Relationships

Every brand function generates a different type of relationship with specific expectations and needs. Bremer's research for SWOCC (1998) makes a comparison between the functions of relationships between people and the functions that (relationships with) brands fulfill for consumers. This is illustrated in Figure 10.3.

Figure 10.3 **Functions of Brand Relationships**

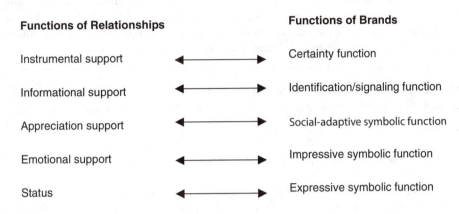

Functions of Relationships   **Functions of Brands**

Instrumental support ⟷ Certainty function

Informational support ⟷ Identification/signaling function

Appreciation support ⟷ Social-adaptive symbolic function

Emotional support ⟷ Impressive symbolic function

Status ⟷ Expressive symbolic function

Source: SWOCC, Bremer (1998).

1. Instrumental support or security function
Relationships can offer instrumental support in the form of direct, practical help. The security function of brands is about the practical help that a brand gives in the decision process when consumers buy a product or choose a certain service provider. The brand is seen here as someone or something that helps the consumer make a quick, easy decision.

2. Informational support or identification-signaling function
This points to practical information, as well as information that partners receive indirectly by comparing their own experiences and ideas with those of others, in order to reduce uncertainty. The function can be compared with the identification or signaling function of brands. In both cases, this is about information that the other—in this case, the brand—can give. This is the brand as adviser.

3. Appreciation support or social-adaptive symbolic function
This is about recognition and appreciation of the other. In relationships between people, brands can fulfill a symbolic function. People buy and use certain brands in order to get recognition and appreciation from certain social reference groups. Here the brand is someone or something that offers access to reference groups.

4. Emotional support or impressive symbolic function
Emotional support can be described as affection, acceptance, warmth, and trust. Some brands, such as a glass of Remy Martin, a Cuban cigar, or a cup of Celestial Seasonings tea, have an indulgence function for their users. This is the brand as someone who spoils you.

5. Status or expressive symbolic function
The relationship brings a certain (derived) status with it. In psychology, this is known as "reflected glory," the self-enhancement one seeks by associating with successful, competent, or attractive people (Lippa 1994). This is the brand as someone who helps express your identity and whose presence adds to your status.

Depending on the function the brand fulfills within the relationship with the consumer, the nature of the relationship can differ in its expectations, durability, and emotional intensity, as well as the expectations of the personality of the partner. It is quite possible that, as the function becomes more instrumental, the capacity to enter into deep, emotionally intense relationships with consumers is more reduced than with brands that have a more ego-related function.

Principle: Depending on the function that a brand fulfils within a relationship with consumers, brand personality has a more central or more peripheral meaning.

Types of Relationships and Types of Personalities

It is still assumed, and wrongly so, that there is always a correspondence between the personality of consumers and that of the brands they use. D. Aaker (1996a) posits that even though some people do not have the personality or even the aspiration to be competent leaders, they do want a relationship with someone like that, certainly when they need a banker or an attorney. A reliable, conservative personality may be somewhat boring, but it could nonetheless radiate traits that people value in a financial adviser, garden maintenance service, or even a car (a clear example is the brand personality of Volvo). Aaker believes that the concept of a relationship between a brand and a person (analogous to a relationship between two people) provides insights into how a brand personality could work.

As described, depending of the core function it fulfills, a relationship generates specific expectations, which can be related to personality traits. The brand function, the binding factor of the brand relationship, can form the point of departure for the formulation of a brand personality concept.

The relationship-based model of D. Aaker (1996a) is based on the assumption that the nature of the relationship between person and brand determines the customer's appreciation (suitability, relevance) of the brand personality attributes. In turn, brand personality attributes can give direction to the type of relationship that develops between customer and brand (distant, formal, open, egalitarian, etc.). The same happens in relationships between people. For a doctor, for instance, traits such as extravertedness, exuberance, and sophistication are probably not too relevant in relationships with patients; the function of the relationship between the doctor and the patient makes certain personality traits more relevant and desirable than others. The following list (based on D. Aaker 1996a) illustrates how various brand personality types, compared to human personality types, can generate different types of relationships.

- *Sincerity: down-to-earth, family-oriented, genuine, old-fashioned.* This might describe brands like Kodak and Coke. The relationship could be similar to one with a well-liked and respected member of the family.
- *Excitement: spirited, young, up-to-date, outgoing.* In the soft drinks category, Pepsi fits this mold more than Coke. Especially on a weekend evening, it might be enjoyable to have a friend with these personality characteristics.
- *Competence: accomplished, influential, competent.* Hewlett Packard and the *Wall Street Journal* might fit this profile. It parallels a relationship with a person whose accomplishments you respect, such as a teacher, minister, or business leader. Perhaps that is what a relationship between a business computer and its customer should be like.
- *Sophistication: pretentious, wealthy, condescending.* This would be a BMW, Mercedes,

or Lexus (with gold trim) as opposed to a Mazda Miata, a Beetle, or a VW Golf. It would be similar to having a relationship with a powerful boss or rich relative.

- *Ruggedness: athletic and outdoorsy:* Nike (versus LA Gear), Marlboro (versus Virginia Slims), and Wells Fargo (versus Bank of America) are examples. When planning an outing, a friend with outdoorsy interests would be welcome.

What Does the Brand Think of Me?

When it comes to brand personality, people tend to treat the brand as a passive element within the relationship. The focus lies on consumer perceptions, attitudes, and behaviors toward the brand. The attitude and perceptions of the brand itself remain hidden behind the closed doors of the organization. The relationships between people are influenced not only by what or who the other person is, but also by what one person thinks of another. The same way, the brand-consumer relationship has an active partner on each side, that of the brand and that of the consumer.

To understand the nature of the relationship between consumer and brand, Blackston (1993) believes it is crucial not only to measure the perception of the brand personality by the consumer, but also to research what consumers think the brand thinks of them. In addition to the well-known "attitude toward the brand," Blackston introduces the concept of brand attitude, arguing that both types of information are necessary to characterize the emotional interaction between consumer and brand. He states that the link between brand attitude and purchasing behavior is explained mainly by what the consumers think that the brand thinks about them (brand attitude). In other words, the brand (as expressed in its marketing communication) may suggest that its customers are hip and cool or sophisticated or old-fashioned and conservative.

A way to identify the brand attitude is to ask respondents what the brand would say if it were a person. The answer brings to the fore information that remains hidden when only the brand personality perception is measured.

Principle: A person-brand relationship has two sides to it and both provide insight into the brand relationship. From the consumers' perspective, we can see their "attitude toward the brand"; from the brand's perspective, there is a "brand attitude toward the consumer."

Brand Personality and Communication

We have talked about the function of brand personality in memory and in the construction of relationships. This last function looks at the role of brand personality in brand communication. In communication between brands and people, the personality of the brand plays a critical role. Brand personality gives a brand a face, adds emotion to a lifeless object, makes communication more personal and appealing, and creates a bond when the personality is likable.

Together with the emotions they are associated with (sympathy, rejection, etc.), brand personality associations in the memory of consumers can influence how consumers perceive manifestations of the brand. The representation of a brand in the memory colors the consumers' perceptions. The emotional response to the personality of a brand thus influences how consumers deal with subsequent communication from the brand: the attention they pay to it, how well they remember it, and so on (Franzen and Bouwman 2001; du Plessis 2000; Berg 2000). This is comparable to the way you perceive and communicate with a person you love, as opposed to someone you do not know or someone you dislike. What you think others think of you also plays a role here.

Brand personality makes it possible to communicate in a "human voice." It goes without saying that it is more pleasant to communicate with a brand that approaches a human tone. This way, brand personality facilitates communication between brands and people. This is how the Dutch advertising agency Kessels Kramer (1999) describes the role of personality in the communication between brands and people:

> If we give a brand all the aspects of a human being, the brand will become more real. More engaging and personal. A consumer can then relate to and talk with a brand. A brand that opens up. In communication, a brand can talk about itself all the time, which gets annoying, or a brand can converse about a wide range of topics. . . . A brand can have an opinion on everything from the ozone layer to window-shopping. The more dynamic and alive a brand is, the more interesting it becomes.

Not only can brand personality make communication more attractive, alive, and inspiring, it can also contribute to the recognizability of various manifestations of a brand. Brand personality integrates everything a brand says and does—in short, the whole marketing communication mix.

Principle: Brand personality integrates everything a brand says and does.

Brand Personality and Symbolic Brand Functions

People communicate not only with brands but also through them. Some brands play an important role in relationships between people; they form the "words" of a symbolic vocabulary with which people communicate. In Chapter 4 we called this the symbolic function of brands and distinguished three variants: an expressive, an impressive, and a social-adaptive function. In this role, the brand is a lubricant in the myriad social processes in which people are entangled.

Some brands are purchased primarily because of their symbolic meanings. They are used by consumers to express their identity (for themselves or others), as is the case with certain clothing brands and fragrances. Brand personality associations are part of the symbolic meaning of a brand. In symbolic brands, brand personality associations determine the usefulness of the brand in expressing identity and consequently have a direct influence on the brand preference. In such brands, consumers relate brand personality to their own personality. Symbolic brands are used to endorse the consumer's own personality (identification) or to bring the ideal, desired personality closer (aspiration).

In marketing and scientific research into brand personality, the implicit assumption is often made that all brands fulfill a symbolic function. Experts investigate the degree to which brand personality corresponds with a consumers' perception of their own personality. In many cases, little or no connection is found (J. Aaker 1999; Plummer 1985; Sirgy 1982). That should not be surprising. After all, we have described how brands can have different types of functions. Not all brands have a symbolic core function—personalities of brands with other functions can be found to be attractive without resembling the personality of their users.

Brand Personality and Social Communication

Personality plays a central role in social communication between people. People are always trying to estimate the personality of others in order to determine their social position. Consciously or otherwise, they pick up all kinds of verbal and nonverbal signals from each other. Based on these multisensory perceptions, they ascribe personality traits to each other, thus forming an image of the personality of people around them. This image determines the tone of the mutual communication process.

RESEARCH INTO BRAND PERSONALITY

To develop an effective brand personality strategy, insight is needed not only into the brand personality associations of a brand, but also into the degree of influence that these associations have on the positioning of the brand in memory and on the choice behavior of consumers. This goes beyond making an inventory of brand personality associations, as is still done in much image research.

Insight is needed into the role of brand personality within the associative structure: the degree to which a brand is associated with personality traits and the degree to which these are characteristic of that brand. It is also necessary to acquire insight into the evaluation of brand personality associations. Do consumers consider them important, and to what extent do they evaluate brand personality associations positively or negatively? By establishing a connection with brand attitudes, purchasing intentions, and, if possible, actual purchasing behavior, it becomes possible to determine whether brand personality really has an influence on purchasing behavior.

This procedure was followed by a SWOCC study of the associative structure of twelve brands (Timmerman 2001). No connection was found between the brand attributes reported by respondents on the one side and brand attitude and purchasing intention on the other. However, a clear connection was found between the evaluation of the brand attributes and brand attitude and purchasing intention. This associative connection is thus not just about the bare brand personality associations per se, but mostly about their emotional evaluation by the consumer.

To really get insight into the role of brand personality in the development of a specific brand, it is necessary to first find out whether consumers associate the brand with symbolic meanings—especially brand personality—and the extent to which these meanings play a role in the choice process of a specific segment. To this end, it is necessary to investigate the following issues:

- *whether* the brand is associated with personality traits;
- *which* personality traits these are;
- *how* these personality traits are evaluated;
- *whether* the personality associations are related to brand attitude, purchasing intention, and purchasing behavior.

If brand personality proves indeed to be an important, distinguishing characteristic of the brand, the next step would be to find out what position the brand takes on the basis of its personality among other brands in the competition field. As we have said before, brand personality can be an important differentiating characteristic that lends strength to a brand.

THE PROCESS OF BRAND PERSONALITY DEVELOPMENT

To gain insight into the possibilities for strategic application of brand personality, it is necessary to examine whether a real possibility exists of extending brand personality from plain brand attribute into a brand asset with a decisive influence on brand choice and purchasing behavior. Let us consider now the roles that the brand personality can fulfill in the process of brand strategy development.

Strong brands do not emerge spontaneously, and the same applies to their personality. Brand personality is made up of everything a brand is, says, does, and shows. All contacts between consumer and brand can contribute to this total effect. All contacts with the brand itself, the packaging, the advertising, employees, and so on form the basis for the consumer's brand personality perception. People slowly get to know the brand and its personality. In the course of time, the brand creates a trusted position as consumers learn what the brand is and what it can do for them. Obviously the perception of personality lies within the mind of the consumer; however, as with the brand image, the brand manager must manage the communication system that delivers the brand personality cues.

> *Principle:* Brand personality is not created in an instant. Over time, the brand develops a personality and creates a position of trust with its customers.

Before brand personality can be communicated by means of brand-person meetings, it must become clear which personality traits best represent the brand. What is the brand, what is its vision, what are its core meanings, what is its history, what does the brand consider important, what does it stand for? In short, what is the identity and soul of the brand? Next, the role of brand personality within the brand strategy has to be determined: does it remain limited to a communication level, or can it play a role at a strategic level? The primary brand functions and the related nature of the relationship can serve as a point of departure for creating a brand personality concept. Several phases can be distinguished in bringing a brand personality into life and full growth.

Phase 1: Determine the Status Quo

- Identify existing symbolic associations (brand personality, user image, values) with the product category, the brand, and competing brands in the market.
- Identify the existing personality associations with the brand.
- Determine the key brand function. What does the brand essentially do for the consumer? What is its claim to existence?
- Typify the nature of the relationship between brand and consumer (brand as friend, partner, slave, inspiration, admirer, hero, etc.).

Phase 2: Determine What the Brand Should Be

- Determine what the brand should mean for consumers.
- Determine the ideal relationship between the brand and consumers.
- Determine what developments the personality should go through in order to grow into the new desired personality.
- Decide whether there should be an abrupt break between the current personality and the introduction of a completely new personality, a reincarnation as was done several years ago for Camel, or a gradual transformation of the existing personality into the desired brand personality.

Phase 3: Develop a Brand Personality Concept

- Determine what kind of personality the desired relationship will support optimally.

Phase 4: Transform the Concept Into Design

- Identify the existing visual codes and metaphors of the brand.
- Depict the desired brand personality attributes with strong, distinctive visual signs (metaphors).
- Create a symbol at the brand strategic level. A strong symbol provides the visual brand identity with coherence and structure, making it easier to generate brand recognition and recall. The symbol can be everything the personality of the brand represents: a pay-off, a character, a visual metaphor, a logo, a color, a piece of music, a package, and so on.

Phase 5: Implement the Plan

- Make the brand personality concept the driver of strategic, tactical, and creative decisions.
- Make sure that each element from the marketing communication mix plays a role in brand personality development. The successful creation of brand personality strongly depends on all these different powers working synergistically.

Phase 6: Monitor the Effects of the Brand Personality Strategy

- Follow the effects of the brand personality strategy through time.
- If there are no effects, or if they go the wrong way, take appropriate action in time.

In summary, brand personality plays important roles at both the strategic and the tactical levels. On the strategic level, brand personality is important for the following reasons:

- Brand personality can be a mental brand asset (driver of brand equity).
- Brand personality can improve positioning.
- Brand personality can be a means to differentiate the brand from functionally identical brands in the market.
- The brand makes it possible to provide expressive consumer needs (the symbolic brand function).
- Brand personality can help develop relationships between consumer and a brand as friend, adviser, expert, inspiration, and so on.

Brand personality is also a key dimension of brand meaning that operates at the tactical level in the following ways:

- Brand personality gives direction to the content, tone, and execution of all forms of brand communication (advertising, packaging, displays, etc.).
- Brand personality thus fosters the recognizability of the brand as sender of communication manifestations, ensuring a clear link with the brand.
- Brand personality is a connecting thread that integrates the various manifestations in the communication mix.

Table 10.4

Personality-Driven Brand Strategies

	Strategic focus	Strategic challenge
Communication	Brand identity	Reconizability
	Saliency	Visibility and importance
Competitive advantage	Differentiation	Uniqueness
	Position	One of a kind
Relationships	Customer connection	Emotional bond
	Self-expression	Personal identity
	Friend	Humanizing, personalizing
	Relationship	Liking, loyalty
	Familiarity	Consistency anchor

- Brand personality makes communication with consumers more human, reflecting the human voice.
- Brand personality makes brand communication salient (noticeable, eye-catching).

We can summarize all these strategic dimensions of brand personality as a set of strategic approaches that are designed to create and amplify the brand personality. Table 10.4 summarizes these strategies.

THE VOLKSWAGEN BEETLE AND BRAND PERSONALITY

The original Beetle was successful in the 1960s because it was the opposite of everything a car was supposed to be and look like and its iconoclastic personality appealed perfectly to the counterculture mentality of young people of that time. It was small and cheap when other cars were large and expensive; it was short and round when its competitors were long and streamlined; it was a gasoline miser when other cars were gas-guzzlers; and it did not change its style when its competitors unveiled their new designs every fall, quickly making last year's model obsolete.

From our list of brand personality components, we could characterize the personality of the original Beetle as creative, likable, gentle, sincere, honest, and real. In the era of huge fins and excessive chrome, the little bug was an icon for the peaceful revolution of its flower-children followers.

The restyled Beetle that took to the streets in the 2000s maintained much of the original bug's personality, including the bold, noncar-like colors. To restate its link with the earlier era of innocence, the new bug even has a vase on the dashboard for a flower. The primary link between the two cars is the Beetle personality, which can be characterized using the same adjectives for both the original and the restyled version. Both the old and the new Beetle speak of a quiet revolution against excess.

NOTE

This chapter for the most part is based on a study by Marieke van den Berg for SWOCC (Institute for Scientific Research into Commercial Communication).

1. The Brokken list is a Dutch inventory of 1,203 personality items, developed in 1978 by Frank B. Brokken on the basis of the Van Dale Dutch dictionary and studies of 200 couples of men and women rating each other.

CHAPTER 11

BRAND MEANING AND BRAND PHYSIQUE

In Chapter 3 we made a distinction between the brand as it is present in reality, its representation in the mind and strategy of its managers (the brand concept), and its representation in the mind of the consumer or stakeholder (the brand image). In this chapter we will deal with the brand as it is present in the memory of consumers and stakeholders—that is, the point where it transcends strategy, becomes a physical reality, and takes on brand meaning for consumers. Our premise is that a brand becomes a brand only when it takes on meaning and therefore exists as an entity in people's memory. Starbucks is a relatively new brand that has achieved immense success in creating brand meaning.

STARBUCKS: REDEFINING CAFÉ SOCIETY

The Starbucks Coffee Company was founded as a coffee roaster in Seattle in 1971. In 1982, Howard Schultz was appointed manager of operations and marketing. In 1984 he tried out the espresso bar concept he had learned about in Milan. Based on this success, he took over the business in 1987 and opened its first branches in Chicago and Vancouver. By the end of that year, Starbucks had 17 branches, then 84 in 1990, 676 in 1995, 4,400 in 2001, and 10,500 in 2005, of which 3,500 were outside North America. By 2006 it had operations in 37 countries. By the end of 2007 Starbucks had 8,505 company-owned outlets worldwide, and 6,500 joined ventures and licensed outlets. Over the twenty-year period since the first coffee bar opened, Schultz's figures for traditional advertising had not reached $20 million.

"Our brand is based on the experience that we control in our stores," says Schultz, who believes that a company that creates a relevant, emotional, and intimate experience builds trust with the customer. "We have benefited by the fact that our stores are reliable, safe, and consistent, where people can take a break."

That was not necessarily the plan when Schultz first moved the coffee roaster into retail stores, but Starbucks evolved that way through customer demand. This has given the brand tremendous value, he says. Through coffee, which is a universal drink, Schultz says Starbucks has created a universal language. He is convinced that "we couldn't have created that through traditional advertising." The company attracts its customers through word of mouth. Starbucks has chosen to spend its money on employee benefits. It was one of the first companies in the United States to offer part-time employees equity and health benefits. According to the Starbucks mission statement, the company's goal is to "establish Starbucks as the premier purveyor of the finest coffee in the world while maintaining our uncompromising principles while we grow." To "help us measure the appropriateness of our decisions," Starbucks management follows six guiding principles:

- Provide a great work environment and treat each other with respect and dignity.
- Embrace diversity as an essential component in the way we do business.
- Apply the highest standards of excellence to the purchasing, roasting, and fresh delivery of our coffee.
- Develop enthusiastically satisfied customers all of the time.
- Contribute positively to our communities and our environment.
- Recognize that profitability is essential to our future success.

Starbucks also "is committed to a role of environmental leadership in all facets of our business," a commitment it fulfills by

- Understanding of environmental issues and sharing information with our partners.
- Developing innovative and flexible solutions to bring about change.
- Striving to buy, sell, and use environmentally friendly products.
- Recognizing that fiscal responsibility is essential to our environmental future.
- Instilling environmental responsibility as a corporate value.
- Measuring and monitoring our progress for each project.
- Encouraging all partners to share in our mission.

Besides building trust with the customer, Schultz identifies two other "attributes that are more relevant than ever before in terms of these new standards of engagement for brands." The company works to "build hope with our people, the people who do the work and the people who represent the company. More than ever before, people want to have a relationship with a company, and the company is represented by its people." Schultz's third attribute is community, "a sense of benevolence. A company today has to have a balance, and that balance is benevolence: giving back to the community and building community."

Schultz argues that if a company can "maintain trust with your customer, hope with your people, and build community, you're not going to need the traditional forms of advertising. Because innately in the equity of the brand there has to be this reservoir of goodwill. And that is how Starbucks has built its business." Although the Starbucks brand is "deeply rooted in coffee, obviously," it has become "much, much more"—what Schultz calls the "third place" in all the communities in which the company does business, "the place between home and work. We have delivered something to the customer that's very important in their lives, and that is a great cup of coffee. We've also become a gathering place. And the romance of coffee and what we do has become an extension of people's front porch in the way they use our stores."

Schultz admits that "we're in a fortunate position" because "most people start their day drinking a cup of coffee: either at home or hopefully in a Starbucks store." More than 35 million customers visit Starbucks every week, and the average customer returns eighteen times a month. The company has used this customer base to expand. Schultz says, "We believe that the relationship that we built with our customers in our stores can be leveraged for other products in other channels of distribution"; for example, "we have the lead position in bottled Frappucino, and now we're bringing Starbucks to the grocery aisle." Another strong Starbuck product is ice cream. "We have the number one coffee ice cream in America," Schultz declares. "We've created flavors that bring a smile to people's faces when they eat, and enjoyment to their life. It's a little thing, but that carton of ice cream on the table with the family means that we are part of people's lives. And we want to continue to do those kinds of things. We don't want to be a one-dimensional component of their life, we want to share moments with them." In 2003 Starbucks started selling breakfast sandwiches, a line that is gradually expanding and might give the company a whole new area of growth.

Advertising may be able to play a greater role in Starbucks' international expansion by reinforcing its "message about the passion, care, and integrity of the coffee," says Schultz. Although acknowledging that "it's very challenging to get big and stay small," he insists that brands and companies can be successful by trying to create new opportunities for customers: "One of the great things about the future is that there are no rules. It's a very exciting time; you don't have to take the road that has been traveled before. Breaking the rules is part of the Starbucks culture; we like it, we enjoy it. We don't want to do what has been done before."

Sources: Adapted from Holmes (2001); H. Schultz (2000); Starbucks (2001); Delfeld (2006).

BRAND STORIES AND BRAND MEANING

Starbucks takes on meaning as a brand because it has a compelling brand story. We explained the importance and role of brand stories in Chapter 9, but it is important in this chapter on brand meaning to remember that the brand story is the container of meaning—the way consumers put their brand impressions into words. The brand story articulates what the brand represents and how it relates to consumers' lives.

Compared to Starbucks, there are thousands of brand names out there that nobody has ever heard about or whose brand story has never been told or is highly forgettable. This happens frequently with private labels, as retailers tend to qualify such names as their house brands, but they are usually nothing more than what the word *label* implies. Brand names that are linked in our memory to all kinds of other elements, including a story about the meaning of the brand, are what we call brand representations.

There was a time when consumers had no idea that some day they would go through life with information on a good ten thousand brands in their heads. Fortunately, most people are not really bothered by all this brand information. The storage capacity of human memory is enormous—comparable to 100,000 computer hard disks—and one brand more or less will not make a difference in people's lives.

Still, there are people for whom these brands are important. In addition to people who are loyal to their favorite brands, millions of professionals earn a living with brands by building, maintaining, and communicating about them. They are very interested in the content of consumers' memories in relation to the brand they are responsible for. A large part of their workweek centers around the meanings (in the broadest sense of the word) the brand is associated with, or knowledge of the mental brand representation in the memory of a specific consumer group. The main reason behind their interest in the contents of consumers' memories is the assumption that the representation in the mind has an influence on people's brand purchasing behavior.

Although adults have information in some form on thousands of brands, there are large differences between the quantity, content, and strength of the brand information. A person may just know a brand's name or logo, whereas another brand stirs up a whole gamut of associations that range from nostalgia and other emotions to imagery, smells, and sounds.

BRAND IMAGE: THE MENTAL BRAND

Northwestern University professor Sid Levy coined the term *brand image* in 1955. He defined it as the ideas, feelings, and attitudes that consumers have about brands. It is an image in customers' minds that reflects what they think and feel about a brand—how they value it. Brand personality (see Chapter 10)—the idea that a brand takes on familiar human characteristics, such as friendliness, trustworthiness, or snobbery—is an important part of an image. Levy and his colleagues at the SRI research center in Chicago found that a brand's image and personality could be just as important as the product's performance or price.

However, the mental brand, the representation of a brand that consumers carry in their minds, also exists as a brand concept in the strategy of its managers. Ideally, the customer's brand representation and the manager's brand concept match. Effective brand strategy could be defined as achieving this match when the meaning of both brand perspectives is the same.

Also, a brand has both physical and psychological dimensions. The physical dimension, which we refer to as the brand physique, consists of the physical characteristics of the product itself; the design of its identity system—the package, logo, and other graphics, such as letters, shapes, art, and colors—that defines the look and style of the brand; and all the physical manifestations of the brand organization, such as offices, cars, and brochures (see Chapter 6 on brand identity). These elements create the public face of a brand, providing the recognition signals customers use to identify specific brands, but they also cue psychological meanings.

The psychological side builds on the brand's identity (Chapter 6) to complete the brand representation. The psychological side includes the emotions, beliefs, values, and personalities that people ascribe to the brand. For example, when we talk about the brand image of Hershey's, we are talking about the chocolate itself and also about the distinctive brown package and the lettering of the name (the physical side). However, there is also the multitude of impressions and values (the psychological side) conveyed by its history and embodied in its slogan "the all-American candy bar."

The transformative power of branding, where the brand takes on character and meaning, is particularly important for parity products, those for which there are few if any major differences in features. Salt is an example of a parity product. Though the products are undifferentiated in the marketplace, salt can be differentiated in the minds of its users through the development of a brand image, as Morton Salt has demonstrated, even to point of creating total category dominance just because of the powerful image. What enhances the difference between one type of salt and another is meaning conveyed through the brand image. So how is this brand meaning created?

MEANING THROUGH ASSOCIATION NETWORKS

In the foreword to the book *America's Greatest Brands*, Stephen Smith writes, "A great brand is not merely a maker's mark. It is almost an heraldic symbol, carrying with it a whole web of positive associations" (2003). The power of associations and the symbolic meanings they elicit—both cognitive and emotional—determine the profile of a brand as it is inscribed on a customer's memory.

Components of Brand Association

The current views on representations in memory are based on the idea of a structure of neural connections that constitutes the foundation of mental associations between "memory elements" or "nodes." These connections or associations are the end products of learning (and forgetting) processes. All encounters between a person and the manifestations of the brand serve as didactic material: the brand article or the service, the advertisement, the employees, the buildings, publicity (positive or otherwise), the use of the brand by others, and so on. Memory is an endlessly large associative system in which everything is interconnected.

When we speak of brands, associations tend to be seen only in the narrowest sense of connections between cognitive knowledge elements, but in fact the concept has a broader meaning: it is about everything that can be interconnected in our brain, including connections between brands and emotions, attitudes, and behavioral tendencies (habits). Based on the theoretical models of associative memory, we can distinguish several types of brand associations (see Figure 11.1). These are the seven components of brand association networks as presented in *The Mental World of Brands* (Franzen and Bouwman 2001):

1. *Brand awareness and familiarity:* The presence of a brand and its related identification features (name, logo, color, etc.) in long-term memory and the ability to recall this information into working memory.
2. *Brand meanings:* The mental connection of a brand name to cognitions in long-term memory.
3. *Brand emotions:* The mental connection of a brand name to emotions that can be distinguished on the basis of their nature (positive, neutral, and negative) and intensity.
4. *Brand positioning:* The classification of a brand in a group or subgroup of other brands on the basis of the most characteristic common properties and the distinction of a brand from other brands within the group or subgroup on the basis of its most characteristic differences.

Figure 11.1 **Components of Brand Association Networks**

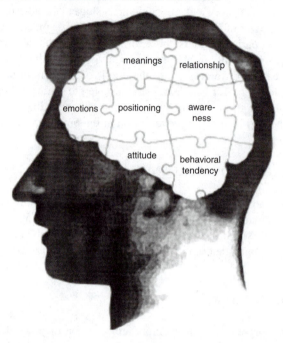

5. *Brand attitude:* The long-term evaluation of a brand, based on the consideration of its positive and negative characteristics, which has consequences for consumer behavior relative to the brand.
6. *Brand behavioral tendency:* The tendency, embedded in memory, to keep buying a brand (the acquired purchasing habit).
7. *Brand relation:* The two-way involvement between a consumer and a brand, consisting of interaction, communication, reciprocity, and continuity.

Principle: A brand's association network contains all the connections of brand features (name, logo, color, etc.) together with other memory elements such as meanings, emotions, attitudes, and behavior.

How Associations Create Brand Meaning

The meanings that people allocate to brands can be of different natures and intensities. The physical product is often a source of associations. In many fast-moving brands, the meaning emanates directly from the product and category it is linked to. Sometimes, however, an abstract or symbolic meaning, or a combination of both, is attached to the brand through image-building communication.

The meaning of a brand can stem from any perception of or experience related to the brand. Every contact with the brand can result in forming an association with the brand in memory. Many authors have made inventories of the brand association categories that can be distinguished. Based on an analysis of all these lists, Timmerman (2001) developed the Inventory of Brand

Figure 11.2 **Inventory of Brand Association Categories**

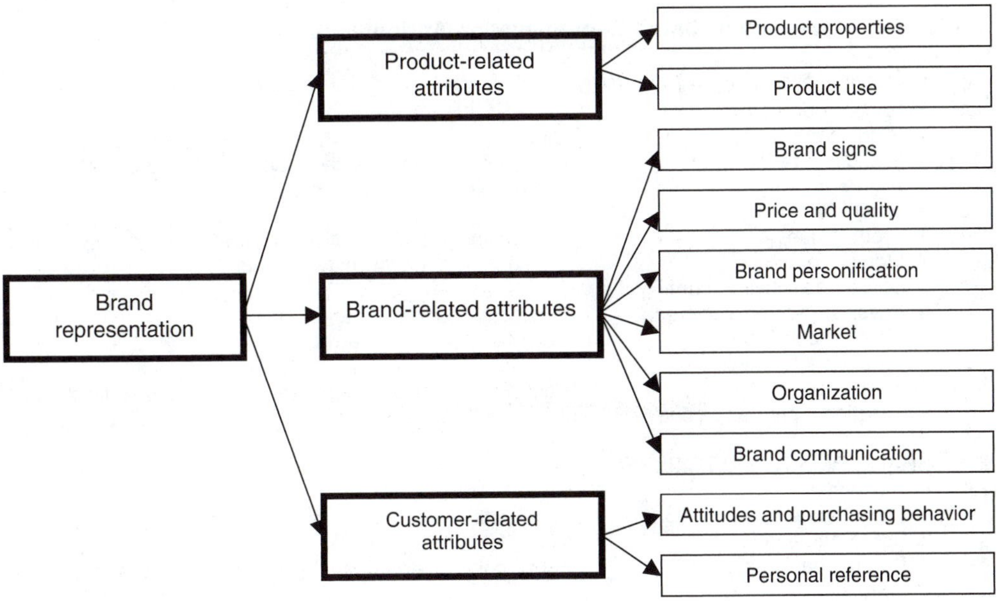

Source: Timmerman (2001).

Representation Attributes (IBRA) for SWOCC, in which he distinguishes three main categories and ten subcategories. Figure 11.2 shows the categories; Table 11.1 shows the subcategories and describes their content.

IBRA gives a good overview of all possible associations that people can have with brands. Not all these associations are equally relevant for all brands. To develop an effective brand strategy, it is useful to research what associations consumers have with the brand in question and which of these associations plays the lead role in the evaluation process of consumers. Insight into the mental status of the various brand meanings is very important, as this determines whether the meanings play a role within brand choice. And what that role is. Without this insight, it is difficult to determine which brand associations have to be strengthened, weakened, or added in order to reinforce the position of the brand.

Hierarchical Levels of Brand Associations

A brand is an associative network, a system in which everything connects. Depending on the situation and the cue being faced, certain parts of this network can be activated and enter a consumer's working memory. Some experts suggest that the knowledge stored in memory is organized in some way so that people have easy access to it. These sets of knowledge are known as "meaning structures" and they are expressed as either hierarchies or networks. The meanings can be found in words, images, concepts, feelings, or patterns (small–big, light–heavy, etc.).

Several models have been developed to describe the meaning structures in our memory (Pieters 1989). Almost without exception, they distinguish different levels that are ordered in a continuum from abstract to concrete. Timmerman (2001) gives as an example: animal → bird → sparrow. In a brand representation, the lowest level consists of the most concrete: the representation of the

Table 11.1

The SWOCC Inventory of Brand Representation Attributes (IBRA)

1   PRODUCT-RELATED ATTRIBUTES
1.1   Product properties

1. Product indication	Class, type, variants
2. Product exterior	Form, color, smell, touch, sound, taste, ingredients/composition, product history

1.2   Product use

1. Product use	Use procedures, work, effect, application, user convenience
2. Moment of use	Season, time, day/week/weekend
3. Social user environment	
4. Physical user environment	Outdoors, indoors, location
5. Physical condition	Condition, physical needs
6. Purpose and effect	
7. Product use image	Age, character traits, appearance, status, sex, lifestyle
8. Functional pros and cons	

2   BRAND-RELATED ATTRIBUTES
2.1   Brand signs

1. Brand name	Informant, metaphorical meaning, sound
2. Brand name/logo	Color, form, typography
3. Product packaging	Form, color, material, package variants, packaging style

2.2   Price/quality

1. Generic product quality	Dimensions: objective/perceived and comparable/non-comparable, performance, characteristics, reliability, durability, style and design
2. Brand article quality	Dimensions: objective/perceived and comparable/non-comparable, performance, characteristics, reliability, durability, style and design
3. Generic product price	Dimensions: exact/indicative price and comparable/non-comparable, evaluative
4. Brand article price	Dimensions: exact/indicative price and comparable/non-comparable, evaluative
5. Brand article	Price-quality ratio

2.3   Brand personification

1. Brand personality	Age, character traits, external appearance, status, sex, lifestyle
2. Values	
3. Brand ideology	
4. Brand relation	Partner quality, affection, intimacy, binding with self-concept, nostalgia, personal commitment, passionate binding
5. Affection	Positive versus negative affect, low versus high intensity
6. Self-image: impressive function	
7. Self-image: expressive function	
8. Brand user image	Age, character traits, external appearance, status, sex, lifestyle

2.4   Market

1. Competition	Leader/follower, market pressure
2. Uniqueness (singularity)	
3. Actuality, contemporary	
4. Shop, branch, availability	
5. Market: local, global	

2.5   Organization

1. Provenience (geographical)	Country, region, location
2. Characteristics	History, founders/personalities, culture, reputation, relation with consumers, media exposure, real estate

(continued)

Table 11.1 *(continued)*

	3. Competence	Overall success, service, competence, innovativeness, expertise, brand-product relation
	4. Social responsibility	Vision, ideology
	5. Alliances	
2.6	Brand communication	
	1. Campaign	Style, type of medium, time, content
	2. Pay-off/slogan	
	3. Endorser	Celebrity, expert, stereotype personality, "character"
	4. Promotions, campaigns, gadgets	
	5. Sponsoring	
	6. Attitude toward advertising	
3	CONSUMER-RELATED ATTRIBUTES	
3.1	Attitude and purchasing behavior	
	1. Product purchasing behavior in the past	
	2. Brand purchasing behavior in the past	
	3. Overall product attitude	
	4. Overall brand attitude	
	5. Social norm in relation to product	
	6. Social norm in relation to brand	
	7. Product purchasing potential	
	8. Brand purchasing potential	
	9. Product purchasing intention	
	10. Brand purchasing intention	
	11. Brand preference/rejection	
3.2	Personal reference	
	1. Social reference	Participation, automation, anticipating and negative group references
	2. Self-reference	Personal experience, life course, important experience moments
	3. Sources of information	Customer reports, media

Source: Timmerman (2007).

brand's identity signs themselves, such as the name, brand logo, color, and packaging. The highest level consists of central value orientations, such as striving toward harmony or power. The value of these models lies with their instrumentality: to what degree do lower meanings contribute to higher ones? Which meanings are instrumental in realizing people's higher goals and values? This is why these structures are given the name of means-end chains (Chapter 9).

Within these models we can distinguish various levels (see Franzen and Bouwman 2001). To create a practical application tool, these are the following four meaning levels—brand signs, product-related meanings, symbolic brand signs, and organizational associations. Within each of these four main levels we can also distinguish several association categories. This creates a hierarchy that consists of the following four levels.

Level 1. Brand Signs

- The recognizable signs of a brand: name, style of writing, color, logo, sound, smell, visual style, packaging

Level 2. Product-Related Meanings

- Physical (sensory) and abstract product properties
- The products and product variants the brand is associated with (e.g., Heineken and beer, Thermos and thermos bottles)
- Concrete product properties: the visible, tangible, sensory characteristics of the products (e.g., the smell of coffee)
- Abstract product properties: the summary of the product properties in comprehensive meanings (e.g., "family car," "sports utility vehicle")
- Functional consequences: the observable, direct consequences of the use of the product for the consumer (e.g., quick, strong, easy, durable)

Level 3. Symbolic or Abstract Meanings

- The association with feelings that the brand (or product) evokes during its use, also known as impressive values (e.g., cozy, intimate, cheerful)
- The personality traits the brand is associated with (e.g., young, individualistic, no-nonsense)
- User association: the image of the stereotyped users of the brand
- Personal values: the ideal representation of the personal life with which the brand is associated (e.g., freedom, independence, health, wisdom)
- Social values: the ideal representation of the society consumers live in and with which they associate the brand (e.g., peace in the world, a cleaner environment, a fair society)

Level 4. Organizational Associations

- Provenience of the brand: country, region, location, and maker
- Organizational characteristics: founders, history, activities, scale, culture, and branches
- Organizational capabilities: competencies, reputation, reliability, and degree of success, authority
- Societal outlook (ethics, ideology): activities and reputations in relation to societal issues, position vis-à-vis stakeholder groups

This classification system deserves some explanation. First, there is the question of whether brand meanings are indeed structured according to such a hierarchy. Meaning structures are infinitely more complex than the hierarchical order suggested above. Researchers rarely find them arranged so neatly. Mostly, researchers create a hierarchy by arranging the order of the questions they ask consumers or by arranging the results afterward. The levels found with techniques such as laddering (see the discussion of the means-end chain in Chapter 9) can be the result of the research method, in which the association process is steered deliberately into increasingly higher and more abstract levels of meaning.

Another concern is the level at which the meaning hierarchy stops. This is difficult to determine with laddering, because the method forces respondents to make a connection between brand associations and their value systems. This process could produce artificial associative connections that are constructed on the spot, rather than being present in memory naturally.

A third concern is the obfuscation of the core meanings of a brand, which can be the result of the research method used. Results of laddering research provide no insight into which are the core meanings of the brand. It is mainly on the basis of these core meanings that consumers classify brands into catego-

Figure 11.3 **The Direction of Associations**

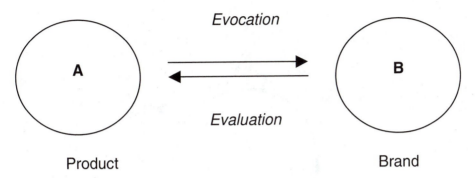

ries and thus distinguish them from other brands. The core meanings also constitute the fundamentals in the formation of a brand concept, which will be discussed below. Most laddering research we are familiar with does not distinguish between the "meanings" of the brand meanings distinguished.

Despite these reservations about the hypothesis of hierarchical levels of meaning, practicing professionals could benefit from grouping the associations of their brands according to the indicated classification and linking goals to these associations. This procedure creates the possibility of deepening the meaning of brands without neglecting the embedment of the physical product.

> *Principle:* A distinction is made within brand meaning structures at various levels, in a continuum that ranges from concrete to abstract. This is known as a means-end chain.

Association Evocation

When professionals deal with brands—for example, when doing research into the knowledge, feelings, and attitudes of consumers toward brands—they tend to implicitly presume associations about a specific brand. For instance, they ask, "What is the image of our brand?" However, associations have a dual structure: there are not only associations between a brand and certain meanings, there are also associations between other memory elements and brands. This is represented in Figure 11.3.

Associations toward a brand is almost never investigated. In fact, this only happens when measuring brand familiarity: "Which bicycle brands do you know, even if just by name?" We establish the association between the bicycle element in the memory and brands and call it brand awareness. This concept sets us in the wrong direction, though: it is not about brand awareness at a high abstract level, but about a very concrete association. We could also ask consumers which brands come to mind when they think about healthy margarine? Or safe detergents? Alcohol-free beer? Clothing stores for young people?

Association Strength

The relative strength of a brand is based on the strength of its associations, as well as the factors that have contributed to its stability over time. An association elicits a connection between a search

Figure 11.4   **The Strength of Associations**

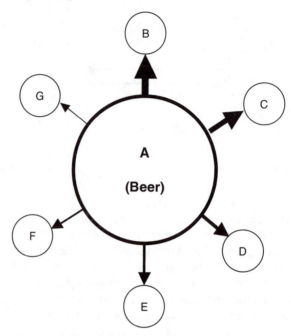

cue and a brand, a connection that exists as the result of learning and forgetting processes through time. Brands that stand at the cradle of their category, as it were, enjoy the major advantages of having been the first to bring this connection into being and of having had the most time to maintain and even strengthen that connection. This is probably the main explanation for the stability of so many large brands with which current generations have grown up.

Woodside and Trappey (1992), studying the connection between the associations of brands and the purchasing behavior of consumers, arrive at the conclusion that only a few of these associations are major explanatory factors for purchasing behavior. The research of Holden (1993) also leads to the conclusion that inclusion of a brand in the consideration set strongly correlates to the response time after the consumer is given a relevant search cue. In other words, strong brands in a category come quickly to mind or come to mind first.

A great deal of market research (see, among others, van Westendorp in Franzen and Bouwman 2001) shows a strong relationship between spontaneous brand awareness and purchasing behavior. If we read this as "strong spontaneous product category → brand association" (that which actually gets measured), this relationship lends support to that principle.

Spreading Activation Theory

There is a theory that describes the course that the association process follows after the evocation of a cue: this is the theory of spreading activation. It is based on the fact that connections in the human brain are of varying strengths (in neurobiological terminology, the neurotransmitters are fired off more easily by the presynaptic neurons and let in more easily by the postsynaptic neurons; see Franzen and Bouwman 2001).

Figure 11.5 **Spreading Activation Theory**

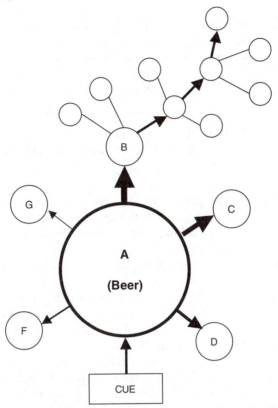

Figure 11.4 represents this concept. The chances of a brand being activated in the evocation phase are dependent on the relative strength of the connection between search cues and that brand rather than competing brands—in other words, from "beer" the association moves first toward brand B, then C, and so on. In cases of low involvement, the strength of the association of a product category or attribute with a brand exerts a dominant influence on brand choice.

This process takes place in supermarkets in a few seconds. In the Netherlands, the time between a shopper's arriving at a supermarket shelf and pulling a brand from the shelf to place it in the shopping cart amounts to 3.0 seconds for margarine, 3.4 seconds for beer, 5.2 seconds for coffee, and only 1.2 seconds for milk (Brouwer and van der Weyde 1998).

In choice decisions where there is a higher level of involvement and consideration, the degree of initial automatic activation of a brand serves as a heuristic to activate the knowledge stored in the associative network. This can elicit a more extensive network and, if necessary, stimulate the processing of more external information as well. The strength of the connections with a brand serves here as a gatekeeper. If a consumer activates beer brand B, other elements that are connected to B will then be activated. Elements of the representation of beer brand B enter the consciousness, as is depicted in Figure 11.5.

The spreading activation theory implies that what is activated first is cue- and content-dependent. The activation then shifts toward following elements on the basis of the relative strength of the individual connections, but it decreases exponentially with time and the distance covered.

CORE ASSOCIATIONS

The core associations determine the accessibility of brand elements in memory and are the associations that first come to mind when given a certain cue—when it comes to cream cheese, many people think first of the Philadelphia brand. The combination of product cue and context influences the saliency of the brand. When people think of beer for weekday consumption, a different brand may come to mind than when they consider buying beer for a party.

> *Principle:* Connections between memory elements have a strength that determines their accessibility. A high relative accessibility denotes the more salient associations.

Although very different elements can be part of a brand representation, Greenfield (1995) posits that memories are made of memory elements that are activated from an "epicenter"—imagine this as a relatively small fabric of elements with a lasting interconnection that determines how they are activated. All kinds of other elements, usually designated as "gestalts," by psychologists, can be activated from there. The strength of the mutual connections and the distance in the chain determine what is part of these gestalts.

An extension of this theory would be to speak of an association core when discussing brands. This denotes the first responses a person has when confronted with a brand or a brand signal, or the first brand associations that enter consciousness. These can be cognitive meanings (Heineken → beer), affective reactions (L'Oréal → "because you're worth it"), attitudes (McDonald's → not for me), and behavioral tendencies (Virgin Airlines → I always take it).

We can imagine a brand metaphorically as a spherical space in which the core associations are located in the center, encircled by a space with associations that are decreasing in intensity. The core contains the main distinguishing marks of the brand, often the brand name and its regular external characteristics (e.g., a certain color, logo, style of typography, and packaging image). The core also contains most primary associations—that is, the first thing a customer thinks of about a brand, such as a product and a dominant property, an application, or an image of the users (e.g., young people). What exactly is in the core is individually determined and varies from brand to brand.

All kinds of other associations can become active from this core, depending on the situation in which consumers find themselves and the stimuli that reach them. Each element could be the core for a new set of associations. These are determined through focused questions in an interview situation or internal responses when seeing an advertisement or packaging in a shelf. The spherical space is shown graphically in Figure 11.6.

We assume that the value and attitude development in relation to a brand is largely based on the core associations of the brand. This linkage seems strongest when consumers are faced with simple choices in which the alternatives are evaluated for only one or several attributes. In many countries, for example, Duracell is the master brand because it has a small but extremely strong association core. Duracell is intensely associated with the product group of alkaline batteries, with extended durability as its main product property, with the quality-suggesting colors of black and gold, and with the reassuring sound of a heavy closing door. For more than forty years, these core associations have been developed in the memories of new generations of battery users and constantly strengthened by the experiences of those consumers who already know the brand. Still, not all brands have such a strong, simple, easy-to-understand, unique association core.

Figure 11.6 **Core Associations**

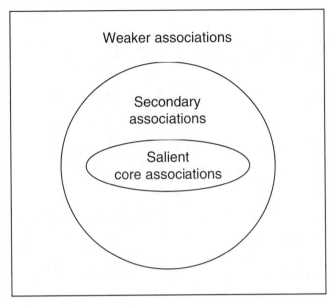

Researching Core Associations

In his research for SWOCC, Timmerman (2001) searched for the core associations of twelve different brands in the Netherlands: coffee brands Van Nelle, Kannis & Gunnik, and Max Havelaar; detergents Persil, Omo, and Ariel; and Philips, Sony, Grundig, Volvo, BMW, and Nissan. He used two research methods—the free association method and the focused free association method (Timmerman calls this the informed association method).

In the free association method, the respondents wrote down all the associations that came to mind after reading a brand name. In the focused free method, they reported the brand associations they got after reading cues that corresponded with the association categories from IBRA. The most noticeable result was that the product-related associations were found in nearly all brands. To illustrate, here is a diagram of the distribution of the answers in the focused free method for two other competing brands—Heineken and Grolsch.

For Heineken, the association categories of product properties, product use, brand communication, and attitude and purchasing behavior appear relatively frequently. The categories for Grolsch are the product properties, brand personality, and attitude and purchasing behavior. It should be mentioned that the research methods used can lead to an advantage for the more concrete brand associations, which apparently are more easily accessible to introspection. Still, abstract meanings can be less present in these research results than in methods in which the respondents are given these meanings in verbal and/or visual form to evaluate a brand, as is the case in most image research.

Tables 11.2 and 11.3 show to what degree associations of nine brands in a study distinguish themselves from the averages in their product categories as far as frequency (with which they are mentioned by respondents) goes. A plus sign means that the associations in that row for that brand were mentioned more than the average of the brands together. No differences were found with detergents (not included here). This could indicate that the detergent associations are determined

Figure 11.7 **Free Associations for Heinken and Grolsch**

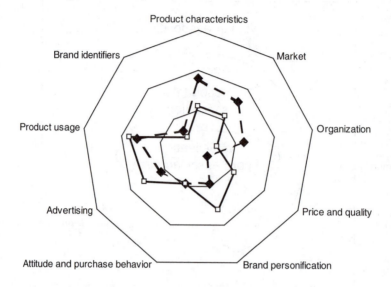

Source: Timmerman (2001).

Table 11.2

Differences in Brand Association Structure From Free Association

	Van Nelle	Kannis and Gunnik	Max Havelaar	Philips	Sony	Grundig	Volvo	BMW	Nissan
Product properties						−			−
Product use	+		−				+		−
Brand signs	−	+							
Price/quality			+				+	+	−
Brand personification	−	−	+				+	+	−
Market organization		−	+	+					+
Brand communication	+	+	−		+				+
Attitude/purchase behavior									
Personal reference		+							+

Source: Timmerman (2001).
Note: Items with a plus or a minus indicate significant contributions to the cue effect; a plus means a relatively high number of answers, a minus a relatively low number.

Table 11.3

Differences in Brand Association Structure From Focused Association

	Van Nelle	Kannis and Gunnik	Max Havelaar	Philips	Sony	Grundig	Volvo	BMW	Nissan
Product properties		+	−				+		−
Product use		+	−	−	+				
Brand signs									
Price/quality			+				+		
Brand personification	−	−	+					+	
Market organization		−	+	+			−		+
Brand communication	+								+
Attitude/purchase behavior	−			−				+	
Personal reference									

Source: Timmerman (2001).
Note: Items with a plus or a minus indicate significant contributions to the cue effect; a plus means a relatively high number of answers, a minus a relatively low number.

mainly by the types of associations in the core of the detergent product category. In the coffee, audiovisual, and automobile categories, brands seem to distinguish themselves more from the average in their product category.

Timmerman's research illustrates that there are important differences in the meaning structures of brands within the same category. The type of associations in the brand core can vary per brand, even in brands within a category. The big question is, of course, which meanings have to be present in the brand core so that the brand can perform optimally when competing out in the world.

Principle: A brand has an association core that largely determines its position in memory.

Category or Product Associations?

The degree to which the products and services or the manifestations of the brands themselves are emphasized as main input for the brand association varies per product category. In categories in which products remain the same for decades and thus have no more secrets for the consumer, like Heineken beer and Nivea crème, associations and manifestations at a brand level are by far the most influential variables (which does not mean that the associations at a product level should be neglected). In fact, a marketer of the Heineken company wondered whether the brand Heineken does not by now stand more for entertainment (music) than for beer (Evers 2000). In this vision, Heineken has risen from a product brand to a brand that claims the entertainment domain, a domain whose original product is merely one element. Heineken has now introduced its own record label in the United States.

In some product categories, like cars and mobile phones, research, product development, and design still lead to differentiated products. In these categories, which still have room for real innovation at a product level, product-related associations have a relatively important influence on the brand associative network. A good example of a brand that has become strong on the basis of perceptions and experiences of the product itself is Starbucks.

Associations as Brand Assets

Not all associations with a brand have a direct influence on the attitude and the purchasing behavior. How does one determine which brand associations are the core meanings of the brands and whether they have the ability to create a strong brain position in memory for the brand and thus motivate purchase?

All types of image research have been carried out, and the purchasing behavior of consumers has also been mapped. Sometimes these are linked and the difference in associations between the buyers and the nonbuyers of a brand is examined. Usually, though, causal relations between image and behavior constitute a personal hypothesis that is seldom made explicit. Chapter 13, which is about the saliency of a brand, shows how relative the influence of the brand image on purchasing behavior can be.

In a study of the connection between brand associations and brand choice (Schuring et al. 1999), all the brands in the Dutch margarine, beer, and coffee markets were subjected to 125 image statements and the brand choice (preference) was measured with the constant sum method. Principal component analyses (a factor analysis method) and partial-least-square analyses (a regression method) were carried out on the data file. The analyses showed that a considerable part of the variance in brand choices in these markets could be explained with a relatively small number of (perception) variables. These findings support the view that the success of a brand depends on a limited number of core meanings.

These behavior-influencing brand meanings are what we call brand assets. There are also negative assets—brand meanings that are evaluated negatively and constitute reasons not to buy the brand. The various brand meanings are represented in Figure 11.8.

Not all brand associations within a brand associative system belong to the brand core concept, and brand associations within the brand core concept are not always assets. It is very important to be

Figure 11.8   **Brand Meanings**

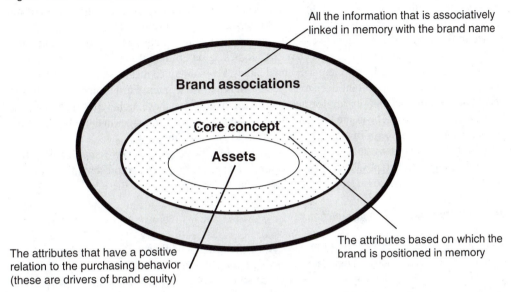

All the information that is associatively linked in memory with the brand name

Brand associations

Core concept

Assets

The attributes that have a positive relation to the purchasing behavior (these are drivers of brand equity)

The attributes based on which the brand is positioned in memory

aware of these distinctions. Ultimately, the goal is that consumers will experience the core meanings of the brand as relevant. Only then can brand core meanings achieve brand asset status. Large brands like BMW, Coca-Cola, and Mars are often present in the memory of many people who have certain associations with these brands. Everyone has (core) associations with Coca-Cola, the product, the bottle, the history, the red color, the logo, "Always Coca-Cola," "The real thing," and so on. However, these associations are not relevant for everyone and thus are not assets to everyone either.

In Chapter 16, which discusses brand equity from the consumer's viewpoint, we will look at these brand assets in more detail. Assets are only those meanings within the core concept of a brand that have a positive, logical relation to the needs, desires, and longings of a certain group of consumers and are therefore reasons to prefer and buy the brand.

CORE BRAND MEANING, ARCHETYPES, AND MYTHS

We have been talking about the way brand meaning is constructed through the process of association. Another way to analyze brand meaning is through the concepts of archetypes and myths.

The psychologist Carl Jung and Joseph Campbell, an expert on cultural myths, were both fascinated by the fact that they kept encountering the same (or very similar) symbolic motifs and meanings in the stories of old civilizations and contemporary primitive societies, in all religions, in medieval alchemy, in the visual arts, literature, and theater, in dreams, and even in the delusions and hallucinations of psychotic patients. Jung called these meanings archetypes and Campbell called them mythologies.

Brand Archetypes

Jung's archetypes are increasingly appealing to the imagination when it comes to brands (e.g., Pawle 2000; Mark and Pearson 2001; Wertime 2002). Jung believed that behind every concrete symbol there is an intangible collective idea, image, or concept. The symbol itself can, of course, be a conscious one, but the thought behind it is unconscious. People do not realize that these ideas are present in their minds. Why is it that the Marlboro man has come to represent the idea of the American West and the independence of the solitary cowboy? Moreover, all those meanings coalesce in the minds of consumers in all cultures, on a global level, not just in the United States.

Jung saw these unconscious, collective archetypes as determining behavior and influencing attitudes and views as well as preferences and dislikes. He maintained that these universal symbols play a role in all the important decisions people make in their lives. Furthermore, he believed that character and personality are formed by the relative power these archetypes have over the unconscious. Everyone, he argued, carries these archetypes, ideas, or images in their minds—now as well as 5,000 years ago, in New York as well as in New Guinea.

It is striking that many successful brands, such as Marlboro, seem to represent meanings that tally with Jung's archetypes. That is because these deeper meanings also represent the essence of the category and resonate on a primal level with the consumers who buy these brands.

Brand Archetypes and Brand Functions

Pawle (2000), Mark and Pearson (2001), Wertime (2002), and Millward Brown (2006c) together distinguish nineteen archetypal brand core meanings (Jung himself was convinced that the number of different archetypes is countless). Though the labels sometimes differ, these researchers link a primary brand function to each archetype, describing the relationship between people and the archetypal brand meaning. They see archetypes as forming what some might call the "software of the psyche."

These archetype programs resonate with consumers' self-image and the way they classify people and objects they encounter. In *The Hero and the Outlaw*, Mark and Pearson explain that some people live continuously in the personal image of the Explorer archetype ("I'm on a journey," "Get out of my way," "Don't restrict my freedom," "I own the road") or the Ruler archetype ("I'm in charge," "Get the job done or you're history").

Brands that are associated with one of these archetypes give a good feeling to people who also radiate such an archetype, creating resonance by giving meaning to their lives in a special way. Table 11.4 presents a compilation of the most common of these archetypes and their main functions in people's lives.

According to Mark and Pearson (2001), a strong archetypal brand meaning is always anchored in an archetypal product meaning. They describe Starbucks, for example, as a classic Explorer brand; they point not only to its name, which is a reference to *Moby Dick*, but also to the sea goddess logo. The company's emphasis on finding the best coffee from all over the world also contributes to the archetype.

An archetype symbolizes something, and by standing for something bigger than just a product, it becomes iconic. The Marlboro Man is an iconic image because of the richness of its symbolism and the way symbolism deepens the meaning of the brand. Similarly, Starbucks has come to stand for the best coffee and the best coffee-drinking experience. But the iconic meaning can also rest with a product or category. Consider the tuxedo and everything it represents. The makers of champagne have labored for years to break away from its iconic meaning as a celebratory drink in order to move the product into more general use. Because its iconic meaning is so deep-seated, however, no amount of advertising can change the image of champagne.

All the brands discussed in the opening stories in this book are iconic in the sense that they have become strong brands as a result of their archetypal meanings. Some of them have been more successful than others—Levi's is a good example of a brand whose troubles are exacerbated by inconsistency in its deeper meaning. Consider the following examples:

Table 11.4

Brand Archetypes and Their Functions

	Archetypes	Functions
1. The Innocent	Desires purity, goodness, and simplicity.	Retain or renew faith
2. The Explorer	Wants the freedom to discover him/herself by exploring the world. Wants the freedom to experience a better, more authentic, more fulfilling life.	Maintain independence
3. The Sage	Seeks to discover truth. Uses intelligence and analysis to understand the world.	Understand the world
4. The Hero	Desires to prove his or her worth through courageous and difficult action. Wants to exert mastery.	Act courageously
5. The Outlaw	Aims to find identity outside the current social structure. Wants to disrupt society, to shock, to destroy what does not work. Iconoclastic.	Break the rules
6. The Magician	Seeks the fundamental laws of how things work. Hopes to make dreams come true.	Affect transformation
7. The Regular Guy/Girl	Wants to connect with others, to belong and fit in.	Be okay just as one is
8. The Lover	Hopes to attain intimacy and experience sensual pleasure. Wants relationships with people, work and experiences.	Find and give love
9. The Jester	Wants to live in the moment, with full enjoyment. Wants to have great time.	Have a good time
10. The Caregiver	Tries to protect people from harm, to help, and to give to others.	Care for others
11. The Creator	Yearns to create something of enduring value to give form to a vision, to create culture.	Craft something new
12. The Ruler	Wants to have control, to take responsibility, and to exert leadership.	Exert control
13. The Siren	The sexual being in each of us. The power of attraction linked with the possibility of destruction.	Be sexually stimulated
14. The Anti-Hero	The evil in each of us, which symbolizes faithlessness and the lack of repentance. Goes against the grain.	Be contrarian
15. The Change-Master	The desire to be master of one's own destiny.	Control one's destiny
16. The Friend	The shoulder to cry on. The embodiment of trust, loyalty, and reassurance.	Be socially connected
17. The Enigma	The desire for fascination, mystery, and suspense, represents the world of imagination.	Be fascinating
18. The Mother	Is giving life. A nourishing, timeless feeder. Protects and maintains a condition of well being	Being protected
19. The Maiden	The materialization of virtue and perfection. The object of platonic love.	Being virtuous

Diesel: Antihero
Lego: Creator, Caregiver
Swatch: Jester
Gillette: Loyalist
Red Bull: Explorer
Harley-Davidson: Outlaw
Levi's: Explorer (also flirted with Regular Guy, Outlaw, and Hero)
Pepsi-Cola: Jester
Volkswagen Beetle: Innocent, Antihero
Apple: Outlaw
Martha Stewart: Creator
Virgin: Explorer
Nestlé: Loyalist
Ivory: Innocent
Samsung: Change-master
Cadbury Schweppes: Caregiver
BMW: Explorer

Brand Mythologies and Brand Stories

The concept of myth is important to brand meaning because mythologies represent sacred stories that illustrate basic truths. As we said earlier, the brand story is the container of the brand meaning, and most brand stories are designed to connect with these deeper truths. These themes, such as coming of age, conquering an impossible task, rags to riches, Cinderella and the prince, and the ugly duckling who becomes beautiful, express various types of human dramas. They reflect universal dreams and struggles. Because the themes are embedded deep in culture—the universal cultural experience—consumers recognize them easily and link their meaning to a brand.

In Coke's classic "Mountaintop" commercial, its meaning of universal brotherhood is immediately understood without any announcer proclaiming the obvious. Apple's "1984" commercial, in which a woman athlete throws a hammer through the screen, obliterating the image of Big Brother, mirrors the David and Goliath story, and its message is understood even though it is largely nonverbal.

Stories are powerful because they invite people to immerse themselves in an affective, personal, meaning-making experience. The key word here is affective. Recent research into perception and the workings of the brain has shown dramatically that the emotional response comes first (A.M. Barry 1997, 2005). Furthermore, such research suggests that brand choices are driven more by emotion than rational thinking. Therefore, brand stories, which are embedded in personal emotional experiences, open the door to people's souls and link them to the soul of the brand.

A classic example is the Nike women's campaign, which reaches its female target by moving away from the highly competitive athletes and sports stars showcased in the brand's more male-targeted advertising. The campaign strikes a chord because it speaks to women in language that resonates with their personal values and self-image:

A magazine is not a mirror.
Have you ever seen anyone in a magazine who
Seemed even vaguely like you looking back?
(If you have, turn the page.)
Most magazines are made to sell us a fantasy of what we're supposed to be.

They reflect what society deems to be a standard
However unrealistic or unattainable that standard is.
That doesn't mean you should cancel your subscription.
It means you need to remember
That it's just ink on paper
And that whatever standards you set for yourself
For how much you want to weigh,
For how hard you work out,
Or how many times you make it to the gym
Should be your standards,
Not someone else's.

How Does Meaning Work?

When an idea emerges in a person's mind or an image or symbol resonates on a personal level, we say it takes on meaning. How does that happen? First of all, making meaning is an experience. As S. Diller et al. (2006) explain, people have the strongest ties to products, services, and brands that evoke meaningful experiences for them. Meaning, they say, is a framework for assessing what we value, believe, criticize, and desire.

Making meaning operates at a deep level in the human psyche. People are constantly in a search for meaning—for sense making. As McCracken (2005) explains, however, this is not meaning with a capital M but rather the small meanings of daily life—what it means to be a man or a woman, what it means to be a member of a community or a country. When the consumer looks at ads, McCracken says, they are looking for symbolic resources, new ideas, and better versions of old ideas with which to advance the meaning-making project.

Meaning experience can be passive (relatively unconscious) or active (when people have to concentrate on sense-making). Most of Jung's archetypes and Campbell's mythologies operate first on the unconscious level, where they connect with deeply buried experiences. People intuit meaning that they find hard to express. Putting this connection into words, then, is done by concentration. The process is like art appreciation—museum-goers may initially like or dislike a painting, but they have to think about it beyond their superficial encounter with its appearance in order to articulate the symbols and various levels of meaning. Mark and Pearson (2001) liken this active method of meaning making to peel an artichoke, stripping the flesh from the outer leaves and discarding them until the heart of the artichoke is uncovered. But either way—passive or active—the meaning experience results from an encounter.

We have discussed how meaning is created through association. An important aspect of that pattern of mental links is association with needs and values. In Chapter 9 we outlined various types of needs and values, but it should be clear that archetypes and mythologies express these need states and values. Archetypes represent underlying values through symbols and icons; mythologies represent them through stories. We will continue this discussion of making meaning as we develop the concept of the mental brand.

THE DEVELOPMENT OF THE MENTAL BRAND

Brand development is basically about the creation or emergence of meanings in the memory of consumers. Restall and Gordon (in Franzen and Bouwman 2001) state that, after all, brands do not exist in the factory, in the studios, in the sales points in an advertisement, or on the supermarket shelves, not even on the television screen—they exist only in the minds of consumers. The development of the mental components of brands is thus an important element of the management of a brand system.

But there is more to the mental representation than images conveyed through advertising. Individuals have their own unique experiences on the basis of which they develop a unique memory content. At the same time, individual interpretation of the brand meaning is strongly colored by the social interpretation of the brand within the culture or subculture. As it became clear in our discussion in Chapter 2, people are programmed collectively by the culture in which they live. The meanings that the members of a culture ascribe to a brand resemble each other strongly and can therefore serve as culturally understood symbols. In that chapter we also described the extent of this social influence on brand-meaning construction and brand use. People often learn to know and use brands through important others in their social environment.

Brand communication generally plays a mere supporting role in this process. By making brands, advertising, and other communication part of the social context of people's lives, companies increase their chance of playing a role in the game of meaning construction.

Brand strategy is manifested in the attempts that strategists make to positively influence their brand's system of meaning. Remember, however, that the meaning-making process cannot be managed 100 percent by the marketer due to the system's own internal logic. Of course, this does not mean that brand systems are completely unmanageable, but rather that insight is needed into the essential components and, especially, the relationships between intended and perceived associations and meanings. To influence the behavior of a brand system, changes in these components themselves or the relationships between them are required. The question is, thus, which components lie within the sphere of influence of brand management and what instruments can be deployed to this end.

Linking Brand Mentality and Brand Physique

The connecting element between the different manifestations of a brand is the personality, values, or the mentality of the brand. This is an immaterial or intangible aspect, which is not to say it is less important than the tangible aspects of a product. From a strategist's perspective, the intangible dimensions of the mental brand are the driving force behind everything a brand is, says, and does—the intangible element provides the connecting thread between the brand story and the brand performance and between the marketer's intended brand image and the customer's brand meaning.

The mental brand concept is a way of thinking about a brand image from a manager's perspective. It is an inclusive term for concepts that we have discussed throughout the book, including brand vision, brand identity, and brand function. Consumers may or may not feel addressed by this mental concept but, at some point, they must develop a similar mentality if the brand is to be successfully communicated.

Some mentalities are shared by many products (at least potentially), others are much less attractive; every brand has its own fan club. The mentality can even surpass the physical manifestation of the brand, just as with people. It is what distinguishes brands like Nike, Swatch, Diesel, Virgin, Absolut, Harley-Davidson, Caterpillar, and Ben & Jerry's. It involves brands with a meaning, a story. This meaning can relate to social issues, as is the case with Benetton, Diesel, or The Body Shop. It can also relate to a specific domain, as Bertolli shows in its vision of Italian cooking, as Sanex shows in its embodiment of healthy body care, and as easyJet shows in its insistence on providing no-nonsense, accessible, easy, and affordable services.

easyJet: Fully Integrated Mentality and Physique

In November 1995 Stelios Haji-Ioanmou started an airline in Great Britain, naming it easyJet. He began operations with two leased Boeing 737s, flying from London to Glasgow and Edinburgh. The company's rapid growth was accelerated by its merger with €0-fly in 2002, which made easyJet Europe's largest low-cost airline. In 2007 easyJet carried 40 million passengers in a fleet of 137 aircraft flying 289 routes to about in 21 country airports. It is now expanding outside Europe.

The secret of easyJet's successful formula is its no-frills position and cheap pricing structure. The position is based on insights into the fundamental values of a large segment of the airline industry's customers. They make their choice based on getting the best deal they can find in travel. However, since flying is also seen as potentially dangerous, they do not want to trade off safety considerations. easyJet understands those values and has addressed them effectively with its business model.

To satisfy its customers' desire for cheap travel, easyJet cuts corners every way it can to keep costs down. Tickets can be reserved only by telephone or on the Internet, not via expensive travel agents or another company. *Ticket* is actually the wrong word, because travelers flying easyJet get nothing on paper, only a reservation code by e-mail or telephone. At the airport there are no boarding passes to be torn or magnetically read, only a plastic card with a number customers submit while boarding. Customers with low numbers are the first ones allowed to choose a seat; the higher ones follow. Costly paper piles are eliminated this way.

Austerity is the word on board too. There is only one class of passengers, and everybody pays for drinks and snacks. "The trip is less important than the destination," says founder Haji-Ioanmou. "What would you rather say when you arrive at the office on Monday: I went skiing in Switzerland this weekend, or I had a great meal on the KLM?"

There are two things not subject to savings: airplanes and pilots. easyJet claims to be convinced of the vulnerability of its reputation. "Airplane maintenance is expensive, but not as expensive as an accident," says Haji-Ioanmou. The current fleet of eighteen 737s, with their average age of four years, is one of the youngest in the world. This is how easyJet recruits pilots from renowned companies.

The no-frills formula fits the times, Haji-Ioanmou believes. His success story confirms his belief—the $3.5 billion sales in 2007 with a pre-tax profit of $396 million, and the growing number of Internet reservations, now 80 percent, from the success of two brand extensions—easyCar (car rental via the Internet) and the easyEverything chain of Internet cafés.

Sources: Steketee (2000a); Kirsnar (2002); Osborne (2006).

It is important to translate this brand mentality into the components of the brand system that are perceived through the senses (the physical reality of the brand). After all, this external reality is the source of association forming and brand-bonding. Seeing, hearing, feeling, smelling, and tasting all the possible manifestations of a brand leave traces in memory, and the result is a brand representation.

Synergy and Integration in the Mental Brand

All the possible ways in which a brand manifests itself to consumers play a role in the development of the mental brand in their memory. In Chapter 1 we distinguished a material, a human, and a behavioral component within external brand reality. Of these three, the material component—the brand physique—can be influenced most directly. Manifestations like products, services, advertising, packaging, events, and buildings are, in principle, all pliable and can be deployed as a means of communication. The brand physique is therefore the most important instrument in the construction of brand meaning, as it forms the raw material for brand experience.

The challenge lies in being able to link all these manifestations in one way or another, so that they form an integrated whole whose strength is greater than the proverbial sum of its parts. The synergy between all these different physical parts or manifestations of a brand does not happen overnight. It is a dynamic process whose explanation is likely to be found not by studying the separate elements (e.g., product, communication, packaging) but in their combination. Not only the physical components and their designers are involved in this process, but also the consumers and the people surrounding them.

Integrated Branding and the Total Brand Concept

The secret of strong brands lies in synergy—in the linking or merging between mentality and brand physique whose core is formed in many cases by the products and services the brand represents. When they come together, they form a total brand concept. What these successful brands, such as Nike, have in common is that they all succeed in concretizing and realizing their mentality. They are not empty stories, they really do it—the story and the performance are in balance.

This is why the relationship between brand mentality and brand physique deserves special attention. Concretizing the mentality of the brand with things that can be perceived through the senses is a crucial aspect of brand development (brand management, brand strategy). The success companies have in transforming vision, values, and personality into products, services, and even buildings, shops, and interiors determines the degree to which brand physique can serve as an expression of the mentality. After all, consumers and other stakeholders do exactly the opposite: they experience only the physical manifestation of a brand and on this basis form for themselves an image of its underlying mentality. Consumers and other stakeholders of the brand will never notice anything about the existence of a brand mentality if the company does not succeed in making it resonate through its physical manifestations.

The physical manifestation of a brand is essentially unlimited, but it would be useful to have an insight into the elements that are essential within it. Meanings differ with regard to the differences in importance between the physical manifestation forms. Franzen and Bouwman (2001) see products and services as central, but Geursen (1994) posits that, in the form in which a brand appears, no difference in degree of importance is made in principle between the physical product (behind the brand) and every other manifestation. In other words, if a brand is an idea, this goal approves all the means that can bring that idea to life.

Given the proposal in Chapter 4 that all brands are essentially service providers, the core function of a brand may provide a foothold toward determining the essential components within the brand physique. It is clear that products and services are very important for brands that are bought primarily for the functionality of the products (product-related core function). This is probably the case for most of the fast movers, but with brands that are increasingly independent of physical products (e.g., Greenpeace) or brands whose mentality determines brand choice behavior (e.g., Nike, Harley-Davidson), products may be at a lower rank in the hierarchy of the brand physique—provided they meet the basic quality requirements. Here the core question always remains: what is the right to existence of a brand and what is it based on?

Finding the Right Balance

Existing brands vary enormously in their mentality and physique and the integration of both. To illustrate, the following variants can be distinguished.

Brands that are mentally poor. In many fast-moving brands, the mentality components seem to be lacking or are poorly developed; the brands have no personality, values, or vision. In general, such brands have not yet risen above the stage of "product with a brand name." Large brands that have existed for generations are usually loaded with meanings and emotions, but these tend to have emerged (for instance, in the social application context) rather than been drafted intentionally that way by producers. The origins of brands like Nivea, Heineken, Quaker Oats, and Knorr lie in the product and not so much in a mentality.

Brands in which the link between the mentality and the brand physique is lacking or unclear. In some brands, a mental component is formulated on paper but is not successfully transformed into the physical aspects of the brand, as a result of which it is not perceivable by consumers.

Brands with a nonintegrated appearance. In attempts to make brands out of existing names without the basis of a developed mentality or vision, the physical manifestation of the brand risks being disjointed. There may be no recognizable link between the products that hang under the brand name, between packaging and advertising, between product quality and price, between sponsoring and other activities, and so on. A perfect example is the attempt by Philips to combine light bulbs, hairdryers, and toasters with DVD recorders, mobile telephones, and MRI scanners.

Within the framework of brand strategy and management of the mental brand, it is important to keep track of the development of the mentality, the brand physique, and, especially, the balance and the link between both, managing them when necessary to create coherence in the way they ultimately contribute to the consumer's brand choice and brand loyalty.

THE CONSUMER RESPONSE PUZZLE

As was mentioned in Chapter 1, an important dimension of the brand system is its "black box" character. Much of the brand system—and the strategy that drives it—comes together in the form of a consumer response, which is sometimes more puzzling than predictable. We know that consumers are sensitive to the brand system and respond to the brand's actions and messages; however, the way that response process works is largely hidden from the brand manager, who can approach consumer response only through trial and error. There is no magic wand. That is why consumer research is so important in strategy development. Yet, at best, research is only a surrogate, giving mere glimpses into the way a customer views a brand, feels and thinks about a brand, and approaches a brand decision.

Ideally, the result of a brand strategy is the creation of a brand preference that leads customers to make a purchase and a repeat purchase, eventually becoming brand-loyal or, at least, including the brand in their brand repertoire.

In the ideal world of brand-focused strategy development, the puzzle is easy to put together and the pieces are all precut and matched. In customer-focused brand analysis, however, purchase behavior is affected by a large number of other, uncontrolled factors that also affect the brand system, making the end result agonizingly unpredictable. When the focus is on the consumer, rather than the brand plan, the end result—the consumer's response—may look like an unfinished puzzle, with missing pieces and pieces that cannot be made to fit no matter how you turn them.

Consumer behavior is the arena where these puzzles are contemplated, and account planners are the professionals who specialize in puzzling out insights into consumers' attitudes and decision-making processes. Account planners use a variety of qualitative and quantitative research methods with the aim of acquiring a deeper insight into the relationships between people, product, and brand.

Consumer Insight Into Brand Meaning

Gathering insight into brand meanings is important for any marketing or brand manager, but it is particularly critical for people working in marketing communication. A brand's relationships with its customers are driven by its communication: what it says and does not say, how it invites customers to contact the company and how the company responds, and what others say about it.

In the process of planning these message opportunities, account planners play the role of the voice of the customer. In order to be effective in that role, they must have valid insight into the feelings, motivations, and attitudes that drive their customers' behavior. They cannot make it up; they cannot read their own lives and meanings into the customer's response. They have to be truly in touch, in synch, and inside the lives of their typical customer. That person—the typical customer—has to be the planner's friend, adviser, mentor, and critic. How else can you have a dialogue with someone?

According to Steel (1997), the role of a communication strategist, particularly an account planner, should be to embrace consumers as partners in the process of market development in order to use their input in evaluating the ensuing campaign. This approach aims at understanding and gathering insight.

Lisa Fortini-Campbell (1998) discusses the problems of marketers who are so focused on their products and their jobs that they are unable to see the consumer insights that would shed light on strategies relating to brand meaning:

> Our problems as marketers start with the way we describe our targets and how quickly and easily we leap from simple demographics to what we think is an insight. Target descriptions that refer to nothing more than general demographics and simple purchase history statistics are trite, superficial and far too common. We think we know a lot because we know the target consumer is a woman 25–54, with a $40,000 plus income and three plus children, who buys one or more gallons of orange juice a week. And there we stop, rather than begin the really hard process of internalizing our consumer's perspective.

Often we are satisfied with only the most rudimentary and superficial understanding of the consumers with whom we are trying to communicate, and we act on that shallow understanding without bothering to delve any deeper. Our skills of consumer understanding are weak and flaccid. We think to know a little is to know enough.

We do such a poor job of getting into our consumer and achieving the true insight and understanding that requires, and then we start our work in the form of a product, an advertisement, or some other marketing program. And then we are surprised that our consumer targets don't get it. Our work betrays the fact that we have neither understanding nor real empathy for them. They don't identify with the characters in our spots and they think our clever ads are bizarre or off-putting. Or they simply ignore what could not possibly be intended for them. Obviously, if consumers are not persuaded, they don't buy. And when they don't buy we even blame them for their stupidity.

On the other hand, successful marketing programs are characterized by the exact opposite, by the ability of the people behind them to achieve real empathy with their consumers, to think from their point-of-view, to experience the product or service as they would and then to act on that knowledge to design every element of the consumer's experience service and support.

Qualitative Research Techniques

Uncovering brand meanings requires probing techniques, such as ethnographic or motivational research, that move below the surface of consumer survey research. Focus groups are useful, but the methods used by account planners tend to be more observational and interactive. The account planner is looking not for people's reports on their attitudes and behavior, but rather for insights into why they feel, believe, and act as they do, particularly concerning brand choice.

Ethnographic Research

Some planners find insight into brand meanings by studying the way people live and interact with products and brands. This form of research comes from anthropology and is called ethnography. Ethnographic methods are useful to move beyond the self-reported data gathered from surveys and focus groups. Abrams (in Khermouch 2001) emphasizes the need to get to know consumers closely:

> As products mature and differences in quality diminish, marketers are anxious to hook into subtle emotional dimensions that might give them an edge. This up-close approach can also help marketers figure out how different ethnic and demographic groups react to their products, especially important in a fragmenting marketplace. . . . Knowing the individual consumer on an intimate basis has become a necessity. And ethnography is the intimate connection to the consumer.

The true feelings and views of people are more evident from their deeds than their words. Researchers who try to discover how consumers relate to a brand and construct brand meanings start by looking carefully at what they do, as behavior is often the most important source of information about the knowledge and attitude of consumers. Account planners manage access to consumers' kitchens, bathrooms, cars, and offices, registering precisely what happens there. Sometimes they accompany consumers on shopping trips. The consumers' behavior is sometimes recorded on videotape and then used later to elicit explanations about what caught the consumers' attention and why, what they were thinking at a particular time, and why they behaved as they did in certain situations. Mariampolski (1999) explains the value of ethnography as follows:

> Ethnography cannot reasonably be classified as just another single method or technique. In substance, it is a research discipline based upon culture as an organizing concept and a mix of both observational and interviewing tactics to record behavioral dynamics. Above all, ethnography relies upon entering respondents' natural life worlds—at home, while shopping, at leisure, and in the workplace. The researcher essentially becomes a naïve visitor in that world by engaging respondents during realistic product usage situations in the course of daily life. Herein lies the power of ethnography.
>
> Whether called on-site, observational, naturalistic, or contextual research, ethnographic methods allow marketers to delve into the actual occasions and situations in which products are used, services are received, and benefits are conferred.
>
> Going from focus groups to ethnography is somewhat like moving from black and white to color—the immediacy of the smells, textures, tastes, heat, sounds movements, and muscular strain all stimulate an enriched level of understanding. If the research objective is to understand consumer-shopping patterns, the ethnographer can tag right along at the supermarket or department store. If we need to understand home cleaning patterns and products, ethnography allows the researcher to sniff the air around the home, stare at hairballs on the sofa—actually see the success or failure of product performance and share the consumer's look of satisfaction and pride after a job well done. Ethnography takes place not in laboratories but in the real world.
>
> Consequently, clients and practitioners benefit from a more holistic and better-nuanced view of consumer satisfactions, frustrations, and limitations than any other research approach. Laboratories such as telephone banks and focus group studios are limited in their ability to capture the human dimension. In contrast, naturalistic ethnography can offer insights into consumer practices, language, myths, and aspirations that cannot be deduced elsewhere. The main task of ethnography is not only to watch but also to decode human experience—to move from unstructured observations to discover the underlying meanings behind behavior; to understand feelings and intentions in order to deduce logical implications for strategic decisions.
>
> Observation provides the discipline to bring depth and richness to research findings because utterances alone are not the source of data—our understanding is enlarged by an appreciation of nuance and context.

Principle: Observation of displayed consumer behavior (ethnographic research), supplemented with motivational research into the underlying motives of this behavior, is increasingly being used in brand strategy development.

New Forms of Motivational Research

In the middle of the twentieth century, the concept of motivational research came into vogue, later, however, gaining a stigma as speculative psychology. The Dutch research bureau Censydiam succeeded in making it respectable again and published in 1999 a book on it titled *Motivational Marketing Research Revisited* (Callebout et al. 1994), a psychodynamic approach to consumer behavior. The book describes motivational research as "aimed at gaining insight into the fundamental motivational frame of reference and mapping the various groups of needs":

- The basic needs consistent with each motivational segment.
- The analysis of the way in which these basic needs are translated into a choice of specific products, product variants, and brands and also into actual buying behavior.
- The analysis of the way in which products do or do not succeed in entering into a constructive relation with one or more of those groups of needs.
- The analysis of the way in which communication (packaging or advertising) is or is not supportive with regard to this relationship.

Mark and Pearson (2001) illustrate archetypal-focused motivational research with the American automobile industry as an example:

> In a major study we conducted for the automotive industry, we were determined to avoid the usual rationalizations and clichés common to asking drivers about what they want from an automobile brand. Instead, we began with a framework of fundamental psychological needs: achievement, aggression, belonging, independence, sexuality, status, etc. For each need, we generated adjectives, phrases, images, and descriptions of situations that were then incorporated into a questionnaire. In the actual interviews, respondents were first asked to free associate, recalling their earliest memories of first getting behind the wheel of the car, putting the key into the first car that they ever owned, and the like. Following this exercise, they responded to the battery of questions derived from the psychological needs framework, indicating the degree to which each word, phrase, or image described how they related to the experience of driving. Finally, they were asked to indicate which car brand or nameplate they associated with these situations, images, and feelings.
>
> The results were quite astounding. Drivers who, in more conventional approaches, might have talked about gas mileage and sticker prices, offered memories of early driving experiences that were far richer and more authentic than surveys of customer preferences generally yield. One man simply recalled hot summer nights, blondes, cops, [and] the color red.
>
> The response that was most overwhelming and intense with respect to the deep meaning of cars and driving related to the Hero and the Explorer archetypes. In reacting to the words and phrases, many drivers indicated that, for them, the experience of driving was about testing themselves, driving in bad weather, rising to challenges, and overcoming obstacles. No insulated living-room-on-wheels experience for them—even though this type of experience is often featured in automotive advertising and emphasized at the showroom. Their earliest memories of cars and driving conformed to this finding and helped to explain the fundamental importance of cars in our culture. It was clear that for many Americans—especially, but not exclusively, men—cars and driving are our first true loves, and the act of earning one's driving license is one of the few true rites of passage in our culture, marking our passing into adulthood. . . .
>
> Cars have meanings that can be used to differentiate brands: status, luxury, rebellion, and sophistication, for example. But each of these meanings must be understood within the larger context of the essential meaning of the category and, ideally, should be fused with it. In this category, the spirit of the Hero and the Explorer is the tailwind that can provide an unexpected source of energy and velocity in the marketplace.

Information for a consumer-based brand strategy using methods similar to ethnography can be developed as a type of developmental research or "presearch" (Moens 1999). It is geared toward understanding consumers' motives and behavioral mechanisms and intended as a systematic thought framework regarding consumer needs. It is not so much a control or evaluation instrument as a source of inspiration for brand positioning and communication strategy.

Stoop (2000) proposes "insearch" as an umbrella term for research that feeds the advertising process by gathering exhaustive consumer insights in early stages, thus finding the effective "clicks" between brand or product and consumer, and between strategy and execution. Within this context, Unilever speaks of acquiring insight into the consumer by identifying that one element, relative to everything the company knows about the target consumers and their needs in this competitive environment, on which the relationship between customer and brand is built.

Principle: For an effective brand strategy, companies need research into the role of products and brands in the life of consumers and into their perception of the alternatives. The goal is to gather insights into consumer attitudes and behavior: how does this product or brand fit into the life of this consumer?

Elicitation Techniques

An important methodological contribution was provided in 1995 by Zaltman and Coulter's introduction of the Zaltman metaphor elicitation technique (ZMET). ZMET is not a new technique—it is a hybrid research approach that combines various techniques that were already in existence, such as laddering, repertory grid, photosort, and collage. ZMET helps strategists get a better insight into the image that consumers have of a brand or product, bringing out deeper motivations.

Compared to other research methods, the ZMET method has the following aims:

- Providing deeper understanding about consumers as a basis for advertising and other marketing-mix decisions.
- Doing a better job of eliciting latent and emerging needs.
- Providing better guidance for capturing consumers' attention and further engaging their thought processes.
- Codifying and organizing nonverbal data more effectively.
- Facilitating the presentation of findings by researchers in ways that more closely resemble the end products their clients must develop, e.g., visual advertising.

An important element of ZMET is that consumers themselves gather the stimuli that are used during the research. It is they who have to look within their environment for images with which they can express the world they experience. Sometimes they are given a video camera so they can record this world. The research then proceeds in eight steps:

1. *Storytelling:* The respondents describe the chosen images.
2. *Missed images:* The respondents describe images that they would have liked to find but could not.
3. *Sorting:* If there are more than twelve pictures, the respondents are asked to sort them.

4. *Construction elicitation:* The interviewer selects random pictures and asks how these differ from other pictures in relation to the research subject.
5. *Metaphor elaboration:* The interviewer uses specific criteria to select two or three pictures, and the respondents choose additional pictures that are complementary or contradictory.
6. *Sensory images:* The respondents are asked about nonvisual sensory aspects—sounds, smells, and so on—that are or are not representative of the subject.
7. *The vignette:* The respondents are asked to imagine a short film that describes their feelings about the subject.
8. *The digital image:* The respondents make a summarizing montage that best expresses the subject.

The ZMET method has much to offer. Experience shows that the results of ZMET are consistent with those of other methods, with the addition of a deeper insight into the underlying motives and perceptions of consumers. Nevertheless, for all studies consisting of interviews by researchers and introspections by respondents, the question remains as to the degree to which the actual causes of behavior can be brought to the surface.

Quantitative Techniques

In recent decades, many techniques have been developed to measure brand image. For an overview, see Franzen and Bouwman (2001). These very different techniques are based on four basic approaches:

Free methods
1. *Free association methods:* The respondents report everything that occurs to them spontaneously after hearing or reading the brand name.
2. *Focused free association methods:* The respondents report everything that occurs to them spontaneously in relation to a brand on the basis of a series of guiding instructions, such as "what product does this brand make you think of?"

Choice methods
3. *Free choice method:* The respondents are presented with a series of association meanings, in verbal or visual form, and may indicate with which brands they associate them or put them aside as irrelevant.
4. *Forced choice method:* The respondents are presented with a series of meanings and indicate for every brand to what degree they associate the brand with the meaning. This method tends to make use of ranking and scaling techniques.

In the free methods, the risk of influencing (biasing) by a researcher or question is minimized. These methods provide a good insight into the accessibility of the brand associations. However, experience shows that in these methods it is mainly the very concrete brand associations that are activated, like those related to products, product properties, advertisements, price, and quality. Abstract meanings, like symbolic attributes (brand personality associations, values, etc.) are named spontaneously to a much lesser degree.

In the choice methods, respondents are more likely to associate brands with symbolic meanings. The free choice method produces a relatively low nonresponse of 40 to 50 percent (Winchester and

Fletcher 2000) and therefore discriminates better between brands. In the forced choice method, there is a risk of not measuring autonomous associations in long-term memory, as opposed to temporary links being established in working memory as a result of the reflection process. This could lead to the construction of nonexistent associations.

In the choice methods, associations are observed that do not occur to that degree in the free method. This is particularly the case with symbolic associations. Because, when positioning brands, brand management strategists increasingly look for solutions in the development of a brand personality, the preference in research goes largely to these choice methods.

The large, and in our view still unanswered, question is whether the free methods fail to activate the less explicit, more abstract, or deeper associative links, or whether choice methods lead to measuring meanings that have an extremely weak or no long-term connection with a brand. We therefore believe that it would be worthwhile for researchers to deploy free methods as well as choice methods in order to obtain as complete a picture as possible of the meanings a brand is associated with and their relative strength.

In addition to the difference between free association methods and choice methods, there is an important second aspect that deserves attention: the difference between associations from the brand and associations toward the brand. In the first case, respondents get the brand name as cue and are asked which associations they have with the brand (the free association methods) and secondly to what degree they associate the brand with provided meanings (as is done in the choice methods).

It could also be useful to find out which meanings respondents associate with a product or product category, service, or other domain, especially which brands they name as first in that context. This would provide insight into the saliency of a brand within a certain category (also known as top-of-mind awareness). Chapter 13 is dedicated to the importance of saliency.

Principle: Research into brand associations distinguishes between free methods (in which respondents associate freely) and choice methods (in which respondents react to cues provided). A comprehensive study should include both.

BRAND STRATEGY IMPLICATIONS

Insight into the core concept of a brand and the part of it that influences choice behavior—the brand assets—is necessary for a responsible brand strategy. The brand strategist will have to consider whether the existing core associations should be strengthened or adjusted. For new brands, the strategist must determine the appropriate product or category connections and the other symbolic and organizational associations that will create meaning for the brand. Table 11.5 summarizes the basic strategies focused on the creation of brand meaning in consumers' minds.

In established brands there is less room for flexibility. Strongly anchored associations are permanent in memory—they cannot easily be broken down. The only way to change them (a process we called repositioning in Chapter 8) is to develop new associations next to the existing ones. The new associations must then be strengthened so, in the course of time, they will be stronger than those that formed the core of the brand. This is often a lengthy and expensive operation that tends to be underestimated by optimistic brand managers. Marketing history is full of failed repositioning operations.

Above all, research into associations and brand representations alerts managers to the fact

Table 11.5

Meaning-Driven Brand Strategies

Associations	Existing	New
Product/category	Strengthen or change	Establish link
Core associations	Strengthen, change, establish new	Establish link
Symbolic	Strengthen, change, establish new	Establish link
Organizational	Strengthen, change, establish new	Establish link
Association network/structure	Simplify, strengthen, change	Establish system of links

that meaning entails a complex set of associations and that the strongest brands are the ones with the simplest association structure. Today's communication society, which is characterized by an unimaginable information overload, calls urgently for limitation of the informational content of messages. The attention span of the recipients of individual advertising expressions is becoming increasingly shorter and more superficial. The more messages offered in an advertisement, the smaller the chances of any of them getting sufficient attention. From a message planner's perspective, concentration on an extremely limited number of core messages that set up a simple, clear association network is recommended.

STARBUCKS AND BRAND MEANINGS

Starbucks means . . . coffee, first of all. It also means strong coffee or even European-style coffee. And it means a nice place to drink the coffee, a place to meet friends and visit with neighbors, a social experience based on the enjoyment of a cup of quality coffee. But Starbucks means even more than a social coffee drinking experience—it also means a company that supports its local community, its employees, and the environment. There are other meanings, of course; some customers think the coffee is too strong or too bitter, and some are appalled to see this global company moving in on local, small-town businesses.

Not every customer holds all these associations in mind, but one measure of the global success of Starbucks is that many of its customers equate most of the positive associations to the meaning of the Starbucks brand. And most of those associations are so positive that they bring customers back to Starbucks frequently. Starbucks fans are as committed to Starbucks coffee as its network of employees and management are committed to maintaining and protecting the rich association network of the brand.

BRAND RELATIONSHIPS AND REPUTATION

Regis McKenna (1991b), who wrote one of the first books on the theory and practice of relationship marketing, asks, "What is a brand but a special relationship?"

Like the bonds in a friendship or marriage, the connections between customers and their favorite brands are special. The brand relationship concept is a metaphor and at its heart are the connections that define partnerships, friendships, marriage, and family. The idea is that people connect with their favorite brands based on personal and emotional links. These deep relationships are not true of all brands, but rather reflect, as McKenna says, a "special relationship" with a well-loved brand.

An example of a strong brand relationship is the bond that the Apple Macintosh has established with its customers. The brand's initial slogan, "The computer for the rest of us," defined both its target and its competitive advantage and contributed to an extreme level of loyalty among Macintosh users. The company's subsequent "Think different" slogan focused on the computer's creative applications and state-of-the-art design. The image of this brand—not to mention the quality of the product—has created emotional bonds in a high-tech category where such strong feelings of liking are relatively unknown.

THE APPLE BRAND STORY

Apple Computer is a good example of a brand that would have died off long ago, but for the power of its customer brand relationships. Its initial position as innovator in the personal computer market was usurped by IBM; it never made much headway in the business machine market; its proprietary operating system kept partners away from developing and extending product reach; and it stumbled for years with a series of miscues in distribution, pricing, and product development. So why, then, is it still alive—and why does it have a near cult-like following among loyal Macintosh users?

Its success is based on the integration of two compelling brand stories. Apple is, as the legendary positioning statement proclaims, "the computer for the rest of us." Its ownership of the ease-of-use position in a high-technology marketplace has kept its fans in the fold in spite of problems with its marketing mix and its high prices. And that easy-to-use, easy-to-learn position was reinforced for years by its ownership of the educational market, particularly at the lower levels of instruction in elementary schools. That is changing now as lower-priced personal computer (PC) manufacturers are nibbling at Apple's dominance of this market. But everyone knows how to use a computer now, so where is the power in this continuing storyline?

Interestingly, Macintosh has buttressed its innovation position with an additional storyline about creativity. Serious graphic designers and serious artists use Macs. The brand has set the standard in the design market, with PC systems trying to keep up with Apple's continually evolving platform. Inside the box is a state-of-the-art design tool that has allowed the Mac to maintain a loyal following among artists, graphic designers, digital video producers and editors, and audio producers and sound designers.

The design story, however, is not buried inside the box; it is also a product design statement. The iMac and PowerBooks have won raves, as well as awards, for their product design. The iMac, instead of being cold, hard, dull, square, gray, and computer-like, proclaimed its fun brand personality through its distinctive profile, which is curvy, colorful, and almost cuddly. It is sculpture for the desk, a story concept expressed visually in a magazine ad that shows a circle of various colored iMacs and the headline, "Yum." It has also become a visual icon for computers in general, showing up in other ads, TV sitcoms, magazines, comic strips, and movies whenever a symbol of computerness is needed. So the Mac is not just for the rest of us—for people who are not geeks—but also for people who are creative, people who are artists, people who have taste and appreciate good design.

The coolest innovation is the iPod and its iTunes downloadable music system, which dominates the portable music market. The success of the iPod and its continuing product improvements and innovations (Mini, Shuffle, Nano, as well as the iPhone) has polished the Apple brand and, surprisingly, driven new customers to the computer line. It has made the Mac cool again with a new generation of users.

It is true that the powerful brand storyline with its twin themes of innovation and ease-of-use has not given Apple dominance in the computer market, but it has kept Apple and Macintosh alive even in times of trouble. Although IBM lost its dominance in the personal computer market because it permitted its technology to be cloned by other manufacturers who then became serious competitors, the PC-based system has a hammerlock on the business desktop. Given the structural power of the PC platform, Apple will probably never be able to overcome its position as David versus the PC Goliath.

But lending strength to its customers' loyalty is the powerful and universal mythology embedded in that David archetype and how those meanings are signaled in the Macintosh brand story. Apple users are proud to support the underdog, the iconoclast, the revolutionary. As in the legendary "1984" commercial that launched the Mac—the one that shows a runner throwing a sledgehammer through a screen image of Big Brother—Macintosh is not afraid to break the rules and liberate its customers through innovative design.

Sources: www.Gartner.com; www.Apple.com; Swartz (2007); Consumer Goods (2006).

WHAT IS A RELATIONSHIP?

This chapter will explain the phenomenon of brand relationships—how people make long-term commitments to inanimate objects that they buy and use, as well as help make, sell, and distribute. Of course, we know that a brand is not capable of having feelings and notions of affiliation. That prerogative resides in its managers, who are the keepers of the brand's associations and affiliations, and its users, who sometimes even feel ownership of the brand—as in "my Coke." However, in keeping with the relationship metaphor, we will also refer to the brand, the marketer, or the company as a functional partner in a parasocial relationship, and we will speak of the brand as if it were a partner playing a role in this relationship.

Interpersonal Relationships

To better understand the metaphor, it is useful to look to the literature where theories about interpersonal relationship can be found. As Barnes (2001) explains, the word *relationship* has a special meaning for most people and is used in those special situations where there are strong feelings and an emotional connection between—in most cases—two people. He admits that this special feeling can extend to brands—that the emotional links, feelings of closeness, and interactive communication are typical even of a parasocial relationship.

From a review of interpersonal literature, Fournier (1998, 344) identifies four conditions that typify "the brand as partner." The following four characteristics personalize a brand relationship and move it away from passive anonymity:

- A reciprocal exchange between partners who are both active in the construction of the relationship.
- A purposive effort that delivers meaning to both partners.
- A multidimensional effort that provides a range of benefits.
- A process that evolves and changes over time.

Expanding on the personal relationship metaphor, Fournier compiles a typology of fifteen different forms of relationship that describe how the people in her study felt about the brands they use: arranged marriages, casual friendships or buddy relationships, marriages of convenience, committed partnerships, best friendships, compartmentalized friendships, kinships, rebounds or avoidance-driven relationships, childhood friendships, courtships, dependencies, flings, enmities, secret affairs, and enslavements (1998, 362).

In truth, however, we know from psychology that the number of close relationships that most people have is relatively low and that those they do have vary in strength (Baumeister and Leary 1995). A person may have many acquaintances, but is genuinely bonded to few people—generally close friends and family. Closeness is the defining factor and that certainly applies to brands, as well as interpersonal, relationships.

What Is Relationship Marketing?

When the relationship metaphor was adopted by marketing theorists in the 1980s, the concept was described but rarely defined. Pinning down a definition continues to be a problem as scholars, business executives, and consultants all talk about relationship marketing and then find they are all talking about different things.

In looking back over the evolution of the term, the scholars at Britain's Cranfield School of Management in the 1980s tracked the emergence of a definition of relationship marketing in the 1980s as "the development and cultivation of longer-term profitable and mutually beneficial relationships between an organization and its customers" (Peck et al. 1999, 2). The Cranfield group modified this original view of relationship marketing by describing it as a convergence of marketing, customer service, and the total quality movement (Christopher and Ballantyne 1991). So these early definitions emphasized that a quality brand relationship was customer-oriented, long-term, and reciprocal (mutually beneficial).

In a more recent version, Tony Cram (1994, 19) continues to emphasize those key notions as he adds several new dimensions: "Relationship Marketing is the consistent application of up-to-date knowledge of individual customers to product and service design which is communicated interactively, in order to develop a continuous and long-term relationship, which is mutually beneficial." In addition to customer focus, long-term connections, and reciprocity, Cram's definition adds knowledge about customers and interactivity. The customer knowledge factor reflects the emergence in the 1990s of databases as a key to customized marketing and marketing communication; interactivity is included as a result of the explosion of electronic communication technology and the Internet.

A systems approach can be seen in the definition of relationship marketing given by Gummesson (1999), which spells out in a simple statement his view of the key requirements: "Relationship marketing is marketing seen as relationships, networks, and interactions." He explains that a relationship requires at least two parties who are in contact with each other. A network is a complex set of these basic relationships, and the connections between the various parties in the network are represented by interactions. Although he does not specify the notion of mutual benefit, it is clear that Gummesson's network of interactive relationships is describing a system of reciprocity.

Mutual Benefit

Why do customers choose to relate to a brand—what benefit do they get? Ideally, savvy marketers design products that solve consumers' problems and serve their needs more effectively than in the past. Beyond these basic requirements of customer-focused marketing, satisfaction with a brand experience means there is less risk in choosing that brand again, so familiarity anchors reliability and reduces risk. On a personal level, a brand can be a badge that allows customers to express their personality and aspirations. A brand relationship can also provide an affective motivation through the pleasure that comes from affiliation with something customers like.

For the marketer, a successful brand relationship reduces marketing costs by making it easier to sell to a satisfied customer. Brand relationships also lead to loyalty and, in the aggregate, contribute to the goodwill that is associated with brand equity. As Duncan and Moriarty explain in their book *Driving Brand Value* (1997a, xii), "Brand equity is determined by the quality of a brand's relationships with its customers and other key stakeholders."

It should be noted, however, that there are all kinds of relationships—some positive and some dreadful. As in personal relationships, brand relationships can be dysfunctional. Some people, for example, might identify their relationships with their banks, airlines, or other service providers in that way. Sometimes we are locked into relationships that increasingly seem to lack positive benefits—so it is important to remember that not all brand relationships are necessarily good or strong.

The Relationship-Building Process

How does all this relationship building work? In a major study of brand relationships, researchers at the SWOCC center in Amsterdam (Tolboom 2004a) identified a series of steps that characterize the development of a consumer-brand relationship:

- A series of interactions occur during a time period.
- During these interactions there is an exchange.
- During the exchange the brand influences the consumer.
- The consumer attaches a meaning to the interaction and the evaluation.
- This meaning can lead to positive, neutral, or negative emotions.
- The emotions lead to a level of bonding.
- On the basis of the strength of the bonding, future interactions are considered.

We will be discussing aspects of this process throughout this chapter. But first, let us consider the characterization of a brand relationship as a series of interactions.

A Classic Paradigm Shift

Many companies think of sales transactions as isolated events that deliver short-term results, rather than the first step in building long-term relationships with their customers. This is a shortsighted approach that rarely leads to a sense of brand loyalty in the customer. The concern for brand loyalty and, at a higher level, brand equity, has led to a major paradigm shift that Blattberg and Deighton (1996) describes as replacing exchange and transactional theories of marketing with relationship theories. This shift moves the industry from the short-term sales focus to a long-term customer focus.

The definitions of relationship marketing that mandate a mutually beneficial condition constitute an oppositional approach that sets up relationship marketing as an alternative theory to transactional marketing, with its emphasis on short-term objectives, 4Ps strategies, and consumers as targets. In contrast, relationship-marketing focuses on long-term connections with customers through strategies that better identify and satisfy their needs.

This customer-focus requirement is the mantra of the United Kingdom's Cranfield School of Management, where Adrian Payne, Martin Christopher, David Ballantyne, Helen Peck, and their colleagues call for a new relationship approach. Payne (1995, 32) outlines the differences as follows. Transaction marketing focuses on a single sale. It is characterized by orientation to product features; little emphasis on customer service or customer commitment; short-term, moderate customer contact; and quality as a concern of production. In contrast, relationship marketing focuses on customer retention; orientation to customer values; high customer service and long-term customer contact; and quality as everyone's concern.

In other words, relationship marketing reinvigorates the old customer-focus orientation of the original, but infrequently applied, marketing concept. Payne describes his view of relationship marketing as customer-focused management. In order to deliver that customer focus, relationship marketing requires more than just marketing responsibility; rather it demands an organization-wide perspective operationalized through cross-functional management (1995, 19).

Calls for a new relationship-based marketing philosophy emanate from the United States and Australia, as well as from Cranfield. In the United States, Len Berry, who is known for his contributions to the development of the ServQual methodology at Texas A&M, is credited with being the first to use the term *relationship marketing* (1983). Jag Sheth's Center for Relationship Marketing at Emory University also made significant contributions to the development of the field.

The boldest challenge to traditional (transactional) marketing, however, came from the Nordic school of services marketing. Grönroos (1998) makes the point that there is a range of contacts between the service firm and its customer that are beyond the traditional 4Ps of the marketing mix. He also articulates a new relationship-focused definition of marketing (1990): "The purpose of marketing is to establish, maintain, enhance, and commercialize customer relationships (often, but not necessarily always, long-term relationships) so that the objectives of the parties involved are met. This is done by the mutual exchange and fulfillment of promises."

Gummesson (1999) argues that the 4Ps represent supplier-controlled activities for manipulating customers primarily using mass marketing, an approach that is no longer appropriate in the modern world of business. Even though the theorists agree that a customer focus is essential in relationship marketing, there are still managers who think of relationship marketing merely as more intensive supplier-controlled communication. For example, the senior vice president of marketing for Feld Entertainment (which operates Ringling Brothers, Barnum & Bailey Circus, and Disney on Ice) describes her company's relationship program as "communicating through e-mail and direct mail, and using our database to track customers' preferred seating, types of customers, and their contact information." Although the use of e-mail opens up opportunities for dialogue, we still wonder how this company answers customers who ask, "What's in it for me?" (Robertson 2006).

The Real Meaning of Customer Focus

"What's in it for me—today and tomorrow?" is the question that drives relationship programs that are truly customer-focused (Hornstein 2006). The concept of customer focus has shifted with the maturation of relationship marketing. When the concept emerged in the 1980s, the focus was primarily on the supplier side of the equation; the goal was to identify how the marketer could benefit by knowing more about customers—similar to the view of the Feld marketing vice president.

More recent work in the 1990s redefined brand relationships as two-way commitment and communication (Duncan and Moriarty 1997a, 1998). Hennig-Thurau et al. (2000), also tracing the growing recognition of mutually beneficial reasons for customers to participate in brand relationships, developed an integrative theory of customer motivations. The point is that in modern marketing, a customer focus means that the marketer is as concerned about fulfilling customer needs as it is about its own business performance, realizing that a true customer focus will naturally optimize sales.

What brands do for their current or potential customers with each and every contact helps build or break customer relationships and, in the end, creates or destroys customer loyalty to the brand. Relationship marketing, then, is the way to create a true customer-focused marketing program. A customer focus is even more important now that there has been a worldwide shift from goods to services marketing, with services accounting for an even greater percentage of sales, profits, and gross domestic product.

As a way to summarize a brand relationship from a customer's viewpoint, Duncan (2000) developed the Customer's Bill of Rights, a list of critical behaviors designed to help companies articulate the respect and concern they have for their customers. This list reminds managers that customer relationships are at the heart of marketing and that customer-centric strategies should protect customers from the dehumanization, coldness, and high-tech veneer of modern business:

---

1. Customers have the right to contact a company twenty-four hours a day, seven days a week (and, at the least, be able to leave a message).
2. Customers have the right to select from a variety of ways (phone, fax, e-mail) to contact a company.
3. Customers have the right (e.g., option) to talk to a human being without being subjected to multiple levels of an automated voice-response system.
4. Customers have the right to talk to a person with enough authority to make a decision.
5. Customers have the right to talk to a knowledgeable person who has immediate access to information necessary to answer any reasonable question or complaint.
6. Customers are right 98 percent of the time—the other 2 percent of the time, they have the right to a sensitive and empathetic explanation of why they are not right.
7. Customers have the right to receive an "immediate" response, relative to typical use of the product (e.g., if product is used twenty-four hours a day, then response should be available twenty-four hours a day).
8. Customers have the right to be rewarded in proportion to their support of a company (e.g., buying, referring others, following procedures).
9. Customers have the right not to be subjected to intrusive phone calls and spam e-mails.
10. Customers have the right to privacy regarding their transactions (e.g., the option to control the selling of their names to other companies).

Source: Duncan (2000).

Relationship Management

Earlier we noted that Payne used the phrase *customer-focused management* to call attention to the mutually beneficial nature of brand relationships. That leads us to the concept of customer relationship management (CRM), which, one might think, is a practice that leads to more customer-focused relationship programs.

Building on Cram's requirement of customer knowledge in his definition of relationship marketing, CRM uses information technology and databases to target the right customers with the right products or features to meet their needs. Databases allow companies to identify their customers' needs and wants, likes and dislikes, behaviors and personal information, such as demographics and contact information. These databases can also be used to drive communication with customers and keep track of their interactions with a brand. However, they also open up the brand relationship to privacy challenges as companies struggle to identify the permissible use of customers' personal data.

Originally CRM was designed as software to help sales managers in "contact management." In some cases, CRM was simply another term for sales automation that integrated back-office record-keeping, production, and fulfillment operations with the information needs of front-line sales staff. These software packages made it possible to contact prospects more frequently and provide them with more information—in some cases, more contacts and more information than customers needed or wanted to receive.

The objective of CRM, then, is to use practices like data mining to target new customers and to drive sales growth from current customers. In order to increase share-of-customer wallet, traditional CRM identified the most profitable or "high-value" customers and prospects in order to provide them with special attention. Burnett, in his book on CRM for business-to-business organizations, calls these key customers or key accounts (2001).

The problem with the early CRM programs is that they were designed by computer experts for computer experts, so managers were slow to launch the programs throughout the company. Sales and marketing people sometimes found the systems difficult to use in their own areas. So CRM got criticized for promising efficiency when, in fact, it added more levels of complexity.

There are some unfriendly concepts embedded in CRM. For example, customers that do not provide an adequate return on the company's investment in the relationship are targeted for programs intended to increase their level of business with the brand or they are relegated to a maintenance level where their needs are met to the extent their business is considered profitable. Some customers may be dissuaded from doing business with the company if it is clear they are not profitable and never will be. The problem is in making that determination. The story used to be told that IBM did business only with large customers with a sufficient budget to justify the huge company's business. Unfortunately, that meant small companies were discouraged from doing business with IBM. As these smaller companies grew and their business became more attractive, IBM discovered they were committed to other suppliers. Whether or not the story is true, the point is that targeting has to be based on indicators of potential and business growth, as well as current size.

Obviously the roots of CRM and some of its practices, while important in terms of customer knowledge, are contrary to the customer-focused philosophy of a true relationship-marketing program. These tools rely on targeting and strategy in the military sense to capture information, as well as customers. Barnes (2001) is particularly critical of such programs, observing that both parties must want the relationship and that maintaining the relationship is grounded in feelings and positive experiences. Nobody wants to be in a relationship that is managed by others for their own purposes.

More recent developments in CRM are transforming information technology into relationship technology with the goal of building stronger long-term relationships that encourage more meaningful interactions. Newell (2000, 7–8) describes this as a big change from traditional database marketing to data-driven communication. Traditional database marketing focused on targeted promotion, which Newell admits was company-centric, rather than on customers' benefits and values in a true customer-focused strategy.

But even with that goal, the corporate viewpoint still dominates. Consider a recent definition in a CRM book by Swift (2001): "Customer Relationship Management is an enterprise approach to understanding and influencing customer behavior through meaningful communications in order to improve customer acquisition, customer retention, customer loyalty, and customer profitability." This definition needs work before it can be seen as focusing on the support of a mutually beneficial relationship, two-way communication, and a true customer focus.

PARTICIPANTS AND PARTNERS

A relationship strategy, by definition, involves more than a simple one-time transaction. Such a strategy drives a long-term commitment and a series of interactions between at least two parties— usually a marketer and a customer, although others can also participate in supporting and maintaining the relationship. Managers cannot impose a relationship on customers; customers have to believe that they are partners who have a stake in the brand, perhaps even ownership of the brand. Coke discovered the power of the perception of brand ownership when its loyal customers rebelled against the imposition of "New Coke."

A System of Stakeholders

Relationship marketing theory evolved from research in two primary areas: customer service and supplier/vendor/distributor relationships. In particular, channel relationships were analyzed through the frame of business-to-business marketing, where successful customer service operations are essential. As relationship marketing practices moved into more general consumer marketing, the objective became to create a bond between a brand and its customers, a connection that encourages them to feel as if they are partners or even part of the brand's family.

More recent views of relationship marketing consider all the company's stakeholders as important partners—whether employees, channel members, suppliers and vendors, agencies, investors and others in the financial community, the media, governmental and regulatory bodies, activist and consumer groups, members of the local community, and even competitors who sometimes become business partners. In their definition of relationship marketing, Payne and his Cranfield colleagues insist that the customer-marketer dyad be expanded to include all the stakeholders that have an impact on the customer relationship. In other words, relationship marketing is about more than just customer relationships (Christopher and Ballantyne 1991).

In keeping with our systems theme, this broad set of stakeholders creates a network of interactive relationships in which brand-related communication is passed among all these participants, as Duncan and Moriarty (1998) illustrate in their model of relationship-based marketing.

The stakeholder concept has its roots in public relations, but it has been adapted to the marketing world as a means of engaging all the powerful loyalties that support a brand's performance. B. Murphy et al. (1999) have developed a concept they call stakeholderism, which they define as nurturing mutually beneficial long-term relationships between an organization and its various stakeholders, such as customers, employees, suppliers, the community, and shareholders. The basis of these relationships is the ethical values of affirmation, integrity, efficiency, and equity, which lead to sustainable value for all stakeholders. With its socially responsible undertone, the Murphy definition reflects a clear win/win philosophy of relationship management.

Some stakeholders are more important than others, depending upon the brand's marketing situation. Customers, of course, are the focus of many relationship-building programs that aim to create and cement brand loyalty. These customer relationships often are driven by one-to-one marketing programs based on relational databases, data-driven direct contact, and personal attention. But in a sense all stakeholders have an impact upon customer relationships because these varied groups of people interact with and influence customer brand perceptions. Employees are a key stakeholder group, particularly in service positions, because they present the face and personality of the brand in their interactions with customers. Rosenbluth and Peters (2002) argue in their book *The Customer Comes Second* that successful brands put their employees first, even before customers. Rosenbluth comes from the service industry and that is one reason he believes so strongly in superior service as the foundation of a positive customer relationship. His driving principle is, "The highest achievable level of service comes from the heart." Therefore, the company that keeps its employees happy will keep its customers happy.

Markets and Players

Reflecting this broader focus on stakeholders, rather than just a customer focus, a number of experts emphasize the breadth of the relationship network. The Cranfield School of Management proposes six key markets that need attention in a relationship-marketing program (Payne 1995, 31). Customers are at the center, but surrounding that key market are stakeholders grouped in the following categories:

- internal markets (employees)
- supplier markets
- recruitment markets (the source for good employees)
- influence markets (those who influence business practices, such as government and financial bodies)
- referral markets (those who recommend or advocate a brand)

The Murphy model of relationships (B. Murphy et al. 1999) is a stakeholder pentagon that calls attention to five groups: customers, suppliers, shareholders, community, and employees. Kotler (1992) developed a concept he calls "total marketing" in which he identifies ten key players in a company's business environment. He classifies them into two groups: the microenvironment, which includes suppliers, distributors, end-users, and employees, and the macroenvironment, which includes the financial community, the government, the media, allies, competitors, and the general public.

A true stakeholder map will vary with the brand. Some product categories are subject to government regulation; others may find the financial community to be critical—or the local community, or activist groups, or the media. The important thing to remember, from a communication perspective, is that these groups can overlap, so there needs to be consistency in the core brand messages. Employees, for example, may be shareholders; they may live in the community, where they may serve on governmental bodies that regulate a company's actions; and they also may be involved with a consumer group. No doubt they talk to friends and they may even be interviewed by the media.

Brand Communities

Sometimes relationship efforts are not only initiated by customers, but they involve bonds between customers. The classic example is the Harley Owners Group (HOG), which was created by Harley owners. This group is a self-directed brand community that has endured for years and maintains its own Web site, activities, and presence within the motorcycle market. Harley-Davidson managers keep their eyes on this group but do not attempt to manage it.

How are brand communities defined and identified? Muniz and O'Guinn (2001) define a brand community as a "specialized, non-geographically bound community based on a structured set of social relations among admirers of a brand." Two brand communities that Muniz and O'Guinn identify are users of Apple computers and drivers of Saab cars. The researchers identify three "markers" of brand communities:

- *Consciousness:* a feeling of connection not only to the brand but also to other brand users.
- *Legitimacy:* rituals and traditions used to differentiate between true members and marginal members.
- *Opposition:* a sense of community based on opposition to competing brands, which creates a brand loyalty derived from a moral responsibility.

Online communities have reshaped the way brands interact with their customers, as well as how customers interact with each other. Intel found that out when challenges to its chip circulated online and overwhelmed the company's attempts to control, or even respond to, these very public complaints.

An Extensive Network of Relationships

Gummesson's (1999) extensive list of thirty relationships includes types of relationships, as well as parties in relationship dyads. He classifies these thirty relationships into classic market or special market relationships, which are further grouped into mega (external) and nano (internal) relationships. Here is his system of relationships (abbreviated as R):

Classic market relationships

R1   Marketer and customer
R2   Marketer, customer, competitor
R3   The distribution network

Special market relationships

R4   Full-time and part-time marketers (people in marketing and sales departments)
R5   Service providers
R6   Other business organizations (customers and suppliers)
R7   The customer's customer
R8   Close versus distant relationships (personal versus mass)
R9   Dissatisfied customers
R10   Monopoly relationships (customers as prisoners)
R11   Customers as members
R12   Electronic relationships
R13   Parasocial relationships (connections to symbols and objects)
R14   Noncommercial relationships (families, public sector, nonprofits)
R15   Green relationships (opinion leaders, activists in environment and health-related communities)

R16   Law-based relationships (legal contracts and litigation)
R17   The criminal network (organized crime, illegal business ventures)

Mega relationships (external and above-the-market relationships)

R18   Personal and social networks
R19   Mega marketing (governments, legislators, influentials)
R20   Alliances
R21   The knowledge relationship (information sources)
R22   Mega alliances (European Union, NAFTA, and others beyond nation and industry)
R23   Mass media relationships

Nano relationships (relationships inside the organization)

R24   Internal market mechanisms (profit centers)
R25   Internal customer (and supplier) relationships
R26   Quality community and providers inside the company
R27   Internal marketing (the employee market)
R28   Two-dimensional matrix relationships (marketing and sales)
R29   External marketing service providers (agencies, freelancers)
R30   Owner and financier relationships (investors, partners)

Gummesson's list illustrates the complexity of the relationships that surround a brand. Not only is there a vast group of stakeholders involved in relationships with a brand, but also all these groups are interacting in a network of communication about the brand. Because of the breadth and depth of his stakeholder analysis, Gummesson has leveraged his thirty relationships into a concept he calls "total relationship marketing," which he believes is a fundamental factor in effective brand marketing.

A Compilation of Brand Relationships

Building on the work of these relationship experts, we believe that various types of relationships can be positioned as a field, set, or network (Figure 12.1). This classification system provides a guide to the key relationships that need to be considered in the development of a brand strategy.

- *Macroenvironment:* the financial community, industry groups, the government (regulators, agencies, legislators), the media, activist groups, opinion leaders, and the general public
- *Microenvironment:* suppliers, distributors, allies and partners, competitors, agencies, and other specialized service providers
- *Internal environment:* employees, other divisions and departments, shareholders
- *Market environment:* customers and end-users, prospective customers, buyers, purchase decision influencers, brand communities

As we have said, all stakeholders are important, but contemporary research and theory tend to focus on the marketer-customer dyad. In recognition of the special role that employees and channel members play in maintaining and supporting this key relationship, the research is

Figure 12.1   **A Field of Brand Relationships**

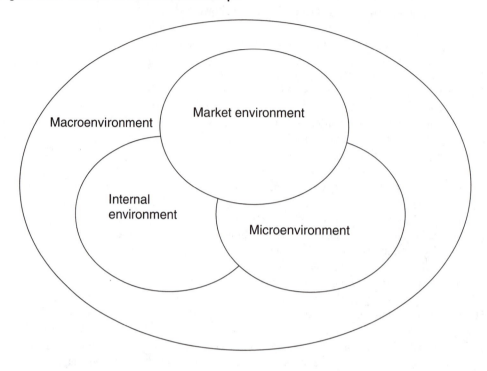

sometimes expanded to include triads, such as marketer-customer-channel or marketer-customer-employee relationships. The area where they have the most impact on customer relationships is the brand promise.

THE RELATIONSHIP BETWEEN BRAND AND CUSTOMER

In his criticism of many relationship marketing programs, Barnes (2001) observes not only that they are not customer-focused, but that they are missing two-way interaction, as well as a critical emotional link—both of which he believes are required for any type of relationship.

Research has determined that Barnes is right about the emotional connection. Regardless of the structure of the relationship, it is always based on an emotional bond, which can be analyzed using such bipolar adjectives as positive/negative, caring/uncaring, liking/disliking. Some critics might be inclined to wonder if the relationship metaphor is too strong for the favorite-brand phenomenon and to doubt the emotional connection that people develop for brands.

In her groundbreaking study of brand relationships, Fournier (1994, 363) analyzed all the brand relationships in a set of in-depth case studies. Based on that research, she asserts, "At the core of all strong brand relationships was a rich affective grounding reminiscent of concepts of love in the interpersonal domain."

To answer the question, then, people can develop strong bonds with their favorite brands even if only a few brands develop such a link. So besides emotion—caring, liking, disliking—what are the other critical factors in a customer-brand relationship?

The Brand as a Promise

Communication is a basic requirement of any relationship, whether personal between friends or parasocial between a customer and a brand or company. In a sense, a brand is a platform for communicating with a customer. The platform itself is a promise, a covenant, between the partners in the relationship. A brand's reason for being, then, is to make a promise to a customer. Zhivago expresses the principle of the brand promise (Auken 2000) when she says, "A brand is not an icon, a slogan, or a mission statement. It is a promise—a promise your company can keep." Grönroos (1990) redefines marketing as a relationship concept and also includes the requirement of a promise: "Marketing is to establish, maintain, enhance, and commercialize customer relationships so that the objectives of the parties involved are met. This is done by a mutual exchange and fulfillment of promises."

A brand is a promise that the product will deliver a satisfactory performance and meet the customer's expectations. It is a mental formulation of what the brand will do for a consumer in an instrumental as well as symbolic sense. A brand promise includes a sense of continuity, a commitment extending from the past to the present and future, setting up expectations for both partners.

The promise also carries with it some notion of what makes the brand superior to its competing brands. For Harley-Davidson, such a promise could be expressed as follows: "Only Harley-Davidson delivers you the fantasy of complete freedom on the road and the comradeship of kindred spirits" (Auken 2000). The brand promise must influence and be observable in all the manifestations of a brand. It should be expressed as much as possible at every moment of contact and in every situation in which consumers are confronted with the brand.

Zhivago (Auken 2000) outlines the analysis that brand managers need to conduct to identify and strengthen their brand promise, "First you find out, using research, what promises your customers want companies like yours to make and keep, using the products, processes, and people in your company." The benefit of such an analysis is that it verifies the brand's competitive position. Then, she explains, "You look at your competition and decide which promise would give you the best competitive advantage. This is the promise you make and keep in every marketing activity, every action, every corporate decision and every customer interaction. You promote it internally and externally." We have mentioned the importance of a shared brand vision—the brand promise is another way to integrate the vision throughout the company. Zhivago explains, "The promise drives budgets and stops arguments. If everyone in the company knows what the promise is, and knows that he/she will be rewarded or punished depending on the personal commitment to the promise, politics and personal turf issues start to disappear."

An example of a brand that successfully exploited a brand promise is Lexus, a car brand that was brought into the American market by Toyota in 1989 to compete against brands like Mercedes, BMW, Jaguar, Saab, and Cadillac. Three years after its introduction, Lexus sales surpassed those of other high-end cars in the United States. In seven out of eight years, Lexus rated highest in customer satisfaction. Consider the story about Lexus and its brand promise.

The brand promise comes alive in the central communication theme. In this context, Keller (1999a) points to the use of mantras, formulas loaded with power that originated in Hinduism and related spiritual movements. He sees "brand mantras" as short, three- to five-word phrases, similar to slogans, that embody the essence of the brand vision—for example, Nike's "just do it," BMW's "the ultimate driving machine," Federal Express's "the world on time," Coca-Cola's "the real thing." Mantras are oversimplifications, their purpose being to summarize the essence of the brand's promise in a simple, memorable way that can connect easily with consumers' needs and wants.

Lexus

Toyota started with the premise that it would build the best luxury car and surround it by unprecedented customer service. The essence of the brand was formulated as the relentless pursuit of perfection, a promise voiced in its slogan: "We pursue perfection . . . so you can pursue living."

Jim Press, Lexus CEO in the United States, expressed the Lexus promise as offering a total experience that reflects a sincere, uncompromising striving toward excellence. Lexus ensures that all facilities, systems, and procedures are customized to the needs and wishes of the customer. The company's professional approach emerged from an honest involvement of everyone working at Lexus. Everything is about efficiency, functionality, and professionalism, says Press. To make good on its promises, three goals were formulated for Lexus: manufacturing products with the best quality in the world, solving problems the first time they appear, and providing a level of service and convenience that Lexus buyers had never experienced before. Press describes Lexus customer service as a way of life, treating people as they want to be treated—it is a sort of "say yes" culture. Lexus enables its employees, front office personnel, and dealers to always find a way to say yes.

The success of the brand promise is demonstrated in the car's sales, which surpassed 300,000 for the first time in 2005, making it the top-selling luxury brand in the United States for the six preceding years. In 2007 Toyota sold 329,177 Lexus cars. Lexus has maintained steady growth through the years, which the company attributes to its constant pursuit of perfection and its total focus on positive customer experiences.

Sources: Auken (2000); Knapp (2000); Lexus press releases, www. toyota.com/about/news/corporate/2008/01/03.

Dimensions of Brand Relationships

In marketing terms, the brand relationship is defined as customer-focused, as well as product-focused—in other words, it is reciprocal. This is the heart of the marketing concept, which establishes customer needs as the platform for product and brand development. The partners influence each other mutually in a two-way or symmetrical relationship. But reciprocity is more than meeting needs; it also recognizes shared ownership of the brand. That was the heart of the New Coke crisis in the 1990s when the Coca-Cola managers decided, based on consumer research, that the taste of Coke needed to be modified. An uprising of loyal Coke customers demonstrated to management that they had a stake in the ownership of that brand and that management had moved beyond its authority in manipulating the flavor of the original Coke.

Because a relationship is like two hands clapping, there are factors that affect the management of the relationship, as well as factors that govern the perception of the relationship. Some of them overlap and some are specific to the perspective. Table 12.1 shows some key company and customer-brand relationship drivers.

Table 12.1

Relationship Drivers

Company perspective	Customer perspective
• Trust: Follow-through, deliver on promises	• Trust: Belief and confidence in brand to deliver brand promise; familiarity, risk reduction
• Interaction: The brand envisions communication as a dialog; it knows how and when to listen; it personalizes the experience	• Interaction: Practical, emotional, and social experiences related to use; willing to initiate communication
• Sincerity: Honesty, integrity	• Commitment: Conviction, loyal, bonded to the brand, willing to advocate on behalf of brand
• Intimacy (psychological closeness): The brand gives the feeling of being close to the consumer and in tune with needs	• Intimacy (love): Moves beyond liking and generalized positive feelings; the emotional attachment that drives bonding
• Involvement: Degree of attachment to product experiences that create positive participation in the brand's promotion and delivery	• Involvement: Degree of attachment to brand; self-identification; personal interest; saliency and relevance to consumer's life
• Appreciation support: Recognition, reaction, appreciation of customer	• Satisfaction: Evaluation of brand experiences as positive fulfillment of want or need; delight and surprise
	• Excitement: Delivers energy, vitality, or arousal leading to belief formation or action

The Connection Components

The "stuff" of brand relationships includes the factors that create connections between people—and between people and inanimate objects, such as brands and companies, such as these brand relationship drivers (Figure 12.1). Duncan and Moriarty (1997a, 46) suggest there are three types of brand connections: links, ties, and bonds. Links result from technical, administrative, and marketing activities. Think of links in the online sense, as a way to connect with another source or supplier. Ties result from exchanging and sharing resources—both tangible (equipment, facilities) and intangible (budgets, knowledge). Collaboration is a form of tie that is particularly important in business partnerships. Bonds are between people—and brands in the parasocial view of brand relationships—and result from positive interactions. Bonds are the cement that holds these social and parasocial relationships together.

A System of Bonds

Staying within the parasocial metaphor, the factors that create a strong or weak relationship are complex and multidimensional and represent all the different ways and reasons people connect to each other and to the brands they use. The drivers identified in Table 12.1 are a place to start. The following list, although not inclusive, also identifies the most important characteristics of the connections between people and their favorite brands, grouped into two categories—functional/cognitive and emotional/experiential.

Functional/Cognitive

- *Self-identification:* Consumers like to identify with the brand's image.
- *Familiarity:* Consumers are familiar with the brand and therefore can rely on it.

- *Reciprocity:* The partners influence each other mutually, both gaining from the relationship.
- *Symmetry:* In a win/win relationship, the control is symmetrical, with neither partner having power over the other.
- *Involvement:* The brand is part of the lives of the consumers, and they are part of the brand.
- *Communication:* Consumers come in contact with a brand and can send or receive a message.
- *Recognition:* The company knows who its best customers are, and its information system makes it possible to identify and recognize those customers when they contact the company.
- *Openness:* Consumers can communicate with the brand and its managers, who listen to all suggestions, complaints, and compliments.
- *Responsiveness:* The brand listens to consumers—its people provide answers to questions and solve customers' problems.
- *Recourse:* The company explains clearly how it deals with product problems—by replacing the product, fixing it, refunding money, or providing some type of incentives or rewards to encourage the customer to remain loyal.
- *Continuity:* There is a past, present, and future expectation.

Emotional/Experiential

- *Trust:* The basis of any relationship—consumers believe in the brand and that it is operating in their best interests; they believe it will deliver on its promises.
- *Psychological closeness:* The brand gives the feeling of being close to consumers and to their needs, wants, and values.
- *Personality:* Consumers like this person or brand—they are comfortable with it.
- *Respect:* Customers are not targets; they are partners.
- *Integrity:* The brand does what it says; it does not promise too much; it stands for something that is good for society.
- *Commitment:* Consumers believe in the brand and have developed a passion or intensity about it; the brand is equally committed to honoring its customers' needs and values and putting their interests first.
- *Dependency:* Consumers depend upon relationships that are important to them.
- *Interaction:* Practical, emotional, and social experiences related to use govern brand perceptions.
- *Consistency:* All the brand messages from all contact points say the same thing. Product performance and service are predictably the same.

In his analysis of the characteristics of enduring brand relationships, Barnes (2001) points out that commitment, trust, and likability are critical. He also mentions attractiveness, closeness, similarity, mutuality and reciprocity, interdependence, reliability and dependability, understanding and empathy, shared values, respect and sincerity, awareness of history, two-way communication, intimacy, interest in needs, knowledge, responsiveness, keeping promises, social support, and competency.

Relationship Building Blocks

Relationship bonds not only define the nature of the connection between a brand and its customers, but also constitute the building blocks of brand loyalty. They thus figure prominently in customer retention strategies. Familiarity, trust, and liking are the three most important drivers of brand loyalty. When a brand delivers a successful performance on its promise, then a customer has the rationale for feeling satisfied. This positive emotional response, when intensified or reinforced through experience and confirming messages from others, is transformed into liking for the brand.

Familiarity

A brand creates a feeling of familiarity by making a product known. The recognition of identity cues transforms a product into a well-known brand. Because the brand is familiar, consumers feel comfortable or even pleased to buy it again. This process of transforming a product into a familiar face is the secret behind the success of Ivory, Levi's, and Coke. The soap, jeans, and soft-drink brands have familiar and comfortable images, and consumers know from experience that they offer dependable quality. By creating these memorable images, branding hopes to establish preferences, habits, and loyalties. But more than that, brand relationship programs hope to add the elements that create bonding, such as trust and liking.

Trust

Some branding experts feel that trust is the most important factor in a brand relationship (Hart and Johnson 1999). Consumers need to be convinced that the brand they have tried and liked will perform as it has previously. Furthermore, the brand communication does not promise too much or set expectations beyond what the brand can deliver. From the producer's perspective, that means the brand delivers on all its promises and there are no unpleasant surprises. Furthermore, if there is a service failure, the company will solve the problem and try to overcome the negative feelings that might be left because the brand did not meet expectations.

The reason trust is important is because it represents the reduction of risk that comes when first buying something unknown. Consumers tend to trust what they know—that is, they trust the familiar brands they have purchased in the past. Successful branding is sometimes referred to as creating "trustmarks," such as the brand name AT&T and the swish logo for Nike. Business relationships are always based on a bond of trust between people, even if one partner is a company or brand.

Liking

We have mentioned the importance of the emotional component. Liking is more intense than satisfaction and is the basis for preference—that is, moving a brand into the category of a "favorite" brand—thus providing the emotional and cognitive foundation for brand loyalty. Some take it a step further and claim that positive experiences can move liking to love. Retired founder of Southwest Airlines Herb Kelleher proclaims that the way he built a unique corporate culture and a company that was able to withstand the airline industry's economic tailspin after 9/11 was by using love to "pump juice into how we do business." Similarly, Kevin Roberts, the CEO of the Saatchi & Saatchi advertising agency, insists that instead of trademarks, companies should think of brands as "lovemarks," a way to capture the depth of feeling that consumers can develop for their favorite brands.

Brand personality is a key factor in liking. The Dutch study by Smit et al. (2006) determined that brand personality is an important determinant in establishing the "old friend" feeling for a brand. In fact, that study found that brand personality was more important than product category: "As with people, some brands possess certain traits that make relationships with them—as friends or as lovers—easier."

Table 12.2

Strength of Brand Relationships

		In percent		
Users of brand	Category	Does experience a relationship	Does experience a bond, but not a relationship	Does not experience relationship or a bond
1. BMW	Cars	25.5	59.9	14.6
2. Volkskrant	Daily	5.4	45.6	49.0
3. Telegraaf	Daily	7.1	37.6	55.3
4. Vodafone	Mobile phone	8.2	46.9	44.8
5. Albert Heijn	Supermarkets	13.9	61.7	24.4
6. Heineken	Beer	5.5	45.5	49.1
7. Grolsch	Beer	8.2	53.3	38.5
8. Postbank	Bank	11.0	67.4	21.5
9. ING	Bank	12.7	55.8	31.5
10. Becel	Margarine	7.4	45.3	47.3

Source: Tolboom (2004a).

Brand Relationship Quality

Research by SWOCC (Tolboom 2004a) measuring the desirability and the quality of the relationship between users and their brands in the Netherlands revealed that only 10.5 percent of users experienced a personal relationship with their brands in the study. Another 52 percent experienced a bond with the brand, but not a personal relationship; 37.5 percent did not experience either a relationship or a bond (see Table 12.2). Only one in three brand users experienced a quality relationship or bond, and 50 percent stated that they were indifferent to having a relationship with any of these brands.

There is a difference between an interaction and a relationship. Customers may interact with a company and its brand personnel, but that does not mean they see themselves as being in a relationship with the brand. So what conditions create a relationship in the mind of the customer?

In her multidimensional model of brand relationship quality (BRQ), Fournier (1994, 1998) identifies seven key facets of a brand relationship: intimacy, personal commitment, passionate attachment, love, self-concept connection, nostalgic connections, and brand partner quality. This SWOCC research showed that there is a high correlation between Fournier's seven relationship facets with one factor explaining 66 percent of the variation within the facets.

Based on Fournier's work, SWOCC researchers (Smit et al. 2006) developed an instrument that evaluated a number of other variables. In addition to the seven BRQ factors, the SWOCC instrument added brand involvement, degree of use, relationship proneness, intentions of use, and demographics. By indexing the responses, the researchers found two underlying dimensions: the BRQ connection items as well as passionate attachment and intimacy, and the brand partner quality dimension combined with trust. This study of the extended list of relationship factors found that different brands achieved different levels of relationship quality, but "expressive" brands used by consumers to reflect or mirror their self-images were particularly strong in creating brand relationships. The reason is that the image of the brand intersects with and reinforces the users' self-image. The study also found that differences in brand relationship quality could be explained most often by brand personality—higher brand relationship quality was associated with brands perceived as distinguished or conveying excitement. Consumer satisfaction was also a critical factor, as were frequency of use and length of commitment.

CONTACT POINTS THAT TOUCH THE CUSTOMER

When people think of communication in relation to marketing and branding, they usually think of advertising and promotion. Brand communication, however, involves much more than these traditional forms. Almost all facets of marketing—including product design and performance, distribution, and pricing—are forms of communication that affect a customer's brand relationship. That is because everything a brand does, and sometimes what it does not do, delivers a message (Duncan and Moriarty 1997a). The slowness and navigation problems of a Web site are messages; the personal address, or lack thereof, on a solicitation says something about the organization; the length of time it takes to respond to an inquiry by phone or e-mail speaks volumes about the importance of a customer; the appearance of delivery trucks and stores, as well as the attitudes of drivers, sales clerks, and receptionists, become the public face of a company or brand.

Everything communicates even if there is not an explicit message. Marshall McLuhan's theory that the medium is the message is often the reality of contact point communication, where the experience itself speaks volumes about a company's attitude toward its customers, even if the message is not framed explicitly in words.

Zhivago (Auken 2000) insists that all contact points must deliver consistently on the brand promise: "Certainly the brand promise drives your marketing communications and your brand identity standards and systems. But it must do much more than that. Your products and services, every point of contact your brand makes with consumers and the total consumer experience your brand creates, must reinforce your brand's promise." Communication at this level moves beyond marketing communication and into a concept we call integrated branding, which, among other things, recognizes the structural challenges implicit in analyzing and managing communication throughout a complex system. As Zhivago explains, "This has tremendous organizational implications. How can an organization deliver against its promise if its front line employees don't know (or care about) what its brand stands for?"

In recognition of the need for strategic consistency, not all messages will be the same at all contact points, but they will all be anchored by the brand's core concept and values. When Apple Computer, for example, began using the "think different" slogan (which co-opted and one-upped IBM's old 'think' slogan and position), it drove all Apple's operations and interactions—the easy-to-use operating system, the distinctive designs, its corporate culture, and its advertising, which focused on creative genius.

The Field of Contact Points

In most cases, a brand's system of contact points is huge, and the challenge is to identify the key communication opportunities and then analyze the messages being delivered at these points of contact in order diagnose consistency problems. Davis and Dunn (2002) suggest that managing touch points through integrated branding involves identifying, prioritizing, and controlling the touch points of each stakeholder.

Table 12.3 illustrates the breadth of the contact point communication system and the many ways it touches the lives and minds of consumers. The list is organized using Duncan and Moriarty's (1997a) contact point classification system of intrinsic (product and service experiences), unplanned, customer-initiated, and planned marketing communication. This is not a complete list but rather a thought-starter for managers seeking to analyze their brand's contact points. The extent of the list, however, dramatizes the many possibilities of consistency problems.

Analyzing Contact Points

The analysis of contact points typically begins with an ethnographic study that mirrors the way various stakeholders go about their business and daily lives. As researchers follow these people around, they note points where the person comes in contact with the brand or a competing brand. A similar analysis from the viewpoint of employees can extend the list in ways that might not show up in a customer's usual activities. Davis and Dunn (2001) suggest that there are four categories of contact points and that each one represents a different type of customer-brand relationship.

1. *Prepurchase contact points:* the contact points that influence whether prospective customers will place the brand into their consideration set. These points usually include advertising, word of mouth, direct mail, and the Internet.
2. *Purchase contact points:* the brand contact points that move customers from considering the brand to purchasing it. These include field sales, stores, clerks, and customer representatives.
3. *Postpurchase contact points:* the brand contact points that reinforce the purchase decision after the sale. In addition to use of the actual product, these include installation, customer service, warranty and rebate programs, customer satisfaction surveys, regular maintenance, and reminders of product innovations.
4. *Influencing contact points:* the brand contact points that indirectly make an impression of the brand on its customers and other stakeholders, such as annual reports, analysts' reports, word of mouth by current and past customers and employees, and recruiting materials.

To deepen the analysis of the effectiveness of these contact point experiences, Chermatony (2001) suggests that researchers use the following six questions to analyze the quality of the contact point experience:

1. How did consumers become aware of your brand?
2. How do stakeholders further develop opinions about your brand through interactions with each other?
3. When then deciding to have further dealings with your brand, what routes do they follow?
4. Do all the brand communicators reinforce the brand's core values?
5. What roles do staff and technology play throughout the stakeholders' journeys—do they support the brand's core values?
6. What mechanisms are in place to reinforce the brand's value after the transaction?

Touch Points and the Affective Dimension

In addition to the idea that everything delivers a message, everything and everyone related to the brand can "touch" the customer. Davis and Dunn (2002) define a brand touch point as any of the instances where a brand interacts with stakeholders. However, although the terms *contact point* and *touch point* often are used interchangeably, there is more to a touch point than mere contact.

Table 12.3

The Field of Contact Points

I. Intrinsic (product/service experience) message sources
Shopping experience
Customer experience
Aftermarketing
Customer interactions
Customer service
Tech support
Call centers
Attendants
Sales clerks
Reception
Reservation
Ordering
Check-in, check-out
On-hold messages
Voice mail
Marketing mix messages
Pricing
Distribution
Product design
Product performance
Company messages
Building design
Store ambiance
Grounds and landscaping
Delivery trucks
Staff appearance, attitude
Order forms
Tracking systems

II. Unplanned messages
News investigations, media questions
Gossip, rumors
Whistle blowing
Blogs
Crisis, disasters
Protests

III. Customer-initiated messages
In-bound phone calls
In-bound e-mails
Fan, user clubs
Hotlines
Word-of-mouth
Testimonials
Referrals, advocacy

IV. Planned marketing communication messages
Print
House magazines, newsletters
Magazine ads
Newspaper ads
Advertorials
Classified ads

(continued)

Table 12.3 *(continued)*

    Directories, directory ads
    Co-op ads
    Special reports
    Annual reports
    Brochures, flyers,
    Sales, product, collateral literature
    Statement stuffers
    Newsletters
    Newsletter/magazine inserts
    Calendars
    Books
    Perfume cards
    Pop-ups
    Talking cards/inserts with chips
Broadcast/film/video
    TV ads
    TV infomercials
    Screen crawls
    Radio ads
    Cinema ads
    Corporate/brand videos, audio cassettes, CD ROMs, DVDs
    Video news releases
    Video interviews
    Product placement
    Advertainment
Outdoor
    Bus, taxi signs, and posters (interior and exterior)
    Outdoor boards
    Transit stop/subway posters
    Bumper stickers
    Gas station pump ads
    Balloons
    Airplane banners
    Inflatables
    Painted vehicles
Electronic
    Web site
    Banners
    E-mail (permission, spam)
    Online product movies
    Newsletters
    Catalogues
    Wireless
    Instant messaging
    MP3 player messages
    Handheld devices
    Blogging
    Video games, product games
Packaging
    Package design (functional, aesthetic)
    On package information, coupons, ads
    In-package ads, coupons, literature
    Bonus packs
Sales promotion (consumer and trade)
    Coupons
    Rebates

(continued)

Table 12.3 *(continued)*

    Sampling
    Loss leaders
    Cross promotions
    Gifts (baskets), gift vouchers, incentives, rewards, points
    Competitions
    Contests, sweepstakes
    Prize drawings
Sponsorships
    Athletes and stars
    Athletic events
    Cause marketing
    Mission marketing
Events
    Sponsored events
    Special (celebratory) events: grand openings, ribbon cuttings
    Breakfast, lunch meetings
    Seminars, workshops
    Parties, receptions
    Private unveiling or showing
    Previews
    Conferences, meetings
    Sales meetings
    Trade shows
    Exhibits, displays
    Festivals, fairs
    Telethons, marathons, walkathons
Direct
    Direct mail
    Mail order
    Direct advertising
    Response cards, tear-outs, clipped forms
    Outbound telemarketing
    Catalogs: print, online, CD Rom
    E-mail ads (permission/spam)
    Fax ads (permission/spam)
Place-based media
    Restaurant placements
    Table toppers
    On-site signage
    Shelf talkers
Specialties
    Matchbook advertising
    Tschotkes: pens, mugs, caps, t-shirts, tote bags, etc.
    Postcards, note cards
Public relations
    Press releases
    Press conferences
    Tours, road shows
    Interviews
    Fact sheets
    Publicity kits
    Pitch letters
    Media advisories
    Special reports
    Letter to editor
    Commentary, op-ed

(continued)

Table 12.3 *(continued)*

    Columns
    Models (physical replications)
    Donor/volunteer programs
    Fundraising
    Talk shows
    Junkets
    Endorsements
    Public service advertising (PSAs)
    Advocacy, point-of-view ads
    Testimonies
    Underwriting
    Employee communication programs
    Internal marketing
    Training programs
    Crisis plans, rehearsals
Relationship programs
    Cross-branding
    Partnership programs
    Awards, recognition
    Frequency programs
    User clubs, events
    Meetings
    Breakfasts, luncheons, dinners
    Selective entertainment (events)
    Channel marketing communication
    Supplier/vendor marketing communication
Personal contact (targeted)
    Personal sales
    Sales presentations
    Personalized letters, thank yous
    Speeches
    Trade show booths, exhibits
    Surveys
    Door-to-door sales, canvassing
Interactive contact
    Expert consultations
    Teleconferences
    Toll-free numbers
    Hotlines
    URLs and e-mail addresses
    Word-of-mouth, buzz
    Referrals
    Booths
New/alternative media
    Toilet stall posters
    Street chalk messages
    Painted buildings
    Balloons
    Fly-over banners
    Guerilla marketing stunts
Retail/store
    Store boards, posters, banners, windows, aisle displays
    Point-of-purchase displays
    Bag stuffers
    Shopping bags
    On-site store signage

(continued)

Table 12.3 *(continued)*

    Store window displays
    Counter displays
    Display cards
    Dump bins
    Plastic stickers
    Shelf talkers
    Check-out line posters, displays, videos
    Product demonstrations, sampling, trial
    Aroma management (coffee, baking, perfume)
Brand communication
    Brand identification: logo, signature, trademark, colors, slogans, audio tags
    Brand characters
Corporate communication
    Corporate identity programs
    Culture: tone, style, personality, values
    Financial relations programs
    Annual report
    Employee relations programs
    Community relations programs
    Government relations programs
    Lobbying
    Labor relations programs
    Public affairs communication
    Media relations programs (proactive, reactive)
    Crisis communication plans
    Recruitment programs
    Consumer/activist programs
    Museums, traveling exhibits
Organizational/administrative
    Stationery
    Business cards
    Memos
    Order forms
    Database maintenance messages
Communication infrastructure
    Phone answering
    Phone menus
    E-mail response
    Web site reply system
    Intranet, extranet systems

Touch points have an emotional impact, lending an affective dimension to the brand perception.

Brand management can be seen as the process of managing all these customer contact points in order to increase the value of the brand by cementing the customer-brand relationship and by intensifying the positive brand experience in ways that customers find meaningful.

Another dimension of touch points is experience. The concept of experience marketing has evolved to help managers understand this crucial interaction between customer and brand in meaningful ways. Although any brand interaction is an experience, such activities as sponsorships, special events in public relations programs, and event marketing are particularly rich in the kind of involvement that delivers engaging, affect-laden experiences.

The idea of brand contact points summarizes all these varied ways in which a customer can come in contact with a brand. Each contact point creates a brand experience and delivers a message, either positive or negative, about the brand. Service, for example, is a communication experience. The creation of positive experiences at this touch point creates and strengthens relationships as it also builds competitive advantage. The accumulation of these brand experiences creates value and ultimately contributes to brand equity (Duncan and Moriarty 2006).

Critical Touch Points

Because touch points are so varied, it stands to reason that their impact on relationships between brands and customers or stakeholders will also vary. Many touch points are service-related and add value to the brand experience, which in turn can cement or rupture a customer-brand relationship. Some touch points are even more critical because they are more directly related to future purchase decisions. Critical touch points (CTPs) are observed when customers connect with a brand on an emotional level (Duncan and Moriarty 2006, 240). In other words, the contact infuses the relationship with positive or negative emotions.

Jan Carlson, former SAS Airlines CEO, calls these CTPs "moments of truth" and describes them as the contacts that keep customers satisfied or drive them away. He estimates that 50,000 moments of truth occur every day in the airline business, so all employees, from the reservation agents to the pilots, have to be committed to service quality. By focusing on these critical touch points, SAS moved from red ink to black with an $80 million swing in profits (Goldsmith et al. 2003)

Because these CTPs have significant impact on customers, these "touching experiences" must be carefully designed and strategically managed. Unfortunately, these experiences are often embedded in operations and may be completely missed by a brand's communication managers. Yet one good or bad experience may have more impact on brand perceptions than a million dollars in advertising.

Interactive Communication

As in all relationships, brand relationships are driven by interactive communication. The effectiveness of two-way communication is a major factor in determining the strength of the brand. Grönroos and Lindberg-Repo (1998) developed a model of relationship marketing called the relationship communications globe, which depicts the interplay of company-driven marketing communication and customer-driven or word-of-mouth communication.

Word of mouth has become increasingly important as marketers realize they are communicating with brand communities, as well as individual customers. Research, for example, has found that the average dissatisfied customer tells nine or ten people about the experience. Furthermore, 13 percent of dissatisfied customers spread the news to more than twenty people, so the damage may be far greater than a single lost sale (Sonnenberg 1993).

The success of one-to-one marketing (Peppers and Rogers 1993) lies with its ability to personalize communication and speak directly to the interests, needs, and values of customers—as well as listen to and respond to those customers' concerns. The development of the Internet has created an explosion of interest in interactive communication by e-businesses.

New advances in the theory and practice of customer relationship management are also making interaction a more accessible platform for maintaining effective brand relationships. As Newell (2000, 26) explains, "From the customer point of view, everything from the paper stock to the salutation to the layout of a questionnaire communicates how little or how much you know about them and how much you value them as customers."

And with the development of the Internet and more savvy consumers, two-way communication is forcing companies to respond to, rather than just create, messages aimed at their customers. The increase in customer-initiated communication forces a company to do a better job of listening and responding as a partner in a dialogue, rather than as a source in a targeted communication effort.

Dialogue is the key to successful commercial relationships. Grunig's (1992) theory of symmetry, one of his principles of excellence in public relations, is an important insight into how relationships are supported and maintained through two-way communication. In his theory, asymmetrical relations, such as are found in advertising, are based on one-way communication from the source—the marketer—to the target audience. In a true relationship, however, the communication is interactive, providing the foundation for a more open, symmetrical relationship between the two parties. The Internet, among other technological advances, has opened up new opportunities for symmetrical relationships that use interactive communication.

CRM and Data-Driven Communication

In order to achieve a level of bonding sufficient to create a customer-brand relationship, the marketer has to develop what Duncan and Moriarty (1997a) call "relationship memory"—the marketer is as informed about past customer-brand interactions as the customer is. The goal, in other words, is to create a relationship memory for the marketer that reflects the brand experience as seen through the eyes of the customer. If someone buys a new coat and calls with a complaint, then the next time that customer interacts with the company, the person at the point of contact (sales associate, customer service representative) should be able to refer back to the original phone call and check whether the customer's concern was dealt with satisfactorily. This level of memory can be achieved only through strategic use of databases that not only maintain customer information, but also track customer interactions.

We discussed earlier the difficulties that customer relationship management has had in moving into a relationship focus. This application is one way that CRM can be used positively to help in customer-focused relationship management. CRM is useful, in other words, for other reasons than just identifying high-value customers.

Newell (2000) makes the argument that loyalty programs are effective to the extent that the company knows its customers and can develop targeted programs to meet their individualized needs. What does the customer value in the brand relationship? One of the most important benefits to the customer, for example, is communication based on a previous dialogue with the company. This only happens with a CRM program that provides relationship memory and insight into consumer behavior, as well as numbers.

The Service Dimension of Relationship Marketing

Some marketers and marketing theorists argue that all marketing is now service, even the marketing of goods. In other words, what consumers buy when they buy a computer is the expertise of the salesperson and the technical support and customer service that come with the product. In some purchases, the service support may be more important than the product itself.

This service-dominant approach was the premise of the service marketing movement that began in the 1980s with the work of Len Berry and his colleagues, who developed the SERVQUAL instrument (Parasuraman et al. 1988). It was also an important component in marketing's intersection with the quality movement, also during the 1980s. More recently, the emphasis on service has emerged as its own theory, referred to as "service-dominant logic" by Vargo and Lusch (2004), and Lusch and Vargo (2006), who have written extensively on this topic.

Service quality is a customer perception that is determined by the gap between the level of service customers expect and their impression of the service they receive. The SERVQUAL instrument identifies five core dimensions that affect positively or negatively a customer's perception of service:

- *Tangibles:* physical facilities, equipment, and appearance
- *Reliability:* delivery of the promised service
- *Responsiveness:* willingness to help and provide speedy service
- *Assurance:* knowledge and courtesy of employees, ability to inspire confidence and trust
- *Empathy:* caring and individualized attention

This emphasis on service quality in customer retention has made the previously ignored area of customer service a new player in marketing programs. Christopher (1991) investigated this new synthesis between quality, customer service, and marketing in their first book on relationship marketing.

Internal Branding

The concern about service has also increased the attention on internal branding, which designs communication, incentive, empowerment, and brand-supportive training programs for employees. The theory is that happy employees tend to positively influence customers and thus increase the level of customer satisfaction and loyalty (Rosenbluth and Peters 2002). Employees are the front line in customer contacts and their performance and loyalty can make or break customer loyalty. Research by Reichheld and others suggests a strong link between positive service experiences, employee satisfaction, and customer retention (Payne 1995, 46; Schneider and Bowen 1985), which can lead to a dramatic increase in profitability (Reichheld and Sasser 1990).

BRAND LOYALTY

Marketers are intensely concerned about brand loyalty even though the literature is confused about the importance, as well as the relative consequence, of loyalty as a brand-relationship measure. Some writers, such as Weilbacher (1993), feel that the explosion of similar products makes it very difficult for customers to develop brand loyalty and has led to an overall decrease in the amount of brand loyalty.

Other experts believe that customers are rarely loyal to a specific brand, but rather to a group of preferred brands within a category. Typically they will switch among the brands in this set depending upon such marketing factors as availability and price, as well as service and the customer's previous experiences with the brand and competing brands within the set. The objective of a marketing manager, then, is not necessarily to build a high level of brand loyalty, but rather to get onto the list.

But regardless of whether the details are in dispute, the concept of brand loyalty is useful in that it still represents the best manifestation of a successful, enduring brand relationship. As Reichheld (2001, 1) explains, the lack of loyalty "stunts corporate performance by 25 to 50 percent, sometimes more." In contrast, his research at the Bain & Company consulting firm has found that "businesses that concentrate on finding and keeping good customers, productive employees, and supportive investors continue to generate superior results."

How Brand Loyalty Works

The theory behind brand loyalty is based on an acquisition-retention continuum. Customer acquisition is focused on getting as many new customers as possible to try a brand. It is often the focus of programs that are driven by short-term, transactional objectives resulting in one-time sales. At the other end of the continuum is customer retention, which is driven by an emphasis on creating and maintaining customer relationships over time by building high levels of commitment and bonding.

The theory is that acquiring and selling to new customers costs more than selling to current customers. The longer the relationship, the more the initial costs of acquisition can be spread over multiple purchases and thus increase the profitability of the customer. Most of these computations are based on estimates of the cost of making the first sale versus the cost of making a repeat sale. The rule of thumb is that it generally costs five to ten times as much to get a new customer as it costs to keep an existing customer. Direct-marketing companies that estimate cost per sale have developed the models for making these comparisons. One problem is that these models do not consider the lost investment in acquisition that occurs when a customer defects (Duncan and Moriarty 1997a, 43).

The Loyalty Ladder

The Cranfield School developed a model called the relationship-marketing ladder (Payne 1995, 4), also known as the loyalty ladder, that explains how loyalty evolves over time and after the accumulation of significant experiences with the brand. This continuum begins with the identification of a prospect; moves through the interim stages of customer, client, supporter, and advocate; and ends with a customer who has become a brand partner. Payne notes that moving customers up the loyalty ladder is not simple unless the marketer knows its customers very well and can tune the offering to best meet their individual needs, wants, and motivations.

Levels of Bonding

Another, related model that identifies five levels of bonds characterizing the nature of the brand-customer relationship was presented by Cross and Smith in their book, *Customer Bonding: Pathway to Lasting Customer Loyalty* (1995, 54–55). Their theory is that the depth of the bond between customers and a brand increases with the customer's brand experiences. If relationships are properly strengthened over time, the percentage of customers who move into the top three levels should increase.

- *Advocacy:* Customers recommend the brand to others.
- *Community:* Customers talk to each other.
- *Relationship:* Customers initiate communication with the company.
- *Identity:* Customers proudly display the brand.
- *Awareness:* Brand is included on customers' menu.

Satisfaction, Retention, and Loyalty

Better service in all areas of the delivery of the brand promise is important in retention. Much of the literature on customer retention, as well as loyalty, focuses on satisfaction. The idea is that the more satisfied the customer, the more long-lasting the brand relationship. Satisfaction results from positive brand experiences, such as good product performance, useful features not offered by competitors, confirmation of positive brand experiences from others, and the company's effective response to complaints or inquiries.

The other side of retention is defection, which, presumably, results from an unhappy brand experience. In order to build a retention program, it is also necessary to understand the reasons why people leave the brand. In addition to taking their business elsewhere, dissatisfied customers may increase the customer-service workload and say bad things about the brand to others.

Recovery programs are designed to turn around a bad service experience. Recovery programs usually result from consumer complaints, but what happens depends upon whether the front-line staff is empowered to make things right—to make reparation, give refunds, find replacements, and provide incentives. Customers often will forgive a bad experience if the company attempts to make it right, and the more surprising the effort, the more impact it will have on the customer's brand perception.

The problem with satisfaction, however, is its lack of predictive power. As Reichheld points out, "Satisfaction, a fleeting attitude that lacks durable staying power, is a poor substitute for loyalty and sets far too low a standard of excellence" (2001, 4–5). The point is that people can be satisfied with a product and still switch to another brand. There is more to loyalty than mere satisfaction. Reichheld's standards of excellence for loyalty (17) are based on six principles that drive compensation, organization, strategy, and measurement:

1. *Play to win/win:* Profiting at the expense of others is a lose/lose situation.
2. *Be picky:* Membership in a brand's club is a privilege.
3. *Keep it simple:* Complexity defeats speed and responsiveness.
4. *Reward the right results:* Set worthy goals and reward worthy partners.
5. *Listen hard, talk straight:* Relationships require honest, two-way communication and learning.
6. *Preach what you practice:* Actions speak louder than words—together they are unbeatable.

Loyalty Programs

Loyalty programs are designed to maintain a connection between a brand and a customer over time, a link that delivers repeat sales and other manifestations of a positive relationship, such as advocacy, testimonials, and referrals. For example, a construction company in California spends most of its marketing communication budget on low-cost goodwill efforts that spawn referrals and repeat business. For example, the company sends "Pardon our dust" letters to every home near a client's remodeling site and asks neighbors to call if they have complaints. Instead of complaining, many neighbors call to ask the firm to bid on their projects. Kitchen remodeling customers get gift certificates to a nearby restaurant when their kitchen is about two-thirds completed and a handwritten note of apology for their personal upheaval. The result of such efforts is that more than 70 percent of the company's business comes from referrals by past customers.

One common type of loyalty effort is a frequency program, such as frequent buyer or frequent flyer programs, which lock customers into an ongoing brand relationship through rewards and incentives. The airlines developed this approach, but retailers have also learned how to encourage their customers to sign up for program membership that allows them to get discounts on purchases. Competitors, however, are usually quick to follow. In the Netherlands, 40 percent of all retail chains offer a client card. They hope to buy loyalty by giving rebates, but they do very little with the shopping data. The average supermarket invests 75 euros per cardholder, but only realizes 275 euros in additional sales (Bijmalt in Heijden 2006).

Research Into Brand Loyalty and Bonding

The question is, to what degree can brand-loyal purchasing behavior be traced back to a customer's underlying commitment (bond or attachment), or does it happen out of sheer habit? In other words,

Figure 12.2   **Relation Between Attitude and Loyalty** (in percent)

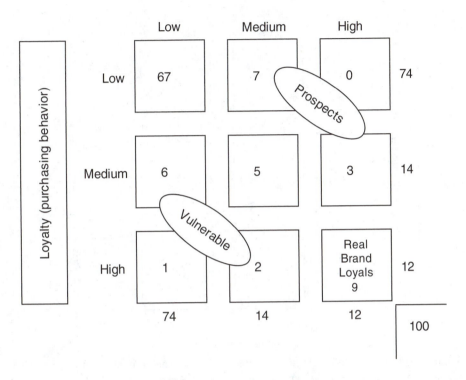

Bonding (attitude)

Source: Baldinger and Rubinson (1996).

to what degree is there a "real" brand loyalty? And to the degree that there is one, how durable is the behavioral component? How unfaltering are consumers in their loyalty to brands? And can brand loyalty behavior be predicted from brand attitude?

In order to make substantiated statements about these questions, panel research can be used in which all brand purchases in a category are registered over a long period (at least one year) and in which attitude measurements are also taken periodically for the same spot check. This results in a matrix in which buyers of a brand are segmented based on both characteristics—behavior and attitude.

Baldinger and Rubinson (1996) reported on such panel research and the corresponding analysis carried out in the United States for twenty-seven brands of fast-moving consumer articles. Buyers were classified into three classes according to behavior (low, medium, and high loyals) and attitude (strong, medium, and weak). The result was a three-by-three matrix with nine segments (see Figure 12.2).

In this research, a strong connection was evident between behavior and attitude: among those buyers with a weak attitude (74 percent), only 1 percent showed high brand loyalty. Among the buyers with a strong attitude (12 percent), three-quarters (9 percent) showed high brand loyalty. At the same time, 85 percent of the buyers of the average brand had a weak-to-medium attitude toward the brand as well as a low-to-medium brand-loyal purchasing behavior! The durability of

Figure 12.3 **The Durability of Brand Loyalty** (in percent)

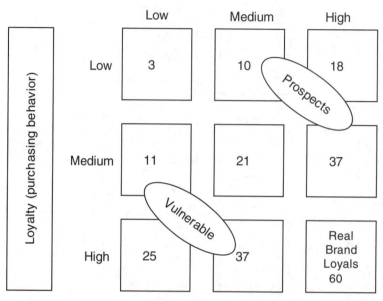

Source: Baldinger and Rubinson (1996).

the brand loyalty was not too high either. Figure 12.3 gives the percentage of buyers in each of the segments who were still in the same segment after one year.

Only 53 percent of brands with high brand-loyal buyers showed a share-of-requirements level higher than 50 percent after one year. (Also known as share of customer, this term refers to the share of the customer's purchase or spending within the category.) Only 60 percent of the brands with "real loyals" (strong bond with the brand in combination with a share of re-quirements higher than 50 percent) in the first year also stayed in the same category the second year, but 40 percent of this group showed a decline in the strength of the attachment level or share of requirements. Of the high loyals (share of requirements higher than 50 percent) with an average attitude, only 37 percent stayed as high loyals the second year. In other words, the durability of both attachment level and share of customer is very limited, even within a period of only one year.

Bonding and Market Share

Finally, Baldinger and Rubinson analyzed the extent to which developments in attitudes were pre-dictive of developments in the market shares of the researched brands. To this end, two subgroups were followed: *prospects*, the buyers whose attitude is stronger than their brand-loyal purchasing behavior, and *vulnerables*, the buyers whose attitude is weaker than their purchasing loyalty. The scope of both groups was 10 to 11 percent of the average brand's customers. The ratio between the two groups corresponded with the development of the market share in two-thirds of the researched brands. The main conclusions of this analysis were as follows:

- Of all buyers of a brand, only a small part (12 percent) showed a share of requirements higher than 50 percent.
- An equally small part (12 percent) experienced a high degree of bonding or attachment to the brand.
- There was a strong link between the two: three-quarters (9 percent) of this last group of buyers seemed to be really brand-loyal, at least at the moment of the study.
  - Of all high loyals, only 53 percent showed a share of requirements higher than 50 percent after one year. The durability of the brand loyalty was therefore very relative.
  - The attitude developments in two-thirds of the brands correlate with the development of the purchasing behavior and consequently with the market share too. Between these a two-sided causal relationship exists: purchasing behavior and attitude influence each other mutually, albeit not in a durable way.

This study suggests that the importance of bonding cannot be overstated. Bonded users are the basis of a strong brand. This is manifest in the following characteristics of bonded users compared to other users:

- They spend a large part of their expenditures in the category on their brand (high share of requirements).
- They are willing to pay a higher price for the brand.
- They remain loyal to their brand longer.
- Less marketing effort is needed to keep them.
- They are more open to communication about the brand.
- They are less open to communication about other brands.
- When the product is out of stock, they are more likely to postpone the purchase.
- They are less sensitive to price offers of competitors.
- They sometimes act as ambassadors of their brand.

Brand-loyal customers have established a bond with a brand, even if only within a set of acceptable brands in a category. Although positive attitudes driven by familiarity, liking, and trust are the bedrock of these bonds, the commitment is still based on a sharing of values. Consequently, to understand the depth of consumer response to a brand, a manager must also understand the values of the targeted segment and the way those values intersect with the brand's mentality.

Brand Loyalty and Brand Growth

Research on brand loyalty has consistently found that pure brand loyalty rarely exists, but rather that customers are loyal to a set of favorite brands. For the sake of simplicity in this discussion, we will continue to refer to brand loyalty, but please remember that the loyalty usually is spread among a set of brands.

Brand managers must understand what motivates loyalty for the category, the set of brands, and a particular brand. Is the loyalty rate of a brand's customer base indicative of the growth and strength of the brand? Table 12.4 shows the analysis by Sylvester et al. (1994) of the growth of a hundred brands in the United States. The researchers were able to distinguish five brand typologies on the basis of the composition of their dominant users group.

Here is a summary of the key insights from this study:

Table 12.4

A Typology of Brand Motivators

	Brands chosen by dominant buyers group		Segment's contribution to brand growth	
Brand buyer segments	Number of brands		Penetration (in percent)	Purchasing frequency (in percent)
Price-driven	29		75	25
Rotators	20		68	32
Light buyers	19		100	0
Deal selectives	17		50	50
Bonded buyers	15		43	57
Total	100		Average: 75	Average: 25

Source: Sylvester et al. (1994).

- *Bonded buyers:* Only fifteen of the (growing) brands were dominated by bonded buyers. Their sales grew due to the increase in both purchasing frequency and penetration.
- *Light buyers:* Brands that depend mostly on light buyers, who make a purchase only once or twice a year in the category, owe their growth entirely to the increase in penetration.
- *Rotators:* Brands that are dominated by "rotators," hot switch brands on the basis of product performance, know how to attract new buyers as well as increase their purchasing frequency through product improvements.
- *Deal selectives:* These brands are dominated by buyers that buy mainly on the basis of price but within a small brand repertoire. Growth comes equally from increases in penetration and frequency.
- *Price-driven buyers:* People who buy only on the basis of price form the most important buyers' group for twenty-nine of the growing brands. These brands grow predominantly in response to increasing penetration.

The Sylvester study demonstrates that on average penetration increases are responsible for 75 percent of the growth of brands, and frequency increases for 25 percent. But this proportion varies, dependent on the dominant user groups. Frequency growth was particularly important for the brands dominated by bonded users and deal selectives. For the other brands, growth came mainly from increased penetration—that is, finding new buyers.

Most literature on this issue confirms that growth is a result of increases in both penetration and frequency, with penetration most often the dominant factor. Growth is also a product of a more qualitative factor, which is usually referred to as brand or corporate reputation.

BRAND REPUTATION

Brand loyalty is dependent upon brand reputation, which is the esteem, even admiration, with which stakeholders regard a company or brand. Reputation differs significantly from brand image, which is a representation derived from brand communication, such as advertising. Image is what a brand says about itself; reputation is what others say about it (Duncan and Moriarty 1997a). Reputation is built on performance—how well a company delivers on its brand promise—rather than advertising. It results not from what a company says, but rather from what it does. Of course, a reputation can be good or bad, depending upon the organization's performance and the buzz about it among its stakeholders. Apple, for example, has a good reputation as a leader in innovation, not only in the design breakthroughs it has brought to the computer industry, but also in its related music product line, led by iPod and iTunes and the iPhones.

Although we talk about brand reputation, inevitably this discussion migrates to corporate reputation, since the company behind the brand is the source of the behaviors that lead to a positive or negative reputation for a brand. That is why, in his analysis of successful companies, Kay (1993) includes reputation as one of the three foundations of corporate success. The other two are innovation and architecture, and by architecture he is referring to the system of relationships within the firm or between the firm and its stakeholders and the company's leadership in building and maintaining these relationships.

Reputation—the degree to which a company is admired for its excellence—has a dollar value. It relates directly to the goodwill represented in brand equity. Cannon and Schwaiger (2005) explain that reputation equates with goodwill: companies that win the confidence of customers can command premium prices by reducing consumers' perceived risk. In other words, strong brands develop a positive reputation and where such a reputation exists, there is value.

Components of Reputation

What exactly does reputation represent? The Harris-Fombrun Reputation Quotient™, which was developed at the Reputation Institute at New York University's Stern School of Business in partnership with Harris Interactive, is a research tool used to evaluate corporate reputation and the firm's source credibility. The survey uses twenty items in six dimensions to define reputation:

1. *Emotional appeal:* Consumers have a good feeling about the company; they admire, respect, and trust it.
2. *Products and services:* The company stands behind its products and services; it is known for innovations, high quality, and good value.
3. *Financial performance:* The company shows profitability, offers low-risk investment, promises future growth, and outperforms its competition.
4. *Vision and leadership:* The company demonstrates leadership and clear vision in seizing market opportunities.
5. *Workplace environment:* The company is well-managed, good to work for, and has good employees.
6. *Social responsibility:* The company supports good causes, is environmentally responsible, and treats people well.

To this list we would add word-of-mouth because a brand or corporate reputation exists to the degree that people talk about the brand.

Mission and Cause Marketing

The social responsibility component in the Harris-Fombrun Reputation Quotient is particularly critical for brand reputations because it directly engages a sense of the brand's integrity. At the most basic level, a brand or company performs with integrity when it treats its employees and community with respect, delivers on its marketing promises, and keeps its customers' best interests in mind in developing its strategies and programs. This is the platform B. Murphy et al. (1999) advocate as a foundational marketing principle in their concept of stakeholderism.

Brand integrity also benefits from a commitment to a socially responsible business platform. What does the company stand for, besides making a profit, and why does good corporate and brand citizenship matter to its customers and other stakeholders? Apple, for example, has dedicated itself to computer literacy, liberating nontechies from the need to know a lot about computers in order to benefit from them. The company launched the Macintosh with the classic position that became a brand slogan, "The computer for the rest of us." That computer literacy mission also drove Apple into the educational market, which it has always dominated.

Why should companies care about social responsibility? The power of affiliation with a good cause has been documented for years as positively influencing consumer-purchasing patterns. Findings from ongoing national surveys conducted by Roper Starch Worldwide and Cone Communications have uncovered the motivational power of social responsibility. The benchmark study of 2,000 U.S. adults in 1994 (Carringer 1994) found that when given a choice between two brands of equal price and quality:

- 78 percent of respondents would be more likely to buy the one that supported a cause they cared about;
- 66 percent would switch or would be likely to switch brands to support a cause;
- 62 percent would switch retailers;
- 54 percent would pay more for a brand that supported a cause they cared about.

Ten years later, the 2004 Starch-Cone study found that 80 percent of respondents said that corporate support of good causes wins their trust, which was a 21 percent increase since the interim 1997 version of the study. The 2004 version (DaSilva 2004) also asked how people would respond to a company's negative performance on social issues:

- 90 percent said they would consider switching brands;
- 81 percent would speak out against the company to family and friends;
- 80 percent would consider selling their stock in the company and 80 percent would refuse to invest in the company;
- 75 percent would refuse to work for the company;
- 73 percent would boycott the company's products or services.

There are three ways that a brand can publicly express its commitment to good works—philanthropy, cause marketing, and mission marketing.

Philanthropy, or charitable giving, is a standard practice in most U.S. firms. However, if a company uses a scattergun approach, contributing to dozens or even hundreds of charities, then it is difficult for relationship partners to develop a sense of the company's good works. An audit of a local sporting goods chain, for example, found that the company was supporting so many varied causes that no one, including the president and top management, knew how much was being spent or where it was going (Duncan and Moriarty 1997b). When companies unify their philanthropy and strategically focus it on a cause that reinforces their mission and business, their involvement is generally large enough to have a presence and to make a real difference, thus making it more likely to gain stakeholder attention and appreciation. Concentration of effort creates impact.

Cause marketing means adopting a good cause and supporting it financially and with resources and staff time. This can be a short-term effort used for public relations reasons to present a positive image to consumers. This highly public *cause de jour* approach is often supported by advertising and public relations and designed to focus the attention of stakeholders on the company's

adopted cause for a short time. Because of the marketing communication support, cause marketing can generate some resistance from consumers who see the effort as self-serving rather than
good works. In the 1994 Starch-Cone study, for example, 58 percent of the respondents said that
marketing promotions are done just to improve the company's self-image. This negative attitude
is changing, however, with 86 percent of the respondents in 2004 saying they want companies to
talk about their social issue activities, although 60 percent said that companies are not doing that
well. If not handled with sensitivity, cause marketing may be seen as merely exploiting popular
causes, as well as consumers' social consciousness.

Mission marketing (Duncan and Moriarty 1997a), in contrast, aligns the mission of the company
with some area of social concern. It is a philosophy of business that permeates the company and
reinforces the brand position. Stakeholders are proud to associate with the company or brand because of its mission. Apple, for example, owns computer literacy. Ben & Jerry's, Tom's of Maine,
and The Body Shop are committed to helping the environment, as well as local and third-world
suppliers. Home Depot has adopted Habitat for Humanity and has made significant efforts to help
with the reconstruction of the Gulf Coast after Hurricane Katrina.

Mission marketing proves that a company has a purpose in addition to generating sales and
making a profit. In all these cases, the business platform of the company is associated with a
related cause in a long-term connection, sometimes even an association that defines and directs
the firm's operations. For mission marketing to work, stakeholders must become aware of it and,
ideally, involved with its implementation. But more than communication, the company's mission
and identity are embedded in and surrounded by the cause.

BRAND RELATIONSHIP COMPONENTS AND STRATEGIES

Brand strategies that seek to strengthen customer relationships focus on a number of critical
components that have an impact on brand meaning and the construction of the mental brand. It is
important to manage these customer and stakeholder relationships strategically because positive
relationships contribute to brand equity.

In terms of components, the first effort involves identifying stakeholders and their interaction
networks, as well as the content and value of their communication experiences within the network.
These brand relationship components can be summarized as follows:

- stakeholders
- contact points
- brand messages
- interactions (with the brand and other stakeholders)
- brand experiences

In order to build effective relationship-focused strategies, all these components need to be
analyzed. Are the stakeholder relationships as effective as they might be? What needs to be done
to increase the power of these stakeholder relationships? Next, strategy development identifies
other customer contact points and assesses their importance in order to determine which ones are
critical. Contact point analysis also looks for touch points that carry emotional weight in order to
identify their positive and negative impact.

Related to stakeholder and contact point strategies is an analysis of the nature of the relationship bonds, as well as the structure of the connections that customers have with a brand.
In particular, this effort looks for the emotional bonds that cement the relationship and lead to

Table 12.5

Relationship-Driven Brand Strategies

Relationship component	Focus
Stakeholders	Who has a stake in the brand's performance?
Interaction networks	Who talks to whom about the brand and who has influence on brand
Structure of influence	decisions?
Contact points	How can points of contact be strengthened or expanded?
Touch points	How can emotional impact be used, refined, strengthened?
Critical touch points	Which touch points control messages that drive brand decisions?
Bonds	What is the basis of the connection that links the customer to the brand?
Emotional links	How can emotional experiences be designed to better cement relationship bonds?
Brand loyalty	What are the factors that affect loyalty and how can they be strengthened?
Reputation	What are people saying about the brand? How can "buzz" be created? How can referrals and advocacy be intensified?

loyalty. These strategies focus on determining which bonds are critical and how these bonds can be strengthened.

An analysis of the loyalty of brand customers considers not only the bonds, but also the factors that might rupture the connection and lead to brand switching. Such an analysis may also consider factors that lead the loyal customers of other competitive brands to switch. Satisfaction, of course, is a critical factor that brand strategies can address. Finally, brand reputation is analyzed to discover what is being said about the brand and whether the word of mouth accurately reflects the brand's performance and ideal mental brand. Brand relationship strategies, then, are designed to address problems and opportunities in all of these areas, as Table 12.5 illustrates.

EVALUATING BRAND RELATIONSHIP EFFECTIVENESS

With the emphasis on accountability, marketers are demanding more reliable ways to assess the impact of all marketing programs, including relationship marketing. Gummesson (1999, 183) has proposed a return on relationships (ROR) measure to evaluate the effectiveness of relationship programs. He defines ROR as "the long-term net financial outcome caused by the establishment and maintenance of an organization's network of relationships." There are a number of ways to approach the accountability problem, including satisfaction levels, relationship audits, and relationship metrics.

Satisfaction Levels

One of the oldest forms of relationship evaluation is the customer satisfaction survey. Research by Fornell (1992) found that customer satisfaction does predict future profits. The problem, however, is that satisfaction has low correlation with loyalty, so such tests are more useful as red flags than as relationship metrics. As Gummesson (1999, 184) explains, most brand switchers say that they are satisfied with their current brand, yet they switch for a variety of reasons, such as competitors' marketing programs, word of mouth from friends or family, or the desire to try something new.

However, surveys have found that those who respond that they are "very satisfied" are more likely to be loyal than those who are simply "satisfied."

Another factor, the "service paradox," states that the less profitable customers are, the more satisfied they are likely to be (Gummesson 1999, 185). On the other hand, the more profitable customers are, the less satisfied they are likely to be. In other words, satisfaction may not relate to loyalty because the more satisfied are also more critical and have higher expectations.

Relationship Audits

Customer and employee loyalty is the test of a long-term customer-brand relationship. Reichheld (2001, 5) and his colleagues at Bain & Company, working with Walker Research, have developed a loyalty survey as a relationship report card. Reichheld has benchmarked the loyalty test by testing it with a group of what he calls "loyalty leader firms" (firms recognized as having the highest levels of customer loyalty). He also administered it to a representative national sample of over 2,000 employees. Firms can compare their results against the benchmark rates in his database. Sample surveys, as well as variations for business-to-business marketers, channel members, and investors, are available at www.loyaltyrules.com. Reichheld's book, *Loyalty Rules!* (2003), also includes some survey questions.

Murphy et al. (1999) have developed a stakeholder relationship audit based on their concept of stakeholderism best practices, derived from research conducted by Research Consultants Ltd. in New Zealand. The first step in their methodology is to identify the key stakeholders for a brand and then develop a set of key value issues relevant to each group. A representative sample from each group is then asked to evaluate the brand on four central questions:

- *Importance:* How important is this issue in an excellent organization?
- *Performance:* How well does the organization perform on this issue?
- *Competition:* How well does the best other organization perform on this issue? What is the name of that organization and why was it chosen?
- *Improvement:* How can the organization improve its performance on this issue?

A performance gap is computed from the difference between the Importance and Performance ratings. A best practices gap is computed from the difference between the Performance and the Competition ratings. The results are also aggregated to determine a stakeholder relationship index that can be benchmarked against the scores of different companies as well as different stakeholder groups that have participated in the company's relationship evaluation program.

Brand Relationship Metrics

In theory, it is possible to estimate the ROR of a relationship program by evaluating the behavior of two key groups: heavy and midrange purchasers (Newell 2000, 56). In practice, it is difficult to establish ROR for relationship programs because of the many variables that affect these customer behaviors. The difficulty is further complicated by the long-term time span. There are, however, a number of ways to estimate the value of these efforts. The most common are retention and defection rates, customer profitability estimates, RFMD indices (recency, frequency, monetary, and duration), lifetime customer value (LTCV), share of wallet, and referral rate.

Retention and Defection Rates

Actual behaviors, such as the continuation of loyalty as evidenced in customer and employee retention, is a useful benchmark. Tracking studies can compare year-to-date behaviors and provide comparisons with industry and competitor rates. Retention is measured by the percentage of customers who remain with a brand for a year; defection is the percentage of customers who switch to a competing brand and no longer buy from the original brand.

Customer Profitability

One of the selling points of CRM programs is the ability to identify the most profitable customers in order to focus more marketing efforts on them. The point is that not all customers are worth the costs of a relationship program. Some do not buy enough or they buy only on price, some cost too much in hand holding and customer service, and some are constantly sending negative messages to other consumers. No matter how much business these customers do with a marketer, there is no point in extending the relationship if it only contributes to red ink. Research has found that it is not uncommon, for example, for close to 50 percent of a bank's customer base to be unprofitable (Storbacka 1994; Storbacka et al. 1994). CRM software provides the information from its databases that lets a manager assess whether a customer's profitability level justifies a continuing relationship effort.

According to Newell (2000, 40), the determination of profitability is a two-step process. The first step is to separate the transaction buyers (customers who buy once) from those who have a viable brand relationship. Database software systems make it possible "to track customers by their individual gross margin contribution or the average discount percent of their cumulative purchases." Newell then suggests separating those who have been identified as potentially profitable into three groups based on a monetary analysis: (1) those who are clearly the most profitable (10 percent); (2) those who have the potential to become top-profitable customers (40–50 percent); and (3) those who are only marginally profitable (40–50 percent).

RFMD Indices

The recency, frequency, monetary, and duration measures track actual customer behavior and predict relationship effectiveness based on changes in these indices. Recency tracks when the customer last purchased something, frequency tracks the number of purchases the customer made within a specified time period, the monetary measure looks at the amount the customer spent within that same time period, and duration tracks how long a customer has been a customer. The theory with these indices is that the more people buy, the more often they buy, the more they spend, and the longer they have been in the relationship, the more likely they are to buy that brand in the future.

LTCV

The primary benefit of focusing strategy on customer relationships is increasing retention and optimizing lifetime customer value (LTCV). Some companies rarely think of a bad brand experience as a glitch in the process of building a lifelong customer relationship, which means they either have not or cannot compute the lifelong value of that relationship. Software programs are available to do this based on the product category and the cost associated with servicing customers in that category.

Basically, LTCV is determined by multiplying the average length of time a customer stays with a brand times that customer's average annual contribution to profit, minus the cost of maintaining the relationship. To determine the relative value of a customer, companies need the data to build an estimate of the customer's lifetime customer value. For example, Cadillac estimates that an existing customer is worth $332,000 over his or her lifetime (Gummesson 1999, 183).

The analysis is usually done using quintiles that divide customers into five equal groups based on their profitability profiles, or their monetary index, multiplied by the average customer "life years" for the brand—that is, the average length of time a customer continues to buy the brand. In the top group would be the 20 percent with the highest LTCV and in the bottom group, the 20 percent with the lowest LTCV. If, for example, the top quintile's average annual profitability is estimated at $100 and the average number of life years for that group is six years, then the LTCV is $600. In contrast, if the lowest quintile's average profitability level is $50 and that group's estimated number of life years is only four, then their LTCV is $200 (Duncan and Moriarty 1997a, 263).

Share of Wallet

Because the most profitable customers often buy multiple brands, one objective is to increase the brand's percent of share of these category purchases. Scanner data can be useful in determining these changes in behavior, particularly for packaged goods categories. A share-of-wallet (also called share-of-customer) estimate is useful to determine the level of increase in purchases made by the midrange segment, as well as heavy users. The midrange segment is presumed to have more room for expansion in its business profile through cross-selling programs.

Referral Rate

Some relationship experts believe that the type and frequency of referrals is a valuable indicator of relationship bonding. Satisfied customers are happy to make recommendations to family, friends, and colleagues. As an example of the importance of referrals, the Cranfield School experts, identify referral networks as a key market arguing that these types of relationships are a largely underutilized competitive advantage for a brand (Peck et al. 1999, 6).

Referrals not only demonstrate a willingness to advocate on behalf of a brand, but also engage the persuasive power of word of mouth. This personal communication between friends anchors the intention-to-buy in conviction based on the testimony of someone who is perceived as having higher credibility than the company behind the brand. Referrals and recommendations are not easy to track. Consumer panels can estimate referral levels, but it is more useful to actually document the behavior with referral cards or responses on questionnaires. Both sides of the referral can be surveyed—the provider of the information as well as the receiver.

PEELING THE APPLE MYSTIQUE

One of Apple's billboards used for the launch of the iMac proclaimed, "Chic. Not geek." That line says a lot about Apple's position in the marketplace, and it also says a lot about the loyal users who identify with Apple's long-running slogan, "Think Different."

Surprisingly, Apple has never been a market leader or even a dominant player in the computer market. As a halo effect of its iPod and iPhone successes, Apple's worldwide share in the computer market has been steadily climbing every quarter since 2005. It has been estimated at around four percent over 2007. In the U.S. Apple has moved into third place, with an estimated share of around

8 percent points in 2007, an increase of 32 percent over 2006, and still climbing (Gartner). The relatively still small worldwide market share has only fueled the loyalty of its fanatical users, who are almost irritating in their defense of Apple and its Macintosh computer line. They talk it up, they celebrate its new launches, they join Mac clubs, they proselytize, and they refuse to believe that any other computer works as well or as simply. Others—the people they try to convert—sigh, shake their heads, and refuse to believe that anyone could be so pigheaded.

So what is it that makes Apple such a consummate example of a great consumer brand relationship? The answer is not a database or a loyalty program or rewards or attempts by Apple to keep in touch with its fans, although the company has started using e-mail to announce product news to its customers. Apple's over-the-top brand loyalty starts with a good product, of course, which is supported not only by a willingness to dump outmoded, redundant technology, but also by an eye for the fine art of product design. The cool factor has always been Apple's competitive advantage. Yet, in the end, the intense loyalty is anchored by Apple's revolutionary, creative, iconoclastic image. It appeals to people who are not geeks and resonates with people who think outside the box—outside the gray PC box, to be exact. It appeals to the self-image of people who, like the slogan, "think different"—a perfect match between image and self-image.

Source: www.Gartner.com.

PART IV

BRAND EQUITY

EXPANSION AND INTEGRATION

CHAPTER 13

BRAND STRENGTH AND BRAND SALIENCY

Part III brings together the two parallel systems of the management-driven brand concept and the customer perception of brand image. It recognizes that managing a brand involves both planning strategy and manipulating meaning. The end result, when effectively managed, is a powerful brand.

But what makes a brand powerful? What makes it enduring? This chapter will look at the issues surrounding brand stability and attempt to determine what factors make a brand a survivor, as well as strong and salient. The discussion begins with the Martha Stewart story about a brand in trouble and how it survived challenges to the integrity of its founder.

MARTHA STEWART: BRAND STRENGTH AND SURVIVAL

Martha Stewart, the diva of domesticity, is the founder of the company that bears her name, Martha Stewart Living Omnimedia. A celebrity in her own right, she created a brand that stands for how-to ideas and inspiration, as well as high-quality products that bring style, usefulness, and affordability to middle-class homes. The ideas are disseminated through her media empire, which includes magazines, Web sites, television shows, and a satellite radio program. The products are distributed through Kmart, bringing an element of style and class to the discounter's home fashion departments.

But the high-flying Martha Stewart brand crashed when Martha Stewart the person was investigated by a U.S. government agency and charged in June 2003 with insider trading. This is the story about how external forces (the stock market, government regulators, the court system) almost destroyed the brand, while the internal forces (the history and identity of the brand, its branding competency, the business scope and organization, the corporate culture, and the brand image and reputation) protected the brand and, ultimately, allowed it to survive.

The Martha Meltdown

In March 2004, Martha Stewart was found guilty of obstruction of justice and lying to federal investigators about her sale of shares in ImClone Systems in 2001. She was sentenced to a five-month jail term and reported to prison in October 2004.

It was a difficult time for her personally, as well as for her corporate empire and for the company's investors, who were thrown into a panic. Commentators predicted that the company was dead because there was no way the Martha Stewart brand could survive the negative splashback from this legal disaster. Advertisers and media planners deserted her and some TV affiliates dropped her shows. The Omnimedia company struggled to keep afloat, losing, according to analysts' estimates, 50 percent of its value in 2003. In 2003, advertising pages fell 35 percent, followed by an even more dramatic freefall in 2004 when ad pages fell 47 percent. The low point for the brand's flagship magazine, *Martha Stewart Living*, came in January 2005 when the previously bulky publication appeared with only twenty-six pages of ads.

After Stewart was charged, the company's share price dropped from $49 to $5.26 as the company lost an estimated $54 million in the first six months of 2004. In the third quarter of 2004, Omnimedia announced that revenue had dropped 24.4 percent from the previous year.

Brand Survival Strategy

The big question during Stewart's trial and prison term was how to manage the association between Martha Stewart the person and the Martha Stewart brand and company. Throughout this disaster, *Martha Stewart Living*'s editorial department stayed focused on the brand's mission and readers generally stayed with the magazine in spite of the advertising community's abandonment.

Under the guidance of Omnimedia CEO Sharon Patrick, the initial strategy was to do the obvious thing, creating some distance between the brand and the person and lessening the dependence upon the founder's name and face. The Martha Stewart name was reduced in size on the cover of *Martha Stewart Living*. The company also launched a new food magazine, *Everyday Food*, in the fall of 2003 with no links to the Martha Stewart name or image. Apparently this strategy was unacceptable to the company's founder, who, from prison, replaced Patrick with Susan Lyne, former head of ABC Entertainment, as president and recording industry executive Charles Koppelman as chair.

In spite of the dire predictions of the experts, consumer support helped keep the brand afloat during the dark prison days. Loyal consumers flocked to the MarthaTalks.com Web site to hear Stewart's words from prison, and another support group formed around SaveMartha.com. No one predicted that the brand would roar back the way it has, but it only happened because of the Martha loyalists.

The Martha Brand Rehab

On the personal level, rebuilding the Martha Stewart brand began with Stewart's release when she was photographed leaving prison in a poncho crocheted by another inmate as a gift. That little bit of publicity ballooned into a campaign of its own, connecting on a personal and emotional level with women who knit and crochet. The poncho was sold on the company Web site and on eBay, and the Lion Brand Yarn Company gave away the pattern on its Web site. The free poncho pattern also was featured on ABC's *Good Morning America* program; the response totally overwhelmed the Lion Web site.

Martha Stewart walked out of prison leaner but nicer and with a goal to be positive, humble, and willing to talk about her experiences in prison and the women she met there. She went from a superbusinesswoman to a gentler, more dignified, and empathetic real person. She became more believable in her knowledge of a broad cross-section of women and their concerns. The transformation deepened the level of emotional connection with her market. The unintended strategy worked: her disgraced image changed to one of bravery and honor.

On the business side, the Martha brand launched a blizzard of new initiatives, including a satellite radio program with round-the-clock programming catering to women's interests and two new NBC television programs: *Martha*, a branded entertainment program for daytime TV, and *The Apprentice: Martha Stewart* in prime time, based on the highly successful Donald Trump program. Other initiatives were three new books, a joint venture with a home-building firm that launched a collection of Martha Stewart designer homes, and a series of home-decorating DVDs.

Martha Stewart Living's business fortunes rode upward on the euphoria of these initiatives. In 2005, it reported an unheard-of increase of 38 percent in ad pages sold. In the fourth quarter, its business increased a phenomenal 133 percent, creating a 57 percent increase in revenues for the publishing division of the company. Circulation also increased, with the highest renewal rates in the magazine's history in 2005. The success of the Omnimedia ventures helped the company recover in the investment community. By August 2005, the Martha Stewart Omnimedia share price had climbed back to $30.

Brand Strength and Resilience

So how did the Martha Stewart brand and Omnimedia manage this comeback despite the predictions of doom? There are two secrets to the successful rehabilitation. The first is the strength and power of the Martha Stewart brand relationships and the second is the resiliency of the brand position. In terms of relationships, Kmart and Stewart's suppliers stayed by her side. More important, however, was the connection with her consumers, who maintained their loyalty. In terms of positioning, the company found that the brand itself had its own meaning, standing for a good life and a distinctive lifestyle. The brand continued to deliver on its quality-of-life promise in spite of the founder's personal problems.

There are other explanations, of course. Although Martha Stewart got caught lying in an investment scheme, it was considered a victimless crime. And to some of her housewife fans, the stock deal was a symbol of her success in a man's world. Her fans believed she was victimized by a system that was having a much harder time convicting and punishing the Tyco and Enron executives. According to a Gallup poll released in 2005, Martha Stewart was more popular than she had been before her legal trouble.

Sources: Tony Case, "Back in Business," *Brand Week Special Report,* March 6, 2006, p. SR1–7, 27; Gail Schiller, "A Tale of Two Marthas for Brand Partners," *Hollywood Reporter*, September 12, 2005, www.insidebrandedentertainment.com/bep/article_display.jsp?vnu_content_d=1001096364; David Carr, "Martha Stewart: The Business and the Brand," *International Herald Tribune*, August 30, 2005, www.iuht.com/bin/print_ipub.php?file=/articles/2005/08/29/business/stewart.php; Whisper Brand Strategy Consultants, "Martha Stewart's Brand Research," March 11, 2005, www.whisperbrand.com; Claude Singer, "Brand Elites Beware, Martha's Back!" Mediaweek.com, March 7, 2005, www.mediaweek.com/mw/search/article_display.jsp?schema=&vnu_content_id=1000827859; BBC News, "Martha Stewart Brand Bounces Back," April 27, 2004, http://news.bbc.co.uk/go/pr/fr/-/1/h/business/3664431.stm; CNNMoney.com, "Martha Quits Company Board," March 15, 2004, money.cnn.com/2004/03/15/news/companies/martha_trademark/?cnn=yes.

SUPERBRANDS: WHAT MAKES THEM STRONG?

Corporate managers long for strong brands that dominate their categories and set the standard for the competition. Is that just wishful thinking or is it, in fact, achievable, at least by some brands in some categories? A superbrand gains its power from the convergence of all the fragments of meaning that are cued by its strategy and experienced by its customers.

Although management decisions underlie the development of a powerful brand strategy, the power of a strong brand is exhibited through customer attitudes and actions. Marcel Knobil (1998), chair of the Brand Council in the United Kingdom and editor in chief of the Superbrands series of publication, defines a superbrand as one that "offers consumers significant emotional and/or tangible advantages over its competitors which (consciously or sub-consciously) consumers recognize and want." The characteristics that lead to the superbrand designation have been carefully analyzed by the Brand Council and its judging panel over the years. This chapter looks at these characteristics in terms of how they contribute strength, stability, and saliency to great brands.

Superbrands and Powerbrands: The Elite Brands

Knobil writes that 70 percent of British people think that their favorite brands would be better at running the country than the government. And 66 percent of consumers feel that Britain's top brands are more trustworthy than the major political parties—the majority even believe that brands are more likely to live up to their promises than political parties. In other words, successful brands are seen as reliable, efficient, and worthy of respect. They inspire confidence, loyalty, and trust.

The Brand Council brings together a panel of well-respected judges from all areas of marketing who evaluate the effectiveness of branding to determine Britain's strongest brands. The 2003 Superbrands edition (Knobil 2003) featured seventy-four brands deemed Superbrands by the panel. And research by the J. Walter Thompson advertising agency, which was also reported in the Superbrands book, identified the Top Ten Elite brands in the United Kingdom as Gillette, Marks & Spencer, BBC, McDonald's, Nike, Nescafé, Heinz, Kellogg's, Whiskas, and Colgate. Many of those names are also known outside the United Kingdom, suggesting that one of the characteristics of powerful brands is that they tend to be in more international markets than their competitors.

What do these brands have in common? For one thing, they dominate their categories. In some cases they created the category; in most cases the brand is practically synonymous with the category. That is because one of their fundamental principles is to offer a really good product and never move away from that position of core competence in the category.

Another characteristic is that they have more customers—that is, more share of the market—than other brands and their customers are more bonded to the brand; they have a higher level of loyalty than other competitive brands.

Another reason for these brands' success is that they are differentiated from competitors based on brand "values," a sense of brand character and integrity. And that values position has remained consistent across time, across product categories, and across borders.

Even with consistency in core values, these leading brands also tend to be innovators in their categories. The brand dynamic is not to sit back and rely on its leadership position but to maintain and protect that position by reading the market, listening to customers and other stakeholders, and adapting the brand and its product offerings to a changing market.

Consistency also means that their success is built over time. A superbrand is an enduring brand. Hamish Pringle, director general of the Institute of Practitioners in Advertising (IPA), says that the Superbrands collection celebrates great brands whose total value proposition satisfies discerning customers over and over again (Knobil 2003).

The Power of a Brand Story

One characteristic that stands out in the Superbrands collection is that the meaning of a powerful brand comes together as a brand story. And this story touches the hearts, heads, and hands of its customers and other stakeholders in such a way as to make them faithful to the brand. The story brings the brand to life and creates passion in its loyal followers, similar to the response of the Martha Stewart loyalists to all her legal travails.

A powerful brand, then, is built on a compelling brand story that marries all aspects of the brand strategy with customers' experience of the brand. As Howard-Spink (2003) points out, a brand is more than a jumble of unrelated adjectives used to profile a personality. He speaks of the need to connect a brand with the universal motivations and feelings found in cultural myths and fairy tales. They express the archetypes of character in ways that are cross-cultural and hardwired deep in our psyches. Scott Bedbury (2002), who has been in charge of marketing at both Nike and Starbucks, describes a brand as "a metaphorical story that connects with something very deep."

We opened Chapter 12 with the Apple brand story and observed that its success—actually, its survival, given all the management problems—is owing to the power of its twin stories of an easy-to-use computer that opens the door to creativity.

THE LONG-TERM STABILITY OF BRANDS

Except for the rare case of a new brand that succeeds (Starbucks, Diesel), a powerful brand is also enduring. The branding consultancy firm Interbrand, which specializes in creating brands and calculating their financial value, published a book in 1996 titled *The World's Greatest Brands* (Kochan 1996). The book contains short descriptions of hundreds of major brands. Among them, we note that 38 percent have existed for more than a century and 44 percent were introduced between 1900 and 1950, 14 percent between 1950 and 1975, and only 4 percent more recently than that.

Golder (2000) carried out a historical analysis of the brand stability over a period of seventy-five years (1923–1997) of 650 brands in a hundred product categories in the United States. The analysis determined that 23 percent of the market leaders in 1923 were still market leaders in 1997, and 25 percent were still among the top five brands in their category in 1997 (see Table

Table 13.1

Stability of Top Five Brands, 1923–1997

Position in 1923	Sample	Position in 1997 (in percent)			
		Number 1	Number 2	Number 3	4+5
Number 1 brand	97	23	8	9	8
Number 2 brand	70	11	9	3	4
Number 3 brand	43	5	7	2	5
Number 4 brand	26	4	4	4	4
Number 5 brand	12	0	0	25	0

Source: Golder (2000).

Table 13.2

Position in 1999 of the 1975 Brand Leaders and Runners-Up

Position in 1999	Brand leaders in 1975	Runners-up in 1975
Market leader	19	2
Runner-up	2	10
Other brand—share > 2% share	4	7
Other brand—share < 2% share	0	2
No longer for sale	1*	5*
Total number of brands	26	26

Source: Buck (2001a, b).
*Six of the number 1 brands from 1975 do not exist anymore. This is usually the result of mergers and product-line cuts.

13.1). With 39 percent of food and drink product brands maintaining a leadership position, their stability proved to be considerably greater than that of brands of durable products.

In 1996, ACNielsen compiled the age of the top hundred brands of fast-moving consumer goods in England. Among these brands, 83 already existed before 1980; in the last sixteen years, only seventeen new brands made their way into the top hundred. Seen globally, only one brand per year succeeded in taking a place among that top hundred (Franzen and Bouwman 1999).

Buck (2001a, b) analyzed the market share development of all brands in 126 categories of fast-moving consumer goods in the United Kingdom between 1975 and 1999 (see Table 13.2). Of the twenty-six market leaders in 1975, nineteen (73 percent) were still market leaders in 1999; of the twenty-six brands in second position in 1987, only two became market leaders and ten maintained their runner-up position.

The market research company Millward-Brown (2006a), analyzing the market share changes of seventy-one brands in England from year to year, concluded that the share for forty brands was absolutely stable. For twenty-seven other brands, the changes were limited to less than 1 percent of the yearly market share. There were major changes in only four of the seventy-one brands. Likewise, Dekimpe and Hanssens (1995), in a meta-analysis of 419 published marketing cases, determined that, among those brands whose market share developments were published, 78 percent were stable.

Table 13.3 presents the development of the market shares of Dutch beer brands, indexed at 1995 = 100. The share of the average brand changes on an average of only 0.3 percent per year.

Table 13.3

Market Shares of Beer Brands (Food Channel)

	1995	1996	1997	1998	1999	2000	2001	2002	2003
A	100	97	96	95	95	96	92	98	91
B	100	99	98	96	95	94	86	86	81
C	100	99	96	97	105	104	102	101	99
D	100	99	110	109	97	92	85	72	74
E	100	100	96	100	113	113	117	130	139
F	100	104	100	104	100	104	111	115	122
Other brands	100	107	105	109	108	113	132	131	146

Source: ACNielsen Nederland.

Limited Success of New Brands

Against the stability of these large brands, we can observe the limited success of scores of new brands. ACNielsen Nederland found out how many new brands and brand extensions in the fast-moving consumer goods area were successful in the short term between 1990 and 2000. There were initially only twenty-seven successful new brands—that is, three per year—of which only seventeen continued their success until 2000. In short, long-established brands tend to be very stable, whereas the chance of success of new brands is minimal. What could be the cause?

Order of Introduction

Brands that are introduced at an early stage of the development of a category can maintain a high market share for many years. Analyses of various databases in which the development of market shares was followed for many years all point in the same direction:

- PIMS data (W. Robinson and Fornell 1985) show that the market share of the pioneer brands reaches an average of 29 percent in the course of time, the early followers 16 percent, and the latecomers 11 percent.[1]
- ASSESSOR data on 129 brands (Urban et al. 1986) point out that the first follower reaches only 71 percent of the share of the pioneer and the second follower only 58 percent. Urban and colleagues estimated the market share of pioneers in a set of three brands at 43.6 percent, in a set of four brands at 35.7 percent, and in a set of five brands at 30.8 percent (see Table 13.4).
- BASES data lead to similar conclusions: the second brand reaches a share of 67 percent of the first, the second follower 45 percent, and the third 43 percent (Ernst & Young et al. 1999). The development of the shares is shown in Table 13.5.

Pioneers and First Movers

All these analyses point out that pioneer (first mover) brands have a substantial advantage in the long term, as long as they are managed properly. However, the data also show that this success is not a sure thing: a considerable percentage of market leaders slide after a few decades to a lower rank; almost half disappear from the top five after seventy years (Golder 2000). The early followers can take over the leading position especially when they succeed in developing

Table 13.4

Expected Market Share for the Following Numbers of Brands

Number of brands	1	2	3	4
First brand	100	58.5	43.6	35.7
Second brand		41.5	31.0	25.4
Third brand			25.4	20.8
Fourth brand				18.1

Source: Urban et al. (1986).

Table 13.5

Market Share for the Following Number of Brands

Number of brands	1	2	3	4
First brand	100	61	49	39
Second brand		39	29	25
Third brand			22	19
Fourth brand				17

Source: ACNielsen (2001).

relevant innovations, when they have developed an effective position, or when they can and want to invest excessively in market share development. According to Golder and Tellis (1993), the evolution of products shows that each company that could not or was not inclined to deploy the means necessary for market leadership was surpassed by another company that was capable and willing. The authors arrive at this conclusion after analyzing the development of 500 brands in fifty product categories.

Min et al. (2006) analyzed 264 new industrial product markets and concluded that innovation has a considerable impact on new-product survival and success. Pioneers that start a new market with a really new product had much lower survival rates than pioneers that launched an incremental innovation. Early followers in these new markets can learn from the pioneer's mistakes and have a better survival rate. In existing product markets, the pioneers that introduce incremental improvements have a considerably higher survival rate than early followers.

The advantage of first movers and early followers has several causes. This advantage can stem from building capacities and a financial head start that derives from the products' early introduction. Both make it possible to keep leading the further development of a category and consolidating the starting position of the brand. The head start makes it possible to allocate communication budgets that cannot be afforded by those joining later. This results in share-of-market/share-of-voice ratios that, in turn, work to the advantage of the first movers and early followers. D'Aveni and Gunther (1994) summarizes the advantages of being a first mover:

- *Response lags.* In the time it takes for second movers to reach the market, the first mover can earn substantial rents as a temporary monopolist.
- *Economies of scale.* The first mover has to achieve economies of scale before later entrants arrive. First movers tend to have significantly broader served markets.

- *Reputation and switching costs.* The first mover can establish brand loyalty first, so followers must convince customers to bear the costs and risks of switching to an untried, unknown late entrant's brand. The first mover is also helped by the cost of evaluating switching to a new product, which often leads to customers buying from the market leader.
- *Advertising and channel crowding.* By the time later entrants arrive, it may be hard for them to find uncluttered advertising space and distribution networks.
- *User-base effects.* Some products, such as telephones, increase in value as the number of users increases. By arriving first, the innovator can set the standard and build a stable, large user base that provides funds for the next leap in products.
- *Producer learning.* The innovator can move down the production and technology experience curve faster than competitors.
- *Preemption of scarce assets.* First movers have their choice of unique natural resources (e.g., nickel mines with the lowest extraction costs), valuable land (e.g., McDonald's restaurant locations), or shelf space (e.g., Procter & Gamble's control of supermarket displays and shelving).

Principle: If they are properly managed, pioneers and early followers have a sub-stantial long-term advantage.

Brand Learning

An important explanation for the stability of already established positions of the large brands in a category is the way consumers learn about brands and the resulting relative saliency of brands.

Two aspects of learning processes work to the advantage of the pioneers and the early follow-ers. First, a pioneer sets the basis for the category scheme. By scheme we mean the connecting structure of concepts that represent a phenomenon—in this case a product category—in memory (see Franzen and Bouwman 1999). For example, the phenomenon of the temporary employment agency was introduced in the Netherlands by Randstad. The way Randstad has manifested itself since then has determined what the Dutch see as the concept of a temp agency. Randstad formed the core meanings of this scheme in their memory and taught them which basic values they can expect from temp agencies. Randstad has thus become the prototype brand for temp agencies in the Netherlands. Every temp agency that the Dutch have subsequently got to know (Manpower, Adecco, Vedior, Start, Unique, etc.) is linked in their memory with the cognition of temp agency and is evaluated on the basis of the fundamental values that cognition has become linked to, thanks to Randstad.

The second phenomenon of the learning process is the relative strength of the connection be-tween the category scheme—for example, temp agency—and the various brands that are part of a category. The primacy effect in cognitive psychology means that material that is learned first is remembered better and has more of an effect than material that is learned later as part of a series. This works strongly to the advantage of brands that have stood at the basis of their category or have at least settled in memory as first representative of a category. Such a position may not be untouchable, but if well protected does bring important advantages with it. In Chapter 8, which discussed positioning, we looked at the strategies that will allow brands entering the market later to acquire an acceptable position behind the prototypical brand.

The important point, however, is that the long-term stability of a brand, which is based to a certain degree on the primacy of its introduction, is an indication of the brand's strength in the marketplace.

Principle: The advantage of pioneers and early followers can be largely traced back to the primacy effect when people learn new material. That which is learned first is remembered better.

Penetration and Consideration Sets

Because of the limited scope of consideration sets (usually no more than one to five brands), in many markets only a small number of brands account for a high percentage of the purchases. An analysis by ACNielsen (Van der Ouderaa 1994) shows that, measured over ninety product groups in the Netherlands, the three largest brands represent an average of 60 percent of the category turnover. These brands included, among others, food, nonfood, drinks, small household articles, and do-it-yourself products. The average mutual ratios between the turnover shares of these three brands measured over all categories are 4:2:1.

We can therefore speak of a pattern in which the nuance should be mentioned that the exact ratios depend on the degree of product differentiation and market segmentation. The pattern manifests itself in several countries, including the United States, the United Kingdom, and the Netherlands, and appears in many different product categories. The average over the ninety analyzed categories in the Netherlands was 4:1, 1:9, and 1:0 (the average shares of the numbers 1, 2, and 3 top-selling brands are 35.1 percent, 16.3 percent, and 8.6 percent, respectively). These ratios show much consistency through time.

By manipulating the external variables (sales promotions, measures to change positions on the shelves), suppliers can bring about some temporary changes, but the initial situation almost always restores itself in a short time. By far, most people fall back into their routine purchasing habits. Structural changes are in fact only possible when the saliency of a brand changes in the memory of consumers in relation to that of the alternatives. The relative saliency of the brand has to increase in order for the brand to become part of the customers' consideration set.

Principle: In most markets, the three largest brands account for a high percentage of the purchases—an average of 60 percent of the money. The ratios between the turnover shares of these brands averages 4:2:1.

BRAND SALIENCY

The psychological concept of saliency is not well known in the marketing world and thus requires some definition. The psychology literature in which the concept is discussed is not particularly clear on its meaning either. Reber (1997) defines saliency as clarity, conspicuousness, pronouncedness.

The term is used in the study of perception and cognition to indicate parts of a stimulus that stand out for some reason, such as visibility, importance, or relevance. During perception, certain aspects of the visual field are selected and then may or may not be given further attention based on the viewer's interest. What motivates that selection process is saliency, or, rather, a salient feature tends to get selected and attended to more than other features that have less saliency for the perceiver. Saliency could also be described as the process by which something enters a person's consciousness.

So what makes a brand stand out within its field of other brands and other related product categories? In brand theory, standing out means a brand begins to exist as an entity—it has an identity and it takes on importance. Miller and Berry (1998) state that brand saliency refers to the brands consumers reflect about, rather than what they think of those brands or how positively they evaluate them. Sutherland (1993) describes brand saliency as the possibility of a brand entering a person's consciousness at any random moment of life. Saliency thus refers to attributes of external stimuli, as well as the presence of entities in memory itself. It follows that there is internal and external brand saliency.

Internal and External Saliency

Internal saliency has to do with the relative accessibility of a brand representation in memory. This saliency is the result of the relative strength of the synaptic connections from cues directed toward a brand in contrast to cues directed toward competing brands. This accessibility or impact of a brand representation exerts a large influence on the perception of a brand.

Within the brand associative network, there is saliency of the various meanings to which a brand is connected. Salient meanings, for example, are those that stand out the most and enter consciousness earlier. The saliency of the category toward the brand association, combined with the saliency of certain brand meanings, largely determines whether a brand will become part of a consideration set and the prominence within that set relative to the other brands.

External saliency entails the manifest presence of a brand in the surroundings of a consumer. Here another distinction is made, between perceptual saliency and social saliency. Perceptual saliency refers to the degree to which a stimulus constellation distinguishes itself from competing stimuli—for example, to what extent packaging stands out on a shelf at a store. Social saliency has to do with the degree to which a brand is present in and gets attention from the social surroundings. The concept is close to the notion of popularity defined by Webster as being related to the general public and being suitable for the majority. A brand becomes socially salient as it becomes more and more emphatically present in the surroundings—for example, a drink becomes salient in shops and bars as people use it or talk about it.

Impact of Saliency on Perception

There is an exchange between internal and external saliency. Brands that have internal saliency are perceived more often, thus strengthening the connections to them in memory. This, in turn, influences the perception of brands in the surroundings.

The saliency of a brand influences the choice and purchasing behavior of consumers. Ehrenberg et al. (1997) are even convinced that a brand's success depends upon it. They claim that there is seldom a real difference between competing brands, since all innovations that stimulate their sale tend to be quickly borrowed. By the same token, brand advertising of similar brands does not usually and clearly radiate a different image or different values, regardless of what people may say.

Why are market shares of similar brands so dissimilar, then? The discrepancy has to do with the large differences in numbers between the groups of people for whom certain brands are salient—that is, the brands that resonate with them or give them a positive feeling. Market share, then, represents the power of an emotional response. This feeling can be developed, maintained, and/or stimulated through advertising. Ehrenberg and colleagues (1997) ask why a market leader is often ten times bigger than the seventh brand and conclude that this is *not* the result of differentiation. Users of a brand do not see their brand as very different—the only thing different is the number of people for whom the brand is salient.

Principle: Brand saliency is the relative conspicuousness of a brand in its surroundings. To make a brand internally salient, the brand representation in memory must be accessible; to make it externally salient, the presence of a brand in the physical and social surroundings must be manifest.

The Beer Market: An Example

There are quite a number of beer brands in the Dutch market: large brands like Heineken, Amstel, and Grolsch; mid-size brands like Bavaria; and smaller brands like Brand, Dommelsch, Gulpener, and Hertog Jan. They all have very different images. These are illustrated in Figures 13.1a, b, and c.

The value positioning of Dutch beer brands was examined (Centerdata 1999) with the help of the SWOCC value measurement instrument, developed by Sikkel and Oppenhuisen (1998a). For each brand, a determination was made of the degree to which it was associated with the six value dimensions found in the fundamental SWOCC research (see Chapter 9 on brand values). This resulted in three maps that, together, represent the perceptual space. They show, among other things, that Grolsch distinguishes itself from other brands in the dimension of "own identity" and "carefreeness," Amstel is strongly associated with "family life," and Heineken with "having a career'" and "independence from the judgment of others." The results reflect meanings that lie inside the measuring instrument—in this case, values. Another measurement instrument may provide a different perceptual space.

In 1997, these brands combined spent as much as 54 million euros in mass media advertising (BBC 1998), in addition to tens of millions of euros in other forms of marketing communication. Globally seen, their share of voice was equal to their share of market, with only Heineken and the small brands, Brand and Dommelsch, having a considerable higher share of voice; Grolsch had a lower one (see Figure 13.2).

At the beginning of this chapter, we noted that the market share of the average beer brand in the Netherlands changes only at about 0.3 percent per year. The market shares of the brands, however, differ enormously according to the geographical area. In Table 13.6, the shares for 2003 are indexed for each brand, setting at 100 the highest share reached in a beer area for a brand. From this it follows that in other areas the share is usually considerably lower, sometimes amounting to not even one-tenth of the highest share that the same brand has in its strongest area. The situation can thus be summarized as follows:

- The brands have different images.
- All the brands have campaigns in the national media, especially on television.
- The brands allocate large budgets to marketing communication.
- In general, their share of voice is equal to their share of market.
- Almost all the brands have national distribution.
- The brands hardly succeed, or not all, in having their market shares grow.
- The brands show large differences according to area.

Figure 13.1a–c **Value Associations of Beer Brands in the Netherlands**

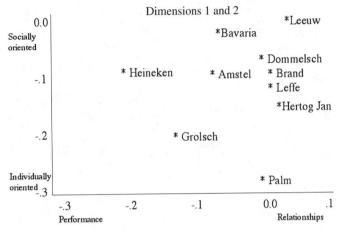

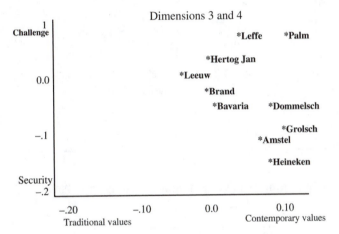

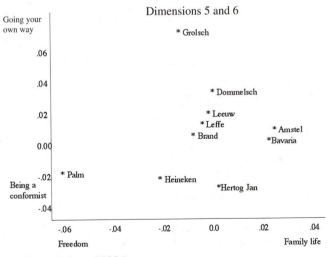

Source: Sikkel and Oppenhuizen (1998a).

Figure 13.2   **Share of Voice Versus Share of Market of Home-Use Market Beer Brands**

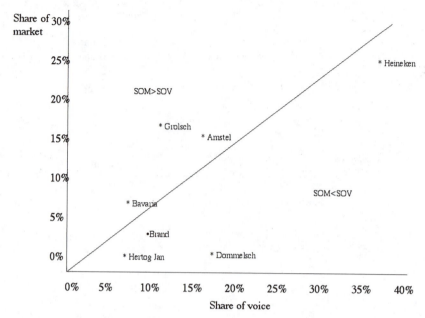

Source: FHV/BBDO (2001).

Table 13.6

Market Shares of Beer Brands in the Netherlands per Area in 2003

Brand	1	2	3	4	5	6	7
A	54	100	38	12	97	24	9
B	32	49	32	100	71	31	13
C	100	35	77	3	65	20	18
D	5	15	5	4	16	100	12
E	40	85	35	9	77	100	9
F	48	71	32	9	100	16	7

Source: ACNielsen (2003).
Note: Shares indexed on the basis of area with highest share = 100.

What is the explanation? The answer is saliency.

Sources of Internal Brand Saliency

There are three important sources of internal brand saliency:

- consumer usage and experience of a brand;
- the perception or presence of a brand in the physical and social environment;
- the perception of communication manifestations of a brand.

Figure 13.3 **Sources of Internal Brand Saliency**

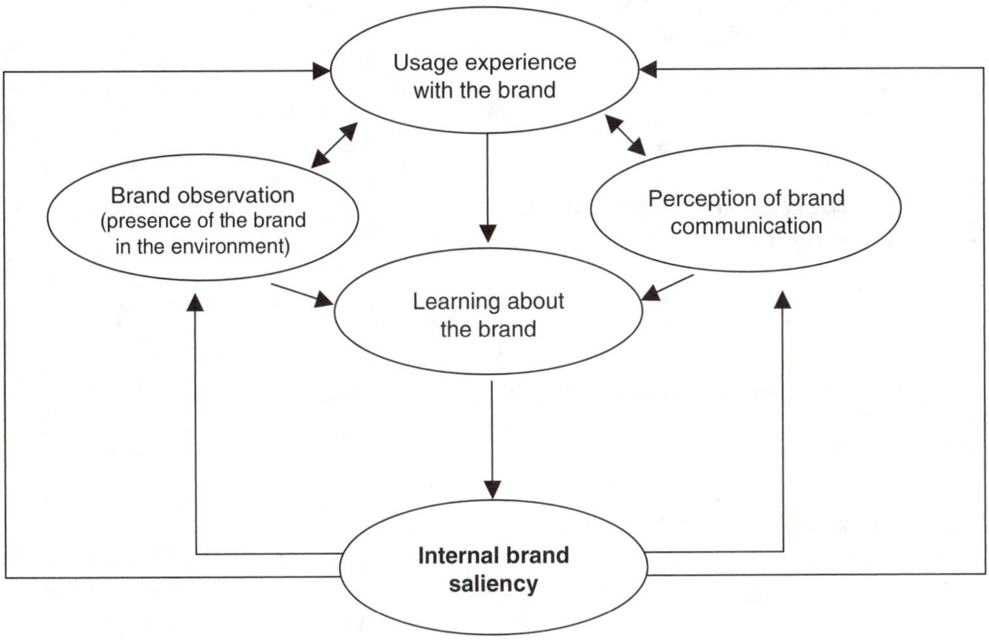

All three sources lead to learning processes in consumers that result, among other things, in internal brand saliency. In turn, this influences the degree of attention given to those sources. The result is the emergence of a system in which cause and effect can no longer be distinguished. This system is depicted in Figure 13.3.

Advertising: Image or Saliency?

How does advertising work—via brand saliency or brand image? In past decades, most advertisers and scholars were convinced that advertising works mainly by influencing brand image. Questioning this consensus, Miller and Berry (1998) argued that perhaps advertising works mainly by influencing brand saliency. They had a database of car rental agencies (Avis, Hertz, etc.) in the United States at their disposal that gave the market share development, advertisement expenditures, and brand and advertising data over an eleven-year period. The researchers carried out two different regression analyses (see Figure 13.4) and calculated the net effect of the share-of-voice and share-of-market changes, calculating the percentages back to 100 percent. Thus emerged a model of advertising effects (see Figure 13.5).

The analysis leads to the following conclusions:

- The effects of the advertising share (share of voice) on brand familiarity and advertising memory are much bigger than those on the content of the brand image.
- Brand familiarity has the greatest influence on the market share.
- The image also has a considerable influence on the market share, but is not strongly influenced by the share of voice.

Figure 13.4   **Research Approach of Miller and Berry**

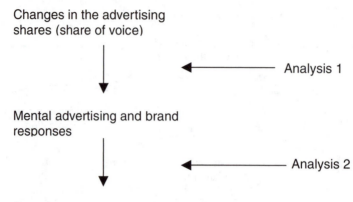

Source: Miller and Berry (1998).

Figure 13.5   **Advertising Effects** (in percent)

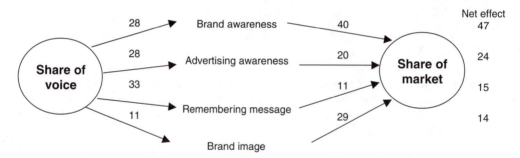

Source: Based on Miller and Berry (1998).

- Advertising awareness has a relatively large effect of 24 percent on the market share changes.
- The effect of the recall of the content of the advertising message on the market share is rather limited.
- Of the net effect on market share changes, 47 percent is explained by brand awareness and only 14 percent by image changes.

In short, in this market, which probably has a high instrumental and commodity character, brand awareness (read: brand saliency) is the most important advertising effect variable, and the meaning of the advertising message and its influence on the content of the brand image are marginal (Miller and Berry 1998).

If an advertising strategy has successfully positioned a new brand, the same strategy is then usually expected to improve that position over time. Since this is rarely possible, most advertising for established brands produces relatively low persuasion scores, and the advertising on behalf of one brand tends to be offset by its competitors' advertising. New brands quickly settle into a market-share pecking order with the competition and rarely move up as advertising is asked to improve perceptions.

Not only do established brands rarely improve their market share, unless the product is reformulated, but the average brand actually loses about a third of a share point each year to new entrants.

Advertising for an established brand, particularly a well-differentiated one, will be much more effective if it exploits the brand's positioning. Specifically, advertising should focus on the elements that differentiate the brand from competing brands in a set. For example, if consumers use a brand of toothpaste to prevent tooth decay, and some of these consumers also use other brands for other reasons, advertising alone will not improve perceptions of the brand's decay-fighting ability, but it can and should make decay prevention more important as a decision factor.

The key to more effective advertising is to understand exactly what it is about the brand that is both differentiating and important to current users. Often the driving elements of a brand's positioning are not what marketers assume because they may lie below the threshold of cognitive response.

This chapter has made clear how large the influence of the past on the position of the brand is. The large world brands have existed for more than half a century already, and chances of new brands successfully penetrating the established order are not very high. When developing a new communication strategy, marketers should be aware of the limited possibilities of exerting influence in the development of a brand. There is almost always a status quo that is difficult to break through.

An analysis by the Leo Burnett agency of 1,251 U.S. brands (Sylvester et al. 1994) indicated that 605 did not show growth but declined instead. For brands that did grow, the growth was usually minimal. Only 95 brands (7.6 percent of the researched brands) showed an annual turnover growth of more than 20 percent.

Of course, the entire marketing mix is influential in this process. Relevant product improvements that are well communicated can help a brand break through the status quo and bring about growth. However, in stabilized markets where there are no significant innovations at a product level, the development of brands depends completely or predominantly on their communication strategy, and as the communications expenditures are a reflection of existing market positions, it is exceedingly difficult to realize market share growth.

Ehrenberg et al. (1997) believe that, in this situation, the emphasis should lie not on influencing the content-wise brand perceptions (the image), but on the saliency of the brand. Ehrenberg makes a passionate plea for advertising that is aimed primarily at attracting attention toward the brand:

> The closer and more substitutable the brand is with its competitors, the easier it is for creative and effective "Here I Am" publicity to maintain, reinforce, and/or nudge the brand's salience and consumers' purchase propensities. There are then no differentiating functional (or emotional) values that the advertising would have to overcome (like greatly preferring shredded wheat to a muesli, say). Only consumers' habitual brand-choice propensities (and their consequent feelings for Brands A or B: "I use it, therefore I like it") may inhibit moving between directly competitive brands.
>
> The less brands are differentiated, the more readily advertising can nudge choice behavior. But the greater challenge, therefore, is the need for defensive reinforcement of the brand.
>
> This explains the role of advertising to try to nudge the brand's impact and the even greater need to defend the brand's customers from its many competitors' encroachments. Most advertising and marketing for established brands seems in practice to be geared to counter the competition and defend one's market share from its close competitors.
>
> Advertising a well-established brand to experienced consumers can seldom if ever imbue it with new, highly differentiating attributes, or with more liking than before, because these things are features of the product-type and generally vary little from brand to brand anyway. Nor does it seem likely that consumers' attitudes can be changed readily just by seeing a

few advertising messages. In contrast, simply to *publicize* the brand well *can* lead to more people being aware of the brand, feeling *assured* about it, bringing it into their consideration set. The brand's name and package are its distinctive features by which it is known. Hence the overwhelming importance, we think, of publicizing the brand name. Many ads, and perhaps most, do just that, either as:

"Here I Am" (e.g., "*Coke is It*"), or

"I'm a good example of the product category" (e.g., "*Domestos kills all known germs dead*").

The advertising copy has to be distinctive to be noticed and leave memory traces. But in practice this is not in order to attach a different message or image to the brand (or certainly not *necessarily*). To change people's attitudes or feelings greatly and/or lastingly is quite widely accepted to be very difficult or near impossible.

In this situation, what is most important is to influence the evocation of a brand by strengthening the association from the relevant choice-cue to the brand. Concentration on this connection should be carried out in such a way that the communication manifestations get as much attention as possible.

Khermouch (2001) analyzed the communication strategies of established brands in the United States that have managed to realize a larger perceived popularity than their market share would lead one to suspect. Examples are Budweiser and Nike. Although their share of voice is important, it does not usually surpass their market share, but their communication strategy has several striking characteristics:

- a large number of different executions, sometimes several simultaneous campaigns;
- the use of nontraditional media, like event sponsoring;
- zeroing in on popular culture events;
- the use of icons from the music, movie, and sports worlds.

In short, these brands ensure there is a penetrating omnipresence.

STRENGTH AND SALIENCY IN BRAND CHOICE

The most important behavioral response that indicates brand strength is brand selection or choice. In high-involvement situations, consumers may investigate a brand or product category, establish mental choice criteria, and develop positive or negative attitudes toward various brands, leading to preference or an intention to try or buy a certain brand. Subsequent evaluation of the product's performance leads to a decision to either buy or not buy a second time.

In low-involvement situations, consumers may decide to buy a product on impulse and then evaluate the decision, leading to a yes or no on a repeat purchase. Feelings about the brand may contribute more to saliency and thus brand choice than rational thoughts. Several repeated purchases can lead to habit or loyalty. How does this work and what is the role of saliency in both low- and high-involvement brand choices?

Brand Evocation and Brand Evaluation

As mentioned in the discussion of consideration sets, two phases can be distinguished in the choice and purchasing process of consumers that reflect or affect the strength and saliency of a brand: the evocation phase and the evaluation phase. In the evocation phase, the available alternatives are reduced, consciously or unconsciously, to a limited number from which the final choice is made.

Table 13.7

Use of Information Sources

Duration and nature of the choice process	Use of information sources		
	Mainly internal information	Interaction between internal and external information	Mainly external information
Short and routine-like	Margarine, cola	Specialty beers	Frozen pizza
Limited scope and duration	Desserts, facial crème	Foreign cheese	Quality wine, books
Lengthy and extensive	Perfume	Car, PC	Travels

This number of brands is called the consideration set. In the evaluation phase, a choice is made for one single alternative (or several) within this consideration set.

This process can be short and routine, as is the case with purchase actions that are impulsive or repeated often and involve little risk. It can also be lengthy and extensive when it comes to important and more risky choices in categories in which product costs are high or their features are constantly renewing themselves.

Beach (1993) also emphasizes that consumers go through two different processes: "screening" and "choice," in his terminology. He also proposes that screening is not just a preliminary step to choice, but a *different* process from choice—the consideration set is brought about in a different way than the final choice in the choice phase. The saliency of a brand based on feelings and a limited set of associations has a dominant influence in this screening process. For the final choice, brands within the consideration set can be evaluated against more elaborated choice criteria—one could speak of postconsideration information here and previous experiences. Examples are very specific product attributes (handling, durability) or the perceived price-value ratio of brands.

In simple, routine choice processes, choices can be made just on the basis of information in the long-term memory—again dominated by feelings and experiences. In choices with larger perceived risks and insufficient information present in memory on the (new) alternatives, the need increases for gathering and processing external information. The interaction balance between the two dimensions, the type of information and the duration of the choice process, are sketched in a matrix in Table 13.7.

Based on these two dimensions, the brand choice matrix includes various possibilities that are classified into two phases.

Principle: The brand choice process consists of two phases: an evocation phase, in which the available alternatives are unconsciously reduced to a small number, and an evaluation phase, in which a final, more conscious choice is made.

The evocation phase involves a lot of unconscious processes, in which the goals lead to the activation of associations in long-term memory of what are known as search cues ("I need healthy margarine, Italian pasta, something for cocktails Sunday afternoon"). From these search cues, the memory makes automatic connections with brands, sometimes only when a person arrives at the corresponding shelf at the supermarket.

Figure 13.6   **Brand Evocation and Brand Evaluation**

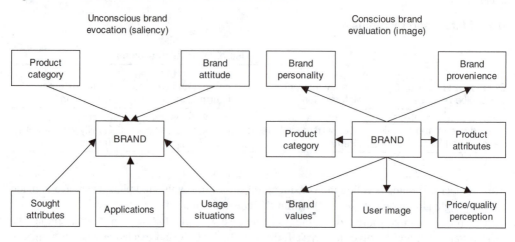

When there is a high degree of involvement, the unconscious processes set boundaries within which a more conscious brand evaluation takes place. For example, people spend more cognitive energy when choosing which ice cream flavor or which French cheese to buy than when choosing a brand of toilet paper. The essential question is, to what extent do they fall back on experience-based knowledge in their memory, and to what extent do they supplement this knowledge with external information during the purchasing process? In general, the effects of long-term memory are so strong that the influence of external information may be limited. The two processes are presented in a diagram in Figure 13.6.

Different Routes to Brand Choice

Until recently, it was assumed that people are aware of what happens in their brains and that they can steer what happens there. Even the most common theories of consumer behavior were based on this assumption. According to this implicit belief, Homo sapiens have free will with which they make conscious choices from the possibilities that the world and life hand out to them. Furthermore, the common view of brand choice was that it results from cognitive processing and follows a logical, linear decision path with predictable steps, such as those outlined in the early twentieth-century AIDA model (attention, interest, desire, action).

Marketing and advertising decisions continue to be viewed through this lens of logical decision making, even though theorists have argued for the past fifty years that this model is not adequate to explain how decision making works in a range of product categories and situations. In this section, we will discuss the traditional rational or cognitive approach, the routine or habit approach, and the affective approach.

The Rational Approach

Peter and Olson (1994) state that the point of departure in both marketing and advertising is the vision of consumers as having goals they want to achieve and problems that need to be solved.

Consumers make decisions as to which behavior they will exhibit in order to realize their goals. In this sense, decision making (seen as a choice among two or more alternative actions) is a purposeful process of problem solving. Stephan and Tannenholz (1994) call this the process theory of brand choice and describe it as follows:

1. The experience consumers receive from using a brand solidifies their perceptions of it. These fixed perceptions can rarely be changed through advertising alone.
2. How consumers perceive each of the different brands in a category determines which ones are used and which ones are not. If consumers perceive different brands to be superior according to different desirable attributes, this results in switching around within a set of brands rather than using a single brand.
3. Consumers' fluctuating wants and desires cause them to switch from one brand to another.
4. In many categories, brand use itself causes consumers' desires to fluctuate. Consumers may temporarily satisfy certain desires by using one brand but deprive themselves of other satisfactions they could have received from a competing brand.
5. As consumers' desires fluctuate relative to their fixed perceptions of brands, a consistent process of brand switching results over time.
6. Advertising and promotion intervene in the process by temporarily changing the probability of a user purchasing the brand the next time.
   a. Advertising intervenes by temporarily intensifying the consumer's desire for some benefit the brand is already perceived to provide.
   b. Price promotion intervenes by temporarily changing the perception of the price/value relationship.
7. New brands, line extensions, product improvements, price changes, and restages of existing brands change consumers' perceptions and permanently alter the process of brand choice for some category users.
8. Most advertising by brands will never improve their users' perceptions, but new competitors can diminish these perceptions over time.

Figure 13.7 presents a rationalistic model of consumer choice and decision making with several basic stages of processes that reflect the vision of Peter and Olson (1994) and Engel et al. (1990). The process results in a decision plan that consists of one or more behavioral intentions, such as to test drive, visit a showroom, search online for more information, or actually try the product or service. The usage experience is fed back into the process and leads to repetition of the purchase or reexamination of the alternatives.

The Routine or Habit Approach

It has gradually become clear that this rational model is only applicable to a limited number of consumer decisions. Researchers have realized that many automated purchasing behavior processes are carried out without thought, intention, or even awareness. People react automatically to the things that influence their behavior without even noticing them. The result is a decision to buy things on impulse.

The role of free will is one issue. For example, when solving problems or when evaluating and assessing alternatives, many people are aware only of the results, not of the underlying thought processes. They cannot indicate properly what influences their behavior either. Their statements

Figure 13.7   **General Model for Consumer Problem Solving**

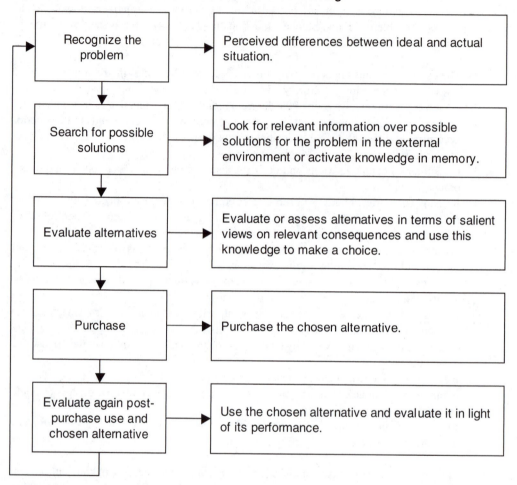

Source: Based on Peter and Olsen (1994).

on the subject tend to be mere after-the-fact attributions based on naive personal assumptions. Quite often, what seems to be a free-will decision is just a conspiracy between biological needs, inner motives, and learned memory combined with external stimuli. Homemakers, for example, may find themselves buying the same brands that their mothers' bought. Some research even shows that when you feel the intention to stand up, it can be as much a side effect of the action during its execution!

The question is thus whether there is anything such as free will at all, or whether people just have mental conditions that influence behavior directly while they experience them as free will. Bargh (1997) expresses his views on the subject as follows:

> Life is full of automatisms that play an important role in the creation of a situation from which subjective experiences and their ensuing conscious processes arise. Our perceptions, evaluations and the goals we strive for can be determined by our surroundings, and that is what really occurs. Because neither these interpretations based on perception, preferences

and dislikes, nor the reasons for our behavior can be experienced consciously, we try to understand them by translating them into aspects we are aware of and into our theories about the how and why of our feelings and actions. Our understanding of what we think, feel and do is largely formed after the fact. It may be that the conscious exists in order to enable us to establish logical connections, so that we get a feeling of stability and control.

Bargh believes that the step-by-step plan, which assumes that perceptions precede conscious evaluation and thought processes, which then precede reactions, is the reason that we underestimate the mediating role of unconscious processes. This "meta assumption" is based on the idea that conscious recognition and thought processes precede a decision and that they practically form a blockage for affective reactions or behaviorist responses. In the current parallel models, contrary to the step-by-step models of the 1960s, proceeding thought processes are not necessary in order to bring about a perceptual, evaluative behavioral effect. Attributional assessments are largely unconscious, spontaneous, and lacking in presupposed intentions.

Zajonc (1980), supported by subsequent research, claimed that affective reactions can precede, act almost simultaneously, or even be entirely independent of the most elementary conscious processes, such as stimulus recognition. Goals and plans and the thought processes and behaviors to pursue these goals can become automatisms without involving a conscious choice or consultation.

The Affective Approach

The most dramatic departure from the rational model is seen in the work emanating from neurobiology in which emotion is seen as the driving force behind many, if not most, brand decisions and behaviors. As we mentioned earlier, brand saliency is often a function of something so simple as having a positive feeling about a brand. David Penn (2006), founder of Conquest Research, a U.K.-based brand research company, has followed the newly developing area of neuroscience and its sibling, neuromarketing, and explains that "brain science suggests that emotions powerfully influence much of our brand choices."

According to Ann Marie Barry (1997), who has made an extensive study of the role of emotion in advertising and visual communication, the perceptual approach to communication theory acknowledges the primacy of emotions in processing all communication. Visual communication, which is central to understanding the impact of advertising, is particularly dependent on emotional response. She reports that "neurological research reveals that visuals may be processed and form the basis of future action without passing through consciousness at all." Although the advertising industry is still dependent on the cognitive processing model of advertising with its rational consumer targets and linear decision making, some practitioners have intuitively understood the power of visuals to generate the emotional responses that they sometimes refer to as "hot buttons."

Another aspect of the new brain science approach is a deeper understanding of the way low-attention processing actually works as a form of unconscious, intuitive decision making. In the discussion of the routine or habit approach, we noted the lack of conscious thought about many decisions. That is true also for decisions that are driven by emotions and feelings.

Mitch McCasland, planning director for Moroch Partners advertising agency, and Nicole Davis, brand manager for Samsung Telecommunications, analyzed a group of studies (2005) and determined that in each category they investigated, including such unemotional products as telecommunications and appliances, as well as antidepressants, cereal, insurance, soft drinks, and even doggie diapers, "we discovered emotional components in brand purchase considerations." The discovery led them to the insight that strategy should be based on an understanding of the role of passion in branding. They observe that, for many brands, passion is essential. This is particularly true for aspirational brands or status symbol brands They conclude, "A brand's emotional realm is often where the greatest distinction and differentiation can be found, particularly for brands in mature categories."

Penn (2005) says that marketers focus too much in research and strategy development on what consumers remember about advertising. In his view, what is more important is the impact of communication on brand perception. "What this means," he suggests, "is that, ultimately, brand response is more important than ad response" and that brand response is often driven more by feelings than thoughts. As Penn explains, "A lot of our 'thinking' about brands and advertising is unconscious and not easily accessed via standard (conscious) questioning."

Brand experiences can be based on rational reflections about features, benefits, and performance, but emotional values may be the brand's most important point of difference in a category. The Dove campaign with its very real worldview of feminine beauty tapped into a deeper insight that moved beyond the idea that all women aspire to be beautiful. The brand's secret is that it exploded the stereotypes of beauty and actually expressed the idea that there is beauty in everyone, using real women, not models, to make that point.

Bottom-Up and Top-Down Processes

To reconcile the various approaches, Schneider and Shiffrin presented as early as 1977 what is known as the "two-processes theory," an interaction between processes that take place unconsciously and automatically, outside free will, and processes that humans are aware of and that they can control and study. These can also be referred to as bottom-up and top-down processes.

Some choice processes seem to be under the control of free will. The situation is as people experience it themselves because they are aware of it (by being aware we mean a cognition that is reachable through introspection). These choice processes are focused: it seems as if people are making their decision autonomously. The big problem is that nobody knows what is responsible for this "center of control" in the human brain. Despite various hypotheses and speculations, the question remains whether there is a sort of center in the brain that leads things, determining what people pay attention to and taking the initiative in instigating behavior—for example, deciding to buy a different brand of beer tomorrow.

Taylor of the University of London posits that the mind has a passive and an active component, generally corresponding with the bottom-up and top-down processes. The passive component is receptive, input-driven. It reacts automatically to external stimuli and has a limited capacity. It is based on competition in memory. The active component is reflective, focused, and controlled. It is response-driven. Behavior could be a mixture of these two processes, since the influence of each one can vary. A considerable part of behavior allegedly arises from the passive component and takes an automatic course; a smaller part may be steered from the active component, in which goals, values, and attribute evaluations lead to decision plans.

Swaab, former director of the Dutch Brain Institute, argues that consciousness

> has no free will at all. What's more, it lags behind the facts. Tests show that, when people move their fingers, the motor centre of the brain gets activated first. Only afterward is the test subject aware of it. "You may think that you have moved your finger consciously, but in fact the decision has been taken by the motor centre. Awareness only comes a couple of hundred milliseconds later."

Swaab once went with a colleague to the Metropolitan Museum in New York. "We asked ourselves then: are we here out of free will or not? Does that visit come forth indeed from an education with love of art from an early age?" Walking through the halls we arrived at the conclusion that it really doesn't matter. There are so many factors that determine the structure and the decisions of the brain! If one knows the brain in all its facets, it is possible, in principle, to predict what will happen. There is no reason whatsoever to assume that we do things out of free will. At best, one becomes aware after the fact of the calculations made in the brain. . . .

Still, there is a way in which our consciousness can influence our decisions. Consciousness comes after the decision to do something, but that consciousness can influence the next decision that is taken. This is also why it makes sense to punish people. (Spiering and Thijssen 2001)

Visser (1999) interviewed several Dutch scientists on this matter. They are unanimous in their views. Edward de Haan of Utrecht University believes that "consciousness is the end result of a selection process at a lower neural level. It seems as if you think of something, but it is a sort of 'survival of the fittest' between behavioral alternatives." Bob Bermond, biopsychologist at the University of Amsterdam, posits that reflection serves to make a conscious choice between behavioral alternatives produced by the unconscious. Max Sutherland (1993) suggests that the ultimate choice when weighing out alternatives depends not only on the consumer's preference, but also on the order in which the various alternatives are categorized in memory:

What determines which alternatives one really considers? Let's look at a consumer decision that we probably make every day: it's the middle of the afternoon, and you're getting hungry and ask yourself, "What will I have for today?" All kinds of alternatives come to your mind, and you evaluate them as they come up. The process goes something like this:

Shall I have a mince pie?
No, I had that yesterday.
A sandwich?
No, the sandwich shop is too far and, besides, it's raining.
I can always drive to McDonald's.
Yes, that's what I'll do.
(Or, on second thought. . . . I could have lunch at Pizza Hut.)

Two things should be noted here. First, your mind provides alternatives, one by one. In this case, the mental list of alternatives follows an order:

1. mince pie
2. sandwich
3. McDonald's
4. Pizza Hut

The second remark is that the order in which the alternatives are classified is the same as that in which they are generated by the brain. This order may end up influencing the final choice. It may be the case that you like Pizza Hut more than McDonald's, but in the example you went to McDonald's and not to Pizza Hut. If instead of stopping at the third alternative (McDonald's) you had continued the thought process, you would have probably gone to Pizza Hut, but since Pizza Hut was number five in your mental list of lunch options, chances are more reduced of going there frequently. You did not go to Pizza Hut because you hadn't thought about it before running into a satisfying solution—McDonald's. You didn't go because it did not come to your mind. Even when we like something, chances are we will not go for it if it is not relatively high in our mental list.

Another scientist interviewed by Visser, Hans Crombach, law psychologist at the University of Maastricht, says that evolution has brought human consciousness. With it, people try to bring their behavior under control. They may have succeeded to a small degree. Crombach points out that most behavior looks intelligent and focused, but in fact runs its course automatically. He does not believe that the mystery of mental cause will be solved quickly. One of the problems he mentions is that people are unable to conceive of the question in other than dualistic terms. Although many philosophers state nowadays that the Cartesian distinction between mind and body is outdated, Crombach has yet to hear anyone say something convincing about it in different terms. "Even if we try to speak as objectively as possible by using concepts such as mental and neural processes, we keep falling into expressions of dualism. And it couldn't be any other way: we seem to have a mind that steers our body." Is the causal consciousness an illusion, then? Maybe, says Crombach, though why do we have that illusion?—in other words, it is crazy that nature provides illusions that appear *as* illusions. Because of this type of question, Crombach does see causal consciousness as a real possibility, even if there is little reason for it (Visser 1999).

Principle: Brand choice is the result of two processes: a bottom-up, unconscious, automatic process outside the reach of free will, and a top-down, consciously reflective, focused, and controlled process.

The Heuristics of Brand Choice

The more widespread theories of choice processes are based on the assumption that consumers evaluate the alternatives according to specific choice criteria. They "search" for certain attributes, find out to what degree a brand has them, and apply a "choice rule" to them. Consumers integrate their choice criteria (e.g., symbolic meanings and preferred product attributes) into this outlook, thus arriving at a final choice. Scholars have formulated several decision rules that have by now become standards for the study of consumer behavior (Bettman 1979; Engel et al. 1990; Assael 1987).

1. *Compensatory processes.* According to the multiattribute model, perceived weakness or negative evaluation of one criterion can be compensated by a positive evaluation on another criterion. Separate evaluations for each choice criterion are combined (merged or averaged) to arrive at a general evaluation of each alternative. The highest-scoring alternative is then chosen.

2. *Noncompensatory processes*

   - Conjunctive. The consumer sets a minimum level of acceptability for each choice criterion. An alternative is only accepted if the criterion equals or exceeds the minimum level.
   - Disjunctive. The consumer poses acceptable norms for each criterion. A product is acceptable if it comes up with at least one criterion above the minimum level.
   - Lexicographic. The consumer categorizes choice criteria in order of importance, first choosing the best alternative according to the most important criterion. If two or more

alternatives are evaluated as equivalent, the choice goes to the best possibility according to the second most important criterion, and so on.

- Elimination of aspects. The consumer sets a minimum level for each choice criterion, electing a criterion and eliminating all alternatives that do not reach the minimum level. This process of elimination of alternatives continues until one single alternative remains and is chosen.

3. *Combination processes.* The customer mixes compensatory and noncompensatory processes, combined on the spot as an adjustment to environmental factors.

Already in the 1970s, Tversky and Kahneman (1973) argued that these theories are too rationalistic. People usually have insufficient insight into their own choice criteria and insufficient information to be able to properly evaluate the alternatives. In many cases, the choice is not important enough to merit the allocation of much cognitive energy. In other cases, consumers are overwhelmed by the enormous overburdening of information they are exposed to. Still, since they have to make choices anyway, they apply heuristics: abbreviated approaches, rules of thumb, memory aids. They are not so much aiming at optimizing the choice as trying to avoid the risk of making a wrong choice. Here are some well-known heuristics:

- *Awareness heuristic:* Customers choose brands they know above unknown brands.
- *Familiarity heuristic:* Customers choose the brand they feel more familiar with.
- *Popularity heuristic:* Customers choose the brand that most people in their surroundings also choose. This includes choosing what is "in" also.
- *Authority heuristic:* Customers choose what the experts choose (for example, on the basis of other consumer comments).
- *Reliability heuristic:* Customers choose the brand that seems most reliable or has a reputation of reliability.
- *Representative heuristic:* Consumers choose the brand that is experienced as most representative for its category or subcategory.
- *Quality heuristic:* Customers choose the brand that is known as the best in its class.

It is plausible to believe in a connection between the strength of the associations and the evaluation of a brand on the basis of several of these criteria. Researchers at the Centre for Adaptive Behavior and Cognition in Berlin (Evans 2001) have shown that applying the familiarity heuristic is often conducive to a better result than choosing on the basis of an elaborated comparison of the alternatives.

Principle: The relative strength of the associations from a search cue toward a brand largely determines what brands consumers choose. In more weighed-out choice decisions, this strength serves as a heuristic that allows consumers to more extensively evaluate an alternative.

The Role of Segmentation in Brand Choice

Regarding segmentation, Ehrenberg and Goodhart (1978) conclude that, in new brands and brand extensions, marketers often believe that being different is enough to make the brand succeed.

Accordingly, they try to breed a specific client need that differentiates a considerable consumer subgroup from the rest (for example, by claiming that the subgroup prefers a more durable or less perfumed product). A new brand or brand extension with the required characteristics is then offered to that segment, and most members of that target group may be attracted to the new brand because it offers them something that research shows they deem important. However, chances are small that the power of attraction will be strong or exclusive enough to determine brand choice: purchasing behavior shows that those consumers have been buying brands without those specific characteristics and will probably continue to do so.

As we discussed previously in the section on brand loyalty, the general pattern is that of a brand repertoire, a set of brands between which consumers switch back and forth. Within that repertoire, each brand has a specific share of customer that goes together with its relative saliency, its distribution, and the quality of its presence in shops.

Deviations from this general pattern reflect the existence of certain specific subcategories. When products are bought for specific purposes (for example, herbal tea to allow buyers to fall asleep at night in addition to black tea to drink during the day), brands in these subcategories can show higher duplication levels with the "large" brands. When brands at a product level are not very differentiated (Coca-Cola and Pepsi-Cola, Hellmann's Mayonnaise and Kraft Mayonnaise), the markets are hardly segmented. In other words, there is little difference in the composition of the buyers' groups of the different brands. Those buyers that are 100 percent brand-loyal are generally the very light users of the product category, who have less opportunity or reason to switch.

Research Into Brand Saliency

As has already become clear, saliency is the accessibility of a brand in memory that results from the relative strength of the connections from (goal) cues toward a brand association network compared to that of competing brands. The saliency of core meanings plays a role here: the strength of the connections of the brand name with the meanings that represent the essence of the brand is critical. A brand whose core meanings are perceived as the most relevant by the consumer is salient within the mental category and has a platform for category dominance.

Brand saliency can best be determined by measuring the associations from search cues toward the various brands, as well as the order in which the brands are mentioned and the time elapsed between the cue and the mention of the different brands. Identification of the proper cues is crucial. Brand-image measurement should be aimed at uncovering the core meanings of a brand and measuring their relevance.

Penn (2005) says that brand research needs to drill down deeper than the superficial responses that many consumers give to questions about recall and feelings: "that approach may mislead, because unconscious processes cannot easily be accessed by introspection." Rather, marketers might investigate the linkage of unconscious emotional responses with brand perceptions. Penn suggests shifting from recall, which reflects a conscious state, to recognition of advertising as a more appropriate tool to evaluate brand response, because it "seems to invoke emotional memories . . . buried in the limbic system, even before our conscious brain registered the fact." However, researching the deep structure of emotional brand responses is difficult. Because "emotions are simple, unconscious impulses," Penn points out that marketers need to use simple choices to measure emotional brand responses—ideally, nonverbal scales designed to encourage intuitive and associative links to brands. If people are "thinking it through," they are not reacting emotionally. That is why photo sorts, such as Zaltman's ZMET and Ameritest's "Flow of Emotion" techniques in television commercial research, are useful.

Figure 13.8   **Share of Penetration and Purchasing Frequency in Volume Growth**

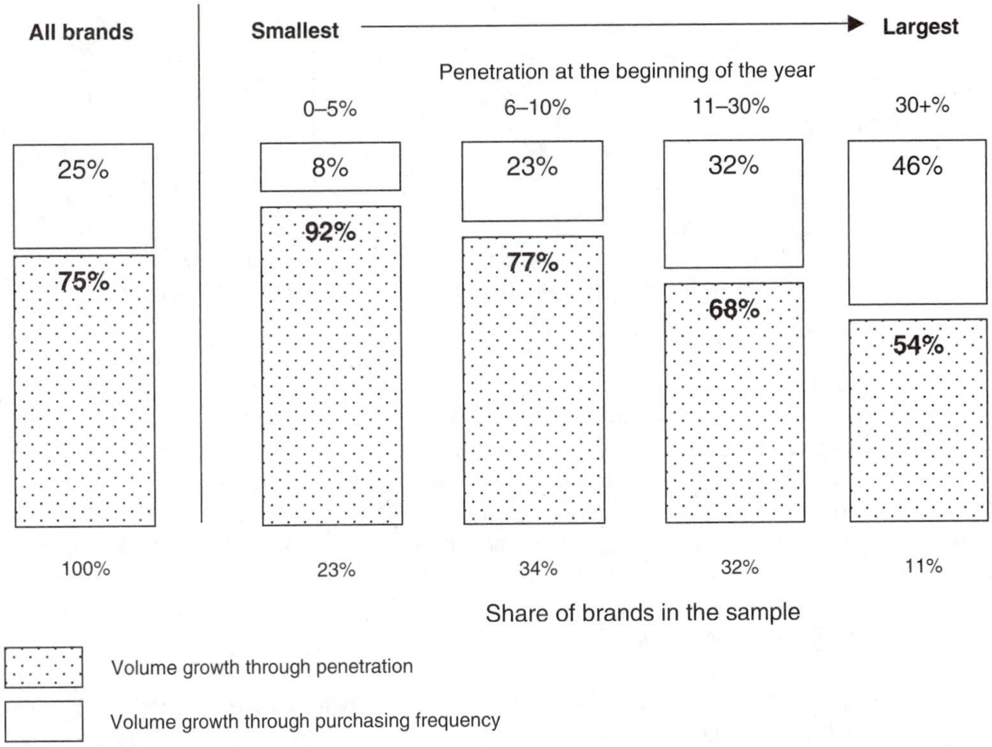

| All brands | Smallest ——————————————————————→ Largest | | | |

Penetration at the beginning of the year

	0–5%	6–10%	11–30%	30+%
25%	8%	23%	32%	46%
75%	92%	77%	68%	54%
100%	23%	34%	32%	11%

Share of brands in the sample

Volume growth through penetration

Volume growth through purchasing frequency

Source: Sylvester et al. (1994).

WHERE DOES GROWTH COME FROM?

Healthy brands show growth or are, at the very least, stable. What are the factors or components of growth? The literature on superbrands, as well as brand saliency research, identifies and investigates a set of qualities that provide some clues about the important factors that create brand strength. They include penetration, frequency of purchase, brand loyalty, familiarity, and popularity.

For example, the American advertising agency Leo Burnett carried out a study of growth among 1,251 brands (Sylvester et al. 1994). For 60 percent of the brands there seemed to be no growth, but decline instead. In 60 percent of the brands that did grow, the growth was lower than 20 percent per year. Finally, an analysis was done of 95 brands, classified according to penetration class. The result is depicted in Figure 13.8 (Sylvester et al. 1994). For the classification of the brands according to size, the penetration at the beginning of the year was used.

Is It Penetration or Frequency?

From studies like this, it seems that an average 75 percent of the volume growth in these brands can be attributed to penetration growth and 25 percent to an increase in purchasing frequency. Part of this increase in frequency flows autonomously out of the penetration increase, as a result of the double jeopardy effect.

Figure 13.9 **Loyalty of Brand Users**

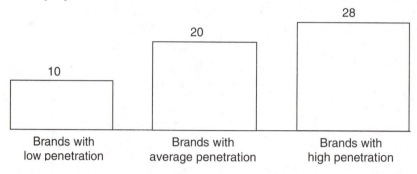

Source: Davenport and Hallward (1999).

Small brands have a 92 percent dependency on penetration increase for their growth. As the penetration increases, so does the contribution of the frequency increase to the growth. It is only for the very largest brands (with a penetration above 30 percent) that penetration and frequency increases contribute more or less equally to the growth. Marketers should nonetheless keep in mind that the penetration change is the result of the inflowing and outflowing buyers of the brands, thus involving conversion as well as retention.

The Double Jeopardy Phenomenon

As we have already shown, large brands are large because they have many buyers who buy the brand often, and small brands are small because they have fewer buyers who purchase the brand slightly less often. An analysis of 200 brands in the United States (Davenport and Hallward 1999) showed yet again that loyalty to a brand increases with its penetration (see Figure 13.9). The theoretical explanation for the occurrence of this double jeopardy phenomenon is the asymmetry in the familiarity with or the exposure to issues (like products and brands) that are equal to each other but whose popularity is not the same.

> *Principle:* In the double jeopardy phenomenon, large brands are large because they have many buyers who buy the brand often, and small brands are small because they have relatively few buyers who buy the brands a bit less often.

The double jeopardy phenomenon appears in all brands and in every product category. Usually, brand articles in stabilized markets present hardly any functional differences between them. Only a real aficionado would taste the difference between an Amstel and a Bavaria beer, between Coca-Cola and Pepsi, between Maggi and Knorr chicken broth cubes, between Kellogg's corn flakes and the supermarket brand corn flakes. Nonetheless, there are differences in sales and it is assumed that some brands are stronger than others. According to Ehrenberg and Uncles (1996), this is not the case. He claims that some brands are just more popular and, therefore, have a larger market share. Thus, Amstel beer is more popular than Bavaria, and its popularity expresses itself in the difference in market shares.

Ehrenberg believes that brands are essentially large or small. As a result of this double jeopardy effect, the large brands are more successful in measurements of purchasing behavior, brand loyalty, and attitude than the small brands. The pattern-like relationship between penetration, purchasing frequency, and duplication with other brands has led to what is known as the Dirichlet formula,[2] by which the purchasing frequency of brands can be accurately predicted.

Is It Habit or Penetration?

Based on purchasing behavior research over a period of more than thirty years in more than fifty different product categories of fast movers and in several countries, Ehrenberg and Uncles (1995, 1996) showed that the more people buy a brand, the more it seems to have the character of a habit. Table 13.8 gives an overview of several average scores (year averages over five to ten largest brands in twelve categories in four countries).

Although the buying patterns vary per individual and per household, the aggregated behavior at a market level of all buyers together answers to the same patterns for different products and brands. These patterns apply mainly to markets that are in balance and in which market shares remain more or less stable for one year. The patterns apply not only to fast-moving consumer goods but also to categories as different as medicines, choice of shops, television programs, gasoline, and cosmetics. The same patterns can be determined even in the purchases of car brands over a longer period.

The buying patterns and brand penetration in all these markets can be described as follows:

1. The number of consumers who buy a specific brand in a specific period—for example, one year in one category—varies per brand. In other words, the penetration of different brands varies.
2. There is a strong correlation between this penetration and the market shares of the brands.
3. The average frequency with which the different brands are acquired by their buyers does not differ much. On average, large brands are acquired by their buyers only slightly more often than small brands: this is the double jeopardy phenomenon, in which small brands are bought by fewer people who also do this less often.
4. Large brands are thus large mainly because they have many buyers and, on average, are also bought a bit more often by those buyers.
5. Most buyers of a brand buy it infrequently.
6. The number of buyers who purchase a brand increases with the length of the period over which the measurement is made. The penetration thus depends on the time period along which the measurement is taken (usually one year).
7. The average number of repeat purchases, measured per trimester, is relatively low, but measured per brand the repeat purchase rates are closer together.
8. In general, repeat purchasing levels are stable over time. This means that consumers have stable purchasing patterns.
9. The average amount bought per purchase does not differ much from brand to brand.

Table 13.9 illustrates these patterns using an example from the instant coffee market in the United States (Ehrenberg and Uncles 1995).

The patterns that come out of the research of Ehrenberg and Uncles seem to apply mainly to short-term market developments. Ehrenberg ignores the fact that, in markets that seem rather stable from year to year (like the Dutch beer market), the long-term developments (such as those

370

Table 13.8

Average Scores of Brands

Category/country/year	Average penetration of brands (percent)	Average Purchases	Percent one-time buyers of brands	100 percent brand-loyal customers (percent)	Duplicates with brand (percent that bought it too)		
					Largest	3rd	5th
Toothpaste, Germany, 1990	38	3.3	37	16	58	40	19
Gasoline, UK, 1990	34	8.7	34	0	62	48	51
Toothpaste, Japan, 1983	28	2.5	52	7	67	34	10
Cereals, UK, 1968	27	6.3	24	12	74	11	15
Orange juice, USA, 1984	26	3.4	49	17	59	35	10
Liquid detergents, Japan, 1983	24	2.0	57	15	46	31	28
Paper towels, USA, 1992	23	2.7	54	4	55	46	43
Detergents, Germany, 1990	20	2.6	48	16	32	27	10
Cleaning products, UK, 1988	14	1.9	61	14	44	37	7
Cheese, UK, 1988	12	2.9	54	12	42	28	20
Beer (domestic use), UK, 1992	10	3.7	56	10	19	13	11
Paper towels, UK, 1988	8	2.8	52	19	40	11	12
Average	22	3.6	49	12	50	13	20

Source: Ehrenberg and Uncles (1995).

Table 13.9

The Instant Coffee Market in the United States, 1981

	Percent market share	Percent penetration	Average number of purchases per buyer		Share per consumer
			Of the brand	All brands	
All brands	100	67	—	7	—
Maxwell House	19	24	3.6	9	40
Sanka	15	21	3.3	9	37
Taster's Choice	14	22	2.8	9	31
High Point	13	22	2.6	8	32
Folgers	11	18	2.7	9	30
Nescafé	8	13	2.9	11	26
Brim	4	9	2.0	9	22
Maxim	3	6	2.6	11	24
Other brands	13	20	3.0	9	33
Average brand	11	17	2.8	9	31

Source: Ehrenberg and Uncles (1995).

measured over a twenty-year period) can be quite substantial. Brands can present downward or upward developments, which lead to only small changes from year to year but over a long period can result in important changes in the market position.

Is It Brand Loyalty?

Ehrenberg's proposition that brand loyalty emanates from penetration, with a double jeopardy correction, is also debatable. When analyzing 117 brands, Baldinger and Rubinson (1996) determined that the penetration of a brand explains on average 50 to 66 percent of the variance in the share of customer in a product category. This figure may well support the double jeopardy law, but at the same time shows that the share of customer contributes independently to the market share and that this contribution increases with the market share.

Seen over a longer period, few buyers end up being 100 percent brand-loyal. Most buyers of a certain brand tend to buy other brands too. Seen over several product categories and several brands, these purchasing duplications also show major similarities. The degree to which buyers of brand A also buy brand B is a function of the penetration of brand B—or, since penetration and market share are highly correlated, a function of the market share of brand B. Table 13.10 presents an example of the duplication of brand purchases in the American instant-coffee market.

It should be remarked that purchasing behavior is the result of supply and demand. The degree to which and the quality with which brands are present in the retail location (for example, the height at which they are placed on the supermarket shelves) have as great an influence on the ultimate purchasing behavior. In marketing slang, we are dealing here with a push as well as a pull process.

Is It Saliency or Market Share?

These general patterns indicate that the performance of a brand in the market—in terms of penetration, purchasing frequency, repeat purchases, and purchasing duplication with other brands—largely

Table 13.10

Instant Coffee Brands in the United States, 1981

Buyers of	Percentage that also bought							
	Maxwell H.	Sanka	Tast. Cho.	High Pt.	Folgers	Nescafé	Brim	Maxim
Maxwell House	–	32	29	32	38	26	13	13
Sanka	36	–	32	40	25	23	20	11
Taster's Choice	31	32	–	36	28	20	17	14
High Point	34	38	34	–	31	22	18	10
Folgers	51	30	35	40	–	25	15	11
Nescafé	48	39	34	40	34	–	15	8
Brim	33	45	39	44	27	20	–	16
Maxim	52	38	51	39	34	17	25	–
Average brand	41	36	36	39	31	22	17	12

Source: Ehrenberg and Uncles (1995).

reflects the working of one single factor. Ehrenberg believes that this factor is the market share of a brand. This conclusion would make the market share not the result of other marketing factors but the most important explanatory factor of all brand performance. It is not surprising that marketing people have great difficulty accepting this conclusion. They tend to see brand familiarity and brand image as the causes of a brand's market position. They have great difficulty thinking in terms other than cause-effect relationships, and they are unwilling to see the patterns in the revealed purchasing behavior as pure acts of habit (as exposed especially by Ehrenberg). Still, the facts cannot be ignored.

The explanation should be sought not only in the market share, as Ehrenberg suggests based on the purely statistical relationship he finds, but also in brand saliency, which is the intensity of the representation that the brand has gained in the course of its history in the memories of its users and its position in the distribution channels. One single component does not explain everything. The total system is the explanation. The fact that it is extremely difficult and probably impossible to illustrate this in numbers, such as scores for research questions, is an entirely different matter. The truth has to do with the complexity of human memory, which we can approach analytically, but cannot dissect and certainly cannot represent with one single factor.

In Chapter 15 on brand equity, we will take a more detailed look at the relationships between the mental position of brands, purchasing behavior, and market positions. These relationships help make branding such a dynamic system.

Principle: Seen per brand, there is a strong correlation between penetration, purchasing frequency, repeated purchases, and duplication with other brands. They reflect to a large degree the working of the total brand system.

Is It Brand Popularity?

Anschuetz (1997) concluded that brand popularity (the number of households that buys a brand = penetration) leads to a higher frequency of brand purchases, a greater number of heavy buyers, stronger brand loyalty (share of customer), and a larger market share, and that within a specific marketing budget, maximizing penetration is a must in order to achieve maximum profitability.

After reviewing a number of studies, Weilbacher (1993) arrived at the conclusion that successful brand marketing depends on two factors. First, a relatively higher market penetration arises not from brand loyalty but is clearly the result of marketing activities, particularly those that ensure that the new brand is tried out by a wide consumer group during the introductory period. The more a marketer succeeds in making a brand seem valuable to the consumer, the more likely that the consumer will try the brand during the first phase.

The second factor Weilbacher cites is that the development of brand adoption on a scale as broad as possible should have the highest marketing priority. Adoption does not equal decisive preference, but membership in the brand repertoire. The larger the number of consumer repertoires a brand belongs to, the larger the market share will probably be. The purpose of marketing activities per se is not to convince the customer of brand superiority, but to make the brand at the very least acceptable for as large a number of consumers as possible. According to Weilbacher, the more a marketer succeeds in making a brand valuable to the consumer, the more acceptable that brand will probably be and the larger the number of brand repertoires the brand can belong to. The Andrex story demonstrates the importance of brand popularity.

Andrex: Soft, Strong, and Very Long

Andrex is an English brand of toilet paper, introduced in 1942. The product was based on Harrods disposable handkerchiefs and was much softer than regular toilet paper.

In 1961 Andrex became market leader, a position it has kept for more than forty-five years. In 1972 an advertising campaign was launched in which a Labrador puppy carrying a roll of Andrex roamed through a house to demonstrate that Andrex is "soft, strong, and very long." The puppy developed into one of the most beloved brand icons in the United Kingdom, and can be still seen on television.

In the more than thirty-five years that have passed since, more than 110 puppy commercials have been made. Andrex is not only market leader in toilet paper, but its sales have reached a top-ten position among all brands of the fast movers channel, even though it has been priced at a premium compared to the market average since the beginning of the 1970s. The British have taken the puppies into their hearts. Andrex may well have become the most salient—and popular—brand in British society.

Sources: Knobil (2003); Stow (1992); Biel and Lannon (1993).

Brand popularity hinges on people's tendency to watch their surroundings and the behavior of other people. The degree to which others show a certain behavior can constitute the most important criterion for what is seen as proper behavior. Normally speaking, this tendency works well: a person makes fewer mistakes when acting in correspondence with most others than contrary to them. It is a fact that in the phase of life in which young people develop independence and their own consumption habits, they tend to play it safe and choose those brands that most people in their social surroundings choose. What we call the "perceived popularity" of a brand is one of their most important choice criteria.

In the BRANDZ project, a study of 30,000 global brands by Millward-Brown for the advertising agency holding company WPP, perceived popularity seemed to be the most important attitude driver of market leaders (Meer 1999). Market leaders that are also seen as larger-than-life trendsetters score especially high in this dimension. Clear examples of such brands are Starbucks and Nike.

People learn the most from the things they do. Through the constant interaction of the use of a brand and the processing of its communication manifestations, an increasingly richer and stronger associative network comes into being. Ehrenberg et al. (1997) gives an example of how this process works for cereals in England. The scores for "liked by the whole family" vary for users and non-users, as seen in Table 13.11. Of all cereal users, 15 percent said that Sugar Puffs was liked by the whole family. For users of Sugar Puffs this is 51 percent, for non-users only 11 percent. Positive attitudes thus arise mainly through usage experiences. Consumers always find that brands they use are in most ways better than those they do not use. Their internal saliency increases and the attitudes toward the used brands are strengthened.

These mechanisms are well illustrated by the situation we described earlier in this chapter about the Dutch beer market. The brand choice of young people who begin drinking beer is to a large degree influenced by what they observe in their social surroundings. If most people drink a specific brand, youngsters will strongly tend to conform. Once they drink a certain brand, the user experiences start exerting a major influence on the internal saliency of the brand.

As a result, manifestations of that brand are also given more attention than manifestations of other brands. The ensuing situation, presented in Tables 13.8, 13.9, and 13.10, is nearly impossible to break through: even important differences in image seem to have no or hardly any influence on the market positions of the different brands.

The three sources of brand saliency vary in the degree to which they can be manipulated. Causing brand use by means of stimulating trial purchases is probably the most effective route to take. We will look at this process in more detail in Chapter 15, on brand equity.

In any event, marketers should be aware of the modest influence of communication on this process. The competition should not be underestimated either. Communication expenditures are usually derived from the realized or expected turnover, which makes them a reflection of existing market positions and leads to a confirmation of the status quo. A great deal of the competition in the market can be traced back to competition in the memory of consumers. This leads to the large stability of established major brands we have described.

Principle: Many choice decisions are not the result of extensive comparison of the alternatives, but come about with the help of heuristics, strong, abridged approaches based on a general criterion.

The Overpowering Importance of Penetration

This review of the components of brand strength has determined that growth comes from a set of factors that are sometimes interrelated but always difficult to separate. The lead factor seems to be penetration, but its impact is modified or enhanced by other factors. A model then might be constructed that demonstrates these components (see Figure 13.10).

The consequence of the double jeopardy phenomenon is that the sales of a brand depend largely on the brand's penetration. There is indeed a brand-loyal purchasing behavior, but this also evidences the double jeopardy characteristics—that is, the purchasing frequency of large brands surpassing that of small brands. There are exceptions (see, for example, Dowling and Uncles 1997), but they are far from becoming the rule. These exceptions are as follows:

Table 13.11

Belief Scores for Users and Non-Users

Cereals	Corn-flakes	Weeta-bix	Rice Krispies	Shredded Wheat	Sugar Puffs	Frosties	Special K	All-Bran	Average Brand
Percent buys regularly	48	29	13	12	10	9	7	7	17
Percent liked by whole family									
• users	83	70	65	67	51	54	43	34	55
• non-users	40	14	13	6	11	7	4	3	8
Average	61	31	20	13	15	12	6	5	15

Source: BMRB, 1964 and 1984, Field Control, 1973 and 1974, in Ehrenberg et al. (1997).

Figure 13.10   **The Components of Brand Strength**

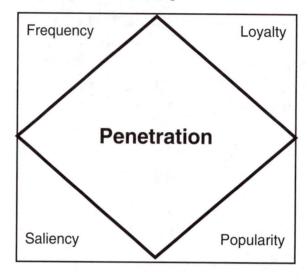

- *Superloyal brands:* very large brands that have more brand-loyal users than those predicted by the Dirichlet formula;
- *Niche brands:* brands that answer to very specific expectations of small buyer segments and realize a high purchasing frequency there;
- *Alternate brands:* brands that are bought for specific situations or moments, like alcohol-free beer; they show a much lower purchasing frequency than that predicted by the Dirichlet formula.

These three types of brands occur less frequently than the regular large and small brands that do answer to the Dirichlet laws. Increasing the penetration is usually the most effective way to make a brand grow. The connection between penetration and market share is represented in Figure 13.11, based on an analysis by Jones (1995) of sales for 142 brands in the United States over a period of one year. The connection between penetration and market share increases, the connection becoming stronger as the penetration rises. This is the effect of the double jeopardy phenomenon, in which high penetration is also accompanied by higher purchasing frequency.

Martha Stewart as Superbrand

Powerful brands—Harley-Davidson, Microsoft, Kraft, Ben & Jerry's, MTV—are powerful because everyone knows what they stand for: they consistently deliver on their promise to their customers. The strengths and quality of their products are well known and their customers have had good experiences with these products and think fondly of them. These brands are locked into their customers' memories. The bond is demonstrated in high levels of brand loyalty.

Superbrands are powerful in the sense that they dominate their categories; in some cases they created the category and continue to be the leader in innovative thinking for that category. They have differentiated themselves based on the value they deliver to their customers—functional, psychological, or both. And that promise and the core values it represents remain consistent over time.

The consumer connection is the primary reason the Martha Stewart brand was able to survive the legal difficulties of its founder. But behind the company's defense of the brand was the corporate

Figure 13.11   **The Relationship Between Market Share and Penetration**

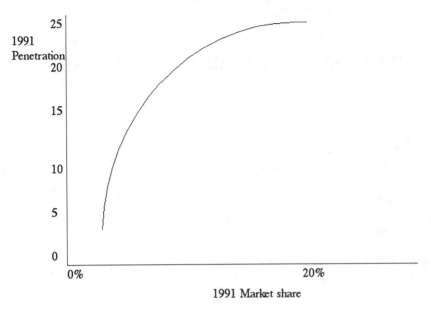

Source: Jones (1995).

decision to maintain true to its brand values. The survival of the Martha Stewart brand is an example of faithfulness on both sides of the brand equation—corporate and consumer. Customers, for example, kept Martha Stewart afloat even when the advertising and media communities concluded that the brand was dead. The brand's strength was found not only in its familiarity and saliency, but also in the empathy produced by the threatening (and, according to some consumers, unfair) legal situation. This emotional brand response to high corporate drama cushioned the fall of Martha Stewart the brand, even as Martha Stewart the person overcame the negative aura of a prison sentence.

NOTES

1. The Profit Impact of Market Strategy (PIMS) database was set up in 1972 by the Marketing Science Institute in the United States. About 450 companies participate in it, periodically reporting information on finances, market, customers, and quality for more than 3,000 business units. The researchers then determine the correlations and trend developments. The PIMS database is the only database in the world that contains strategic information on a large variety of companies. Several subdatabases are analyzed to identify the effects of all kinds of strategic variables, including advertising expenditures. Connections are always established between and among the final financial results, such as the profits, the returns on invested assets, and the cash flow. The PIMS database is now maintained by the Strategic Planning Institute.

2. The pattern-like connection between penetration, purchasing frequency, and duplication with purchases of other brands and market share is expressed in the Dirichlet formula. This is a mathematical formula through which predictions can be made on the average purchasing frequency of a brand and the duplication with other brands, on the basis of the market share of that brand. In addition to knowledge of the market share, numerical knowledge is needed of the number of households that bought the product type in a year, the average purchasing frequency of the product type, and the number of brands that is bought on average per household. There seems to be a correlation larger than 0.9 between the predicted purchasing frequency of a brand and the purchasing frequency that is perceived in the market.

CHAPTER 14

BRAND SPAN AND BRAND EXTENSION

Brands come in a myriad of types and sizes and can be classified in many different ways. An important approach is the way suppliers (producers, manufacturers) combine their brands and products. Some companies have numerous brands. In 2000 Unilever had 1,600 different brands worldwide, 3M maintains 1,500 product brands, and Nestlé as many as 7,500. Roughly three-quarters of the Fortune 1000 consumer goods companies manage more than a hundred brands each (Carlotti et al. 2004). Other companies, such as HSBC, Microsoft, and Samsung, bring to the market nearly everything they offer under the umbrella of the corporate brand. Another example is Virgin.

VIRGIN EVERYTHING

Virgin, a brand that is not yet very well known in the United States, is one of the most respected brands in the United Kingdom.

It started in 1970 in the music business with the Virgin record shop, followed in 1973 by the launch of the Virgin record label. Virgin was founded by Richard Branson, then a young Briton with an irrepressible drive for adventurous undertakings. Branson's words illustrate his daredevil attitude:

> I've always liked a challenge! I've been involved in a number of world record-breaking attempts since 1985. My first success was in 1986 with my boat *Virgin Atlantic Challenger II*.

I wanted to rekindle the spirit of the Blue Riband by crossing the Atlantic Ocean in the fastest ever recorded time. A year later I crossed the same ocean, by hot-air balloon this time. The *Virgin Atlantic Flyer* was not only the first hot-air balloon to cross the Atlantic, but also was the largest balloon ever at 2.3 million cubic feet. It reached speeds in excess of 130 miles per hour.

In January 1991, I crossed the Pacific Ocean from Japan to Arctic Canada at the furthest distance of 6,700 miles. Again, this broke all existing records. The balloon measured 2.6 million cubic feet with speeds of up to 245 miles per hour.

Between 1995 and 1998 I made a number of attempts to circumnavigate the globe by balloon. In late 1998 we made a record breaking flight from Morocco to Hawaii but unfortunately, our dream of a global flight was shattered by bad weather.

The same drive made Branson start new businesses under the umbrella of the Virgin brand almost every other year. By 2005 the Virgin group counted 200 companies worldwide, all tied together by Branson's charisma and the values of the Virgin brand:

- *value for money:* simple, honest, and transparent pricing;
- *good quality:* high standards; attention to detail;
- *customer service:* friendly, human, and relaxed; professional but not corporate;
- *innovation:* challenging convention; modern, stylish design;
- *competitiveness:* fighting the big competition;
- *fun:* providing the public and the customers with a bit of entertainment.

In fact, Virgin tries to break all the rules that have become common practice in the field of brand extension. Its timeline of extensions looks like this:

1970	Virgin Records Mail Order
1971	Virgin Record Shop
	Virgin Computers
1973	Virgin Record Label
	Virgin Credit Cards
	Virgin Vision film and video distribution
1984	Virgin Atlantic Airways
1985	Virgin Holidays Travel agency and tour operators
1987	Virgin Mastertronic computer games
	Virgin Airships and Balloon flights
1988	Virgin Broadcasting
	Virgin Hotels
1989	Virgin Megastores, CD, DVD, and games retail chain
1991	Virgin Books publisher and retailer
1993	Virgin Radio station
1994	Virgin Vodka
	Virgin Cola
1995	Virgin Direct Financial Services
1996	Virgin Trains Railway Service
	Virgin Net
	Virgin Brides bridal wear shop

1997	Virgin Vie Cosmetics
	Virgin Clothes
1998	Virgin One Banking
1999	Virgin Mobile Phone Service
	Virgin Jeans
	Virgin Audio Health Club
2000	Virgin Cars
	Virgin Money
	Virgin Wines
	Virgin Mobile Phones
	Virgin Energy gas and electricity
	Virgin Travel Store
2001	Virgin Bikes
2003	Virgin Pulse Electronics
2004	Virgin Digital Service music retailer
	Virgin Galactic space flights
2006	Virgin Fuel
	Virgin Comics
	Virgin Animation
2007	Virgin Health Bank for storing stem cells
	Virgin Media/Virgin 1 cable television, broadband and mobile telephone

Taken as a whole, Virgin is a success both in sales and in admiration by the British public. But it is not surprising that much went wrong along the way, as we will see at the end of this chapter.

Sources: Brown (1998); Deutschman (2004); D. Taylor (2004); www.virgin.com/uk.

The totality of brands brought to the market by an organization is called its *brand portfolio*. The relation between a brand and the number of product categories it is linked to is called the *brand span*. When a company attaches one of its brands to a new product category, this is called *brand extension*. A product may also be given several brand designations (labels), each adding its specific meanings to the product—for example, Heinz Tennessee Hickory Mesquite Flavored Jack Daniel's Grilling Sauce. This link of one or several brands to a product or series of products is known as *brand architecture*.

The branding strategy of a company involves decisions about all four issues: brand portfolio, brand span, brand extension, and brand architecture. Since these concepts are all interrelated, a strict division of topics is difficult. In this chapter we will first present an overview of the types of brands that can be distinguished in terms of basic categories. We will then discuss the related concepts of brand span and brand extension. Chapter 15 will deal with the problems and opportunities of brand portfolios and brand architecture.

TYPES OF BRANDS

Based on the number of product categories a brand is linked to and the degree of connections between these product categories, brands can be classified into three different span classes: category brands, domain brands, and multidomain brands.

Category brands are associatively linked with just one product category, but the strategy includes two types of brands:

Product brands (monobrands), are linked to just one product variant, like Snickers or Q-tips, and *line brands*, which include several variants of the same product but with different composition, amounts, packaging, or other features. Examples are Pampers and Marlboro.

Domain brands, also known as family or umbrella brands, are brands linked to a group of different product categories that have one or several common properties, which create an interconnectedness. The common elements can consist of a product property (nonsaturated fats), an application area (skin care), a symbolic meaning (antiestablishment), or a target group (family). Examples are Becel Margarine and Nivea body care.

Multidomain brands are linked to several very different product categories that often have little or no common ground—for example, various kinds of electronic equipment or different food articles. Philips and General Electric are examples of such brands. Philips sells hair dryers, lightbulbs, MRI scanners, DVD recorders, and cell phones. Very often these brands mainly present a provenience—"by Philips."

> *Principle:* The brand span points to the relation between a brand and the number of different product categories to which it is linked.

Main Brands and Brand Combinations

Main brands are those perceived by consumers as the main meaning carriers within a brand architecture. The main brand establishes the basis and carries an extensive set of meanings that contain most of the information about the brand article being offered. As a representative of the brand concept (see Chapter 5), a main brand plays the largest role in the evaluation process of consumers. Within the category of main brands there are corporate brands and individual brands.

A *corporate brand* is the name of the company itself or of a division of it that is used to identify its products, as is the case with Microsoft, Miele, and Nike.

An *individual brand* is a name that is independent of the company's name, such as Pampers, Dove, and Snickers.

Brand combinations are combinations of two or more brands that are linked to a product or series of products, each contributing its specific meanings. Combinations usually involve adding subordinate or superordinate brands to the main brand, each adding its specific meaning to the combination in the consumer's perception. We call them *sub-brands* and *endorsement brands*, respectively. Examples of sub-brands are Apple Macintosh and Volkswagen Golf. Examples of endorsement-brands are Motta (by Nestlé) and John West (by Heinz).

The combination of two different main brands, such as the Philips Alessi line of small household appliances, is called *co-branding*. When an ingredient brand (Intel) is combined with a main brand (Dell), we call this *ingredient branding*.

Corporate Brands

The most important branding decision to be made by a company is whether it will brand its products with its corporate name or with an individual name.

A corporate brand is always linked to an organizational unit and is perceived as such. Organizational associations are thus part of its association network. Table 14.1 shows an overview of the types of brands and how they can be differentiated according to their input in different markets.

Table 14.1

Brand Types

	Brand span		
	Category brands	Domain brands	Multidomain brands
Brand architecture **Main brands**	Product/line brands	Umbrella/family brands	Provenience brands
Corporate brand (division brand)	Microsoft	Buitoni	Heinz
	Pepsi-Cola Heineken Robeco	ABN-AMRO Nike Gillette Miele Kodak	Verkade Philips 3M Virgin
Individual brand (house brand, stand-alone brand, furtive brand)	Philadelphia Duracell	Dove Kleenex	Calvin Klein
	Pampers Whiskas Marlboro	Jockey Nexxus	
Brand combinations			
Dual brand (co-brands, "parent" brands)	YSL/Poison	Kellogg's/Corn flakes	Braun/Oral-B
	Volkswagen/Golf		Nike/Apple iPod
Sub-brand*	Pampers (Ultra Dry) Pepsi (Max) Renault (Megane)	Kleenex (Velvet) Microsoft (Explorer) Nivea (Visage) Nike (Air)	Philips (Softone) Mitsubishi (Colt) Calvin Klein (CK)
Endorsement brand*	Opel (GM) Post-it (3M)	Motta (Nestlé) John West (Heinz)	AEG (Electrolux)
Ingredient brand	Dell (Intel)* Loewe (Goretex)		

*Sub-brands, endorsement brands, and ingredient brands are in parenthesis following the main brands.

A *full corporate brand* such as Nestlé and Sony operates in the marketplace, the labor market (employees), and the financial markets, whereas a *limited corporate brand* such as Procter & Gamble is not used in the marketplace—that is, in the communication with the end customers.

A *division brand* is generally linked to an organizational unit that has a business role and is perceived as such, but does not operate independently in the financial market. This can be a subsidiary or an autonomous business unit. Some holding companies aim at placing their division brands (like Nestlé's Buitoni, Gillette's Braun, or Akzo Nobel's Organon) in the limelight of the marketplace while the holding company itself is visible only in the financial markets, as is the case with Procter & Gamble. Other companies prefer using their corporate brand in all three markets, as British Airways and Siemens do.

For branding strategy purposes, it is important to determine whether a brand is perceived to some degree by consumers as an organizational entity and whether this is a conscious goal of the supplier. Organizational associations are more abstract than product-related associations and therefore provide more room for extension policy. They can also offer a perception of differences that are less perceptible or not perceptible at all at a product level.

Principle: Depending on the use in the retail market, three types of corporate brands can be distinguished: full corporate brands, limited corporate brands, and division brands.

Individual Brands

Individual brands are those not linked associatively with a company. The provenience is sometimes indicated in small print on the back of the package—as a sender—but the supplier intentionally wants to stay in the background. Unilever puts its logo in very small print on the bottom of the Omo detergent packages. Consumers usually have no idea where these individual brands come from. There are three categories of individual brands: house brands, stand-alone brands, and furtive brands.

House brands. These represent a provenience (the "house" of the manufacturer or seller) for a collection of products, but are not (or no longer) associated with an organizational unit. In the past, they may very well have been corporate brands that became integrated into the new company that took them over—for example, through mergers. An example is Maggi, which was founded in 1870 by Julius Maggi, taken over in 1947 by Nestlé, and then gradually absorbed into the Nestlé Company. It now is one of Nestlé's important house brands.

Stand-alone brands. Such brands are neither linked nor associated by consumers with an organizational unit. A stand-alone brand serves as a main brand but does not refer to a company. Companies that exploit these brands often have good reasons to remain anonymous. For example, they could be putting several competing brands into the market (in the Benelux market, the detergents Persil, Dixan, Dato, Witte Reus, Color Reus, and Fleuril are all brands of Henkel) while trying to give each of those brands a position as independent as possible. Sometimes a corporate brand or house brand is added to a stand-alone brand as an endorsement (KitKat by Nestlé, Persil by Henkel).

Furtive brands. These are an extreme form of individual brands. Here the supplier intentionally wants to avoid the association between the brand and the supplying company, usually because the brand is better regarded than the company and indicates its name (in small letters on the back of the package) only to comply with legal requirements.

Principle: Individual brands are those brands that are not perceptibly linked with a company. There are three types of individual brands: house brands, stand-alone brands, and furtive brands.

BRAND SPAN

Brand span refers to the number of product categories related to a particular brand. Kraft, for example, refers to food categories as diverse as salad dressing, candy, and cheese, so it would be considered a wide brand. Narrow brands are closely associated with one product category, such as Whiskas, which applies only to cat food.

Brand span and brand architecture can be combined into a matrix in which every type of brand can be classified. Table 14.1 demonstrates the richness and complexity of options a company has in formulating its branding strategies. These strategies also mirror a brand manager's understanding of consumer decision making relating to the category or categories related to the brand span.

For branding strategy it is crucial to have insight into the influence that the mental representations of various product categories, as well as the systems of brand meaning embedded in the brand architecture, exert on consumer decision making. We believe that inaccurate understanding of the interplay of these systems is a big factor in the 90 percent of product introductions that either fail or do not meet the marketers' expectations—for example, Grolsch's amber-colored beer, Biotex main-wash detergents, and Philips cell phones.

Brands serve consumers to the extent that the meanings rooted in their association network meet consumers' information needs during the buying process. The choice process of consumers begins in most cases with a product need, not with a brand. A person needs espresso coffee, wants new soccer shoes, or has become interested in cell phones. The consumers search their own memories for information, but also find relevant information in their environment, encountering brand articles in the purchasing environment or consulting consumer guides, friends, family, and colleagues. This internal and external information influences the final choice to various degrees and in different ways. The choice process can last 5.2 seconds, as is the case when buying coffee in the supermarket (Brouwer and van der Weijde 1998), or several months, as tends to be the case when buying a car.

BRAND-PRODUCT ASSOCIATION

In Chapter 13 we discussed the *spreading activation theory*, which is relevant when trying to understand the effects of the size of the brand span on consumer choice.

This theory states that when a concept, such as a brand name, is activated in memory, the activation spreads along the paths of the brand association network. There is a limit on the amount of activation that can be spread from the brand name—the more elements associated with the brand name, the less activation will spread to any particular element. An element will enter into consciousness in an amount of time that is inversely related to its level of activation. The "fan effect" is the name given to this increase in reaction time related to an increase in the number of elements associated with the brand, because the increase in reaction time is related to an increase in the fan of elements emanating from the brand name (Anderson 2000).

> *Principle:* The more elements associated with a brand, the slower the retrieval of any one of them.

The consequence of the fan effect is that the more product categories that a brand is attached to, the slower the retrieval of any one of these product categories from memory. The activation will first activate the category that is most strongly linked with the brand name. Most often this is the category on which the brand was founded, such as lightbulbs in the case of Philips and copying machines for Xerox.

Products that were introduced early in the brand's lifetime may subsequently be activated, such as radio and television for Philips. Products introduced later in a growing series of brand extensions usually have a harder time developing a strong memory link to the brand. For Philips this difficulty may have played a role in its cell phone disaster, and for Xerox in its computer flop. Creating new brand-product associations is not, of course, impossible, but it will demand an exceptionally strong effort. Just putting a well-known brand onto a new product category and believing that will suffice often leads to trouble.

Also, market research has produced strong indications that the relative strength of the product-brand associations has an important influence on brand choice (Franzen and Bouwman 2001). By relative strength we mean the relative power of the synaptic connections in the brain between a product code and the brands—and brand architectures—that are part of the product association network. In research, this power is seen when posing a brand familiarity question in which the product indication serves as a stimulus: "Which brands of muesli do you know, even if just by name?" The order in which brands are named at this point (and each brand's place in the list) and the time elapsed between the question and the spontaneous naming of a brand are indications of this association strength. The association strength has a solid correlation with purchasing behavior (and a high aggregated level with the market share) of the individual brands in product categories that are purchased routinely (Franzen and Bouwman 2001).

With products in which the choice process is wider and lengthier, the influence of external information on the brand choice increases.

There are strong indications that the strength of product-brand association also has considerable influence on its inclusion in the consideration set and thus on the final brand choice. A brand that is strongly associated with a product category also tends to be more linked with product-related meanings, as a result of which the evaluation becomes easier. Thanks to this principle, familiar brands (i.e., brands that are strongly linked to a product category) reach higher levels of valuing and preference with both consumers and retailers (Rindfleisch and Inman 1998).

Principle: The relative strength of the product-brand association has a large influence on the brand choice.

BRAND EXTENSION

Brand extension is the process by which a new product category is brought to the market under an established brand that until then has not been attached to that category. It probably is the most favored option in the unfolding of a branding strategy.

As a result of extension to other product categories, a product brand usually develops into a brand that spans a whole category of products. It becomes a category brand. From there it may develop into a domain brand, spanning a series of different categories that fall under a broadly defined domain, such as financial services or body care. When a brand is extended to basically unrelated domains, such as Philips shavers, Philips television, and Philips MRI scanners, it develops into a multi-domain brand.

Brand Extension Effects

The development from product brand to ultimately a multi-domain brand has a number of consequences. Its presence in the market increases, which enhances its familiarity and perceived reliability. At the same time the brand's association network becomes more complex. The association from individual product category to brand and vice-versa usually gets weaker. The meanings of the brand develop into a higher abstract level. Often this also happens to the values associated with the brand. As a result the brands' association network loses sharpness and gets more diffuse. It may end up merely representing the provenience of the products—that is, "made by Philips." Figure 14.1 summarizes the effects of brand span broadening.

Figure14.1 **Brand Extension Effects**

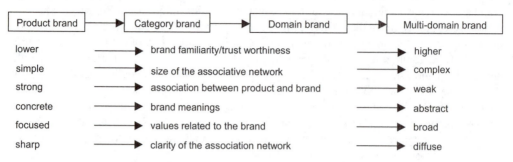

Brand Familiarity and Reliability

As a brand moves from product brand to ultimately multi-domain brand, its visibility in the market increases and likewise its turnover-base. This allows for increased marketing-support that also boosts the overall brand-awareness. The increased presence of the brand may also create an image of acceptance by others, and of familiarity, reliability, and trustworthiness.

The brands' function as a heuristic to reduce potential losses of time, monetary and social/ psychological facing the consumers when they purchase a product is enhanced (Del Vecchio 2000). For many brands this is their core-function.

It is often argued that the addition of more diversified categories to the brand family acts to dilute the strength of the brand, because it leads to a fuzzier set of brand beliefs, and to more abstract brand meanings. This explains the one-sided emphasis on "fit" when researching brand-extensions. But research by Del Vecchio (2000) provided evidence in support of the importance of the number of categories affiliated with the brand to increase the ability of the brand to reduce risk associated with a purchase. He demonstrated that consumers would be more favorably inclined toward brands that are associated with a greater number of products.

Brand Meaning

Brands are mental containers of meanings and serve as information sources for buyers. They fulfill that function to the extent that the meanings rooted in their association network meet consumers' information needs during the buying process. The choice process of consumers begins in most cases with a product need, not with a brand. A person needs espresso coffee, wants new soccer shoes, or has become interested in cell phones. People search their own memories for information, but also find relevant information in their environment. One encounters branded articles in the purchasing environment or consults consumer guides, as well as friends, family, and colleagues. This internal and external information influences the final choice to various degrees and in different ways. That choice can last 5.2 seconds, as is the case when buying coffee in the supermarket (Brouwer and van der Weijde 1998) or several months, as tends to be the case when buying a car.

This development into more abstract core meanings when a brand expands does not necessarily have to be negative. It very much depends on the relevance of the adjusted core meanings for the consumer's choice process. When the choice is brought about largely on the basis of external information, as is the case with many durable products, a high abstract meaning like "a reliable company" can have a positive influence (Dacin and Smith 1994). The risks of higher abstractions of brand meanings are greatest in choice processes based on merely internal information, as happens with most product categories in what are known as fast-moving consumer goods (FMCG) in Europe and package goods in the United States.

Multidomain brands often have a hard time with product categories in which they have to take on more focused category brands (see the Nike story below). When Philips links its brand to 200 different product categories, to what degree can consumers develop strong associations with all those different categories? Philips is an ultimate multidomain brand.

This problem also occurs with line brands in segmented markets. When competing brands are strongly associated with a certain subcategory, it is often difficult for category brands with a broader line of product variants to build a meaningful position in that subcategory. For example, the amber-beer subcategory in the Netherlands is dominated by the Palm brand. Traditional Pilsner brands like Grolsch play no significant role here. In this context, Chernatony (1999) quotes a study that shows that 68 percent of consumers prefer buying brands they perceive as specialist.

Nike: From Specialist to Generalist

The Nike brand was introduced by Philip Knight and Bill Bowerman in 1971 as a specialist in running shoes. Nikes were light shoes made of durable nylon, with an in-between, shock-absorbing layer and a special waffle sole for a good grip on any surface. The Nike Air System was introduced later. Within a short time, Nike succeeded in becoming the preferred brand of serious runners and one of the most celebrated brands in the marketing world.

The first step into brand expansion followed rapidly, with the introduction of basketball and tennis shoes. Knight then decided that running shoes would no longer form the core of Nike ("leave them to Reebok and Adidas"), but that Nike would transform itself into the world's best sports and fitness company. In 1979 a clothing line was added, followed shortly afterward by leisure-time shoes. In 1982 Nike brought out football shoes and in subsequent years articles for golf, aerobics, skiing, and skating, sports watches, sunglasses, and a children's clothing line. Nike developed from a specialist brand for running shoes into a broad generalist for sports articles and sports clothing.

Two specialists in running shoes have emerged since: Saucony and Asics. They are completely devoted to the world of serious runners. Saucony positions itself as a niche brand, with the right models for different types of runners. Asics also focuses on the functional runners market, among other things, through selective distribution—that is, via specialty shops for runners.

In the late 1990s in the Netherlands, Asics became indisputable market leader within the functional use niche with a share higher than 50 percent, followed by Saucony with a share of about 20 percent. The share of Nike with serious runners dropped to around 10 percent even as its share of the athletic product market as a whole has expanded. Nike was no longer taken seriously by the runners' group, but it has made up for that lack of product association in one specialized category by expanding across many other related categories of performance athletics. Nike is by far the largest brand within the casual segment, although it is losing ground there too.

Sources: Adapted from Kieft (2000); Klein (2000).

> *Principle:* Brand expansion results in the development of the core meanings of a brand into a higher abstraction level. Because of this, brands serve less well as internal information sources over individual categories.

Brand Diversification

An extreme form of brand extension takes place when a brand enters a domain that has no relation with the domains to which it was originally linked, such as is the case with the Virgin brand. This relatively recent phenomenon, known as brand diversification or concept transfer, enjoys much interest among brand specialists.

Another example is Sainsbury's. This major English supermarket chain, which was established in 1869 in London, decided in 1997 to go into financial services with a Sainsbury Bank. The company took this step at a time when things were going less well financially with its supermarkets, even with its solid relationship with 12 million customers. This relationship was supposed to constitute a sufficient guarantee for the market success of simple banking services. The reactions of experts were quite mixed, however. Paul Edwards, director of the renowned Henley Centre, a consulting firm that specializes in research and corporate vision, was quoted as saying in the *Sunday Times* (March 11, 1996) that Sainsbury was taking too large a leap at once and that it might be trying to keep up with Tesco. The banks' financial results were bad for a number of years. In 2006 it still was losing money at a rate of 20 million dollars a year (www.j-sainsbury.co.uk).

Extension Considerations

Various kinds of extension strategies are valued because they deliver economies of scale benefits to the marketer. In order to make that work, several key variables have to be factored into the brand extension strategy. The first is a question of consistency and fit, the second involves leverage, and the third involves budget issues.

Fit

Ninety-five percent of product introductions consist of line and brand extensions (J. Murphy 1997), 80 to 90 percent of which fail. This is due to several reasons. An important one is undoubtedly an overoptimistic estimate of brand extension possibilities. Research into the potential of a brand in unexplored categories has to be geared toward two essential issues:

- the *fit* between a brand and a new category, which depends mainly on product feature similarity and the consistency of the brand concept (Park et al. 1991); and
- the *leverage* of a brand against the competing brands that are already established in that category.

Various theories suggest that the perceived similarity of brand-affiliated products facilitate the transfer of knowledge, affect and buying intentions. The more similar two objects are, the more likely the transfer from the well-known object to the lesser-known object. The question however is: which is the basis of perceived similarity? Research by Martin and Stewart (2001) revealed that this is a multidimensional construct, and that the dimensions are different when the consumer goals are different. The results show that the presence of a set of shared goals can link non-similar products together. When there is a lack of similarity in goals, consumers may focus on some other cue such as usage situation similarity. When two products share a set of goals, the transfer of meaning and affect may be more elaborated. When the two products are less goal congruent, their elaborations are shorter and less detailed and focused more on "why the extension doesn't make sense." In relationship with brands, the goals that consumers pursue have been defined in the context of this publication as "brand-functions," to which Chapter 4 has been devoted. It will demonstrate that the dimensions of similarity can be very different from brand category to brand category. Deep understanding of a brand's key function is a first condition for estimating the similarity between an extension and the parent brand.

Since Park et al. and Martin published these principles, it became clear that the principle of "fit" is a bit more complicated, because fit can apply to more different brand-dimensions. Based on extensive literature analyses, the following bases of fit can be distinguished:

1. *Product attribute based fit:* the attribute-associations are relevant in the extension-category. Dove soap's one-quarter hydrating ingredients enabled it to extend to a number of other categories in which this attribute is relevant.
2. *Style based fit:* although style is a product attribute, it should have separate attention, because of its importance for a large number of brands. For typical design-brands, for "signature-brands" and for other brands for which the "look" of their products is characteristic, style based fit is an important extension-consideration.
3. *Capabilities based fit:* the capabilities and experiences of the brander in producing the parent-product(s) fit those that are perceived as required for the extension category. It confers believability's to the brand.
4. *Product-usage-associations based fit:* the complimentarily between the usage situation and usage moments of the parent product and the extension leads to perception of coherence and fit. This also applies to an extension that substitutes the parent product.
5. *Symbolic fit:* When the symbolic brand associations are relevant for the new category this can be a strong basis for fit—especially when they complement attribute based fit.
6. *Users group-identity based fit:* for brands with a narrowly defined user group, with which the participants identify, an extension may be perceived as fitting on the basis of perceived understanding of and adapting by the brand to the identity and culture of the group.
7. *(Country of) Origin based fit:* brands that represent the culture of a country of origin, can be extended to more different categories that are associated with this country. Bertolli can stretch to all kinds of food-categories that fit "the Italian gusto for life."
8. *Quality-perceptions based fit:* brands which are known as providing and maintaining a high degree of quality can be gradually extended into more diverse categories, as long as a high degree of quality is maintained across extensions. (Dacin and Smith 1994)
9. *Value for money based fit:* brands which primarily represent a value-based proposition, as the Virgin brand discussed before, can more easily be extended to categories in which established brands under perform in important generic product or service dimensions.

Fit judgments are holistic, not compositional. Boush and Loken (1991) suggest that fit-judgments are a form of holistic categorization, and allow for gradations in fit. Different associations carry different importance.

Since symbolic brands are more abstract than functional brands, they are able to accommodate more diverse sets of products sharing fewer features.

The core associations of a brand thus have a paramount influence on its extension potential. The more a new extension corresponds with the brand concept, the greater the chances of its success. When an extension corresponds less with a concept, chances of rejection increase. This rejection can lead to an adjustment of the brand concept—the consumer changes the concept of the brand in such a way that the new extension can belong to it again. This happens especially when a brand is linked to a new product category.

The central principle for accepting several or many product variants under the same main brand is that of cognitive consistency. Consumers look for a link, a correspondence through which they can fit those different products into their concept of the brand. When this happens to be easy, the brand concept can be strengthened and become more accessible, and the extension is accepted more quickly (Dacin and Smith 1993).

Differences between brand concept and product perceptions can result in a development of the brand meaning into higher abstraction levels. Each new addition of a product category to a brand assortment makes a customer redefine the essence of the brand. A brand that is initially defined by product-related meanings can easily shift to a concept in which symbolic meanings are central. This shift can ultimately lead to the brand merely representing a provenience. The organizational associations will then constitute the core of the brand.

There are different theories concerning the influence of new information on existing concepts. Two of them—the bookkeeping model and the typicality model—are discussed here.

Loken and John (1993) studied situations in which specific product properties of extension products may weaken the actual brand association. Their results support the accuracy of both models. They also conclude that unsuccessful brand extensions can indeed damage the brand considerably.

The *bookkeeping* model posits that association can change slowly through new, inconsistent information received by the consumer. Therefore, when an existing brand is used for a new product category, this can influence the specific beliefs associated with the brand name. For example, when the Dutch temporary employment agency Randstad decided to carry out personnel recruiting along with its flexible personnel services, the Randstad brand changed. The strong association with the category of temporary employment agency weakened.

According to the *typicality* model, the effect of inconsistent information depends on the degree to which the brand is seen as typical of a product class. In general, inconsistent information will have a more negative effect the more the brand is seen as a prototype of a product class.

In general, it can be assumed that an incoherent product assortment does not fit with a reliable brand in the eyes of consumers. To get an insight into the extension possibilities of a brand, a company needs to identify the relative strength of the brand associations, especially their core meanings that constitute the brand concept.

To research the potential extensions of a brand, Oakenfull et al. (2000) propose a method based on a holistic assessment of a brand's fit with a broad selection of conceivable extensions. This evaluation asks respondents to identify products that fit with the brands, as well as products that do not. Respondents are then asked to classify the two resulting selections and to identify the extensions they see as most and least fitting. To find out which perceptions determine their evaluations, a "why" question is always asked. A systematic analysis of the answers sheds light on the core meanings of a brand—what it is and what it is not in the eyes of the consumer—and the degree to which those meanings are found to be relevant for new extensions.

Principle: Cognitive consistency is the central principle for accepting different products under the same brand. Coherence strengthens the brand evaluation. An incoherent product range can harm the perceived reliability of a brand.

Leverage

Even more important than fit to the success of an extension is leverage. It seems that fit has the character of a precondition, but leverage is the most important success factor. A telling example is Dreft, for years a leader in the Dutch market category of handwash dish detergents. When penetration of dishwashers increased in the 1990s, Dreft introduced a line extension for that market. We can hardly imagine a clearer example of a fit. Still, the extension failed because it was competing against Sun, a Unilever brand that had positioned itself as specialist in dishwasher detergents years before. The Dreft brand proved to have insufficient leverage to compete successfully against Sun.

Another example is Philips mobile phones. For years, Philips had been the component supplier to manufacturers of mobile phones and had all the necessary technology at its disposal. When the market exploded in the early 1990s, Philips in 1996 decided to make end products too, aspiring to break through to a position between the top three brands (Nokia, Ericsson, and Motorola at that time). Five years later, Philips had not even managed to reach the top ten. Independent production was halted in 2001. The adventure had a cumulative loss of almost 1.5 billion euros. The fit was certainly appropriate, but there was no leverage at all.

Considering the high failure percentages of brand extensions, it is important not to overestimate the importance of a perceptual fit between a new product and an established brand. Tauber (1993) goes as far as designating the concept of fit as deceiving: as consumers are able to imagine more different products under the same brand, the relevance of that brand for the individual extension becomes more limited.

But even more important is the leverage of a brand in a new category, the advantage it represents in the perception of consumers against the brands already established in that category. Many recent studies indicate that consumers tend to base their evaluation of an extension on the relevance of brand meanings in the new category (Bridges et al. 1997; Broniarozyk and Alba 1994). A pan-European study by Ernst & Young and ACNielsen in the FMCG markets (1999) showed that 80 to 90 percent of introductions fail, not because the brand or the product is not good, but because consumers feel bonded with the brands they already use. Introducing a new product is like trying to break up a good marriage.

Budget Advantages

When consumers choose a brand extension over a new brand, expectations often play a role that can be met with nominal communication efforts. Analysis by D.C. Smith (1992) and D.C. Smith and Park (1992) showed that, as a rule, such situations have considerably lower advertising budgets: 10 percent of the sales as against 19.3 percent for new brands. However, this example seemed to depend very much on the degree of coherence between the new products and the existing ones. The more a new product deviates from the brand concept, it follows that even less budget advantages are realized. The advantage also turned out to be lower to the degree that consumers were able to evaluate the new product and thus depend less on brand trust. Other studies also show that the

Figure 14.2 **Factors That Determine Success or Failure of Brand Extensions**

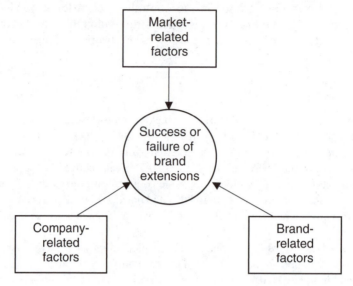

Source: Blom (2005).

effect of brand extensions is greatest with so-called experience products, such as sporting events and theme parks (Erdem 1998).

An older study by Peckham (1973) also indicated that within FMCG markets, companies get pretty much what they pay for—lower budgets are voted more for brand extensions than for new brands, but brand extensions also reach lower market shares (there was hardly any difference between extensions and new branding in realized market shares per invested dollar.)

SUCCESS AND FAILURE FACTORS

Based on Nielsen data on fast-moving consumer goods in the Dutch supermarkets over a nine-year period (1994–2003), SWOCC, the Netherlands-based institute for marketing research, analyzed 100 brand extensions of thirty-one leading food and nonfood brands. It turned out that only 41 percent of them had been really successful, in the sense that three years after their introduction they still had respectable sales (Blom 2005).

To determine the success and failure factors behind these brand-extensions, SWOCC also executed a meta-analysis of more than 100 publications (Blom 2005). Three groups of factors that determine the success of brand extensions were identified as market-, company-, and brand-related factors.

Market Factors

- Competition: A large number of competitive brands in the new category seems to have a negative influence on the success rate of extensions. Most extensions offer little meaningful differentiation, and established brands are fast in following with a similar product.
- Retailers' benevolence: Retailers decide which extensions they will initially make room for on their shelves. The retailers' benevolence toward the company influences their decisions.

Company Factors

- Experience of the company: The marketing experience of a company has a big influence on the success rate of extensions. Companies that have built up a body of knowledge on product development, product introductions, and branding have a better chance of success.
- Success rate of earlier extensions: Earlier failed extensions diminish the chance of success because they cast a negative aura over the brand; earlier successes have a positive influence on new extensions.
- Size of the company: Big companies on average have more successful extensions than smaller ones.
- Brand span: Wide brands that already are established in a number of different categories are easier to extend than narrow brands that are closely related to one specific category.
- Distance of extension to brand: The extension should share an attribute with the other brand or products. Too great a distance can be overcome by introducing intermediate stepping-stones; too little a distance limits the possibility of future extensions to more distant categories.
- Rank order of entering a new category: Extensions that are introduced early in a new category have a better chance of success; later extensions, however, can benefit from increased insight.
- Introduction budget: The size of the advertising and promotion support influences the success or failure of extensions. Campaigns specifically supporting the extension increase the chances of success.
- Distribution: The strength and breadth of distribution obviously have an impact on the success rate of an extension. Distribution is also a factor that is dependent on other factors.

Brand Factors

- Consumer brand equity: In Chapter 15 the concept of brand equity will be discussed. Here we will equate it with the strength of the brand in the mind and the behavior of consumers. Big and strong brands have a larger chance of extension success than smaller and weaker brands.
- Brand equity of competing brands: Smaller and weaker brands have a hard time extending to categories that are dominated by big and strong competitors.
- Focus of brand: Brands that are strongly associated with one very specific subcategory are more difficult to extend to a new category. (See the Xerox box on page 395.)
- Perceived quality of the brand: Brand perception is an important success factor for extensions. A perception of quality reduces perceived risk and stimulates trial purchases.
- Brand loyalty: Consumers who are loyal to a brand in other categories are more open to a new extension if it is relevant to them.
- Product associations: Brands that are strongly associated with specific product attributes are difficult to extend to unrelated categories or subcategories.
- Symbolic associations: Brands that are well associated with symbolic meanings have a bigger chance of success when extending to new categories.
- Perceived level of difficulty: Extensions that are regarded as difficult to produce have a better chance of success for a brand with the right perceived capability.
- Brand believability: Credibility is dependent on the perceived capability and reliability of a brand. When these are considered important in a new category, the believable brand has a better chance of success.

The Strength of Core Associations

The strength of a brand's core associations has a considerable influence on the development of new associations. Different associations compete constantly against each other in memory. This can cause what is known as *proactive interference*, through which old associations complicate the development of new ones. This happens especially when an attempt is made to link a brand affixed to a certain product category with another category or subcategory. In the Netherlands, the Brinta brand is so strongly associated with porridge that it really cannot be connected to anything else. For this reason, its parent brand, Honig, was wise to bring its breakfast drink into the market under a new name, Wake-Up. Biotex, a brand of Sara Lee in the Netherlands, has such strong associations with soaking and prewash that the introduction of a Biotex detergent for the main wash turned out to be a complete flop.

When a brand is so strongly determined by a single association, the direct extension possibilities are limited to products that are perceptually very close. In that case, a sub-brand can sometimes produce a solution because it can be linked with the new meanings. Still, what is then, in fact, being developed is a new main brand, as is the case with Brinta's launch of Wake-Up. The series of failed extensions of the Xerox brand demonstrates how a brand can become a prison (see page 395).

Principle: A fit between a brand and a new product category has the character of a precondition. The brand response is largely determined by the leverage—that is, the assessment of a brand against those brands that are already established in the category.

To get insight into the leverage of a brand in a new category, research is needed into the relative evaluation of a brand-product concept in relation to the brands already established in that category. Various research techniques are available for this purpose (see, e.g., Franzen and Bouwman 2001). A combination of brand purchasing intention questions and the constant sum method to measure attitude can be enlightening when trying to find out an extension's relative potential. Marchant et al. (1994) show that having respondents rank their brand purchasing intention produces a valid prediction of an extension's market potential.

Such research certainly does not cover every branding situation, though. The entire marketing mix behind a new brand-product combination influences its chances of succeeding. Long-term support plays a particularly important role here. The chapter on brand equity discusses this topic further.

VIRGIN: BRAND STRATEGY OR EGO TRIP?

The enormous costs involved in the development and maintenance of brands make it very tempting to stretch megabrands further and further.

Little is known at this point about the influence of brand diversification on the strength of brands like Virgin. Lab research has studied the effects of brand extensions on the perception of brands, but when it comes to their influence on market positions in unrelated markets, the business community has made few contributions. We are assuming that most companies have limited insight into this issue.

Xerox: Prisoner of an Association

When we think of Xerox we think of . . .

Right. The word *Xerox* even figures in Webster's dictionary with the meaning "to copy on a xerographic machine."

The brand and the word stem from *xerography*, which is derived from the Greek words for "dry" and "writing."

The first automatic plain paper copier was introduced by Xerox in 1959 and became one of the most successful products ever marketed in the United States. As its technology was well patented, Xerox owned the category until the Federal Trade Commission forced the company to license its technology in 1972. This dramatically changed the situation, with low-cost Japanese competitors, such as Canon and Ricoh, taking a huge chunk of Xerox's share of the market.

In 1970 Xerox tried to broaden its base by entering the computer market. But few customers could relate the brand to anything other than copying, even though Xerox invented the world's first personal computer in 1973. In 1975 Xerox ended its production of mainframe computers. In 1978 Xerox introduced Xten, a business network that was unsuccessful. In 1979 Xerox tried to expand again with the introduction of telecopiers, with very modest success. In 1981 Xerox introduced a personal computer, which flopped. In the minds of its customers, "Xeroxing" was not "computing," but simply "copying."

And then came laser printers. Xerox had started work on laser printers in 1969. By 1977 it was selling the 9700 printer, a huge monster, costing $350,000. In 1982 Canon brought out the first desktop laser printer, followed in 1984 by Hewlett Packard with its Laserjet, which captured the largest market share. Now, with a personal computer on everyone's desk, printing documents on a laser printer began to replace Xeroxing. Copies made on laser printers now exceed copies made on copiers.

Xerox found itself on the brink of bankruptcy. Having failed to capture a relevant market position in the printer market or the data-processing market, it lost market share in the U.S. copying market to around 15 percent and its share price plummeted from a high of $64 in 1999 to $4 in 2004 To a large degree, Xerox was a victim of its own core meaning.

Xerox is now executing a new strategy under the mantra "Xerox, the document company." Its objective is to turn into a service company helping large corporations operate their document management processes from paper to digital efficiently. Under this new philosophy, Xerox managed to stabilize its operating revenues in 2005 for the first time since 1995.

Sources: Trout (2001); Xinxin (2005).

The Virgin case can best be seen as a large-scale, in-market experiment for determining the limitations of brand diversification. Virgin has broken all the rules that have become common practice in the field of brand extensions and that have been discussed in this chapter. The question is: Are the rules inappropriate, or is Richard Branson's Virgin a balloon? Most experts think the last is the case, pointing to all the extensions that have ended up in trouble. Virgin Cola, Virgin Vodka,

Virgin Clothes, and Virgin Jeans disappeared silently from the market. Virgin Money, Virgin Vie Cosmetics, Virgin Wine, Virgin Brides, Virgin Cosmetics, and Virgin Cars did not fulfill Branson's predictions. The original investors in Virgin Express, V2, and Virgin Blue all lost money. In 2000 all the Virgin businesses except airlines and rail were losing money

According to Forbes Global, "Virgin's image is suffering." Branson admits that the image of Virgin has been diluted. "Hopefully we learn from our mistakes," he says. "Most of our businesses do succeed. But if something completely fails, as long as we bow out gracefully and pay off all our debts, and nobody gets hurt, then I don't think people disrespect Virgin for trying."

Contrary to most business practices, the secret of Branson's success is his failures, according to his publisher, Mick Brown—although a good many of Branson's ventures fail, he just keeps on going. But most branding experts are critical of Virgin's approach to brand stretching. "A brand can't stand for music stores, airlines, mobile phones, colas, financial services, and on and on," says Peter Sealey, former head of marketing at Coca-Cola. "There is no brand that can do that. That's ego." A common criticism is that many of the extensions seem poorly thought out. One key reason for the failure of a number of Virgin extensions may be a misunderstanding about the type of brand that Branson has created. Branson has managed to create compelling and competitive products and services in markets such as airlines, where established brands have been overcharging and underperforming. In other markets, he has been much less successful.

Sources: Virgin.com; Bower (2005); M. Brown (1998); Deutschman (2004); D. Taylor (2004).

BRAND PORTFOLIO AND BRAND ARCHITECTURE

The management of the brand portfolio and the related brand architecture are critical issues in brand strategy development. The brand portfolio includes all the brands used by an organization, including main brands, sub-brands, endorsement brands, co-brands, and ingredient brands. Brand architecture refers to the combination of brands used to identify a product or a group of products.

The two concepts are very much interrelated, in the sense that the brand portfolio determines the options for the architecture strategy. Some authors even declare them to be the same. To complicate matters further, both brand portfolio and brand architecture strategy are determined by the decision either to use the corporate name as the main brand or to use individual brands. These are usually referred to as a *branded house* strategy versus a *house of brands* strategy.

In this chapter we will untangle these subjects as much as possible. We will first discuss the portfolio strategy. Companies that have historically chosen in favor of individual brands usually have large portfolios with sometimes thousands of brands, as the following account of Nestlé illustrates.

MANAGING THOUSANDS OF BRANDS IN THE NESTLÉ BRAND STABLE

The Nestlé empire began with the invention of the first formula for milk powder by the Swiss chemist Henri Nestlé in 1867. It was an immediate success. In 1875 a friend of Henri Nestlé, Daniel Peter, discovered the first formula for making milk chocolate and formed the business of Peter Cailler Kohler Chocolat Swiss. Nestlé first acquired a chocolate company, Swiss General, in 1904 and Cailler twenty-five years later.

In 1938 Nestlé succeeded in drying coffee beans and making a soluble product: Nescafé. After World War II Nestlé began a series of acquisitions. The Maggi soups and seasoning business was acquired in 1947, followed by Crosse & Blackwell preserves in 1960, Findus frozen foods in 1962, Vittel mineral water in 1969, Libby's fruit juices in 1971, and Stouffer's frozen foods in 1973. In 1974 Nestlé bought a 49 percent stake in Gesparel, the holding company for L'Oréal cosmetics. Pharmaceutical developer Alcon Laboratories was added in 1977, Chambourcy in 1979, Carnation in 1985. British chocolate maker Rowntree Mackintosh and Italian food company Buitoni were added in 1988. In 1992 Nestlé took over the bottled water manufacturer Perrier and Clarke Foods; in 1994 it acquired the Alpo pet food company and in 1998 Spillers.

By the end of the twentieth century, Nestlé had a stable of thousands of brands. The previous CEO Peter Brabeck-Letmathe summarized the situation:

> Nestlé has ten worldwide corporate strategic brands, including Nestlé itself, as well as Nescafé, Maggi, Friskies, Buitoni and Carnation. Additionally, we have 45 different strategic worldwide product brands, among them KitKat, Coffeemate, and Crunch. Then there are 25 regional corporate strategic brands . . . together with about a hundred regional product brands. Each corporate brand has its own territory into which the local brands will fall. We also have some 700 local strategic brands that are important to particular countries, like Brigadeiro in Brazil. Then there are 7,500 purely local brands.
>
> Our first principle is to consolidate all our resources behind the key corporate strategic brands. Whatever the product brand or range brand, it has to be supported by one of our corporate brands. . . . Rowntree had a "one product, one brand" policy: KitKat, Smarties, Rolo, After Eight. No mention of Rowntree. When we acquired the company, we applied our system, and KitKat became Nestlé KitKat.
>
> Nestlé is a brand in its own right. For consumers, the relevance of Nestlé as a company comes first of all through contact with products that are branded Nestlé. If we want to be perceived as the world's leading food company, we have to offer consumers an increasing amount of products that they can identify as Nestlé. The choice of products that we will [group] under the Nestlé brand depends on the way these products enhance the Nestlé image—not on what Nestlé brings to its products. Therefore each of these products has to have deep roots. Take infant cereals, for example. This is the only product that has an

automatic right to the Nestlé brand because it is with infant cereals that Nestlé began. Next come baby food and infant formula, powdered, condensed, and refrigerated milk products, chocolate, confectionery, breakfast cereals, and ice cream. All are basic Nestlé territory positioned under nourishment and enjoyment. They have earned the Nestlé brand too.

Today, about 40 percent of total turnover is from products covered by the Nestlé corporate brand. Every day, consumers are in contact with Nestlé-branded products.

For products that don't carry the Nestlé brand, we have created a Nestlé Seal of Guarantee to put on the back and linked to Nestlé by a short note like: "All Maggi products benefit from Nestlé experience in producing quality foods all over the world." But we have to strike a balance between making purchasers aware of Nestlé and preserving the distinct personalities of our other strategic corporate brands. Where we have a relevant core competence combined with a specific brand territory, as we do with Maggi and Buitoni for example, it is better to keep a separate brand identity. We do not combine Nestlé/Buitoni, because Buitoni is more than a product—it represents the authentic Italian lifestyle. Nor do we have Nestlé/Maggi. Maggi offers local recipes to suit local tastes, even though it belongs to a multinational.

Nestlé is the world's biggest food manufacturer. Its top six brands generate more than 70 percent of its revenues; the Nestlé brand itself, being the biggest of them all, is responsible for 40 percent of the company's revenues.

Sources: Parsons (1996); Adbrands Company Profiles (2006a); Nestlé Web site, www.nestle.com.

BRAND PORTFOLIOS

Brand portfolios vary enormously in size and composition. Many companies have opted for a very limited set of brands—as we saw in the Virgin case history in the previous chapter. Richard Branson decided to brand all his businesses with the Virgin name, from record shops and airlines to jeans, wines, and bridal shops. The same portfolio strategy is adhered to by General Electric (GE), Philips, Dell, Microsoft, Deutsche Bank, Vodafone, and many thousands of other companies around the world. They may add sub-brands (Apple Macintosh, Apple iPod), but the corporate brand is the main or master brand.

Portfolio Drivers

Large brand portfolios, such as Nestlé's, are mainly the result of takeovers in the company's history. As Nestlé acquired companies in a range of different markets, each acquired company added its own brand portfolio to the overall Nestlé portfolio, which grew ultimately to thousands of brands. This collection poses a huge strategic problem to the company management—how can all these brands be classified and managed strategically according to their importance for future corporate growth? A board cannot keep track of hundreds or even thousands of brands, but it usually can manage the few brands that define a company's wealth. As the opening story shows, Nestlé identifies seventy of its most important brands as "strategic brands" in its portfolio, which still is a huge number to manage.

As is the case with Nestlé, a company's history is doubtless the main driver underlying its brand portfolio, but there are a number of other important drivers. Douglas et al. (1999) identifies three groups: (1) company-based drivers, (2) product- and market-based drivers, and (3) environment-based drivers.

1. Company-Based Drivers

History. Brand portfolios and brand architectures reflect the imprimatur of previous generations of managers. Of particular importance is the growth strategy of a company—organic or via acquisitions.

Organizational structure. The balance between centralization and decentralization has an impact on the brand portfolio. In decentralized organizations, subsidiary managers tend to cherish their "own" brands. This is the case with Nestlé. Highly centralized organizations such as Sony and Siemens tend to adopt corporate branding strategies and to have fewer brands. They also tend to extend these brands into international markets.

Corporate identity. Companies that place a strong emphasis on corporate identity tend to operate under their corporate brand—for example, Apple, IBM, and Nike.

Product diversity. The diversity and interrelatedness of a company's activities play a big role. Companies with closely related product lines that share a common technology or competencies emphasize corporate brands. Very diversified companies tend to use brands to identify these differences. Akzo Nobel, which is big in pharmaceuticals, coatings, and chemicals, uses a roster of different company brands.

2. Product- and Market-Based Drivers

Market segmentation. Brands are used to appeal to different market segments. In highly segmented markets, this leads to the use of more brands, as we see in the confectionery and soft drink markets. Relatively homogeneous markets are usually covered with one single brand.

Market integration. Where markets are fully integrated and the same competitors compete worldwide, such as in air travel and computers, companies tend to operate with a very limited number of international brands. Globalization tends to reduce the brand portfolio.

Cultural embeddedness. For products that are deeply culturally embedded, such as foods, local brands are still important. This leads to the larger number of brands in the portfolio of companies such as Unilever and Nestlé.

3. Environment-Based Drivers

Political and economic integration. Increasing integration of markets, such as in the European Union, stimulates brand alignment across borders and so reduces the number of local brands.

Infrastructure. The arrival of global media, such as the Internet, is a catalyst to the spread of international brands.

Internationalization of retailers. The growth of global retailers facilitates and stimulates the use of international brands. As retail power increases, producers tend to put their marketing funds behind a limited number of brands in order to increase their counterweight.

Consumer mobility. Increased international travel exposes consumers to brands in other countries. It enhances the awareness of and trust in international brands and so stimulates harmonization of branding across borders.

Most of the drivers stimulate the reduction of the number of brands in the large portfolios of big global companies such as Nestlé. They are also the main considerations behind the reduction of the number of brands in the Unilever portfolio from 1,600 to 400 early in the twenty-first century and the phasing out of more than 1,000 brands by Procter & Gamble in the same period. Economic considerations also play an important role. A limited percentage of brands in the portfolio usually are responsible for a large share of total revenue. In the case of Unilever, 25 percent of its 1,600 brands generated 84 percent of the company's 2001 revenues.

Conglomerization

Sometimes the current management of long-established companies finds a portfolio of brands in its stable for which the strategic reasoning and decision making remain largely a mystery. In their drive for expansion in the fourth quarter of the twentieth century, many companies acquired businesses with brands far removed from their original areas of competence. They developed into conglomerates with a primarily financial orientation. In essence, they were not very different in nature from investment companies. Often this status had a negative impact on their profit margins. A dramatic example is Sara Lee Corporation, a bakery firm by origin, which developed into a broad food and beverage company and then diversified into the household, personal care, and apparel businesses (see page 402).

In the first decade of the twenty-first century, investment companies, venture capitalists, hedge funds, and pension funds began to exercise strong pressure on these large corporations to stick to their roots, split off unfamiliar businesses, and sell underperforming units. The idea was that as far as investment was concerned, they could do better as a corporation than as a conglomerate of enterprises. They could at least eliminate a lot of administrative holding costs. Corporate managers began to consider some crucial questions:

- What is the true nature of the company?
- Which are its areas of core competence?
- What is the added value of the combination of different categories?
- On which brands are the company's fortunes based?
- What is the synergy between newly acquired businesses and the present key brands in the portfolio?
- Do all brands perform at top level or do some of them, at least, negatively influence the company's returns on investment?
- What is the long-term outlook of the underperforming brands? Would selling them improve the company's financial performance?

Refocusing the Company

Under this mounting pressure from the financial community, CEOs and boards of directors of diversified corporations began to take a new look at their businesses and brand portfolios and redefine a leading concept or mission for their businesses. Unilever, for example, came up with "vitality" as its leading principle and as a result sold off its perfume brands and some unhealthy food brands, such as Mora Snacks in the Netherlands. Philips settled on "sense and simplicity" and tried to figure out what this mantra would mean for its portfolio. Nestlé in 2008 announced that it would concentrate on food, health, wellness products, and sell all subsidiaries that do not fit with this principle, such as its eye-lens business. And Sara Lee decided to bid farewell to all its apparel brands, which constituted 40 percent of its business, and a large number of underperforming local brands in the household and personal-care markets.

Thus these companies shifted away from the role of investment companies and toward a narrower focus on their true mission—their point of excellence.

Sara Lee Bids Farewell to a Hundred Brands

Sara Lee started in 1939 with the purchase of C.D. Kenny Company, a small wholesale distributor of sugar, coffee, and tea in Baltimore. Since then its history is best described as a continuous process of acquisitions. In 1958 the company acquired "Kitchens of Sara Lee," a company famous for its cheesecakes.

It adopted this brand as its company name in 1985. But before then it had already entered the apparel market by acquiring Gant and the household products segment by acquiring Erdal in the Netherlands. In 1978 it made an initial investment in Douwe Egberts, a leading European tobacco and beverage company. In the last quarter of the twentieth century, Sara Lee developed into a huge conglomerate with a global portfolio of more than 200 brands that could be classified into five different business areas:

1. *Food:* Sara Lee, Jimmy Dean, Aoste, Ball Park, Bimbo, Bryan, Earth Grains, Hillshire Farm, Stegeman, Duyvis, Lassie, Natrena
2. *Beverages:* Douwe Egberts coffee, Senseo, Maison du Café, Pickwick tea, Chock Full O'Nuts, Hills Bros., Van Nelle
3. *Apparel:* Bali, Champion, Dim, Hanes, Playtex, Unno, Wonderbra, L'eggs, Coach, Aristoc, Elbeo, Gossard, Nur Die
4. *Household products:* Ambi Pur, Kiwi, Tana, Endust, Biotex, Vapona, Cruz+Verde, Goodnight, Hit
5. *Personal care:* Sanex, Delial, Zwitsal, Prodent, Badedas, Brylcreem, Monsavon, Radox, Zendium

By 1998 sales had reached $20 billion.

At that point, sales growth stagnated at about 1 to 2 percent per annum and the earnings and stock price began to fall. In 2005 Sara Lee's sales totaled $19.2 billion, its growth was negative, and net income plummeted by 43.5 percent. Shareholders complained. Their analysis: (1) the product line had become far too diversified and unmanageable, (2) too many businesses underperformed, especially in the apparel and household sector, (3) there were no synergies between the diverse businesses, and (4) there was too much overhead in the headquarters.

Although the company had been restructuring and promising better results for seven years, it had not managed to turn around its financial fortunes. "Sara Lee is headed towards a break-up," wrote *Business Week* back in 2001; "it should define its core business and sell what doesn't fit with it." And in 2003: "The best way to unlock value may be to dismantle Sara Lee, by creating three separate companies." *USA*

Today voiced the same criticism in 2005: "Wall Street has too long awaited Sara Lee's return to its pound cake roots."

In 2005, under pressure from investment funds, hedge funds, pension funds, and other important investment companies, the new CEO, Brenda Barnes, gave in. She introduced a bold new strategy and a five-year implementation plan. Her mission: "To bring the Sara Lee back to Sara Lee, from a collection of companies to a single operating enterprise, a premier consumer products company focused on food, beverage, and household and personal care." The company decided to sell off its apparel business and underperforming national brands without real growth potential, such as Hills Bros. in the United States; Stegeman, Duyvis, and Lassie in the Netherlands; and household and body-care products such as Kiwi and Dobbelman in other non-U.S. markets. The company's managers hoped to end up with about a hundred brands. Whether this change will turn Sara Lee into a prosperous enterprise again, only time will tell.

Sources: Scardino (2005); Forster (2001); Horovitz (2005); www.saralee.com; Gogoi (2003).

The Brand Portfolio Audit

Most brand portfolios are the heritage of past generations of managers and, until recently, were regarded as just facts of corporate life. As the examples of Nestlé, Unilever, Procter & Gamble, and Sara Lee illustrate, this attitude changed in the late 1990s, reflecting the emerging recognition of the value of brands as assets. Now brand portfolio management is an important concern of most CEOs. It has become an integral part of business strategy, which it needs to reflect and support.

An overcrowded brand portfolio can result in marginal brands absorbing financial and managerial resources at the expense of the strategic brands in the portfolio. In this first decade of the twenty-first century, many companies have come to realize that their portfolio contains too many brands and that the time has come for a strategic brand consolidation. A systematic audit of the utility and strength of all the brands in the portfolio results in a decision to eliminate or consolidate many of the brands and to prioritize them for the allocation of funds.

As the brands are supposed to support the corporate strategy, a deep understanding of where the company is today and where it should be going in the near future is a prerequisite for a successful brand portfolio audit. The key questions for a brand portfolio audit are "What is the business strategy and how do the company's brands support it?" More specifically, managers need to consider the following questions:

- What are the core competences of the company?
- In which new domains should the company be active?
- Which domains should be abandoned?
- How should categories be defined?
- Which categories should the company be in?
- Which subcategories can be distinguished? Do they need separate brands?
- Do the company's businesses deliver synergy? Do the brands support this?
- Do the brands strategically fit with the direction the company intends to take?
- What are the strategic brands in the key categories?

Figure 15.1 **Brand Equity**

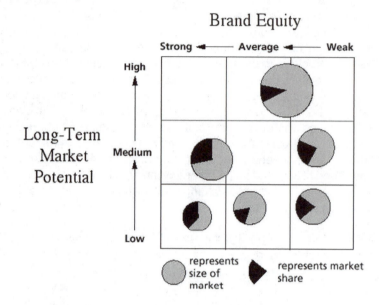

- What brands should be supported for further growth?
- What brands should be managed for cash to support the strategic and growth brands?
- What brands should be sold or deleted?
- What brands should be identified as candidates for acquisitions?
- What brands could be extended to other categories?

The Attractiveness Matrix

A typical approach to a brand portfolio audit is to rate each market the company is in today or could enter in the near future according to long-term market potential and brand equity. Each brand is positioned in a matrix (see Figure 15.1) according to a series of indicators of these two dimensions. Each organization has to identify the factors underlying these two dimensions and find a way to measure them and combine them.

The most common measures for market attractiveness are market size, annual market growth rate, historical average profit margins, competitive structure, and technological requirements. The key brand equity questions to be answered for all the major brands and sub-brands in the portfolio are these:

- What are the core perceptions of the brands? What do they stand for?
- What is the relevance of the brands from the consumers' perspective?
- What is the consumer's commitment to the brand?
- What is the market share and the market share trends of the brands?
- What is their distribution position?
- What is the contribution to the company's earnings?
- What are the extension potentials of the brands?
- What are their limitations?

Figure 15.2 **Strong Brands Represent a Large Proportion of Total Revenues**

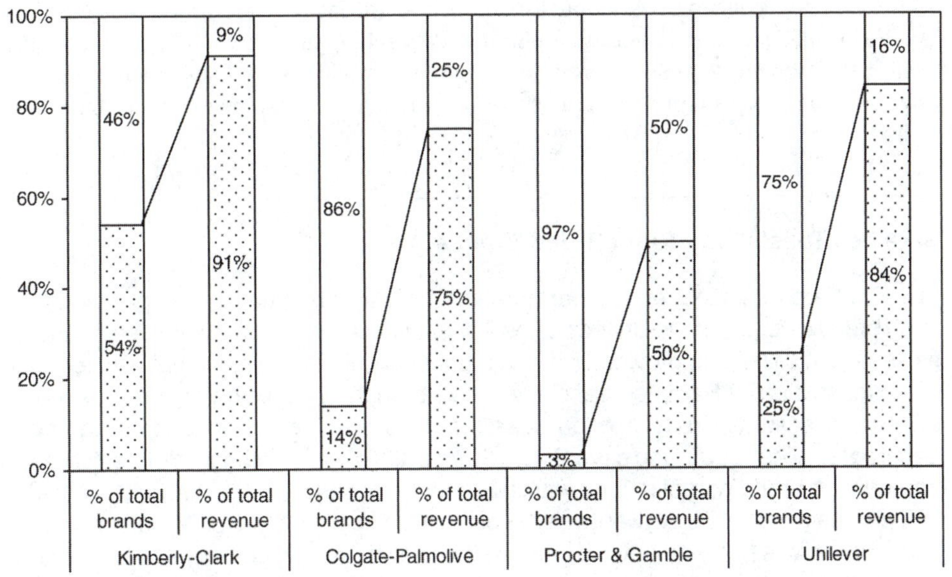

Source: Lippincott Mercer Management Consultants (2002).

Downsizing the Portfolio

A strong relationship exists between the ranking of brands in a category and the pretax return on investment that they generate. In the PIMS database, the number one brands on average showed a return on investment before tax of 32.9 percent; the number two brands of 17.8 percent; the number three brands of 14.1 percent; and the number four brands of 9.1 percent (Buzzel & Gale 1987). This relationship is the reason managers set the goal of being number one or two in a market; otherwise, they withdraw.

Inevitably, this analysis of the brand's market position also will lead to a reappraisal by big international companies of their brand portfolio policy. They realize that a very large part of their total revenue is generated by a small number of their brands (see Figure 15.2). Eliminating weak brands leads to direct cost reductions from savings in marketing, manufacturing materials, and distribution. In the case of Unilever, 25 percent of its 1,600 brands generated 84 percent of the company's revenues in 2001. Eliminating the other 75 percent would lead to a sizable reduction of costs and a more manageable portfolio. The company projected that after this operation the 400 leading brands would account for 95 percent of Unilever's total revenues. As Nial Fitzgerald, former Unilever co-chair, stated in 2002, "We dissipate our energy and resources on far too many brands. We recently had 1,600 brands and between 5,000 to 10,000 stock keeping units per business group, which led to fragmented delivery systems to our customers. So Unilever decided that it would prune its stable of brands and focus its $6 billion advertising and promotion budget on roughly 400 power brands" (Lippincott Mercer 2002).

Many companies also aggressively try to acquire other companies with a strong brand portfolio even as they are eliminating many of their own underperforming brands. Procter & Gamble, for example, acquired Clairol, Ralston Purina, Tambrands, Max Factor, Betrix, Wella, and Gillette. Likewise, Unilever acquired Cheseborough-Pond, Slim-Fast, and most recently Best Foods (Knorr and Hellmann's). Secondary brands were eliminated by selling them or transferring the products sold under those brands to another power brand in the portfolio. In 2001, for example, Sara Lee divested fifty-eight of its eighty American bread brands in order to create a more manageable portfolio.

Sara Lee Toasts Fifty-Eight Bread Brands

In 2001, Sara Lee acquired the Earthgrains Company, the number two player in the fresh bread category in the United States. The purchase quadrupled Sara Lee's bakery sales to $3.4 billion and provided it with a premier distribution system that accelerated the extension of the Sara Lee franchise. It also brought a profusion of brands, almost all of them regional—from Chicago Hearth to Rainbo and from Iron Kids to Grandma Sycamore's. The acquisition gave Sara Lee a portfolio of eighty brands of fresh bread and buns. A brand portfolio audit was an absolute necessity.

This analysis found that twenty-seven of the brands accounted for 95 percent of the company's gross sales dollars and gross margins. Research by Lippincott Mercer brand consultants led to the observation that only a handful of the company's big brands—including Sara Lee, Iron Kids, and Earth Grain—promised sustained growth.

Sara Lee concluded that it could maintain a forceful national presence with a few "pillar" brands, several super-regional brands, and a small group of strong regionals. This smaller, stronger portfolio would yield substantial marketing cost savings yet offer retailers greater flexibility for promotions and private labeling. The management team lost no time in acting on the recommendations: by May 2003, fifty-eight bread brands were toast and nearly 2,000 SKUs had been eliminated.

Source: Lippincott Mercer Company, *Sense Solving the Puzzle of Complex Brand Portfolios*, company brochure (2005).

A brand portfolio audit should end up with a classification of the brands in a portfolio according to their strategic importance and the desirable allocation of financial resources to each one. Such a classification could distinguish between the brands as follows:

1. *Strategic investment brands* that will be allocated substantial budgets to further develop them.
2. *Support-and-grow brands* that will receive budgets to sufficiently support them for future growth.
3. *Sustain brands* that will be allocated just sufficient budgets to consolidate them.
4. *Manage-for-cash brands* that will be maintained only to earn money for the other categories
5. *To be divested brands*.

As we saw earlier, Nestlé has been prioritizing the brands in its portfolio for a long time. Each of its ten worldwide corporate strategic brands is centrally managed by a top executive who serves as a "brand champion" and has final approval over major brand-building efforts. Beyond those, the forty-five strategic worldwide product brands and the twenty-five regional corporate strategic brands receive management attention from the Swiss headquarters.

BRAND ARCHITECTURE

There is confusion about the nature of brand architecture stemming from the perspective from which it is viewed. Seen from the position of the producer, brand architecture is the organizing structure of the brand portfolio. It defines and orders the relationship between the corporate entity, all of its brands, and its families of products and services. Seen from the position of the consumer, it is the combination of brands that represents and identifies a specific product or family of products. It guides their perception, evaluation, and choice process.

These two approaches are intertwined. A company's brand architecture has to address and meet complex corporate needs. At the same time, a company cannot lose sight of the fundamental function of branding: influencing consumer choice.

Brand architecture consists of a hierarchy of several elements whose meanings complement one another and that, together, represent a complete information package about the underlying product or products. The most important element is the main brand, or master brand as the main bearer of brand equity. It presents an extensive set of meanings that contain the relevant information on the brand. As a representation of the brand concept, the main brand plays a dominant role in the choice process of consumers.

In brand architecture, superordinate and subordinate brands are added to the main brand, each contributing with their specific meaning to the perception of consumers. As discussed in Chapter 14, they are called endorsement brands and sub-brands, respectively. An endorsement-brand is a provenience brand, such as Kraft, that adds a certain reputation to the main brand (Philadelphia). A sub-brand specifies the capacity of one or more products from the total product range under the main brand. It can add an attribute, a benefit, an application, a personality, or a target group.

Sometimes product descriptions are added to the architecture in regular language (generic product names or product descriptions) in order to communicate the specific capacity and properties of the individual product (e.g., Celestial Seasonings Honey Ginger Peach Wellness Tea). In dual brands, two more-or-less equivalent brands are combined. The following overview gives an indication of the various combination possibilities:

Variant 1	Main brand only (corporate or individual)
Variant 2	Main brand + product name
Variant 3	Main brand + sub-brand
Variant 4	Main brand + main brand
Variant 5	Endorsement brand + main brand
Variant 6	Endorsement brand + main brand + product name
Variant 7	Endorsement brand + main brand + sub-brand
Variant 8	Endorsement brand + main brand + sub-brand + product name

Before considering the many factors that play a part in deciding on one or the other of these possibilities, let us take a look first at a striking brand architecture case in Western Europe. It concerns the French telecom provider France Telecom.

France Telecom Paints the World Orange

France Telecom (FT) is one of the world's leading telecommunication carriers, with more than 147 million customers on five continents (220 countries and territories). In Europe it is the second biggest telecom group.

In the early 1990s it still was a state-owned, primarily fixed-line telecom corporation, operating as a monopolist provider almost exclusively in France. It invested heavily in promoting independent daughter brands such as Ola, Loft, and Mobicarte, each addressing a specific target with a discreet reference to France Telecom. In 1995 it launched a cellular telephone brand under the name of Itineris and subsequently an Internet service provider under the brand Wanadoo.

The complexity of its brand portfolio can be seen in the way FT grouped its corporate business services under the Equant brand. Its portfolio included a host of other individual brands, such as the Voila search engine, Alapage books and music sites, Marcopoly electronic appliance site, the Page Jaunes and Europages printed directories, Globe Cast satellite content distributor, Oleane Internet solutions for small companies, and Sofrecom communication consultancy.

When the telecom markets in the European Union opened up to competition in 2000, FT acquired the British Orange mobile service, becoming the second largest mobile operator in Europe and the number one in France. In 2000 Wanadoo took over the British Internet provider Freeserve, which in 2004 was rebranded to Wanadoo. In 2005 FT also was Europe's second largest Internet provider and the number one in France.

Gradually, however, it had become clear that this overly complicated brand architecture badly needed simplification. In 2001 FT decided to rebrand its various mobile brands such as Itineris, Ola, and Mobicarte into Orange. In 2005 it launched NEXT, a three-year transformation program for new telecom services in Europe, "giving customers access to a single portal, providing a simpler interface to the group's services." These services were sub-branded under the following names:

- *Family Talk:* communication between a family's fixed and mobile devices
- *LiveCom:* communication software integrating voice, video telephony, and instant messaging to communicate with computers, fixed-line terminals, cell phones, and videophones
- *Livephone:* broadband telephone that announces incoming e-mails and provides access to practical services
- *Mobile & Connected:* combined mobile and Internet access
- *Photo Transfer:* a service that transfers photos stored on a cell phone through the Livebos to the photoblog of the consumer's choice
- *LiveMusic:* wireless transfer of music from a computer to a high-quality sound system or home cinema
- *Live Zoom:* enables remote surveillance of the home through a mobile or a computer
- *Home Care:* combines a range of services to allow consumers to stay in contact with family and friends and to access social and medical services
- *Mobivisit:* an interactive mobile guide providing location-specific information when on the move (sites, restaurants, events, etc.)

In 2006, when research showed that the Orange brand meant more to consumers than Wanadoo, France Telecom decided to also rebrand Wanadoo as Orange. It surrendered its traditional name in the interest of creating a single global brand that stands for convergence of IP (Internet Protocol), IT (information technology), and mobility. Equant was also brought under the Orange brand. FT's group executive vice president explained, "Our goal is to be the reference service provider in Europe. We want to provide a new experience in telecom, which can be life changing for our customers. . . . We can create a single unified user experience that encompasses mobile and desktop."

Sources: Reid (2005); Wilson (2005); Donegan and Lunden (2005); France Telecom Web site, francetelecom.com.

This case history illustrates the emerging trends in brand architecture strategy. France Telecom came to the conclusion that employing a large number of individual brands, however different in its various European markets, was not an efficient and effective strategy. By combining all its mobile services under the strong Orange house brand, it built a stronger competitive position versus the other big European providers such as British Vodafone and German T-Mobile. At the same time it recognized that its individual services need identification too and opted for giving them descriptive product names. It refrained from using the corporate France Telecom brand as an endorser.

We will now discuss the most pregnant architecture issue a company is confronted with—the choice between the use of the corporate brand(s) and individual brands as main brand(s) or a combination of both.

Corporate and Individual Brands

The key difference between corporate and individual brands is that the corporate brand concept tends to be grounded in the values, opinions, and attitudes of the company founders, owners, managers, and personnel, whereas individual brands are mainly the product of marketing and advertising strategists (Balmer and Gray 2002). Corporate brands are the representation of corporate identity, which includes answers to such questions as "Who are we?" and "What are we?" (see Chapter 6). Personnel play a critically important role in transmitting and fulfilling the brand's promise. They provide the interface between the internal and external environments. This is especially the case in service brands, which tend to also be corporate brands.

Another difference is that corporate brands are geared toward different stakeholder groups, such as financial markets (the shareholders, private investors and investment funds, professionals in those markets, the media), the labor market (employees, potential employees, the workers' council, unions, the general press), and the retail market (retail channels, dealers, salespeople). Individual brands are geared more to prospects and customers. As a consequence, corporate brands are the concern of top management, whereas individual brands are primarily a concern of marketing management.

As the justification of the existence of a company ultimately rests with its customers and consumers, one would assume that the choice between corporate branding and individual branding would be based mainly on consumer behavior, but in reality a company's sense of identity is often so strong that this is what most influences its branding decisions. The values, vision, and convictions of the company senior management form the most important point of departure. It is not without reason that a great many brands are named after their founders' family names, such as Gucci or Liz Claiborne. See also Table 4.1 in Chapter 4.

Interaction Among Consumer, Labor, and Financial Markets

The choice for corporate brands is connected to assumed interactions among brand representations in the financial, labor, and consumer markets. Members of all these markets perceive the corporate brand from the point of view of their specific role and as citizens of society, but they combine both these outlooks, storing all the perceived information in memory and linking it to one and the same brand. Consumers are not only customers; they are also environmental activists and investors. They have become the largest shareholders of companies via their pension and investment funds and the share portfolios of their insurance companies. This creates an interaction among the various components of the corporate brand, influencing the functioning of this brand in the perceptions of people in these three most important markets.

Put simply, investors base their strategy partly on the familiarity of a brand, which is strongly influenced by its presence in the marketplace. When choosing a job, potential employees are also influenced by the saliency and attractiveness of a brand and its perceived financial performance. Haigh (1998) concludes from an English study that the financial market is paying increasing attention to companies' marketing policies. People are more aware that brands have a large influence on stock market values. For the Coca-Cola Company, the stock market value at the end of 1997 amounted to almost twenty times its fixed assets. The value of its brands accounted for 95 percent of the stock market value of the company.

Although not much research has been done on the interactions between the three markets, the individual perceptions and assumptions of the company's senior management play an important role in the formulation of brand architecture strategy.

There are three approaches: (1) a deliberate choice for the monolithic corporate branding strategy (the branded house strategy) based on assumed synergistic effects, (2) a deliberate separation between brands in the consumer market and the corporate brand (the house of brands strategy) based on what is known as the contrast effect: the risk that poor performance or an occasional fiasco in the consumer market will damage the position in the financial market and vice versa. A compromise can be reached by (3) the mixed approach, in which one or some of the product categories carry the corporate brand and the other categories an individual brand.

Rao et al. (2004) analyzed the relationship between the stock exchange performance of thirteen American brands over a five-year period and their managers' choice of one of these three branding strategies. The researchers' conclusions were that the monolithic corporate branding strategy correlated more positively with the stock value of the brands than the house of brands and mixed strategies. Referring to a study by Friedler and Subrahmanyam (2002) that showed that the perceived quality of brands and brand familiarity influence investment decisions, Rao et al. presume that the financial community has a better knowledge of corporate brands and feels more familiar with them, resulting in a more positive expectation of the future profit development of these companies.

Not every company is entirely free in this choice—a corporate brand usually needs a holding structure and the history of a company limits that freedom. Consolidated Foods, parent company of, among others, the Dutch coffee company Douwe Egberts, renamed itself Sara Lee Corporation, after one of its large consumer brands in the United States. The company is now known in the Netherlands as Sara Lee-DE (Douwe Egberts). The VMF holding company in the Netherlands traded its name for that of its most famous subsidiary and historical origin—Stork. Fortis, a financial holding that emerged out of the Amev Insurance Company, has replaced most of its bank brands (including Generale Bank, VSB, ASLK, parts of Mees-Pierson) by Fortis Bank. ING (Internationale Nederlanden Groep) replaced the NMB and Postbank banking brands, but continued other brands like Nationale-Nederlanden (insurances).

In contrast is the story of Nutricia, a leading European producer of baby food under the Nutricia brand, which renamed itself Numico. Klaas de Jong, one of the company's top executives, said that when the company experiences a product problem in Portugal, the Dutch press reacts with "Nutricia under fire," which causes mothers to worry unnecessarily about the Nutricia baby food and creates undesirable stock exchange fluctuations (*De Volkskrant* 1999c).

There are many examples of negative publicity surrounding corporate brands. Influenced by the failure of important product introductions, often poor financial results, and confusing reorganization measures, the image of Philips weakened in the European consumer market between 1968 and 1993 (Litjens 1996). Even in the Netherlands, Philips's home country, the image of Sony became more positive. As a result, on a bad day, the Philips stock exchange rate in the financial market has been known to drop under its intrinsic value.

Stock prices of Coca-Cola, the largest and strongest brand in the world, dropped from $87 to $52 (the level of late 1996) between mid-1998 and October 1999, a period when the sky was the limit for stock prices in the United States and Western Europe. This minicrash was the result of a ruling in Italy based on violation of antitrust laws, some children in Belgium becoming ill after drinking from contaminated Coca-Cola cans, and a ruling by French authorities to take over the soft drink producer Orangina. The pharmaceutical company Merck had to withdraw its arthritis and pain relief drug Vioxx from the market and was confronted with over a thousand legal challenges. Fortunately, Vioxx was not a corporate brand name.

Considering the all-prevailing interest that the position of brands in consumer markets represents for a company, managers must give extremely careful consideration to both opportunities and threats. The synergistic positive effects on sales, market share, and brand reputation, when things are going well can be very tempting. Unique talents are attracted by successful companies. Stock prices rise because investors expect even more success, and the image in the consumer market reacts along with all the positive news in the media. However, at some point in the life of every business, the wind starts inevitably blowing against it. A brand that once seemed unassailable (Philips, Coca-Cola, Merck, Nike) may be vulnerable nonetheless, and the negative publicity that breaks loose can seriously harm the consumer market image.

Principle: Monolithic corporate brands can be encumbered in their retail markets because of failure to perform in their financial markets, and vice versa.

House Brands and Division Brands

To avoid these risks, some companies deliberately separate their corporate brand from their consumer brands. The corporate brand (Ahold) is reserved for the financial markets; the division brands (Albert Heijn, Etos, Gall & Gall, Stop & Shop, Giant Landover, Tops) are used as house brands by the consumer and employee markets.

Division and house brands take an intermediate position between pure corporate brands and individual brands. Many of them were once corporate brands and now are the family or umbrella brands in the portfolio of the corporation. Fast-moving producers in the United Kingdom, however, see such brands as compromises (i.e., less successful) between the economic advantages of real corporate brands and the differentiation advantages of pure individual brands (Laforet and Saunders 1999).

Division and house brands offer more freedom in tactical adjustments to risky short-term trends that may negatively affect the corporate brand. They also make it financially feasible to carry out a brand strategy in product categories and product variants that represent by themselves insufficient sales potential for the financing of a brand operation.

Branded House Versus House of Brands

In corporate branding strategy, two extremes can be identified that Kitchen and Schultz (2001) call the "branded house" and the "house of brands" strategies. In the branded house, all activities carry the corporate brand; in the house of brands, the business units carry their own brands. Between these two extremes there is a continuum of endorsement from high corporate visibility to very low corporate visibility. Basically, four levels can be identified.

Branded House

1. Pure corporate branding: All activities carry the corporate brand. The corporate brand is highly visible and there is a high degree of identification of management and personnel with the corporate level. Brand management is the responsibility of the CEO. Headquarters makes all branding and communication decisions.
2. Corporate branding combined with sub-branding: The corporate brand still functions as the main brand and is highly visible. Useful sub-brands are added to represent specific business units, product categories, or domains. Business units tend to have a strong influence on brand management and communication.

House of Brands

3. Individual branding with corporate endorsement: The individual brands fulfill the function of main brand and wherever suitable the corporate brand is added at a secondary level as a seal of approval. It usually has a low degree of visibility. Branding decisions are made by the management of the business unit.
4. Pure individual branding: The individual brands stand-alone. Only when legally required or sensible from a consumer perspective are the company name and address added in small print to identify the legal sender. Branding decisions are the domain of marketing management.

Hybrid Branding Strategies

5. Combination of corporate and individual brands: Many companies choose to make one of their important brands their corporate brand. Coca-Cola for instance uses its Coca-Cola brand worldwide, but also has a number of individual soft drink brands, such as Sprite, Fanta, Minute Maid, Tab, Canada Dry, Powerade, Dasine, and 450 other brands in over 200 countries. Consolidated Foods; the parent company of Douwe Egberts switched to Sara Lee Corporation as its corporate brand, using its main individual brand in the U.S. also as its corporate brand. The Dannon brand represents both the corporation, and their yogurt brand, but Dannon also owns Lu, Evian, Kronenbourg, Volvic and a longer list of individual brands.

Individual branding gives each brand the opportunity to have its own unique identity, values, and personality and, therefore, to be positioned quite precisely in the target group's memory. Viagra is more precise than Pfizer. Moreover, if the brand is connected with a marketing disaster, the bad news does not influence the other businesses of the company. Corporate branding adds the same corporate identity, values, and personality to each product, limiting the possibilities of positioning them precisely. It gives them the insurance of quality and authenticity and it is expected to save on advertising and promotional spending.

There seems to be a positive relationship between these strategies and the intangible value of the company. The branded house model seems to lead to higher shareholder-value, possibly because of a higher perceived visibility within the financial markets. Many companies therefore choose to make one of their important brands their corporate brand, as Consolidated Foods did when switching to Sara Lee Corporation.

Perceived Risk

The consumer's perceived risk when buying a product or service plays an important role in decisions regarding the balance between corporate and individual brands. When there are high perceived risks, people have the need to know and trust the supplier. This is especially the case with business-to-business markets and when people purchase durable consumer articles. With services, due to the impossibility of prepurchase product evaluation, the emphasis lies strongly on the trust people put in the supplier. The trust in the corporate-endorsed individual brand is higher in the following circumstances:

- when the number of endorsed individual brands increases;
- when the individual brands have the same level of quality;
- when there is a clear connection between the individual brands;
- when consumers have an a priori trust in the endorser.

In particular, suppliers have to guarantee the consistency in an endorsement strategy. Quality principles play an important role in this respect (Jansen 1999b).

The choice of individual brands is most common in low-involvement consumer products when the choice process is extremely short and habitual and when the brand representation has to contain all the information that makes it possible to carry out the purchasing action with a minimum of cognitive effort. Chiquita bananas is an example.

When there is a conflict between the values underlying the choice of different products of a manufacturer, the choice for individual brands can be the best option. Toyota has deliberately not linked its corporate brand to its high-end cars, introducing instead the Lexus brand. Similarly, General Motors (GM) launched Saturn as a stand-alone car brand complete with its own dealers. (This strategy has since been changed as GM is now bringing Saturn into the GM brand stable, hoping that the car's good reputation will transfer back to the manufacturer and its family of brands.) A high-tech brand is probably better off introducing its low-tech products under a different brand.

Other Considerations

To analyze the factors behind the choice of a level of corporate versus individual branding, Riel (2003) developed the "Sidec" model, consisting of five consideration areas: strategic fit, internal organization, driving forces, environmental assessment, and corporate branding strategy.

1. *Strategic fit:* To what degree do the operational businesses augment or complement the parent company's strategy and thus make identifiable contributions to the parent company's financial and nonfinancial goals?
   - Is there complementarity in the scope of the activities among the company's various divisions?
   - Is there complementarity in the way in which the company's objectives are implemented?
2. *Internal organization:* To what extent are the cultural and administrative practices and the characteristics of the business units in harmony with the company's strategy?
3. *Driving forces:* Is there congruity between individuals and management concerning the values of the company? Do individuals identify with the company personally?
4. *Environmental assessment:* When business units operate in significantly different environments from other business units or from the corporate environment, a uniform corporate branding approach will likely be undesirable. The following questions must be answered:
   - Are there differences in the environment between business unit and corporate level, and between the individual business units?
   - Are there differences in how the parent company and the business units are regarded by the environment?
   - To what degree does the environmental forces want to know the company behind the business units?

For the Netherlands-based SWOCC research group, Cramer (2005) executed a meta-analysis of literature on factors that influenced the level of corporate branding, using the determinants found in interviews with managers from companies in the financial and temping markets in the Netherlands. Nine determinants, detailed below, were found to be the most important according to these managers:

1. *Employee commitment:* Although this factor was deemed very important, it was not related to a specific brand architecture strategy. Employees' commitment to their own, individual brand is equally desirable as commitment to the corporate brand.
2. *Functional fit:* Services that differ from the core business of a company are more often represented by an individual brand name (multibranding) than services comparable with core business.
3. *Symbolic fit:* Services that differ from the corporate values of a company are more often represented by an individual brand name (multibranding) than services fitting the corporate values (monobranding or endorsement branding).
4. *Segmentation:* When companies wanted to serve several segments, the corporate endorsement strategy was mostly used, thus gaining the advantages of both individual brands (differentiation) and the corporate brand (brand leverage).
5. *Brand association transfer to services:* If companies wanted to link corporate brand association to a service, they mostly used monobranding.
6. *Risk avoidance:* Negative reactions to an individual product or service can dilute the corporate brand and so spill over to other categories. Avoidance of such risks leads to the use of individual brands.
7. *Attracting employees:* This determinant did not lead to a specific strategy. On the one hand, presenting a firm by its corporate brand can provide a strong, reputable image. On the other hand, it can lead to an excessively broad, undifferentiated image.

8. *History:* Companies attaching importance to their historical roots more often used corporate branding or endorsement branding than individual branding.
9. *Brand association transfer between the corporate brand and the individual brand:* If companies wanted to link corporate brand associations to their individual brands, they mostly used endorsement branding.

Another important determinant mentioned by the managers was internal politics. The interviews showed that, in some of the companies, internal politics were sometimes more decisive than other influences. Internal politics often govern which brand portfolio and architecture strategy is used in organizations. Since internal politics are personal and situation-specific, they generally do not point to the direction of a certain brand architecture strategy.

ENDORSEMENT BRANDING

Endorsing literally means to sanction, approve, recommend, and add strength. It is a widely applied strategy that makes use of the strength of the main brand, whose name may appear inconspicuously on the back of the package, such as the name Bristol-Myers in small print on the back of a Clairol shampoo bottle, or be very much present visually, as is the Nestlé logo on the upper left corner of a KitKat package. Like corporate branding, endorsement branding is used to reduce consumers' perceived risk.

The literature tends to ascribe significant importance to the use of endorsement brands. However, research by Laforet and Saunders (1999) has shown that entrepreneurs in the British fast-moving consumer goods market ascribe little power to such brands. In general, they do not expect the subordinate referral to the company (or house brand) to have much influence on consumer choice and brand loyalty. The way endorsement brands are presented is illustrated by Unilever, which introduced a new visual brand logo, which it put on the back of all its products. Vindi Banga, its head of foods, said that Unilever was not trying to create a superbrand, and had no plans to give the Unilever brand prominence over its individual brands.

> Ten or twenty years ago, in an age where you might have product recalls or a brand might be damaged because of some issue, there would have been a school of thought that said you would be better off avoiding any connection being made between brands because if one. Unilever product has a problem consumers might think they all had that problem.
>
> In this day and age, we need to be open with our consumers and not try to hide behind brands. We need to stand up and say quite unashamedly, Yes all of these brands are ours. That does mean that occasionally there might be some downsides. But overall, I believe the benefits outweigh them. (Noonan 2001)

Unilever may no longer be hiding behind its individual brands, but it certainly is not yet using its corporate brand as a true endorser.

According to research by Riezebos and Alleman (1997), marketers are concerned about the potential negative effects of endorsements—that is, watering down the endorsement brand or causing a negative spillover on the main brand's image. Countering these concerns are the advantages of quicker acceptance of the endorsed brands by retailers and consumers, as well as lower financial risks. Most experts do not believe, however, that an endorsement strategy allows for a lower marketing budget.

Figure 15.3 **Cognitive Consistency in Endorsement**

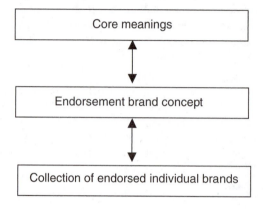

Conditions for Successful Endorsement

If an endorsement brand is to fulfill its function properly, a number of conditions should be met:

- The endorsement brand should be present in the memory of the target group and linked with clear meanings.
- These meanings should be relevant to the evaluation of product categories to which the brand is given.
- The endorsement brand should be part of the association network of the main brand (PlayStation is by Sony).
- The endorsement brand should be perceived on the package or on the product as it appears in the orientation and purchasing phases. For example, the Nestlé brand is very visible on Crunch, KitKat, and Lion candy bars.

Many endorsement brands do not meet these conditions and are therefore nothing more than a meaningless graphic element on the packaging of the main brand. In this case, what we have are "senders," or subordinate mentions of the producer. Lingens Blond and Kylian, for example, come from the Heineken breweries, but almost no consumers perceive this corporate relationship or have any idea who is behind these brands.

Cognitive Consistency

An endorsement strategy has to be based on the recognition that the individual brands belong to one family. Cohesion among the various product categories is therefore important. When the discrepancy between these categories is too great, uncertainty arises over the meaning of the endorsement brand. There should be a unity in diversity. In turn, the endorsed individual brands influence the meaning of the endorsement brand. This is the most important endorsement principle for Nestlé.

Cognitive consistency is thus the central concept behind the application of the endorsement principle. In an endorsement brand, the core meanings and the brands they are added to have to fit within this concept (see Figure 15.3). This is precisely the reason why Akzo Nobel links its logo to that of Sikkens (the world's largest coating brand), but not to that of Organon medicines (a leading producer of contraception brands and veterinary pharmaceuticals).

Formulating a strategy for endorsement brands is not always easy, among other reasons because the responsibility usually lies at the corporate level and is rarely linked to a function there. Another reason is that the principle of the definition of the endorsement brand concept is not understood. Likewise, safeguarding the consistency of the main brand with the endorsed brands is difficult. The balance in the degree to which endorser and endorsed brands should serve each other tends to lead to internal tensions, especially in decentralized organizations.

Individual brands are being used increasingly as endorsement brands: BonBonBloc praline chocolate by Côte D'Or, Mastro Lorenzo coffee by Jacobs, and Grape-Nuts cereal by Post are brought to the market by Kraft Foods. These individual brands usually have more concrete category meanings than the corporate brand and would therefore ensure better cohesion with the endorsed brands at a product level.

> *Principle:* The effects of the use of an endorsement brand depend on the strength of the brand, its relevance for the product category, and the perceptual saliency of the packaging or product.

DUAL BRANDING

An analysis of 400 brands in the food industry in the United Kingdom showed that in 50 percent of the products at least two brands were represented prominently in the packaging (Laforet and Saunders 1994). The function and meaning of each of these brands in the architecture depends on the nature and strength of the memory representations of each brand and on the perceptual saliency (weight) of each brand on the product or the packaging.

It is often difficult to determine what is the main brand and which is the sub-brand or endorsement brand. Therefore, we have come to speak of *dual brands*, more or less equivalent combinations of two different brands with each contributing its own specific meaning to the brand architecture. A dual brand can be two brands of the same company in which one represents provenience (Kellogg's) and the other a product capacity (All Bran). It can also refer to one specific domain expertise (Oral B for oral hygiene) combined with product expertise (Braun for small electrical appliances). The last two brands are the property of Gillette (now a division brand of Procter & Gamble), which in this case chooses to stay anonymous.

Mihailovic and Chernatony (1994) state that the strategic binding of a corporate brand with an individual brand can be one of the most powerful brand strategies that a company can consider. Mitchell (1993) agrees that two strong brands working together can accomplish more than each brand separately. Based on lab research, Saunders and Guogun (1996) also conclude that the combination of two brands is almost always assessed as better than the use of merely one brand as a stand-alone. They also believe that the exclusive use of a corporate brand or of an individual brand is at the very least a suboptimal possibility, given that in ever growing and changing markets consumers feel better with the totality of two brand values of a corporate name and a brand name than with each name separately.

The intended added value is reached not by the joint use of two brands, however, but through their holistic fusion. A duality has to emerge in the perception of consumers: Apple iPod and Ralph Lauren Polo are two examples. The strategy seems ideal, but the results depend on each brand's contribution to the perception of the combination. The question is, are the two brands more or less equally strong, and has a certain degree of symbiosis taken place through which the combination is perceived and experienced as a duality?

> *Principle:* In half of the products of the food industry, at least two brands are prominent on the packaging. Two powerful brands working together accomplish more than each brand separately.

One particular form of dual branding is what Kapferer (1992) calls "family name brands." This is the combination of a family name and a first name. Descendants of a family name brand have their own first names, but are linked to the dominating family spirit. The concept of a family name or mother brand is recognizable in each of the daughter brands. The brand Yves Saint Laurent is the mother brand of Rive Gauche, giving the daughter brand a distinction and cachet.

Another form of dual brands is co-branding, in which two brands of different companies are joined together. In the combination of Philips and Alessi, Philips represents the product technology and Alessi the design expertise. This dichotomy can make a difference, or even add confusion, to the consumer perception: is this a Philips or an Alessi product?

Adding an ingredient brand to a main brand can also be seen as a form of dual branding—for example, Hewlett-Packard with Intel Inside, Diet Coke with NutraSweet, or Haägen-Dazs with Baileys.

The strategic combination of a corporate brand and a category or domain brand can constitute a strong brand strategy. The domain brand represents the product-related meanings; the corporate brand contributes the company's competences and reputation—for example, Saturn and GM.

SUB-BRANDING

As the span of a main brand increases, its core meaning inevitably moves to a higher abstraction level. The information that lies enclosed in the memory representation of the brand thus answers to the information need of consumers during the evaluation and purchasing process of individual products but to a decreasing degree. On its package, for example, the brand Nivea says little about its specific contents. To balance this lack, the main or umbrella brand can be linked to a sub-brand, which in turn is linked to the additional product information needed. For instance, Vital is used as a sub-brand of Nivea for facial skin care products for mature skin.

Sub-brands tend to be used to specify the capacity of one or more products from the total product range under the main brand. Mach 3, which denotes a razor made up of three razor blades, is a sub-brand of Gillette.

A sub-brand is always related to something else—a main brand or master brand—and determining the nature of that relationship is a critical factor in brand architecture strategy. Most desirable is a master brand that encompasses a large number of sub-brands. For example, Microsoft is a powerful master brand that permits a variety of software and hardware extensions, including Microsoft Word. In contrast, WordPerfect, which preceded Microsoft Word and was a strong player in the word processing market, has fallen behind because its master brand is much more limiting than Microsoft's and has had a harder time evolving in the software market (Hirsch 2003).

Sub-Brands or Direct Extensions

Research by Jun et al. (1995) found that a combination of two brands with mutually complementary meanings is assessed more positively than when the same product is introduced as a direct extension of one of these brands. A sub-brand is assessed differently than a direct extension of the main brand because the additional brand changes the saliency (prominence) of the main brand.

When a main brand is insufficiently consistent with a new product variant or category, a greater perceptual saliency can lead to a less positive evaluation. By adding a sub-brand, the saliency of the main brand can be reduced, whereas the sub-brand can activate tentative product expectations that would not come up if only the main brand was used (Sheinin 1998). In a good fit between brand and extension, the prominence of the main brand should be increased and direct brand extensions are a good choice. In a weak fit, the saliency of the main brand has to be reduced by adding a sub-brand. Sub-brands thus tend to be necessary for extensions that do not fit well within the main brand concept.

When a new product is added as a direct extension to a main brand, the product perceptions can influence the perception of the main brand and its other related brands, a factor referred to as the "halo effect." Sometimes this is a positive relationship and sometimes it is negative. Hirsch (2003) explains this strategy this way: for some product audiences the sub-brand is an extension of the master brand (Apple Macintosh), but for others it is the brand (iPod). Toyota introduced the Lexus and GM introduced the Saturn with the positive halo effect in mind. In both cases, the parent car company wanted a more positive or different association for the new car model than the parent brand could confer and therefore disassociated itself by using separate dealerships and downplaying the brand ownership. As their success evolved, both car makes reflected positively back on their parent companies. Saturn brought a sense of quality production and consumer focus to GM, and Lexus brought a more upscale orientation to Toyota.

When the extension is not sufficiently consistent with the main brand, it can damage that brand. This is known as a backward negative association transfer toward the main brand. This happened to Apple when it introduced the Newton handheld electronic business assistant. The effect seems to be especially damaging when the quality perceptions of the extension remain behind those of the main brand. Deploying a totally unrelated sub-brand can therefore reduce this risk. Sub-brands act as a necessary buffer when an extension is inconsistent in some way and to a certain degree with the meaning of the main brand.

A sub-brand does remain a brand, though. Just like the main brand, it has to be present in the memory of the target group and be linked there with relevant meanings. It is not just a product indication described in plain language. As a result of insufficient communication budgets, many sub-brands languish in the shadow of the main brand, with only minor visibility and weak associations (Farquhar et al. 1992). They have a hard time competing with main brands that are solidly associated with their corresponding categories or subcategories.

Countless misunderstandings have occurred as the result of a lack of clarity in the meaning of sub-brands. In the Netherlands, the sub-brand Boncafé as a coffee variant of Douwe Egberts led to constant problems in its functioning because the exact meaning of Boncafé was not clear. Only when it was replaced by Mildcafé did the product communicate clearly to Dutch consumers.

In the United States, Kohli and La Bahn (1997) studied the goals that drive companies when developing new brand names. Most respondents seemed to be of the opinion that a new brand name had to say something about the product. Communicating the product positioning (61 percent) and establishing product differentiation (41 percent) and a clear product segment (41 percent) were by far the most important goals. Supporting a distinguishing image (20 percent) followed at quite a distance. No major difference appeared between consumer products and industrial goods.

> *Principle:* For a good fix between the main brand and a new product, a direct extension tends to be a good choice. In a weak fit, a sub-brand can reduce the saliency of the brand and activate the desired product expectations. Still, a sub-brand is only a brand to the degree that it is present in the memory of consumers and linked with the relevant meanings.

Sub-Brands or Generic Product Names

The balance between using a sub-brand or a generic product name usually tilts toward the second option for economic reasons. In the Dutch market, the sub-brand Roerbakmix (stir fry mix) is dominant on the new Honig packages, although the brand Honig itself has been moved to the upper left corner as a mere endorsement brand. Especially in subcategories with relatively low sales, it is nearly impossible to develop a sub-brand with its own consumer equity. A compromise is often found by introducing a sub-brand with an autonomous relevant linguistic meaning, but imitation from the competition never lags far behind. Here we can illustrate with examples from the Dutch market: Mildcafé was followed by a competitive product Milde Koffie, and Unilever's flavoring mix Aardapel Anders (Potatoes Differently) preceded the competitor's Aardapel Idee (Potato Idea).

Choosing a sub-brand over a more generic product indication as an addition to the main brand can result in a greater perceived unity. The iPod has a much stronger identity and suggests more unique associations than a name like, say, MP3 Player. A sub-brand can be so strong that it acquires a meaning that deviates from the main brand but hardly lags behind in intensity of experience in the process. The Volkswagen sub-brand Golf has practically become an independent main brand, perfectly illustrating the concept of dual brands.

Several interconnected brands thus have a link to a product or series of products within the brand architecture. Leaving out product specifications of a more descriptive nature, which are used to distinguish product variants from one another, no more than three elements are usually involved—a main brand, a sub-brand, and an endorsement brand. The character and strength of each brand's contribution to the combination can vary, as well as the degree to which they are mutually associated in memory.

A brand communication strategy should possess clarity regarding the relative influence of each architectural element on the perception of consumers and their choice decisions. Many marketing problems are the result of faulty estimates in this area, especially in the introductory phase of new product-brand combinations. Marketers tend to underestimate the investments necessary to develop a new brand or sub-brand and to have excessive expectations about the influence of an endorsement brand.

POSITIONING THE MAIN BRAND IN THE BRAND ARCHITECTURE

The most important questions in brand architecture are which brand serves or should serve as main brand and to what degree this brand is associated with the endorsement brand above it and/or the sub-brand under it.

Consumer perception plays a role here. When there is a high degree of involvement and extensive attention toward external sources of information, the use of three or more levels is not usually a problem. Young people do manage to find out what Nike Alpha Project Air Cross Trainer

II means. Things are different in a supermarket, where the contents of the shelves must become clear within a few seconds. Here the maximum number of levels would be two and, perceptually speaking, both levels should be sufficiently salient in order to be perceived together.

What is often missing, too, are the financial means to develop sufficient familiarity and meanings at three levels. This is another reason there is a trend toward reducing the number of levels. A generic product name is added to the main brand, as in Kellogg's Frosted Flakes or Kraft Macaroni and Cheese. In the introduction phase of a new brand, the endorsement brand is strongly emphasized until the new brand is strong enough to stand on its own—for example, Gillette's Mach 3 or Nabisco's Oreo (now owned by Kraft).

In the United States, Kellogg's and Post follow two different strategies (Keller 1998). Kellogg's works mainly with the combination of main brand and sub-brand, whereas Post prefers the endorsement principle. In a study into the provenience of ten breakfast cereals, in 86 percent of all cases Kellogg's brands were correctly attributed by consumers to Kellogg's, with only 44 percent for Post brands. Insight into brand strength and the nature of consumers' responses to the various elements of a brand architecture is a precondition for a solid communication strategy.

Blurring the Main Brand

When too many sub-brands are added to a main brand, it becomes difficult for consumers to remember all those additions and their meanings. The brand risks losing clarity. Farquhar et al. (1992) suggest that companies should focus on brand competencies, given that even a large umbrella can cover only so many items. This is the risk that Virgin faces with its use of the Virgin name across so many disparate categories. At this point, the brand maintains an identity based on its strong graphics and the personality of Branson, which lends personality to the various products. But the connection can be tenuous and the result could very well dilute the meaning of the Virgin brand if these product category extensions slip away from the core iconoclastic personality.

Product-Brand Associations

Brand associations from specific goal-related cues (product category, attribute, application, etc.) have a great influence on whether a brand is taken into a consumer's consideration set or not. If a brand wants to take an important position in a market or market segment, a strong association with the most important choice cues toward the brand is a precondition. This is about the relative strength of the associative connection from the goal-related cues toward brands as against each other. Which brands come to mind first when consumers think of mobile telephones, white beer, or healthy margarine? As we discussed in Chapter 13, activating brands in long-term memory and their entry into consciousness is a process that takes place largely outside a person's conscious control.

Only where brand and product fall together, as in the monobrands, is the strategy choice a given. In brands like Head and Shoulders, KitKat, Rolo, Philadelphia, and Post-it, the question of which product-brand association to develop does not arise. That question does become an immediate issue, however, when the brand has to represent several product variants. When, in addition to its regular premium Pilsner beer, Grolsch introduces a beer with a lower alcohol content (2.5 percent instead of 5 percent), the question immediately arises regarding the degree to which the association "light beer equals Grolsch 2.5 percent" has to be developed. And when Camel, originally associated with a flavorful, nonfiltered, plain cigarette, wanted to build a market share in the segment of light filter cigarettes, its brand managers had to ask themselves what needed to be added to the brand's association network, and to what degree?

Volkswagen Phaeton or Volkswagen Phiasco?

Of all European car brands, Volkswagen (VW) is seen as the most sympathetic. Its values are classlessness, openness, authenticity, humanity, clarity, and good quality. Its product range starts with a small car, Lupo (Fox), and until a few years ago ended with the midsize Passat. The name Volkswagen means "people cars," and that is what the brand represents—an absolute mainstream brand.

What made VW decide to develop a premium-end model that would enter into direct competition with Europe's most prestigious brands such as the Mercedes C-class, the BMW 740, and the Audi A8? The answer is unclear, but that is what the company attempted to do with the launch of the Phaeton. Some 700 million euros were invested in the development of the car, and for another 200 million euros, a state-of-the-art transparent glass plant was built for it in Dresden.

The Phaeton was unveiled at the Geneva Motor Show in 2002. It was priced at almost 100,000 euros. The company announced that it expected to sell 30,000 units a year. The model met admiration by the automotive media. Journalists driving the Phaeton agreed that it was a magnificent machine. But at the same time they expressed doubt that people who can afford to pay 100,000 euros for a car would buy a Volkswagen. Why had Volkswagen not chosen to sell the car under one of its own prestige brands, such as Audi, Bugatti, Bentley, or Lamborghini?

The answer seems to be that VW hoped that the Phaeton would enhance the image of its other models, underscore their high quality, and allow the company to increase its price premium. But the Phaeton was not a success. Sales forecasts were soon scaled back to 15,000 a year and then to 10,000. The results in the United States were particularly disappointing—Phaeton sold only seventy units per month. In 2005 the company decided to terminate Phaeton sales in America altogether. And it postponed the plans for development of a midsize luxury car.

Sources: www.wintonsworld.com; www.automobile.com; Hofmann (2004).

The problem gets more complex with domain brands. When Nivea, originally an all-purpose cream for skin care, developed into a master brand with an ever-extending series of body care specialty products (Nivea Body Care, Nivea Visage, Nivea Sun, Nivea for men, Nivea Shower and Bath, Nivea Hair Care, Nivea Deo), managers had to consider carefully the consequences that might arise for the development of product-brand associations.

In multidomain brands, like Samsung and Philips, these are usually very difficult strategy choices. Managers generally rely on the familiarity and reputation of the brand, trusting that they will be a sufficient precondition to make a brand extension into a success. This strategy, however, tends to lead to problematic situations in markets where the category association is dominated by other brands. Philips, for example, faced competition from Braun and Nokia in its attempts to sell electric toothbrushes and mobile phones. Depending on the company's ambitions and goals when entering new markets, a communication strategy will have to be created that is aimed at developing and strengthening the specific category-brand association.

Image Factors

Brands are perceived in relation to the products and services to which they are linked. The capacity of those products and services has an influence on the abstract (symbolic) meanings with which the brand is associated. Depending on the intended image, the effect can be positive or negative.

Products that reflect to a large degree what the brand wants to stand for can fulfill a flagship function. Products that cannot be reconciled with the intended core meanings of a brand can cause damage. An example of a flagship product is the swing-top bottle of Grolsch, symbolizing the authentic, old-fashioned image of the brand. In contrast, Grolsch cans could influence this image negatively given that they stand for factory-made products. The segment of 45/50-centiliter bottles under which the Grolsch swing-top bottle falls has been under pressure for decades. There was an initial shift toward the thirty-centiliter cork bottle, and more recently can sales have increased significantly. The question of which variants have to be communicated with which strengths cannot be easily answered in such situations.

Also, symbolic associations can limit the possibilities to extend a brand to product categories with conflicting meanings. A car brand that is primarily associated with small, popular cars will not easily be linked to values such as prestige and status, as Volkswagen experienced with its Phaeton prestige model.

MANAGING THE COMPLEX NESTLÉ BRAND ARCHITECTURE SYSTEM

Nestlé is an organizational nightmare for any brand architect who might be hired to bring order to the company's huge stable of brands. Nestlé company has a number of key products identified under its ten worldwide corporate brands, another set of products are grouped under its forty-five worldwide product brands, and then there are thousands of local brands. In terms of architecture, this is probably the most complex brand system in the world and the one with the widest product span.

And, of course, Nestlé is a powerful corporate brand in its own right, and, since 40 percent of the company's sales come from products identified by the Nestlé brand, this corporate brand structure is crucial to the success of the Nestlé empire. Nestlé brand management, therefore, has to decide what brands carry the Nestlé name—as well as any of the key corporate or product brand names. Or is the product a strictly local offering that justifies having an individual brand name unrelated to the Nestlé strategic brand structure? And if the product is offered under the Nestlé name, will it support Nestlé's position, associations, and image—or blur the Nestlé brand?

In addition, for the individual brands, is there a need for Nestlé identification at all? If so, how is this multiple layering of brand names handled? What is the appropriate balance between the corporate and individual brand names and identities? When is it a good strategic decision to launch or maintain a distinctive brand personality for an individual brand? These questions are complicated by the globalization trend that sees previously local brands moving to a global stage.

This Nestlé story demonstrates that there are no easy answers or simple rules for the construction and management of a modern system of global brand architecture. We learn most from the experience of managers like former Nestlé CEO Peter Brabeck-Letmathe, who is willing to share his company's experiences and strategies, such as the use of a Nestlé Seal of Guarantee to connect Nestlé with freestanding brands such as Buitoni.

CHAPTER 16

CONSUMER BRAND EQUITY

Development of the brand phenomenon affects not only the consumers' mental brand, but also, and more important, at any rate for the marketer, the observable behavior related to it—the continued purchase of products and the use of the services connected to the brand. These concrete behaviors lead to sales, market position, profits, and growth.

Logically, marketers' interest is very much related to the strength of their brands, usually referred to as *brand equity,* and to the observable economic consequences of branding, referred to by the financial community as *brand value.* In this and the following chapter, we will discuss the brand equity concept first in terms of the consumer and then in terms of the marketplace. In Chapter 17 we will tackle brand value. To understand brand equity and the impact it has on brand value, consider the story of Ivory Soap.

IVORY FLOATS ABOVE IT ALL

In Victorian times, the benchmark for quality soap was the highly expensive Castile bar—a pure white soap from the Mediterranean that was made from the finest olive oil and imported in small quantities by merchants who carried only the finest products.

The average household soap was made from lye and fats. In rural areas of the United States during the 1700s and 1800s, it was generally made at home by women using their fireplace ashes and cooking grease. It was a soft, jelly-like, yellowish soap that would clean things adequately, but if it fell to the bottom of a pail, it dissolved into mush. A harder soap could be produced by using soda rather than ashes, but soda had to be purchased and was more prized for cooking than cleaning.

William Procter and James Gamble, who emigrated to Cincinnati, Ohio, from Ireland and England in the 1830s, became partners in a candle-making operation. Fats and ash were by-products that the company used up by making bars of soap. A formula was discovered that finally produced a uniform, predictable bar of soap. During the Civil War, the company provided wooden boxes of these yellow bars to both armies, thus bringing the uniformity of mass production to this household product and opening up a huge market when the soldiers returned to their homes with a demand for the soap bars.

But the bars were still yellow and they still sank to the bottom of the washbasin. Procter's and Gamble's sons, who were college educated and interested in research, hired a chemist to develop a white bar that would be the equivalent of the legendary castile bar. In 1878, after three years of work, P&G White Soap was invented.

It was a modest success initially, and then, the story goes, P&G started getting requests for "the soap that floats," which made no sense to anyone in the front office. Apparently one of the workers had gone to lunch without turning off the beaters that whipped the ingredients together, and the extra whipping added enough air to make the bars lighter than water. So someone who dropped the soap into a pail of dirty water or a pond or river would be delighted to have the bar pop to the surface. The production accident led to one of the world's greatest statements of a product benefit—"It floats." However, P&G historians maintain that James N. Gamble made the discovery himself, in 1863. He wrote in his diary: "I made floating soap today, I think we'll make all our stock that way."

In 1879 a Procter cousin attending church was listening to the scripture "All thy garments smell of myrrh and aloes and cassia out of ivory palaces" when it struck him that Procter & Gamble White Soap should be renamed Ivory Soap, an inspiration that led to one of the world's greatest and most enduring brand names. At the time consumers simply went to the store and asked for soap—soap was soap. But Ivory was different because it was white, it was wrapped in a package to keep off the dust from the grocer's shelves, and it had a name. Ivory Soap marked the beginning of individual brands.

Harley Procter, a cousin of the founders' sons, was determined to match the quality of the legendary castile soap. Turning again to chemists, he asked them to determine the purity of both Castile and Ivory. This research determined that the total impurities in Ivory amounted to only 0.56 percent, which actually was lower than the Castile bars they tested. By turning that percentage to a positive, Harley came up with a purity rating of "99 and 44/100 percent pure," which became one of the most famous slogans in branding history.

Sources: Adapted from Goodrum and Dalrymple (1990) and Crain (1998).

Brand equity is a hugely important factor in determining the financial health of a corporation. Analysis of Equi Trend's studies by Total Research Corporation showed that firms experiencing the largest gains in brand equity saw their return on investment (ROI) average 30 percent; those with the largest losses in brand equity saw their ROI average a negative 10 percent (Petromilli and Morrison 2002a). For that reason, we will focus now on the financial contributions of a brand to a firm's financial position.

THE FINANCIAL VALUE OF A BRAND

The reason brands, particularly superbrands such as Ivory, are important to companies is that they add value for their owners, as well as for their customers. But what is that value and how is it determined?

In economic terms, the answer is that a brand affects the demand side by making it possible to charge a premium price for the product. Furthermore, a well-known brand establishes a huge barrier for other companies wanting to enter that market. The brand affects the supply side by increasing business opportunities as the brand is stretched across related products and categories. But how does this add to corporate value? Does a brand really add anything that the financial side of a company can enter on a balance sheet?

In 1989 Philip Morris paid $12.9 billion for Kraft. In financial terms, this was six times the value of the company's tangible assets. So what was being purchased that justified this inflated price? The answer is the intangible value of the Kraft brand, what it represented to its customers, its suppliers and distributors, its employees, its shareholders, and others that had some reason to value it—that is, its field of value. Philip Morris CEO Hamish Maxwell explained that his company needed a portfolio of brands that had strong brand loyalty that could be leveraged to enable the tobacco company to diversify into the retail food industry. In other words, Kraft's customer loyalty, as well as the investor, financial, and trade relationships tied to the brand, created the intangible value that led Philip Morris to pay billions more for Kraft than its physical assets could justify.

Another example of the value of a brand was observed in 1996 when the initial public offering (IPO) for Donna Karan International, a popular designer of women's and men's upscale clothing and accessories, opened at $24 and immediately jumped to $28. The IPO generated over $250 million; however, the shareholders did not own assets other than product inventories, because there was no physical company. The Karan company is not a manufacturer. *Barron's* magazine described the parent Karan company as "an originator and purveyor of image." The IPO investors did not even own the brand name or trademark, both of which were retained by the parent company. They invested over $250 million in a licensing agreement to use the Donna Karan name; in effect, the shareholders were "renting" Karan's brand equity.

Like Donna Karan, Nike, one of the world's most recognized brands, does not exist as a company with tangible assets, other than offices. Everything is outsourced; the Nike company itself does not manufacture anything. Nike is a marketing machine whose sole purpose as a company is to protect and expand the Nike brand. Given Nike's status as a superbrand, we can only conclude that there must be a great deal of equity in the Nike brand franchise, an equity that may be so valuable that it is actually inestimable (Aaker and Biel 1993; Haigh 1997; Duncan and Moriarty 1997a). These are just a few examples of major companies in which brands became a financial asset.

Brand Equity

Brand equity is a measure of the strength of a brand that impacts the financial contribution the brand makes to the parent company's balance sheet. It represents the intersection between the marketing and finance disciplines and, as David Haigh (1997), CEO of Brand Finance explains, "It supports the notion that branding is a creative practice that, if done successfully, generates financial returns for companies and their shareholders."

In ways that go beyond brand image or brand identity, brand equity represents the point at which the company objectives converge with customer interests. As Haigh observes, "A brand is what the customer buys. Brand equity is what the company owns." He also points out that brand equity includes all the brand description factors of image and identity, as well as the components subject to brand measurement

Figure 16.1 **The Power Grid**

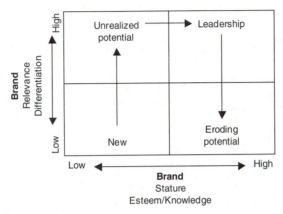

Source: Consult Brand Strategy (2004).

(price elasticity, demand volume, purchase frequency, attitude or awareness levels, repeat sales, share of category, etc.) and the way these factors combine to create or predict brand monetary value.

Y&R's Four Pillars of Brand Equity

Chapter 4 introduced the building of brand equity as the primary function of branding from the company's perspective. There are a number of ways to analyze the building blocks of brand equity. The approach used in this book separates the components into two big categories—consumer-focused brand equity, discussed in this chapter, and market-focused brand equity, discussed in the chapter that follows. But, first, let us look at the "four pillars" approach of the Y&R advertising agency.

The advertising agency Y&R uses a brand equity research instrument, the Brand Asset Valuator, to assess the development of strengths and weaknesses of 20,000 brands in forty-four countries. The Brand Asset Valuator shows that successful brands are developed over time based on four pillars. Each pillar is derived from various measures that relate to different aspects of consumer brand perception. These pillars are:

1. *Differentiation:* Measures the degree to which the brand is seen as different from others. It states the brand's reason for being.
2. *Relevance:* Measures the appropriateness of the brand to the individual consumer. The differentiation must be relevant to consumer needs and wants.
3. *Esteem:* Measures how well the brand is regarded and respected. In short, it measures how well the brand is liked.
4. *Knowledge:* Measures how familiar and intimate consumers are with the brand. It measures how well established the brand is.

Combining differentiation and relevance provides a measure of brand vitality. Brand vitality can be seen as a measure of the brand's potential for growth. Combining esteem and knowledge provides a measure of brand stature. Brand stature indicates the current strength of a brand. Brand vitality and brand stature have been integrated into the PowerGrid (see Figure 16.1).

The PowerGrid depicts the stages in the cycle of brand development—each with its characteristic

Figure 16.2 **The Concept of Brand Equity**

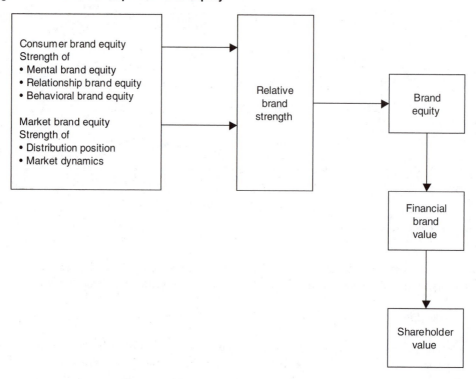

pillar patterns in successive quadrants. The grid provides a clear snapshot of a brand's health. A brand generally begins its life in the lower left quadrant, as the brand differentiates itself. As the brand develops relevance, its brand vitality increases and it rises into the area of unrealized potential. As brands develop brand stature, they move into the leadership area of the PowerGrid. The strongest brands can be found in this quadrant. Successful brands that fail to maintain their vitality will decline to the eroding potential area. Brands can decline even further, eroding both brand stature and brand vitality, becoming unfocused and ultimately fading from consumers' consciousness.

A Systems Model of Brand Equity

Based on our analysis of the complexity of brand systems, we have identified the critical components of brand equity as (1) customer-focused, meaning mental, relational, and behavioral factors, and (2) market-focused, meaning distribution position and market dynamics. These categories of brand equity components are summarized in Figure 16.2. Brand equity, then, represents the strength of a brand and gives insight into the degree to which a brand performs (scores) in these five critical areas compared with competing brands.

1. *Mental brand equity:* A network in people's memory that consists of everything a person associates a brand with including brand cognition and brand evaluation. The mental brand is related to brand behavior and vice versa.
2. *Relationship brand equity:* Relationship brand equity is about the emotional connection

between a consumer and a brand, partly on the basis of acquired experiences: "What does it mean to me? How important is it to me? Does the brand know me?"

3. *Behavioral brand equity:* Behavioral brand equity is the conscious or unconscious repeat purchase of a brand in response to category need. The average share that a brand assumes in its category need is the share of customer (share of requirements, share of wallet). Behavioral brand equity thus has two basic components: brand penetration (the percentage of category users that buy the brand with some regularity) and the average share of customer. Buyers can be classified into three levels according to share of customer.

4. *Distribution position:* Distribution position refers to the position of the brand in the shops. In-store marketing, category management, and trade marketing are all directed at getting a better position within retail outlets. Issues like weighted distribution, shelf position and number of facings, promotion, and retailer testimonials all affect the relative situation of the brand. Over time, distribution position has gained in importance, and it is now an important driver of brand equity.

5. *Market dynamics:* Market dynamics refers not only to the brand's market share, the seasonality of its market share, sales, and value, but also to such things as price elasticity, media elasticity, and the brand's vulnerability to competitor activities. Penetration, sales, turnover, market share, and price premium are observable developments in market position. Market dynamics is an independent driver of sales, and size itself is a driver of brand equity.

These components identify the primary factors that drive the establishment of a brand's financial value. These five areas of brand strength are the ones that brand managers must concern themselves with if brand equity is to develop effectively and sufficiently to meet the company's business goals.

They also are a set of interrelated systems. The goal of strategic brand development is to strengthen the position of a brand in all five areas. The systems through which a brand operates cannot be disconnected from one another: fundamental strengthening in one area will permeate into the other areas over time. Within each of these five components, we can distinguish sublevels, which are summarized in Figure 16.3.

Brand development efforts can result in strengthening the competitive position of the brand in all five areas or in weakening its position. Based on the components of brand equity as distinguished above, brand equity development can be described as a positive or desirable change in these five areas leading to a stronger competitive position. This is expressed not only in an increase of sales, income, and return on investments but, ultimately, in the financial value of a brand.

Brand Assets

In all five-brand equity areas, characteristics can be specified that determine or influence the competitive position of the corresponding brand in that area. The characteristics of a brand that have a positive effect on its competitive position are called *brand assets*. They are the drivers of brand equity. An asset is something that a company owns, or has rights to, that has future economic benefit. Webster's dictionary (Gove 1993) defines it as "a quality, condition, or entity that serves as an advantage, support, resource, or source of strength." Brand assets are the sources of brand equity.

1. *Mental assets:* The part of the network of brand meanings and emotions in the memory of consumers that has a positive effect on purchasing behavior.

2. *Relationship assets:* The network of personal relationships among stakeholders, as well as the relationship of customers to the brand (loyalty).

Figure 16.3 **The Components of Brand Equity**

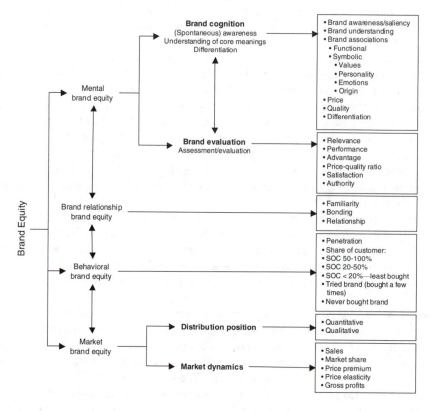

3. *Behavioral assets:* Characteristics of consumer purchasing behaviors that determine the market position of the brand.
4. *Distribution assets:* Characteristics of the distribution position of a brand that determine the opportunity to buy the brand.
5. *Market assets:* Characteristics of a market position of a brand that determine its financial-economic results, market share, price premium, and price elasticity.

People may have an endless number of associations with a brand in their memory. Not all associations from such a brand associative network are equally relevant for consumers with respect to their brand-related needs. Brand associations differ in status as to the degree to which they are related to choice and purchasing behavior. The associations that have a positive relationship with purchasing behavior and that constitute the drivers of brand equity are called *mental brand assets.* They form the basis of mental brand equity.

Research has shown, for example, that the brand Heineken is strongly associated with the attribute "international," but that the attribute plays no role at all in the assessment or valuation of the brand in its home country—the Netherlands. Brands can also be associated with advertising campaigns or slogans that have no bearing on their evaluation. In short, people can have many associations with brands but do not come close to using all these associations to the same degree as criteria for their evaluation of the brand. The associations that play a main role here are called mental brand assets. They are those brand associations on the basis of which the brand competes

Figure 16.4   **Three Brands in a Random Mental Category**

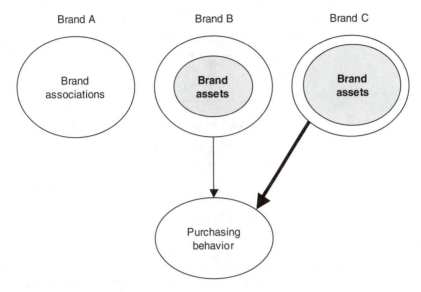

with other brands for the preferential position in the memory of the consumer. These are the perceived advantages of the brand in relation to other brands in the (mental) category.

To determine to what degree a brand has mental assets and what these are, the relationship between brand attributes and choice (behavior) has to be established. There can also be negative assets—those associations that are evaluated negatively and become reasons not to buy a brand. The influence of brand associations in the choice behavior can vary from negative to neutral to strongly positive, as depicted in Figure 16.4.

- Brand A is a brand without mental assets; none of its brand associations present in memory has a positive influence on purchasing behavior; there is no "internal motivation" for the behavior. The result is a very weak or absent mental brand equity.
- Brand B is a brand with some limited mental assets and its brand meanings have a positive influence on purchasing behavior.
- Brand C is also a brand with mental assets. Compared to the competing brand B, the assets of this brand have a stronger relationship with behavior. The mental brand equity of brand C in this example is the strongest.

MENTAL BRAND EQUITY

Brand cognitions are about the presence of the brand name in long-term memory and the concept of what the brand means, in essence—"What does it stand for?" Brand evaluation is about the assessment of the brand based on its core meanings—"What do I think about it?" Brand relationship is about the mental connection between a consumer and a brand, partly on the basis of the experiences the customer has with it—"What does it mean to me? How important is it to me?"

Mental brand equity is related to those elements of the memory representation of a brand that influence the choice behavior of consumers. Mental brand equity is not the same as the memory representation or the image of a brand—it has to do with the strength of the mental brand assets.

Figure 16.5 **Basic Dimensions of Mental Brand Equity**

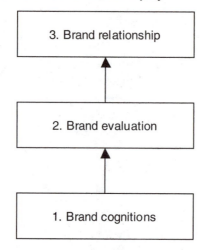

Although in some sense there is a hierarchy of effects among these three levels, it should strongly be emphasized that there is also an interaction. In the next section we will elaborate further on each of the three basic dimensions (Figure 16.5).

Brand Cognitions

Cognition is about the awareness of a brand and the notion of what it basically stands for—its core meanings, or the core concept, as discussed in Chapter 5. Figure 16.6 illustrates these aspects of brand cognition.

Brand Awareness

The awareness of a brand refers to the presence of the brand name and other features of the brand in long-term memory and the ability of consumers to bring them to consciousness—for example, after a market researcher asks, "Which brands of margarine do you know?" An important factor is the relative intensity (saliency, strength) with which a brand is present in memory, manifest in the interval of time between the question and the arrival of the brand in consciousness, as well as in the ranking the brand takes among other activated brands (does it come up first in consciousness, or second, third, etc.). In research terms, this is called top-of-mind awareness, which represents total spontaneous awareness and average ranking (see, e.g., Franzen and Bouwman 2001). Measurements of relative spontaneous brand awareness give a good indication of the saliency of a brand—that is, its prominence in memory. Regarding mental equity development, the saliency of a brand name is important, but what is more essential is the understanding of what a brand stands for—the brand meaning.

Brand Understanding

Research carried out with different measurement instruments (Agres and Dubitsky 1996; Flores and Walker 1999; Dyson et al. 1996) indicates that understanding of the brand concept has to be in place before the brand representation can be of influence to purchasing behavior. Under brand concept we understand the collection of core meanings that determine the categorization and

Figure 16.6 **Brand Cognitions**

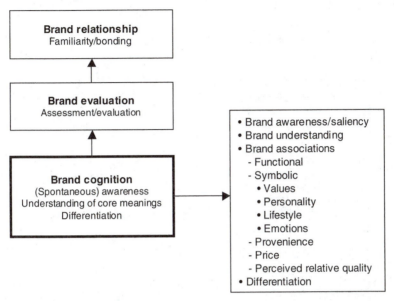

positioning of the brand in memory—those meanings based on which a brand wins a position in the brain of the consumer against competing brands. The quality (in terms of saliency, relevance, and evaluation) of the core meanings determines the quality of the brand position. It is a precondition for the existence of a brand and an important factor for the successful introduction of new products. People will not easily buy a brand if they have no idea what it stands for.

Principle: To influence purchasing behavior, the core meanings of the brand have to be identified, understood, and recognized by customers.

Brand Associations

The types of meanings that form the core of the brand representation differ from brand to brand, even between brands within the same category. Based on these meanings, different types of brand concepts can be distinguished (see Chapter 5). The most important meanings are these:

- *Functional meanings*, such as the categories a brand is associated with, the product characteristics, and applications.
- *Symbolic meanings*, such as associations with brand personality, values, and emotions.
- *Provenience and history*, such as associations with the history of the brand, where it comes from, who is standing behind it. This also includes the organization's associations.
- *Price* as against alternatives.
- *Perceived relative quality*, which is the quality perception of the brand in comparison with other brands. It is a general impression about the brand that directly influences purchase decisions and supports a premium price. It has a proper impact on the profitability of the brand.

Figure 16.7 **Brand Evaluation**

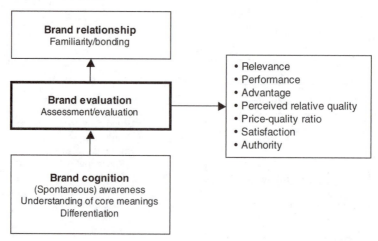

Brand Differentiation

A fourth aspect of brand cognition has to do with uniqueness—that is, the differentiation of a brand and the degree to which it distinguishes itself from similar brands, as described in Chapter 8 on positioning. In various brand equity measurements, uniqueness comes forth as the most important equity driver. Differentiation is the basis of the success of new brands and of their claim to existence in the long term. However, many new brands that do get high scores for differentiation seem not to be experienced as relevant because consumers do not understand, identify, or recognize what the distinguishing characteristics can mean to them (Agres and Dubitsky 1996).

In this context, a distinction should be made between descriptive and evaluative brand attributes. Descriptive attributes are those that can be highly specific for a certain brand but are of little influence to its evaluation (for example, "Saab is Swedish"). Evaluation attributes imply an evaluation of a brand ("Saab is stylish"). Evaluation attributes imply an evaluation strongly correlated with the use of a brand, while descriptive meanings tend to be more or less present to the same degree in users and in non-users. Descriptive attributes have little predictive capacity for the brand choice. They can be distinguishing, but brands are not evaluated on these attributes. Evaluative attributes, on the other hand, have a "what do I think about it" character. Blackston (1995) makes a distinction here between the *objective brand*, which contains the meanings over which there is a broad consensus, and the *subjective brand*, which answers the question of what makes the brand valuable for a specific person.

Theories of attitude development—for example, Fishbein (1967); Fishbein and Ajzen (1980); Ajzen and Fishbein (1975)—are based on the claim that the attitude regarding an object is based on the salient experiences related to that object's core meanings in our terminology. The strength with which people cling to these salient experiences is relevant. The evaluation of salient experiences is the third component of attitude models.

Brand Evaluation

The core meanings of a brand are evaluated by consumers in the light of personal needs, goals, values, and convictions. The very first consideration concerns the degree to which the brand is relevant in light of these evaluative criteria (see Figure 16.7).

Figure 16.8 **Connection Between Core Concept of the Brand and Consumer Needs**

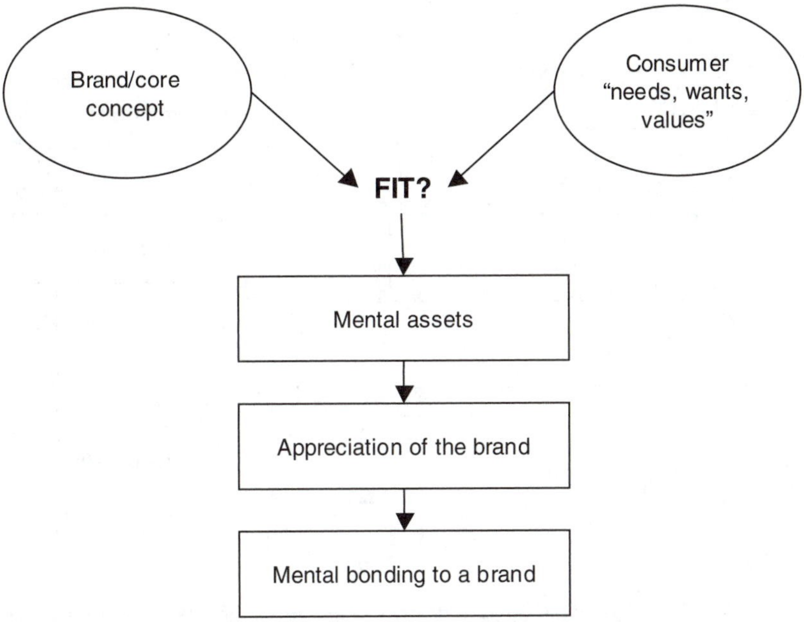

Source: Based on Dyson et al. (1996).

A brand is experienced when a logical connection is observed between the core concept of the brand and the needs, goals, and evaluative criteria of the consumer (this is illustrated in Figure 16.8). Of those brands people know fairly well, nearly half are seen as irrelevant (Dyson et al. 1996). In addition, a clear relationship has been established between relevance scores and the penetration of brands (Agres and Dubitsky 1996). Brands that have managed to achieve a high level of perceived differentiation in combination with a high level of relevance are the most successful. They often define the category or subcategory.

The alternative brands within a category are tested according to the evaluative criteria and a relative evaluation is formed. This is not an extensive cognitive process, but rather a superficial evaluation that usually takes place implicitly.

Ego involvement plays an important mediating role here. With product categories that have a minimal meaning for an individual, evaluation goes no further than establishing whether an alternative possesses the sought-for characteristics. In cases of high ego involvement, as in the choice of clothing or cars, comparison of the alternatives can be more rigorous, but this is more an exception than the rule.

Principle: A brand is experienced as relevant when the core concept answers to the evaluative criteria of consumers.

Brand equity research shows that the following aspects and factors also influence brand evaluation:

Figure 16.9   **Hierarchical Connection Between the Basic Dimensions of Brand Equity**

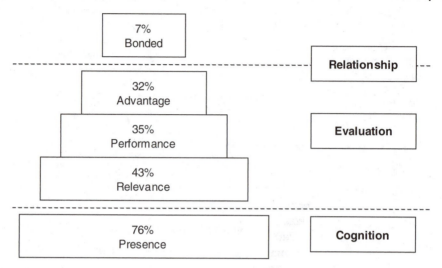

Source: Dyson et at. (1996).

- *Brand performance:* How does the brand perform in light of the most important choice criteria? This question relates to every function that is expected from a brand. For some brands, it is about the functional performance of a product, for others about the symbolic meanings of the brand, and so on. Perceived product performance remains an important driver of brand appreciation. Many brands that find themselves in trouble can attribute their problems to the lack of innovation at a product level.
- *Brand advantage:* How does this performance rate compared to that of other brands? Are they better, the same, or less good?
- *Brand price quality ratio:* What is the ratio of quality assessment against the price of the brand? In research instruments this ratio is generally translated into a question of the degree to which a brand offers its money's worth. Together with the willingness to pay a higher price for the brand, it is an important result of this brand evaluation.
- *Brand satisfaction:* Are people satisfied with the performance of the brand in its use?
- *Authority and respect:* How reliable is the brand and do people respect it? This evaluation goes together with a perception of high quality and of leadership. It indicates how highly a brand is valued and is mainly a characteristic of winning brands. Young brands do not get high scores here yet.

Relationships Between the Dimensions of Mental Brand Equity

It is generally assumed that there is a hierarchical relationship between the basic dimensions of mental brand equity. Research by Millward-Brown using its consumer value model for brand equity measurement (Dyson et al. 1996; Millward-Brown 1995) supports this hypothesis. Figure 16.9 shows that the average scores for presence (a combination of spontaneous brand awareness and understanding of the brand meaning) amount to 76 percent, while the average score for bonding (when the brand is the only accepted one) only amounts to 7 percent. These factors can be explained as follows:

Figure 16.10   **Span and Depth of Mental Brand Equity**

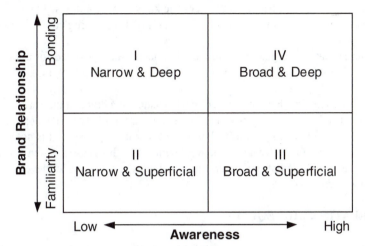

- *Bonded:* A brand is the only one accepted by the consumer.
- *Advantage:* An evaluation of the degree to which the brand represents a unique proposition in a functional or symbolic sense, in combination with direct questions related to uniqueness, supremacy, and level of enthusiasm.
- *Performance:* An evaluation of the performance of the brand article compared with the competition.
- *Relevance:* An evaluation of the degree to which a brand answers to the core criteria of the consumer (functional and/or symbolic) and the degree to which its price is acceptable.
- *Presence:* A factor constructed on the basis of spontaneous awareness, remembered trial use, and active understanding of the brand promise.

Span and Depth of Mental Brand Equity

A span and a depth dimension can be distinguished in the development of mental brand equity. The span dimension is the percentage of persons in the market who know the brand and who know what it means. The depth dimension relates to the percentage of people who have a certain degree of bonding with the brand. Brands can be typified on the basis of the span and the depth of their mental equity. Insight into the position of a brand with regard to both dimensions can provide a focus for marketing and communication activities. The diagram in Figure 16.10 is an abstract representation of this concept.

- Quadrant I in this figure represents strong segment and niche brands; they are known to a relatively small portion of the market, but their users are characterized by a relatively high degree of bonding. Examples are Illy, the Italian brand of espresso coffee, and Ben & Jerry's ice cream.
- Quadrant II includes starting brands and weak segment and niche brands; not many consumers in the market know the brand yet, and the consumers who know it do not yet feel bonded to it. The cholesterol-lowering spread Benecol illustrates such brands.

- Quadrant III includes the broad (well-known), but superficial brands, such as Kmart, Keds tennis shoes, and Buick cars: everyone knows them, but few have a feeling of deep mental bonding with them. They have lost their distinguishing capacity and are often on their way out.
- Quadrant IV has the large, strong brands that have usually existed for a long time already (Tampax, Ray-Ban) and the winning, upcoming brands (Diesel, Nokia).

It is important to realize that the scores or performance of a brand at the various levels of mental brand equity can be partly category-specific. People are unlikely to develop a deep emotional involvement with a brand of light bulbs, but when a service organization is not standing behind its brand, it can be a sign of weakness or weakening. For this reason, when formulating goals for mental equity development, marketers should always consider which levels are feasible and desirable in the corresponding category.

BRAND RELATIONSHIP EQUITY

When consumers evaluate brands, they can take two different perspectives: a performance perspective and a relationship perspective (Raggio and Leone 2005). In the performance perspective, consumers tend to draw on the product attribute information stored in memory (e.g., how well a brand of detergent cleans or whitens) and how these attributes give rise to certain benefits. In the relationship perspective, consumers tend to focus on the brand as a whole and what it means to them. Raggio and Leone found that a combination of favorable impressions based on a high-level relationship perspective is needed to achieve high brand equity.

As described in Chapter 7, the brand relationship has to do with the feeling of mental bonding of the consumer with the brand. The way the relationship is personally experienced by consumers is influenced to some degree by their perception of the evaluation of the brand by important others. This influence can be summed up in the concept of the social norm. The two factors do not equally influence behavior in relation to a brand. In some categories, such as products that are used in an intimate atmosphere, behavior is based predominantly on personal evaluation and feelings in relation to a brand. In other categories, such as brands that are socially visible—watches, drinks, clothing, cars—the perceived evaluation by others plays a larger role.

The personally experienced relationship can vary from very superficial to very deep, from awareness to a truly felt relationship. Figure 16.11 gives an overview of the elements of brand relationship, which are explained below.

Brand Familiarity

A great deal of research (Rindfleisch and Inman 1998; Chavda and Cary 1999; Ahlers 1997; Davenport and Hallward 1999) shows that familiarity stands out as an important aspect of a brand relationship. Familiarity varies from mere "bare name familiarity" to a feeling of extreme psychological closeness. Brands that reach high levels of familiarity also attain high scores for appreciation and preference. Familiarity is one of the explanations for the permanency of so many old brands that have managed to keep their prominent place in society for generations. It is also an explanation for the difficulty that many young brands have in being accepted as a full alternative. People know about them, but have not yet become familiar with them. These brands need more time.

Figure 16.11   **Elements of Relationship Brand Equity**

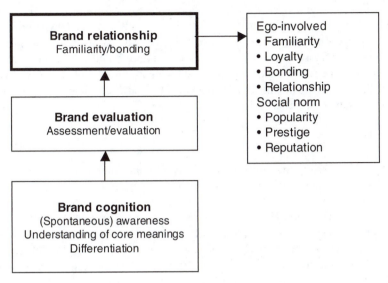

Principle: Familiarity is about experiencing psychological closeness to the brand. It is one of the explanations for the permanency in society of many long-established major brands.

There are three levels in brand familiarity: brand loyalty, brand bonding, and brand relationship.

- *Brand loyalty:* Brand loyalty is a deeply felt commitment to buy the brand on an ongoing basis in the future, as a result of which the brand is repurchased, despite situational influences and competitors' efforts to enforce brand-switching behavior. Brand loyalty has an attitudinal as well as a behavioral aspect. Brand commitment forecasts future brand buying behavior (Oliver 1999).
- *Brand bonding:* When customers perceive goal compatibility between themselves and a brand that they use, they may develop a degree of emotional bonding to that brand. They may use the brand to add meaning to their lives. This bond often has the character of a one-sided connection—the brand itself being passive.
- *Brand relationship:* Customers may enter into a true relationship with a brand. For such a relationship, interdependence between the person and the brand must be evident: the brand has to assume an active role—and the consumer should recognize this role. As discussed in Chapter 12, Fournier (1998) has developed six facets that define the quality of the person-brand relationship: behavioral interdependence, love and passion, nostalgic connection, intimacy, self-concept connection, and partner quality. These six facets may lead to a certain level of commitment where the consumer intends to improve and maintain the relationship over time. The consumer feels guilty when the relationship is compromised—in extreme cases, not accepting of any other alternative. Research by SWOCC in the Netherlands on the basis of Fournier's relationship measurement instrument (Tolboom 2004a) showed that only a very limited percentage of brand users have developed a true relationship with their brand.

Familiarity, commitment, bonding, and brand relationship lead to the inclusion of a brand in the consideration set of consumers and the degree of preference that is achieved within it. An analysis of the market leaders in the English markets of tea, coffee, toothpaste, and margarine showed that, on average, 36 percent of those who consider such a brand would only buy the market leader. For the second brand, the figure was 22 percent, and for the third brand 17 percent (Farr 1996). It is the consumers who are really bonded to the brand who are responsible for its market position. They form the motor behind the distribution position of a brand, which is again greatly influential on the choice of indifferent, noninvolved category buyers.

Social Standing

The bonding or relationship that users experience with their brand is influenced by the brand's social standing, which includes such factors as popularity, prestige, and reputation.

- *Brand popularity:* Sociologists started looking long ago at the fact that there is such a thing as social phenomena. In other words, there are human behaviors that do not allow themselves to be reduced to individual manifestations of the will, but which develop on the basis of perceived social desirability. People have a strong tendency to adjust their behavior to what is usual in their environment for classmates, friends, family, or colleagues. They even tend to make concessions to their own evaluations. In the chapter on saliency, it became clear how great this influence is on choices such as beer brands. In much brand equity research, this perceived popularity also comes forth as a very important driver of brand equity. This seems to be the most important characteristic in large, established, successful brands. In brands that are foundering, it is mainly the perceived popularity that seems to be receding (Meer 1999). As can be expected, this factor plays a less important role with small brands, as they depend more on their distinctiveness.
- *Brand prestige:* In addition to perceived popularity, the prestige a brand is associated with is an important factor whose role is more relevant with some smaller brands. Here the idea is not adjustment to the social norm, but impressing important others in the surroundings. It is the rationale behind brands like Cartier and Gucci.
- *Brand reputation:* Brand reputation can be defined as "the overall value, esteem, and character of the brand as seen or judged by people in general" (Chaudhuri 2002). It is a separate construct from brand attitude and plays an intervening role in the effects of brand advertising on market share and relative price.

BEHAVIORAL BRAND EQUITY

Behavioral brand equity is the conscious or unconscious repeat purchase of a brand by consumers to meet their category need. The share that a brand assumes in the category is the *share of customer* (also called *share of requirements*, *share of wallet*). Behavioral brand equity thus has two basic components: the penetration of the brand (the percentage of category users that buy the brand with some regularity) and the average share of customer.

- *Penetration:* Penetration of a brand is of paramount importance for its sales and market share. An analysis by the Leo Burnett advertising agency of the relative influence of penetration and buying frequency on volume growth showed that on average 75 percent of volume growth is attributable to penetration growth and 25 percent to an increase in buying frequency. For

Figure 16.12   **Classification Into Three Levels**

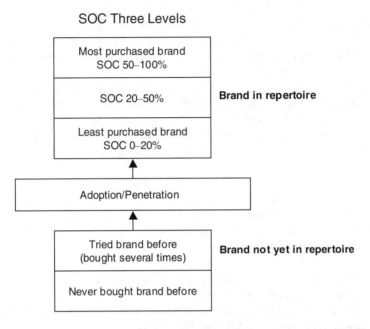

small brands, these figures are 95 percent and 5 percent respectively. The more penetration increases, the more also the buying frequency increases (Sylvester et al. 1994). Anschuetz (1997) concludes that penetration leads to a higher purchase frequency, a higher percentage of heavy buyers, a higher share of customer, and a higher market share. Within a given marketing budget, maximizing the penetration is a condition for maximizing profitability.

- *Share of customer:* The buyers of a brand can be classified into the level of their share of customer, as discussed in Chapter 7 on market segmentation. A classification into three levels is common (see Figure 16.12).

Chapter 7 on market segmentation explained how the share of customer correlates with the size (penetration) of a brand, but to a limited degree also contributes independently to the market share. In the United States, NPD/Nielsen (Johnson 1991) followed the development of the share of customer of fifty brands over a period of fifteen years (1975–1990) and determined that it can increase and decrease considerably, chiefly as a result of marketing decisions. The most important finding was that the average share of customer over this period had slightly declined, but that this decline was much smaller than was generally assumed—on an index basis from 100 to 92. Seen per brand, the changes were important indeed: in twenty-six brands, the share of customer grew or stayed equal; in twenty-four brands, it declined. The connection with important developments in the marketing mix of the brands was then looked into.

Here are the main conclusions of Johnson's research:

1. Where the share of customer declined, the decline tended to be caused by the manufacturer's own strategies (such as increased segmentation or reduced advertising support relative to category expenditures), not by any underlying behavioral changes in consumer purchasing behavior.

2. Most marketers' conception of share of customer (brand loyalty) was that on average it had decreased significantly. This was not true, at least among historically important brands. It was the marketing perception that was wrong.

3. Smaller brands were not apparently living up to the historical standards of the brands used in this study. For major, historical brands, the decline in brand loyalty (share of customer) was apparently not inevitable.

4. While promotion expenditures were growing tremendously, they were not adversely affecting brand equities that were being effectively supported by manufacturers.

5. Switching generally took place within a consumer's traditional repertoire of brands, thus leading to no sizable change in their overall share of customer. These trends also affirm that there was still such a thing as strong brand equity.

Johnson hypothesized that promotion is in no way a strategic marketing tool. Instead, promotion is basically a tactical pricing tool, although it can have other uses, such as purchasing distribution, purchasing facings on the shelf and special displays, or tying in with selected marketing strategies and programs. Put another way, instead of an advertising-and-promotions budget, a marketer should consider two separate budgets:

- *a long-term strategic budget:* an equity-building budget, focused on advertising and a few selected, consumer-oriented promotions;
- *a short-term tactical budget:* a promotional budget, tied into pricing and aimed at managing the amount of sales revenue at different price levels.

Promotions should not be considered a business-building expenditure but rather part of the income equation—specifically, how much price reduction is acceptable to meet volume needs and to respond to localized situations. Thus, in this framework, the promotion expenditure is simply a short-term business response tool that employs very little more than tactical price reductions to control where the brand is priced on the traditional economics demand curve. Brand equity protection and development remain marketing issues involving product development, communication, positioning, imagery, product characteristics, and packaging. Most promotional expenditure is not a part of this side of the equation.

Trial Rate and Repeat Rate

Repeat purchases of a brand (Figure 16.13) are preceded by a "check-out" stage. In fast-moving consumer goods, this takes the form of repeated trial purchases. The success of a brand (or a brand extension) is largely determined by two factors:

- The percentage of category buyers that try out a brand (*trial rate*).
- The percentage of buyers that remain after one or several trial purchases and thus include the brand in their repertoire (*repeat rate*).

Principle: Behavioral brand equity consists of the percentage of buyers who buy the brand with some regularity and the share the brand reaches in the purchase of these buyers.

Figure 16.13   **Repeat Purchases After Introduction of a New Product**

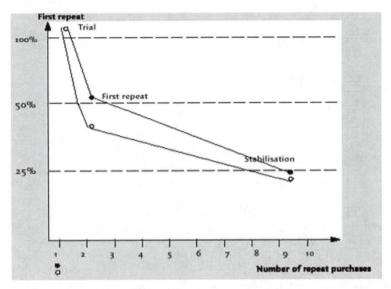

Source: Ernst & Young/ACNielsen Bases (1999).

Table 16.1

Development of the Percentage of Buyers

	Percent
First purchase	100
Second purchase	50
Third purchase	33
Fourth purchase	25

Source: Ernst & Young/ACNielsen Bases (1999).

Analysis of more than 1,000 product introductions by ACNielsen Bases in Europe has shown that, even in the most successful introductions, about half of the consumers who bought a new brand/product combination do not buy it a second time (Ernst & Young/ACNielsen Bases 1999). About one-third of the consumers who do buy a second time do not repeat the purchase, leaving only one-third of the original trial buyers. Of these, about one-quarter make no fourth purchase. This process goes on until after the eighth purchase another 5 percent of the remaining buyers fall through (see Table 16.1).

The trial rate is very much determined by brand awareness: there is an almost linear relationship between these two variables (see Figure 16.14). The second variable of great importance to the trial rate is distribution (see Figure 16.15). For both variables, doubling the scores leads to a doubling of the trial rate.

Research into the underlying variables that determine the success of new brand-product combinations brought forth three important factors:

Figure 16.14 **The Relationship Between Trial Rate and Brand Awareness**

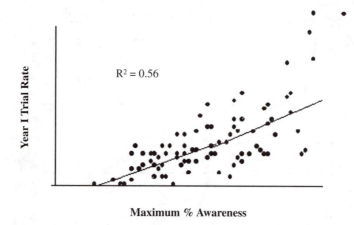

Source: Ernst & Young/ACNielsen Bases (1999).

Figure 16.15 **The Relationship Between Penetration and Distribution**

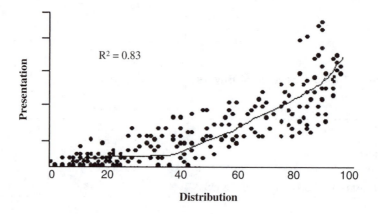

Source: Ernst & Young/ACNielsen Bases (1999).

- *Concept liking:* Obviously, the quality and relevance of the product idea play an important role. Weak concepts tend to be unsuccessful.
- *Product performance:* There is a very strong relationship between the repeat rate of new brand-product combinations and the perceived product performance during the trial phase.
- *Long-term support:* Premature reduction of support is one of the most important causes of the lack of success of nearly 80 percent of product introductions in the first year: 43 percent fail fully within one year, 37 percent try to keep up (see Figure 16.16). According to Information Resources Inc., only one in seven introductions succeed. Of the 700 yearly introductions in everyday consumer articles, only 200 remain in existence after one year (29 percent) and only 130 (19 percent) after two years (Stroeken 2001).

Figure 16.16   **Success Ratio of Brand Extensions, Line Extensions, and Me-toos in Western Europe**

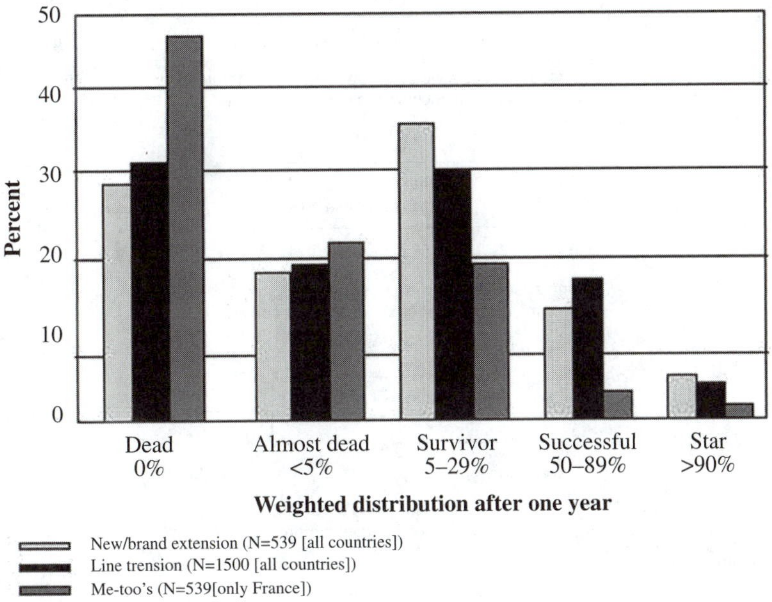

Weighted distribution after one year

New/brand extension (N=539 [all countries])
Line trension (N=1500 [all countries])
Me-too's (N=539[only France])

Source: Ernst & Young (1999).

Principle: Of those consumers who try a brand at some point in time, only about 25 percent are left after four purchases.

The fact that, of all trial buyers of a newly introduced product, an average of only 25 percent stay on is by far the most important explanation of the low market shares of most brands. The predominantly low brand loyalty also plays an important role. In Chapter 7 we saw how the share of customer of brands in the fast-moving consumer goods categories averages between 25 and 30 percent. The ultimate consequence of a low penetration and a relatively low share of customer of most brands is that the sales of a brand become mainly dependent on a small core of loyal customers.

INTERACTION OF MENTAL, RELATIONAL, AND BEHAVIORAL BRAND EQUITY

In brand equity research, it is necessary to establish the relationships between mental relationship and behavioral responses and to follow their development. Especially in the introduction stage of new brands or extensions of existing brands, it is important to establish the degree to which the brand has succeeded in taking on the most important hurdles, repeated trial use and adoption in the brand repertoire. The ATRB model (awareness, trial, reinforcement, bonding) describes the development of the mental and behavioral response at an individual level with purchasing behavior as point of departure (see Figure 16.17).

Figure 16.17 **From Awareness to Bonding**

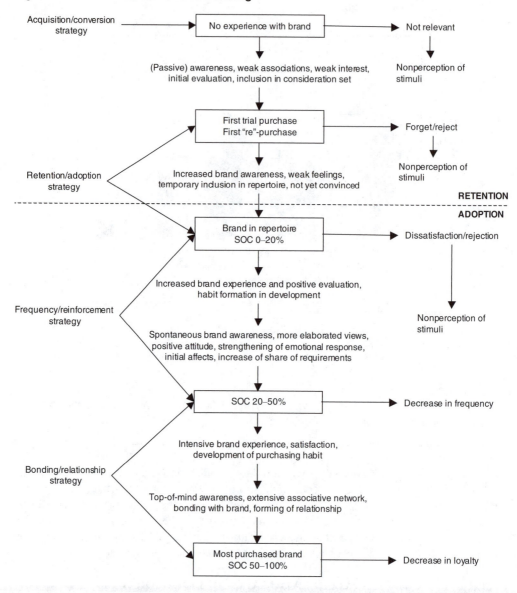

Consumers developing into loyal buyers of a brand or brand extension move through a series of stages in which mental and behavioral variables interact. Consumers gradually move from having no experience with the brand, and probably only weak associations with it, to buying the brand for the first or second time, developing increased awareness and weak feelings. The consumers may temporarily include the brand in their repertoire. Subsequent purchases of the brand and increased usage experience may lead to an increase in positive feelings and tentative habit formation. Gradually, through more elaborate brand knowledge and a strengthening of emotional response, a stronger positive attitude may develop, and the customers may give the brand a larger

Table 16.2

Connection Between Financial SOC and Mental Brand Equity (in percent)

	Consumer share	Average SOC
Bonded	7	38
Evaluation		
Advantage	32	20
Performance	35	19
Relevance	43	17
Presence	76	13

Source: Millward-Brown (Dyson et al. 1996).

Table 16.3

Connection Between SOC and Bonding (in percent)

Degree of bonding	Share of customer
Bonded	81
Loyal	69
Hesitant	45
(Near)-leaver	30

Source: Research Surveys Inc. (Hofmeyr and Rice 2000).

share of their category requirements. Finally, the consumer may develop an intense bonding or even a relationship with the brand and buy it more often than any alternative brand.

This process may also terminate along the way as a result of the forgetting process, less positive usage experiences, or the appearance of new, possibly more attractive alternatives.

From the brand strategist's point of view, segmenting the target market according to these mental and behavioral stages and tracking the awareness, attitude, and share of customer levels will help allocate resources in one of five basic strategic directions:

1. an acquisition strategy
2. a retention/adoption strategy
3. a reinforcement/frequency strategy
4. a bonding/relationship strategy
5. a winning back strategy

For a large number of brands whose equity is measured with the consumer value model, Millward-Brown (Dyson et al. 1996) established a correlation between the financial share of customer and the various levels of mental brand equity (see Table 16.2). Hofmeyr and Rice (2000) also established a correlation between commitment scores and share of customer for brand users in two product categories in nineteen countries (see Table 16.3).

The research company IPSOS-ASI also investigated the relationships between mental brand equity (BE), behavioral BE, and market performance (Hallward 2001). An analysis of 350 different brands in seventy-five different categories in Canada showed a strong and exponential correlation between mental and behavioral BE (see Figure 16.18).

Figure 16.18   **Relationship Between Mental and Behavioral Brand Equity**

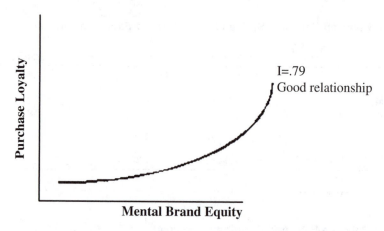

Source: IPOS-ASI (Hallward 2001).

But not all brands with good mental BE earn a high behavioral BE nor perform well in market. Brands with uncompetitive high pricing and brands that are highly substitutable experience weaker behavioral BE. Especially, some old brands had good mental BE, but tended to lose their uniqueness. Such brands need to invent a unique differentiating feature or benefit, such as a new product form or package format. IPSOS found a certain order of effects in building behavioral and market BE.

1. Brand familiarity, understanding what the brand stands for and is about, is the first step. It is the price of entry. Many brands with high aided awareness have below-norm scores of familiarity.
2. As familiarity increases, relevance becomes key. It contributes most to purchase loyalty and market BE. It is the key dimension that differs the most between users and non-users of the brand.
3. Uniqueness or differentiation is somewhat important but is the lowest factor for equity overall. Too much uniqueness correlates negatively with purchase loyalty.
4. Value is key, not costs. Overall price has little to no correlation with purchase loyalty. It is value that makes a brand competitive.
5. Actual product performance is most important—it has the strongest correlation with overall BE scores. It drives relevance and quality.
6. Popularity helps when all else is equal—it correlates with purchase interest.
7. Price affects familiarity and popularity—it makes a brand more approachable and easier to try. This boosts familiarity.

These findings show a high correspondence to the findings by Millward-Brown with its consumer value model (see Figure 16.9).

Principle: There is a strong correlation between mental brand equity and behavioral brand equity.

Table 16.4

Market Share Development

Market share classification	Number of brands	Decline	Equal	Growth
Large and weak	15	8	4	3
Large and strong	14	1	5	8
Small and weak	41	4	35	2
Small and strong	4	1	2	1
Total	74	14	46	14

Source: Millward-Brown (Farr and Hollis 1997).

Brand Size and Brand Strength

Brand equity measurements provide insight into the strength of the brand responses at a specific frozen moment in time. Ehrenberg et al. (1997) and Ehrenberg and Uncles (1995, 1996, 1999) point out constantly that the market share is an adequate measure for brand equity because it expresses the connection between penetration and share of customer. They add that the share of customer is influenced by the double jeopardy phenomenon: large brands are large because they have more users, who also buy these brands a little more often. In these researchers' vision, there are only large and small brands, and not a division between strong and weak ones.

Insight into the status quo of a brand is important for brand strategy development, but the sometimes small movements in the equity of a brand and its competitors are more interesting. After all, it is those movements that can indicate long-term growth or strengthening possibilities.

Millward-Brown (Farr and Hollis 1997) analyzed the relationship between the scores with the Brand Dynamics equity measurement instruments and the changes in market shares for seventy-four brands in the United States and the United Kingdom. Sixty-two percent of the brands had a stable market share, 19 percent showed decline, and another 19 percent showed growth. There was growth in only three of the forty-five small brands. In eleven of the twenty-nine large brands the market share increased; in nine it decreased. This evidenced a clear relationship with the brand equity scores.

So in addition to large and small brands, strong and weak brands do exist.

In the view of Millward-Brown, strong brands distinguish themselves by a relatively high conversion from awareness toward evaluation and bonding. In weak brands, a low conversion takes place: they are much less successful in converting their awareness into bonding. A parenthesis should be made here to point out that conversion can only be properly determined by time sequences. Farr and Hollis (1997) arrived at their conclusions by comparing individual brands with a category average. This analysis shows once again how difficult it is for small brands to be strong too. Only one of forty-five small brands presented a "high voltage" that also led to growth of the market share (see Table 16.4).

Brands can win or lose market share gradually, reflecting their strength or weakness. As we have seen, most brands see only small changes per year, usually no more than 0.5 to 1 percent. Seen over a longer period, small changes can lead to more dramatic ones. In the early 1980s, the brand Heineken had a market share in the Netherlands of 45 percent, which decreased in subsequent years at a steady pace of about 1 percent per year. By 2003, Heineken's market share had dropped to 22 percent. Next to large and small brands, there are strong and weak brands indeed, in the sense of growth or decline: Heineken used to be large but not strong, so it was vulnerable.

Figure 16.19   **Mental Brand Equity Development Phases**

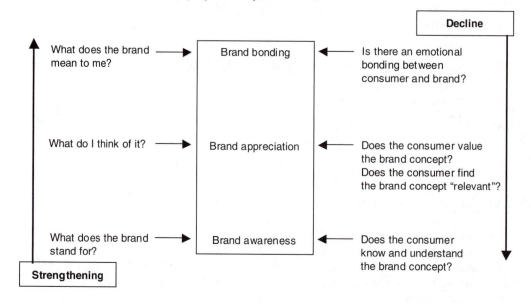

STRATEGIES FOR BUILDING CONSUMER BRAND EQUITY

The two main goals of brand strategy are: (1) strengthening the brand representation that results in an increase of the mental equity, and (2) strengthening the purchasing behavior patterns. This leads to behavioral equity. Insight into the way mental and behavioral equity interconnects as part of a brand equity system constitutes the basis for effective strategy development.

Brand Development Phases

We have seen the hierarchical relationship between brand cognitions, brand evaluation, and brand relationship. Without ignoring the interactions between these dimensions, we can also see them as three theoretical brand development phases, which are summarized in Figure 16.19.

1. *Knowledge phase:* People get to know a brand name and other distinguishing features. At first they may not have an image of what these features mean. For the proper functioning of a brand, consumers need to understand exactly what they can expect from it and how it distinguishes itself from comparable brands: "What does the brand stand for?"
2. *Evaluation phase:* Based on the brand's core meanings, consumers implicitly evaluate whether the brand fits individual needs and values: is it relevant to the person? It is tested based on the person's own evaluation criteria and compared with similar brands: "What do I think of it?"
3. *Relationship phase:* A relationship gradually arises between person and brand. This relationship can take on the character of familiarity, as something that is just part of life;

it can be experienced as a degree of emotional bonding with the brand; or it can lead to a feeling of a strong emotional relationship, as is the case with Harley-Davidson riders (see Chapter 10): "What does the brand mean to me?"

Mental brand equity is not a static fact; it is subject to constant change. From the very beginning, brands go through influences that contribute to their strengthening and/or decline. There is a clear parallel with the development of living things, which go through a cycle of birth, development, growth, adulthood, decline, and death. Many authors have posited that, contrary to the product life cycle, there is no such thing as a brand life cycle. In an absolute sense, this is correct: in the case of brands there is no law of nature that says that their life is finite or that a brand always achieves adulthood. Brands are products of human activity and as such are manageable to some degree.

This does not preclude the development of brands from being subject to a process of strengthening and decline, as Figure 16.19 illustrates. Within this process, bare name awareness is the first condition that has to be met, and a mental, as well as emotional, relationship between people and the brand is the ultimate value that can be achieved. The degree to which a brand succeeds in having consumers flow from one level to the next is an important indication of its strength. This is expressed in the brand equity scores at the aggregated level.

A Typology of Mental Brand Equity Strategies

Brands can be classified on the basis of their performance scores at the various mental equity levels. An analysis of Millward-Brown (Farr 1999) of the scores of 3,500 brands based on a Brand Dynamics measurement instrument produced seven brand types. It is partly on this basis that we distinguish the following eight types of brands.

1. *Beginners.* Beginning brands are those still at the early stages of their brand equity development. These can be brands that have been introduced recently (such as Tarly, a precooked wheat product introduced in the Dutch market by Honig) or brands that have already been in the market but have not yet succeeded in earning a steady place in the minds of consumers (like Daewoo). They are characterized by low spontaneous brand awareness, the lack of clear core meanings, and accompanying low scores for distinguishability. At this stage, few people value them positively or find them relevant. Their sales depend very much on push activities.

2. *Upcoming brands.* Upcoming brands are those that have succeeded in earning a solid basis in the memory of consumers. They mostly owe this place to their distinguishing characteristics, which allow them to keep attracting attention from more involved category users. Their spontaneous brand awareness is advanced and on the rise. Increasing numbers of people have learned what they can expect from these brands, experiencing them more and more as relevant and evaluating them as interesting and positive. The mental bonding is not large yet, but it is growing. Relationships are burgeoning, although we cannot speak of a deep bonding at this point yet. These brands are in an ideal situation for further positive development. The brand strategy should focus on strengthening brand awareness and an understanding of the core meanings. It may be necessary to make clear how these brands can contribute to the lives of the users. These brands also have to increase their trustworthiness. If they fail to reduce the physical distance, further growth remains difficult. The position of such brands can be vulnerable, as threats to further development often come from the

inside. Premature withdrawal of the communicative support can cause development stagnation, and the brand will slip behind again. These are brands that demand investments. Examples from the Dutch market are Lingens Blond beer and Coolbest fruit juice.

3. Winners. Winners are brands that have succeeded in earning a prominent position in their category. They are usually the brand (or one of the brands) that stood at the cradle of that category and were able to build their initial success through aggressive product development and communication. They are seen as trendsetters, having succeeded in realizing high spontaneous brand awareness and a good understanding of their distinguishing proposition in their target group. For most category or subcategory users, they are relevant. Their scores for "respect" increase. They have a higher perceived popularity and growing success in developing a relationship of bonding with their users. Examples of winning brands are Nokia mobile telephones, PlayStation computerized games, and Asics running shoes. The strategy of these brands has to be constant innovation at a product level in order to validate their relevance, support the brand's dominant presence, and maintain customer relations. The risks of such brands also come from the inside: a perception of arrogance (Microsoft) can develop, as well as the tendency to place the brand in an unrelated product category, which can undermine the core meaning.

4. Old and trustworthy brands. Old and familiar brands are those really large brands whose origins usually date from the nineteenth and first half of the twentieth centuries. Current generations have grown up with them. Everyone knows them and knows what to expect from them. Their evaluation is relatively positive. They are bought pretty much on automatic pilot and attain high scores for perceived popularity. Relationships with such brands are often superficial, though: there is some bonding, but it is usually not too strong. These brands may be large, but they may also be vulnerable. Their owners tend to consider their position as self-evident or even as a "legitimate property," as a result of which they develop few novel initiatives. The greatest threat here is loss of distinction: little happens that is new, and what does happen is half-baked. Agres and Dubitsky (1996) found signals of decreasing distinguishability in brands that were at the beginning of their foundering. Such brands are at a constant risk of becoming uninteresting. The strategy of old, familiar brands should be geared mainly toward actualization, giving new impulses through innovation and the stimulation of saliency and relevance. Examples from the Dutch market are Douwe Egberts coffee and the various Honig packaged food products.

5. Dying brands. Dying brands are those that have not succeeded in remaining current and relevant, so they are on a gradual decline. They often retain a high spontaneous awareness, but a clear concept of their essential meaning is no longer there, and they have lost their distinguishability. They usually pay in perceived advantages over other brands. Subsequent brand evaluation tends to be negative. These brands are not (or no longer) seen as popular, and there is hardly any bonding left over. They typically end up in a downward spiral in which decreasing returns make it increasingly difficult to give them a new impulse. This can often induce a strategy aimed at milking anything that is left out of them, at which point the emphasis shifts increasingly to a promotional strategy, leading to further erosion. The big question about these brands is whether reanimation is still possible or even desirable. Is there still a core of more or less bonded users? How are these brands perceived by other category users? Is there still a residue of positive meanings that can be reactivated? In general, when a brand has been showing a negative development for several years, it is hard to get it out of the slump. Examples in the Dutch market are Oranjeboom beer, Droste chocolates, Van Nelle coffee, and Bokma gin.

6. No-nonsense brands. No-nonsense brands are those bought primarily for their low price, and awareness functions as a signal for reasonable quality. These brands are well known, but have few or no really mentally bonded users. They are largely dependent on their distribution position and promotional strategy. Examples from the Dutch market are Dobbelman detergent, Bavaria beer, and Kanis & Gunnik coffee. Examples from the American market are Hershey chocolate and Kmart shops.

7. Cult and niche brands. In addition to the previously described types of brands based on their development stage, there is another group of brands that owes its exclusive placement to a strong position with a small group of users. These are small segment and niche brands, or brands with a high cult content. They are characterized by the fact that they are only relevant to a small group of consumers, among whom they tend to be quite well known and very positively assessed. Outside that group they are less known and are seen as irrelevant. Cult brands exist by the grace of their mystique, and their main risk is an overextension that could damage this mystique. Niche brands can become threatened by extensions of broader brands, due to which their distinguishing capacity can be affected. For both, the big question is to which degree they can expand, increasing their awareness and acceptance without losing their strength and thus alienating the hard core of their users. Pierre Cardin is a remarkable example of a brand that overstretched. Once a top fashion and cosmetics brand, it lost its mystique because of an unbridled franchising strategy that linked the brand with 800 product categories. Examples of typical cult brands are Marc O'Polo, Versace, MaxMara, and Gucci. The cult-like following of the *Star Trek* television programs, both original and spin-offs, and the stream of *Star Trek* movies is an example from the entertainment field.

8. Retro brands. In recent times, the market has seen several long-abandoned or undermanaged brands taken off the shelf, polished up, and refitted into the market as a hip, new contemporary brand. One of the most successful has been the Mini, which captured the imagination of the swinging Brits in the 1960s with its associations to the fashion model Twiggy and the fashions of Barnaby Street. The New Beetle and Chrysler's PT Cruiser are other automotive examples of retro marketing. In the category of fast-mover or package goods, Breck shampoo, Brylcreem, and Charlie perfumes are good examples of retro brands. The objective is to retain the aura of authenticity and the original brand personality while at the same time modernizing the product to the standards of the new times (S. Brown et al. 2003).

Brand Equity Effects on Advertising Response

In the 1980s, theories on advertising effects assumed an effects hierarchy that started with exposure to advertising and ended with purchasing behavior, as presented in Figure 16.20. Behavior, particularly buying the product, is a critical response for brand managers and one that has direct impact on brand equity. In the last two decades, however, it has become clear that, in most cases, there is no such one-sided sequence at all. It became especially clear that brand behavior itself has a major influence on communication processing and that there are two-way causal relations between the three basic levels (Figure 16.21).

Ehrenberg (1974) and Castleberry and Ehrenberg (1990) indicate that association development with brands is more the result of this behavior than its producer: users of a brand have a wider association network than non-users. Table 16.5 gives an impression of the degree to which brand associations go together with brand use to create brand strength. Measured over four very different product categories, the average preference score for regular users is more than twice as high

Figure 16.20 **Traditional Effects Hypothesis**

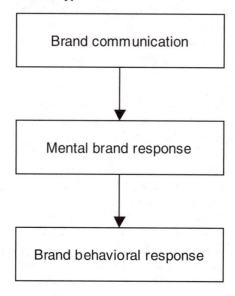

Figure 16.21 **Modern Effects Hypothesis**

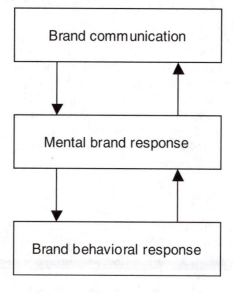

as for those who never use the product (Castleberry and Ehrenberg 1990). For breakfast cereals, these scores are even more far removed from each other. In Table 16.6 an average score has been calculated over three attributes for each brand. We see that people have more brand associations when their use of the brand becomes more frequent. The average score for regular users is 55 percent, and 7 percent for non-users. In short, the more consumers use a brand, the richer their association network.

Analyses of advertising effects research show that there is also a strong connection between

Table 16.5

Average Percentage of Persons With a Preference for a Brand by Use Frequency

	Use frequency			
	Regularly	Occasionally	Infrequently	Never
Breakfast cereals	38	30	21	15
Detergents	58	33	25	17
Fast-food restaurants	55	47	36	30
TV news programs	56	47	35	28
Average	37	39	29	22

Source: Adapted from Castleberry and Ehrenberg (1990).

brand use and brand attitudes on the one side and advertising effect scores on the other. Based on a measurement of 20,000 television commercials, du Plessis and Foster (2000b) established that an average of 27.8 percent of the users of a brand remember having seen a commercial, as against 19.4 percent of the non-users. An analysis of twenty-five studies of television campaigns with the help of the conversion model (see Chapter 7) led to the connections illustrated in Table 16.7.

Users of a brand thus remember the preceding advertising much more than non-users. Their brand attitude influences their willingness to process advertisements and their appreciation for the publicity. What we have here is an interactive process: the brand representation influences the perception of the advertising, and the advertising influences the representation of the brand. This process brings about a high correlation at an aggregated level between the number of users of a brand and advertising effectiveness. Given the fact that large brands have more users, this works very much to their advantage. Correspondingly, communication for smaller brands gets less attention—another effect of the double jeopardy phenomenon. To compensate, a share of voice is needed that is considerably higher than the share of market.

Given the relatively large impact of brand behavior (buying and using) on the mental brand response, push activities aimed at directly inciting or tempting consumers toward trial-and-repeat behavior are essential to the development of mental brand equity. Without these activities, chances are great that no (or insufficient) conversion toward behavior will take place—that is, consumers will know the brand, but will not buy it). Push activities facilitate behavior, and behavior leads to brand knowledge and brand attitude.

> *Principle:* There is a two-way connection between communication effects and purchasing behavior. Users of a brand are more receptive to communication about it than non-users. This leads to a correlation between the size (penetration) of a brand and advertising effectiveness.

IVORY'S TREMENDOUS BRAND EQUITY

The Ivory brand now is more than 125 years old, and an excellent example of brand equity building and maintaining. In the course of time the position of Ivory was threatened by the introduction of Dove by Unilever and Dial by Dial Corporation. Dove has moisturizers that soften the skin. Dial has an antibacterial agent that kills germs. Both were sold at a premium price.

Table 16.6

Table of Usage and Image Attributes

	Corn Flakes	Weetabix	Rice Krispies	Oatmeal	Sugar Puffs	Frosties	Special K	All-Bran	Ave
Buys brand regularly	79	64	54	61	50	58	48	35	55
Buys brand sometimes	55	36	32	27	32	22	25	18	31
Familiar with use of brand	41	24	18	11	12	25	13	13	18
Has tried brand	40	11	12	7	13	12	9	9	14
Has never tried brand	28	8	5	4	5	3	2	2	7
Total (weighted)	61	61	21	16	16	13	10	10	22

Source: Adapted from Barwise and Ehrenberg (1985).

Table 16.7

Percentage of Memory of Advertising Spots

	Users		Non-users	
	Attached	Non-attached	Potential joiners	Rejecters
Claimed recall	62	46	50	36
Verified perception	26	21	23	16
Brand commitment	46	40	42	29
General reaction				
• very good	9	25	37	29
• attractive	73	57	88	57
(top 3 boxes)				
• interesting	64	45	61	47
(top 3 boxes)				
• believable	69	54	58	47
(top 3 boxes)				

Source: Research Surveys Inc. (Rice and Hofmeyr 2000).

Procter & Gamble decided not to match them with similar formulas for Ivory, but to compete on value for the dollar. Today advertising for Ivory almost always stresses its caring quality by featuring young mothers and babies, together with its price. Ivory is the least expensive branded soap on the market. Procter & Gamble has made a tremendous success of its strategy and sells more soap than Dove and Dial.

Of course, Ivory is still the premier example of soap branding. Aaker (1991) estimated that Ivory sales from its introduction in 1879 up to 1987 totaled $25 billion, generating an annual profit in that period between $2 and $3 million.

CHAPTER 17

MARKET BRAND EQUITY

In Chapter 17 we describe brand equity as a measure of the strength of the brand. That strength is derived from the consumer's brand relationship and culminates in the market strength—such factors as sales, market position, profits, and growth. To understand brand equity, particularly as it is manifested in the market, consider the story of Samsung.

SURPRISING SAMSUNG

In 1938 in South Korea, a new company was founded: Samseong, meaning "three stars." Initially it occupied itself with sugar production, insurance, department stores, and newspaper publishing. In 1969, thirty-six of its employees started to produce electric fans. The company changed its name to Samsung Electronics Co. Ltd. in 1984, as a subsidiary to the Samsung Group. By the early 1990s Samsung had become a successful producer of cheap commodity electronics, selling them under a range of sub-brands, such as Plano, Tantus, Yepp, and Wiseview. It excelled at identifying new technologies and business opportunities early and then seizing control of the market with overwhelming production volume.

In 1996 a number of fundamental decisions were made. The company migrated to a premium brand strategy, ditching low-end products. It bade farewell to its sub-brands and decided to focus solely on building Samsung into a global masterbrand. It introduced a new corporate identity program. The name was now written in English, and the new design of the elliptical logo symbolized the world moving through space, conveying an image of innovation and change.

The company transformed its mission statement to keep pace with its growing global operations and escalating competition. It declared, "We will devote our human resources and technology to create superior products and services, thereby contributing to a better global society." Its management philosophy represented its strong determination to contribute directly to the prosperity of people all over the world: "The talent, creativity, and dedication of our people is key to our efforts and the strides we've made in technology offer endless possibilities to achieve higher standards of living everywhere."

Samsung adopted a holistic approach to global brand communication in order to reposition the brand in consumers' minds, concentrating on flagship products such as cell phones and rear projection TVs. It increased its advertising budget to 5 percent of total sales. But most of all it invested in building its technological know-how, spending 7.5 percent of revenues on research and development and employing more and more researchers, to a total of 32,000 in 2006. It planned to invest $40 billion in R&D during the five years from 2006 to 2010. It became one of the world's top ten companies in U.S. patents.

Samsung increased its focus on product design and increased its number of designers from about 100 in 2000 to 450 in 2005. It now has design centers in Los Angeles, Tokyo, Shanghai, and Milan. Moving to a multisensory approach to design, Samsung aims at a consistent black or silver look in all its products. It tries to express its brand's essence by bringing the three elements of "technology, design, and human sensation" together so all the products work in synchronicity.

To showcase the brands as quality, Samsung moved its products from budget stores like Wal-Mart to more specialized retailers. Samsung managed to become world leader in a number of product categories, such as flat screen TVs, microwave ovens, memory chips, and LCD display. Today Samsung is also one of the leading manufacture's of plasma displays and cell phones.

Sources: Rusch (2003); Samsung (2006); *Business Week Online* (2005); Fackler (2006).

DIMENSIONS OF MARKET BRAND EQUITY

Samsung managed to develop the equity of its brand to a position of number 20 in Interbrand's 2005 ranking of the hundred largest global brands. It did so by heavily investing in the mental equity of its brand, which resulted in a strong global market position ahead of Sony, Siemens, and Philips. As we will see, mental brand equity and market brand equity are like yin and yang—they form an intertwined system.

Figure 17.1 **Brand Push and Pull System**

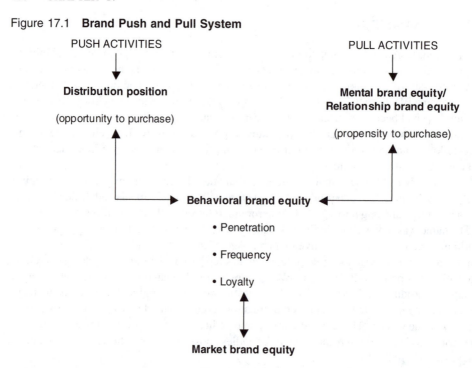

We now take a closer look at the market components of brand equity. Market brand equity consists of two dimensions: distribution position and market dynamics. Within each of them we can distinguish a number of factors.

DISTRIBUTION POSITION

Distribution position involves the following:

- *Span of distribution:* Span refers to the weighted percentage of the sales points where the brand is available (the span component of distribution).
- *Depth of distribution:* Depth refers to the position of the brand within the sales points where it is available (the quality component of the distribution).
- *Quality of distribution points:* For prestige brands, the quality of the distribution points is an important factor.

People's purchasing behavior emerges during an interactive process of mental and purchasing-environment interaction. On the one hand, people are steered from the inside out by their evaluation of brands present in memory. On the other hand, their choice is strongly influenced by what they find and hear during the purchasing process in the purchasing environment.

Push and Pull System

The different elements of the marketing mix are essentially aimed at influencing consumers' propensity and opportunity to purchase. Effective brand strategy requires steering both pillars of brand equity:

the mental equity of the brand and its market equity as based in its distribution position. The main objectives of the strategic input of marketing mix elements would then be the following:

- *Pull activities:* generating acceptance of and a conscious and active preference for a brand by influencing its perception and the feelings about it, the desired result being inclusion of the brand in the purchasing repertoire of consumers and a relatively high share in their category purchases (share of customer requirements).
- *Push activities:* activating brand use by creating favorable conditions for the purchasing possibilities for consumers by influencing supply factors such as degree of distribution and quality of the point-of-purchase position of the brand.

Distribution Span and Depth

Distribution position has two dimensions: the span and the depth of the distribution (J. Oliver and Farris 1989). The span is expressed in the "naked" weighted distribution of a brand—the percentage of all sales points where the category can be obtained and that offers the brand, after weighting for their share in the total category sales. It is a good measure of the percentage of consumers who are offered the opportunity to buy the brand.

The depth of the distribution involves the quality of the presence of the brand at the sales points. For everyday consumer products, it is the place at the shop, shelf placement (e.g., at eye level or near the floor), and the space on the shelves (the number of facings). For durable articles, the attitude and service of the sales personnel play a large role.

Brands with a wide and deep distribution confront consumers often and noticeably, thus reaching high levels of repeat purchases. Such distribution is probably the most important explanation for the double jeopardy effect described in Chapter 13—the fact that large brands generally reach a higher share of customer than smaller brands. The relative brand preference of consumers is modified by the relative span and depth of the distribution of the different brands. Large brands benefit from the relatively weaker distribution position of smaller brands. When smaller, weaker brands are not offered, buyers without strong brand preferences switch easily to larger, stronger brands that are available. In addition, smaller brands get less attention in the shop (fewer facings), as a result of which their presence is less prominent—they are less salient and thus are less visible.

This is how patterns of purchasing behavior arise that in turn influence mental brand representation and distribution. They lead to an interrelated system of effects that works to the advantage of the large brands and to the disadvantage of the smaller ones.

In categories with low involvement, which makes brand repertoires larger, the influence of distribution is more significant than in categories with a more pronounced brand preference (i.e., in which the mental brand equity is larger). An important aspect of brand strategy development is the determination of the optimal balance between pull and push activities. This balance depends on the relative strength of the mental equity of a brand (commitment) and of its distribution position. Based on these two dimensions, a matrix can be constructed in which the position of a brand can be expressed and the priorities for the strategy determined (see Figure 17.2).

In push strategies, a larger portion of the available means are deployed to strengthen the distribution position—category management support, higher margins for retail, trade promotions, and in-store activities, such as demonstrations. In pull strategies, more means are allocated to strengthen the mental brand equity. Both strategies are always necessary for the development of a brand. Small brands often have a difficult time generating both push and pull activities. This

Figure 17.2   **Combinations of Mental Equity and Distribution Position**

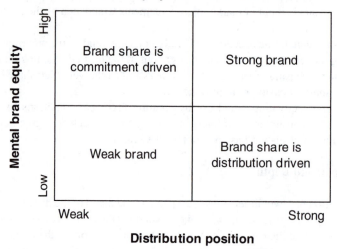

difficulty may very well be the most important cause of the failure of 80 to 90 percent of product introductions and thus the indirect cause of the considerable stability of the position of large established brands too.

Quality of the Distribution Points

Next to the span and depth of the distribution, the quality of the distribution points (shops) can contribute to the creation of favorable conditions for brand purchasing behavior. Channel design and management are becoming increasingly important for brand equity development. Distribution through shops with a favorable image has a positive effect on the quality perception of a brand (Dodds et al. in Yoo et al. 2000). The quality of a brand is perceived differently depending on the retailer that offers it.

MARKET DYNAMICS

Market dynamics includes the following:

- *Sales:* the sold amount in units and in monetary value in a certain period.
- *Market share:* the share of the brand in the total sales of its category or subcategory in a specific period.
- *Price premium:* the difference between the average price of a brand and the average price for the category (sometimes the price distance between a brand and a store brand is used as a criterion).
- *Price elasticity:* the percentile increase or decrease in sales as a result of the increase or decrease of 1 percent in the price.
- *Gross profits:* the sales ex-factory of the brand minus the purchase costs.
- *Net profits:* the gross profits minus production, marketing, sales and overhead costs, and interest on long-term loans.
- *Profit margin:* net profits expressed as a percentage of the sales.

Table 17.1

Average Absolute Financial Market Shares for the Three Largest Brands in the Netherlands (90 product groups, 6 branches)

Branch	No. 1	No. 2	No. 3	Total 1, 2, 3
Food	37.3	15.1	8.8	61.2
Non-food	28.0	16.5	10.2	54.7
Total food plus non-food	32.6	15.8	9.5	57.9
Liquor	24.1	11.1	7.9	43.1
Small domestic electrical appliances	43.0	22.9	11.4	77.3
Do-it-yourself	39.0	18.9	9.4	67.9
All branches	34.4	17.0	9.5	60.9

Source: Positioneringsgroep (2000).

- *Return on investment:* net profits expressed as a percentage of the invested own capital and the long-term loans.

Often brand equity is found only in psychological dimensions, as explained in the preceding chapter. But the performance of a brand in the market not only reflects its mental position, but, to a certain degree, is also an independent factor that impacts the brand standing and development. We call the totality of these equity dimensions market dynamics.

Market Share

The relative strength of brands is manifest at its best in the market shares in money because the relative prices are included here. Measured over many markets in several countries, the money shares of the three largest brands stand at a ratio of roughly 4:2:1. Nielsen in the Netherlands analyzed these ratios for ninety product groups in six different branches in early 1994. As Table 17.1 shows, an average ratio was found over all product groups of 34.4, 17.0, and 9.5 percent.

An analysis of 2,000 business units in the PIMS databases in the United States showed that market leaders on average had 38 percent share of market, those in the number two spot controlled 21 percent, those in the number three position had 12 percent, and those in the number four position had 6 percent (Stevenson 1985).

Interaction Between Distribution and Market Share

There is a two-way causal relationship between distribution position and market share. That distribution leads to market share is self-evident—the larger the availability of a brand, the more opportunities consumers have to buy it. We have seen how this leads to biases for the large brands because their chances of being bought increase in the absence of smaller brands. The competition between retail chain stores also leads to a concentration of promotions on the popular brands, increasing their presence even further. Both mechanisms lead to an increase of the market share as a result of distribution growth.

The fact that market share also leads to distribution is less obvious. This is an indirect result of the higher marketing efforts and larger budgets that are made possible by higher market shares. It sets off a higher perceived pull strength in category managers of retailers and a greater willingness to include the brand. Smaller retailers are forced to limit their assortment and to focus on the

Figure 17.3   **The Connection Between Market Share and Distribution**

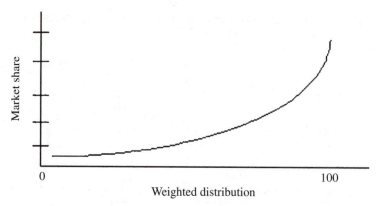

Source: Reibstein and Farris (1995).

large brands. This takes place mostly in what is known as the gray channels. A meta-analysis of studies into the nature of the relationship between market share and distribution points to a convex function (Reibstein and Farris 1995). With small brands, the relationship between distribution and market share has a restraining effect on the development. The connection works very much to the advantage of the large brands, especially in low-involvement categories (see Figure 17.3).

> *Principle:* There is a mutually influential causal relationship between distribution and market share.

Quality and Market Share

Loyal brand-purchasing behavior is based on users' valuing of a brand. There is an interaction here between getting to love what one buys and uses, and buying what one loves. Attitude and behavior influence each other mutually. This manifests itself in the strong relationship between the market share and the quality evaluation of brands. Alleborn (1994) arrived at the following ratio for the United States (see Figure 17.4).

Research into product evaluation has also shown the enormous effect that brand awareness exerts on the quality perception of consumers. The example in Table 17.2 (based on Chernatony and McDonald 1994) shows the preference of the British for Diet Coke and Diet Pepsi. The brand preference in the blind situation, in which people did not know which of the two sodas they were drinking, was compared with the situation in which people did know. The preference for Diet Pepsi more than halved when consumers were aware of the brand.

Price Premium

Evaluation of a branded article (product and brand) influences the price people are willing to pay. As a result, producers of branded products can set prices higher than for generic articles. A Nielsen analysis shows that the average price paid for branded articles in the daily consumer products sector in the Netherlands is 28 percent higher than for comparable private labels.

Figure 17.4 **The Relationship Between Market Share and Quality**

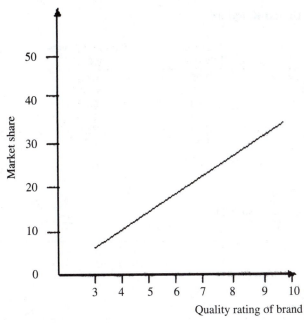

Source: Adapted from Alleborn (1994).

Table 17.2

Brand Preference (in percent)

	Blind	Aware
Prefer Diet Pepsi	51	23
Prefer Diet Coke	44	65
No preference	5	12

Source: Chernatony and McDonald (1994).

As Table 17.3 shows, an analysis by Taylor Nelson Sofres (in Buck 2001b) also indicates that in Great Britain people pay a 28 percent surcharge for premium brands over standard private labels. The difference between premium brands and the basic private labels amounted to as much as 210 percent. Price and volume impacts are often achieved at the same time.

Price Elasticity

Price elasticity, the percentage-wise change of sales and market share resulting from 1 percent price changes, is the marketing variable with the largest influence on purchasing behavior. In an analysis of 118 brands in twenty-four categories of package goods over six years in the United States, Ailawadi et al. (2001) calculated an average price elasticity of –0.541. The researchers found that price elasticity decreases when the market share grows. In other words, the market share of large brands reacts less strongly to price changes than that of small brands. As Table 17.4 shows,

Table 17.3

Brand Prices in the United Kingdom

	Premium brand (£)	Standard private label (£)	Basic private label (£)
White beans in tomato sauce	0.32	0.23	0.11
Carbonated soft drinks	1.17	0.59	0.21
Dish detergents	0.78	0.66	0.07
Corn flakes	1.59	1.19	0.49
Powder detergent	2.54	2.08	0.75
Tea	1.57	1.17	0.44
Toilet paper	2.36	2.15	1.27
Packaged bread	0.59	0.42	0.20
Average over eight categories	1.36	1.06	0.44

Source: Taylor Nelson Sofres (Buck 2001b).

Table 17.4

Price Elasticity

Price elasticity	Index
Number 1	87
Number 2	100
New brand	140
Average of all brands in 1991–1994	100

Source: Taylor Nelson Sofres AGB Superpanel (Buck 1995a).

Buck (1995), taking figures from Taylor Nelson Sofres AGB Superpanel, also observed that the price elasticity of market leaders is considerably smaller than that of brands that are number two and that the price elasticity of new brands is very large.

Gross and Net Profits

The large sales volumes that are generated by the really big brands in the world lead to substantial economies of scale. Research and development costs and marketing costs are compensated by high revenue streams, as a result of which these costs per unit are reduced. And the large production volumes lead to efficiencies in the production processes. No one in the world seems to be able to produce a Mars bar at the cost that Masterfoods does. These economies of scale not only help to lower the price of the product, but also simultaneously increase the gross profit margins of the marketer.

The strong market position that the producer has acquired, thanks to the brand, also leads to a higher share of the total margin on the products (the difference between production cost and consumer price). All these brand effects result in a positive influence on the net profits margin of the marketer. Chernatony and McDonald (1994) found the ratios outline in Table 17.5 for the everyday consumer articles market in Great Britain.

A marked example of this relationship between market share and profitability was the situation in the market of mobile phones in the first quarter of 2006. Nokia, with a market share of 42

Table 17.5

Market Share and Net Profits

Market share hierarchy	Net profits margin in percent
Number 1	17.9
Number 2	2.8
Number 3	−0.9
Number 4	−5.9

Source: Chernatony and McDonald (1994).

Table 17.6

Market Share and Operatunal Margins (first quarter 2006)

	Units sold (000,000)	Percent share	Percent operational margin
Nokia	75.1	42	14.4
Motorola	46.1	26	11.0
Samsung	29.0	16	10.0
LG Electronics	15.6	9	−0.4
Sony Ericsson	13.3	7	5.4
	179.1	100	

Source: Maarsen (2006).

percent, scored an operating margin of 14.4 percent, whereas Sony Ericsson, with a market share of 7 percent, recorded a margin of only 5.4 percent (see Table 17.6).

This relationship is the reason many producers set the goal of being number one or two in a market; otherwise, they withdraw.

Return on Investment

In the end, all these factors lead to a stronger relationship between the market position and the return on investment (ROI) of a brand. Analysis of the PIMS database in the United States showed that the pretax return on investment of the number one brands averaged 32.9 percent, of the number two brands 17.8 percent, of the number three 14.1 percent, and of the number four 9.1 percent. "Number four brands have two things in common," says Larry Light; "they are hard to name, and it's hard for them to make a profit" (Stevenson 1985).

The market position can be expressed in different ways—in the market share, the order of the market share, the ratio between the market share and that of the largest competitor, and in the market share in relation to the three largest competitors. All four ways present a strong relation between the market share and the ROI. This relation is present in all the different product and service categories, as Table 17.7, based on the same PIMS database, shows.

CONSUMER BRAND EQUITY AND MARKET BRAND EQUITY

The market research company ACNielsen analyzed the relationship between mental brand equity and in-market performance for a large number of brands in the package goods, durables, and

Table 17.7

Brand Leadership and Returns on Investment

Market position	Industry	Services	Durable products	Non-durable products
Dominant leaders	31	48	38	37
Marginal leaders	26	37	25	29
Numbers 2	20	24	21	24
Numbers 3	18	20	10	13
Numbers 4+	13	18	11	7

Source: Buzzel and Gale (1987).

Figure 17.5   **Mental Brand Equity and Market Share**

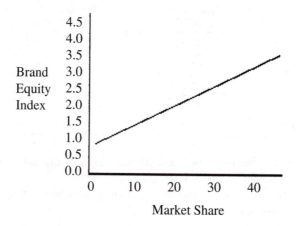

Source: ACNielsen (2001).

services sectors. The company's research instrument for mental brand equity is called Brand Equity Index or BEI.

BEI is an overall equity score, between 0 and 10. It is based on a preference measure and a measure of the consumer's willingness to pay a price premium for a brand compared to other brands in the category. To identify the sources of mental brand equity, the BEI scores are regressed against brand awareness, consideration, and brand associations. ACNielsen found a strong relationship between BEIs and market share (see Figure 17.5).

The mental brand equity of most brands is a strong indicator of their market share. But ACNielsen's analysis demonstrated that there are deviations from this equilibrium so it should be monitored. For this purpose, in consumer research the "brand last bought" is often used as a proxy for market share. When this measure is offset against a relevant measure for mental brand equity, such as an overall likelihood of purchase or disposition toward a brand, it becomes possible to contrast consumer brand equity with market brand equity. This results in the brand equity (BE) matrix illustrated in Figure 17.6.

This analysis leads to four different positions:

Figure 17.6 **Market and Mental Brand Equity Matrix**

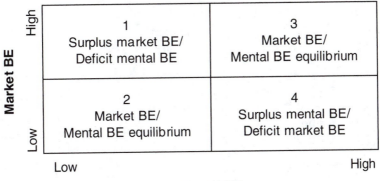

Source: ACNielsen (2001).

1. *Surplus market BE (or deficit of mental BE):* A portion of the users of the brand do not feel particularly well disposed toward it. The brand might be in danger of losing market share. The issue is how such a decline might be prevented.
2. *Mental BE and market BE both low:* Brands in this quadrant are weak, which usually means that they have to be strengthened or will gradually be eliminated by the market.
3. *Mental BE and market BE both strong and in balance:* This is the situation that most long-established and successful brands find themselves in. Managing them is a maintenance job, although it still calls for regular product innovation and communication support at a level in proportion to the standing of the brand.
4. *Surplus mental BE (or deficit of market BE):* A larger portion of category users has a positive disposition toward the brand than is currently using it (or is using it more occasionally). The key issue for the brand strategy is how the surplus mental BE can be exploited or the deficit market BE eliminated. Frequently there is a weak marketing fundamental, such as distribution, pricing, or targeting that should be addressed.

Analyzing the brand equity drivers can provide understanding of how to continue to strengthen market share. Weaknesses in brand familiarity indicate awareness and trial-building strategies. Weaknesses in brand associations indicate positioning issues, a need to refocus on favorable and unique associations, or potentially the need to explore target consumer issues.

The Stabilizing Effect of the Market

In most literature on brand development, the growth possibilities of brands are seen as self-evident. A closer look at the situation sheds a different light, though. In many saturated markets, the growth possibilities for a brand are limited because the market shares are at a deadlock. In some markets, the purchasing behavior of consumers has pretty much become habitual behavior and the marketing efforts of the various brands only keep each other in balance, so only minimal shifts take place in the market shares. With the exception of the few cases that are peaking, the growth possibilities of a brand should always be seen within the preconditions that the reality of the brand sets.

The market position of brands in developed markets is the result of several interacting factors,

Figure 17.7 **The System of Interacting Marketing Factors**

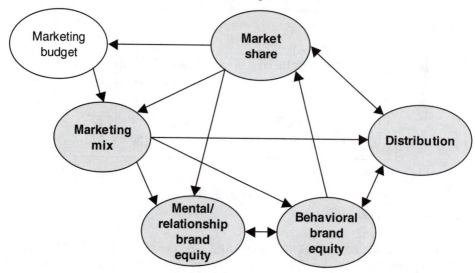

which together form a system, which has a stabilizing effect. These relationships are shown in Figure 17.7. The most important relationships are the following:

- *Market share:* The market share is highly determinant to the available marketing budget, certainly in the slightly longer run. It also leads to prioritizing within the marketing mix (push/pull). As we have seen, the market share influences distribution span and depth. It is also a measure for the popularity of a brand and thus influences purchasing behavior, especially with the less involved consumers.
- *Marketing mix:* The marketing mix aims at influencing brand position by proportionately strengthening the mental brand equity, the behavioral brand equity, and the distribution position.
- *Mental, relationship, and behavioral brand equity:* There is a strong two-way connection between mental and behavioral brand equity. The influence of purchasing behavior on the mental brand equity deserves special attention.
- *Behavioral brand equity and distribution:* The number of buyers (penetration) and the average purchasing frequency influence distribution. In turn, distribution span and depth influence purchasing behavior.

Market shares are, of course, relative. Considering that marketing budgets for established brands are almost always derived from the market shares, the marketing efforts of the various competitors tend to be a reflection of the existing market positions, thus confirming the status quo.

The stability of well-established brands is expressed in the fact that market shares for a specific year can be largely predicted on the basis of the shares of the preceding year. Through the interactions of the influencing factors, market positions of established brands tend to be stable. In Chapter 8 on brand saliency, we already established that market shares for roughly 75 to 80 percent of brands are stable or close enough (Farr 1998; DeKimpe and Hanssens 1995).

Table 17.8

SoV Relative to SoM for Three Brand Groups

Brand groups based on performance between 1975 and 1999	Average SoV-SoM 1975	Average SoV/SoM 1975
Losers	1.6	1.0
Static	2.1	1.2
Winners	11.1	1.6

Source: Buck (2001b).

Table 17.9

SoV Versus SoM Related to Brand Share Trends (1995–1999)

Brands grouped by SOM changes (1995–1999)	Average SoV–SoM 1975	Average SoV/SoM 1975
Falling by 2 or more share points	−1.5	1.1
Falling by up to 2 share points	−0.3	1.0
Rising by up to 2 share points	+11.4	1.6
Rising by 2 or more share points	+21.8	1.9

Source: Buck (2001b).

For growth of the market share, a disturbance of the equilibrium is needed, and that can only be caused by special circumstances: an important competing brand can make major mistakes, a brand introduces a very relevant product improvement, or a brand develops a very effective communications campaign.

Advertising and Market Share

Ipsos-ASI, analyzing the drivers of behavioral brand equity for 350 different brands, concluded that advertising plays an important role in building behavioral brand equity. Advertising builds familiarity and highlights the brand's performance. And when done well, it correlates with uniqueness. In many categories where several brands offer similar product performance, advertising plays an important role in differentiating the brand (Hallward 2001).

Buck (2001) analyzed the market share developments in twenty-six categories of fast-moving consumer goods in the United Kingdom between 1975 and 1999, also investigating the connection with advertising share. Classifying the brands into three groups—losers, statics, and winners—Buck concluded that, in 1975, the winners had an average advertising share of 1.6 times their market share, the losers of 1.0 times (see Table 17.8). Measurements over a short time span (1995–1999) also showed a strong connection between loss of growth of market share and the relationship between market share and advertising share. The brands with strong growth had an advertising share of 1.9 times their market share (Table 17.9).

Buck is correct in pointing out that success depends on more marketing mix elements than just advertising expenditures, but the results indicate that advertising serves as an important booster for this success. The results point to a causal link, because the high advertising shares of the winners precede the growth of their market shares.

RESEARCH INTO BRAND EQUITY

In the world of marketers, researchers, and scientists, the brand equity concept is a multiheaded monster. At an abstract level, people agree that equity stands for the relative strength of a brand. However, this definition raises the question of the brand dimensions that equity affects. Depending on the choice of these dimensions, there is an ample variety of definitions with practically no common ground.

We have avoided the problem by distinguishing five main dimensions in advance and deriving equity definitions at a secondary level. If we are to study the relative strength of a brand, the question of the dimensions on which the research should focus immediately arises—consumer brand equity or market brand equity?

Many of the brand equity instruments offered by market research agencies only measure the strength of the mental and relationship brand equity. But the ultimate function of brands for their owners is to generate future cash flow, to reduce the risk of decline of this cash flow, and to promote the likelihood of growth in this cash flow. Measures of mental brand equity can give insight into the scale and depth of a brand's market presence and the likelihood that a brand will make it into the customer's consideration set, but they are usually poor in explaining the final purchase decision and therefore do not provide a reliable measure of a brand's ability to generate cash flow (Knowles and Olins 2006). To capture the true strength of a brand, measures of behavioral brand equity have to be included as "outcomes." A complete measurement system should also include measures of market brand equity.

Brand managers need insight into how the components influence each other in a concrete situation and which marketing mix strategy is likely to be the most effective.

The strength of a brand is always relative. The brand equity score gives information only when it is compared with that of competing brands in the same market. With brands that operate in different markets, the equity can vary considerably according to the market. It would be difficult to say anything useful about the equity of a brand like Philips, which is much stronger in the lighting category than in mobile telephones.

At an aggregated level, the differences in brand equity will balance out and it is not possible to take an average of the equity scores of all the markets in which the brand is active. Brand equity research, therefore, focuses on the brand and the competing brands in a specific category. Philips television sets compete with brands like Sony, JVC, Panasonic, Samsung, and Loewe, whereas Philips cell phones compete with Nokia, Motorola, Samsung, Siemens, and Sony-Ericson. This difference in markets has consequences for the brand equity score.

Standardized Brand Equity Measurement Instruments

Many market research agencies offer standardized instruments to measure consumer brand equity. A number of them are briefly described below (Knowles and Olins 2006; Franzen 2006).

Brand Dynamics (Millward-Brown)

The notion of a pyramid of engagement is echoed in the BrandDynamics™ methodology developed by Millward-Brown. This approach characterizes the relationship that a customer has with a brand into one of five stages: presence, relevance, performance, advantage, and bonding. "Presence" customers have only a basic awareness of the brand, while "bonded" customers are intensely loyal, at least in their attitudes. The underlying premise is that the lifetime value of customers increases the higher they are in the pyramid.

Equity Engine (Research International)

Equity Engine^SM, developed by Research International, expresses brand equity as a combination of the functional benefits delivered by the brand (performance) and the emotional benefits (affinity). Underlying each of these macro constructs is a further layer of analysis that expresses performance as a function of product and service attributes, and affinity as a function of the brand identification (the closeness customers feel to the brand), approval (the status the brand enjoys among a wider social context of family, friends, and colleagues), and authority (the reputation of the brand). Equity Engine^SM incorporates a form of conjoint methodology that establishes the price premium that a brand's equity will support while still maintaining a "good value for money" rating from customers.

Equity*Builder (Ipsos-ASI)

Equity*Builder, the methodology developed by the Ipsos Group, is uniquely focused on establishing the emotional component of brand equity. It situates a brand's attitudinal equity (measured in terms of differentiation, relevance, popularity, quality, and familiarity) in the context of the degree of customer involvement with the category in question. Similar to Equity Engine^SM, Equity*Builder also explicitly addresses how brand equity translates into perceived value and price.

BrandAsset® Valuator (Young & Rubicam)

The BrandAsset® Valuator, developed by Young & Rubicam, eschews the category-specific approach taken by other brand equity methodologies, seeking instead to establish a pure measure of brand equity independent of category context. All brands are rated on the same forty-eight attributes and four macro constructs of differentiation, relevance, esteem, and knowledge. The constructs of differentiation and relevance are then combined into a single metric of brand strength. The constructs of esteem and relevance are combined to form brand stature, which is correlated to current market share but not potential for growth.

Equitrend (Harris International)

Equitrend, developed in 1989 by Total Research Inc. and now a part of Total Research/Harris Interactive, originally concentrated on measuring perceived quality within the consumers that know the brand. In 2004 the system was enhanced to provide a more comprehensive diagnostic. It now has five key measures: (1) familiarity, (2) quality, (3) purchase intent, (4) brand expectations, and (5) distinctiveness. In the system, brand familiarity forms the foundation for the brand; the momentum is measured by the promise of quality and purchase potential. These three aspects are combined in an equity score. Brand expectations and distinctiveness are treated as diagnostic variables.

CBBE Model (Kevin Lane Keller)

Although not available as a commercial methodology, Kevin Lane Keller's consumer-based brand equity (CBBE) model is worthy of mention because of Keller's authority within the brand equity measurement arena. His model mirrors the Equity Engine^SM approach by seeing the brand as a blend of the rational and the emotional, measured in terms of performance characteristics and imagery. Customers' relationship to a brand can be plotted according to their attitude on the pyramid of engagement and their relative bias toward a rationally dominant or emotionally dominant relationship. Procter & Gamble based its proprietary brand tracking system on the levels of Keller's CBBE pyramid: (1) salience, (2) performance and brand imagery, (3) judgments and feelings, and (4) resonance.

Brand Equity System (Burke)

Burke distinguishes two key drivers of the customer acquisition and retention dynamic: brand recognition and brand regard. The brand regard metric is composed of measures from six dimensions. Specific ratings from these dimensions, combined with brand recognition, are used to construct an overall brand equity score. The model is designed to be combined with a loyalty measure: the Burke Secure Customer Index. Burke claims that its brand equity scoring system correlates with real-world market share and brand value in dollars.

Brand Potential Index (GfK)

GfK's Brand Potential Index (BPI) measures ten different components of brand attitude in the context of the brand's competitive set: brand identification, brand awareness, uniqueness, quality, empathy with the brand, trust in the brand, willingness to recommend the brand, buying intention, brand allegiance, and acceptance of premium pricing. The index combines the component scores into an overall score on a scale from 0 to 100. GfK combines this measure with financial metrics (basically a variant of the discounted cash flow method) to arrive at an estimation of the brand's financial value.

Brand Equity Monitor (Brandmarc)

The Brand Equity Monitor (BEM) is an instrument that explains reported purchasing loyalty as a dependant variable using six different association categories: relative brand awareness, product performance, brand personality, brand values, price/quality evaluation, and commitment.

The BEM distinguishes between descriptive and causal brand equity. In descriptive brand equity, brand assets are defined as the percentage of consumers who have an association with the brand that is relevant to their purchasing behavior. It follows that the higher the percentage of consumers with an association, the higher the asset. In addition to this descriptive modeling, the BEM uses causal brand equity to explain purchase loyalty by means of association categories. Brand equity is not solely defined by the brand's assets but also by their relevance for purchase loyalty. Brand assets, the percentage of consumers with the association, and importance, the percentage of purchase loyalty explained by this asset, together make up for the total contribution of the association categories.

All the aforementioned approaches suffer from the fact that they are attitudinal in nature and have yet to establish the definitive relationship between measures of attitudinal engagement (or loyalty) and observed behavior.

Winning Brands™ (ACNielsen)

Winning Brands™ is the methodology developed by ACNielsen. In contrast to the attitudinal approach to brand equity measurement embodied in the methods described above, Winning Brands™

begins with an observation of behavior. Brand equity is measured in terms of a customer's frequency of purchase and the price premium paid. Once favorable behavior is observed, the methodology seeks to analyze the attitudinal characteristics of those customers.

Brand Power (TNS/NIPO)

TNS/NIPO combines measures of market and mental brand equity. The key elements for market brand equity are quality of distribution, relative price paid, and market share. Market factors are defined by category. For measuring mental brand equity, TNS/NIPO uses the Conversion Model™, originally developed by Hofmeyr and Rice and discussed in Chapter 7, which basically measures commitment and segments customers and noncustomers into four attitude groups.

A COMPLETE SYSTEM OF EQUITY MEASUREMENTS

In view of the number of different definitions and measurement instruments available, it is not strange that Davis (1998) arrived at the conclusion that 80 percent of American companies are not satisfied with how the strength of their brands is measured. He rightly pleads for a combination of various instruments that would, in fact, contain the entire spectrum of the dimensions that have been discussed. Such a combination would involve the establishment of cause-and-effect relationships between the various brand equity levels; the market equity dimensions are the dependent variables and the consumer brand equity the independent ones. A complete system of equity measurements would contain the following components:

- *Mental brand equity measurement at an individual level:* This would include cognitions, evaluations, and intentions.
- *Relationship equity measurement at an individual level:* This would include quantitative and qualitative measurements of familiarity, bonding, commitment, recency, frequency, loyalty, satisfaction, and referrals.
- *Behavioral equity measurement at an individual level:* This would include trial, brand repertoire, and share of customer measurement.
- *Distribution position:* This would include measurements of both the quantitative and qualitative components of the brand's distribution system—span, depth, and quality.
- *Market dynamics:* This would include the performance of the brand in the market, including market share, price premium and price elasticity, profit margins, and ROI.

Principle: A comprehensive brand equity study should focus on the connection between the three basic components of brand equity: mental, behavioral, and market brand equity.

Such a total brand equity measurement system was applied in Canada for 200 brands in forty categories (Davenport and Hallward 1999). Modeling techniques were used to calculate the connection between the independent mental equity scores and the dependent behavioral scores (a 0.87 correlation) and the in-market parameters (a 0.75 correlation). Here are the main conclusions that this large-scale study produced:

Figure 17.8 **Loyalty (SOC) and Relevance**

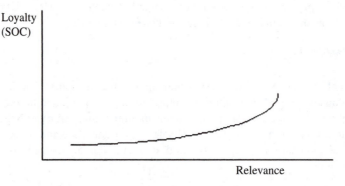

Source: Davenport and Hallward (1999).

- The mental variables of understanding and familiarity, popularity, distinguishability, relevance, and perceived quality correlate with share-of-customer scores.
- Understanding and familiarity should be present before a correlation is active between the other mental variables and the share of customer. Brands that do attain a high score for aided brand awareness but not for understanding or familiarity perform moderately or poorly.
- The most important variable is relevance—the share of customer increases exponentially with the increase of relevance (see Figure 17.8). The double jeopardy phenomenon was confirmed—a strong connection between penetration and share of customer was found. There is also another, independent equity effect: in brands with comparable penetration, a higher equity leads to an additional higher share of customer.
- Large brands score lower on differentiation—they are familiar, popular, high quality, but less unique.
- Low involvement in a category leads to a more minimal influence of the mental brand equity on brand loyalty.
- The availability of acceptable alternative brands has a negative influence on market brand equity. Large, established brands have to keep trying to distinguish themselves through constant product development.
- Measuring the willingness to pay a surcharge contributes to the connection between measurements of mental brand equity and purchasing behavior or share of customer.

Implications for Marketers

The following summarizes the recommendations based on these results and their implications for marketers (Davenport and Hallward 1999).

1. Marketers can and should measure and seek to leverage brand equity with the objective of strengthening in-market performance.
2. Marketers should focus on strengthening equity in order to build a brand that is profitable in the long term instead of focusing on purchase loyalty, which often puts emphasis on promotional activity, discounting, and reward programs.
3. For small brands, marketers should concentrate on familiarity, not just awareness. Until familiarity is established, equity and purchase loyalty will not be strong.

4. For medium-sized brands, marketers should focus on "brand promise" (uniqueness and relevance). This will best serve to build a healthy brand because it will justify brand choice and avoid substitutability.
5. For large brands, relevance is a key characteristic. Marketers should avoid focusing on narrow target or customer segments and instead ensure that the brand proposition has the broadest appeal possible.
6. Large brands tend to soften on uniqueness (and relevance) and thus have a greater reliance on brand salience (familiarity and popularity). Sustaining brand salience requires constant marketing support (the quintessential scenario for "recency media planning").
7. Brand equity initiatives alone will be sharply hampered if the quality of product delivery is lower than the competition, if price is viewed as unreasonable, or if substitutability is an issue. These issues need to be addressed independently of any particular brand positioning campaign. In particular, some brands with a strong mental position perform poorly in markets due to high substitutability. Often unique secondary benefits (such as form, flavors, or packaging) can reduce substitutability with another brand.
8. Brand equity initiatives have less leverage in low-involvement categories. Instead, building salience is likely to be more important.

In practice, many brands will not be able to collect accurate and reliable data on all five consumer and market brand equity dimensions on a regular basis. Exposing and following the relationship between mental scores and the performance of a brand in the market remains a problem.

In many markets there is a lack of registration of consumer behavior at the category and brand levels. In these circumstances, brand equity research remains necessarily limited to forms such as surveys in which responses are measured at an individual level on a one-time basis. It is therefore essential to have an optimal approach to purchasing behavior in the category and in relation to the brands and to determine its relationship with the mental equity dimensions through factor and regression analysis.

Necessity of Flexibility

A complete brand equity measurement system will combine the factors of consumer brand equity and market brand equity and investigate all five of the critical factors: mental brand equity (cognitions and evaluations), relationship brand equity, and behavioral brand equity, as well as distribution position and market dynamics.

It is advisable to have flexibility regarding the dimensions of mental brand equity that are included in a measurement instrument. In particular, the core meanings of brands can be so diverse that measuring them with one and the same question is not always justified. With corporate brands, for example, the organizational associations should be part of a brand equity instrument.

When measuring behavioral equity, marketers need to distinguish between purchases that are made weekly and purchases that are made, say, once every ten years. It would therefore be helpful to start out with broad questions, expose the underlying meaning structures by means of factor analysis (techniques such as principal component analysis), and then analyze the connection between the found factors and behavior. The measurement instrument can then be compressed into the limited number of equity drivers found.

Brand images tend to be quite stable. They do change gradually, but little change is noticeable in the short term. For that reason, it would be useful to follow the development of brand equity continuously with a very compact measurement instrument that would monitor only the relative awareness, commitment, and purchasing behavior, adding a perception measurement at larger intervals.

The development of brand equity scores can now be related to measurements of market brand equity, as offered in standardized form by companies like ACNielsen, Information Resources, and GfK. Haigh (1997) affirms that large companies are now realizing that all measurement instruments should be collected, evaluated, and prioritized within a structured market research approach and considered as a whole within the brand control process.

Customer decisions are made for many different reasons and with differing degrees of conviction. Each product category has a specific set of performance and symbolic benefits that contribute to brand success. And each brand has its own specific association profile. Measures used for one brand may not be applicable to another brand. Most experts therefore conclude that brand equity measures to a certain extent should be uniquely designed for each brand and that multiple measures are required to provide a true assessment of brand equity.

Measurement is defined by how one defines a brand's equity. That definition should have pragmatic value, effectiveness, and efficiency: the brand equity scores should give guidance to improve the branding.

Some experts argue in favor of just one measure. Ehrenberg (1997) states repeatedly that there are only large and small brands and no strong and weak ones. He sees market share as an adequate measure. We agree that it is the most important measure, but it usually is rather volatile, strongly influenced by short-term price promotions. Moreover, to arrive at a market share, the product class and competitive set have to be defined, often a difficult task that is dependent on subjective opinions.

Aaker (1991) argues that customers' willingness to pay a price premium may be the best measure of brand equity available because it directly captures the loyalty of customers in a most relevant way. Fred Reichheld, the author of *The Loyalty Effect* (1996), *Loyalty Rules* (2001), and *The Ultimate Question* (2006), claims that the "willingness to recommend the brand to a friend" is the single most reliable measure of brand equity. Specifically, the "net promoter score," the number of people willing to recommend the brand less those who are not willing to do so, would provide an accurate predictor of a brand's growth prospects.

All of these single measures probably give a good indication of a brand's strength and therefore could be candidates for a compact brand equity tracking system. We are not aware of proper validation against market performance (i.e., market share, price premium, penetration, share of customer), however. Their limitation is that they do not provide any insight into the drivers of brand equity and their development. Ultimately a brander wants to know these—to be able to formulate strategies and execute programs to maintain and possibly improve on a brand's performance. A brand equity measurement system should therefore distinguish between drivers and outcomes, as expressed in Figure 17.9.

The key measure of a brand's equity should reflect an overall purchase likelihood or overall disposition toward a brand in the minds of the category users and within a competitive context (Baker et al. 2005). This can be measured by a disposition scale that permits respondents to state the status of a brand in their purchase repertoire: is it the only brand considered or one of several? Relative preference can be measured on the basis of a constant-sum method by asking respondents to divide a set of points among the considered brands in a category reflecting their preference levels. These scores are then aggregated and repercentaged to yield a "brand share of mind." Regression analysis is applied to uncover the relative influence of the mental equity drivers. And the brand share of mind is then contrasted with the behavioral outcomes, such as

Figure 17.9 **Mental BE Drivers Versus Market BE Outcomes**

MENTAL BE DRIVERS   MARKET BE OUTCOMES

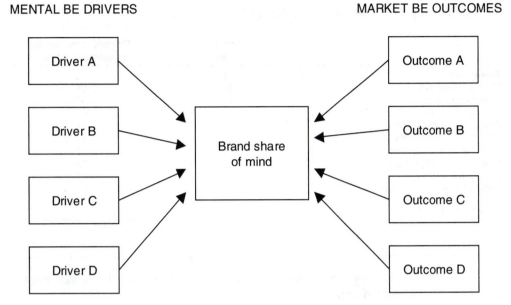

penetration, share of requirements, and share of market. Often the brand last purchased is used as a proxy for market share.

To identify the mental equity drivers, a thorough exploratory research stage is required. As we have seen, there are many different candidates.

Brand Performance Scorecard

A disciplined approach to the matter of measurement could consist of the composition of the brand performance scorecard, in which the most important components of brand equity are specified and tested at regular intervals. Such a scorecard could consist of a selection of the variables presented in the overview of Table 17.11. The composition of the scorecard is, to a certain extent, category- and brand-dependent.

A brand metric is a good one when a manager can use it to make real business decisions. "Nice to know" information has to be distinguished from "need to know" information. Sexton (2005) interviewed twenty brand managers to investigate which measures they considered "most important" and which they considered "absolutely essential" to use in the scorecard. The measure they rated most highly was *perceived value*. Other measures they considered most important were name recall, differentiation, relevance, trust, trial, satisfaction, and recommendation. Based on a survey of 200 top marketers and finance executives, Ambler (2000) describes the measures actually practiced in the United Kingdom, contrasting them with the measures considered to be important for assessing performance.

The scorecard can be supplemented with marketing-mix input variables, through which the exposure of the relationship between marketing investments and brand development materializes in the long term. It is the experience of the author that, in most brand operations, a large amount of data is available, but there usually is a complete lack of systematic recording and analysis.

Table 17.10

Most Commonly Used Metrics (United Kingdom)

	Percent firms using measure	Percent rated top for assessing performance
Awareness	78	2
Market share (volume or value)	78	36
Relative price	70	37
Complaints (dissatisfaction level)	69	45
Consumer satisfaction	68	46
Distribution/availability	66	18
Total number of customers	65	40
Perceived quality/esteem	64	35
Loyalty/retention	64	67
Relative perceived quality	62	62

Source: Ambler (2000).

Principle: A disciplinary measurement and analysis of brand equity development demands a scorecard approach.

BRAND EQUITY STRATEGY IMPLICATIONS

The brand equity position is of decisive importance for the strategy of a brand. Ideally, an analysis of the mental, relational, behavioral, and market brand equity position of the brand is the basis for the formulation of brand goals.

Overall brand equity research, such as that conducted by Millward-Brown (Farr and Hollis 1997), finds that brands under conditions of stability typically do adhere to the double jeopardy relationship. However, it is possible for brands to create a stable and potentially long-lasting deviation from that underlying relationship. This can be the result of either structural market advantages or attitudinally based consumer equities.

The findings of Millward-Brown's research have important implications for all of us involved in marketing brands, even if only to remind us of some important facts of life. Farr and Hollis (1997) summarize a number of these implications below.

1. If you are responsible for an established brand, do not be too optimistic that your marketing activity will change the standing of your brand in the short term. There are many forces that work to obviate change, both market and consumer driven. Much marketing activity serves to maintain the status quo in the face of competition rather than change it. This needs to be better recognized as a positive end in itself, since, as we have seen, brands can decline if existing consumer equities are not supported.

2. Major changes in the status quo will usually result from some form of disruption. This usually takes the form of innovation of one form or another, for example, price segmentation, new creative strategy, repositioning, new product formulation, etc. Saturn's entry into the small car market was a classic example. Careful research and planning identified drivers' needs for a

Table 17.11

Brand Performance Scorecard

Measurement instrument	Measure according to
Mental basic brand equity • Awareness • Price/value • Involvement	• TOMA/rank order • Price trade-off • Relevance • Consideration • Relative preference • Purchasing intention
Mental intermediate brand equity • Product performance associations • Symbolic associations • Brand positioning • Differentiation	• Brand understanding • Brand differentiation • Perceived quality • Perceived value • Brand personality • Brand value
Relationship brand equity • Familiarity • Loyalty/commitment • Bonding • Reciprocal relationship • Social norm	• Familiarity • Relative satisfaction • Loyalty/commitment • Partner quality • Intimacy • Perceived popularity • Reputation • Prestige • Affection
Behavioral brand equity • Penetration • Retention • Share of customer	• Ever bought (penetration) • Bought last • Bought last versus bought previously • Defections • "Share of customer"
Market brand equity • Weighted distribution • Depth of distribution • Relative price • Market share	• Weighted distribution • Facings/support • Market share value • Market share volume • Market share within distribution • Price premium • Price elasticity
Brand value • Net sales • Operating earnings • Future cash flows • Capital employed • Discount rate • Brand monetary value	• Total value of sales • Sales growth rate • Sales less cost of sales • Cash flows

friendlier buying experience and a company that stood behind its product. The result was not only a successful launch but also a basic change in the way the category was viewed.

3. It is easier for a new brand to disrupt a category than an established one for three basic reasons. First, there may be a consumer "straight jacket" based on existing perceptions of established brands. Radical changes are just as likely to disenfranchise existing buyers as bring in new ones. Second, competitors are unlikely to ignore innovations made by an established brand and will try to match them. They may be less threatened by completely new brands that take time to create a presence. Third (and linked to the first), the marketing teams of established brands (and their senior managements) may simply be hesitant to deviate from the existing successful formula and experiment with new approaches.

4. Although new brands will find it easier to disrupt a category, once the initial impetus is lost the new brand is likely to be locked into the new category relationship in the same way it was locked into the old. In other words, the launch is a one-shot opportunity to establish the brand's position in the marketplace. It is critical that it be successful. This supports the typical Procter and Gamble strategy of introducing a new product: Identification of a new relevant and differentiating benefit, followed by heavy weights of advertising to establish that differentiation as a category advantage, at the same time maximizing penetration.

5. There is an important corollary to the previous point. Once disruption occurs, established brands must be prepared to respond quickly. In our examination of case-history material, established brands often decline simply because the competitive context changes, not because they make active marketing errors. A failure to match or defend against new claims can be fatal.

6. Consumer perceptions do matter, but only if they create a strong predisposition toward the brand. We would identify the following broad ways in which a brand can create a strong attitudinal bond with the consumer:

- stronger relevance to people's needs than other brands;
- better perceived product performance;
- stronger emotional appeal;
- stronger saliency;
- stronger perceived popularity, either in terms of growth or in absolute terms;
- better perceived pricing.

Obviously, there is a multitude of ways in which brands can create these differentiating perceptions, and a brand might be strong on several counts. However, we would suggest it is important to identify which approach offers most leverage for your brand. This will differ from brand to brand, category to category, and country to country. Strong and consistent brand communication is then necessary to turn these basic strengths to advantage.

7. Creating a strong attitudinal bond with your consumer is fundamental to your brand's long-term success. The creation of this bond is not a guarantee of growth, but a brand that fails to maintain this equity will be more vulnerable to competitive actions than otherwise. Equally, attitudinal strength alone is not enough to ensure success. Both push and pull mechanisms will affect a brand's standing over time, and the marketing team must successfully leverage both to ensure its brand's longer-term health.

Survey research tools, as discussed above, can provide insight into both the strength of a brand and what to do to make it stronger. Clearly, brands that consumers feel to have either rational, emotional,

Figure 17.10   **Behavioral Brand Equity and Brand Strategy**

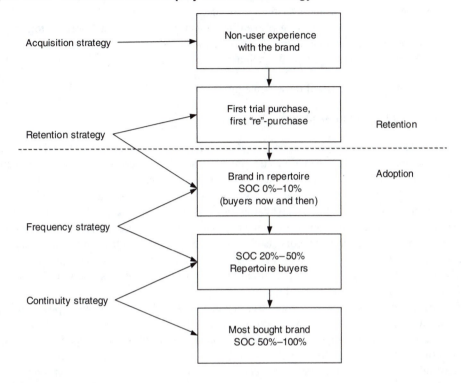

or saliency-based advantages are likely to be worth more to their owners in the future than brands that are bought purely on the basis of availability or pricing. Overall, this provides continued evidence for the value of long-term brand-building activity. In other words, marketers can help their brand grow up big and strong by understanding how to manage effectively the total brand system.

Behavioral Impact

In the end, marketing strategy is focused on the purchasing behavior of consumers. The goal is to get a brand included in the repertoire of category users, to reach the highest possible share of customer within this repertoire, and to maintain brand loyalty over time. In fast-moving consumer goods, trial use almost always precedes it; with cars, this happens through visits to various dealers and test-drives.

The most important strategic consideration is the one between programs that are directly aimed at influencing behavior and those in which influencing brand representation is foremost. The starting point is the behavioral brand equity of a brand and how its development profile looks, as depicted in Figure 17.10.

We distinguish five basic strategies aimed at influencing the brand buying behavior of category users:

1. *Acquisition strategy:* aimed at attracting first-trial users for the brand.
2. *Retention strategy:* aimed at getting first-trial users to try the brand again (as we saw in Chapter 16, about half of the first-trial users do not buy the product a second time).

3. *Frequency strategy:* aimed at getting consumers to add the brand to their buying repertoire and increasing the brand's share of customer.
4. *Continuity strategy:* aimed at preventing defection, winning back lost customers, and increasing or consolidating the share of customer.
5. *Winning-back strategy:* aimed at winning back lost customers.

We will briefly discuss each of these strategies.

Acquisition and Retention Strategies

Penetration is the most important component of the market share of a brand. Every brand has to focus on it because a brand's future depends on attracting new users. So, in addition to penetration, acquisition and retention strategies always form an important part of a brand development strategy.

The possibilities of an acquisition strategy depend on the development stage of a market: to what extent is there an influx of new category users, or to what extent does a brand have to convert users of competitive brands? In young markets for new categories, a brand will obviously concentrate on potential new category users. In established markets, the emphasis is naturally on conversion. The possibilities of a successful conversion strategy depend on four factors: (1) involvement in the category, (2) level of bonding with competing brands, (3) ambivalence, and (4) expectations that a brand knows how to awaken.

To generate initial or repeat trial purchases, a balance has to be found between push- and pull-oriented activities. The most important consideration is the quality and relevance of the brand's concept and potential messages. Does the pull strategy offer sufficient perspective, or should trial be stimulated through promotional activities (such as spreading samples, price discounts, or demonstrations)? Research into the effectiveness of television commercials in generating trial use shows that the following statements show a strong correlation with it (Olsen 1984):

- The commercial showed that the product offers certain advantages.
- The product is important to me.
- The commercial reminded me that I am not satisfied with the product I'm using now, and that I'm searching for something better.
- During the commercial I was thinking in which way could that product be useful to me.
- The commercial gave me the feeling that this is the right product for me.

Commercials with a low trial effect scored low on these aspects. Trial-generating communication has to awaken curious expectations about the product. When a brand concept has insufficient pull strength, mass communication will have little effect.

Frequency Strategies

A strategy aimed at existing brand users has to weigh frequency against continuity. As Chapter 7 on strategic market segmentation made clear, the evidence on the possibility of increasing the share of customer by means of a so-called loyalty program is, at the very least, conflicting. Research into the influence of advertising campaigns and promotions on purchasing behavior also gives a variable picture (Franzen et al. 1999):

- Campaigns can be very effective in influencing consumer purchases in the period that directly follows the confrontation with a television commercial.

- There is ample spreading in the degree of this campaign effectiveness.
- A positive effect within one year also has a positive influence on the sales volume for the two subsequent years.
- In a considerable percentage of the campaigns, there is no real positive influence on purchasing behavior in the period directly following advertising confrontation.
- When there is no such short-term effect, no long-term effect will appear either (that is, there will be no "sleeper effect").
- In a large number of campaigns that do manage to create a positive short-term effect, the attained effect gets lost before the trial year is over due to a lack of continuity.

From the above evidence we can derive that, to achieve a durable increase of the share of customer, an advertising campaign has to exert a direct influence on behavior and needs a high degree of continuity to consolidate this effect. In an analysis of the effects of the "everyday low prices" strategy of Procter & Gamble, it was established that an active price promotion strategy is indeed influential to the penetration of brands (especially retention), but hardly to the share of customer. In this comprehensive analysis, advertising does not seem to have an effect on the share of customer either. Considering all the empirical information on the subject, we arrive at the conclusion that the possibility of substantially increasing the share of customer should not be overestimated.

Continuity Strategies

A continuity strategy aims at maintaining and strengthening the position with consumers who already are loyal buyers of the brand. In terms of the conversion model, these are users who are bonded to the brand as well as loyal users who have no deep emotional bonding with it.

For this strategy it is desirable to have insight into the mental brand equity and the equity drivers, which can be identified on the basis of the former. A weighing out has to be made as to which equity dimensions need strengthening.

Often the continuity strategy is labeled customer relationship building. Research into brand-person relationships by SWOCC in the Netherlands (Tolboom 2004b) shows, however, that only a small minority of the users of a brand is susceptible to forming a relationship with their brand. This conclusion applies about equally to fast mover (package goods), durable, and service brands. On average, only about 10 percent of the users of the researched ten leading brands feel a relationship, and about 6 percent more would appreciate a relationship; about 50 percent are indifferent about such a relationship, and 34 percent even reject the possibility of one. Of those brand users who do not feel a relationship, about 52 percent do feel an attachment to the brand, however. The overall conclusion is that a true brand relationship often is "a bridge too far"—but creating and strengthening a bond is always a useful alternative objective.

Winning-Back Strategies

As we saw in Chapter 7, companies do lose customers every year: estimates range from 20 to 40 percent of them. Often a company has a better chance of winning back former customers than creating new ones. Insight is needed into why they defected. Were they dissatisfied, or just lured away by a competitor by offering them a better price for instance?

One should not wait until the relationship is completely broken to develop a winning-back strategy and such a program should make it easy for them to return. This strategy calls for a well-aimed, well-planned effort based on sound information from the brand's own database. Typical diagnostic questions include the following:

- What are the sources of dissatisfaction?
- What can be done to ameliorate these feelings before they cause a rupture?
- Are these customers worth the extra effort to retain them?
- How much damage can they do to brand perceptions if they leave?

The main goal is to reinstate trust. One has to let customers know that the company values their business, and point out how things may have changed on the company's side. Perhaps it can make a special offer for a re-trial. Sometimes following a complaint registered through customer service, a personal note from a senior-level executive is sufficient to convince them that the company cares, listens, and is willing to improve. If nothing else, it leaves the customers with a better feeling for the company. Also the new supplier may make mistakes, which might encourage them to return to the brand.

Addressing the Bottlenecks

McKinsey & Company (2003) studied over 220 brands in twenty-six industries to ascertain how well a brand succeeds in driving customers through the stages of purchase. The McKinsey researchers distinguished "door openers"—the ratio of those considering a brand to those aware of it—from "deal closers" (trying versus considering) and "retention drivers" (deliberately buying versus occasional use). McKinsey then examined, by industry, the brand messages identified with best-in-class brands at each stage of the hierarchy to determine how different messages can have greater impact as door openers, deal-closers, or retention drivers. In contrast to commonly held beliefs, McKinsey established the following conclusions:

- Predictors of brand performance differ dramatically among industries and change from point to point along the hierarchy.
- Focusing both spending and brand messaging on overcoming the highest-impact bottlenecks at different stages of the hierarchy will open up consumer bottlenecks and drive sales.
- By combining a bottom-up approach with overall top-down brand aspirations, financial services marketers can provide a solid platform for future growth while maximizing marketing spending effectiveness.

McKinsey's research also established that "many financial services marketers fail to focus their message where they can have the most impact on brand bottlenecks, instead falling into one of two traps that reduce spending effectiveness":

- *The brand vision trap:* in which financial institutions expend disproportionate energy and resources against an aspirational brand promise. While brands must be built with a vision in mind, the resulting brand promise may be too broad or too far removed from the customer's existing understanding of the brand and so does not effectively move customers through existing bottlenecks.
- *The general brand health trap:* in which brand messaging and spending are measured by—and focused on—general health metrics like quality or uniqueness instead of attributes specific to the brand's bottlenecks.

Many marketers believe that spending their marketing dollars at a high level of the hierarchy or, generally, across all points in the hierarchy will have the greatest impact. McKinsey's findings strongly contrast with this belief. They indicate that predictors of brand performance change from point to point along the hierarchy and differ dramatically between industries. As a result, marketers who focus their marketing dollars specifically on opening up the bottlenecks will have a greater effect on sales. To accomplish this goal, marketers should identify what McKinsey calls "high-impact attributes" for their industries: the rational and emotional brand benefits, values, images, and personalities that drive customer conversion from awareness to trial to loyalty.

SAMSUNG: THE WORLD'S LEADING ELECTRONICS BRAND

Over a span of about ten years Samsung managed to reinvent itself as a brand with a reputation for quality, despite decades of consumer perception that it manufactured low-end, cheap knock-offs. The company has become the third largest electronics maker in the world, behind Sony and Matchusita and before Philips and Siemens. Today consumers take Samsung seriously.

In Interbrand's annual ranking of the hundred largest global brands, Samsung steadily moved ahead, from number 42 in 2001, to 34 in 2002, to 21 in 2004, (which it still occupies in 2007). By then it had overtaken Sony (26 in 2006) and was way ahead of Siemens (44 in 2006) and Philips (48 in 2006). In 2006 it had a market value exceeding $96 billion. In fact, Samsung was *the* success story in Interbrand's ranking of brand values in the last six years, posting the biggest gain in value of any global 100 brands with a 186 percent surge.

BRAND VALUATION

As we have seen, the phenomenon of brands goes back to about the beginning of the nineteenth century. The brand concept developed in parallel with the Industrial Revolution and the emergence of national distribution systems. But until the mid-1980s there was nothing like a body of knowledge about the function of brands in the society. The first books on brands appeared around 1990.

Brands began to attract focused attention because some managers of large consumer companies became aware of their importance as key value drivers. These managers began to realize that there might be more value in their brands, called "goodwill," than in their material assets. And they started to acquire other companies and to incorporate these brands into their own portfolios.

Since then a worldwide hunt for strong, established, international brands has developed, culminating in takeovers such as Nabisco by Philip Morris, which paid $15.2 billion for the goodwill in its brands (plus $4 billion of Nabisco debt), the goodwill primarily consisting of brand reputation. The excess in purchase price over the estimated net assets was $16.8 billion. That means that 75 percent of the total assets of Nabisco was goodwill. Unilever paid 25.5 billion euros for Best Foods, essentially only to acquire worldwide brands like Knorr and Hellmann's. In 2005 Procter & Gamble paid $57 billion for the Gillette company with its brands, such as Gillette, Duracell, Braun, and Oral B.

This brand hunt, of course, raised the question of how to determine the value of brands. It also raised the issue of whether these brand values should be included on the official corporate balance sheets of their owners. One of the first companies to tackle these issues was the British company Cadbury Schweppes.

CADBURY SCHWEPPES CAPITALIZES ITS BRANDS

The heritage of Cadbury Schweppes starts back in 1783, when Jacob Schweppes perfected his process for manufacturing carbonated mineral water in Geneva, Switzerland. And in 1824 John Cadbury opened a shop in Birmingham, England, selling cocoa and chocolate. In 1879 a new factory was completed in Birmingham, and milk chocolate was introduced. After World War I, mass production began in earnest. Cadbury's Dairy Milk became a household name in Great Britain. In 1938 the brand named Roses was launched.

In 1969 Cadbury merged with Schweppes and in 1986 Canada Dry was acquired. From then on the company became a major acquirer: in 1989 alone the company made twelve separate acquisitions. It increased its brand portfolio in a frenzy of takeover activity that heavily affected the company's balance sheet. Accounting standards dictated that the excess amount paid over and above the net assets of the acquired businesses would have to be written off against shareholders' funds in the company's account, which would make Cadbury Schweppes look like a company in financial difficulty and possibly lead to lower credit ratings and problems with debt covenants.

The management considered that a significant part of the goodwill it had bought was in brand values, which, provided they are supported, tend to increase in value. The managers believed that amortization over a period of twenty years—that is, reduction in value over time—was not necessary. They decided to review these brand values annually and reduce them in the balance sheet only when it was apparent that they had suffered diminution in value. The capitalization of the brands improved the balance sheet significantly and helped to reduce its level of gearing (the relationship between money loaned and share-capital). It also set a process in motion to develop a sophisticated brand valuation system, which led to the discounted cash flow review procedure, to be discussed later in this chapter.

By 2006 Cadbury Schweppes had become the world's largest confectionery company, with a strong presence in beverages in the Americas and Australia.

Sources: Haigh (1999); J. Murphy (1989); www.Cadburyschweppes.com.

MONETARY BRAND VALUE

A former Coca-Cola president once said that, if all the Coke properties were destroyed, he could assemble the worldwide financial support needed to put the company back together again based only on the fact that he held the rights to the Coca-Cola brand name—and the secret formula it represents.

Obviously there has to be value in well-known and highly respected brands such as IBM, Unilever, Sony, Colgate, Nokia, Virgin, Ralph Lauren, and Mercedes. Stephen Smith, chair of the American Brands Council, observes, "Recent surveys indicate that brands may account for 50 to 70 percent of the total value of the company" (S. Smith 2003). In what might be seen as a classic understatement, he concluded that brands might be worth billions of dollars.

The effects of a brand on the market position and the financial results of companies have led in the last ten years to a realization that brands represent a financial value that is often greater than that of the tangible assets on the company's balance sheet. In some takeovers of very large companies with several well-known branded products, a goodwill amount has been paid that was five to six times higher than the worth of the tangible assets, such as production facilities and equipment. A 50 percent to 100 percent premium on the stock exchange value is not uncommon. Philip Morris paid as much as twice the stock exchange value for Kraft and for General Foods.

Diageo, one of the world's largest alcoholic beverage and package food companies, sells some thirty-five brands, including Bailey's, Smirnoff, Guinness, and Johnnie Walker, in 170 countries. Its 2001 annual report showed a total net book value of its brands of $5.213 million. This is more than 1.6 times the net book value of its other intangible assets of $3.176 million (Garcia-Gonzáles 2002).

Although the U.S. market and its accountants have been slow to develop methods for brand valuation, it is a procedure that has been conducted for decades in Europe by such brand management specialists as Interbrand and Brand Finance. Some estimate that the average market value of U.S. companies is at least 70 percent higher than their replacement value. Again the difference lies in the intangible value of the companies' brands. This notion of the value of the brand became even more important, despite the reluctance of accountants to establish values for intangibles, with the mergers and buyouts of the 1990s that led to such examples as those in the opening story.

Estimates of Brand Value

In 1987 the Interbrand consultancy introduced a methodology for brand valuation, and in 1988 it conducted the world's first public brand valuation study for the RHM Group in the United Kingdom, followed in 1989 by a landmark brand valuation of the Pillsbury brand portfolio for Grand Metropolitan acquisition. Since then Interbrand has applied its system on thousands of brands worldwide. Every year it reports the value of the top "most valuable" brands in the world as shown in Table 18.1.

Obviously, the financial value of brands can contribute significantly to the stock exchange value of a business and thus forms one of the most important assets of many companies. The following table shows that, according to Interbrand, the value of the McDonald's brand in 2002 represented 71 percent of the stock exchange value of the fund.

Interbrand reports that in 2001 brands on average accounted for 33 percent of all shareholder value of the companies it valuated, other intangibles 39 percent, and the tangible assets only 28 percent (see Figure 18.1).

Many published analyses have reported a link between branding and the financial performance of a firm. A study by Aaker and Jacobson (1994) found a positive relationship between scores on EquiTrend's eleven-point perceived product quality measure as a brand equity indicator, and stock price as a firm value indicator. Firms experiencing the largest gains in brand equity saw their stock return average 30 percent; conversely, those firms with the largest losses in brand equity saw stock return average a negative 10 percent. And brand equity impact was distinct from that of return on investment—the correlation between the two was small. In contrast, there was no impact of advertising on stock return, except that it was captured by brand equity (Aaker and Joachimsthaler 2000).

An analysis by Interbrand and Citibank found that heavily brand-dependent companies outperformed the FTSE 350 index over a fifteen-year period by between 15 percent and 20 percent (Butterfield 1998).

Madden et al. (2006) analyzed the relationship between estimates of brand value, as provided by Interbrand, and the stock market performance of 111 companies for the period 1994–2000. They concluded that firms that have developed strong brands create value for their shareholders by yielding returns that are 50 percent greater in magnitude than a relevant market benchmark, and do so with 20 percent less risk.

Kerin and Sethuraman (1998) for 55 publicly held U.S. consumer goods firms with 143 brands researched the relationship between their brand value, as calculated by Interbrand, and their share-

Table 18.1

Brand Value of "Twenty–five Most Valuable" Brands, 2007

Rank	Value (in million dollars)
Coca-Cola	65.324
Microsoft	58.709
IBM	57.091
GE	51.569
Nokia	33.696
Toyota	32.070
Intel	30.954
McDonald's	29.398
Disney	29.210
Mercedes	23.568
Citi	23.443
Hewlett-Packard	22.197
BMW	21.612
Marlboro	21.283
American Express	20.827
Gillette	20.415
Louis Vuitton	20.321
Cisco	19.099
Honda	17.998
Google	17.837
Samsung	16.853
Merrillynch	14.343
hsbc	13.563
Nescafé	12.950
Sony	12.907
Pepsi	12.888

Source: Interbrand (2007).

Table 18.2

Brand Contribution to Company Capitalization

Company	Brand value (in billion US$), 2002	Brand contribution to market capitalization of parent company (in percent)
Coca-Cola	69.6	51
Microsoft	64.1	21
IBM	51.2	39
GE	41.3	14
Intel	30.9	22
Nokia	30.0	51
Disney	29.3	68
McDonald's	26.4	71
Marlboro	24.2	20
Mercedes-Benz	21.0	47

Source: BusinessWeek, Interbrand/JP Morgan league table, 2002.

Figure 18.1 **Contributions to Shareholder Value**

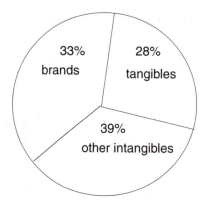

Source: Interbrand (Cole 2002).

holder value as expressed in the ratio between a company's book equity and the market value of its stock over the years 1995 and 1996. They found that firms with higher accumulated brand values have higher market-to-book (M/B) ratios. On average the accumulated brand values explain as much as 40 percent of the variation in the M/B ratio. The functional form of the relationship turned out to be concave with decreasing returns to scale: a given increase in a firm's brand value relates to a larger increase in a firm's M/B ratio when its accumulated brand value is small, and to a smaller increase if a firm already has high accumulated brand values.

Also Barth et al. (1998), in analyzing for 183 publicly traded U.S. firms the relationships between brand values and share prices, found that brand value estimates are significantly positively associated with equity share prices.

The management consultancy Booz Allen and Hamilton and the brand consultancy Wolff Olins carried out research among marketing executives across Europe. They concluded that "brand-driven companies"—those that actively use the brand to drive business decisions and manage the company—significantly outperform their rivals. They have profitability margins nearly twice the industry standard. But less than 20 percent of the companies put the management of their brand at the heart of their business systems and capabilities.

McKinsey Germany found that brand-driven companies realized a 2.6 percent higher total return to shareholders compared to the market average and that companies with weak brands stayed 6.9 percent behind the market average.

This financial advantage is the reason companies are refocusing their brand portfolios and concentrating on the brands that create the most value for their business.

BRAND VALUE ON THE BALANCE SHEET

A strong brand constitutes an important asset for a company and thus a strong argument exists that this value should be reflected on its balance sheet. In the United States, the United Kingdom, Germany, France, and the Netherlands, however, brands legally cannot be included on balance sheets unless the brand was acquired. In other countries, including Australia, Canada, New Zealand, and Japan, the value of "home-grown" brands can be reflected as intangible assets on balance sheets.

Both U.S. and international rules (respectively, Financial Accounting Standard 141 in the

United States and International Financial Reporting Standard 3 from the International Accounting Standard Board) require that all identifiable intangible assets of an acquired business be recorded at fair value. This rule ends the previous practice of treating the excess of the purchase price over the net tangible assets acquired as a single goodwill figure.

Now there is a requirement that this single goodwill figure will be broken down into a number of specific intangible assets, leaving only a small residual amount of unidentified goodwill. The types of intangible assets that are now to be expressly recognized include technology-based assets, such as patents; contract-based assets, such as leases and licensing agreements; artistic assets, such as plays and films; customer-based assets, such as customer lists; and marketing-related assets, such as trademarks and brands (Haigh and Knowles 2006).

But the internally generated brands should still be treated as expenses when they are recurred.

The financial world is recognizing that goodwill is not an amorphous accounting "difference," but a sum covering a range of identifiable and separate assets, such as brands. The supporters of brand valuation argue that the next logical step would be the inclusion of a statement of brand values, including both acquired and internally generated brands, as a separate part of the annual financial statements (Haigh 1999b).

To Value or Not to Value?

The present non-inclusion of homegrown brands reflects the uncertainty or lack of consensus on brand valuation methods. It leads to the strange situation that the McDonald's brand does not appear on the company's balance sheet, even though it represents 71 percent of its stock market value (Lindeman 2004).

Given the enormous value of megabrands such as those reported in Table 18.1, the difference in treatment between acquired and internally generated brands is very unsatisfactory for all parties that have an interest in the proper valuation of companies. Proper valuation of a company's brands would provide a more truthful representation of the company's financial situation. Executed on a continuous basis, it also would enable managers to assess the effects of brand expenditures on the value of their brands and to better manage the stockholder value of their companies. Proper, standardized brand valuation would also bring accounting and marketing closer for the purpose of improving strategic brand management decisions. It would enable managers to compare brand-based results across divisions, product lines, and countries and to judge their results against those of comparable companies and industries.

Brand valuation also allows holding companies to charge a royalty for the use of brands to the operating companies, enabling a portion of the profits of these operating companies to be shielded from local taxes (Haigh and Knowles 2006).

In the case of mergers, acquisitions, and divestitures, having a real value for brands would result in a more realistic and fair evaluation for whatever the purpose—buying, selling, or joining to third parties (Garcia Gonzáles 2002).

> *Principle:* A strong brand is an important corporate asset whose value should be reflected on the company's balance sheet.

Given the big advantages of brand valuation, why has this not yet developed into a standard accounting principle, at least for companies whose stock is traded on the stock exchange? The basic problem is the concept of value itself. Babcock (in Garcia Gonzáles 2002) describes value as "expressible in terms of a single sum of money considered as payable or expected at a particular point in time in exchange for property, that is, the right to receive future benefits beginning at that particular time point." This definition in principle is related to future benefits, which in fact can never be known, but at best can be roughly estimated by extrapolating from the past and considering changes. But the problem is that what the past can tell about future stock price developments, especially as the 2001–2003 period reminds us, is often less than we would like.

A second problem is that brands are intangible assets, like know-how, patents, and customer and other stakeholder relationships. As opposed to tangibles, like production facilities, inventories, and claims for which an organization can provide verifiable quantitative data, the value of intangibles is, to a large extent, dependent on subjective opinions, for which accountants often have little appreciation.

We will now first briefly discuss the different approaches to brand valuation and then return to its complexities.

Approaches to Brand Valuation

Experts in the field of brand valuation distinguish seven approaches: market value, historic cost, replacement cost, royalty relief, price premium, economic value added, and economic use.

Market Value

This method basically measures the value of a brand based on the prices paid for similar brands in the recent past. It is an estimation of the amount for which a brand could be sold. However, given the absence of an actual and real market for most brands, a proper estimation is very difficult. Since markets in which companies operate are very different, and since brands are unique, a satisfactory brand valuation on this basis would require a large database of transactions. This is not yet available.

Historic Cost

This approach consists in adding the expenses incurred in the development of brands, including initial investment and subsequent maintenance costs. The method is essentially backward looking, ignoring the future benefits that the brand may represent which are of primary interest to all parties involved. Moreover, the method meets all kinds of problems in establishing the true net costs, after deduction of the income that the brand already generated in the period considered. In most companies these historical data are not readily available and many costs are not devised over the proper cost centers like brands. Therefore it is difficult to identify the costs that were not directly attributable to the brand, but were expensed in general support of it.

Moreover, what time period should be considered for brands like Coca-Cola or Ford, which have been in the market for over a century?

Replacement Cost

This method implies the calculation of the net costs to create, design, market, and build a brand over a predefined period of time in order to achieve a similar contribution as the actual brand under investigation has. This calculation would include all expenses involved—for example, the research and development costs of the product, market testing, continued advertising and promotion, and product improvements—and an estimation of the income that the brand would already generate during the period.

Basically the method shares the same problems as the historic cost approach: it would require a lot of guesswork to determine what is needed to build from scratch brands such as Pepsi, Ivory, Volvo, and American Express. Although the method complies with standard accounting practice for valuating assets and as a result is often favored by accountants, it calls for too many subjective estimates to be useful for brand management.

Royalty Relief

This method is based on what royalty a company would have to pay for the use of a brand in case it did not own it. To determine the appropriate royalty rate, a comparative study is conducted of publicly available royalty agreements in a given sector. The value calculation would be a saving of not having to pay such royalty. The method involves estimating future sales, applying an appropriate royalty rate to arrive at the savings, and then discounting these back to a net present value (Haigh 1999b).

It is a fairly simple method and therefore often preferred by tax authorities. A problem, however, is that the license fees are extremely difficult to identify. Often they are more a consequence of the value of a brand than vice versa.

Price Premium

This system is based on the price premium a brand realizes over the price of a comparable unbranded product. The price premium can be established in market studies or via conjoint-analysis. To arrive at a brand value, this price premium is then multiplied by the sales volume of the brand. The brand value is based on the additional earnings that are achieved as a sole result of the brand. A forecast is made of the number of years over which these additional earnings will be realized. The net present value of the brand is calculated by discounting these back, by applying an appropriate discount rate.

The approach has the attractiveness of simplicity—any brand-manager can execute it. But the problem is identifying an unbranded product that is fully comparable to the one the brand represents. This may not constitute a real problem for a toilet-paper brand, but it may be very difficult for other categories, such as a car brand or perfume. Moreover, the method tends to ignore the cost structures of the brands that are being compared—and thus offer only a partial comparison. For a proper brand valuation, the cost side cannot be disregarded, and it can be very difficult to arrive at a proper cost structure for the unbranded product used in the comparison.

Economic Value Added (EVA)

The Stern Stewart accounting firm developed the EVA methodology used by companies such as Coca-Cola and General Electric. It is based on the concept that "the value of the company depends on the extent to which investors expect future profits to exceed or fall short of the cost of capital." Current performance is already included in the actual share price. It is the continuous improvement in EVA that brings continuous increases in shareholder value. EVA is defined as net operating profit after taxes less a charge for the use of capital. It is a measure for excess return.

Economic Use

This method bases the value of a brand upon its income-generating capability over time and so is probably the best indicator of the real value of a brand. It is also in harmony with the definition of value that will be discussed under the "Brand Valuation Complexities" heading below. This approach is based on future benefits. In essence, this method adds all the cash flows (sum of net earnings and depreciation) for a predefined period and then calculates the present worth through a discount rate. The method therefore is often referred to as the discounted future cash flow (DCF) method. It is the most widely used method for brand valuation, applied by specialized companies in the field, such as Interbrand and Brand Finance. Therefore, we will discuss the DCF method in more detail.

Steps in the DCF Method

The DCF approach uses projected cash flows after making a fair charge for the tangible assets employed for producing and financing the brand. The result is earnings attributable to the intangible assets as a whole. The brand has to be valued in each segment, and the sum of the segment valuations constitutes the total value of the brand.

Subsequently a charge is made for tax. The resulting "excess earnings" are discounted back to a net present value of the brand.

The method calls for identifying a discount rate, which takes the risks inherent in the predicted cash flow into account. A highly risky cash flow—for example, on sales of Nintendo games—would be discounted more heavily than the cash flow from a less risky brand such as Heineken beer. The method operates with three basic variables:

- the future cash flow that is expected to be generated by the brand;
- the expected duration of such cash flow;
- the associated risk, expressed in terms of a discount rate.

A brand valuation procedure using the DCF methodology typically includes five steps:

1. *Market segmentation:* To distinguish the different markets in which a brand operates.
2. *Brand financial analysis:* To identify branded business earnings.
3. *Brand driver analysis:* To determine what proportion of business earnings is attributable to the brand or brand value added (BVA).
4. *Brand risk analysis:* To assess the security of the brand franchise both with customers and with end-consumers (in business-to-business brands, the customers of customers). To estimate this risk, the strength of the brand has to be determined. For this purpose, different systems are employed, which we will briefly discuss below (Haigh 1999b; Lindemann 2004).
5. *Brand value calculation.*

Step 1—Market Segmentation

Brands only have value in the context of a specific market, both in a product category and in a geographical sense. As a consequence, brand valuations have to be executed for every market (segment) and geographic area in which a brand operates; these have to be aggregated. Homogeneous, non-overlapping markets and market segments have to be identified to ensure that the valuations are relevant to the defined markets.

Figure 18.2   **Average Role of Brands in Various Industries**

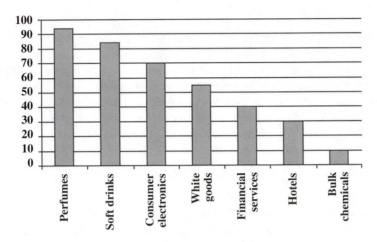

Source: Cole (2002).

Step 2—Brand Financial Analysis

This step involves forecasting future cash flows over a five- to ten-year period and discounting them back to present value. Trends for both volume and value for the market as a whole, and for the brand in particular, have to be taken into account. It may be appropriate to estimate price elasticity to predict the effect of price on sales.

Also, operating cost development has to be forecasted and the projected costs have to be allocated to the segments that have been distinguished. The same applies to the allocation of capital and the resulting charges for capital. Costs and charges for capital and overheads have to be deducted from the brand's earnings streams in order to arrive at a forecast for economic value added.

Step 3—Brand Driver Analysis

Different businesses rely in varying degrees on branding to generate and support sales. This makes it necessary to distinguish and estimate the demand drivers in a specific industry. Interbrand (Cole 2002) has calculated the average role of branding for a number of industries, as depicted in Figure 18.2. This shows that brands account for 95 percent of perfume sales and 10 percent of the sales of bulk chemicals. So the role that the brand plays in driving demand in the markets in which it operates has to be assessed, and the percentage of intangible earnings that is attributable to the brand has to be determined. Interbrand calls this the "role of branding" index. Brand Finance calls it the "brand value added (BVA)" index. It is the heart of brand valuation.

The procedure is to first identify drivers of demand for the branded business—that is, what influences customers to buy the product or services in a category. This is usually done by means of management workshops. It is preferable, however, to eliminate subjectivity as much as possible by using customer-based research and trade-off analysis. This can be done at a number of levels to determine the influence of the brand on the purchase decision between one brand and another, one time period and another, one sub-segment and another, and one product class and another. The information can be valuable also for planning future resource allocation.

Step 4—Brand Risk Analysis

The fourth step in brand valuation is to determine the appropriate discount rate that reflects the risks of the expected future earnings. It is measured by an index referred to as the brand strength score and is usually expressed as a score from 0 to 100.

The Brand Finance consultancy starts from the ten-year risk-free borrowing rate in the geographic markets under review. A brand strength score of 50 implies that the brand offers average investment risk and therefore has a "brand beta score" of 1. This means that the discount rate used in the valuation will be the average rate for the sector. A score of 10 implies a theoretically risk-free brand, which would be discounted at the risk-free rate. A score of 100 implies a weak brand, which doubles the equity risk premium.

Step 5—Brand Value Calculation

Brand value is the net present value (NPV) of the forecasted brand earnings discounted by the brand discount rate. In the valuation example by Interbrand (Lindemann 2004) in Table 18.3, the company profit tax is 35 percent, the charge for capital is 8 percent, the role of branding index is 79 percent, the brand strength score is 66, and the brand discount rate is 7.4 percent.

This calculation is made for each segment identified and added up.

DETERMINATION OF BRAND STRENGTH

For calculating the performance risk, different brand valuation consultancies have developed different sets of key indicators of brand strength.

Interbrand, the pioneer valuation consultancy since 1988, uses a range of seven key attributes that it identified and defined early in its practice:

1. *Market:* This represents 10 percent of brand strength. Brands in markets where consumer preferences are more enduring would score higher. So, for example, a food brand or detergent brand would score higher than a hotel or clothing brand because these latter categories are more susceptible to the swings of consumer preference.
2. *Stability:* This is 15 percent of brand strength. Long-established brands in any market would normally score higher because of the depth of loyalty they command. Ford, for example, would score higher than Kia.
3. *Leadership:* This is 25 percent of brand strength. A market leader is more valuable: being a dominant force and having strong market share matters. So, for example, on this score it is likely that the Coca-Cola brand would outperform Pepsi on a global basis.
4. *Profit trend:* This is 10 percent of brand strength. The long-term profit trend of the brand is an important measure of its ability to remain contemporary and relevant to consumers.
5. *Support:* This is 10 percent of brand strength. Brands that receive consistent investment and focused support usually have a much stronger franchise, but the quality of this support is as important as the quantity.
6. *Geographic spread:* This is 25 percent of brand strength. Brands that have proven international acceptance and appeal are inherently stronger than regional brands or national brands as they are less susceptible to competitive attack and therefore are more stable assets.

Table 18.3

Sample Brand Value Calculation

	Year 1	Year 2	Year 3	Year 4	Year 5
Market (Units)	250,000,000	258,750,000	267,806,250	277,179,469	296,890,750
Market growth rate		4%	4%	4%	4%
Market share (Volume)	15%	17%	19%	21%	20%
Volume	37,500,000	43,987,500	50,383,188	58,207,588	57,376,150
Price ($)	10	10	10	11	11
Price change		3%	2%	2%	2%
Branded revenues	375,000,000	450,871,875	531,983,725	621,341,172	625,326,631
Cost of sales	150,000,000	180,348,750	212,793,490	248,536,469	250,130,653
Gross margin	225,000,000	270,523,125	319,190,235	372,904,703	375,195,979
Marketing costs	67,500,000	81,156,938	187,524,263	111,941,411	112,559,794
Depreciation	2,812,500	3,381,539	3,989,878	4,660,059	4,689,950
Other overheads	18,750,000	22,543,594	26,599,186	31,067,059	31,266,332
Central cost allocation	3,750,000	4,509,719	5,319,837	6,213,412	6,253,266
EBITA (Earnings before interest, tax, and amortization)	132,187,500	158,932,336	187,524,263	219,022,763	220,427,638
Applicable taxes 35%	46,265,625	55,626,318	65,633,492	76,657,967	77,149,673
NOPAT (Net operating profit after tax)	85,921,875	103,306,018	121,890,771	142,364,796	143,277,964
Capital employed	131,250,000	157,805,156	186,194,304	217,469,410	218,864,321
Working capital	112,500,000	135,261,563	159,595,118	186,402,351	187,597,989
Net PPE	18,750,000	22,513,594	26,599,186	31,067,059	31,266,332
Capital charge 8%	10,500,000	12,624,413	14,895,544	17,397,553	17,509,146
Intangible earnings	75,421,875	90,681,606	106,995,227	124,967,243	125,768,819
Brand strength score 66 Brand discount rate 7.4%					
Discounted brand earnings	55,477,916	62,106,597	68,230,515	74,200,384	69,531,031
NPV (Net present value) of discounted brand earnings (Years 1–6) Long-term growth rate 2.5%	329,546,442				
NPV of terminal brand value (beyond Year 5)	1,454,475,639				
BRAND VALUE	1,784,022,082				

Source: Interbrand (Lindemann 2004).

Table 18.4

Brand Beta-Indicators

Time in market	Score
Brand awareness	(0–10)
Brand preference	(0–10)
Loyalty	(0–10)
Perceived quality	(0–10)
Share of voice	(0–10)
Distribution	(0–10)
Market share	(0–10)
Sales growth	(0–10)
Price premium	(0–10)
Total brand rating	(0–100)

Source: Brand Finance (2006).

Table 18.5

GfK's Brand Potential Index

Brand awareness
Uniqueness
Empathy with the brand
Trusting the brand
Brand identification
Willingness to recommend the brand
Buying intention
Brand allegiance
Acceptance of premium pricing
Quality

Source: GfK (Hupp and Powaga 2004).

7. *Protection:* This is 5 percent of brand strength. Securing full protection for the brand under international trademark and copyright law is the final component of brand strength in the Interbrand model.

The Stern Stewart accounting firm bases its Brand Economics valuation methodology on the brand vitality and brand stature scores in the BrandAsset® Valuator system developed by the advertising agency Young & Rubicam (see Chapter 17).

The Brand Finance consultancy uses a template of ten different indicators that carry equal weight. These indicators may vary for each business as appropriate (see Table 18.4).

For its advanced brand valuation model, the European research company GfK uses its Brand Potential Index (BPI) as a key metric of strength of brand equity. BPI is measured in the context of the brand's competitive set, using a scale from 0 to 100 generated from ten different attitudes scores (see Table 18.5).

Millward-Brown developed a brand valuation instrument called Optimor, based on its Brand Dynamics™ instrument for measuring brand equity, as discussed in Chapter 16 (see Figure 16.9).

Brand Dynamics distinguishes five basic dimensions of brand equity: presence, relevance, performance, advantage, and bonding.

BRAND VALUATION COMPLEXITIES

The execution of a brand valuation following the discounted future cash flow methodology includes a number of complexities that increase the difficulty of the procedure. For example, a marketer needs to isolate the brand-specific revenues and costs, reliably forecast future earnings, account for the mental brand factor, determine the appropriate discount rate, account for necessary environmental variables, estimate brand extension opportunities, and evaluate the various brand equity approaches and methods.

- *Isolating brand-specific revenues and costs:* The intangible value of a brand may partly be dependent on tangible assets, such as the research and development capabilities of an organization, making the separation between brand and nonbrand factors almost impossible to determine objectively. Other nonbrand-specific revenues may result from a distribution benefit, from product features, or from a high level of promotion spending.
- *Forecasting future earnings:* Another question is how to arrive at dependable estimates of future earnings. Often current revenues are extrapolated and cost structures are considered to be constant without sufficiently taking market developments, trends, and brand positioning into account. Forecasting requires making all sorts of assumptions about the future, many of which will turn out to be wrong. Buying and selling things on the basis of forecasts (e.g., shares) has an element of gambling about it (Feldwick 2002).
- *Accounting for the mental brand equity factor:* The scoring templates of both Brand Finance and Interbrand demonstrate that neither has incorporated a mental brand equity factor, as opposed to approaches followed by the Stewart accountancy and by GfK, which use the BrandAsset® Valuator and the Brand Potential Index, respectively. This raises questions about the relative reliability of the factors employed.
- *Determining the discounting rate:* To determine the present-day financial value of a brand, the estimated future brand value added has to be discounted back by an appropriate discount rate. This rate has a big impact on the resulting brand value. A one percent higher or lower rate results in a sizable increase or decrease of the resulting brand value. As far as we can see, there is not yet a rational method for determining the discount rate.
- *Accounting for the brand environment:* Brands do not operate in isolation but interact with other parts of the brand system. The value of a brand for a prospective buyer may be very different from the value it represents for the current owner. The particular skills, abilities, and market positions of an acquiring company may justify a considerably higher estimate of a brand's value than it has for the current owner. The tremendous price premiums over the stock market value that world leaders, such as Nestlé, Unilever, Procter & Gamble, and Philip Morris, have been paying for companies like Rowntree, Best Foods, Wella, Nabisco, and Gillette are spectacular cases in point.
- *Estimating brand extension opportunities:* It is striking that in the methodologies used by Interbrand and Brand Finance, no reference whatsoever is made to the extendability of the brand to other product categories. A study by Sattler (2000) found that 50 percent of the total brand equity could be due to extension options, so this seems an issue that cannot be overlooked.

Table 18.6

Brand Value Estimates, 2006 (in billion $)

	Millward-Brown Optimor (April 2006)	Interbrand (2006)	Difference (in billion $)
Microsoft	62	57	5
General Electric	55	49	6
Coca-Cola	41	67	26
Marlboro	39	21	18
Google	37	12	25
IBM	36	56	20
Citibank	31	21	10
Intel	25	32	7
Disney	22	28	6
Dell	18	12	6
Apple	15	9	6
Honda	14	17	3
Yahoo	14	6	8
Ford	14	11	3
eBay	13	7	6
Samsung	12	16	4
Starbucks	11	3	8
L'Óreal	11	6	5
Motorola	9	5	4
Budweiser	7	12	5
ING	6	3	3
Lexus	5	3	2
Nescafe	4	13	9

Source: Business Week (2005), Millward-Brown (2006c).

The Search for a Perfect Solution

In Chapters 16 and 17 it became clear that there are many different proprietary approaches and systems for measuring brand equity. There has not yet developed a general accepted practice—particularly one that could be universally adopted by accountants. Lack of agreement about something this fundamental says much about the state of the branding discipline. A general problem of many brand equity measurement instruments is a lack of focus on business outcomes. Brand equity measures should focus on particular customer behaviors that lead to market outcomes. One of the key questions still to be addressed is the relationship between equity scores and brand financial value. According to Haigh (1999b), "Brand valuations will only be credible if they are based on reliable forecasts and reliable forecasts must be informed with statistical valid historical data. The use of market research tracking data to link 'soft' marketing measures with 'hard' financial measures is one of the fast growing areas of market research. . . . The search for a perfect solution goes on." So until a consensus is reached on brand equity measurements, brand valuation will still be plagued by differences in brand equity schools and approaches.

The deviating subsystems used in the DCF method, for example, make the end results rather incomparable. Table 18.6 presents a comparison of the value in 2007 of 22 worldwide brands as calculated by two reputable companies—Millward-Brown as a subsidiary of WPP and Interbrand as a subsidiary of Omnicom. With differences as great as $26 billion for Coca-Cola, $25 billion for Google, and $20 billion for IBM resulting from the various methods, accountants

Figure 18.3 **Brand Value Versus Brand Earnings Development Matrix**

		Decrease	Increase
Long-term change in brand value	Increase	IBM Toyota	Starbucks Samsung GE
	Decrease	AT&T Kodak Ford	Nike Coca-Cola

Short-term brand-related earnings

Source: Agres et al. (2003).

for the time being will abstain from including these values in the balance sheets of the respective corporations.

Until an international consensus emerges on the procedures and standards regarding the valuation of brands, legislation in most western countries will continue to prohibit the inclusion of homegrown brands into the balance sheets of companies. The result is that Cadbury Schweppes, for example, includes only acquired brands, such as Canada Dry, Dr Pepper, 7-Up, Snapple, and Orangina, in its balance sheet, but not the value of its original brands—Cadbury, Roses, and Schweppes. Moreover, the increase in the value of the acquired brands cannot be incorporated. The consequence is a balance sheet that does not provide a reliable representation of the true value of the company's brands.

Value Earnings Matrix

The goal of every corporation is sustainable, profitable growth. Growth itself is not enough; it must be profitable. And profitable growth is not enough; it must be sustainable. This means that a corporation has to find a balance between short-term financial performance and longer-term growth of brand value, with the aim of growing, or at least maintaining, expected future cash flows. Often, short-term financial performance takes priority over building long-term brand value.

The relationship between brand value and brand earnings development can be expressed in a matrix as in Figure 18.3. Agres et al. (2003) analyzed the situation of a number of major brands based on the Interbrand valuations for 2000–2002. Brands in the upper left corner were growing brand value but not earnings. Both IBM and Toyota were investing in brand value and in growth of future cash flows. Brands in the upper right corner were growing value and earnings simultaneously. Starbucks and Samsung were enjoying the benefits of years of brand building. GE was favoring value growth, but maintaining earnings growth. Brands in the lower right corner were in trouble. Earning growth still continued but brand value declined. Nike and Coca-Cola were in this dangerous situation. Brands in the lower left corner were in trouble with earnings and brand value both in decline. AT&T, Ford, and Kodak had lost their way.

A value-earnings matrix can also be used to plot all the brands in a category in order to assess the developments and potentials of competitive brands.

VALUATION FOR STRATEGIC BRAND MANAGEMENT

Recognition of the economic and financial value of brands has increased the demand for effective management of the brand as an asset. Given the current situation with regard to brand valuation for accounting purposes, it should primarily be approached as a brand management tool. It is a logical extension of brand equity monitoring and it helps bridge the gap between marketing and financial management.

The valuation process focuses brand management on economic value creation. Companies as diverse as American Express, IBM, Samsung, Accenture, United Way of America, BP, Fujitsu, and Duke Energy have adopted brand valuation to help them focus their business decisions on their brands and to create an economic rationale for branding decisions, such as brand investments, licensing the brand to subsidiaries, turning the marketing department in a profit center, allocating financial resources to brands in the portfolio, selling brands, and using brands as securities against debt facilities (Lindeman 2004).

CADBURY SCHWEPPES AND BRAND VALUATION

The capitalization of its acquired brands enabled Cadbury Schweppes to acquire Dr Pepper and 7-Up in 1995, to buy the rights to Hawaiian Punch for the United States in 1999, to acquire Snapple and Orangina in 2000, and to purchase the Adams confectionery business in 2003. Upon acquisition, Cadbury Schweppes assesses the useful economic life of the brands and intangibles. It does not amortize over 99 percent of its brands by value. In arriving at the conclusion that a brand has an indefinite life, management recognizes that Cadbury Schweppes is a brands business that expects to acquire, hold, and support brands for an indefinite period. It supports its brands through spending on consumer marketing and through significant investment in promotional support, which is deducted in arriving at revenue. Many of its brands were established more than fifty years ago and the company continues to protect the legal rights that arise from these brand names indefinitely in the absence of any regulatory, economic, or competitive factors that could truncate the life of the brand name. The cost of brands and other intangibles with a finite life are amortized using a methodology that matches management's estimate of how the benefit of the assets will be extinguished. Each year it reevaluates the remaining useful life of the brands and other intangibles. If the estimate of the remaining useful life changes, the remaining carrying value is amortized prospectively over that revised remaining useful life.

The brand valuation process, moreover, led to an important shift in the internal management of the company.

CHAPTER 19

GESAMTKUNSTWERK
THE ART OF BRAND INTEGRATION

In the introduction to this book we described a brand as a product of both science and art. The science dimension involves the management of the complex set of systems encompassed by the strategies of branding and the complex consumer responses to a brand. The art referred to the metaphoric concept of *Gesamtkunstwerk*, which, like a beautiful building or work of art, represents the aesthetics of "goodness of fit"—the beauty that comes from a parsimonious yet perfect solution to a functional problem. Consider how this aesthetic vision led to the development of grand cathedrals in medieval times.

LIGHT: THE CORE PRINCIPLE IN CATHEDRAL DESIGN

Let us take you back to the Abbey of St. Denis, near Paris, in the year 1122, when the monk Suger was appointed as the new abbot. The abbey had been founded in the seventh century, and by the time Suger stepped in, it had grown into the symbol of royal power. He started a renovation that in a decade would transform the cloister into the first large cathedral in Europe.

    Suger was someone who thought big. His goal was to make the abbey "shine in the greatest splendor, to the highest glory of God." The central principle was that "*God is Light*" and that the ascension of Christ into heaven was a passage from material light to spiritual light. On this founding idea he based the entire renovation of the abbey. He placed three portals so the light of the sunset could penetrate deep into the building. Above the portals he put the first rose window in a Western church. At the other end of the building he situated the choir as the lighting center, the place of the most blinding closeness to God, where the rising sun threw its rays inside.

Under his direction, a cross vault was built that made it possible to remove the dividing walls, allowing the light to enter deep into the building. In this way, Suger tried to make the church transparent to daylight by getting rid of anything in the way. He installed new window openings in the lateral walls that reached as high as possible. The entire church was now bathed in an uninterrupted light that fell inside through the clear windows.

The cathedral was built so it aimed at heaven, with a roof that reached to the clouds. Straight lines on the outside reached to the steeples, making the cathedral shine even higher. The exterior was made even lighter with gables, pinnacles, and finials.

In the twelfth century, Suger and other church figures assumed that a godlike aura concentrated on certain objects, especially precious stones: their glitter would enhance the power of the light that poured into the church through the window openings. They placed reliquaries adorned with gemstones in the middle of the church, where they could get as much light as possible. He then replaced the clear windows with stained glass, intended to refine worldly light, symbolizing the Divine Light that spreads through space. Suger himself speaks of the miraculous light creating the holiest windows.

Later on, the color blue would dominate in these windows, purposely contrasted with red. To prevent color obfuscation, thin strips of white glass were placed between the blue and the red. This often resulted in a dramatic effect, lending an almost explosive power to a window. Light poured from all sides into a space that became a homogeneous experience.

This is how a new art was born in St. Denis. It was subsequently given the appellation of Gothic and spread over all of Europe. Cathedrals rose throughout France and all the neighboring countries. Even today, they remain astounding examples of a totally harmonious reality that humans create from a spiritual principle, shaping the immaterial into the material. The Gothic cathedrals inspired by Suger's St. Denis are undoubtedly the most spectacular *Gesamtkunstwerken* of our Western history.

THE DESIGN OF TOTAL HARMONY

The German term *Gesamtkunstwerk* is translated as "total art work"; however, it might also be defined as unity of spirit and unity of style. The idea of unity of vision—the manifestation of light in a cathedral, for example, or a shared brand vision—anchors the meaning of *Gesamtkunstwerk*. This concept applies to branding because, as we have laid out in this book, a brand is a complex set of interacting systems and the brand concept gains coherence when those pieces and parts are integrated and unified according to some central vision.

The unity of a brand concept is what makes successful brands powerful, such as the ones described in this book—Diesel, Ivory, Swatch, Gillette, Red Bull, BMW, Harley-Davidson, Levi's, Pepsi-Cola, Starbucks, the VW Beetle, and Cadbury Schweppes, among others. But these are just a few among many successful brands. Consider the list of the British top ten elite brands developed by the J. Walter Thompson advertising agency for its parent company WPP. That list starts with Gillette but includes Marks & Spencer, BBC, McDonald's, Nike, Nescafé, Heinz, Kellogg's, Whiskas, and Colgate. All these brands find strength through a shared vision of the brand's core concept that governs all its operations.

A *Gesamtkunstwerk* (a unified work of art), just like these successful brands, gives expression to a certain vision, a certain body of thought or mental ideal that can sustain its focus over time. This forms the connecting thread that gives direction to the various disciplines and components involved in the materialization of the work of art, or, as in this case, the brand. All the possible ways in which a brand manifests itself are integrated into the total harmony of an interconnected whole.

The concept of *Gesamtkunstwerk* is a recurrent one throughout history. The word was introduced by Richard Wagner, but its principles have been clear for centuries in various complex but artistic constructions, such as Gothic cathedrals, operas, symphonies, buildings, and the unity of design expressed in the vision of Art Nouveau and Frank Lloyd Wright. Let us leave brands for a moment and further develop the concept of *Gesamtkunstwerk* in various design areas.

Jugendstil and the Art of Inner Meaning

In the late nineteenth century, the concept of *Gesamtkunstwerk* and the ideals it represented were elevated into the central principle of a new cultural movement that would later be known as *Jugendstil,* or Art Nouveau. Artists who followed this movement had a vision to transform people's entire world of experience into a *Gesamtkunstwerk* through central design principles. Art Nouveau became a design concept, a style, and, ultimately, an era.

The idea penetrated all the arts: painting, fashion, graphic arts, sculpture, architecture, interior decoration, applied art, music, and literature. Essential to Art Nouveau was the idea of striving toward beauty in art and in all of life. This was about total renewal, in which everything should harmonize with everything else in its surroundings. Charles Rennie Mackintosh, one of *Jugendstil*'s most famous artists, expressed the ideal of *Gesamtkunstwerk* as a "synthesis or integration of myriads of details," the product of a "discriminating thoughtfulness in the selection of appropriate shape, decoration, design for everything, no matter how trivial" (Escritt 2000).

Typical of *Jugendstil* are the feelings and ideals that it expresses, expressed in art that was youthful, mystical, dreamy, harmonious, lyric, soft, blooming, elegant, precious, and, especially, decorative. *Jugendstil* reacted against advancing technology and the separation of functions. The style followed living nature, the organic, the growth forms of trees and plants. It avoided straight lines; it let lines oscillate. The female body was seen as the "symbol of all beauty" (Fahr-Becker 1996).

Architecture played a particularly important role in *Jugendstil.* Buildings were planned in which everything harmonized with everything else. The floor plans, the distribution of rooms, and the facades answer to the same ideals as the ornaments and the materials applied. In order to arrive at an optimal oneness, architects even designed the wallpaper, carpeting, furniture, stairs and doors, lighting ornaments, and countless objects of daily use. Several buildings in Europe embody the goal of the *Gesamtkunstwerken:* the Sezessions building in Vienna, the Representations building in Prague, the Casa Batlo of Gaudí in Barcelona, and the Stoclet palace in Brussels are just a few examples. In a more mundane application, the Disney theme parks embody the idea of total design that represents the central concept of the brand—youthful fun. Everything in the parks—buildings, rides, events, staff, and characters—expresses the same attitude of spirit and style.

Frank Lloyd Wright and the Principle of Organic Beauty

The visions of a great design we have discussed thus far are based on a number of core principles—light as God, the integration of music and drama, and decoration or lack of decoration. But in all cases there is sense of a unifying vision that brings harmony to the elements of the design. Nowhere is that harmony more evident than in the work of the American architect Frank Lloyd Wright. His legacy is a truly American style of architecture rejecting the forms of the nineteenth century, confronting and shaping the forms of the twentieth century, and expressing an American sense of place—prairies, mountains, water, and open skies. He called his vision organic architecture, a term he began using as early as 1908. By 1939 he had conceptualized his theory of architecture as the master art form, a holistic vision, and described it thus: "Here I stand before you preaching organic architecture: declaring organic architecture to be the modern ideal . . . so much needed if we are to see the whole of life, and to now serve the whole of life . . . exalting the simple laws of common sense. . . . determining form by way of the nature of materials" (Burns and Novick 1998).

Wright refocused "Form follows function," the famous slogan of his mentor, architect Louis Sullivan, to "Form and function are one," using nature as the best example of this integration. Similar to our explanation of the complexity of systems in branding, subordinated within Wright's holistic vision were "the visual arts, the plastic arts, sculpture, any kind of aesthetic experience . . . which leads to a complete spiritual experience of the universe" (Cronon 1998). Wright's work evolved from his sense of nature and the expressive power of simple geometric forms. Impatient with previous architecture that was based on tradition and past classical styles, he scorned the use of imitation Greek temples for plantation houses and bank buildings, and mock English Tudor manor houses grafted onto a contemporary neighborhood or suburb.

Wright did not mean to imitate natural forms, but instead reinterpret nature's forms through intelligent adaptation to man-made forms. His sense of the organic implies a respect for the properties of the materials; the harmonious relationship between the design (the form) and the function of a building; and the integration of spaces, context and landscape, human scale, and structure into a coherent whole. The core meaning is that architecture has an inherent relationship with both its site and its time. He substituted the notion of a building's "character" for the notion of style (Elman 1998).

Wright was not indifferent to other styles even as he rejected imitation of traditional or classical forms. For example, he respected the Arts and Crafts movement because of its commitment to crafting all objects so they were beautiful. Likewise, he respected Japanese culture because he saw it as one in which human action and human objects were integrated so as to make an entire civilization a work of art. And yet, to avoid backward-looking traditions, he continually searched for inventive ways to use new materials and technologies, equating his vision and his search for innovation with that of Leonardo de Vinci.

In pursuit of his sense of beauty, he subordinated all elements to a consistent style that expressed their underlying unity. He articulated his ideal as follows:

> In organic architecture it is quite impossible to consider the building as one thing, its furnishings another and its setting and environment still another. The spirit in which these buildings are conceived sees all these together at work as one thing. All are to be studiously foreseen and provided for in the nature of the structure . . . the very chairs and tables, cabinets and even musical instruments, where practicable, are of the building itself, never fixtures upon it. No appliances or fixtures are admitted as much where circumstances permit the full development of the organic character of the building scheme. (Escritt 2000)

The vocabulary of Wright's aesthetic vision, then, was geometrical consistency, as described by the historian Cronon (1998) in this way: "Geometry was the key to grammatical consistency, which was in turn the key to aesthetic unity, which was in turn the key to beauty, which was in turn the key of God." Striving for the maximum effect of the expression of his personal vision, Wright said, "The product of a principle never dies." Organic architecture must serve the principles that give order to nature and meaning to the human spirit: "The principles that build the tree, will build the man." Similar to our description of a brand, the secrets to a Frank Lloyd Wright building are not found on its surface but in its heart (Cronon 1998).

The Theory of *Gesamtkunstwerk*

To summarize this discussion of *Gesamtkunstwerk*, we argue that the concept counters the trend of separating artistic disciplines, of separating form and function, and of separating art and society in general. The concept of *Gesamtkunstwerk* emphasizes complementariness and the necessary interconnectedness of the various "partial disciplines," leading to the integration of art into the whole fabric of society. Central to the concept is the integrated use of several disciplines and multiple sets of systems and components as raw matter for the development of a worldview or a brand concept. The carmaker BMW provides an outstanding example of *Gesamtkunstwerk*.

BMW: The Most Admired Car Brand in the World

BMW is one of the most well-known brands in the world. The famous blue and white roundel symbol signals that the owner is driving a prestige car (or motorcycle). The symbol also identifies the brand as delivering the finest design, technology, engineering, and quality available in motoring today.

BMW (Bavarian Motor Works), the car brand we know today, really got started in 1961 with the introduction of the BMW 1500, which was welcomed by *Car and Driver* magazine as "an extremely pleasant and sensible automobile, which will outperform more powerful cars including some two seaters." It was the foundation for BMW's future formula: four doors, room for five, a sporty engine, fine handling, neat styling, and high-speed autobahn capability: it could hit 95 miles per hour.

But the history of BMW as a company goes back to the early twentieth century as a maker of bicycles, motorcycles, and aircraft engines. BMW formally recognizes its birthday as March 7, 1916, when the Bayerische Flugzeug Werke (BFW, Bavarian Aircraft Factory) was founded, followed in 1917 by the founding of the Bayerische Motoren Werke. In the early 1920s, BMW successfully launched its line of motorcycles, which won hundreds of races, giving the brand a reputation for engineering excellence and sportiveness. In 1922 BFW acquired BMW; in 1934 BMW Flug Motorenbau was established.

In 1928 BMW licensed the Austin Seven from the British car manufacturer, renaming it BMW 3/15. It came as a two-seater sports car. In 1933 the blue, white, and black spinning propeller logo appeared on the grille and a six-cylinder model was introduced with the twin-kidney front grill—two designs that make every BMW car on the road recognizable today. In this period also the mantra that would set the course of the company was phrased: "Decisions that sacrificed quality for quantity would never be made."

Car production stopped in 1939 as production capacity shifted to airplane engines, hailed as perhaps the best on either side of World War II. The motor technology would become one of the BMW's most distinguishing assets. In 1945 BMW started rebuilding almost from scratch. It struggled to regain focus through fifteen difficult postwar years. After the introduction of the BMW 1500 in 1961, BMW found its footing as a brand. It managed to create a balance between product development and engineering on one side, and brand and marketing management on the other side.

Its strategy was summed up in the words "unpretentious exclusivity." Paul Hanemann, responsible for the brand in those years and known in Germany as "Mr. BMW," aimed for the brand to fill a psychological gap in the market, not just a product gap. He expressed the difference he perceived between Mercedes and BMW this way: "If a businessman has made something of his life in Germany and has to show his neighbor he is something, he can only drive a Mercedes. If, however, he has made something of his life, but feels not the slightest need to show off, then he can buy himself a BMW." Until the start of the twenty-first century, BMW saw the Mercedes as its only rival. The company's ambition was to build a car that was better engineered than the Mercedes.

By 1980, BMW had developed into a worldwide power brand that stood for one thing: sheer driving pleasure. Its dynamic performance combined with peerless design to create a unique appeal. Today, quality, technology, performance and exclusivity are the core values of the brand. Research and development have a high priority within the company, which spends a higher percentage of its profits on R&D than any other automobile maker. Its R&D center in Munich employs 5,000 engineers and designers. From this technological focus, BMW develops automobiles with a character very much their own. For BMW, performance means not just fast acceleration and quick turns, but a balanced, harmonious cooperation of beautifully designed and crafted working parts. The goal is to produce smarter, not flashier, cars each year. BMW aims at classic, coherent, and simple designs that are attractive from every angle and that will age well. Styling has evolved over time, yet the BMW look has always remained recognizable. The company speaks of "BMW-ness," which means that people ought to know a BMW from 20 yards away, even if it is a new design and the logo is not visible.

The BMW identity is tied to the experience of driving the machine. Such details as the feeling of the steering wheel, the lighting of the instrument panel, and the suspension and the reaction of the motor ensure that the next BMW feels the same as the last one. BMW believes strongly in the importance of product provenience.

No small part of BMW's success is attributable to its design orientation, both product design as well as its corporate and brand design. Director of design Chris Bangle, who oversees 220 artists at BMW, says, "We don't make automobiles as utilitarian machines you use to get from point A to point B. We make 'cars,' moving works of art that express the driver's love of quality." BMW has associated itself intensely with the art world by sponsoring art events and asking famous artists, such as Andy Warhol, David Hockney, and Olafur Eliasson, to create a BMW Art Car that is exhibited in museums. The style of the brand is carefully managed in dealer showrooms, trade shows, and manufacturing facilities.

According to Helmut Panke, BMW chair from 2002 to 2006, "The BMW brands stand for a promise of fascinating individual automobiles"; the company promise is "never build a boring BMW." Twenty years ago, BMW in the United States and the United Kingdom expressed its core identity in the slogan "BMW—The Ultimate Driving Machine," and globally the brand shifted to the "Joy of Driving" position. That is precisely how BMW drivers sum up their automotive experience to researchers.

An unwritten law at BMW is that everyone who works at the company has to love driving and has to understand that driving pleasure is what the company is about. Everyone in engineering, development, purchasing, controlling, and manufacturing has to be focused on driving performance. Most members of the board have been motorcyclists at one time in their lives. BMW's headquarters is a revolutionary building that represents the heart of every car engine: four cylinders. The building has four cylindrical towers, twenty-two stories high, connected at the center by a core; a cross-section of the building resembles a four-leaf clover. In 2006 BMW opened BMW World, a customer reception and delivery center near the Four Cylinders Building.

The communication for the brand is characterized by concentration on the product combined with a tone denoting a certain exclusivity and understatement. The use of trendy creative angles and borrowed values is avoided. People do not appear in traditional BMW advertisements because the focus is always on the car. However, the "BMW Hire" film series, which was launched in 2000 as an extended Internet advertising campaign, presented the devoted loyalist's driving experience in a new and involving format that dramatizes not only the engineering, but also the bond between the owner and the car.

Since the beginning of its branding effort in 1961, BMW has shown almost continuous growth. By 1980 it had produced and sold more than 350,000 cars; by 1990, 514,000; and in 2000, 822,000. In the five years ending in 2005, when most carmakers struggled with falling sales, BMW car sales increased 37 percent to 1,276,793 cars in 2007 (along with 102.467 motorcycles). Moreover, by 2000 BMW earned more than twice as much as GM, Ford, Daimler Chrysler, and Volkswagen per car. It made a 9.9 percent operating margin, second only to Porsche's.

Helmut Panke offered good advice to other companies seeking insight from BMW:

Focus on understanding *who* you are, what you stand for. What are the values you believe in for the products and services that you provide. . . . People like to play characters when they are children—but in real life you cannot impersonate other values and characters and basic principles. There is a sentence I often use to crystallize what we are about: and I think it's important to be able to do that. To articulate the one idea in one sentence that everyone understands and believes it.

BMW builds high performance products because BMW is a high performance organization. That is an idea that speaks not just to our products. It is across seemingly unrelated fields and organizations within the company. Striving for better performance than our competitors is something that drives our controllers and our human resources people, not just our designers and engineers.

I believe in what I call the four P's: the right people, passion in the way we do our jobs and work with one another, absolute premium positioning in whatever we do from making cars to making profit, and always we are process driven, not personality driven.

The consistent management of the BMW brand over the last four decades made it the most admired carmaker and twelfth among the most admired global companies.

Sources: Kiley (2004); www.bmw.com; Bangle (2001).

In the course of time, a central theory has developed around the concept of *Gesamtkunstwerk*. The following elements can be distinguished as this theory has evolved (Eckel 2000; Günther 1994):

1. *A utopia:* This is an abstract central idea, a mental construct, a philosophical or even metaphysical ideal that inspires an attempt to (re)create material reality. In terms of brands, we could talk of a brand vision, a set of core values, and a brand personality.
2. *A visionary:* A spiritual father (or mother) takes the utopia beyond an abstract idea, puts it into words, embodies it, sees the shaping of reality to match this idea as a primary mission. In regard to brands, we call such a person a brand steward.
3. *An audience:* This is not only the sum of individual observers, but melts into a community that participates in the realization of the *Gesamtkunstwerk*. This concept of community is also used in brands.
4. *Multimedia orientation:* The *Gesamtkunstwerk* deploys several interrelated disciplines, as can be increasingly seen with brands.
5. *Control:* This represents the subordination to the utopia of the artists who form the group. They recognize and accept the ideal and are willing to submit themselves to its realization. The resistance against it, as is the case with free artists and applied arts such as those in the communication industry, forms the greatest obstacle to the attempt to give shape to the *Gesamtkunstwerk*.
6. *Consistency:* The vision—its central values and core concept—is shared by everyone in the group.
7. *Interdisciplinarity:* The co-creating professionals coordinate their contributions in such a way that the mental construct is expressed in all the material aspects of the work. The "doubling effect" is to be avoided, and the disciplines are to be made as complementary as possible.
8. *Continuity:* The *Gesamtkunstwerk* is approached not as a project that is subject to a system of planning and execution, but as a permanent design and consummation of the work of art in time, based on the starting points of the ideal. With brands, this approach implies the need to work with a sense of historical awareness.
9. *Synesthesia* (literally, co-perception):[1] The members of the group recognize that the activation of the five sense merges into an integrated perceptual oneness.
10. *Interactivity:* This is about mutual involvement between the member artists and an audience. The audience serves as a sounding board for artists as well as for the brand manager.

In sum, we can say that *Gesamtkunstwerk* is the external manifestation of an inner body of thought that can claim to be a coherent and appealing whole. This is a more complete definition of our original notion of *Gesamtkunstwerk* as unity of spirit or design. In brand development, this definition leads to a brand concept that integrates strategy and perception, manager and user, as well as all the systems managed through the strategy and the messages encountered by the user.

> *Principle: Gesamtkunstwerk* is the external manifestation of an inner body of thought that can claim to be a coherent and appealing whole.

It is obviously difficult to bring about a *Gesamtkunstwerk* in complex systems, particularly in an era characterized by increasing functional separation, as well as increasing specialization and individualization. A 1994 conference dedicated to the concept led to the conclusion that creating *Gesamtkunstwerken* has often resulted in disappointment. What remained were explanations about the intended goal, some synesthetic experiments, and ideological projects that have been discredited (Günther 1994). One of the speakers even claimed that "a real *Gesamtkunstwerk* has not come into existence yet. One could even say that there will never be a *Gesamtkunstwerk*. It is equally impossible to make one as it is to make a circle square or make a *perpetuum mobile*" (Allende-Blin 1994). Even Wagner did not succeed in realizing a *Gesamtkunstwerk* in Bayreuth. His dream remained a dream, a utopia—an ideal to strive for.

Still, in spite of this pessimistic idealism, it remains important to recognize the ideal of an inspiring guiding principle and the value of striving toward its harmonious materialization as the most important guideline, not only in design, but certainly in the world of brand development as well.

Gesamtkunstwerk as the Art of Branding

A brand is a dynamic entity, one that must eternally adapt to changing markets, consumers, and competitors. As John Ballington (2003) of Lever Faberge says in the introduction to the 2003 *Superbrands* book, a powerful brand "only has a season ticket to greatness." Snapshots at different points in time inevitably will show the brand operating at different levels of success; however, there is a core brand strength that remains constant. IBM, for example, was dominant until the 1980s, then it had some difficult times, then it was revitalized in the 1990s, and today it continues to be a leader in computers, although now redefined as e-business. Although its product line has changed, IBM's quality in service and product offerings continues to build brand strength.

A brand without a vision or idea is like a person without an opinion, without a soul, without a passion—uninterested and empty. The strength of special brands lies in the blend between their body of thought and their brand physique, thanks to which they succeed in inspiring and motivating people. From the discussions in this book we can distinguish four types of brands:

1. brands suffering from mental poverty;
2. brands in which the relationship between idea and brand physique is lacking or unclear;
3. brands with an appearance that is not integrated;
4. brands as total concepts, as expressed in the concept of *Gesamtkunstwerk*. We refer to these brands as practicing integrated branding.

In this book we have presented an overview of the brand components that together form a oneness, a unity of brand vision, and, ideally, a work of art. We believe that awareness of the "brand as *Gesamtkunstwerk*" metaphor can contribute to the development of powerful superbrands.

In modern times, *Gesamtkunstwerk* is achieved through the application of the principles of integration. In business, such applications can be seen in integrated branding, integrated marketing, and integrated marketing communication. But before we describe those practices, let us first consider the concept of integration.

The Concept of Integration

In systems thinking, integration is used throughout an organization as a tool to strategically manage the varied activities of the organization, which we have described in this book as a complex system of business, branding, marketing, and marketing communication components and activities.

Form and Function in the Bauhaus

The ideal of *Gesamtkunstwerk* has never left us. Creative artists keep going back to the starting points represented by the concept. In the 1920s it became the central objective of the Bauhaus movement.

The Bauhaus was an architectural school founded in 1919 in Weimar, Germany, by architect Walter Gropius. It was a reaction to what Gropius saw as the threat of growing industrialization—with loneliness, anomie, and disorientation as a result. Gropius saw the solution in redemption of the world by art, in a union between art and technique. In his vision, art needed a new moral orientation in which artists had to tear themselves apart from their own egocentricity and focus in a team setting on the design of social phenomena. He saw stations, factories, cars, steamboats, and yachts as the things with which an artist needed to be involved. Gropius argued for an artful design of technical objects, in which "all the non-essential details are subordinate to the large form, which had to become the symbolic expression of the inner meaning of the modern building or design." He summed up his ideal in the mantra "Art and technique—a new oneness."

His dream was that of the *Gesamtkunstwerk* as well, with a reality that had to be shaped from the concept of the object's core function. Gropius gave the name of *Wesensforschung* ("research into the essence") to this method of exposing the object's core meaning. The idea was for these functions to be expressed as honestly and as clearly as possible. He tried to avoid aesthetic discussions of form and to focus entirely on the purpose of the entity. Form had to be the simplest expression of function. Rejecting the ornamentation that had been so characteristic of *Jugendstil*, he advocated instead a minimalist style of businesslike character, clear colors, powerful forms, and transparent structures.

To bring about this oneness, he went back to the idea of the medieval cathedral builders, who worked together in *Bauhütten*. This is where he derived the name of his institute, the Bauhaus. He saw his Bauhaus as a laboratory for the union between art and technique from which emerged prototypes of objects of daily use that could be mass-produced. The buildings that his students designed were to be the result of collective activity in which each artist contributed a personal share to a larger whole, always aware of the individual's relationship to this totality.

The Bauhaus was influenced by the Dutch Style group, which included Theo van Doesburg, Piet Mondrian, and Gerrit Rietveld. Like the Bauhaus, the Dutch Style was looking for *Gesamtkunstwerk* characterized by the weight of elements in relationships, pure colors, total clarity, and harmony. All elements had to have their own function in the totality.

The Bauhaus had so much impact on modern design that the term eventually became a brand of its own—one that represented the products of a specific design studio, but also a style of design that launched the modern era. The Bauhaus movement and the Dutch Style have shown their influence far into the twentieth century, especially in architecture and interior design.

Sources: Fiedler and Feierabend (2000); http://users.compagnet.be/architectaur2./bauhaus.

The basis for integration within an organization is always a shared vision, an understanding that governs all decisions and operations. Adapting this system-based view of integration to business suggests that a shared vision gives direction to all corporate, as well as marketing, decisions and strategies. Let us revisit the *Gesamtkunstwerk* literature and consider how early twentieth-century artists actually created and branded an artistic movement—the Bauhaus.

Jeff Smith (2002), director of Prophet, a leading brand consulting firm, insists that a shared brand vision anchors all business decisions, not just marketing. A brand "should have a leading seat at the strategy table," he says, and "play a driving role in almost all functional areas of the business." He explains that "corporate strategy is driven or, at a minimum, heavily informed by the brand—from sales process, to pricing decisions, and across all delivery and customer touch points of the company." In other words, integrated branding has to be approached from the viewpoint of the whole company and involve all its business operations, not just its marketing communication programs.

Integration is valued by managers because it not only delivers better internal communication and coordination, but also unleashes the power of synergy. The idea behind synergy as applied to marketing and marketing communication is that repeated experiences reinforce a core vision and that multiple coordinated messages saying the same thing will have more impact on brand perception than will the same number of discrete, unrelated messages. When synergy is part of the equation, two plus two can equal five.

As in other areas of brand management, synergy also has two faces. For management it leads to efficiency and cost effectiveness for communication and brand relationship programs; for consumers it leads to reinforcement, confirmation, and the ease of mind that comes from familiarity.

In order to better understand how integration functions as a prerequisite for *Gesamtkunstwerk*, let us consider how integration is employed in branding, marketing, and marketing communication.

Integrated Branding

Integrated branding is the process used to guarantee that the brand is seen by customers as a whole—as a coherent concept, as an image that holds together through unity of vision, and as an entity that has core values and integrity that are expressed in all areas of its operations.

The most important goal of integrated branding is to maintain consistency through all the firm's operations—from the selection of suppliers and targeting of consumers down to the after-sales servicing of buyers. In *Total Integrated Marketing*, Hulbert et al. (2003) argue that the entire value chain of the company must be integrated with the core brand strategy (value proposition), which serves as a touchstone and directive.

In another approach, Mahavaram et al. (2005) bring together a number of concepts that also have been discussed in this book. They organize these components into two primary sets of systems—brand identity factors and brand equity factors. To implement the brand identity factors, they focus on culture, management support, and internal marketing as key components. Supporting the brand equity factors are integrated marketing communication (IMC) programs (interactivity and consistency are particularly important) and evaluation of IMC effectiveness, which culminates in brand awareness and clearly defined image constructs. But integrated branding is more comprehensive than IMC.

LePla et al. (2003) describe an integrated brand as "one in which every part contains the whole, where every action is based on the brand." In other words, the brand concept guides all actions within the company. To attain that goal, they suggest three key areas that must be effectively managed:

Figure 19.1   **A Value-Chain Model of Integrated Branding**

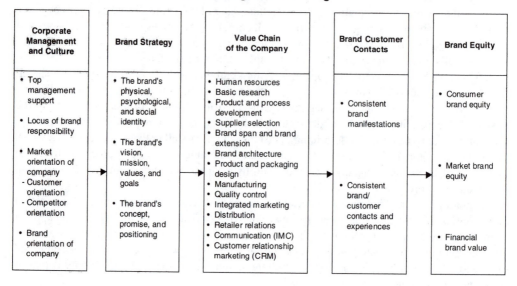

Corporate Management and Culture	Brand Strategy	Value Chain of the Company	Brand Customer Contacts	Brand Equity
• Top management support • Locus of brand responsibility • Market orientation of company - Customer orientation - Competitor orientation • Brand orientation of company	• The brand's physical, psychological, and social identity • The brand's vision, mission, values, and goals • The brand's concept, promise, and positioning	• Human resources • Basic research • Product and process development • Supplier selection • Brand span and brand extension • Brand architecture • Product and packaging design • Manufacturing • Quality control • Integrated marketing • Distribution • Retailer relations • Communication (IMC) • Customer relationship marketing (CRM)	• Consistent brand manifestations • Consistent brand/ customer contacts and experiences	• Consumer brand equity • Market brand equity • Financial brand value

1. *Brand essence:* The company has to know who it is, fully understanding the brand's inherent meaning and articulating it in a way that people can act on.
2. *Company activity alignment:* The company must have organizational alignment if it wants to achieve an integrated brand.
3. *Tell the world who you are:* Communication is the final step, and integration of all marketing communications is a prerequisite. But as Le Pla et al. argue, a brand refers to everything a company does and everything that is experienced or perceived by its customers (and other stakeholders).

In Figure 19.1 we present our model of integrated branding, which focuses on the gearing of all elements of the company's value chain with the brand's strategy, identity, vision, and concept. It encompasses all the business processes, from basic research, product and process development, and human resources to the after-sales service. Effective management of all these processes from a brand platform demands support from top management. With corporate brands, the CEO should be deeply involved in the planning and evaluation of the brand's strategy and the implementation thereof throughout the whole organization. In companies that have a portfolio of individual brands, this task is usually delegated to the chief executive of its business units. Leaving it in the hands of marketing executives often allows the brands to drift, driven by short-term tactical considerations and frequent changes of course as a result of repetitive new appointments. The introduction of a brand-steward function in the organization, performed by an individual who reports to the top management directly, may offer a solution.

In an organization whose fortunes to a significant degree depend on the equity of its brands, a strong emphasis should be placed on the development of both its market orientation and its brand orientation.

Market orientation is an aspect of the culture of an organization that has a far-reaching influence on its branding approach. It refers to the commitment of an organization to the implementation of a consumer-focused marketing philosophy. It centers on the identification of manifest or latent consumer needs and the development of consumer benefits, whether instrumental or emotional. It puts the consumer at the center of the firm's beliefs; all the company's resources are devoted to the continuous creation of superior customer value. This is what we call "customer orientation" (Narver 1990).

But to develop competitive advantages, the organization also has to have good insight into the competencies, strategies, and operations of its competitors—and to take them into consideration when developing its own course of action. This we call "competitor orientation." Because of the organization's limited resources, there is always a tension between its customer orientation and its competitor orientation, with customer orientation usually having the upper hand.

Brand orientation was defined in Chapter 2 as the company's abilities in and dedication to the creation and development of strong brands with the aim to foster their brand equity. A truly brand-oriented company sees brands as the hub around which its strategic processes circle. In Chapter 4 we discussed eight brand orientation factors that have a strong impact on a company's economic performance. Brand orientation should be embedded in all organizational activities.

Both market orientation and brand orientation have an impact on the development of a brand's strategy. A substantial part of this book has been devoted to brand strategy development. In the value-chain model of integrated branding, we included the main building blocks as (1) the brand's vision, mission, values and goals (see Figure 5.1); (2) the brand's concept, promise, and positioning (see Chapters 5 and 8); and (3) the brand's identity (see Chapter 6). Beyond establishing guidelines for the physical dimensions of their brand's identity, many companies do not have a shared vision of their brand's mental and social identities. Although consistency in physical appearance is, of course, essential, the development of a mental and social brand identity as a culture, in an ongoing interaction with customers in the context of integrated branding, is equally necessary. Integrated branding should provide the organization with clear directions and norms for internal behavior and for dealing with external stakeholders.

Drawing on similarities with the notions of market orientation and brand orientation, Madhavaram et al. (2005) call this "brand identity orientation." They argue that firms with a brand-identity-oriented culture will be successful at integrating their brand-related business processes. Integrated branding contributes to consistency in the entire brand's manifestations and so to consistent brand contacts and experience for customers. All these efforts contribute to the strengthening of the brand's equity and financial value.

The Foundation for Fundamental Research on Commercial Communication (SWOCC) at the University of Amsterdam has published a paper on integrated branding that identifies the basic steps to be taken to ensure that stakeholders have consistent contact with a brand (Giling 2006).

1. *Formulate the brand promise:* If an organization wants the brand to be the central point on which all disciplines and departments base their strategy, the brand promise must first be clearly defined.
2. *Integrate the brand promise:* After the brand promise has been formulated, integration and cooperation must be reached between the different disciplines that are directly or indirectly concerned with implementing the brand promise.
3. *Enable the brand promise:* The processes and activities that are responsible for the realization of the brand promise have a great influence on the customers' perceptions and judgment of the service. It is therefore important that brand values be implemented in rules, structures, systems, and instruments.

4. *Carry out the brand promise:* When everything has been settled inside the organization, the brand promise can be carried out externally. The attention of stakeholders can be drawn and brand interest created through advertising, promotion, and sponsorships.
5. *Fulfill the brand promise:* The success of the organization depends largely on the interactions between customers and employees: "the brand builders." The employees' treatment of customers must match the brand values expressed in advertising in order to fulfill the brand promise.

The SWOCC document refers to the "brand promise" as the anchor of integrated branding because a promise represents the basis for the brand-customer relationship. Integrating this brand promise throughout the organization, then, is fundamental to creating a consistent brand impression.

Integration, therefore, provides another way to define a brand—as an integrated perception. Like the unified impression given by *Jugendstil* and Bauhaus design, a brand perception comprises all the messages a customer has received at all the various points of contact with the brand, including personal experiences. Integration is the process by which all these experiences come together to create a coherent brand impression through synesthesia. Integrated brand management is the process of strategically managing this complex system of brand contacts and experiences. As in other forms of *Gesamtkunstwerk*, a brand has integrity when everything it says and does connects and contributes to the brand's core concept.

Principle: A brand has integrity when everything it says and does connects with the customer and contributes to the brand's core concept.

But how does brand integration work in terms of the perception process? Integrating messages from a variety of brand contacts happens without thought by the consumer. It is a natural part of the perceptual process. Brand managers may say they are not concerned about the consistency of brand messages, but, whether they control the process or not, their customers are automatically dealing with these messages by organizing them into something we have been calling the mental brand. Given the way the perceptual process works, consumers will try to integrate the messages in order to make sense of them—but not necessarily in the way brand managers may intend, particularly if there are inconsistencies in the messages and experiences. The important lesson from communication psychology is that you cannot *not* communicate (Watzlawick et al. 1967, 51) because the receiver of the message will make interpretations that lead to an impression regardless of management's intentions.

The only thing that gets in the way of this natural perceptual process is confusion, which can lead to irritation or disinterest. If a customer's experiences with a brand and its messages are not consistent, then the impression may not solidify in a way that creates a coherent, positive perception. The mental brand will not come together or hold together. A brand-loyal customer may forgive some mixed messages, but others do irreparable damage to a customer-brand relationship. Making customers wait in line is an irritation but, depending upon the circumstance, may be accepted as "normal" business. However, saying one thing (this company respects the environment) and doing something else (dumping toxic waste) creates confusion and damages the brand's integrity. Schizoid brands leave gaps between key value-producing customer experiences that would otherwise aggregate to form a coherent mental brand.

The Nokia Brand Building System

Nokia is a good example of integrated marketing used in support of an integrated brand. Nokia's brand essence is based on an understanding of the brand's customer relationship. The brand mission is "connecting people," a commitment that expresses not only the brand's core value, but also its brand promise. The unique expression of that promise is phrased by the company as "warm communion," which describes the moment of uniting, the coming together of consumer and brand. Jorma Ollila, Nokia chairman, explains that Nokia's understanding of "warm communion" is the reason the company's products have become so extraordinarily successful across the world: "All our decision-making, processes, policies, and systems should consciously continue to feed and nurture this quality."

The philosophy of business used by Nokia to implement the brand promise involves twelve insights. Ollila says they are based on an understanding of the following:

- how Nokia customers are motivated
- what customers expect from Nokia
- the Nokia vision
- Nokia's shared values
- the Nokia difference
- Nokia's brand essence
- the Nokia mission, the organizing idea for all its work
- Nokia's unique competence and skill
- how customers uniquely position Nokia
- the core Nokia business model
- the key indicators of success—an integrated dashboard
- the Nokia product—the core design principle

These twelve insights are arrayed in a circle as coordinates based on the Stellar® strategy and identity methodology developed by Angus Jenkinson and Richard Leachman. Like numbers on a clock, each element is precisely in its place with opposites balanced through complementary principles.

According to Ollila, this system of governing principles describes "who we are and what we do, as well as why people buy our products." This systematic approach to the creation of an integrated brand is responsible for creating the special brand relationship that has kept Nokia a highly profitable market leader.

Source: www.stepping-stones.org.

Integrated Marketing

Integrated marketing (IM) is a systems-related term used to describe the philosophy of business advocated by Prophet and other branding consultants. As Hulbert et al. (2003) argue in their book

Total Integrated Marketing, it is a customer-focused approach rather than a specialized staff function. This process manages all a company's or brand's interactions with customers and other key stakeholders—all the systems, as well as their components and interrelationships.

Throughout this book we have identified the multiple systems and components that underlie brand strategy, which could be compiled in a massive model that would demonstrate the complexity of the process but provide little management insight. Figure 19.1 (see page 516) is our simplified version with key components identified.

In addition to a customer focus, the marketing effort begins with a definition of the core concept (essence, DNA, value, promise) of the brand. Then all the mental, physical, and social identity elements are brought together in support of that brand vision. Management systems are put in place to drive the way the brand leader, brand team, and brand apostles spread the brand message and monitor the brand performance through internal branding.

In other words, in an integrated marketing program, the various components merge and mesh in support of a holistic brand strategy, as the Nokia case illustrates. In an ineffective marketing program, these components operate independently with sometimes conflicting systems that undercut the emergence of a coherent brand perception.

In another sense, IM is the process of managing the intangible side of a business beyond the cash, facilities, personnel, and other resources—and increasingly it is the intangible side that delivers brand value and creates brand equity. Similar to the driving principle or concept essential to the design of *Gesamtkunstwerk*, integrated marketing provides the big-picture vision.

In a more formal definition by Burnett and Moriarty (1998, 63), integrated marketing is described as the process of understanding the needs of the customer and other stakeholders, orienting the firm's manufacturing and sales processes to meet those needs, and applying integrated thinking to all marketing decisions based on a shared brand vision. As in systems theory, every decision at every level supports decisions made at all other levels. Consistency in operations, in other words, is a systemic problem, as well as a strategic challenge.

Principle: Every decision supports all other brand decisions. Consistency in operations is a systemic problem as well as a strategic challenge.

Another description of integrated marketing given by Duncan and Moriarty in *Driving Brand Value* (1997a, 9) stresses the organizational underpinnings required to manage a complex system such as a brand: "Integrated marketing is a cross-functional process for managing profitable brand relationships by bringing people and corporate learning together in order to maintain strategic consistency in brand communications, facilitate purposeful dialogue with customers and other stakeholders, and market a corporate mission that increases brand trust." Cross-functional planning and monitoring within the organizational system are essential in order to keep the components working together toward the shared vision. As Duncan says (1995), "You can't be integrated externally if you are not integrated internally."

One of the biggest problems in companies that try to move toward an integrated business platform is departmental silos or stovepipes. As specialization has developed internally in many companies, staff members have become increasingly isolated. Necessary functional divisions turn into fiefdoms and managers subvert integration in order to build and maintain their empires. Cross-functional management is a tool to break down the walls and drive communication more effectively throughout an organization. According to production management expert Dan

Dimancescu (1992), cross-functional management focuses on issues of company-wide importance. These include such processes as quality assurance, cost control, product development, personnel training, and information integration.

Integrated Marketing Communication

In addition to the structural or organizational dimension, communication is another underlying theme in integrated marketing. Communication is the glue that holds an organization together, making it possible to articulate a common vision and transform the vision into operations. But communication is more than a social lubricant; it is also the basis for transaction and interaction. In fact, there is conceptual overlap between the exchange theory of marketing—the idea that customers exchange something of value, such as money, for something they need, such as a product or service—and the theory of exchange in communication. As explained in a *Journal of Marketing* article on the communication dimension of brand relationships (Duncan and Moriarty 1998), marketing exchange could not happen without an exchange of information that leads to mutual satisfaction over the terms of the "deal." This view of brand communication transforms the traditional marketing "exchange" concept from a business transaction to an interactive brand experience that produces value and builds relationships.

Put another way, an underlying theme of this book is that a brand represents a two-way exchange between the source (marketer) and the receiver (customer) and that branding works only to the degree that both parties in the exchange—in both the marketing and communication sense—are in agreement about the brand meaning. IMC at this level parallels integrated marketing. It also represents a paradigm shift moving marketing, as well as marketing communication, from a one-way communication model to a two-way relationship that produces win-win marketing situations.

Two Levels of IMC

The formal or institutionalized approach to the communication dimension in marketing is known as integrated marketing communication or IMC. Integrated marketing communication has two definitions. At its most basic, IMC refers to the strategic coordination of the planned marketing communication areas—advertising, sales promotion, public relations, direct marketing, packaging, telemarketing, event marketing, and so forth—so they all reflect and contribute to a central brand core concept. This is sometimes referred to as a "one-voice, one-look" strategy. All the planned messages are orchestrated to deliver a consistent message on a brand strategy, including such areas as brand identity and image, position, differentiation, and segmentation.

On a higher level—one that is more in line with Prophet's thinking about shared brand vision and the Duncan and Moriarty's view of communication—all brand activities can be seen as a form of communication. More than one-voice, one-look, IMC at this level recognizes that everything a company or brand does, and sometimes what it does not do, sends a message (Duncan and Moriarty 1997a, xii). This type of IMC is defined by Duncan and Mulhern (2004, 9) as "an ongoing, interactive, cross-functional process of brand communication planning, execution, and evaluation that integrates all parties in the exchange process in order to maximize the mutual satisfaction of each other's wants and needs."

Principle: Everything a company or brand does, and sometimes what it does not do, sends a message.

Strategic Consistency

This more advanced approach to IMC also uses a concept Duncan and Moriarty (1997, 70) call "strategic consistency," which acknowledges that message consistency does not mean that every message says the same thing. In fact, different messages are directed at different stakeholders and different target audiences. In an application for government approval of a new cereal, for example, the prospective customer's message will be entirely different from the message directed to investors or employees. However, the brand's core concept and values remain true to the brand essence even though the brand message may vary with the communication situation.

TOUCHPOINTS

In addition to the idea that everything delivers a message, everything and everyone related to the brand can "touch" the customers, impacting their emotions and lending an affective dimension to the brand perception. Brand management can be seen as the process of managing all these customer contact points in order to increase the value of the brand by cementing the customer-brand relationship through positive brand experiences.

The terms *contact point* and *touchpoint* are used interchangeably, although the latter does carry an additional aura of emotion. Davis and Dunn (2002) define a brand touchpoint as any of the instances where a brand interacts with stakeholders.

Another dimension of touchpoints is experience. Experience marketing has evolved to manage this crucial interaction between customer and brand in meaningful ways. Such activities as sponsorships, special events in public relations programs, and event marketing are particularly rich in the kind of involvement that delivers engaging and affect-laden experiences.

In most cases, a brand's system of contact points is huge and the challenge is to identify the key communication opportunities and then analyze the messages being delivered at these points of contact in order to diagnose consistency problems. Davis and Dunn suggest that managing touchpoints through integrated branding involves identifying, prioritizing, and controlling each of the stakeholder's touchpoints.

In recognition of strategic consistency, not all messages will be the same at all touchpoints, but they will all be anchored by the brand's core concept and values. When Apple Computer, for example, began using the "Think different" slogan (which co-opted and one-upped IBM's old "Think" slogan and position), it drove all of Apple's operations and interactions—its easy-to-use operating system, its distinctive designs, its corporate culture, and its advertising, which focused on creative genius.

Table 19.1 illustrates the breadth of the contact point communication system and the many ways it touches the lives and minds of consumers. The list is organized according to the Duncan and Moriarty (1997) contact point classification system of intrinsic (product or service experiences), unplanned, customer-initiated, and planned marketing communication. The list is long, but that is the point. As long as it is, it is not a complete list but rather a thought-starter for managers seeking to analyze their brands' contact points. The extent of the list, however, dramatizes the many chances for consistency problems.

The list also suggests that managers have to move beyond the conventional tools they may be familiar with and attend to activities that may be outside their areas of experience. The reason is that a negative message can be delivered at any contact point, whether it is considered as marketing or marketing communication or simply day-to-day business activity. A negative message about the way a company conducts its business can overpower millions of dollars spent on advertising. Managers who are concerned about their customers' brand perceptions, therefore, have to understand that all these contact points are important, wherever their home in the organization. Managers have to be proactive in ferreting out the source of negative perceptions regardless of administrative lines of responsibility.

In order to manage communication using the higher level of IMC and this broad approach to brand contact points, companies need to identify all brand-related activities that have meaning to customers and other stakeholders. In the traditional 4Ps model of marketing, that means all the product, pricing, and distribution activities, not just the obvious marketing communication functions, are treated as communication sources. This is outlined in Duncan and Moriarty's *Journal of Marketing* article (1998), which also identifies communication contact at different levels between an organization and its customers. This is summarized in Figure 19.2.

Analyzing Touchpoints

The analysis of contact points typically begins with an ethnographic study that mirrors the way various stakeholders go about their business and daily lives. As researchers follow these people around, they make note of points where the person comes in contact with the brand or a competing brand. A similar analysis from the viewpoint of employees can extend the list in ways that might not show up in a customer's usual activities. Davis and Dunn (2002) suggest that there are four categories of touchpoints and that each one represents a different type of customer-brand relationship:

1. *Prepurchase touchpoints:* The touchpoints that influence whether prospective customers will place the brand into their consideration set. These touchpoints usually include advertising, word of mouth, direct mail, and the Internet.
2. *Purchase touchpoints:* The brand touchpoints that move a customer from considering the brand to purchasing it. These include field sales, stores, clerks, and customer representatives.
3. *Postpurchase touchpoints:* The brand touchpoints that occur after the sale and that reinforce the purchase decision. In addition to use of the actual product, these include installation, customer service, warranty and rebate programs, customer satisfaction surveys, regular maintenance, and reminders of product innovations.
4. *Influencing touchpoints:* The brand touchpoints that indirectly make an impression of the brand on its customers and other stakeholders, such as annual reports, analysts' reports, word of mouth by current and past customers (and employees), and recruiting materials.

To deepen the analysis of the effectiveness of these touchpoint experiences, Chernatony (2001) suggests that researchers use the following six questions to analyze the quality of the touchpoint experience:

1. How did customers become aware of the brand?
2. How do stakeholders further develop opinions about the brand through interactions with each other?
3. When then deciding to have further dealings with the brand, what routes do customers follow?

Figure 19.2 **Communication and Brand Relationships**

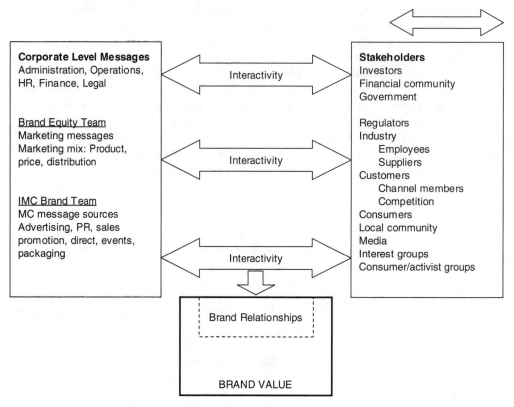

Source: Duncan and Moriarty (1997a).

4. Do all the brand communicators reinforce the brand's core values?
5. Do staff and technology support the brand's core values?
6. What mechanisms are in place to reinforce the brand's value after the transaction?

Critical Touchpoints

Because touchpoints are so varied, it stands to reason that their impact on customer- and stakeholder-brand relationships will also vary. In many cases, these touchpoints are service-related and add value to the brand experience, which in turn can cement or rupture a customer-brand relationship. Some touchpoints are even more critical because they are more directly related to future purchase decisions.

Critical touchpoints (CTPs) are observed when customers connect with a brand on the emotional level (Duncan and Moriarty 2006). In other words, the contact infuses the relationship with positive or negative emotions. Jan Carlson, former CEO of SAS Airlines, called these CTPs "moments of truth" and described them as contacts that kept customers satisfied or drove them away. Because these CTPs have significant impact on the minds and hearts of customers, these "touching experiences" must be carefully designed and strategically managed. Unfortunately, these experiences are often embedded in operations and may be completely missed by a brand's communication managers. Yet one good or bad experience may have more impact on brand perceptions than millions of dollars in advertising.

Interactivity is a product, and also a requirement, of exchange. IMC, with its emphasis on brand relationships, demands new ways of creating symmetrical relationships between the company or brand and its customers. This objective requires interactive communication in order to bring a brand and its stakeholders closer together. The move toward interactivity is also a product of vast, widespread technological changes in communication systems, such as the Internet and wireless telecommunication. The requirement of interactivity has also lessened the importance of traditional mass media-based marketing communication, such as advertising.

The end result of a touchpoint management system that optimizes interactivity is closer customer- and stakeholder-brand relationships, what Duncan and Moriarty (2006, 240) call brand-customer closure. They use the metaphor of a zipper or Velcro closure to illustrate how both sides participate equally in making a strong connection through touchpoints and interactivity. The higher the quality of the brand experience, the stronger and more enduring the bond between customer and brand.

The Integration Triangle and Brand Integrity

We mentioned earlier that a brand has integrity when everything it says and does connects and contributes to the brand core concept. The word *integrity* has the same Latin root as *integration* and, as that linguistic clue suggests, integration is a requirement for brand integrity because it ensures consistency in words and deeds. However, in integrated marketing and IMC, there is another component of consistency and that is found in brand reputation—that is, what other people say about the brand.

The integration triangle (Moriarty and Duncan 1997, 90) is a simple way to illustrate how integrity emerges in customers' brand perceptions. From a customer's point of view, brand integrity exists when a brand does what its maker says it will do and when others confirm that expectation and experience. Duncan and Moriarty express this idea as "say, do, confirm."

This simple model not only illustrates the critical points of brand consistency, but also can be used to uncover inconsistencies or gaps between saying, doing, and confirming that can damage customer-brand relationships. For example, when the brand does not live up to its advertising claims, the *say* messages (brand promises) are out of synch with the *do* messages (brand performance). Likewise, when word of mouth among friends is critical of a brand's claims, then the *confirm* messages are out of synch with the *say* messages. This model is expanded in Figure 19.4 to identify the brand essence as comprising core concept, identity, and position and to show how those components are expressed through three sources of brand meaning—marketing communication, brand experiences, and word of mouth (reputation).

The integration triangle also calls attention to the important role that reputation plays in an integrated brand perception. A brand perception can be cued by planned messages, and the brand's design and performance also make important contributions to brand meaning, but the ultimate test lies in what other stakeholders say about the brand. Ads are important, but employees, channel members, suppliers, consumer groups, and the consumer's friends and family have even more impact on the way the brand meaning is interpreted. Brand reputation carries with it credibility and respect, and the test of these elements of brand strength is found in brand advocacy—when other people say good things about the brand. When "say, do, and confirm" work together, brand integration can be achieved.

Figure 19.3 **The Integration Triangle**

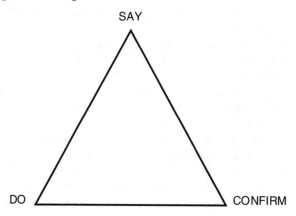

Source: Duncan and Moriarty (1997a).

BRAND STRENGTH THROUGH INTEGRATION

When we delve into the characteristics of superbrands, the *Gesamtkunstwerk* metaphor comes to mind as an explanation for brand power. Both are built on an underlying, intangible premise—a vision, an ideal, or a way of thinking that serves as a driving force behind everything a brand is, says, and does. This vision, which serves as the connecting thread in the brand story, is expressed in all aspects of the physical reality of the brand. In the first place is, of course, the selection of products or categories that are linked to the brand. Then there are the further development of the brand's properties and design; all the communication from the brand; the packaging, buildings, merchandising, materials, and Web sites; and the way complaints and questions are dealt with.

Wagner and *Gesamtkunstwerk*

We started this discussion of *Gesamtkunstwerk* in medieval times with Gothic cathedrals. Let us end in the nineteenth century with one of the great composers of the time—the musician Richard Wagner. Just like Abbot Suger, Wagner also had an ideal in mind: creating a oneness in which all the participating disciplines would flow together on an equal basis in the final work of art. He called this principle *Gesamtkunstwerk* and created operas in the same unity of spirit as Suger created his cathedral.

Wagner reacted against the then-fashionable Italian operas in which music was given a dominant place to which drama was entirely subordinated. Wagner saw this style of opera as a coincidental concatenation of arias, duets, and terzetts—a random conglomerate of autonomous musical elements. The construction of the story was only a rationale for the random arrangement of musical pieces. The art of poetry was subordinated to the singer or to the musical effect. Form dominated over content.

In these operas, Wagner also saw the reflection of the development of society into fragmentation and alienation. Against this, he proposed the ideal of *Gesamtkunstwerk*. He saw *Gesamtkunstwerk* as an interconnected whole, subject to a dominating, fundamental principle or truth, one that strived toward an absolute oneness of action and thought. Wagner based the content of his musical dramas on absolute, timeless material derived from Germanic mythology, which to his mind formed the

Figure 19.4   **The Integration of Brand Essence and Brand Messages**

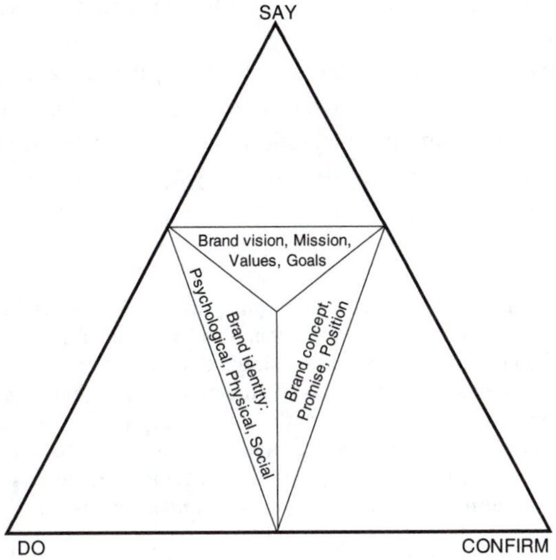

beginning and end of history. His theater pieces do not depict these myths, but re-create them. The arts of music, poetry, and dances were integrated in a meaningful fashion, leading to an "all-inclusive oneness" (Falparsi 2000). Visionary brands, such as Ben & Jerry's Ice Cream or The Body Shop, try to re-create this "all-inclusive oneness" in a commercial setting, centering their business practices on the principles of ecology and respect for others.

Wagner also integrated other disciplines such as performance and theater into his operas. Design, decor, lighting, and every other function had to be subordinate to that oneness of vision. Since such a total oneness was difficult to realize in a traditional opera building, Wagner managed to create a utopian theater: the Bayreuth Festspielhaus. The architecture of this theater was entirely aimed at giving the audience an undisturbed view of the stage. Wagner tried to avoid anything that could distract from the dramatic events on the stage. His musical dramas are still performed there today.

Gesamtkunstwerk in Modern Times

We can see the *Gesamtkunstwerk* philosophy in the Nike brand, for example, a marketing machine that emphasizes the emotion of athletic achievement. In a highly competitive market, the Nike brand stays the same while the Nike company constantly reinvents itself and its products in a spirit of continuous reengineering. What remains the same is Nike's passion for sports and the athletes who embody that passion—everyday people as well as the big-name stars who proudly wear the Nike swoosh logo. The power of that association comes alive in the brand's marketing association but even more so in the events it sponsors and in the Nike stores, where the total brand experience is as important, perhaps more so, than the individual products. Nike's core concept of passion for sports is showcased throughout the store, where shoppers are invited to participate in the achievement of this brand vision.

In integrated marketing and IMC, a basic principle is that everything a brand does, and sometimes what it does not do, sends a brand message. Building a brand as a *Gesamtkunstwerk* demands that every form of contact between a client and the brand be fitted to the brand's inner body of thought. In that sense, the modern notion of brand experience should include not only the events that are organized, but also every sensory experience that a consumer has with a brand. The purpose is for everything in the person and every brand contact to merge into an integrated total perception, in the sense of synesthesia.

A powerful brand, then, is based on understanding that the art of *Gesamtkunstwerk*, with its perfect vision and perfect union of brand and customer, is the magic that surrounds the management of the complex brand system. Through integration, the science and art of branding create brand strength, brand relationships, brand value, brand equity and, ultimately, share holder value.

NOTE

1. In synesthesia, a stimulus that is perceived by one sense induces a perception in another sense. For example, a visual image can generate a sound experience and vice versa. It is based on the hypothesis that the senses do not function autonomously (modularity), but that people have one integrated sensory system that consists of five partial systems (unitariness). The perceptions of the individual senses come together at a specific place in the brain, in order to blend with the total perception into an intermodal experience. It is still unclear whether this process takes place in the hippocampus, an organ of the limbic system, or in the associative memory of the cortex. In any event, the possibility of direct teamwork of the different senses remains an important consideration in striving toward a *Gesamtkunstwerk*.

REFERENCES

Aaker, D. 1991. *Managing Brand Equity: Capitalizing on the Value of a Brand Name.* New York: Free Press.

———. 1996a. "Brand Personality: The Relationship Basis Model." www.haas.berkely.edu/~market/papers/aaker/books/building/brand_personality.html.

———. 1996b. *Building Strong Brands.* New York: Free Press.

Aaker, D., R. Batra, and J. Meyers. 1996. *Advertising Management.* Upper Saddle River, NJ: Prentice Hall.

Aaker, D., and A.L. Biel. 1993. *Brand Equity and Advertising.* Hillsdale, NJ: Lawrence Erlbaum.

Aaker, D., and R. Jacobson. 1994. "The Financial Information Content of Perceived Quality." *Journal of Marketing Research* 31: 191–201.

Aaker, D., and E. Joachimsthaler. 2000. *Brand Leadership.* New York: Free Press.

Aaker, D., and K.L. Keller. 1990. "Consumer Evaluations of Brand Extensions." *Journal of Marketing* 54 (1): 27–41.

Aaker, J. 1997. "Dimensions of Brand Personality." *Journal of Marketing Research* 34 (August): 347–356.

———. 1999. "The Malleable Self: The Role of Self-Expression in Persuasion." *Journal of Marketing Research* 36 (February): 1–21.

Aaker, J., V. Benet-Martinez, and J. Garolera. 2001. "Consumption Symbols as Carriers of Culture: A Study of Japanese and Spanish Brand Personality Constructs." *Journal of Personality & Social Psychology* 81: 492–508.

Aaker, J., S. Fournier, and S.A. Brasel. 2004. "When Good Brands Do Bad." *Journal of Consumer Behavior* 31 (June): 1–16.

Abegglen, M.V. 1995. *Jomini-Einfluss series Strategisschen Denkn.* Zurich: Militarische Fuhrungsschule.

ABN AMRO. 2001. "ABN AMRO missie en waarden." In *Bedrijfsagenda ABN AMRO.*

Abramson, P.R., and R. Inglehart. 1995. *Value Change in Global Perspective.* Ann Arbor: University of Michigan Press.

Academy of Achievement. 2005. New York. www.achievement.org/autodoc/pagegen/newsletter/2005/.

ACNielsen. 2001. *Identificatie van succesvolle nieuwe merken in het levensmiddelenkanaal in Nederland in de periode 1990–2000.* Amsterdam: ACNielsen.

———. 2003. *Analysing of Beer Brands Marketshares per Beer District in the Netherlands.* Unpublished report.

Adamson, A. 2006. "Brand Architecture Trends." Landor Associates. www.landor.com.

Adbrands Company Profiles. 2005. Apple Computer (U.S.). www.warc.com.

———. 2006a. Nestlé S.A. (Switzerland). www.warc.com.

———. 2006b. Sara Lee Corporation. www.warc.com.

Adweek. 2001. "What's the Difference? Not Much If You Ask Consumers." 42 (4): 42.

Agres, S., S. Daiberl, B. Moult, and J. Speath. 2003. "Maximising Shareholder Value by Bridging the Metrics of Finance and Marketing." *ESOMAR* September.

Agres, S., and T.M. Dubitsky. 1996. "Changing Needs for Brands." *Journal of Advertising Research* (January–February): 21–30.

Ahlers, J.B.A. 1997. *De BrandAsset Valuator als ondersteuning bij het ontwikkelen van strategie.* Internal document. Amsterdam: Young & Rubicam.

Ahold. 1998. *De bedrijfscultuur van Ahold.* Company brochure.

Ailawadi, L., S.A. Neslin, and D.R. Lehmann. 2001. "Market Response to a Major Policy Change in the Marketing Mix: Learning from Procter & Gamble's Value Pricing Strategy." *Journal of Marketing* 65 (1): 44–61.

Ajzen, L., and M. Fishbein. 1975. *Beliefs, Attitude, Intention and Behavior: An Introduction to Theory and Research.* Reading, MA: Addison-Wesley.

Alleborn, J.P. 1994. "The Relationship of a Brand's Quality (Value) to a Brand's Sales, Profitability, and Stock Market Performance." Paper presented at the Building Brand Equity Conference of the Advertising Research Foundation: The Leading Role of Research in Managing the Power of Brands, February 14–15.

Allen, D. 2000. "The Acid Test: A Communications Tool for Leadership Teams Who Interact with the Whole Organisation." *Journal of Brand Management* 7 (4): 257–266.

Allende-Blin, J. 1994. "Gesamtkunstwerke: Von Wagners Musikdramen zu Schreyers Bühnenrevolution." In *Gesamtkunstwerk zwischen Synästhesie und Mythos.* Bieleveld: Aisthesis Verlag.

Alonso, S. 2001. "Patrick Morley's geloof in KPN." *NRC Handelsblad* July 6, 14.

Ambler, T. 2000. *Marketing and the Bottom Line.* London: Pearson.

American Food Marketing Institute. 2005. "The World According to Shoppers." https://coke.net/CCRRC/north_america/studies/NA%20Private/KO_CCRRC_2004.pdf.

Anderson, J.R. 2000. *Cognitive Psychology and Its Implications.* New York: W.H. Freeman.

Anschuetz, N. 1997. "Building Brand Popularity: The Myth of Segmenting to Brand Success." *Journal of Advertising Research* (January–February): 63–66.

Antonides, G., and F.v. Raaij. 1994. *Consumentengedrag.* Utrecht: Lemma BV.

APG. 2003. "Creative Planning Awards Shortlist." *Campaign*, special supplement, September 26, 9.

Archer, J. 1996. "Brand Share Wars: Extending the Battleground into Consumers' Minds." ESOMAR 7.

Arnold, D. 1992. *Handbook of Brand Management.* London: Pitman.

Assael, H. 1987. *Consumer Behavior and Marketing Action.* Belmont, CA: Kent.

Auken, B.van. 2000. "Developing the Brand Building Organisation." *Journal of Brand Management* 7 (4): 281–290.

Austin, J.T. 1996. "Goal Constructs in Psychology: Structure, Process and Content." *Psychological Bulletin* 120 (3): 338–375.

Bailey, A., and G. Johnson. 2001. "A Framework for a Managerial Understanding of Strategy Development." In *Rethinking Strategy*, ed. H.W. Volberda and T. Elfring. London: Sage.

Baker, C., C. Nancarrow, and J. Tinson. 2005. "The Mind Versus Market Share Guide to Brand Equity." *International Journal of Market Research* 47 (5): 523–540.

Baldinger, A.L. 1993. *Measuring Brand Equity for Enduring Profitable Growth: The Research Contribution.* New York: Advertising Research Foundation.

Baldinger, A.L., and J. Rubinson. 1996. "Brand Loyalty: The Link Between Attitude and Behavior." *Journal of Advertising Research* 36 (6): 22–34.

Ballington, J. 2003. *How to Remain a Consumer Superbrand.* London: The Brand Council, 6.

Balmer, J., and E. Gray. 2002. "Comprehending Corporate Brands." Bradford University School of Management. Working Paper 02/33, November.

Balmer, J., and G.B. Soenen. 1999. "The Acid Test of Corporate Identity Management." *Journal of Marketing Management* 15: 69–92.

Band, W.A. 1991. *Creating Value for Customers.* New York: John Wiley.

Banens, H. 2000. "Integratie theorievorming ver te zoeken." *Holland Management Review* 70: 66–73.

Bangle, C. 2001. "Marrying Art and Profit at BMW." In *The Ultimate Creativity Machine: How BMW Turns Art into Profit*, ed. C. Bangle. Boston: Harvard Business Review.

Bargh, J.A. 1997. "The Automaticity of Everyday Life." In *The Automaticity of Everyday Life: Advances in Social Cognition*, ed. R.S. Weyer. Mahwah, NJ: Lawrence Erlbaum.

Barlow, R.G. 2000. "How to Court Various Target Markets." *Marketing News* September 10, 22.

Barnard, N., and A.S.C. Ehrenberg. 1985. "Robust Measures of Consumer Brand Beliefs." *Journal of the Market Research Society* 27: 177–187.

Barnes, J.G. 1997. "Closeness, Strength, and Satisfaction: Examining the Nature of Relationships Between Providers of Financial Services and Their Retail Customers." *Psychologie & Marketing* 14 (8): 765–790.

———. 2001. "Establishing Meaningful Customer Relationships: Why Some Companies and Brands Mean More to Their Customers." *Managing Service Quality* 13 (3): 178–186.

Barrett, J., L. Ashley, and P. Venkateswarlu. 1999. "Consumer Perceptions of Brand Extensions: Generalizing Aaker and Keller's Model." *Journal of Empirical Generalisations in Marketing Science* 4: 1–21.

Barry, A.M. 1997. *Visual Intelligence.* Albany: State University of New York Press.

————. 2005. "Perception Theory." In *Handbook of Visual Communication*, ed. K. Smith, S. Moriarty, G. Barbatsis, and K. Kenney. Mahwah, NJ: Lawrence Erlbaum.

Barry, T., and D. Howard. 1990. "A Review and Critique of the Hierarchy of Effects in Advertising." *International Journal of Advertising* 9: 121–135.

Barsalou, L.W. 1993. "Flexibility, Structure and Linguistic Vagary in Concepts: Manifestations of a Compositional System of Perceptual Symbols." In *Theories of Memory*, ed. A.F. Collins, S.E. Gathercole, M.A. Conway, and P.E. Morris. Hove, UK: Lawrence Erlbaum.

Bart, C.K. 1997. "Industrial Firms and the Power of Mission." *Industrial Marketing Management* 26: 371–383.

Barth, M.E., M.B. Clement, G. Foster, and R. Kasznik. 1998. "Brand Values and Capital Market Valuation." *Review of Accounting Studies* 3: 41–68.

Barton, D.J. 2006. *Cola Wars*. New York: Writers Club Press.

Barwise, T.P., and A.S.C. Ehrenberg. 1985. "Consumer Beliefs and Brand Usage." *Journal of the Market Research Society* 27 (2): 81–93.

Bastmeijer, A. 1997. *Waar doe ik het voor?* Amsterdam: Randstad.

Batchelor, A. 2005. "Brand Valuation as a Management Tool." *Market Leader* 29 (Summer): 29–33.

Bateson, G. 1991. *Steps to an Ecology of Mind*. St. Albans, UK: Poladin.

Battelle, J. 2006. "The Innovators." *Business* 20: 124–125.

Bauer, H., R. Mäder, and T. Keller. 2001. *An Investigation of the Brand Personality Scale*. University of Mannheim, Germany. http://marketing.byu.edu/ams/bauer-mader-keller.htm,10–11–2001.

Baumeister, R.F., and M.R. Leary. 1995. "The need to belong: desire for interpersonal attachments as a fundamental human motivation." *Psychological Bulletin* 117 (3): 497–529.

Baxter, M. 2000. *Brand Equity or How to Get On in Market Research*. Paper presented at the Market Research Society Conference.

BBC. 1998. *Reclame bestedingen Nederlandse Biermerken. Niet gepubliceerde data*.

BBDO Austria. 1993. Categorization of detergers by Austrian consumers. Internal document.

Beach, L.R. 1993. "Image Theory: An Alternative to Normative Decision Theory." *Advances in Consumer Research* 20: 235–238.

Bedbury, S. 2002. *A New Brand World*. New York: Penguin.

Beer, P.d. 2004. "Individualisering zit tussen de oren." In *Kiezen voor de kudde: Lichte gemeenschappen en de nieuwe meerderheid*, ed. J.W. Davendak and M. Hurenkamp. Amsterdam: Van Gennip.

Beer, P.d., and P.d. Hoed. 2004. "Wat gij niet wilt dat U geschiedt." In *Verkorte weergave van het WRR-rapport waarden normen en de last van het gedrag*, ed. P.d. Beer and P.d. Hoed. Amsterdam: Amsterdam University Press.

Bennett, P. 1988. *Dictionary of Marketing Terms*. Chicago: American Marketing Association.

Berge, E.v.d. 2001a. *Merkpersoonlijkheid langs de meetlat*. Amsterdam: Stichting Wetenschappelijk Onderzoek Commerciele Communicatie (SWOCC), 21.

————. 2001b. *Ontwikkeling van een meetinstrument voor merkpersoonlijkheid voor de Nederlandse markt*. Amsterdam: Stichting Wetenschappelijk Onderzoek Commerciele Communicatie.

Berg, M.S.v.d. 1999. *Merkpersoonlijkheid: een onderzoek naar de (on)zin van de merk/mens vergelijking*. Amsterdam: Universiteit van Amsterdam, Doctoraalscriptie Communicatiewetenschap.

————. 2000. *De rol van emoties bij communicatie(ver)werking en merkontwikkeling*. Naarden-Vesting: Giep Franzen.

Berner, R., and D. Kiley. 2005. "Global Brands." *Interbrand* July.

Bernstein, D. 1984. *Company Image and Reality: A Critique of Corporate Communications*. Eastborne, East Sussex: Holt, Rinehart and Winston.

Berry, L. 1995a. "Relationship Marketing." In *Emerging Perspectives in Services Marketing*, ed. L.L. Berry, G.L. Shostack, and G.D. Upah. Chicago: American Marketing Association.

————. 1995b. "Relationship Marketing of Services." *Journal of the Academy of Marketing Science* 23 (4): 236–245.

Bettman, J.R. 1979. *An Information Processing Theory of Consumer Choice*. Upper Saddle River, NJ: Addison-Wesley.

Beverage Daily. 2003. "Red Bull Targets Sugar-Conscious Consumers." www.beveragedaily.com.

————. 2005. "Energy Drinks Sector Gaining Momentum." www.beveragedaily.com.

Biel, A.L. 1999. "Exploring Brand Magic." In *How to Use Advertising to Build Strong Brands*, ed. J.P. Jones. Thousand Oaks, CA: Sage.

Biel, A.L., and J. Lannon. 1993. "Steel Bullet in a Velvet Glove? Harnessing 'Visual Metaphor' in Brand Building." *Admap* April.

Blackston, M. 1993. "Beyond Brand Personality: Building Brand Relationships." In *Brand Equity: Advertising's Role in Building Strong Brands*, ed. D. Aaker and A.L. Biel. Hillsdale, NJ: Lawrence Erlbaum.

———. 1995. "The Qualitative Dimension of Brand Equity." *Journal of Advertising Research* (July–August): 9–13.

Blattberg, R., and J. Deighton. 1996. "Manage Marketing by the Customer Equity Test." *Harvard Business Review* 74 (July/August): 136–144.

Block, M. 1991. "Attitudinal Versus Behavioral Segmentation: A Methodological Perspective." Paper presented at the Third Annual ARF Advertising and Promotion Workshop, New York, February 5–6.

Blom, C. 2004. *Success and Failure Factors of Brand Stretching.* Amsterdam: UvA Universiteit van Amsterdam.

———. 2005. *Stretchen in de supermarkt.* Amsterdam: UvA Universiteit van Amsterdam.

Bond, J.R.P., and L. Morris. 2002. "People Are Different If You Know How to Look." Paper presented at the MRS Research conference.

Bottomley, P.A., and J.R. Doyle. 1996. "The Formation of Attitudes Towards Brand Extensions: Testing and Generalizing Aaker and Keller's Model." *International Journal of Research in Marketing* 13: 365–377.

Boush, D.M., and B. Loken. 1991. "A Process Tracing Study of Brand Extension Evaluation." *Journal of Marketing Research* (February).

Bouwman, M.Y. 1999a. *Titanenstrijd.* Amsterdam: Universiteit van Amsterdam, Doctoraalscriptie psychologie.

———. 1999b. *Wat is een merkimago? Presentatie Stichting Wetenschappelijk Onderzoek Commerciële Communicatie.* Amsterdam: SWOCC.

Bower, T. 2005. "Richard's Brand—Branson Hype Has Hidden His Record of Failures." www.guardian.co.uk.

Brabet, J., and M. Klemm. 1995. "De gedeelde visie: bedrijfsmissie van Franse en Britse ondernemingen." *Tijdschrift voor Strategische Bedrijfscommunicatie* 1: 4–15.

Brady, D. 2001. "How Colgate chomps on the Competition." *Business Week* online, August 6, www.businessweek.com/magazine/content/01_32/b3744013.htm.

Brand Finance. 2006. *Current Practice in Brand Valuation.* Company brochure.

Brandmarc. 2000. "Onderzoek naar de positionering van belegginsinstellingen in Nederland." Internal document.

Bremer, D. 1998. *Merkrelaties. SWOCC Publicatie Nr. 8.* Amsterdam: Stichting Wetenschappelijk Onderzoek Commerciele Communicatie.

Brethouwer, W., and A. Lamme. 1995. "De toepassing: Quality Planning geïllustreerd aan de hand van drie cases." *Bladdossier* 9: 7–24.

Bridges, S., K.L. Keller, and S. Sood. 1997. "Communication Strategies for Brand Extensions: Enhancing Perceived Fit by Establishing Explanatory Links." *Journal of Advertising* 29 (4): 1–11.

Broniarozyk, S.M., and J.W. Alba. 1994. "The Importance of the Brand in Brand Extension." *Journal of Marketing Research* 31 (May): 214–228.

Broos, K., and F. Hurts. 1998. *De missie van dienstverleners: van mode naar motor.* Bloemendaal: Corp. Consultants. Internal brochure.

Brouwer, J.D., and J.v.d. Weijde. 1998. *De winkelende consument: beslissingsgedrag in de supermarkt nader bekeken.* Rotterdam: Erasmus Universiteit, Doctoraalscriptie vakgroep commerciële beleidsvorming.

Brown, M. 1998. *Richard Branson: The Authorized Biography.* North Pomfret, UK: Trafalgar Square Publishing.

Brown, S., and K.M. Eisenhardt. 1998. *Competing on the Edge: Strategy as Structured Chaos.* Boston: Harvard Business School Press.

Brown, S., R.V. Kozinets, and J.F. Sherry. 2003. "Teaching Old Brands New Tricks: Retro Branding and the Revival of Brand Meaning." *Journal of Marketing* 67 (July): 19–33.

Brown-Forman. 2007. "Building Enduring Brands." Louisville, KY. Annual Report.

Buck, S. 1995a. "The Decline and Fall of the Premium Brand." *Admap* March, 14–15.

———. 1995b. "Evaluating the Effects of Advertising Through the Use of Consumer Panels." Paper presented at the ADMAP IAA Conference on Monitoring Advertising Performance, London, January 25.

———. 2001a. *Advertising and the Long-Term Success of the Premium Brand.* Oxfordshire, UK: World Advertising Research Center.

———. 2001b. "The Triumph of the Premium Brand." In *Advertising and the Long-Term Success of the Premium Brand.* Oxfordshire, UK: World Advertising Research Center.

Bullmore, J. 1998. *Behind the Scenes of Advertising.* Oxfordshire, UK: Admap Publications.

Bunt, J. 2001. "CRM is gepasseerd station." *Nieuwstribune*, maarti 8, 28.

Burke.com. 2006. "The Burke Approach to Tracking Brand Equity." www.burke.com.

Burnett, J., and S. Moriarty. 1998. *Marketing Communications.* New York: Prentice Hall.

Burnett, K. 2001. *Handbook of Customer Relationship Management.* Upper Saddle River, NJ: FT Press.

Burns, K., and L. Novick. 1998. *Frank Lloyd Wright.* PBS.

Business Plans. 2005. "Mission Statement." www.businessplans.org/Mission.html.

Business Strategy. 2005. "The Fall of Rover." http://icmr.icfai.org/casestudies/catalogue/Business%20Strategy/BSTR166.htm.

Business 2.0. 2006. "The Job Audition." April, 85.

Business Week. 2007. "The 100 Top Brands." August 6.

Business Week Online. 2005. "Samsung Global: Be Like a BMW." www.businessweek.com.

Butterfield, L. 1998. "Economic Benefits of Branding." *Admap* April.

Buzzel, R.D., and B.T. Gale. 1987. *The PIMS-Principles: Linking Strategy to Performance.* New York: Free Press.

Cacioppo, J.T., and R.E. Petty. 1985. "Central and Peripheral Routes to Persuasion: The Role of Message Repetition." In *Psychological Processes and Advertising Effects.* New York: Lawrence Erlbaum.

Callebout, J. 1999. *Motivational Marketing Research Revisited.* Leuven-Apeldoorn: Garant.

Callebout, J., M. Janssens, D. Lorré, and H. Hendrickx. 1994. *The Naked Consumer: The Secret Motivational Research in Global Marketing.* Antwerp: Censydiam Institute.

Campbell, A., and S. Yeung. 1991. "Creating a Sense of Mission." *Long Range Planning* 2: 10–20.

Campbell, J. 1998. *Creating Salience Versus Creating Differentiation: Implications for Marketers and Advertisers.* SMRA Annual Convention.

Campen, C.v. 1996. "Artistieke en psychologische experimenten met synesthesie." *Psychologie & maatschappij* 74 (20): 10–26.

Cannon, H., and M. Schwaiger. 2005. "The Role of Company Reputation in Business Simulations." *Simulation & Gaming* 36 (2): 188–202.

Carlotti, S.J., M.E. Coe, and J. Perrey. 2004. "Making Brand Portfolios Work." *McKinsey Quarterly* November.

Carlotti, S.J., and M.E. Coe. 2003. "Strike Up the Brands." *McKinsey Quarterly* December.

Carlson, B.D. 2005. *Brand-Based Community: The Role of Identification in Developing a Sense of Community Among Brand Users.* Stillwater: Oklahoma State University.

Carpenter, G.S., R. Glazer, and K. Nakamoto. 1994. "Meaningful Brands from Meaningless Differentiation: The Dependence on Irrelevant Attributes." *Journal of Marketing Research* 31 (August): 339–350.

Carringer, P. 1994. "Not Just a Worthy Cause." *American Advertiser* (Spring): 17.

Cary, M.S. 2000. "Ad Strategy and the Stone Age Brain." *Journal of Advertising Research* (January–April): 103–106.

Castleberry, B.S., and A.S.C. Ehrenberg. 1990. "Brand Usage: A Factor in Consumer Beliefs." *Marketing Research* (June).

Censydiam. 1994. *Dossier automobiel 1994: Imagobarometer van 30 merken en 85 modellen.* Brussels.

Centerdata. 1999. "Analyse van de Percepties van Nederlandse Biermerken." Internal document.

Chaudhuri, A. 2002. "How Brand Reputation Affects the Advertising-Brand Equity Link." *Journal of Advertising Research* 42 (May–June).

Chavda, D., and M. Cary. 1999. "Building Your Brand with Brand Equity and Brand-Customer Relationships Through Targeting, Positioning and Advertising." Paper presented at Brand Equity and Advertising Research, an ARF Week of Workshops Event, New York City, October.

Checkland, P. 2000. *Systems Thinking, Systems Practice.* Chichester, UK: John Wiley.

Chernatony, L.d. 1999. "Service Is Key to Success When Considering Brand Extensions." *Brand Strategy* (December): 14.

Chernatony, L.d., and R. Dall'Olmo. 1998. "Modelling the Components of the Brand." *European Journal of Marketing* 32 (11–12): 1074–1090.

Chernatony, L.d., and K. Daniels. 1994. "Developing a More Effective Brand Positioning." *Journal of Brand Management* 1 (6): 373–379.

Chernatony, L.d., and M.H.B. McDonald. 1994. *Creating Powerful Brands: The Strategic Route to Success in Consumer, Industrial and Service Markets.* Oxford, UK: Butterworth Heinemann.

Chernatony, L.d., and M. McEnally. 1999. "The Evolving Nature of Branding: Consumer and Managerial Considerations." *Journal of Consumer and Market Research* 2: 1–46.

Child, L. 1997. "Mission Statements: An Inspiration for Us All?" *Admap* January, 43–46.

Christensen, C.M. 2000. *The Innovator's Dilemma.* New York: HarperBusiness.

Christopher, M., A. Payne, and D. Ballantyne. 1991. *Relationship Marketing: Bringing Quality, Customer Service and Marketing Together.* Oxford: Butterworth-Heinemann.

Cigliano, J., M. Georgiadis, D. Pleasance, and S. Whalley. 2000. "The Price of Loyalty." *McKinsey Quarterly* January 11.

Clancy, K.J. 1991. "The Battle for the Mind Is Often Lost Before the First Strike." *Marketing Revolution* 84–116.

Clancy, K.J., and P.C. Krieg. 2000. *Counter-Intuitive Marketing.* New York: Free Press.

Clancy, K.J., and R.S. Shulman. 1993. *The Marketing Myths That Are Killing Business: A Cure for Death Wish Marketing.* New York: McGraw-Hill.

Clancy, K.J., R.S. Shulman, and M. Wolf. 1995. *Simulated Test Marketing: Technology for Launching Successful New Products.* Lanham, MD: Lexington Books.

Clark, K. 2004. *Brandscendence.* Chicago: Dearborn Trade Publishing.

Clausewitz, C.V. 1932. *On War.* London: Routledge & Kegan.

Clifton, R., and J. Simmons. 2004. *Brands and Branding.* Princeton, NJ: Bloomberg Press.

Cole, S. 2002. "The Interbrand Approach to Brand Evaluation." Paper presented at the GVR-Back to the University Conference, Amsterdam.

Colley, R.H. 1961. "Defining Advertising Goals for Measured Advertising Results." New York: Association of National Advertisers.

Collins, J.C., and J. Porras. 1997. "Visie: ideologie en toekomst verbonden." *Tijdschrift voor Strategische Bedrijfscommunicatie* 3: 4–19.

Colvin, G. 2001. "What's Love Got to Do with It?" *Fortune* November, 60.

Consult Brand Strategy. 2004. *The Brand Asset Valuator.* Internal document.

Consumer Goods. 2006. "Innovation and Technology Awards." www.consumergoods.com.

Coomans, T., and R.v. Veen. 1999. *Het strategievormingsproces.* Rotterdam: Erasmus Universiteit, Doctoraalscriptie.

Cooper, A. 1998. "Brand Equity: A Lifestage Model." *Admap* January.

———. 1999. "Everything You Wanted to Know About Brand Equity Tracking But Were Afraid to Ask." *Journal of Brand Management* 6 (3): 153–160.

Corstjens, J., and M. Corstjens. 1995. *Store Wars: The Battle for Mindspace and Shelfspace.* West Sussex, UK: John Wiley.

CourseWork.com. 2005. "Analysing a Global Player on a Fast Changing Technological Market—Sony." www.coursework.info/i/74485.html.

Court, D. 2000. "Naar een driedimensionale marketing benadering." *Holland Management Review* (72): 52.

Court, D., and M. Loch. 1999. "Capturing the Value." *Advertising Age* November 8.

Crain, R. ed. 1998. *The House That Ivory Built.* Chicago: NTC.

Cram, T. 1994. *The Power of Relationship Marketing.* London: Financial Times.

Cramer, K. 1998. *Reclamestrategieën: een literatuuronderzoek.* Amsterdam: SWOCC (Stichting Wetenschappelijk Onderzoek Commerciële Communicatie).

———. 2005. *Onder moeders paraplu? Determinanten en effecten van merkportfoliostrategieën.* Amsterdam: Universiteit van Amsterdam, Stichting Wetenschappelijk Onderzoek Commerciële Communicatie, Academisch proefschrift.

Cramphorn, M.F. 1991. "Are There Bounds on Brand Equity?" Paper presented at The Challenge of Brands Today and in the Future Conference, Brussels, October 28–30.

Crimmins, J.C. 1992. Better Measurement and Management of Brand Value. *Journal of Advertising Research* (July–August): 11–19.

Cronon, W. 1998. *The Legacy of Frank Lloyd Wright.* www.pbs.org/flw/.

Croon, M. 2001. "Na 25 jaar The Body Shop houdt oprichtster Anita Roddick vast aan haar moreel leiderschap." *NRC Handelsblad* June 9, 39.

Cross, R. and Smith J. 1995. *Customer Bonding: Pathway to Lasting Customer Loyalty.* Lilncolnwood, IL: NTC.

Cytowic, R.E. 1995. *Synesthesia: Phenomenology and Neuropsychology.* http://psyche.cs.monash.edu.au/v2/psyche-2–10-cytowic.html.

Czerniawski, R.D., and M.W. Maloney. 1999. *Creating Brand Loyalty.* New York: AMACOM.

Dacin, P.A., and D.C. Smith. 1993. "The Effects of Adding Products to a Brand on Consumers' Evaluations of New Brand Extensions." *Advances in Consumer Research* 20: 594–598.

———. 1994. "The Effect of Brand Portfolio Characteristics on Consumer Evaluations of Brand Extensions." *Journal of Marketing Research* 31 (May): 229–242.

Dalgic, T., and M. Leeuw. 1994. "Niche Marketing Revisited: Concept, Applications and Some European Cases." *European Journal of Marketing* 28 (4): 39–56.

Darby, N. 1979. *Never Mind the Theory, Only Connect.* London: Advertising Planning Group.

Das, S. 2002. "Balancing on the Seesaw." ESOMAR. Asia Pacific Conference, Singapore. December.

———. 2004. "Building Strong Better Brands: Looking Beyond the Obvious!" ESOMAR Marketing Conference, Warsaw, October.

Da Silva, A. 2004. *Multi-Year Study Finds 21% Increase in Americans Who Say Corporate Support of Social Issues Is Important in Building Trust.* *w*ww.coneinc.com/Pages/pr30html.

D'Aveni, R.A., and R. Gunther. 1994. *Hypercompetition: Managing the Dynamics of Strategic Manoeuvering.* New York: Free Press.

Davenport, A., and J. Hallward. 1999. "The Enigma of Brand Equity Measurement: A Roadmap for Marketers." Paper presented at Brand Equity and Advertising Research, an ARF Week of Workshop Events, New York, October.

David, F.R. 1989. "How Companies Define Their Mission." *Long Range Planning* 22: 90–97.

Davis, N., and M. McCasland. 2005. "Discover the Passion in Your Brand." *Admap* December, 16–18.

Davis, S. 1998. "Do You Know Your ROBI?" *Management Review* October 1, 55.

Davis, S., and M. Dunn. 2002. *Building the Brand-Driven Business.* San Francisco: John Wiley.

Day, G.S. 1986. *Analysis for Strategic Market Decisions.* St. Paul: West.

———. 1990. *Market-Driven Strategy: Processes for Creating Value.* New York: Free Press.

———. 1992. "Marketing's Contribution to the Strategy Dialogue." *Journal of the Academy of Marketing Science* 20 (4): 323–329.

Deephouse, D.L. 1999. "To Be Different, or to Be the Same?" *Strategic Management Journal* 20: 147–166.

Deighton, J., and S. Hoch. 1993. "Teaching Emotion with Drama Advertising." In *Advertising, Exposure, Memory and Choice*, ed. A.A. Mitchell. Hillsdale, NJ: Lawrence Erlbaum.

DeKimpe, M., and D. Hanssens. 1995. "Empirical Generalizations About Market Evolution and Stationarity." *Marketing Science* 14 (3, part 2).

Delfeld, C. 2006. "Starbucks Steams Up Asia." *Forbes*, February.

Delvecchio, D. 2000. "Moving Beyond Fit: The Role of Brand Portfolio Characteristics in Consumer Evaluations of Brand Reliability." *Journal of Product and Brand Management* 9 (7): 457–471.

Deng, B.C. 1992. "The Influence of Individualism-Collectivism on Conflict Management Style: A Cross-Culture Comparison Between Taiwanese and U.S. Business Employees." Master's thesis. California State University, Sacramento.

Dennett, D.C. 1991. *Consciousness Explained.* New York: Little, Brown.

Deseure, A. 1999. "In Search of Understanding." *Admap* December, 34–36.

Deutschman, A. 2004. "The Conzo Way of Branding." *Fast Company* October, 87.

De Volkskrant. 1999a. "Baan." January 5.

———. 1999b. "Coca-Cola beboet in Italië na problemen in rest Europa." December 19.

———. 1999c. "TNT Post Groep? Dan denkt u aan dolfijnen en orakels." November 29.

Diesel. 2001. "Diesel: A State of Mind." www.diesel.com/contact_diesel/downloads/presspack_txt.txt.

Diller, H. 1997. "What Do Customer Clubs Achieve?" In *New and Evolving Paradigms: The Emerging Future of Marketing: Proceedings of Three American Marketing Association Special Conferences*, ed. T. Meenaghan. Dublin, Ireland: AAA.

Diller, S., N. Shedroff, and D. Rhea. 2006. *Making Meaning: How Successful Businesses Deliver Meaningful Customer Experiences.* Berkeley, CA: New Riders.

Dimancescu, D. 1992. *The Seamless Enterprise: Making Cross-Functional Management Work.* Essex Junction, VT: Oliver Wright.

Dixon, N. 1996. *Perspectives on Dialogue: Making Talk Developmental for Individuals and Organizations.* Greensboro, NC: Center for Creative Leadership.

Dolan, K.A. 2005. "The Soda with Buzz." *Forbes* March 28: 126–128.

Donegan, M., and I. Lunden. 2005. "Branded." *Total Telecom Magazine* August, 35.

Douglas, S.P. 1999. *International Brand Architecture: Development, Drivers and Design*. New York: New York University, Stern School of Business.

Douglas, S.P., and C.S. Craig. 2002. "Dynamics of International Brand Architecture: Overview and Directions for Future Research." Paper presented at the Research in International Marketing Conference, CIBER University of Connecticut.

Dowling, G.R., and M. Uncles. 1997. "Do Customer Loyalty Programs Really Work?" *Sloan Management Review* (Summer): 71–82.

Dubow, J.S. 1992. "Occasion-Based vs. User-Based Benefit Segmentation: A Case Study." *Journal of Advertising Research* March–April: 11–18.

Duby, G. 1976. *De Kathedralen bouwers*. Amsterdam: Elsevier.

Duijnisveld, E. 2001. *Succesfactoren merkintroducties in het levensmiddelenkanaal in Nederland in de periode 1990–2000* (Stageverslag SWOCC). Amsterdam: Universiteit van Amsterdam, vakgroep Communicatiewetenschap.

Duncan, T. 1995. "A Macro Model of Integrated Marketing Communication." Paper presented at the IMC conference, Norfolk, VA.

Duncan, T., and S. Moriarty. 1997a. *Driving Brand Value: Using Integrated Marketing to Manage Profitable Stakeholder Relationships*. New York: McGraw-Hill.

———. 1997b. "The IMC Audit: Testing the Fabric of Integration." *IMC Research Journal* 3 (Spring): 3–10.

———. 1998. "A Communication-Based Marketing Model for Managing Relationships." *Journal of Marketing* 62 (April): 1–13.

———. 2000. "The Customer's Bill of Rights." *Integrated Marketing Communication Research Journal* (Spring): 2.

———. 2006. "How Integrated Marketing Communication's 'Touchpoints' Can Operationalize the Service-Dominant Logic." In *The Service-Dominant Logic of Marketing*, ed. B. Lusch and S. Vargo. Armonk, NY: M.E. Sharpe.

Duncan, T. and F. Mulhern. 2004. *A White Paper on the Status, Scope and Future of IMC*. Denver, CO: University of Denver.

du Plessis, E. 2000. "Likeable Ads Work Best, But What Is 'Likeability'?" *Admap* May: 10–13.

du Plessis, E., and C. Foster. 2000a. "Ad Liking and Brand Buying: A Neurological Perspective." *Admap* August, 10–13.

———. 2000b. "Like the Ad. Love the Brand? Chicken, or Egg?" *Admap* December, 35–38.

Dyer, D., F. Dalzell, and R. Olegario. 2004. *Rising Tide*. Boston: Harvard Business School Press.

Dyson, P., A. Farr, and N. Hollis. 1996. "Understanding, Measuring and Using Brand Equity." *Journal of Advertising Research* (January–February): 9–13.

East, R. 1997. *Consumer Behaviour: Advances and Applications in Marketing*. London: Prentice Hall.

Eccles, J.S. 2002. "Motivational Beliefs, Values and Goals." *Annual Review of Psychology*.

Eckel, D.W. 2000. "Konzeption des Gesamtkunstwerks." Paper presented at the Proseminar, 2 St. Theatertheorie. Bochum, Germany, October 14.

Ehrenberg, A.S.C. 1997. "Repetitive Advertising and the Consumer." *Journal of Advertising Research* 14 (2): 25–34.

Ehrenberg, A.S.C., N. Barnard, and J. Scriven. 1997. "Differentiation or Salience." *Journal of Advertising Research* 37 (6): 7–14.

Ehrenberg, A.S.C., and C.J. Goodhart. 1978. *Understanding Buyer Behavior: Market Segmentation*. New York: J. Walter Thompson.

Ehrenberg, A.S.C., and M.D. Uncles. 1995. *Dirichlet-Type Markets: A Review, Part 1: Patterns and Theory*. London: South Bank University.

———. 1996. *Dirichlet-Type Markets: A Position Paper*. South Bank Business School/Bradford Management Centre.

———. 1999. *Understanding Dirichlet-Type Markets: Research Report 1*. London: South Bank University, R&D Initiative.

Elliott, S. 2003. "'Gillette and Dawson' Unite for a Cause." *New York Times Direct* May 6.

Elman, K. 1998. "Frank Lloyd Wright and the Principles of Organic Architecture." www.pbs.org/flw/.

Employee Volunteering. 2005. "The Walt Disney Company—Show Your Character." www.employeevolunteering.org.uk/case.

Energy Fiend. 2007. "The Top 15 Energy Drink Brands." April 12. www.energyfiend.com/2007/04/the-15-top-energy-drink-brands.

Engel, J.F., R.D. Blackwell, and P.W. Miniard. 1990. *Consumer Behaviour,* 6th ed. Chicago: Dryden Press.

Enrico, R. 1986. *The Other Guy Blinked: How Pepsi Won the Cola Wars.* New York: Bantam.

Epstein, S. 1977. "The Self-Concept: A Review and the Proposal of an Integrated Theory of Personality." In *Personality: Basic Aspects and Current Research,* ed. E. Staub. Englewood Cliffs, NJ: Prentice Hall.

Erdem, T. 1998. "An Empirical Analysis of Umbrella Branding." *Journal of Marketing Research* 35 (August): 339–351.

Erikson, E.H. 1963. *Childhood and Society,* 2nd ed. New York: W.W. Norton.

Ernst & Young, Global Client Consulting (GCC), and ACNielsen Bases. 1999. *New Product Introduction Successful Innovation/Failure: A Fragile Boundary.* Internal Report.

Escritt, S. 2000. *Art Nouveau.* London: Phaidon Press.

Evans, D. 2001. *Emotion: The Science of Sentiment.* New York: Oxford University Press.

Evers, J. 2000. "Presentatie Heineken." Paper presented at the Internet en de FMCG branche, Rotterdam, June 6.

Fackler, M. 2006. "Raising the Bar at Samsung." *New York Times* April 25.

Fahr-Becker, G. 1996. *Jugendstil.* Keulen, Germany: Köneman.

Falparsi. 2000. "Wagners Gesamtkunstwerk (1): muzikaal-dramaturgische aspekten van het muziekdrama." www.xs4all.nl~falparsi/Wagner/WagnerGesK1.html.

Falsey, T.A. 1989. *Corporate Philosophies and Mission Statements.* Westport, CT: Greenwood Press.

Farquhar, P.H., J.Y. Han, P.M. Herr, and Y. Ijiri. 1992. "Strategies for Leveraging Master Brands: How to Bypass the Risks of Direct Extensions." *Marketing Research* (September): 32–42.

Farr, A. 1996. "Advertising and Brand Equity." *Admap* April.

———. 1998. "Is Size All That Matters?" *Admap* May, 25–27.

———. 1999. "Does Your Brand Have the Energy to Compete?" *Admap* April, 35–39.

Farr, A., and N. Hollis. 1997. "What Do You Want Your Brand to Be When It Grows Up: Big *and* Strong?" *Journal of Advertising Research* (November–December): 23–36.

Feldwick, P. 2002. *What Is Brand Equity, Anyway?* Henley-on-Thames, UK: World Advertising Research Center (WARC).

Ferguson, M. 1989. *The Aquarian Conspiracy.* London: Paladin.

FHV/BBDO. 2001. *Share of Voice Versus Share of Market in the Dutch Beer Market.* Internal document.

Fiedler, J., and P. Feierabend. 2000. *Bauhaus.* Keulen, Germany: Könemann.

Fishbein, M. 1967. *Readings in Attitude Theory and Measurement.* New York: John Wiley.

———. 1976. "A Behavior Theory Approach to the Relations Between Beliefs About an Object and the Attitude Toward the Object." In *Readings in Attitude Theory and Measurement.* New York: John Wiley.

Fishbein, M., and I. Ajzen. 1975. *Belief, Attitude, Intention, and Behavior: An Introduction to Theory and Research.* Reading, MA: Addisson-Wesley.

———. 1980. "Predicting and Understanding Consumer Behavior: Attitude-Behavior Correspondence." In *Understanding Attitudes and Predicting Social Behavior,* ed. I. Ajzen and M. Fishbein. Englewood Cliffs, NJ: Prentice Hall.

Fishman, C. 2003. "The Wal Mart You Don't Know." *Fast Company* December, 77.

Fisk, P. 2000. "Brand Magnetics." *Journal of Brand Management* 7 (4): 267–274.

Floor, K. 1983. "The Values of Albert Heijn." Internal document, FHV/BBDO.

Flores, L., and D. Walker. 1999. "Measuring the Advertising Contribution to Brand Equity: Integrating Brand Equity Learning into Pretesting." Paper presented at Brand Equity and Advertising Research, an ARF Week of Workshops Event, New York City, October.

Food Marketing Institute. 2000. "Beyond Foodservice: How Consumers View Meals." www.fmi.org.

Ford, M.E. 1992. *Motivating Humans: Goals, Emotions and Personal Agency Beliefs.* Newbury Park, CA: Sage.

Fornell, C. 1992. "A National Customer Satisfaction Barometer: The Swedish Experience." *Journal of Marketing* 56 (January): 6–21.

Forster, J. 2001. "Sara Lee: Changing the Recipe—Again." *Business Week* September 10.

Forsyth, J., G. Gupta, S. Halder, A. Kaul, and K. Kettle. 1999. "A Segmentation You Can Act On." *McKinsey Quarterly* (3): 7–15.

Fortini-Campbell, L. 1998. "Consumer Insight: Getting in Character." *Journal of Integrated Communications* 47–53.

Fournier, S.M. 1994. "A Consumer-Brand Relationship Framework for Strategic Brand-Management." PhD diss., University of Florida.

————. 1998. "Consumers and Their Brands: Developing Relationship Theory in Consumer Research." *Journal of Consumer Research* (24): 343–373.

France Telecom. 2005. Press release, June 29. www.francetelecom.com.

Franzen, G. 1992. *Hoe reclame echt werkt.* Deventer, Netherlands: Kluwer bedrijfswetenschappen.

————. 1994. *Advertising Effectiveness: Findings from Empirical Research.* Henley-on-Thames, UK: Admap Publications.

————, ed. 2000. *Combineren van merken en producten.* Alphen aan den Rijn, Netherlands: Samsom.

————. 2005. *Wat drijft ons? Denken over motivatie sinds Darwin* (What moves us? Thinking about motivation since Darwin). Utrecht, Netherlands: Lemma.

————. 2006. *The SWOCC Book of Brand Management Models.* Amsterdam: SWOCC.

Franzen, G. 2008. *Motivatie: denken over drijfveren sinds Darwin.* Amsterdam: Boom Onderwijs.

Franzen, G., and M. Bouwman. 1999. *De mentale wereld van merken.* Alphen aan den Rijn, Netherlands: Samsom.

————. 2001. *The Mental World of Brands.* Henley-on-Thames, UK: World Advertising Research Center.

Franzen, G., C. Goessens, M. Hoogerbrugge, C. Kappert, R.J. Schuring, and M. Vogel. 1998. *Merken and Reclame: Hoe Reclame-Effectiviteit Brand Equity beïnvloedt.* Deventer, Netherlands: Kluwer Bedrijfswetenschappen.

————. 1999. *Brands and Advertising.* Henley-on-Thames, UK: Admap Publications.

Franzen, G., and F. Holzhauer. 1988. *Het merk.* Deventer, Netherlands: Kluwer Bedrijfswetenschappen.

Franzen, G., and M. Hoogerbrugge. 1996. *Het merk op weg naar de 21e eeuw.* Amsterdam: SWOCC.

Franzen, G., and M.S.v.d. Berg. 2002. *Strategisch management van merken.* Deventer, Netherlands: Kluwer.

Frege, G. 1952. "On Sense and Reference." In *Translations from the Philosophical Writings of Gottlob Frege*, ed. P. Geach and M. Black. Oxford, UK: Basil Blackwell.

Friedler, L., and A. Subrahmanyam. 2002. *Brand Perceptions and the Market for Common Stock.* Los Angeles: Anderson School of Management, University of California.

Frijda, N.H. 1993. "Moods, Emotions, Episodes and Emotions." In *Handbook of Emotions*, ed. M. Lewis and J.M. Haviland. New York: Guilford Press.

Garber, T. 2005. "Marken schaffen konjunkturen." *Absatzwirtschaft* 1–4.

Garcia-Gonzáles, J. 2002. *Establishing the Value of a Brand.* Amsterdam: Esomar.

Gardner, Burleigh B., and S.J. Levy. 1955. "The Product and the Brand." *Harvard Business Review* (March–April): 33–39.

Garten, J.E. 2001. *The Mind of the CEO.* New York: Basic Books.

Gay, V. 1983. "Jack Daniels Builds Big with Nostalgia." *Marketing and Media Decisions*, Spring Special Issue.

Geach, P., and M. Black, eds. 1980. *Translations from the Philosophical Writings of Gottlob Frege,* 3rd ed. Oxford, UK: Basil Blackwell.

Geerts, G.m., and H. Heestermans. 1993. *Van Dale: groot woordenboek der Nederlandse taal (twaalfde, herziene druk).* Utrecht, Netherlands: Van Dale Lexicografie.

Gerber, A., and R. Passikoff. 1999. "Calculating Advertising Expenditure Return-on-Investment: Developing a Brand Equity–Based Evaluation System." Paper presented at Brand Equity and Advertising Research, an ARF Week of Workshops Event, New York City, October.

Gergen, K.J. 1991. *Why am I? Identity Self and Narrative Within Organizational Contexts.* New York: Basic Books.

Gervey, B., and J. Lin. 1999. "Consumer Forecast: Ad Age Polls Nation on Ads, Brands, Internet." *Advertising Age* October 1, 14.

Geursen, G. 1994. *Virtuele Tomaten en Conceptuele Pindakaas: hoe Interactiviteit, Zelforganisatie en Bewustzijnsverruiming de Marketing op zijn Kop Zetten.* Deventer, Netherlands: Kluwer Bedrijfswetenschappen.

Geurtsen, P., and H. Lodders. 2001. "Meer grip op commerciële prestaties." *Tijdschrift voor Marketing*, 56–58.

GfK. 2002. *Euro Socio Styles.* Company brochure. www.Gfk.com.

GfK. 2005. "Wunsch nach Luxus versus Vertrauen auf Gott." Press release, April 3. www.GfK.com.

Giesen, P. 2000. "Rellen helpen." *De Volkskrant* December 16.

Giles, N.P.a.W. 1989. "Making SWOT Analysis Work." *Marketing Intelligence Planning* 7 (5–6): 5–7.

Giling, A. 2006. "SWOCC Integrated Branding Model." In *The SWOCC Book of Brand Management Models*, ed. G. Franzen. Amsterdam: SWOCC.

Gillmore, F.E. 1997. *Brand Warriors: Corporate Leaders Share Their Winning Strategies.* London: HarperCollins Business.

Ginneken, J.v. 1993. *Rages and Crashes: over de onvoorspelbaarheid van de economie.* Bloemendaal, Netherlands: Aramith Uitgevers.

———. 1999. *Brein-bevingen: snelle omslagen in opinie en communicatie.* Amsterdam: Uitgeverij Boom.

Ginsberg, S. 2003. "Coming Apart at the Seams." *Business Times* December.

Glueck, W.F. 1980. *Business Policy and Strategic Management.* New York: McGraw-Hill.

Glynn, M.S., and R.J. Brodie. 1998. "The Importance of Brand-Specific Associations in Brand Extension: Further Empirical Results." *Journal of Product & Brand Management* 7 (6): 509–518.

Gobé, M. 2002. *Citizen Brand.* New York: Allworth Press.

Gogoi, P. 2003. "Sara Lee: No Piece of Cake." *Business Week* May 26.

Golder, P.N. 2000. "Historical Method in Marketing Research with New Evidence on Long-Term Market Share Stability." *Journal of Marketing Research* 37 (May): 156–172.

Golder, P.N., and G.J. Tellis. 1992. "Do Pioneers Really Have Long-Term Advantages? A Historical Analysis." Working paper, Cambridge, MA: Marketing Science Institute.

———. 1993. "Pioneer Advantage: Marketing Logic or Marketing Legend?" *Journal of Marketing Research* 30 (May), 158–170.

Goldsmith, M., V. Govindarajan, B. Kaye, and A. Vicere. 2003. *The Main Facets of Leadership.* Upper Saddle River, NJ: Prentice Hall.

Goodrum, C., and H. Dalrymple. 1990. *Advertising in America.* New York: Harry N. Abrams.

Gove, P.B. 1993. *Webster's Third New International Dictionary.* Springfield, MA: Merriam-Webster.

Greenfield, S.A. 1995. *Journey to the Centers of the Mind: Toward a Science of Consciousness.* New York: W.H. Freeman.

Gregory, J. 2004. *The Best of Branding.* New York: McGraw-Hill.

Griffin, J., and M. Lowenstern. 2001. *Customer Winback: How to Recapture Lost Customers—and Keep Them Loyal.* New York: Jossey-Bass.

Gromark, J., and Melin, F. 2005. "Brand Orientation Index—A Management Tool for Building Strong Brands." Goteborg, Label AB, Internal Report.

Grönroos, C. 1990. "Relationship Approach to Marketing in Service Contexts: The Marketing and Organizational Behavior Interface." *Journal of Business Research* 20 (1): 3–11.

Grönroos, C., and K. Lindberg-Repo. 1998. "Integrated Marketing Communications: The Communications Aspect of Relationship Marketing." *IMC Research Journal* 4 (Spring): 3–11.

Gronstedt, A. 2000. *The Customer Century: Lessons from World-Class Companies in Integrated Marketing and Communications.* New York: Routledge.

Grubisch, T. 2008. "How AOL Can Transform Its Sow's Ear." Annenberg Online *Journalism Review* January 14. www.ojr.org/ojr/stories/080114grubisich/.

Grünig, J., ed. 1992. *Excellence in Public Relations Management.* Mahwah, NJ: Lawrence Erlbaum.

Grünig, J., and T. Hunt. 1984. *Managing Public Relations.* Stamford, CT: Thompson.

Gruyter, C.d. 2001. "Bij Wuustwezel begint het zuiden van Europa." *De Volkskrant* June.

Gudykunst, W.C., and S. Ting-Toomey. 1988. *Culture and Interpersonal Communication.* Newbury Park, CA: Sage.

Gummesson, E. 1999. *Total Relationship Marketing.* Oxford, UK: Butterworth-Heinemann.

Günther, H. 1994. *Gesamtkunstwerk zwischen Synästhesie und Mythos.* Bielefeld: Aisthesis Verlag.

Gürhan-Canli, Z., and D. Maheswaran. 1998. "The Effects of Extensions on Brand Name Dilution and Enhancement." *Journal of Marketing Research* 35 (November): 464–473.

Gutman, J. 1982. "A Means-End Chain Model Based on Consumer Categorisation Processes." *Journal of Marketing* 46 (Spring): 60–72.

Haigh, D. 1997. "Brand Valuation or Brand Monitoring? That Is the Question." *Journal of Brand Management* 4 (5): 311–319.

———. 1998. *Brand Valuation: Understanding, Exploiting and Communicating Brand Values.* London: Financial Times.

———. 1999a. "Brand Valuation in the Food Industry." Company paper of Brand Finance Limited, April.

———. 1999b. *Understanding the Financial Value of Brands.* Brussels, Belgium: European Association of Advertising Agencies (EAAA).

———. 2003. "Brand Equity." In *America's Greatest Brands: An Insight into America's Strongest Brands,* ed. S.P. Smith. Vol. 1. Rye, NY: America's Greatest Brands, Inc.

Haigh, D., and J. Knowles. 2006. "Don't Waste Time with Brand Valuation." www.marketingNPV.com/article.asp?ix=1106.

Haley, R. 1968. "Benefit-Segmentation: A Decision-Oriented Research Tool." *Journal of Marketing* 32 (3): 30–35.

———. 1999. "Benefit-Segmentation: Thoughts on Its Past and Its Future." *Journal of Segmentaton in Marketing* 8 (10): 5–11.

Hall, E. 1976. *Beyond Culture.* New York: Anchor Press.

Hall, M. 1992. "Using Advertising Frameworks: Different Research Models for Different Campaigns." *Admap* March.

Hall, M., and D. Maclay. 1991. *Science and Art: How Does Research Practice Match Advertising Theory?* London: MRS Conference.

Hall, N. 2002. "A Journey to the Center of the Earth." *Business Week* August 5.

Hallberg, G. 1995. *All Consumers Are NOT Created Equal: The Differential Marketing Strategy for Brand Loyalty and Profits.* New York: John Wiley.

Hallward, J.A. 2000. "Attitudinal Brand Equity, Behavioral Loyalty, and Brand Performance: Lessons Learned So Far." Paper presented at Advertising Research Foundation Workshop, October.

———. 2001. "Creators of Equity." Paper presented at Advertising Research Foundation Workshop, October.

Halsall, P. 1996. *Medieval Sourcebook: Abbot Suger: On What Was Done in His Administration.* www.fordham.edu/halsall/source/suger.html.

Hamel, C., and C.K. Prahalad. 1989. "Strategic Intent." In *The Strategy Process*, ed. H. Mintzberg, J.B. Quinn, and S. Ghosal. London: Prentice Hall.

———. 1994. *Competing for the Future.* Boston: Harvard Business School Press.

Hankinson, G., and P. Cowking. 1993. *Branding in Action.* Maidenhead, UK: McGraw-Hill.

———. 1995. "What Do You Really Mean by a Brand?" *Journal of Brand Management* 3 (1): 43–50.

Hansen, F. 1998. "From Life Style to Value Systems to Simplicity." *Advances in Consumer Research* 25, 181–195.

Hansen, F., and A. Kvaerk. 1998. *Value Dimensions: Are They Really That Many?* Copenhagen: Copenhagen Business School.

Harris Interactive. 2006. "Reynolds Wrap Aluminum Foil Ranks #1 in Overall Brand Equity." www.harrisinteractive.com/news/allnewsbydata.asp?newsID=818.

Hart, C., and M. Johnson. 1999. "Growing the Trust Relationship." *Marketing Management* (Spring): 9–22.

Hartnett, M. 1999. "With a Will, There's a Way." *Advertising Age* November 8.

Heath, R. 1997. *Brand Commitment as the Predictor of Advertising Effect.* London: Taylor Nelson AGB.

Heijden, T.v.d. 2006. "De wedergeboorte van de klantenkaart." *Tijdschrift voor Marketing*, October.

Hennig-Thurau, T., K. Gwinner, and D. Gremler. 2000. "Why Customers Build Relationships with Companies and Why Not." In *Relationship Marketing: Gaining Competitive Advantage Through Customer Satisfaction and Cost Retention.* Berlin: Springer.

Henry, M. 1987. "Five P's for Strategy." In *The Strategy Process*, ed. H. Mintzberg, J.B. Quinn, and S. Ghosal. London: Prentice Hall.

Herk, H.v., F. Schelbergen, D. Sikkel, and T. Verhallen. 1995. "Positioneringstechnieken." *Tijdschrift voor Marketing Interface* (January–February): 2–15.

Het Financieel Dagblad. 2001. "Het product als balsem voor de ziel." January 31.

Heylen, J.P. 1990a. "De impliciete persoonlijkheid." *Onderzoek* November 27.

———. 1990b. "Modelling Implicit Dynamics: A More Systematic Approach to Data Gathering and Interpretation." Paper presented at the Seminar on Qualitative Research: How Are We Preparing for the Future? Geneva, November 7–9.

Heylen, J.P., B. Dawson, and P. Sampson. 1995. "An Implicit Model of Consumer Behaviour." *Journal of Market Research Society* 37 (1): 51–67.

Heylighen, F., C. Joslyn, and V. Turchin, eds. 1991. "A Short Introduction to the Principia Cybernetica Project." *Journal of Ideas* 2 (1): 26–29.

———. 1995. *The Quantum of Evolution: Toward a Theory of Metasystems Transitions.* New York: Gordon & Breach.

Hirsch, R. 2003. "Umbrella Brands and Sub-brands." *Admap* October, 37–39.

Hirsh, E.R., and S.B. Wheeler. 1999. "Channel Champions: The Rise and Fall of Product-Based Differentiation." *Strategy Management Competition* 17: 43–50.

Hofmann, T. 2004. "Audi of America CEO Fired for Criticism of Poor Selling VW Phaeton." *Canadian Auto Press* November 18.

Hofmeyr, J. 1990. "The Conversion Model—A New Foundation for Strategic Planning in Marketing." Paper presented at the New ways in Marketing and Marketing Research conference, Athens.

Hofmeyr, J. and B. Rice. 2000. *Commitment-Led Marketing.* Chichester, UK: John Wiley.

Hofstede, F.T., A. Audeneart, J.E.M. Steenkamp, and M. Wedel. 1998. "An Investigation into the Association Pattern Technique as a Quantitative Approach to Measuring Means-End Chains." *International Journal of Research in Marketing* 15: 37–50.

Hofstede, G.H. 1980. *Culture's Consequences: International Differences in Work-Related Values.* Beverly Hills, CA: Sage.

———. 1983. "The Cultural Relativity of Organization Practices and Theories." *Journal of International Business Studies* 14 (2): 75–89.

———. 1991. *Cultures and Organisations: Software of the Mind.* London: McGraw-Hill.

Hoggard, L. 2005. "Why We're All Beautiful Now." *The Observer* January 9: 4.

Holden, S.J.S. 1993. "Understanding Brand Awareness: Let Me Give You a Clue." *Advances in Consumer Research* 20: 383–388.

Holmes, S. 2001. "Starbuck's: Keeping the Brew Hot." *Business Week* August 6.

Hoogerwerf, A. 1984. "Beleid berust op veronderstellingen: de beleidstheorie." *Acta Politica*, April: 493–531.

Hornstein, S. 2006. "The Lure of the Easy Target: Or, Why the CRM Process Gets Lip Service and Often Little Else." *Sales & Marketing Management* March.

Horovitz, B. 2005. "Sara Lee to Shed Clothes, Focus on Food." *USA Today* November 2.

Houtman, J. 2000. "Doelzoekers." *E/Merce* October 1(6): 88.

Howard, T. 2006. "Absolut Gets into Spirit of Name Play with New Ads." *USA Today* January 16.

———. 2005. "Dove Ads Enlist all Shapes, Styles, Sizes." *USA Today* August 28: 3.

Howard-Spink, J. 2003. "Who Is Your Brand? And What Is Its Story?" *Admap* October, 15–17.

How-to.com. 2005. "Mission Statement: How to Create a Mission Statement." www.how-to.com/Operations/mission-statement.htm.

Hubertz, I. 2000. "Die marke auf der Couch: Das wesen der marke und wie man es messen kann." *Planung & Analyse* (February): 26–32.

Huffman, C., S. Ratneshwar, and D.G. Mick. 2000. *The Why of Consumption.* London and New York: Routledge.

Hulbert, J., N. Capon, and N. Piercy. 2003. *Total Integrated Marketing.* New York: Free Press.

Hulsebos, M. 2000. "Philip Kotler over de waarde van oude theorieën in de nieuwe economie." *Tijdschrift voor Marketing* (October): 11–13.

Hupp, O., and K. Powega. 2004. "Using Consumer Attitudes to Value Brands: Evaluation of the Financial Value of Brands." *Journal of Advertising Research* (September): 312–314.

Ihator, A. 1999. *When in Rome: International Business Communication. Communication World.* December. http://findarticles.com/p/articles/mi_m4422/is_1_17/ai_59228569.

———. 2000. "Understand the Cultural Patterns of the World: An Imperative in Implementing Strategic International PR programs." *Public Relations Quarterly* (Winter): 38–44.

Interbrand. 2002. "Brand Contribution to Company Capitalization." *Business Week.*

———. 2004a. 2003 "Global Brands Scoreboard." *Business Week* August 4.

———. 2004b. "Brand Valuation." In *Brands and Branding,* R. Clifton, J. Simmons, S. Ahmad, eds. *The Economist Series.* New York: Interbrand.

Interbrand. 2007. "The 100 Top Brands." *Business Week.* August 6.

Jack Daniel's. 2001. "Jack Daniel's Tennessee Whiskey—Home Page." www.jackdaniels.com.

Jacobs, M.G.P.A., and W.H.G. Maas. 2001. *De magie van Heineken.* Amsterdam: Heineken NV.

Jamieson, D. 1997. "The New Face of Marketing: Targeting Your Efforts More Cost-Effectively to Increase Commitment." *Esomar* (July).

Jansen, M. 1999a. "Succesfactoren voor endorsement branding." *Tijdschrift voor Marketing* (December): 30–31.

———. 1999b. *Endorsement Branding from a Portfolio Perspective.* Nijmegen, Netherlands: Nijmegen Business School, Faculty of Policy Sciences.

Jap, S.D. 1993. "An Examination of the Effects of Multiple Brand Extensions on the Brand Concept." *Advances in Consumer Research* 20: 607–611.

John, D.R., B. Loken, and C. Joiner. 1998. "The Negative Impact of Extensions: Can Flagship Products Be Diluted?" *Journal of Marketing* 62 (January): 19–32.

Johnson, G., and K. Scholes. 2002. *Exploring Corporate Strategy*. London: Prentice Hall.

Johnson, T. 1991. "The Inherent Value of Brands: Results from Over Fifteen Years of Brand Loyalty Data." Paper presented at the Third Annual ARF Advertising and Promotion Workshop, New York, February 5–6.

Jones, J.P. 1992. *How Much Is Enough?* New York: Lexington Books.

———. 1995. *When Ads Work*. New York: Lexington Books.

Jong, H.d., and O. Zeitsen. 2001. "De succesfactoren en obstakels van CRM: one call does it all." *Nieuwstribune* March 18.

Joyce, T. 1991. "Models of Advertising Process." *Marketing and Research Today* November.

Jun, Y.S., R. Gilbert, and C.W. Park. 1995. "The Effectiveness of Composite Branding Strategies." *Advances in Consumer Research*: 252.

Kahle, L.R., P.M. Homer, R.M. O'Brien, and D.M. Boush. 1997. "Maslow's Hierarchy and Social Adaptation as Alternative Accounts of Value Structure." In *Values, Lifestyles and Psychographics*, ed. L.R. Kahle and L.E. Chiagouris. Mahwah, NJ: Lawrence Erlbaum.

Kapferer, J.N. 1990. "Une opposition ideologique: le produit ou la marque?" *Revenue Vinicole Internationale* (March).

———. 1992. *Strategic Brand Management*. New York: Free Press.

———. 1996. *Strategisch Merkmanagement: over het eigen vermogen van merken*. Schoonhoven, Netherlands: Academic Service.

———. 1998. "Why Are We Seduced by Luxury Brands?" *Journal of Brand Management* 6 (1): 44–49.

Kaplan, R.S., and D.P. Norton. 1996. *The Balanced Scorecard: Translating Strategy into Action*. Boston: Harvard Business School Press.

———. 2000. *Strategie in de 21e eeuw*. Boston: Harvard Business School Press.

Karel, J.W. 1991. "Brand Strategy Positions Products Worldwide." *Journal of Business Strategy* (May–June): 16–19.

Kay, J. 1993. *Foundations of Corporate Success*. Oxford, UK: Oxford University Press.

Keller, K.L. 1998. *Strategic Brand Management*. Upper Saddle River, NJ: Prentice Hall.

———. 1999a. "Brand Mantras: Rationale, Criteria and Examples." *Journal of Marketing Management* 15: 43–51.

———. 1999b. "Designing and Implementing Branding Strategies." *Journal of Brand Management* 6 (5): 315–332.

———. 2003. *Strategic Brand Management: Building, Measuring, and Managing Brand Equity*, 2nd ed. Upper Saddle River, NJ: Prentice Hall.

Keller, K.L., and D.A. Aaker. 1992. "The Effects of Corporate Images and Branding Strategies on New Product Evaluations. Stanford University: Jackson Library, Graduate School of Business. Research paper no. 1216.

———. 1997. *Managing the Corporate Brand: The Effects of Corporate Marketing Activity on Consumer Evaluations of Brand Extensions"* (no. 97-106). Cambridge, MA: Marketing Science Institute.

Kennedy, R., and A. Ehrenberg. 2001. "There Is No Brand Segmentation." *Journal of Marketing Research* 13 (1): 4–7.

Kennedy, R., A. Ehrenberg, and S. Long. 2000. *The Customer Profiles of Competing Brands*. London: South Bank University.

Kerin, R.A., and R. Sethuraman. 1998. "Exploring the Brand Value–Shareholder Value Nexus for Consumer Goods Companies." *Journal of the Academy of Marketing Science* 26 (4): 260–273.

KesselsKramer. 1999. "Wat voor persoon is Ilse?" Amsterdam: KesselsKramer. Internal document.

———. 2001. *KesselsKramer 96-01*. Amsterdam: Uitgeverij Bis.

Khandelwal, M., and C. McKinney. 2003. "Comparing Brand Equity Valuation with In-Market Performance." *ESOMAR*.

Khermouch, G. 2001. "Consumers in the Mist." *Business Week* (February 26): 92–94.

Kitchen, P.J., and D.E. Schulz. 2001. *Raising the Corporate Umbrella: Corporate Communications in the 21st Century*. New York: Palgrave.

Kieft, F.v.d. 2000. "De verbreding van Nike en de merkbeleving van Nike Running in de gedachten van de hardloper." PhD diss., Universiteit van Amsterdam.

Kiley, D. 2004. *Driven: Inside BMW, the Most Admired Car Company in the World*. Hoboken, NJ: John Wiley.

Kim, H., W. Kim, and J.A. An. 2003. "The Effect of Consumer-Based Brand Equity on Firms' Financial Performance." *Journal of Consumer Marketing* 20 (4): 335–351.

Kirmani, A., S. Sood, and S. Bridges. 1999. "The Ownership Effect in Consumer Responses to Brand Line Stretches." *Journal of Marketing* 63 (January): 88–101.

Kirsner, S. 2002. "Stelios Makes Growth Look Easy." *Fast Company* November.

Klein, N. 2000. *No Logo.* London: Flamingo.

Klemm, M., S. Sanderson, and G. Luffman. 1991. "Mission Statements: Selling Corporate Values to Employees." *Long-Range Planning* 24 (3): 73–78.

Knapp, D.W. 2000. *The Brandmindset.* New York: McGraw-Hill.

Knobil, M. 1998. *Superbrands: An Insight into 65 of Britain's Superbrands.* Vol. 3. London: Creative & Commercial Communications.

Knobil, M., ed. 2003. *Consumer Superbrands.* London: The Brand Council.

Knobler, W. 1981. "Position Brand in Its Optimal Market Niche by Finding Benefits That Matter to Buyers." *Marketing News* May 15, 14–15.

Knowles, J., and W. Olins. 2006. "In search of a reliable measure of brand equity." www.zibs.com/knowles. shtml.

Kochan, N. 1996. *The World's Greatest Brands.* New York: Interbrand.

Kohli, C., and D.W. LaBahn. 1997. "Creating Effective Brand Names: A Study of the Naming Process." *Journal of Advertising Research* (January–February): 67–75.

Kok, R.A. 1997. "Corporate Branding: merkkeuzes bij AKZO Nobel." *Tijdschrift voor Strategische Bedrijfscommunicatie* 3 (1): 94–106.

Kops, H. 2000. "Ik mis emotie bij de nieuwe generatie." *Elan* November 1 (11): 16.

———. 1992. "Total Marketing." *Business Week Advance, Executive Brief,* February.

Kotler, P. 2003. *Marketing Management.* Upper Saddle River, NJ: Prentice Hall.

Kotler, P., and G. Zaltman. 1971 "Social Marketing: An Approach to Planned Social Change," *Journal of Marketing* July: 3–12.

Kouwer, P.D.B.J. 1963. *Het spel van de persoonlijkheid.* Utrecht: Uitgeverij Erven J. Bijleveld.

Kralingen, R.v. 1999. *Superbrands.* Deventer, Netherlands: Samsom.

Kramer, L. 1999. "Coca-Cola Tells Shops: Capture Magic Moment." *Advertising Age* October.

Krouwel, A. 2004. "De kiezer zweeft stabiel." In *Kiezen voor de kudde: Lichte gemeenschappen en de nieuwe meerderheid,* ed. J.W. Duyvendak and M. Hurenkamp. Amsterdam: Van Gennip.

Krugman, H.E. 1965. "The Impact of Television Advertising: Learning Without Involvement." *Public Opinion Quarterly* 29: 349–356.

Künh, F.K. 2000. "Van afstandelijke bekoorlijkheid naar vermoeidheid door het rationele-eergisteren propaganda, gisteren reclame, vandaag werving, morgen communicatie." In *Bauhaus,* ed. J. Fiedler and P. Feierabend. Keulen, Germany: Könemann.

Laforet, S., and J. Saunders. 1994. "Managing Brand Portfolios: How the Leaders Do It." *Journal of Advertising Research* (September–October): 64–76.

———. 1999. "Managing Brand Portfolios: Why Leaders Do What They Do." *Journal of Advertising Research* (January–February): 51–66.

———. 2005. "Managing Brand Portfolios: How Strategy Has Changed." *Journal of Advertising Research* (September): 314–327.

Lai, A.W. 1995. "Consumer Values, Product Benefits and Customer Value: A Consumption Behavior Approach." In L. McAlister and M. Rothschild, eds. *Advances in Consumer Research* 20: 381–388.

Lane, V., and R. Jacobson. 1995. "Stock Market Reactions to Brand Extensions Announcements: The Effects of Brand Attitude and Familiarity." *Journal of Marketing* 59: 63–77.

Langer, J. 1997. "What Consumers Wish Brand Managers Knew." *Journal of Advertising Research* (November–December).

Lannon, J.C.P. 1983. "Humanistic Advertising." *International Journal of Advertising* 2 (July–September): 195–213.

Lau, S. 2001. "I Want My MTV, But in Mandarin, Please." *Admap* March, 34–36.

Lavidge, R.J., and G.A. Steiner. 1961. "A Model for Predictive Measurements of Advertising Effectiveness." *Journal of Marketing* 25: 59–62.

Law, A. 2003. "VW Phaeton to Top Out at $85,390." *American Auto Press* November 22.

Lee, L. 2000. "Can Levi's Be Cool Again?" http://bwarchive.businessweek.com/.

Leeuwen, R.v. 1998. *Positionering in de automarkt.* Diemen: Netherlands: Van Leeuwen Consulting BV.

Leidelmeijer, F. 2001. "Jugendstil en Art Deco." http://217.18.67.78/05/Articles/Leidemeijer/article.htm.

Leith, A., and N. Riley. 1998. "Understanding Needstates and Their Role in Developing Successful Marketing Strategies." *Journal of the Market Research Society* 40 (1).

Lepeu, C. 2005. Le livre des Grande Marques. London: Superbrands Ltd.

LePla, J., S.V. Davis, and L.M. Parker. 2003. *Brand Driven: The Route to Integrated Branding Through Great Leadership.* London: Kogan Page.

Leuthesser, L., and C. Kohli. 1997. "Corporate Identity: The Role of Mission Statements." *Business Horizons* 40 (3): 59–66.

Levitt, T. 1991. *Thinking About Management.* New York: Free Press.

Liedtka, J.M. 1998. "Strategic Thinking: Can It Be Taught?" *Long Range Planning* 31 (1): 120–129.

Liedtka, J.M., and J.W. Rosenblum. 1996. "Shaping Conversations: Making Strategy, Managing Change." *California Management Review* 39 (1): 141–156.

Ligtelijn, M., and L.v. Buiten. 2000. "Vrienden bepalen de aantrekkingskracht van het merk." *Nieuwstribune* January 25.

Lindemann, J. 2004. "Brand Valuation." In *Brands and Branding*, ed. J. Lindeman. Princeton, NJ: Bloomberg Press.

Lippa, R.A. 1994. *An Introduction to Social Psychology,* 2nd ed. Belmont, CA: Brooks/Cole.

Litjens, E. 1996. "Strategic Brand Communication." PhD diss., University of Amsterdam.

Loken, B., and D.R. John. 1993. "Diluting Brand Beliefs: When Do Brand Extensions Have a Negative Impact?" *Journal of Marketing* (July).

Luik, J.C., and M.J. Waterson. 1996. *Advertising and Markets.* Henley-on-Thames, UK: NTC.

Lusch, B., and S. Vargo. 2006. *The Service-Dominant Logic of Marketing.* Armonk, NY: M.E. Sharpe.

Lyons, A.D. 2001. "Gestalt Approaches to the Gesamtkunstwerk." www.users,bigpond.com/tstex/gestalt.htm.

Maarsen, H. 2006. "Dun is de mode." *Financiële Dagblad* April 22.

Maathuis, O.J.H. 1999. "Corporate Brands: The Value of the Corporate Brand to Customers and Managers." PhD diss., Erasmus University.

Machleit, K.A., C.T. Allen, and T.J. Madden. 1993. "The Mature Brand and Brand Interest: An Alternative Consequence of Ad-Evoked Affect." *Journal of Marketing* 57 (October): 72–82.

Macrae, C. 1991. *World Class Brands.* Workingham, UK: Addison-Wesley.

———. 1996. *The Brand Chartering Handbook.* Harlow, UK: Addison-Wesley.

Macworld News. 2006. "How Apple Beat the Beatles." www.macworld.com/news/.

Madden, T.J., F. Fehle, and S. Fournier. 2006. "Brands Matter: An Empirical Demonstration of the Creation of Shareholder Value Through Branding." *Journal of the Academy of Marketing Science* 34 (2): 224–235.

Madhavaram, S., V. Badrinarayanan, and R.E. McDonald. 2005. "Integrated Branding Communications (IMC) and Brand Identity as Critical Components of Brand Equity Strategy." *Journal of Advertising* 34 (4): 69–80.

Marchant, L., P. Hutchinson, and C. Walker. 1994. "A Ranking Approach to Predicting Sales." Paper presented at the Market Research Society Conference.

Mariampolski, H. 1999. "The Power of Ethnography." *Journal of the Market Research Society* 41 (1): 75–86.

Mark, M., and C.S. Pearson. 2001. *The Hero and the Outlaw: Building Extraordinary Brands Through the Power of Archetypes.* New York: McGraw-Hill.

Marsden, P. 2000. "Brand Selection, Naturally." Paper presented at the Market Research Society Conference.

Martin, J.H., and J.M. Daley. 1989. "How to Develop a Customer-Driven Positioning Strategy." *Business* (October–December): 11–20.

Martin, I.M., and D.W. Stewart. 2001. "The Differential Impact of Good Congruency on Attitudes, Intentions, and the Transfer of Brand Equity." *Journal of Marketing Research.* Vol. xxxviii, 471–484.

May, J. 2000. "Bedrijven met corporate personality zijn zichzelf en daardoor anders." *Holland Management Review* 71: 60–64.

McAdams, D.E. 2004. *The Person: An Introduction to Personality Psychology,* 4th ed. Fort Worth, TX: Harcourt Brace.

McCracken, G. 2005. *Culture and Consumption II: Markets, Meaning, and Brand Management.* Bloomington: Indiana University Press.

McCrummen, S. 2006. "Marketing and Building Communities to Match Values." *Boulder Daily Camera* April 23.

McDonald, C. 1991. "Intended Response." *Admap* July–August.

———. 1992. *How Advertising Works.* Oxfordshire, UK: NTC.

———. 1993. "Point of View: The Key Is to Understand Consumer Response." *Journal of Advertising Research* (September–October): 63–69.

McDonough, J. 1998. "Pepsi Turns 100." *Advertising Age* July 20.

McGuire, W. 1968. "The Nature of Attitudes and Attitude Change." *Handbook of Social Psychology.* New York: Academic Press, 191–229.

McKenna, R. 1991a. "Marketing Is Everything." *Harvard Business Review* (January–February): 65–79.

———. 1991b. *Relationship Marketing.* Reading, MA: Addison-Wesley.

McKinsey, F. 1994. "Winning the Right to Brand." *Brand Strategy Newsletter.*

———. 2003. *Unlock Your Financial Brand: Create Value by Focusing on High Impact Attributes.* Company brochure.

McQueen, J. 1992. "How Advertising Works: Stimulating Long-Term Brand Growth." *Admap* April: 7.

McWalter, A. 2000. "The Brand New World of Marks & Spencer." *Journal of the Marketing Society* 11.

McWilliam, G. 1993. "The Effect of Brand Typology on Brand Extension Fit: Commercial and Academic Research Findings." *European Advances in Consumer Research* 1: 485–491.

Meer, D. 1999. "The Role of 'Popularity' in Creating Great Brands." Paper presented at Brand Equity & Advertising Research, an ARF Week of Workshops Event, New York City, October.

Meertens, R.W., and J.v. Grumkow. 1988. *Sociale Psychologie.* Groningen, Netherlands: Wolters-Noordhoff.

Melin, F. 2005. *Brand Orientation Index.* Götenborg, Sweden: LABELbrand Consultancy AB. Company booklet.

Menkveld. 2000. "The Company Behind the Brand." *Adformatie.*

Mercer Management Consulting. 2002. *Brand Portfolio Economics.* Internal report.

Mihailovic, P., and L.d. Chernatony. 1994. "Categorizing Brand Strategies Using the Brand-Bonding Spectrum." *Journal of Brand Management* 1 (5): 310–318.

Miller, S., and L. Berry. 1998. "Brand Salience Versus Brand Image: Two Theories of Advertising Effectiveness." *Journal of Advertising Research* 38 (5): 77–82.

Millward Brown. 1991. *How Advertising Affects the Sales of Packaged Goods Brands.* Warwick, UK: Millward Brown International.

———. 1995. *Persuasion.* Internal paper.

———. 2004. *Brand Archetype Framework.* Internal paper.

———. 2006a. "Millward Brown Announces a New Ranking of the World's Most Powerful Brands." Press release, April 3.

———. 2006b. *Young Families and Young Couples.* Company brochure.

———. 2006c. *Brandz: Top 100 Most Powerful Brands.* Millward Brown: Optimor. www.millwardbrown.com.

Min, S., K.U. Kalwani, and W.T. Robinson. 2006. "Market Pioneer and Early Follower Survival Risks: A Contingency Analysis of Really New Versus Incrementally New Product-Markets." *Journal of Marketing* 70: 15–35.

Mintzberg, H. 1987. "Crafting Strategy." In *The Strategy Process,* ed. H. Mintzberg, J.B. Quinn, and S. Ghosal. London: Prentice Hall.

———. 1994. *The Rise and Fall of Strategic Planning.* Hertfordshire, UK: Prentice Hall International.

Mintzberg, H., B. Ahlstrand, and J. Lampel. 1998. *Strategy Safari: A Guided Tour Through the Wilds of Strategic Management.* New York: Simon & Schuster.

Mintzberg, H., J.B. Quinn, and S. Ghosal, eds. 1999. *The Strategy Process.* London: Prentice Hall.

Miskell, Peter. 2005. How Crest Made Business History, January 17. Harvard Business School Archive, www.hbswk.hbs.edu/archive/4574.html.

Mitchell, A. 1993. "New Marketing Vision." *Marketing Business* 4 (December–January): 12–17.

———. 2000. "How Rover Lost the Plot." Paper No. 10. Henley-on-Thames, UK: World Advertising Research Center (WARC).

Mittal, B., and W.M. Lasser. 1998. "Why Do Customers Switch? The Dynamics of Satisfaction Versus Loyalty." *Journal of Services Marketing* 12 (13): 177–194.

Moenaert, R.K., and H.S.J. Robben. 1999. "Visionaire Marketing: Concurreren nu, bouwen voor de toekomst." Inaugural lecture, Universiteit Nijenrode.

Moens, J. 1999. "Onderzoek als bron van inspiratie bij strategieontwikkeling." *Effieboek '99: bekroonde voorbeelden van effectieve commerciële communicatie.* Almere, Netherlands: NieuwsTribune Publishing BV.

Moingeon, B., and B. Ramanantsoa. 1979. "Understanding Corporate Identity: The French School of Thought." *European Journal of Marketing* 31 (5–6): 383–395.

Montgomery, J., and M. Lieberman. 2005. "A Compendium of Brand Measurement." *Admap* September: 45–47.

Moore, J. 1993. "Predators and Prey: A New Ecology of Competition." *Harvard Business Review* May–June, 75–86.

Morgan, A. 1999. *Eating the Big Fish: How Challenger Brands Can Compete Against Brand Leaders.* New York: John Wiley.

Morrin, M. 1999. "The Impact of Brand Extensions on Parent Brand Memory Structures and Retrieval Processes." *Journal of Marketing Research* 36 (November): 517–525.

Mos, C.K. 2001. "Richard Wagner." www.composers.net/database/w/wagner.html.

Moseley, D. 2003. "Is Brand Valuation a Threat to Branding?" *Market Leader* (Summer): 21.

MSBBC. 2006. "Beatles' Apple Corps Loses Trademark Suit." www.msnbc.msn.com/id/12685223/.

Mungen, A. 1998. "Wagner's Visual Concept of Music Theater and Its French Background in the Early Nineteenth Century." Paper presented at the Wagner at the Millennium conference, Adelaide, Australia, November.

Muniz, A., and T. O'Guinn. 2001. "Brand Community." *Journal of Consumer Research* 27 (March): 412–431.

Murphy, B., A. Murphy, S. Woodall, and R. O'Hare. 1999. "The Stakeholder Relationship Audit: Measuring the Effectiveness of Integrated Marketing Communications." *IMC Research Journal* 5 (1): 9–12.

Murphy, J. 1989. *Brand Valuation.* London: Business Books.

———. 1997. "What Is Branding?" In *Brands: The New Creators*, ed. S. Hart and J. Murphy. New York: New York University Press.

Muthukrishnan, A.V., and A.W. Barton. 1991. "Role of Product Knowledge in Evaluation of Brand Extension." *Advances in Consumer Research* 18: 407–413.

Myers, J.H. 1996. *Segmentation & Positioning for Strategic Marketing Decisions.* Chicago: American Marketing Association.

Myers, I., K. Briggs, and M.H. McCaulley. 1987. *Manual for the Myers-Briggs Type Indicator: A Guide to the Development and Use of the MBTI.* Palo Alto, CA: Consulting Psychologists Press.

Narver, J.C. 1990. "The Effect of a Market Orientation on Business Profitability." *Journal of Marketing*, 54: 20–35.

Naumann, E. 1995. *Creating Customer Value: The Path to Sustainable Competitive Advantage.* Cincinnati, OH: Thomson Executive Press.

Nechvatal, J. 2000. "On Art and Technology–A New Unity: The Bauhaus 1923–1932 and Bauhaus Dessau-Chicago-New York." A review. www.dom.de/arts/artists/jnech/.

Nedungadi, P., and W.J. Hutchinson. 1985. "The Prototypicality of Brands: Relationships with Brand Awareness, Preference and Usage." *Advances in Consumer Research* 12: 498–503.

Neuman, O. 1984. "Automatic Processing: A Review of Recent Findings and a Plea for an Old Theory." In *Cognition and Motor Processes*, ed. W. Printz and A. Sanders. Berlin: Springer.

Neustadt, R., and E. May. 1986. *Thinking in Time: The Uses of History for Decision-Makers.* New York: Free Press.

Newell, F. 2000. *Why CRM Doesn't Work.* London: Kogan Page.

Nieuwstribune. 1999. "Het merk van de eeuw verkiezing." (46).

Niven, P.R. 2002. *Balanced Scorecard Step by Step: Maximizing Performance and Maintaining Results.* New York: John Wiley.

Noonan, D. 2001. "Red Bull's Good Buzz." *Newsweek* May 14: 63.

Oakenfull, G., E. Blair, B. Gelb, and P. Dacin. 2000. "Measuring Brand Meaning." *Journal of Advertising Research* (September–October): 43–53.

O'Connell, P. 2005. "Samsung's Goal: Be Like BMW." *Business Week Online* August 1, 2005.

Ohmae, K. 1982. *The Mind of the Strategist.* New York: McGraw-Hill.

Olins, R. 1996. "Elastic Brands." *Sunday Times.* March 11: 7.

Oliver, J.M., and P.W. Farris. 1989. "Push and Pull: A One-Two Punch for Packaged Products." *Sloan Management Review* (Fall): 53–61.

Oliver, R.L. 1999. "Whence Consumer Loyalty?" *Journal of Marketing* 63: 33–44.

Olson, D.W. 1984. "Validation of Copytesting Measures Based on In-Market Performance: An Analysis of New Products Ads." *The Characteristics of High Trial New Product raadsverkiezing.* ESOMAR Symposium on Methodological Advances in Marketing Research in Theory and Practice.

Oosterling. 2001. "Gesamtkunstwerk multi-medialiteit en interactiviteit." www.eur.nl/fw/cfk/oosterling/gesamtkw-arnhem.html.

Oppenhuisen, J. 2000. "Een schaap in de bus? Een onderzoek naar de waarden van de Nederlander." PhD diss., SWOCC: Universiteit van Amsterdam. Stichting Wetenschappelijk Onderzoek Commerciële Communicatie.

Osborne, R.L. 1991. "Core Value Statements: The Corporate Compass." *Business Horizon* September–October, 28–34.

———. 2006. "Easy Jet Makes Profit a Priority." *Business Telegraph* February 3.

Ossimitz, G. 1997. "The Development of Systems Thinking Skills: Using Systems Dynamics Modeling Tools." www.uni-ku.ac.at/users/gossimit/sdyn/gdm-eng.htm.

Ouderaa, J.v.d. 1994a. "Hoezo merkenbouwen?" *Niewstribune* October 27, 38–39.

———. 1994b. Positioneringsgroep & (NED), A.C.N. *Studie top 3 merken.* ACNielsen.

Ourusoff, A., M. Ozanian, P.B. Brown, and J. Starr. 1992. "What's in a Name? What the World's Top Brands Are Worth." *Financial World* September 1, 32–49.

Pappu, R., P.G. Quester, and R.W. Cooksey. 2005. "Consumer-Based Brand Equity: Improving the Measurement—Empirical Evidence." *Journal of Product & Brand Management* 14 (3): 143–154.

Parasuraman, A., V. Zeithaml, and L. Berry. 1988. "SERVQUAL: A Multiple Theme Scale for Measuring Consumer Perceptions of Service Quality." *Journal of Retailing* 64: 12–40.

Park, C.W., S. Milberg, and R. Lawson. 1991. "Evaluation of Brand Extensions: The Role of Product Feature Similarity and Brand Concept Consistency." *Journal of Consumer Research* 18 (September): 185–193.

Parker Bradey, R. 2001. "Coca Cola-truc werkt bij éénpersoonssoep." *Nieuwstribune* (22).

Parker Bradey, R., and M. Akerboom. 1996. "Verzekeraars zijn wel degelijk een merk." *Nieuwstribune* October 10.

Parsons, A.J. 1996. "Nestlé: The Visions of Local Managers. An Interview with Peter Brabeck-Letmathe, CEO Elect." *McKinsey Quarterly* May.

Pascale, R., L. Gioja, and M. Milleman. 2000. *Surfing the Edge of Chaos: The Laws of Nature and the New Laws of Business.* New York: Crown Business.

Patterson, M. 1999. "Re-appraising the Concept of Brand Image." *Journal of Brand Management* 6 (6): 409–426.

Pawle, J.A. 2000. "A New View of Global Brand Personality." MRS 2000 Conference Proceedings. 279–291.

Payne, A., M. Christopher, M. Clark, and H. Peck, eds. 1998. *Relationship Marketing for Competitive Advantage.* Oxford, UK: Butterworth-Heinemann.

Payne, A. 1995. *Advances in Relationship Marketing.* London: Kogan Page.

Pearce, J.A., and F. David. 1987. "Corporate Mission Statements: The Bottom Line." *Academy of Management Executives* 2: 109–115.

Pearson, S. 1996. *Building Brands Directly.* London: Macmillan.

Peck, H., A. Payne, M. Christopher, and M. Clark. 1999. *Relationship Marketing: Strategy and Implementation.* Oxford, UK: Butterworth Heinemann.

Peckham, J. 1973. *Wheel of Marketing.* ACNielsen company publication.

Pegasus Communications. 2005. "What Is Systems Thinking?" www.pegasuscom.com/aboutst.html.

Peichl, T. 2004. "What Do the United Consumers of Europe Think?" *GfK Magazine for Staff and Clients* 2: 16–19.

Pelsmacker, P.d., and P.v. Kenhove. 1994. *Marktonderzoek: Methoden en toepassingen.* Leuven, Belgium.

Penn, D. 2005. "Could Brain Science Be Peace Broker in the 'Recall Wars'?" *Admap* September: 33–35.

Peppers, D., and M. Rogers. 1993. *One to One Future.* London: Piatkus.

Peter, P.J., and J.C. Olson. 1994. *Consumentengedrag en Marketingstrategie.* Schoonhoven, Netherlands: Academic Service.

Petromilli, M., and D. Morrison. 2002a. "Brand Architecture: Building Brand Portfolio Value." *Strategy & Leadership* 30: 22–28.

———. 2002b. "Creating Brand Harmony." www.prophet.com.

Pfannenmüller, J. 2003. "Vom eigenen Erfolg überholt." *Werven & Verkaufen* (20).

Piercy, N., and W. Giles. 1989. "Making SWOT Analysis Work." *Marketing Intelligence Planning* 7 (5–6): 5–7.

Pieters, R. 1989. "Laddering: een nieuwe ontwikkeling in segmentatie." *Tijdschrift voor Marketing* (October): 30–41.

———. 1991. "EPM: een positioneringsmodel." *Reclame en Onderzoek*, 108–117.

Pieters, R., H. Baumgartner, and D. Allen. 1995. "A Means-End Chain Approach to Consumer Goal Structures." *International Journal of Research in Marketing* 12 (October): 227–244.

Pikaar, A. 2000. "Merktrouw, hoe (zo) trouw?" PhD diss., Universiteit van Amsterdam.

Pimpl, R. 2003. "Ewige Rätsel um den wert der Marke." *100 Jahre Deutscher Markenverband.* Publication of German Brand Association.

Pine, B., and J. Gilmore. 1999. *The Experience Economy.* Boston: Harvard Business School Press.

Pirrie, A. 2006. "What Value Brands?" *Admap* October.

Plummer, J.T. 1985. "How Personality Makes a Difference." *Journal of Advertising Research* 24 (6): 27–31.

Polet, R.B. 1993. Lecture at Unilever Marketingday.

Polster, B. 1999. *Design Directory Scandinavia.* Bonn, Germany: Howard Buch Production.

Porter, M.E. 1979. "How Competitive Forces Shape Strategy?" *Harvard Business Review* (March–April): 1–10.

———. 1996. "What Is Strategy?" *Harvard Business Review* (November–December): 61–78.

Positioneringsgroep. 2000. Merkpositionering. Personal discussion with Giep Franzen and Marieke van den Berg. October 25.

Prahalad, C.K. 1990. "The Core Competence of the Corporation." In *The Strategy Process*, ed. H. Mintzberg, J.B. Quinn, and S. Ghosal. London: Prentice Hall.

Prensky, D., and C. Wright-Isak. 1997. "Advertising, Values and the Consumption Community." In *Values, Lifestyles, and Psychographics*, ed. L.R. Kahle and L.E. Chiagouris. Mahwah, NJ: Lawrence Erlbaum.

Prue, T. 1994. "The 1994 IPA Advertising Effectiveness Awards: A Frameworkish' Guide to Some of This Years's Winners." *Admap* November.

Prue, T., and A. Cooper. 2001. "Why Monitoring Advertising Performance Is Only Half the Answer." Paper presented at the Monitoring Advertising Performance Conference, London: January 30.

Quinn, J.B. 1980. *Strategies for Change: Logical Incrementalism.* Homewood, IL: Richard D. Irwin.

Raaij, v.F., W. 1990. "Betekenisgeving door categorisatie en differentiatie." *Reclame en Onderzoek,* 147–157.

Raggio, R.D., and R.P. Leone. 2005. "The Theoretical Separation of Brand Equity and Brand Value: Managerial Implications for Strategic Planning." Working paper, Fischer College of Business, Ohio State University.

———. 2006. "Producing a Measure of Brand Equity by Decomposing Brand Beliefs into Brand and Attribute Sources." Zyman Institute of Brand Science. Technical Report Series.

Ramzy, d.A. 2001. *Narrativity and The Briefing.* Amstelveen, Netherlands: FHV/BBDO. Internal document.

Rao, A.R., L. Qu, and W.R. Robert. 1999. "Signaling Unobservable Product Quality Through a Brand Ally." *Journal of Marketing Research* 36 (May): 258–268.

Rao, V.R., M.K. Agarwal, and D. Dahlhoff. 2004. "How Is Manifest Branding Strategy Related to the Intangible Value of a Corporation?" *Journal of Marketing* 68: 126–141.

Rapaport, A., ed. 1982. *Carl Von Clausewitz on War.* New York: Barnes & Noble.

Ratneshwar, S., D.G. Mick, and C. Huffman. 2000. *The Why of Consumption.* London: Routledge.

Reber, A.S. 1997. *Woordenboek van de psychologie.* Amsterdam: Bert Bakker.

Reibstein, D.J., and P.W. Farris. 1995. "Market Share and Distribution: A Generalization, a Speculation, and Some Implications." *Marketing Science* 14 (3): 190–202.

Reichheld, F.F. 1993. "Loyalty-Based Management." *Harvard Business Review* (March–April): 64–73.

———. 1996. *The Loyalty Effect.* Boston: Harvard Business School Press.

———. 2003. *Loyalty Rules! How Today's Leaders Build Lasting Relationships.* Boston: Harvard Business School Press.

———. 2006. *The Ultimate Question: Driving Good Profits and True Growth.* Boston: Harvard Business School Press.

Reichheld, F.F., and W.E. Sasser. 1990. "Zero Defections: Quality Comes to Services." *Harvard Business Review* (September–October): 105–111.

Reid, A. 2005. "Rebranding Wanadoo." *Campaign* August 7.

Reiss, S. 2002. *Who Am I? The 16 Basic Desires That Motivate Our Actions and Define Our Personality.* New York: Berkeley.

Rekom, J.v. 1997. "Deriving an Operational Measure of Corporate Identity." *European Journal of Marketing* 31 (5–6) 410–422.

———. 1998. "Corporate Identity." PhD diss., Erasmus University.

Reuters. 2005. "Market Research Report." Research and Markets. www.researchandmarkets.com.

Reynolds, T.J., and J. Gutman. 1984. "Advertising Is Image Management." *Journal of Advertising Research* 24 (February–March): 27–34.

———. 1988. "Laddering Theory, Method, Analysis and Interpretation." Special Issue: Values. *Journal of Advertising Research* 28 (March): 11–31.

Reynolds, T.J., and C.B. Phillips. 2005. "In Search of True Brand Equity Metrics: All Market Share Ain't Created Equal." *Journal of Advertising Research* 45 (2): 171–186.

Rice, B. 1998. "Loyalty Equals Retention: The Great Myth." Paper presented at the National Convention on Data-Driven Marketing, Melbourne, Australia, November 17–19.

Rice, B., and J. Hofmeyr. 2000. "The Measurement of Commitment." Cape Town: Research Surveys.

Richards, T. 1997. *Buying Loyalty vs. Building Commitment.* Research Surveys of Great Britain.

———. 1998. "Building Customer Loyalty." Paper presented at the Dialogue Marketing Conference.

Richards, T., and J. Bevan. 2000. "Measuring the True Value of Brands: Can You Afford Not To?" www.strategyresearch.com.

Richardson, M. 2000. "Letting the Brand Guide the People." *Journal of Brand Management* 7 (4): 275–280.

Richins, M.L. 1994. "Valuing Things: The Public and Private Meaning of Possessions." *Journal of Consumer Research* 21 (December): 504–421.

Riel, C.B.M. 2003. *Identiteit en Imago.* The Hague: Academic Service.

Ries, A., and L. Ries. 1998. *The 22 Immutable Laws of Branding.* New York: HarperCollins.

Ries, A., and J. Trout. 1981. *Positioning: The Battle for Your Mind.* New York: McGraw-Hill.

Riezebos, R., and J. Alleman. 1997. "De strategie achter corporate endorsements." *Tijdschrift voor marketing* (July–August): 50–51.

Riezebos, R., J. Alleman, H.v. Avendonk, and E. Visser. 1997. "Warm aanbevolen: strategische plaatsbepaling en doelstellingen van endorsement." *Tijdschrift voor Marketing* (May): 50–52.

Riezebos, R., and A. Visser-Hendriks. 1999. "Rokers in cowboy-look." *Tijdschrift voor Marketing* (July–August): 46–48.

Rijkenberg, J. 1998. *Concepting: het managen van concept-merken in het communicatiegeoriënteerde tijdperk.* The Hague: Uitgeverij BZZToH bv.

Rindfleisch, A., and J.J. Imman. 1998. "Explaining the Familiarity-Liking Relationship: Mere Exposure, Information Availability or Social Desirability?" *Marketing Letters* 9: 1.

Robertson, J. 2006. "Questions." *Sales & Marketing Management* March: 13.

Robinson, C.M. 2003. "From Soap and Chocolate to Bleach and Blue Jeans." Brandpapers, www.brandchannel.com.

Robinson, W.T., and C. Fornell. 1985. "Sources of Market Pioneer Advantage in Consumer Goods Industries." *Journal of Marketing Research* 22 (August): 305–317.

Rokeach, M. 1973. *The Nature of Human Values.* New York: Free Press.

Roll, M. 2006. *Asian Brand Strategy: How Asia Builds Strong Brands.* New York: Palgrave Macmillan.

Rosenbluth, H., and D. Peters. 2002. *The Customer Comes Second.* New York: HarperCollins.

Roskies, L. 1999. "The Binding Problem." *Neuron* 24 (September).

Rossiter, J.R., and L. Percy. 1987. *Advertising and Promotion Management.* New York: McGraw-Hill.

Rossiter, J.R., L. Percy, and R.J. Donovan. 1991. "A Better Advertising Planning Grid." *Journal of Advertising Research* (October–November): 11–21.

Rubinson, J., and M. Pfeiffer. 2005. "Brand Key Performance Indicators as a Force for Brand Equity Management." *Journal of Advertising Research* 45 (June): 170–181.

Ruffell, B. 1996. "The Genetics of Brandnaming." *Journal of Brand Management* 4 (2): 108–115.

Rugoff, R. 2000. "Designing the Future." Paper presented at The Spirit of Design conference, Aspen, Colorado, July.

Rusch, R. 2003. "Samsung Shows Its Strength." *Brand Channel*, July 28. www.brandchannel.com/features_effect.asp?pf_id=168.

Russo, E.J., and F. Leclerc. 1994. "An Eye-Fixation Analysis of Choice Processes for Consumer Nondurables." *Journal of Consumer Research* 21 (2): 274–290.

Rustema, C. 1995. *Brand Extension. Monografie Genootschap voor Reclame.* (7).

Ryans, A.B., A.M. Roger, and J.S. Hulland. 1995. "Profitable Multibranding." *Journal of Brand Management* 3 (3): 183–196.

Sampson, P. 1992. "An Examination of Car Image Typologies Using an Implicit Model of Personality." *ESOMAR.*

Samsung. 2006. "About Samsung." www.samsung.com/AboutSAMSUNG/SAMSUNGGroup/TimelineHistory/index.htm.

Sanders, T. 2000. *Merkidentiteit: tussen droom en werkelijkheid.* SWOCC publicatie nr. 15. Amsterdam: Stichting Wetenschappelijk Onderzoek Commerciele Communicatie.

Sara Lee. 2005a. "Sara Lee Corporation Reviews Transformation Plan at Cagny's Annual Conference." *Company Newsletter* February 23, 3.

Sattler, H. 2000. Eine Simulationsanalyse zur Beurteilung von Markeninvestitionen. *OR Spektrum-Quantitative Approaches in Management* 22 (1): 173–196.

Sattler, H., S. Hogl, and O. Hupp. 2002. "Evaluation of the Financial Value of Brands." *Esomar*, September.

Saunders, J., and F. Guogun. 1996. "Dual Branding: How Corporate Names Add Value." *Marketing Intelligence & Planning* 14 (7): 29–34.

Scardino, E. 2005. "Sara Lee Slims Down Portfolio Span." *DSN Retailing Today*, February 28.

Schein, E.H. 2004. *Organizational Culture and Leadership.* 2nd ed., San Francisco: Jossey-Bass.

Schijns, J.M.C. 1998. "The Impact of a Membership Program on Relationship Strength: Results of Exploratory Research." In *New Frontiers in Relationship Marketing Theory and Practice*, ed. J.N. Sheth and A.E. Menon. Atlanta, GA: Emory University.

Schimansky, A. 2003. "Schlechte Noten für Markenbewerter." *Marketingjournal* 5: 44–49.

Schippers, G.M. 2000. *De dynamiek in verslaving. Rede bij de aanvaarding van het ambt van bijzonder hoogleraar Verslavingsgedrag en Zorgevaluatie aan de Universiteit van Amsterdam.* Amsterdam: Vossiuspers AUP.

Schmitt, B. 1999. "Experiential Marketing: A New Framework for Design and Communications." *Design Management Journal* (Spring): 10–16.

Schmitt, B., and A. Simonson. 1998. "Coupling Brand and Organizational Identities Through Partnering." *Design Management Journal* (Winter): 9–14.

Schneider, B., and D. Bowen. 1985. "Employee and Customer Perceptions of Service in Banks." *Administrative Science Quarterly* 24: 252–267.

Schneider, W., and R.M. Shiffrin. 1977. "Controlled and Automatic Information Processing I: Detection, Search and Attention." *Psychological Review* 84: 1–66.

Schocker, A.D. 1995. "Positive and Negative Effects of Brand Extension and Co-Branding." *Advances in Consumer Research* 22: 432–434.

Schrameyer, H. 2000. "Campagne moet Ericsson verder inkleuren." *Adformatie* December 15, 30.

Schramm, W. 1954. *How Communications Works. The Process and Effects of Communication.* Urbana: University of Illinois Press.

Schultz, D.E., and S. Bailey. 1999. "Building a Viable Model of Customer Brand Loyalty in an Interactive Market Place." Paper presented at Brand Equity & Advertising Research, an ARF Week of Workshops Event, New York City, October.

Schultz, H. 2000. "Starbucks Coffee Company." In *The Future of Brands: Twenty-Five Visions*, ed. R. Clifton and E. Maughan. London: Macmillan.

Schuring, R.J., and R. Plug. 2001. "The Brand Equity Monitor®: An Actionable Instrument." Paper presented at "Genootschap voor Reclame." Amsterdam. February 28.

Schuring, R.J., D. Sikkel, and G. Franzen, G. 1999. *The Relationship Between Brand Association and Brand Choice in Three Markets.* BrandMarc internal document.

Schwartz, S.H. 1992. "Universals in the Content and Structure of Values: Theoretical Advances and Empirical Tests in 20 Countries." In *Advances in Experimental Social Psychology*, ed. M.P.E. Zanna. Orlando, FL: Academic Press.

———. 1994. "Are There Universal Aspects in the Structure and Contents of Human Value?" *Journal of Social Issues* 50 (4): 19–45.

———. 2003a. "Basic Human Values: Their Content and Structure Across Countries." In *Valores e trabalho*, ed. A. Tamayo and J. Porto. Brasilia: University of Brasilia.

———. 2003b. "Robustness and Fruitfulness of a Theory of Universals in Individual Values." In *Valores e trabalho*, ed. A. Tamayo and J. Porto. Brasilia: University of Brasilia.

———. 2006a. "Basic Human Values: Theory, Measurement and Applications." *Revue francaise de sociologie* 47 (4): 56–95.

———. 2006b. "One Brick at a Time." *Fortune* June 12: 10.

Schwartz, S.H., and W. Bilsky. 1987. "Toward a Universal Psychological Structure of Human Values." *Journal of Personality and Social Psychology* 53 (3): 550–562.

Screeton, A. 1999. *A Matter of Figures: Third Quarter's Results, 1999.* Philips.

Scrivener, A. 1998. "The Somascope: A Tool for Guided Self-Healing Using Medical Imaging." www.well. com/~abs/Somascope/Somascope.html.

———. 2004. "A Curriculum for Cybernetics and System Theory." www.well.com/user/abs/curriculum. html.

Scroggs, J.R. 1994. *Persoon en Persoonlijkheid: Sleutelideeën uit Persoonlijkheidstheorieën.* Vol. Deel 2. Rotterdam: Uitgeversmaatschappij Ad.Donker.

Seth, J.N., B.I. Newman, and B.L. Gross. 1991. "Why We Buy What We Buy: A Theory of Consumption Values." *Journal of Business Research* 22: 159–170.

Sexton, D. 2005. "Building the Brand Scorecard." *The Advertiser* February: 90–104.

Shani, D., and S. Chalasani. 1992. "Exploiting Niches Using Relationship Marketing." *Journal of Service Marketing* 4 (Fall): 43–51.

Sharp, B., and A. Sharp. 1997. "Loyalty Programs and Their Impact on Repeat-Purchase Loyalty Patterns." *International Journal of Research in Marketing* 14: 473–486.

Sheinin, D.A. 1998. "Sub-Brand Evaluation and Use Versus Brand Extension." *Journal of Brand Management* 6 (2): 113–122.

Sherif, J., and C. Hovland. 1961. *Social Judgment: Assimilation and Contrast Effects in Communication and Attitude Change.* New Haven, CT: Yale University Press.

Sikkel, D., and J. Oppenhuisen. 1998a. *Reader Commerciele Communicatie.* Amsterdam: De SWOCC-Waardeninventarisatie, Vakgroep Communicatiewetenschap, Universiteit van Amsterdam.

———. 1998b. Vrijheid & gebondenheid: de Woorden van Waarden. Amsterdam/Tilburg.

Silverstein, M.J., and G. Stalk. 2000. *Breaking Compromises.* New York: John Wiley.

Sirgy, J. 1982. "Self-Concept in Consumer Behavior: A Critical Review." *Journal of Consumer Research* 9: 287–300.

SMA, and A. Nielsen. 2000. *Productintroducties de feiten op een rij, Brochure Stichting Merkartikel.* Amesterdam: Merkarticle Association.

Smit, E., M. Tolboom, and F. Bronner. 2006. "Brand Relationship Quality: Why Relationships Between Consumers and Their Brands Differ." *Journal of Business Research* May 5.

Smit, R. 2000. "De spruitjeslucht rond Startpagina.nl." *Adformatie* December 15, 57.

———. 2001. "DDB laat merken op vrijersvoeten gaan." *Adformatie* January 18, 14.

Smit, R., and L. Ligtenberg. 2000. "Visionair Durk Jager bij P & G slachtoffer van eigen ambitie." *Adformatie* (5): June 15.

Smith, D.C. 1992. "Brand Extension and Advertising Efficiency: What Can and Cannot Be Expected." *Journal of Advertising Research* (November–December): 11–20.

Smith, D.C., and C.W. Park. 1992. "The Effects of Brand Extensions on Market Share and Advertising Efficiency." *Journal of Marketing Research* 29 (August): 296–313.

Smith, D.P.E., and M.D. Jones. 1998. *Philips No Ordinary Restructuring Story.* Salomon Smith Barney.

Smith, G. 1997. "Can George Fisher Fix Kodak?" *Business Week* (October): 116–120.

Smith, J. 2002. "Brand Metrics: Your Key to Measuring Return on Brand Investment." MarketingProfs. com, April 5.

Smith, S. ed, 2000. *America's Greatest Brands*, Vol. 1. Rye, NY: America's Greatest Brands, Inc.

———. 2003. *America's Greatest Brands.* Vol. 2. Rye, NY: America's Greatest Brands, Inc.

Solomon, Michael R. 2004. *Consumer Behavior*, 6th ed. Upper Saddle River, NJ: Pearson Prentice Hall.

Sonnenberg, J. 1993. "If I Had Only One Client." *Sales & Marketing Management* November: 104–107.

Sony. 2005. "Corporate History." www.sony.net.

Spaeth, J. 1993. "Brand Equity and Advertising: Lessons from Jimi Hendrix." New York: Advertising Research Foundation.

Spiering, H. 2003. "Typisch homo sapiens." *NRC Handelsblad* June 14, 35.

———. 2004. "Volledig modern." *NRC Handelsblad* May 1 and 2: 41.

Spiering, H., and A. Thijssen. 2001. "Wat wil het brein?" *NRC Handelsblad* June 2.

SRI Consulting Business Intelligence (SRI-BI). www.sric-bi.com/VALS.

Stacey, R. 1992. *Managing the Unknowable.* San Francisco: Jossey-Bass.

Stappers, J.G.R., A.D. Reijnders, and W.A.J. Möller. 1990. "De werking van de massamedia een overzicht van inzichten." *De Arbeiderspers,* a monograph.

Starbucks. 2001. "Starbucks Timeline and History." www.starbucks.com/aboutus/timeline.asp.

Steel, J. 1997. *Truth, Lies and Advertising: The Art of Account Planning.* New York: John Wiley.

Steketee, H. 2000a. "Easy Jet gelooft in sober vliegen." *NRC Handelsblad* October 19.

———. 2000b. "Rover leed onder BMW's zig-zag-rijstijl." *NRC Handelsblad* March 17.

Steketee, H., and M.d. Waard. 2000. "BMW verkoopt noodlijdend Rover." *NRC Handelsblad* March 17.

Stephan, S.K., and B.L. Tannenholz. 1994. "The Real Reason for Brand-Switching." *Advertising Age* 12: 13.

Stevenson, D. 1985. "One, Two, Three or Out: Brand Rank Is Everything." *Ad Forum* February, 22–27.

Stockdale, M. 1999. "Are All Consumers Equal? Segmentation: The Statute of Limitations." *How to Use Advertising to Build Strong Brands*. Thousand Oaks, CA: Sage.

Stoop, J. 2000. "Insearch: een onderzoek naar de belemmeringen voor reclamemensen om meer kwalitatief inputonderzoek te doen." PhD diss., Universiteit van Amsterdam.

Storbacka, K. 1994. *The Nature of Customer Relationship Profitability*. Helsinki: Swedish School of Economics and Business Administration.

Storbacka, K., T. Strandvik, and C. Grönroos. 1994. "Managing Customer Relationships for Profit: The Dynamics of Relationship Quality." *Service Industry Management* 5 (5): 21–38.

Stow, M. 1992. "Andrex: Sold on a Pup." IPA Effectiveness Awards" (Institute of Practitioners in Advertising). World Advertising Research Center (WARC) publication.

Strasburg, J. 2003. "Levi's to Close Last U.S. Plants: Struggling Jeansmaker to Cut 1,980 More Jobs." www.sweatshopwatch.org/headlines/2003/levicloses_sept03.html.

Strategy Research Corporation. 1999a. *Conversion Model: Loyalty and Commitment: Two Sides of the Same Coin*. Company brochure.

———. 1999b. *Conversion Model: Understanding Commitment, the Key to Relationship Management*. Cape Town: Strategy Research Corporation.

Stroeken, J. 2001. "Innovaties: Top of Flop?" *Eye* February 1, 4.

Sujan, M., and J.R. Bettman. 1989. "The Effects of Brand Positioning Strategies on Consumers' Brand and Category Perceptions." *Journal of Marketing Research* 26 (November): 454–467.

Sullivan, M.W. 1989. *Brand-Extension and Order-of-Entry: Study of 96 Brands in 11 Markets over 38 Years*. Chicago: University of Chicago Press.

Sung, Y., and S.T. Tinkham. 2005. "Brand Personality Structures in the United States and Korea: Common and Culture-Specific Factors." *Journal of Consumer Psychology* 15 (4): 334–350.

Supphellen, M., and K. Gronhaug. 2003. "Building Foreign Brand Personalities in Russia." *International Journal of Advertising* 22 (2): 203–226.

Sutherland, M. 1993. *Advertising and the Mind of the Consumer: What Works, What Doesn't and Why*. St. Leonards, Australia: Allen & Unwin.

———. 1996. "To Build a Brand, Use Something Old as a Link to Something New." *Journal of Brand Management* 3 (5): 284–286.

Swartz, J. 2007. "Apple's New iPod Could Bolster Music Dominance," *USA Today* January 1.

Swift, R.S. 2001. *Accelerating Customer Relationships—Using CRM and Relationship Technologies*. Upper Saddle River, NJ: Prentice-Hall.

Swinyard, W.R. 1998. "Spiritual Solace on Two Wheels: The Motorcycle Mystique and Rider Segments." *Journal of Segmentation in Marketing* 2 (2): 7–25.

Sylvester, A.K., J. McQueen, and S.D. Moore. 1994. "Brand Growth and 'Phase 4 Marketing.'" *Admap* September, 34–36.

Szeemann, H. 1983. "Der Hang zum Gesamtkunstwerk." www.brock.uni-wuppertal.de/Schrifte/AGEU/Totalkun.html.

Szymanski, D.M., S.G. Bharadwaj, and P.R. Varadarajan. 1993. "An Analysis of the Market Share–Profitability Relationship." *Journal of Marketing* 57 (July): 1–18.

Tait, B. 2001. "Do Gaps in Marketing Theory Make New Brands Fail?" *Admap* June, 40–43.

Tas, W., and E. Sondervan. 2006. Brand Power: over aantrekkingskracht en markbarrières. TNS NIPO, Amsterdam.

Tauber, E.M. 1993. "Fit and Leverage in Brand Extensions." *Brand Equity and Advertising*, ed. D.A. Aaker and A.L. Biel. Hillsdale, NJ: Lawrence Erlbaum.

Taylor, D. 2004. *Brand Stretch: Why 1 in 2 Extensions Fails and How to Beat the Odds*. Chichester, UK: John Wiley.

Taylor, J.G. 1999. *The Race for Consciousness*. Cambridge: MIT Press.

Taylor, R.E. 1999. "A Six-Segment Message Strategy Wheel." *Journal of Advertising Research* 39 (6): 7–17.

Taylor, W. 1993. "Message and Muscle: An Interview with Swatch Titan Hayek." *Harvard Business Review* (March–April): 92–110.

Thornberry, N. 1997. "Een visie op 'visie.'" *PEM* 3: 13–21.

Tilles, S. 1986. "How to Evaluate Corporate Strategy." *Harvard Business Review*, July–August: 112.

Time Warner Website, www.timewarner.com.

Timmerman, E.M. 1998. *Bouwstenen van het merkimago: merkassociaties in het hoofd van de consument.* *Presentatie.* Amsterdam: SWOCC.

———. 2001. "Researching Brand Images: The Nature and Activation of Brand Representations in Memory." PhD diss., Universiteit van Amsterdam.

TNS NIPO. 2006. "Getting Insight in Brand Equity." Amsterdam. Internal Report.

Tolboom, M. 2004a. *A Brand as a Friend?* SWOCC Research Report. Amsterdam: University of Amsterdam.

———. 2004b. *Person-Brand Relationships.* Amsterdam: University of Amsterdam.

Toman, R. 1998. *De kunst van de Gotiek.* Keulen, Germany: Köneman Verlagsgesellschaft mbh.

Tracey, M., and F. Wiersema. 1995. "How Market Leaders Keep Their Edge." *Fortune* 6: 52.

Trochen, B. 1994–1995. *The Pepsi Case.* Paper presented at the Seminar Commercial Communication, University of Amsterdam.

Trommsdorff, V., and C. Zellerhoff. 1994. "Produkt- und Markenpositionierung." *Markenstrategie* November: 508–511.

Trout, J. 2000. *Differentiate or Die.* New York: John Wiley.

———. 2001. *Big Brands, Big Trouble.* New York: John Wiley.

Trout, J., and S. Rivkin. 1996. *The New Positioning.* New York: McGraw-Hill.

Tversky, A., and D. Kahneman. 1973. "Availability: A Heuristic for Judging Frequency and Probability." *Cognitive Psychology* 5: 207–232.

Tyler, K. 1998. "Europe in the Middle Ages." www.ccs.neu.edu/home/romulus/papers/medeur/cathedrals.htm.

Uncles, M., M. Cocks, and C. Macrae. 1995. "Brand Architecture: Reconfiguring Organisations for Effective Brand Management." *Journal of Brand Management* 3 (2): 81–92.

Upshaw, L. 1995. *Building Brand Identity: A Strategy for Success in a Hostile Marketplace.* New York: John Wiley.

Urban, G.L., T. Carter, S. Gaskin, and Z. Mucha. 1986. "Market Share Rewards to Pioneering Brands: An Empirical Analysis and Strategic Implications." *Management Science* 32 (6): 645–659.

Urde, M. 1999. "Brand Orientation: A Mindset for Building Brands into Strategic Resources." *Journal of Marketing Management* 15(1–): 117–133.

Vakrastsas, D., and T. Amber. 1995. "Advertising Effects: A Taxonomy and Review of Concepts, Methods and Results from the Academic Literature." London Business School, Centre for Marketing. Working paper no. 95–301.

Van Dijk, D. 2000. "Nieuwe Jeans moet Levi's weer in het zadel helpen." *De Telegraaf* March 18. Working paper no. 95–301.

Vargo, S., and R. Lusch. 2004. "A New Dominant Logic." *Journal of Marketing* 68 (January): 1–17.

Vaughn, R. 1980. "How Advertising Works: A Planning Model." *Journal of Advertising Research* 20 (5): 27–33.

———. 1986. "How Advertising Works: A Planning Model Revisited." *Journal of Advertising Research* 26 (1): 57–66.

Vavra, T. 1992. *Aftermarketing.* Homewood, IL: Business One/Irwin.

Velding, I. 2001. "Het brein van de CEO." *Management Team*, 102–111.

Verbeke, W. 1991. "Advertisers Do Not Persuade Consumers: They Create Societies Around Their Brands to Maintain Power in the Marketplace." *International Journal of Advertising* 11.

Verhulst, S. 2001. "Ja, ik wil alsnog." *NRC Handelsblad* August 4, 19.

Vinson, D.E., J.E. Scott, and L.M. Lamont. 1977. "The Role of Personal Values in Marketing and Consumer Behavior: Can Personal Values Be Used to Assist Marketers in Determining Consumer Choice Behavior?" *Journal of Marketing* (April): 44–50.

Visser, E. 1998. "Multibranding: Symptom of an Unclear Branding Policy." *Design Marketing Journal* (Winter): 60–64.

Visser, H. 1999. "Zinloos bewustzijn, de invloed van denken op gedrag is omstreden." *NRC Handelsblad* September 11.

Volberda, H.W., and T. Elfring, eds. 2001. *Rethinking Strategy.* London: Sage.

Vriens, D. 1998. *Constructief beslissen: een cybernetische verkenning van het individuele beslisproces.* Delft, Netherlands: Eburon.

Vromen, M. 1995. *Personal Drives Analyses*. Amstelveen, Netherlands: FHV/BBDO.

Vyncke, P. 1992. *Imago-management: Handboek voor reclamestrategen*. Ghent, Belgium: Mys & Breesch.

Waal de, F.B.M. 1999. "The End of Nature Versus Nurture." *Scientific American* (December): 93–99.

Waalewijn, P., R.v.d. Griendt, and B.W.C.M. Kamp. 1996. "Missies Geuit!" *Bedrijfskunde* 68: 74–85.

Wagner, R. 1849. Die Kunst und die Revolution. *Gesammelten Werke*, Band 12.

Watzlawick, P., J. Bavelas, and D. Jackson. 1967. *Pragmatics of Human Communications*. New York: W.W. Norton.

Webber, A.M. 2001. "Life: Adapt or Die." *Fast Company* (April): 130–137.

Weilbacher, W.M. 1993. *Brand Marketing: Building Winning Brand Strategies That Deliver Value and Customer Satisfaction*. London: NTC Business Books.

Wells, M. 2000. "Red Baron." *Forbes Global* July 3, 57–60.

Wells, S., S. Moriarty, and J. Burnett. 2006. *Apple Tops the Charts with Digital Music*. Upper Saddle River, NJ: Pearson Prentice Hall.

Wells, W.D. 1980. *How Advertising Works*. Chicago: Needham Harper Worldwide.

Wernerfelt, B. 1988. "Umbrella Branding as a Signal of New Product Quality: An Example of Signaling by Posting a Brand." *Rand Journal of Economics* 19 (3): 458–466.

Wertime, K. 2002. *Building Brands and Believers*. Singapore: John Wiley.

Westendorp, P.H.v. 1996. *Op weg naar accountability*. Amsterdam: Genootschap Voor Reclame.

Whittlesea, B. 1993. "Illusions of Familiarity." *Journal of Experimental Psychology: Learning, Memory and Cognition* 19: 1235–1253.

Wikipedia. 2005. "Sony Company Profile, History and Culture, and SWOT." www.en.wikipedia.org/wiki/Sony.

Wilson, C. 2005. "France Telecom Unites Brands, Will Sell Services as Orange." www.teleohonyonline.com.

Wilson, I. 1992. "Realizing the Power of Strategic Vision." *Long Range Planning* 25: 18–28.

Winchester, M.K., and M. Fletcher. 2000. "Calibrating Your Brand Image Measurement Technique by Utilising Empirical Generalisations." *Journal of Brand Management* 8 (2): 99–110.

Wind, J., and Main, J. 1998. *Driving Change: How the Best Companies Are Preparing for the 21st Century*. London: Kogan Page.

Winton, N. 2003. "VW Phaeton, Wrong Badge, Weak Market, Phaeton Fated to Flounder." www.just-auto.com.

Wit, B.d. 2000. "Verdeel en heers." *Management Team* September 8, 53–57.

Woodside, A.G., and R.J. Trappey. 1992. "Finding Out Why Customers Shop Your Store and Buy Your Brand." *Journal of Advertising Research* (November–December): 59–78.

Wyner, G.A. 2001. "The Trouble with Brand Equity Valuation." *Marketing Research* (Winter): 4–5.

Xinxin, H. 2005. "Case Study: Xerox Corporation." www.boraid.com.

Yoo, B., N. Donthu, S. Lee. 2000. "An Examination of Selected Marketing Mix Elements and Brand Equity." *Journal of the Academy of Marketing Science* 2: 195–211.

Yoon, C. 1991. "Tears, Cheers and Fears: The Role of Emotions in Advertising." Paper presented at Marketing Science Institute conference, February 14–15.

Yovovich, B.G. 1981. "Not Fancy, Just Phenomenal." *Advertising Age* July 27.

Zajonc, R.B. 1980. "Feeling and Thinking: Preferences Need No Inferences." *American Psychologist* 35: 151–175.

Zakon, A.J. 1994. "Das Boston Consulting Group Strategie Buch." In *Bolko v. Oetinger*. Internal report.

Zaltman, G., and R.H. Coulter. 1995. "Seeing the Voice of the Customer: Metaphor-Based Advertising Research." *Journal of Advertising Research* 35 (4): 35.

Zhang, S., and A.B. Markman. 1998. "Overcoming the Early Entrant Advantage: The Role of Alignable and Nonalignable Differences." *Journal of Marketing Research* 35 (November): 413–426.

INDEX

ABOUT THE AUTHORS

Giep Franzen was founder of FHV/BBDO, a leading advertising agency in the Netherlands, and has worked for several of the largest companies in the country. He was a board member of BBDO Worldwide and a member of BBDO's European management group. In 1989 he joined academia and became a professor at the University of Amsterdam—a position he held until 2002. There he founded SWOCC, a foundation for scientific research into brand communication and branding, funded by the Dutch business community. He serves today as a director of SWOCC. In 2000 the readers of the two Dutch advertising trade journals elected him "advertising man of the twentieth century."

Sandra Moriarty was a cofounder of the integrated marketing communication master's program at the University of Colorado. She also has taught at Michigan State University, the University of Kansas, and Kansas State University, and has worked in government public relations, owned an advertising and public relations agency, directed a university publications program, and edited a university alumni magazine. Professor Moriarty has published widely in scholarly journals on marketing communication and visual communication topics, and the eighth edition of her textbook, *Advertising Principles and Practices*, will be published in 2008. She has spoken to groups and presented seminars in most European countries, as well as in Mexico, Japan, Korea, New Zealand, and Turkey, and is a consultant to Dentsu, the world's fifth-largest marketing communication agency.

575